**THE ANALYSIS
OF INTELLIGENCE**

McGRAW-HILL SERIES IN PSYCHOLOGY

Consulting Editors
Norman Garmezy
Richard L. Solomon
Harold W. Stevenson
Lyle V. Jones

Adams   *Human Memory*
Beach, Hebb, Morgan, and Nissen   *The Neuropsychology of Lashley*
Von Békésy   *Experiments in Hearing*
Berkowitz   *Aggression: A Social Psychological Analysis*
Berlyne   *Conflict, Arousal, and Curiosity*
Blum   *Psychoanalytic Theories of Personality*
Brown   *The Motivation of Behavior*
Brown and Ghiselli   *Scientific Method in Psychology*
Butcher   *MMPI: Research Developments and Clinical Applications*
Campbell, Dunnette, Lawler, and Weick   *Managerial Behavior, Performance, and Effectiveness*
Cofer   *Verbal Learning and Verbal Behavior*
Cofer and Musgrave   *Verbal Behavior and Learning: Problems and Processes*
Crafts, Schneirla, Robinson, and Gilbert   *Recent Experiments in Psychology*
Crites   *Vocational Psychology*
D'Amato   *Experimental Psychology: Methodology, Psychophysics, and Learning*
Davitz   *The Communication of Emotional Meaning*
Deese and Hulse   *The Psychology of Learning*
Dollard and Miller   *Personality and Psychotherapy*
Edgington   *Statistical Inference: The Distribution-free Approach*
Ellis   *Handbook of Mental Deficiency*
Epstein   *Varieties of Perceptual Learning*
Ferguson   *Statistical Analysis in Psychology and Education*
Forgus   *Perception: The Basic Process in Cognitive Development*
Franks   *Behavioral Therapy: Appraisal and Status*
Ghiselli   *Theory of Psychological Measurement*
Ghiselli and Brown   *Personnel and Industrial Psychology*
Gilmer   *Industrial and Organizational Psychology*
Gray   *Psychology Applied to Human Affairs*
Guilford   *Fundamental Statistics in Psychology and Education*
Guilford   *The Nature of Human Intelligence*
Guilford   *Personality*
Guilford   *Psychometric Methods*
Guilford and Hoepfner   *The Analysis of Intelligence*
Guion   *Personnel Testing*
Haire   *Psychology in Management*
Hirsch   *Behavior-genetic Analysis*
Hirsh   *The Measurement of Hearing*
Hurlock   *Adolescent Development*

Hurlock *Child Development*
Hurlock *Developmental Psychology*
Jackson and Messick *Problems in Human Assessment*
Karn and Gilmer *Readings in Industrial and Business Psycholgy*
Krech, Crutchfield, and Ballachey *Individual in Society*
Lawler *Pay and Organizational Effectiveness: A Psychological View*
Lazarus, A. *Behavior Therapy and Beyond*
Lazarus, R. *Adjustment and Personality*
Lazarus, R. *Psychological Stress and the Coping Process*
Lewin *A Dynamic Theory of Personality*
Lewin *Principles of Topological Psychology*
Maher *Principles of Psychopathology*
Marascuilo *Statistical Methods for Behavioral Science Research*
Marx and Hillix *Systems and Theories in Psychology*
Messick and Brayfield *Decision and Choice: Contributions of Sidney Siegel*
Miller *Language and Communication*
Morgan *Physiological Psychology*
Mulaik *The Foundations of Factor Analysis*
Nunnally *Psychometric Theory*
Overall and Klett *Applied Multivariate Analysis*
Rethlingshafer *Motivation as Related to Personality*
Robinson and Robinson *The Mentally Retarded Child*
Rosenthal *Genetic Theory and Abnormal Behavior*
Scherer and Wertheimer *A Psycholinguistic Experiment on Foreign Language Teaching*
Shaw *Group Dynamics: The Psychology of Small Group Behavior*
Shaw and Costanza *Theories of Social Psychology*
Shaw and Wright *Scales for the Measurement of Attitudes*
Sidowski *Experimental Methods and Instrumentation in Psychology*
Siegel *Nonparametric Statistics for the Behavioral Sciences*
Spencer and Kass *Perspectives in Child Psychology*
Stagner *Psychology of Personality*
Townsend *Introduction to Experimental Methods for Psychology and the Social Sciences*
Vinacke *The Psychology of Thinking*
Wallen *Clinical Psychology: The Study of Persons*
Warren and Akert *The Frontal Granular Cortex and Behavior*
Waters, Rethlingshafer, and Caldwell *Principles of Comparative Psychology*
Winer *Statistical Principles in Experimental Design*
Zubek and Solberg *Human Development*

John F. Dashiell was Consulting Editor of this series from its inception in 1931 until January 1, 1950. Clifford T. Morgan was Consulting Editor of this series from January 1, 1950 until January 1, 1959. Harry F. Harlow assumed the duties of Consulting Editor from 1959 to 1965. In 1965 a Board of Consulting Editors was established according to areas of interest. The current board members are Richard L. Solomon (physiological, experimental), Norman Garmezy (abnormal, clinical), Harold W. Stevenson (child, adolescent, human development), and Lyle V. Jones (statistical, quantitative).

THE ANALYSIS OF INTELLIGENCE

J. P. GUILFORD

Emeritus Professor of Psychology
University of Southern California

RALPH HOEPFNER

Graduate School of Education
University of California at Los Angeles

McGRAW-HILL BOOK COMPANY

New York   St. Louis   San Francisco   Düsseldorf   Johannesburg
Kuala Lumpur   London   Mexico   Montreal   New Delhi
Panama   Rio de Janeiro   Singapore   Sydney   Toronto

THE ANALYSIS
OF INTELLIGENCE

Copyright © 1971 by McGraw-Hill, Inc. All rights reserved. Printed in the United States of America. No part of this publication may be reproduced, stored in a retrieval system, or transmitted, in any form or by any means, electronic, mechanical, photocopying, recording, or otherwise, without the prior written permission of the publisher.

Library of Congress Catalog Card Number 78-149714
07-025137-1

1 2 3 4 5 6 7 8 9 0 M A M M 7 9 8 7 6 5 4 3 2 1

This book was set in Press Roman by Creative Book Services,
Division of McGregor & Werner, Incorporated,
and printed on permanent paper and bound by The Maple Press Company.
The designer was Barbara Ellwood;
the drawings were done by John Cordes, J. & R. Technical Services, Inc.
The editors were Walter Maytham and Susan Gamer.
John A. Sabella supervised production.

CONTENTS

Preface	xi
1 Background of the Aptitudes Research Project	1
Origins of factor analysis and factors	1
General plans	9
2 The structure of intellect	17
Nature of the SI model	17
Origins and development of the SI model	21
Implications and uses of the SI model	27
3 The goal of factorial invariance	33
Factorial invariance as scientific reproducibility	34
Approaches to the achievement of invariance	35
Types of factorial invariance	36

	Indices of factorial invariance	38
	Handling of the invariance problem by the ARP	41
4	**Methods of analysis**	43
	Preparation of the earlier data for reanalysis	45
	Application of uniform analytical procedures	46
	Some features of results of the analyses	54
	Additional multivariate techniques	58
	Summary	60
5	**Abilities in reasoning and problem solving**	61
	The reasoning-A analysis	62
	The reasoning-B analysis	90
	The study of general reasoning	93
	Studies of reasoning, creativity, and evaluation abilities	97
	Analysis of abilities in problem solving	103
	The study of symbolic abilities	112
	An analysis of figural-cognition and figural-convergent-production abilities	115
	General summary	121
6	**Abilities in creative thinking and planning**	123
	The first study of creative-thinking abilities	124
	The analysis of abilities in planning	142
	A study of verbal fluency	150
	A study of intellectual flexibility	160
	Creative abilities at the ninth-grade level	165
	Creative abilities at the sixth-grade level	169
	Figural- and symbolic-divergent-production abilities	171
	Figural-, symbolic-, and semantic-DP abilities	176
	A study of transformation abilities	177
	Summary on creative-thinking and planning abilities	186
7	**Evaluation abilities**	189
	The first analysis of evaluation	189
	Semantic-evaluation abilities	205
	Symbolic-evaluation abilities	213
	Figural-evaluation abilities	220
	The targeted-rotation analysis	226
	General concluding remarks	227
8	**Memory abilities**	229
	Analysis of semantic-memory abilities	230
	Symbolic-memory abilities	242
	Visual-figural-memory abilities	250
	Summary and conclusions	255

9	**Behavioral abilities**	257
	Social intelligence	257
	Behavioral-cognition abilities	258
	Behavioral divergent production	269
	Current status of knowledge of social intelligence	277
10	**Some extra-intellectual-aptitude relationships**	279
	Predictions of teachers' ratings of creativity	280
	Predictions of grades in the U.S. Coast Guard Academy	284
	Predicting achievement in higher-mathematics courses	288
	Validation of SI abilities in ninth-grade mathematics	291
	The role of SI abilities in concept learning	304
	Roles of transformation abilities in school learning	315
	Importance of SI abilities as viewed by creative individuals	317
	Relevance of selected abilities in performances of military officers	319
	Relations of SI abilities to other personality traits, in adults	325
	Relations of SI abilities to other personality traits, in children	336
	Summary and conclusions	342
11	**Some general considerations**	347
	Factor analysis as a scientific method	347
	Some findings of general psychological significance	353
	The future of intelligence testing	356
	Conclusions	361
	Appendix A	363
	Appendix B	367
	References	499
	Name index	507
	Subject index	509

PREFACE

This book is an account of a coordinated program of research on intellectual abilities, which became also an investigation of basic intellectual functions or processes, extending over a period of 20 years from 1949 to 1969, in the Aptitudes Research Project (ARP) at the University of Southern California. In a sense, it is a condensation of the series of 41 reports from the Psychological Laboratory at U.S.C. (see Appendix A), but it is definitely much more than that, for it organizes those reports and presents a unified view of events and their outcomes and implications.

The account presents the underlying philosophy of the research methodology and demonstrates how somewhat unorthodox rational applications of multiple-factor-analytical procedures can yield rich results for psychological concepts and theory. As is clearly shown, one may discover how individuals are alike in their mental functioning by discovering the unique ways in which they differ. One demand was overriding—to achieve a taxonomy of intellectual functioning with ability concepts that are invariant over marked changes in analyzed test batteries and moderate changes in subject populations. In this way, the scientific demand for replication of findings was served.

Years of experience in employing factor analysis have shown that no analytical method of rotation of axes that is based upon a mathematical definition of simple structure can give an acceptable degree of invariance. The trouble is that simple structure, itself, is neither a safe nor a sufficient guide to the rotation of axes. It seems somewhat paradoxical that when rotations yield invariant concepts, a simple structure is likely to be achieved; but the converse is not likely to hold. However it is rigorously defined, rotation to a simple structure will not ensure invariant conceptual factors. These matters are discussed in Chapters 3, 4, and 11.

An important unifying frame of reference has been provided by the structure-of-intellect (SI) theory and model. The SI model, a three-way classification of 120 hypothetical intellectual abilities or functions, was developed during the first 10 years of the program's history and was used thereafter to suggest dimensions of intellect yet to be discovered. The pace of demonstration of new abilities was thereby much quickened. By the end of the second 10 years, 98 of these abilities had been demonstrated, and prospects appear excellent for the successful demonstration of the remaining 22, by applying the same procedures. The structure of intellect is explained in Chapter 2, and some of its implications for general psychological theory are mentioned there and in Chapter 11.

The general philosophy of research with factor analysis in the ARP's program placed considerable emphasis upon rational predictions of unique abilities to be expected. Provisional categories of abilities were carried over from traditional taxonomic concepts, in the areas of reasoning, problem solving, creative thinking, planning, and judgment or evaluation. Early findings, and the structure-of-intellect theory derived from them, led to the substitution of another list of operational categories—cognition, memory, divergent production, convergent production, and evaluation.

Studies of reasoning and problem solving brought out abilities mostly in the SI categories of cognition and convergent production, which are, respectively, inductive and deductive in character. Such studies provided the content of Chapter 5. The investigations of creative thinking led to abilities in the operation category of divergent production (fluency in searching) and the *product* category of transformations (intellectual flexibility), which intersect in the SI model. Chapter 6 presents the story of this subject.

Chapter 7 tells that one study of evaluation processes was conducted before the SI theory was developed, leading to the inclusion of a special operation category by that name. Three analyses made after the theory was developed demonstrated 18 of the 24 evaluation abilities in the model, all that were investigated. The investigations of memory abilities, as reported in Chapter 8, were all conducted after the model had become available, and they demonstrated all of the 18 unique abilities to which attention was given.

One of the most novel aspects of the SI model is that it made a place for what E. L. Thorndike called "social intelligence," by hypothesizing a special kind of information (among four content categories) called "behavioral." Only the six hypothesized behavioral-cognition abilities and the six hypothesized behavioral-divergent-production abilities were investigated, but all 12 were demonstrated, as told in Chapter 9.

From time to time, questions arose, more from outside the Project's boundaries than from within, concerning the "validity" of the intellectual abilities that were being demonstrated, and concerning their relations to nonaptitude traits of personality. A small number of studies on such problems were made, and incidental information regarding validity was obtained in a few primarily factor-analytical studies. The outcomes are related in Chapter 10.

Such an extensive program of research is necessarily the work of many hands and many brains. It would be most ungracious and unfair not to mention by name at least those who served as study leaders, each of whom had direct responsibility for conducting one or more major investigations. In alphabetical order, they were Myron S. Allen, Raymond M. Berger, Paul A. Bradley, Stephen W. Brown, Paul R. Christensen, Anna B. Cox, Jack L. Dunham, James W. Frick, Sheldon F. Gardner, Arthur Gershon, Moana Hendricks, Alfred F. Hertzka, John R. Hills, Ralph Hoepfner, Kaaren I. Hoffman, Norman W. Kettner, Alvin Marks, Philip R. Merrifield, Kazuo Nihira, Maureen O'Sullivan, Hugh Petersen, Mary L. Tenopyr, and Robert C. Wilson. Special mention should be made of Paul R. Christensen, Philip R. Merrifield, and Ralph Hoepfner, who also served as assistant director, successively, during the course of the program. Prof. Guilford served as responsible investigator and director throughout.

Enough cannot be said in acknowledgement of the financial support that made the research program possible. The Personnel and Training Branch of the Psychological Sciences Division of the U.S. Office of Naval Research provided continuity by its support throughout the 20 years. The personal interests of Drs. John T. Wilson, Denzel D. Smith, Glenn L. Bryan, John Nagay, and Victor Fields have been deeply appreciated. Other financial support from time to time, with material additions to the total, came from the U.S. Department of Health, Education, and Welfare's Office of Education and from the National Science Foundation.

Acknowledgement is also due to agencies in the Department of Defense for providing material assistance in the administration of test batteries during the early years. Specifically, one of these organizations was the U.S. Air Force's Personnel Research Laboratory, at Lackland Air Force Base, Texas, in connection with which thanks must be given to Drs. John T. Dailey, Lloyd G. Humphreys, J. W. Bowles, and William B. Leczner. Dr. Malcolm J. Williams made possible the administration of two test batteries at the U.S. Coast Guard Academy, at New London, Connecticut. A number of batteries were administered to aviation cadets at the U.S. Naval Air Station, Pensacola, Florida, through the generosity of Drs. Wilse B. Webb, Henry A. Imus, and Rosalie Ambler. One validation study employed officers of the U.S. Marine Corps, at Camp Pendleton, California, as subjects.

Most of the later analyses employed subjects from public high schools in Los Angeles, Claremont, Burbank, Pasadena, Manhattan Beach, La Puente, Riverside, Lakewood, and Fullerton, California. One battery was administered to the students of architecture at the University of Illinois, Chicago Circle Campus.

Numerous subjects for pretesting were supplied from classes in psychology and other academic subjects at the University of Southern California and other local institutions. We are much indebted to persons, too numerous to mention, who thus contributed to progress in the research program. We trust that they and the thousands of examinees who contributed their time to making tests derived some benefits from the experience. Many high school students were furnished some feedback information on how well they had performed. All subjects, military and nonmilitary, earned our gratitude. We only hope that they or their children will benefit from the social values deriving from what they did.

J. P. Guilford
Ralph Hoepfner

ONE

BACKGROUND OF THE APTITUDES RESEARCH PROJECT

Although this book is primarily concerned with the substantive outcomes of approximately 20 years of research on intellectual abilities by the Aptitudes Research Project at the University of Southern California, we shall have to give some attention to the methods and procedures employed. This is true because findings are everywhere best interpreted in the light of methods by which they were derived, and frequent references in this volume will be made to those methods. Most of the information about the method of factor analysis and about the special kinds of application that have been made in the Project research will be given in later chapters. In this chapter we shall consider the origins of factor analysis, the pre-Project applications to the investigation of intellectual abilities, and the general plans and operations that prevailed in the Aptitudes Research Project.

ORIGINS OF FACTOR ANALYSIS AND FACTORS
The Invention of Factor Analysis

Although Charles Spearman has been credited with being the father of factor analysis, and this accreditation still applies so far as factor analysis in psychology is concerned, Karl Pearson (1901) had previously proposed the mathematical basis for this approach to data reduction. Spearman (1904) is well known for his proposal of a two-factor theory of intelligence, or, more precisely stated, a two-factor theory of intelligence tests. He proposed that all tests of an intellectual character have one variable in common, namely a component "*g.*" Every intellectual test measures individual differences in *g* to some extent. Some are stronger or more pure measures than others. The presence of a *g* factor in intellectual tests implies positive intercorrelations among all such tests, no zero or negative correlations being possible except by chance. The other component or variable measured by each test, Spearman originally believed, is a specific component unique to that particular test. No other test shares that component (except another form of the same test), and it contributes nothing to intercorrelations.

It was not long, however, until experiences with intercorrelations among tests showed that some groups of tests intercorrelated more strongly than could be accounted for on the basis of the strengths or loadings of *g* in those tests. The tests of a group thus had something in common other than *g,* and such a variable in common was called a "group factor," since it applies to a certain group of tests. Examples of such groups of tests were those concerned with space problems, knowledge of words, and operations with numbers. The group factors thus differentiated sets of tests usually in accordance with the kind of information involved. In later chapters we shall see that such distinctions are accounted for in terms of a more general theory of intelligence and that differentiations of abilities have gone much further. Spearman and his followers were very much inclined to downgrade the importance of their group factors, and to keep the list of such recognized factors quite small. On the other hand, they played up the importance of *g.* This was especially true of Cyril Burt, Philip E. Vernon, and Raymond B. Cattell.

Multiple-Factor Theory and Methods

There were others who reversed the relative importance of *g* and the group factors. Among them were Maxwell Garnett, T. L. Kelley, and L. L. Thurstone. Garnett (1919) was perhaps first to break with the prevailing doctrine of *g* and the methods of analysis by which the strengths of *g* in various tests were determined from their intercorrelations. With attention focused on the "group" factors, and assuming a state of affairs possibly without *g,* investigators developed new methods for the factoring of correlation matrices (tables of intercorrelations). The most successful of these methods, known originally as the "method of principal components," was developed by Hotelling (1933). Hotelling's method of extracting factors was not employed very much until electronic computers came into use. Today, with modifications, and known as the "principal-factor method," it is the most commonly used procedure.

It was L. L. Thurstone who popularized multiple-factor theory and methods in psychology. Geometrically, the multiple-factor model is a set of dimensions or vectors extending from the same origin, each vector representing a common factor. The dimensions are often considered to be orthogonal (mutually at right angles), but they need not be. When at other angles they are known as "oblique." A set of factor vectors provides a reference frame in an n-dimensional common-factor space. Each experimental test variable is also represented by a vector of its own, lying in mathematical relations to the factor vectors within the common-factor space.

The nearer to a certain factor vector a test vector lies, the greater is the involvement of the test with that factor, the greater is its "loading" on that factor. A factor loading is also the correlation between a test (an empirical variable) and the factor (a purely ideal variable). The number of common factors is expected to be smaller than the number of tests; hence the use of factor scores should provide considerable economy in the quantitative descriptions of individuals. This is one of a number of advantages in the use of factor variables.

A set of tests and their common factors, with the relations between tests and their factors, as indicated by factor loadings, constitutes a "factor structure." The factor structure is largely determined by the intercorrelations among the tests. The intercorrelations are the empirical data, the observed facts. Except for sampling errors in the correlation coefficients, when all common factors are accounted for, the table of factor loadings (known as a "factor matrix") represents all the essential information provided by the correlation matrix. Allowing for the errors just mentioned, the correlation matrix can be readily reproduced from the factor matrix.

But producing the factor matrix from the correlation matrix is *not* so easy. In order to keep the computational steps within practical limits, before high-speed computers were available, Thurstone developed his "centroid method" for extracting factors from the correlation matrix. Burt proposed essentially the same procedure, calling it the "summation method." By whatever method the factors are extracted, including Hotelling's principal-factor method, the factors that emerge are of a purely mathematical nature, probably none representing a psychological variable exactly. It is possible to bring the reference frame given by the factor vectors into positions that do represent the psychological factors rather well, by a process of "rotation of axes." The intercorrelations describe a configuration of test vectors, each vector being more or less close to all the others in its direction from the origin. The mathematical-factor vectors have the same origin, and rotating them about that point as a pivot can bring them into positions that make them psychologically meaningful.

Unfortunately, there are an infinite number of possible positions for the factor vectors, a fact that has caused no end of trouble in factor analysis. No completely satisfactory mathematical criterion has as yet been developed to tell us exactly where the axes should be rotated in order to give a "correct" solution. In dealing with tests of abilities, two guides have been used. The criterion of "positive manifold" means that factor loadings should be positive or zero, not negative, except by chance. The logic for this is that a genuine negative loading would mean that the more of the ability an individual has, the more poorly he would do on the test. It is reasonable to expect that, if they contribute at all, abilities should be positive contributors to success on tests.

As another criterion of where to rotate, Thurstone suggested the condition of "simple structure." In a simple structure, the axes are so located that, in general, there should be a maximum number of zero loadings. The simple-structure criterion also means that each test should be loaded substantially on as few factors as possible. In applying this criterion, loadings between −.10 and +.10 can readily be regarded as zero. In considering the number of factors on which each test is "substantially" loaded, only loadings of .30 and higher are commonly regarded as "significant." Loadings between .10 and .30 are in a kind of twilight zone.

A number of attempts have been made to give simple-structure mathematical specifications; and rotational methods, such as quartimax, varimax, and equamax, have been based upon those specifications. But, in the experience of the writers and others, none gives a solution that is satisfying from the point of view of psychological meaningfulness.[1] More will be said on this point in Chapter 4.

In order to improve the chances of achieving simple structure in rotations, Thurstone proposed the use of "oblique rotations," by which is meant letting factor axes depart from orthogonality. Letting each axis rotate through its own angles is expected to permit a better fit to the test vectors, and it should achieve a greater number of zero loadings. Furthermore, after rotations, each oblique, primary axis is taken to stand for a psychological factor. Since axes at angles other than 90 degrees are correlated (the coefficient of correlation between two factors is the cosine of the angle of separation), a matrix of the intercorrelations of the primary axes, which stand for the "first-order factors," can be factored to find second-order factors, or factors of factors.

Thurstone proposed that Spearman's g should be found as a second-order factor. Unfortunately, usually more than one second-order factor appears in an analysis, which should mean that one of them would have to be selected arbitrarily as representing g, and then it would probably not be universal. One could make oblique rotations of second-order factors, third-order factors, and so on, until there is only one highest-order factor. But this should probably not happen if there were any genuinely zero correlations anywhere in the correlation matrix, as there often are.[2]

The psychological validity of oblique rotations can be seriously questioned, so that the notion of a superstructure of higher-order factors may lack foundation. When the two sets of tests representing two factors tend to correlate nonzero, we do not know that this is not due to faulty test construction, faulty in that tests of the one factor inadvertently contain contributions from the other factor. The two factors may be actually independent, but experimental controls in connection with the tests are not adequate for avoiding such contaminations. When there are such possibilities for yielding an oblique-looking structure, we cannot have much confidence in estimates of correlations between factors that are based upon oblique rotations. Without any other basis for estimating factor intercorrelations, the writers have kept to orthogonal solutions. Orthogonal structures are much simpler to deal with and to think about, and

---

[1] See Guilford & Hoepfner (1969).

[2] Guilford (1964) has demonstrated that as many as 18 percent of the correlations among tests of intellectual abilities can be regarded as zero. See also Chapter 4.

they probably approximate any possible genuinely oblique structures as may be needed when more is known.

Early Sources of Intellectual Factors

Before the initiation of the Aptitudes Research Project, most of the information regarding intellectual abilities found by multivariate factor analysis came from only a few sources. One was the work of Thurstone and his coworkers and students at the University of Chicago. Another was the Aviation Psychology Research Program of the U.S. Army Air Forces during World War II, particularly the contributions of Psychological Research Unit No. 3 at the Santa Ana Army Air Base, directed by Guilford. This unit had been assigned the responsibility for development of aptitude tests for flying personnel in the areas of intelligence, judgment, and information, to use the program's terminology.

Analyses by Thurstone and His Associates Thurstone's first large factor analysis began, as such a study should, by his setting up hypotheses regarding the kinds of distinct abilities to be expected in the domain under investigation (Thurstone, 1938). A number of tests were adapted or constructed in accordance with the conceived nature of the hypothesized abilities. From the results of this classic study, Thurstone concluded that the following abilities were differentiated:[3]

Space	Rote memory
Perceptual speed	Induction
Numerical facility	Word fluency
Verbal comprehension	Deduction
	General reasoning

Four of these "primary mental abilities", as Thurstone called them, have come through as unitary variables, in numerous subsequent analyses, but five of them have been shown by the Aptitudes Research Project experiences to be composites, each of two or more unique abilities, including space, numerical facility, rote memory, induction, and deduction. The factorial components of these variables will be mentioned in later chapters.

Thurstone's classic PMA study was conducted using college students as volunteer subjects. There followed another analysis of a very similar battery of tests given at the eighth-grade level (L. L. Thurstone & T. G. Thurstone, 1941), with generally confirming results. The Thurstones felt sufficiently confident of six of the primary abilities to justify their publishing PMA tests for them at three age levels (Thurstone & Thurstone, 1954). In an analysis of perceptual tests, L. L. Thurstone (1944) uncovered another pair of abilities that are now regarded as intellectual. One has been called "Gestalt perception" and the other "Gestalt flexibility" by French (1951). Thurstone conceived of them as "speed and strength of closure" and "flexibility of closure."

In the years that followed Thurstone's PMA analyses, a number of his students made some contributions, by way of verification of Thurstone's

---

[3]The naming of Thurstone's factors here departs from his own names in some instances, using more commonly employed terminology.

abilities and by additions of new ones. Coombs (1941) focused his attention on the number factor. Karlin (1941, 1942) went into the area of speech sounds and music, uncovering some cognition and memory abilities concerned with sound inputs. Unfortunately, there has been no systematic follow-up of Karlin's work. Taylor (1947) directed his research toward the subject of expression in writing, finding some abilities of verbal fluency that are quite distinct from Thurstone's word fluency. Bechtoldt (1947) gave attention to the area of "perceptual speed," but from the vantage point of today's information, his battery of tests held much greater potential for discovering some new evaluation abilities that became known later. Rimoldi (1951) was concerned about the finding of a g factor in the second-order domain, but, of course, he was also necessarily dealing with first-order factors of the Thurstone type. Botzum (1951) directed his efforts toward factors of closure and reasoning, while Adkins and Lyerly (1951) concentrated on reasoning abilities. Pemberton (1951) was further investigating the "closure" abilities at about the same time. The last three analyses were reported during the early days of the Aptitude Research Project (ARP) program.

There were a few other noteworthy factor-analytical studies, apparently not done by Thurstone's students but no doubt inspired by the efforts of the Chicago group. Blakey (1941) concentrated on a few reasoning abilities. Woodrow (1939) analyzed a large, heterogeneous battery of tests that included parts of the George Washington University Test of Social Intelligence, without finding a separate social-intelligence factor marked by those tests. Carroll (1941) studied verbal abilities, with an emphasis upon fluency factors, which were supported by the Taylor (1947) study referred to above.

Analyses in the U.S. Army Air Forces Aviation Psychology Research The Aviation Psychology Research Program of the U.S.A.A.F. during World War II had the primary responsibility of developing devices for selection and classification of aircrew personnel. Among the recruits for flying training, different groups were to be trained as pilots, bombardiers, navigators, flight engineers, or flexible gunners. Four research units were instituted, of which Psychological Research Unit (PRU) No. 3 had the responsibility for developing tests in the intellectual area. After a general survey had been made on the question of why students failed in pilot training at the primary school level, the following partial list of psychological constructs was drawn up:

1. Judgment
2. Foresight and planning
3. Memory
4. Comprehension
5. Visualization (of flight course)
6. Orientation (in space)
7. Coordination (integration of information)

With the addition of the category of reasoning to the list, PRU No. 3 explored systematically all these areas by factor analysis, a rather full account of which may be found in a volume edited by Guilford and Lacey (1947). The main advancements made in this program included finding a judgment factor that was not very well defined but did show that there are variances in commonsense-judgment tests that are not accounted for in terms of other known factors. This situation called for the investigation of evaluation abilities in several analyses of the Aptitudes Research Project (ARP).

Analysis in the area of planning and foresight revealed only one new unique ability called "planning." It was characterized by visual-figural tests such as have continued to represent an ability found more than once in ARP research. Parallel abilities have been demonstrated in tests with other kinds of information—symbolic, semantic, and behavioral—and a better common name for them would be "foresight" abilities. Planning implies some productive activities, which go beyond mere understanding.

Thurstone's "rote-memory" ability was apparently given some support in terms of a factor whose characteristic tests were of the paired-associates type of memory task. There was some indication of a second factor of this type, in tests in which a name had to be associated with an aerial landmark or with a kind of ship. This differentiation suggests that different associative-memory tests may depend upon two or more associative-memory abilities, depending upon the kind of information that must be recalled or recognized in connection with given information. A quite distinct visual-memory ability of some kind was consistently differentiated from the two associative-memory abilities.

The "comprehension" category, as applied to failures to pass the course in flying training, referred to understanding instructions in either oral or written form. This definition suggested the well-known ability for verbal comprehension, a multiply replicated factor. No other unique abilities were expected to be needed in this area, so no special factor-analytic study was made of it. The verbal-comprehension ability came out incidently as a factor in vocabulary tests and reading-comprehension tests from time to time. Much of the student's comprehension in aviation training, however, depended upon how much mechanical knowledge he possessed. A mechanical-knowledge factor was found a number of times, but it can hardly be classified as an intellectual ability. Tests aimed at mechanical comprehension involved also some variance from the visualization ability, which *is* regarded as an intellectual ability.

In the area of space conceptions, two abilities were differentiated, spatial orientation and spatial visualization, which has suggested that Thurstone's "space" factor was a composite of these two variables, for the two kinds of representative tests were loaded together on that factor. There was also some evidence for a limited spatial-orientation ability for right-left discriminations, which may rest upon kinesthetic input. The distinction made between categories 5 and 6 above was a forecast of the "splitting" of Thurstone's space factor.

One large analysis of tests designed to get at the concept of "coordination" (integration) came out with three factors that, for lack of better psychological interpretation, were labeled as "Integration I, II, and III." Integration I may have been a memory ability—an ability to remember a set of steps given in the instructions. The other two integration factors may have been confoundings of two or more intellectual abilities; there have been no counterparts in ARP research.

Analyses of reasoning, which was added to the original list of A.A.F.

aptitude areas to be investigated, gave some rewarding results. The most verified result was the leading ability in tests of arithmetical reasoning, the ability that became known as "general reasoning." It was given this label because it was found at least as a secondary component in quite a variety of tests, as varied as Mechanical Comprehension, Reading Comprehension, and Picture Integration. Much attention was given to this ability in ARP research, eventually pinning down the nature of the ability involved (Guilford, Kettner, & Christensen, 1956). Thurstone (1938) had probably found much the same factor, for which his test Arithmetical Reasoning was high in the list. But he did not identify it as a reasoning ability, perhaps because he had identified other factors as "induction" and "deduction." He thought the common feature of tests for the ability was thinking under restrictions of some kind. For some reason, French (1951) identified this ability as "deduction" in spite of the fact that Thurstone had used the term "deduction" for another factor that much more reasonably deserved that title.

Two other U.S.A.A.F. factors were thought to represent reasoning abilities, at least because they were found related to tests designed as reasoning tests. One factor was featured by tests like figure analogies, and in the early ARP research it became known as "eduction of figural relations," in deference to Spearman's conceptions of relations. Another A.A.F. factor was labeled "Reasoning III," but judging from present information the factor was probably a weak composite.

Some Postwar Analyses

Two large A.A.F. factor analyses were under way when the war ended. The tests had been administered, and some scoring had been done, even the intercorrelations for one of the analyses. Guilford, Fruchter, and Zimmerman (1952) completed one analysis and reported the results. Not much was added by this study to what was previously known. Roff (1952) analyzed the other battery, which was heavily weighted with perceptual tests, and some new findings were forthcoming in the perceptual area.

Two other investigators analyzed the A.A.F. aircrew classification battery as administered to special populations, the battery tests having been analyzed a number of times with male aviation students as subjects. In a group of women pilot trainees, Dudek (1948, 1949) found the only marked sex difference in factor structure to be the absence of a mechanical-knowledge ability in the female group, which reflected the low degree of variance in this respect in that group. The intellectual abilities differentiated were essentially the same. Michael (1949) compared the factor structures for the same classification battery in Negro and white aviation-student populations. The structures were much the same except that the Negro group showed a factor that was interpreted as "kinesthetic sensitivity," which showed up most strongly in a psychomotor test.

Two analyses involved reworking of the Thurstone PMA data. With selected test variables, Fruchter (1948) examined the possibility that there were fluency abilities in addition to Thurstone's word-fluency factor. He found some evidence that there was an "associational-fluency factor" and possibly a third fluency factor latent in Thurstone's data. Zimmerman (1953) reanalyzed

Thurstone's entire PMA battery. Zimmerman's analysis brought the factors obtained from the PMA-analysis battery much more closely into line with factorial concepts found later in the ARP research. He found a separation of the two space factors (spatial orientation and spatial visualization) in place of Thurstone's one space factor. He found an associational-fluency factor in addition to the word-fluency factor. He found a second memory ability, which he called "memory for observed relationships," which involved meaningful information in contrast to the nonverbal information of the rote-memory tests. He found a factor identified as "classification," foreshadowing a number of such abilities to come in the ARP research, but did not find Thurstone's "induction" ability. Possibly in partial replacement, he found a factor that he called "eduction of relationships," similar to a factor that he also helped to find in one of the early ARP analyses (Reports 1 and 3; Green, Guilford, Christensen & Comrey, 1953.)[4] He agreed with Thurstone with respect to a "deduction" factor and on the findings of verbal and numerical factors. One factor, similar to one ill-defined by Thurstone, Zimmerman identified as "general reasoning," in line with the U.S.A.A.F. and ARP research. The common test that linked the two was Arithmetical Reasoning, an unfailing type of marker test. Inspection of Zimmerman's results, which still show an unusual number of tests (sometimes of varied natures) loaded on each factor, and some hindsight provided by today's information regarding intellectual abilities indicate that there were still undetected abilities latent in Thurstone's battery.

GENERAL PLANS

The ARP's program of research cannot be regarded as merely a continuation of the A.A.F's wartime Aviation Psychology Research Program, although the latter had much to do with its early directions, and the underlying philosophy and the methodology were generally the same. The list of areas of intellectual abilities to be mentioned next will show some differences between the two programs.

Areas Selected for Analysis

The most direct carry-over from A.A.F. research was shown in some initial analyses aimed at reasoning abilities, in an attempt to clear up the distinctions to be made among the three reasoning abilities found in the earlier research. Altogether, four analyses were primarily on this subject, and another analysis on problem solving might be regarded as belonging in that same area. Reasoning abilities have also figured incidentally in some other analyses. The net result has been the discovery of quite a number of abilities that can be regarded as inductive or deductive in nature. But with much clarified interpretations and sharper definitions for those abilities, and because of their numbers and their somewhat heterogeneous natures, it now appears that psychology can well dispense with the term "reasoning" as a technical or systematic concept.

The area of intellectual abilities receiving most attention from the ARP was that of creativity or creative-thinking abilities. This unusual interest reflected Guilford's long-standing conviction that a neglect of creative abilities

---

[4]For a list of the reports, see Appendix A.

had been a serious historical oversight that should be corrected. The interest had led to some motions in the direction of investigation of this area in the A.A.F. wartime research when problems of leadership had come in for examination late in the war. After the war, two semesters of seminars had been devoted to the subject of creative talents and other traits just before the initiation of the ARP, from which had evolved some hypotheses concerning creative disposition. The ARP devoted seven of the analyses specifically to creative-thinking abilities, and an eighth that was on planning abilities can be put in the same category. Almost all the initial hypotheses were supported by factor analysis, and numerous demonstrated abilities categorized as "fluency," "flexibility," "elaboration," and "redefinition" may be regarded as having special claim to being "creative abilities."

The ARP's analyses in the area of evaluation were initially inspired by the A.A.F.'s puzzling "judgment" factor. The first of four analyses in this area found a number of new abilities of this type, none of which was clearly a confirmation of the judgment factor. The three more recent analyses, however, were direct outcomes of the development of the structure-of-intellect (SI) theory and model, which implies 24 evaluation abilities. These studies found supporting evidence for 18 of the evaluation abilities. The A.A.F.'s judgment factor still remains a puzzle.

For a number of years, the ARP had no intention of investigating in the area of memory abilities. But some events during that time led to interest in that area. Two other investigators, Christal (1958) and H. P. Kelley (1964), had shown the possibility of memory abilities over and above those found in the A.A.F. or in other previous research. The structure-of-intellect model called for as many as 24 memory abilities. The ARP's three analyses in this area have supported 18 such abilities, and a study of the remaining 6 should be rewarding in someone's future research.

An entirely new area of research by factor analysis is that including "behavioral abilities." This is the area that E. L. Thorndike called "social intelligence," and for which there had been at least one suggested measuring instrument, the George Washington University Test of Social Intelligence. Structure-of-intellect theory calls for 30 abilities in this area, by analogy to 30 in each of the three other content areas—figural, symbolic, and semantic. The ARP's first investigation was aimed at the six hypothesized cognition abilities, and it demonstrated six such factors. Its second analysis in the area was directed at six parallel divergent-production abilities. Although the construction of tests for such abilities provided many obstacles, it was possible to find evidence that the usual six kinds of divergent-production ability have discriminability.

From recent paragraphs it will be seen that, after the SI theory was developed, the ARP commonly investigated the six hypothesized abilities within single columns of the model.[5] This strategy keeps kind of content and kind of operation constant, varying kind of product. The strategy has been a fairly good one, since it has been found generally more difficult to differentiate abilities differing only as to products. It is usually easier to separate abilities in factor

---

[5] The SI theory and model are treated at some length in Chapter 2.

analysis when they differ in content or in operation. But the strategy has the disadvantage that, if strictly followed, it provides no evidence regarding distinctness of abilities differing in content or operation. There is some evidence for the latter kinds of differentiations in earlier studies where content and operation did vary, but in a more or less random manner. There is some evidence in the more recent six-factor studies from the fact that marker tests were commonly used for abilities in other operation or content categories, e.g., tests for parallel cognition abilities when the main interest was on evaluation or memory abilities.

More extensive information of this kind is forthcoming from the application of a different strategy, that of keeping the kind of product constant and letting content and operation vary. One analysis was aimed at abilities pertaining to classes, and another at abilities pertaining to the product of transformations. More studies using this same strategy are needed in order to complete the picture of discriminability of many of the abilities. Past experience lends considerable confidence that positive evidence will be found. In Chapter 4 information will be presented as to the numbers of times pairs of factors have been separated in the same analyses.

There were a few miscellaneous factor analyses, usually in connection with validation studies of one kind or another. At the U.S. Coast Guard Academy there was interest in experimenting with new tests of intellectual abilities, with the prospect of finding improved predictions of achievement of students in the Academy. On two occasions, batteries of selected tests were administered to entering classes, followed by factor analyses and later correlations with grades and ratings of achievement. The factor-analytic information thus gained was largely of a confirmatory nature (Reports 13 and 14). Information on validation appears in Chapter 10.

On another occasion, a graduate student and reserve U.S. Marine officer elected to study the correlations between tests of some of the intellectual-aptitude factors and rating-criterion measures of leadership performance of Marine officers (Report 21). With each factor represented by at least two marker tests, a factor analysis confirmed the factor structure expected in accordance with theory and previous findings.

Near the end of the 1950s, a study of the relationships of certain intellectual abilities to achievement in ninth-grade mathematics was initiated, for two reasons. One reason was that a number of new primary abilities had been discovered, probably none of which is significantly represented in current academic-aptitude-test batteries, but which seemed to possess properties related to mathematics. Another reason was that it was realized that success in most school subjects probably draws upon weighted combinations of intellectual abilities. The study of ninth-grade mathematics represents the kind of investigation that will need to be made with any subject, if we are to know what intellectual resources are needed and to what degree. There were four levels of mathematics involved, including two of general mathematics and two of algebra. Criteria of success were provided by special achievement examinations (Report 31; Guilford, Hoepfner, & Petersen, 1965). Two factor analyses were done, one for the general-mathematics students and one for the algebra students, in order to determine which tests to use in either case to obtain factor scores. Thus a number of factors demonstrated previously only among young adults were also demonstrated for populations at earlier age levels.

A study of another kind, using factor tests in connection with problems of educational import, was undertaken to determine which of several hypothesized abilities play roles in the learning of concepts (Report 39; Dunham, Guilford, & Hoepfner, 1968). It was suspected that the most relevant abilities would be concerned with the product of class; hence the study of concept learning included a factor analysis that emphasized abilities to operate with classes. A factor structure was determined for the tests, and then it was determined how much loading on each of the factors was needed in order to account for correlations between test scores and learning scores at different stages of practice. The results showed how some factors are relevant and some are not, and how the weights often change systematically with practice. By such methods, it should be possible to determine where learning in different kinds of tasks depends upon certain intellectual abilities. On the basis of such information, teaching procedures could be suggested, taking into account what kinds of operation and of information need to be given attention in particular learning events.

Hypothesis Construction

The last section gave an overview, somewhat in chronological order, of the areas of intellectual abilities investigated by the ARP and of the particular analyses and some related validation studies. We shall next consider how the typical analytical study was approached so as to extract as much psychological meaning as possible. It is sometimes said that "you get out of a factor analysis what you put into it." This is a highly ambiguous statement, which can be used to express two widely divergent views. Stated facetiously, it sometimes means that if the investigator knows exactly what he wants to demonstrate in the way of dimensions of abilities or other personality traits, he can manage this by putting into the analyzed battery of variables just what he needs to accomplish his goal. The authors have never known of anyone who has that much psychological insight in advance (without the aid of a theory such as the SI model), and it is doubtful that, apart from such an aid, such omniscient investigators exist.

There is another interpretation of this statement that has much validity. If one does not put into the analyzed battery at least two different measures of the same factor, there should be no expectation that the factor can be demonstrated, by the ordinary processes of analysis. A successful factor analysis of a number of experimental psychological-measurement variables depends upon an adequate representation of all the psychological factors involved.

Thurstone and others have repeatedly warned against analyzing just any correlation matrix that comes along. Although factor analysis is highly sensitive to underlying variables when they are at all sufficiently represented, it cannot perform miracles; it cannot be expected to yield good psychological sense, starting with randomly selected variables.

As stated earlier, in his first important analysis, Thurstone (1938) started with certain notions regarding the distinct intellectual variables to be expected as a result of factor analysis, and he saw to it that each hypothesized factor was represented by three or more tests that might reasonably be expected to be related to it. From that point on, Thurstone let his customary procedures of extracting factors and rotating axes determine the final solution. He expected that, by following rotational steps that would place the axes so as to satisfy the criteria of positive manifold and simple structure, he would arrive at psychologically meaningful positions for the rotated axes. The implicit assumption was that the tests that one constructs for expected factors would, on analysis, conform to the simple-structure model, a model that was not then rigorously defined and that, in the opinion of the authors, has usually not by itself determined fully meaningful positions for rotated axes. It can always be questioned whether the particular set of analyzed variables, when represented appropriately by vectors in the factor space, should conform to a simple-structure form, or to any other universally prescribed form. Rotational methods that have been based upon different mathematical models that are designed to stand for Thurstone's simple-structure condition may also miss the mark where good psychological significance is wanted, because the prescribed model does not fit the meaningful picture for a particular set of variables.

Questions regarding alternative methods of rotation will be discussed much more at length in later chapters. The point of the discussion of that topic here is that, in determining where to rotate axes so as to achieve the most meaningful set of dimensions, we are left with the need for some degree of freedom to depart from preconceived models. Later chapters will discuss ways in which that freedom can be achieved. We thus lose the advantage of *compelling* factorial solutions, and must be satisfied with *permissive* solutions. We may conclude from such analyses that prefabricated hypotheses regarding psychological factors may be tolerated or they may not, based mostly on intuitive judgment. We cannot very confidently reject particular hypotheses, but we can often decide which of alternative hypotheses have more support.

After the SI theory and model were developed, they became very promptly the source of hypothesized but undemonstrated primary intellectual abilities that invited investigation. Each cell in the model determines the unique combination of properties for a particular ability, by specifying its kind of operation, content, and product. Following such cues has led to ideas for tests that help one another to determine a common factor. Following this strategy in constructing tests for a factor failed to demonstrate that factor completely only two or three times, among numerous successes. Particular tests have failed to load significantly on their hypothesized factors, either by exhibiting higher loadings on some other factors or no significant loadings whatever. Such failures of particular tests belie to some extent the saying quoted earlier—"You get out of a factor analysis what you put into it." One cannot always do so, even when the conditions seem favorable. Such failures often teach us something about test construction and how certain built-in experimental controls fail to work. They sometimes suggest modifications in conceptions of factors or of concepts connected with theory.

Success with the use of the SI model leads us to urge that, wherever possible, a comprehensive and systematic theory be developed as early as possible in the factor-analytic investigation of a particular psychological domain. Even lacking a theory of large scope, much can be done in the generation of logically derived hypotheses. This was the case in earlier studies in the ARP. In such a situation, findings from previous analyses are the best sources of hypotheses. Some examples follow.

At the initiation of the studies of reasoning abilities by the ARP, based upon prior findings and upon speculations regarding them, four reasoning abilities were hypothesized, with alternative conceptions regarding the essential nature of each ability (Report 1; Green, Guilford, Christensen, & Comrey, 1953). These hypotheses and their variations, and the ways in which they were utilized, will be fully explained in Chapter 5.

Hypotheses regarding abilities to be expected in the area of creative thinking, as stated earlier, came from rational consideration of what creative persons have to do in the way of mental operations. Abilities for being fluent, flexible, and original were anticipated, with more than one ability of each kind being recognized as possible. Provisions were made for tests that might demonstrate such underlying intellectual variables. More information on this subject will be found in Chapter 6.

A third example of the use of hypotheses is from the area of evaluation. At the beginning of one analytical study in this area, there were two rival definitions of evaluation. One conception defined evaluation essentially as sensitivity to errors. The other defined it as making decisions under the condition of uncertainty. Somewhat in line with the two conceptions were two kinds of tests. The first conception favored the construction of items with two-choice answers; the subject (S) has to say whether a thing is all right or it is not. The second favored multiple-choice items, in which it is a matter of selecting the best (or worst) alternative. The two kinds of tests performed about equally well in measurement of the obtained evaluation factors, so the issue proved to be irrelevant from this point of view.

Experimental Subjects (Examinees)

Kinds of Subjects At the beginning of the ARP research the kind of experimental subject preferred and the kind used were young men in military service. These subjects were optimal for several reasons. For the most part, in the age range 18 to 25 years most intellectual abilities could be assumed to have reached maturity. For factor-analytic purposes, it is desirable to have subjects whose level of maturity is approximately the same. At younger levels, if there is a range in chronological ages, since abilities generally increase with age, all tests are likely to correlate nonzero because thay are all correlated with age. This situation makes separation of the factors more difficult. Another favorable condition was that the military Ss were all of the same sex. No possible sex-generated variances would tend to confuse the picture of factor structure.

Also preferred as subjects were men who were already earmarked for officer status. This meant that the average IQ was moderately high and the range of IQs was somewhat limited. Such subjects could therefore presumably be depended upon to minimize verbal-comprehension variance involved in tests not designed to measure it. It could be expected that in young adults the differentiation of all intellectual abilities would have been achieved, if that does occur as a function of age, so that they could all be detected by analysis. From experience it was also known that testing conditions are generally very good in groups who are under military regulations. The ARP was fortunate to be given testing time with aviation students in the U.S. Air Force and in the Navy, as well as cadets at the U.S. Coast Guard Academy, and U.S. Marine officers. Full acknowledgements have been made to the various sources in the technical reports.

As time went on, and as many new factor abilities came to light, there was interest in determining whether similar differentiations of abilities apply at younger age levels, particularly in the area of creative-thinking abilities. Accordingly, a number of analyses were carried out with ninth-grade subjects and one with sixth-grade subjects. The successful testing and the good analytical results with such subjects encouraged the ARP to seek further groups for studies in virgin areas. At the same time, military sources were drying up as the rate of recruitment for training diminished during the late 1950s. In all the more recent analyses, therefore, the ARP utilized subjects in senior high schools, in Los Angeles, Orange, and Riverside Counties in Southern California. Since these subjects were of both sexes, a sex-membership variable was included in each analysis, in order to segregate sex-generated variances, which have proved to be generally negligible.

Numbers of Subjects The general goal was to have at least 200 subjects in the sample for each analysis, and with very few exceptions this goal was achieved. The samples ranged from 175 to approximately 400 in size, as reported in Chapters 5 through 9, for various analyses. The total number of subjects from the U.S. Air Force numbered 2,820; from the Naval Air Force, 1,156; from the Coast Guard Academy, 354; and from the U.S. Marine officer group, 204. High schools, including the ninth-grade groups, have contributed more than 3,000, and there were 403 in the sixth-grade group. The total number of subjects used for factor analyses was well above 8,000. In addition, there were numerous small groups of college and high school students who were subjects in pretesting the tests. All new and adapted tests were put through experimental administrations one or more times, to determine technical adequacies.

TWO

THE STRUCTURE OF INTELLECT

The contents of the chapters to follow make frequent references to the structure-of-intellect (SI) theory and to the structure-of-intellect model as the basic frame of reference. It is necessary, therefore, that the reader become acquainted with that conception and its systematic categories. The general nature of the theory will be explained, something will be said concerning its origin and development, and formal definitions for its concepts will be given. In addition, something will be said regarding uses of the model, in psychological research and theory, in education, and in operations of intelligence testing. Much more complete treatment of these subjects will be found in Guilford's *The nature of human intelligence* (1967).

NATURE OF THE SI MODEL
In the historical course of the use of factor analysis to find differentiated intellectual abilities, questions naturally arose concerning possible interrelations

of those abilities. Efforts were made to embrace them all in a single, systematic, logical scheme. The first attempt was that of Cyril Burt (1949), who proposed a hierarchical model. Burt thought of intellectual abilities as having different degrees of generality, Spearman's g having universal generality. The first differentiation under g is in the form of two groups of abilities that he designated as "formal factors" and "content factors." Subdivisions of the formal factors include a general memory ability and a "productive-association ability." Under each of these are abilities of narrower scope, in the form of special memory abilities and special thinking abilities. The other major subdivision under $g-$content factors—includes narrower factors of "imagery," "verbal ability," "arithmetical ability," and "practical ability." Verbal ability encompasses a "word factor" and a "language factor." Practical ability includes as subcategories a "spatial factor" and a "mechanical factor." Vernon (1950) has a similar hierarchical model that he applies to all abilities, including intellectual abilities. He regards the lower-level or "narrow" group factors as being of very little importance.

Parameters of the SI Model and Their Categories

The structure-of-intelligence model is not hierarchical in nature. Instead, it comes in the category of "morphological" models. In more common terminology, it is a cross-classification of the abilities. That is to say, it classifies the abilities in three different ways, and the categories of one way intersect with those of the other ways of classification. As the graphic representation of the SI model in Fig. 2.1 shows, one way of classification is in terms of the kind of mental *operation* involved in the abilities. Each ability involves simply cognition (knowing), memory (or learning "that sticks"), divergent production (generation of logical alternatives), convergent production (generation of logic-tight conclusions), and evaluation (judging goodness of what is known or produced). Each operation category of the model is shown as including 24 different abilities, parallel to those in every other operation category.

The second way of classification is in terms of *content*, or areas of information within which the operations are performed—figural (concrete, perceived), symbolic (signs, code elements such as numbers or letters), semantic (thoughts, conceptions, or constructs) and behavioral (psychological). The more precise nature of these general varieties of information will be given later in terms of formal definitions and examples of abilities. Each set of abilities distinguished as to content includes 30 abilities that are parallel to those in every other content category.

Whereas we may say that the content categories describe the basic substantive kinds of information from the psychological point of view, the *product* categories describe the formal kinds of information. Information takes the form of units (segregated chunks), classes (common properties within sets), relations (meaningful connections), systems (organized patterns), transformations (changes, transitions), and implications (information suggested by other information). Within any area of information it takes different abilities to process information in the form of the various products. Within each product category there is a set of 20 abilities, which are parallel with those in each of the five other product categories.

THE STRUCTURE OF INTELLECT

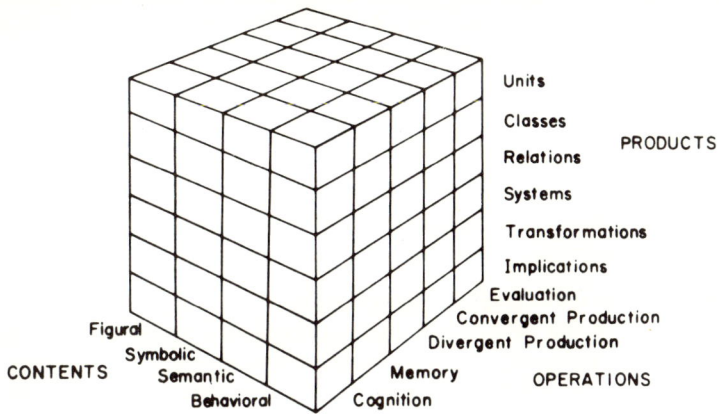

FIGURE 2.1   The structure-of-intellect model. See the text for definitions of terms.

It is by putting all three classifications together in one cross-classification that we obtain the model shown in Fig. 2.1. Altogether there are 120 little cubes or cells in the model, each representing a unique kind of ability. An ability in any cell is unique by virtue of its own combination of one kind of operation, one kind of content, and one kind of product. It may be the cognition of symbolic units, the memory for semantic relations, or the evaluation of behavioral systems. Four times five times six yields 120 such combinations, and theoretically 120 unique abilities.

But it should not be supposed that 120 abilities cover the whole range of intellectual traits or variables. There are reasons to expect more than that number, when investigations have been thorough. Present indications are that at least three of the cells already have two abilities represented in each of them, and a fourth cell has three. The cells for cognition of figural units and for cognition of symbolic units have visual and auditory abilities, which is also true of one of the figural-memory cells. The cell for cognition of figural systems has not only a visual and an auditory ability but also what appears to be a kinesthetic ability. It thus appears that within the cognition and memory operation categories, at least, there may be quite generally differentiation of abilities along sense-modality lines. This may prove to be true in other operation categories, also, for the figural and symbolic areas of content, at least. It will depend upon how much information in the nonvisual senses is processed in terms of the different kinds of products and how much use is ordinarily made of such information in a population's mental economy.

It must not be supposed that, although the abilities are separate and distinct logically and they can be segregated by factor analysis, they function in isolation in the mental activities of the individual. Two or more of the abilities are ordinarily involved in solving the same problem. The fact that they habitually operate together in various mixtures in ordinary mental functioning has been the reason for the difficulty of recognizing them by direct observation or even by ordinary laboratory procedures. It has taken the sensitive and searching procedure of factor analysis to tease those functions out of their matrix of natural operation. Only by constructing special tests, each one aimed at a particular ability, with controls that keep the task from reflecting individual differences in other abilities, can we clearly demonstrate the separateness of an ability. Factor analysis often shows indications of an ability before a unique test can be successfully constructed for it. When such a test is found, it is usually quite simple in its own way. And "its own way" is definable in terms of a unique operation-content-product description.

Definitions of the Parameters and Their Categories

Formal definitions of the parameters and their categories are given below, with examples of abilities representing them and with other elaborations to follow. Letter symbols applied to the various categories are also given here. Their use will be explained later.

Operations Major kinds of intellectual activities or processes; things that the organism does in the processing of information, information being defined as "that which the organism discriminates."

Cognition (C). Immediate discovery, awareness, rediscovery, or recognition of information in its various forms; comprehension or understanding.

Memory (M). Fixation of newly gained information in storage. The operation of memory is to be distinguished from the memory store.

Divergent production (D). Generation of logical alternatives from given information, where the emphasis is upon variety, quantity, and relevance of output from the same source. Likely to involve transfer recall (instigated by new cues).

Convergent production (N). Generation of logical conclusions from given information, where emphasis is upon achieving unique or conventionally best outcomes. It is likely that the given (cue) information fully determines the outcome, as in mathematics and logic.

Evaluation (E). Comparison of items of information in terms of variables and making judgments concerning criterion satisfaction (correctness, identity, consistency, etc.).

Contents Broad, substantive, basic kinds or areas of information.

Figural (F). Pertaining to information in concrete form, as perceived or as recalled in the form of images. The term "figural" minimally implies figure-ground perceptual organization. Different sense modalities may be involved—visual, auditory, kinesthetic, and perhaps others.

Symbolic (S). Pertaining to information in the form of denotative signs having no significance in and of themselves, such as letters, numbers, musical notations, codes, and words (as ordered letter combinations).

Semantic (M). Pertaining to information in the form of conceptions or mental constructs to which words are often applied, hence most notable in verbal thinking and verbal communication, but not necessarily dependent upon words. Meaningful pictures also convey semantic information.

Behavioral (B). Pertaining to information, essentially nonfigural and nonverbal, involved in human interactions, where the attitudes, needs, desires, moods, intentions, perceptions, thoughts, etc. of others and of ourselves are involved.

Products Basic forms that information takes in the organism's processing of it.

Units (U). Relatively segregated or circumscribed items or "chunks" of information having "thing" character. May be close to Gestalt psychology's "figure on a ground."

Classes (C). Conceptions underlying sets of items of information grouped by virtue of their common properties.

Relations (R). Connections between items of information based upon variables or points of contact that apply to them. Relational connections are more definable than implicational connections.

Systems (S). Organized or structured aggregates of items of information; complexes of interrelated or interacting parts.

Transformations (T). Changes of various kinds (redefinitions, shifts, transitions, or modifications) in existing information.

Implications (I). Circumstantial connections between items of information, as by virtue of contiguity, or any condition that promotes "belongingness."

The SI Code System

The code letters for the 15 SI categories and their use will now be explained. Each SI ability is often designated in terms of its special trigram, composed of a letter for each of its parameters—its operation, content, and product, in that order. For example, CMS is a shorthand expression for "cognition of semantic systems," and EFT is the label for "evaluation of figural transformations." Some letters happen to be used twice, but never for categories of the same parameter—for example, MMR means "memory for semantic relations," and NSS means "convergent production of symbolic systems." Keeping in mind the order of the three parameters in a trigram should help the reader avoid confusions. The code system is summarized here for convenient reference:

Operation	*Content*	*Product*
C — cognition	F — figural	U — unit
M — memory	S — symbolic	C — class
D — divergent production	M — semantic	R — relation
N — convergent production	B — behavioral	S — system
E — evaluation		T — transformation
		I — implication

ORIGINS AND DEVELOPMENT OF THE SI MODEL

Observations of Parallel Abilities

To appreciate and to understand the nature of the SI model, it may help to know something about its origin and its development. The original effort was designed to see whether the growing list of abilities could be given some kind of pattern of relationships, as was true for Burt and Vernon, mentioned earlier. By

1955, almost 40 intellectual abilities had been demonstrated by quite a number of factor analyses, by the Aptitudes Research Project and by others, as related in the preceding chapter. A mere listing of the abilities was far from satisfactory as a means of communication and as a guide for remembering them and thinking about them. Some kind of systematic order seemed imperative.

First attempts to classify the abilities and to find relations among them did not suggest any kind of hierarchical order, for two reasons. Although there was some reason to note that the abilities differ somewhat in degree of generality, there was no indication that those of lower generality were subsidiary to those of greater generality. There was no indication of a universal or *g* factor in the whole list; none was loaded significantly in all tests, even all the tests of a single analyzed battery. On the other hand, there were a number of clearly parallel abilities, parallel because in certain pairs of abilities the members of the pair differed in only one respect. The difference might have been in the kind of material involved in the test, i.e., figural versus verbal, or symbolic versus verbal. In some, it might have been in one other respect, later recognized as a difference in operation or a difference in product. Some illustrations will be given.

Abilities Differing as to Content Pairs of abilities differing only in content were most conspicuous. This fact is in line with the early and persistent distinction between verbal and nonverbal tests and between verbal and nonverbal abilities in practices of mental testing. A distinction has been observed for many years in tests of academic aptitude at the college level between verbal and "quantitative" tests, and a verbal-nonverbal distinction was observed by Wechsler in developing his intelligence scales. But these distinctions were not clear-cut, nor were they always of the same kind, and they failed in not going far enough, as we shall see.

One of the earliest pairs of parallel abilities recognized by the ARP was that of "eduction of perceptual relations" and "eduction of conceptual relations."[1] The typical kind of test for either of the abilities of this pair is the familiar analogies test with multiple-choice answers. For the conceptual-relations test, a verbal-analogies item might read

Father is to son as mother is to
A. sister,   B. aunt,   C. daughter,   D. brother.

A parallel figural-analogies test might contain an item such as that in Fig. 2.2. A circle is to its lower-right half as a square is to its lower-right half. In both items the examinee's success depends upon his seeing (cognizing) what relation exists between the first two objects and his showing that he has grasped the relation by completing the second pair of objects so as to involve the same relation. It takes different abilities to do well with the two kinds of items, the only difference being figural relations in the one case and semantic relations in the other. The operation is cognition in both cases, and each product is a relation. In terms of trigram symbols the two abilities are CFR and CMR.

---

[1] The "eduction" terminology was derived from Spearman (1927). Spearman believed that any intellectual act could be classified as an "eduction of relations" or an "eduction of correlates." A "correlate" is a member of a related pair.

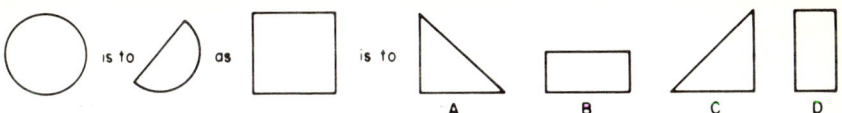

FIGURE 2.2   An example of a simple item from a figure-analogies test.

Another instance of a pair of abilities differing only in content includes the commonly known abilities for word fluency and ideational fluency. A word-fluency task might ask the examinee to list all words that he can that end in "-tion," in a limited time, perhaps 4 minutes. An ideational-fluency task might ask the examinee to list all the things he can think of that are both round and hard, such as coin, button, wheel, ball bearing, marble, poker chip, manhole cover, and so on. In the first of these two tasks, what is given by the examinee must satisfy a spelling specification only. In the latter the responses must satisfy two meaningful class specifications. In each case, units are produced, words as letter combinations in the first case and words representing familiar objects in the second case. The listing performance, with its alternative answers, is an instance of divergent production. The first ability has the SI designation "divergent production of symbolic units" (DSU), and the second is "divergent production of semantic units" (DMU).

Other such pairs, differing in the content variable only, include seeing figural patterns or systems, as when a person is well oriented with respect to visually perceived arrangements of objects in space, and seeing symbolic patterns, e.g., in number series such as 2   3   5   8   12 _____   _____ , as if the person were well oriented with respect to a sequence of numbers. In the latter test, the examinee shows that he has cognized the principle of the system by writing the two numbers that should come next. The two abilities have the SI labels "CFS" and "CSS."

There was also a pair of abilities, in tests of one of which classes have to be cognized among the figures of sets, e.g., figures containing intersecting lines or figures containing parallel lines. In a test of the other, classes have to be cognized in sets of familiar words, e.g., TROUT RADISH CARP SHARK PERCH, and this is shown by telling which object does not belong to the class. These abilities are CFC and CMC.

Abilities Differing as to Operation   Most of the examples given thus far are pairs of abilities involving cognition. A few cases also became known early in which the pairs of abilities belonged to other operation categories. Let us consider now some pairs that differ with respect to kind of operation only. The finding of an ability called "eduction of conceptual relations" has been mentioned, parallel to a figural ability of the same type, and they differ with respect to the kind of information that is related. But it is also parallel to another ability that differs with respect to the kind of operation. Where the ability just mentioned involves the operation of cognition, the parallel ability involves convergent production. A multiple-choice kind of analogies test is typical for measuring the ability to see or to cognize relations. In a test for measuring a production ability, the examinee must *produce* the answers himself. Hence, for the ability now known as "convergent production involving relations" (NMR), we do better by giving a completion form of item and by making the relation between the first two things very easy to see; for example,

    BOAT is to WATER as TRAIN is to _____ .

In answering a multiple-choice item, all the examinee has to do is to recognize which answer fulfills the given relationship, where "relationship" is conceived as being composed of two things and a relational connection. In answering a completion item, the examinee has to recall from his memory store the appropriate answer. Given one member of a relationship and a relation idea derived from the completely given relationship, recall is directed to the idea that will complete the second relationship. It may seem strange that two analogies tests differing only in format could involve two different abilities, but they do. Each type of test may involve both abilities, but each can be expected to involve the one more than the other. Other kinds of tests can be more successful in minimizing individual differences in the one ability while maximizing variance in the other.

    Another example is of a pair of clearly parallel abilities differing only in operation but both involving semantic units of information. Their stock in trade is familiar words. To say "familiar" here means that the printed words readily carry semantic content. One ability of the pair is commonly known as "verbal comprehension" (CMU), which is measured most strongly and purely by a vocabulary test in either multiple-choice or definition form. A multiple-choice item might be

    TO CRITICIZE is to   A. notice, B. find fault, C. decline, D. covet.

The definition form would read

    TO CRITICIZE means _____ .

In the latter case, any response that indicates that the word is familiar to the examinee would be accepted as successful. Since no *particular* statement, worded in a certain way, is required, this form does not become a convergent-production test. But it would do so if we gave a definition that could apply to only one word and that word had to be given to receive credit; for example,

    A missile fired from a 22-caliber gun is called a _____ .

    Another test, suitable for the ability for convergent production of semantic units (NMU), calls for giving "the smallest whole of which each object is a part," e.g.,

    What is the smallest whole of which the eyelash is a part? _____ .

Naming tests are also measures of convergent production of semantic units, especially if the thing to be named is abstract. In one form of naming test the examinee is to state the name of a class, given some members of an obvious class. In another naming test he states the name of a relation that can be readily seen in a trend in a list of objects, such as

WORM LEAF DOG MAN DOOR ELEPHANT HOUSE

The expected answer is "size," the relation of each object to the one before being "larger than."

A more recently discovered evaluation ability is parallel to the two abilities just mentioned. It is defined as the "evaluation of semantic units" (EMU). In a test of this ability, we give already generated answers as to an ideational-fluency task and we ask the examinee whether or not they satisfy the rules of the task, or we ask him to say which of several alternatives comes closest to satisfying the rules. For example, the question might be

> Which of the following objects is both round and hard?
> A. iron, B. button, C. tennis ball, D. yardstick.

B (button) fulfills best the two specifications, "round and hard."

Abilities Differing Only as to Product Some parallel abilities differing only in kind of product are readily seen among those having to do with fluency of production of responses, in the divergent-production operation category. Earlier the ability of ideational fluency (DMU) was mentioned, and the illustrative task called for listing objects that are both round and hard. Other tests involving the listing of words measure abilities known as "associational fluency" and "expressional fluency." A Simile Insertion test presents an item that reads

> The fog is as _____ as a sponge.

The task is to fill the blank with as many different, appropriate words or phrases as time will permit. Examples of completions are "heavy," "damp," "full of holes," "opaque," "soft." Each of these terms forms a connection (relation) between the two objects in its own way. The ability involved is divergent production of semantic relations (DMR).

An Expressional Fluency test presents a standardized sentence-writing task, each sentence being composed of four words, and the same initial letters of the words being specified for each task; for example,

> W_____ c_____ t_____ b_____.

Acceptable answers might be

> Who can that be?
> Willie came to bathe.
> Walruses cannot teach ballet.

The product involved in the ability for this test is a system, a sentence being an organized thought (semantic) system. Hence the ability is divergent production of semantic systems (DMS).

Steps in Development of the SI Model

It may help to relate very briefly the major steps that occurred in development of the SI model. In the first attempt, made in 1955 (Guilford, 1956a), operational categories were distinguished, but with some differences in terminology.

Cognition abilities were under the label "discovery," and convergent-production abilities were simply called "production" abilities. Divergent production was called "divergent thinking." The parallel nature of the two production categories had not yet dawned, only the general contrast between them.

Content categories of figural, "structural," and "conceptual" abilities were differentiated, but only within the "discovery" and "production" operation categories. A special group of "symbolic" abilities was composed of leftovers that seemed to have nothing in common except that they dealt with symbols. The group included the well-known factors for verbal comprehension and numerical facility and two new factors interpreted as "symbol substitution" and "symbol manipulation."

A second attempt followed very quickly (Guilford, 1956b). In this presentation of the theory, there were five operation categories with names more like the current ones, the only exceptions being the use of the terms "divergent *thinking*" and "convergent *thinking*" instead of "divergent production" and "convergent production." The three content categories of figural, "structural," and "conceptual" abilities were recognized as applying within all five operation categories. The product concepts were beginning to appear, but terminology (and conceptions) differed from one operation to another. Six different products were recognized for the categories of cognition and divergent-production abilities, five for convergent production, two for memory, and three doubtfully for evaluation. The names of products differed from those employed at present, as well as from one operation category to another. Those for cognition came nearest to later terminology, with "fundaments" (a term borrowed from Spearman), "classes," "relations," "patterns" or "systems," "problems" (which was later seen as identical with "systems"), and "implications." Transformations were implicitly recognized, but were called "changes" in one operation category and "shifts" in another.

An interim report was made in 1957, taking advantage of additional factorial abilities that had been discovered by the Aptitudes Research Project and one or two others found described in the literature (Report 19). Here the term "production" replaced the former "thinking" term in the divergent and convergent categories. The notion of production of information seemed more operationally descriptive than the fuzzy term "thinking." It was also recognized that "thinking" was sufficiently broad to include both cognition and evaluation, so a more restrictive term was needed.

The three content terms were the same as used previously, including the term "structural" instead of the later term "symbolic." A few more product terms were used, but there was little or no gain in seeing that the same product concepts could be applied in all operation categories.

In the following year, however, the product-concept problem was solved (Guilford, 1958), and the complete model was presented essentially as it appears today. By applying the same product concepts in all operation areas, it was possible to put everything into the solid, cubical figure. Another significant change was the addition of the behavioral content category. This was on purely speculative grounds; there was no empirical basis for the addition, in terms of known behavioral-information abilities. E. L. Thorndike (1920) had suggested that there is such a thing as "social intelligence," and further mention of the idea was made rather incidentally later (Thorndike et al., 1927). Subsequent experiences have given support to this content aspect of the structure-of-intellect theory.

An incidental change in terminology in the 1958 presentation of the model should be mentioned. The former content concept of "structural" was given the new label "symbolic." The reason was that there was danger of confusion with the product term "system." It was realized that a system or pattern has structure. The reference to "structural" as a kind of content had been suggested by the fact that so many tests of symbolic abilities use word material, in which the letter composition is the important consideration, not word meaning. But additional experience showed that numbers and other kinds of symbols (such as geometric forms used as "tokens") were also common in tests falling in the same category. In those tests, structure is not always a feature, except where certain products, such as systems, are involved.

Two 1959 publications showed a regression to the term "thinking" in place of the term "production" in the two operation categories of that kind (Guilford, 1959a, b). The only explanation that can be given is that, in writing for the less technically inclined audiences involved, it was thought that the more familiar term "thinking" would be better understood, in spite of its lower precision.

IMPLICATIONS AND USES OF THE SI MODEL

In Factor-analytical Investigations

The heuristic usefulness of the SI model was apparent even before it was fully developed. In particular, the realization that there are symbolic abilities distinct from visual-figural and semantic abilities, yet parallel to them, instigated a special analysis of such abilities in the operation areas of cognition and convergent production, with some very informative and confirmative results (Report 23). Thorndike et al. (1927) had made much of a distinction between "concrete" and "abstract" intelligences, where the former is probably equivalent to the figural category of SI theory but the latter fails to differentiate the symbolic and semantic classes of abilities. The two-way distinction between verbal and nonverbal tests in the Wechsler scales and elsewhere usually means recognitions of the classes of semantic and figural tests, respectively. The distinction between verbal and quantitative scores in recent and current academic-aptitude tests, however, represents only an implicit recognition of symbolic abilities. The clear recognition of the symbolic category of abilities thus cleared up a formerly muddy picture.

After the SI model was fully developed, it soon became the Aptitude Project's sole source of hypotheses regarding undiscovered intellectual abilities, as discussed in Chapter 1. In an analysis aimed at a particular SI ability, the three aspects of the ability—its operation, content, and product—automatically tell us what kind of tests should be constructed for that ability. This information is not sufficient, but it goes a long way, and in fact, it is essential to the construction of successful tests. Beyond this, minimizing the involvement in other operations, contents, and products often creates other problems, the solutions of which often tax the test writer's skills. For it is often found that if too much latitude is left to the examinee's ingenuity, by inventing strategies he can circumvent the test writer's intentions. The awareness of SI concepts also helps to build preventive measures into a test.

Special problems aside, it can be said that the availability of the SI model has very much facilitated the demonstration of new intellectual abilities, and it has provided a much broadened view that includes intellectual resources hitherto unsuspected. Past and present plans have not extended beyond the 120 hypothetical abilities offered by the model, with restriction to the visual modality of input. There remain the virgin theoretical territories that include many possible auditory and kinesthetic abilities that call for investigation. Where creative-productive activity in the areas of the four content areas of the present model seem to be well accounted for, areas such as musical composition, arranging, and improvising probably rest upon parallel auditory abilities, and areas of the dance and pantomime should rest upon kinesthetic abilities.

In General Psychological Theory

How the SI theory and its concepts can serve as the basis for a new point of view described as an "operational-informational" psychology has been treated at length elsewhere (Guilford, 1967). Only some of the highlights can be mentioned here. There is little doubt that a new tide of cognition theory is growing in psychological affairs. The inadequacies of the simple behavioristic stimulus-response (S-R) model of behavior as a basis of comprehensive theory of behavior are more and more realized. There is more and more talk of the individual as an active, information-processing agent and not as a passive clay waiting for stimuli. There is less hesitation to infer from observed behavior the kinds of processes that occur between stimulus and response and even before the stimulus comes.

A psychology based upon SI theory is very much in line with the new types of thinking. The SI model cannot by itself provide a theory of ongoing behavior. It is a taxonomic model, whereas for the latter kind of theory operational models are needed. Such operational models can be constructed on the basis of SI concepts, and it can be shown how SI abilities play their roles in behavior. It has been proposed (Guilford, 1967) that the 24 content-product categories provide us with a "psychoepistemology." They are the 24 basic kinds of information, which need to be taken into account, in theory and practice. It has also been proposed that the six product categories provide us with the basis for a "psychologic," something for which Piaget has been calling (Piaget, 1953). One of Piaget's major conclusions has been that, in the individual's development, such things as classes, relations, systems, and implications play significant roles, and that thinking develops in the direction of closer following of the rules of modern, formal logic.

Some Traditional Concepts Accounted For An operational-informational psychology is a functional psychology without the influence of Darwinism. It could start by adopting the Darwinian axiom that behavior is adaptive, having the elementary biological goals, but that is not necessary. An operational analysis can proceed without reference to survival or any other such goal. It proceeds much in the spirit of the engineer who makes operational or systems analyses of the phenomena with which he deals. The SI concepts are available and can be useful aids in making operational descriptions of psychological functioning.

Both philosophical and scientific psychology have long been limited in theorizing because they have been dominated by the concept of "association." This term does not appear among the SI concepts, but it is very close in its properties to the concept of "implication," which *is* among them. It is believed, however, that the latter term is more accurate, for it treats the connection between two things (products) as something with distinct informational existence. In defining this kind of product earlier, the synonym "belongingness" was mentioned. An implication is not the "neutral-bond" conception of "association" against which Gestalt psychologists formerly railed. It does involve a connecting link, but it is more than that. The connection and the things connected constitute a mental structure. An implication involves implicitly a statement: "If X, then Y." There is nothing of this character about the prevailing conception of an "association," except for those who added the qualities of "belongingness" or of "expectation."

Having noted that the product of implication takes care of the usual event of association that is said to occur in mental affairs, it should be emphasized that in the SI model there are five other kinds of products. There have been numerous attempts to account for some of those products by applying the associative principle. Classes and their members are sometimes said to depend upon "association by similarity," an interpretation which not all associative theorists accept, but which is as old as Aristotle. Related things are also said to be associated, but the mere fact of a connection, be it conceived as an association or not, cannot account for the great variety of relations that obviously exist. Even if one gave some credence to such lame associative theory in the case of classes and relations, there is even less chance of accounting for the other products—units, systems, and transformations. There is something about each of them that defies associative interpretations. A unit is a thing associated; it cannot be a kind of connection. Nor is a unit any longer accepted as a result of associations of sensations, images, and feelings, as Wundt and Titchener tried to show. A system is a pattern or a Gestalt, not merely a set of associated things. A transformation often involves the breaking up of a product and the forming of a new one. There is nothing in the conception of "association" to account for such an event. It just does not apply.

It is obvious that the six product concepts can account for much more in terms of theory than could the single concept of "association," which, as was shown, cannot even fully account for the product of implication. The list of six concepts is still parsimonious, when one considers the enormous variety of psychological phenomena that must be accounted for. With regard to theory, the phenomena involving products other than implications have been ignored or have been given very inadequate attention.

We have seen how the six kinds of products can replace the time-honored concept of "association" and can go much beyond it in development of psychological theory. Let us consider next the phenomenon of learning, for which "association" has also been the key theoretical concept. From the operational-informational frame of reference, learning is seen as the acquisition of information, which comes about in the form of new discriminations in terms of new products. It is noteworthy that factor analysis has not demonstrated any operation that has been called "learning." Apparently the operations involved in learning, broadly conceived, are the five of SI theory. We cannot say that any item of information has been learned until it has been cognized. That which is learned cannot have any future effects unless it is fixated and retained (memory). Items of information produced (divergent or convergent) in response to new cues may also be fixated and remembered. In attempting to learn, the individual makes errors, and he must discriminate between errors and correct information. This involves evaluation. Evaluation is conceived as playing an important role in reinforcement.

It would clarify problems and interpretations a great deal for those who experiment with human learning and memory if they kept in mind the content and product categories. A crude distinction has commonly been made between "rote" and "logical" memory, without giving specifications of the essential natures or the boundaries of either concept. On the whole, it appears that rote memory pertains to symbolic items of information, which the subject has difficulty relating, on the one hand, and semantic items of information, which the subject can more easily relate, on the other. It is not clear that this is the distinction that is generally meant. The distinction can be sharply defined, as just suggested, in terms of SI concepts.

In investigations of learning there has been little or no distinction made between kinds of products. Again, it has been assumed that associations are the things learned—in other words, implications. The learning of implications is clearest in the case of the paired-associates method of experimentation. But another product is involved—namely, unit. Only recently has it occurred to some investigators of learning that even in the paired-associates method the subject learns units as well as implications. Rarely have learning problems that concern the products of classes, relations, systems, or transformations been attacked, at least knowingly. Investigators of serial learning are actually dealing primarily with systems, for learned order is a system. This does not exclude the possible formation of implications, each one connecting an item with the next. But unfortunately, it has been too easy to conceive of the learning of order of a series of items of information as a matter of forming associations between contiguous items. Intentional studies of the neglected products of classes, relations, and transformations are very much in order.

Other new problems investigated by the factor-analytic methods are concerned with the relation of the SI abilities to learning. This kind of problem has already been given much attention by Fleishman (1966) and others, with some very illuminating results. Whether the learning task involves improvement in psychomotor tasks, the mastery of code signals, or the learning of concepts, it can be demonstrated that a number of SI abilities are involved in individual differences in scores in such tasks, and that the importance of the various abilities shows systematic changes as learning proceeds (Fleishman & Fruchter, 1960; Dunham, Guilford, & Hoepfner, 1968). There are also problems of the relevance of transfer for the development of SI abilities, and of possible principles of transfer within and between SI abilities.

The very old concept of "reasoning" has been worked very hard, but it has never been univocally or empirically defined. Even the modifiers "inductive" and "deductive" have not been pinned down with clear empirical referents. All three terms may just as well be discarded, for it is possible to replace what they probably stood for by much more precise terms from SI theory. "Induction" is in the area of cognition because of its "discovery" properties. "Deduction" is in the area of convergent production because it has to do with drawing firm conclusions. In both cases we could point to six typical instances of each, in accordance with the six product concepts. This kind of differentiation undoubtedly goes beyond anyone's conception of either "induction" or "deduction," however.

Problem solving is a widely investigated phenomenon in psychology, yet it also lacks a unique reference, for a multitude of events of different kinds take place under that heading. A problem is presented to the individual whenever the situation calls for his doing anything novel in order to cope with it, "novel" in the sense of being different from his past behavior. The novelty aspect of problem solving leads us to say that there is something creative about any genuine problem solving and that problem solving has enough in common with creative production to justify treating the two together. Guilford (1966, 1967) has designed an operational model as a generic description of problem solving. The concepts from the SI model fit into the picture very nicely. There are places for all five kinds of operation, and the problem solver needs to deal with almost any kind of information, in any kind of content and any kind of product, depending upon the context in which the problem arises and the kinds of products required in order to reach a solution.

Becoming aware that a problem exists is a matter of cognition, often emphasizing the product of implication. Before progress can be made toward a solution, the problem must be understood; it must be structured, which usually means cognition of a system. Having structured the problem, the individual generates alternative solutions, which is divergent production. If sufficient basis for a unique solution is cognized, there is convergent production. All the way along the problem-solving event there is evaluation, in the form of accepting or rejecting cognitions of the problem and the generated solutions. At any step what happens may become fixated and retained for possible later use, so that memory is involved. When evaluation leads to rejections, there may be new starts, with revised cognitions and productions. Decision making often looks as if it involves evaluation only, but it really belongs in the category of problem solving and frequently involves cognitive and productive steps as described above.

The greater the need for novelty, the more signs there are of creative functioning. This means a greater dependence upon divergent-production abilities, or upon abilities involving transformations, or upon abilities that involve both, where divergent-production and transformation categories intersect in the SI model. Creative potential is therefore not any one thing. It has many aspects and takes many directions. Although problem solving, and creative production, depend upon cognition and therefore upon cognitive abilities, high cognitive abilities alone do not make an individual creative. High IQ is a favorable condition for creative performance, but it is not a sufficient condition. One must also be high in at least some of the divergent-production abilities or transformation abilities, and these are not appreciably represented in the traditional IQ test.

Other Implications It is hoped that these few excursions into theoretical issues in psychology will support the claim of the relevance for an operational-informational approach that is based upon SI theory and concepts. Many special psychological problems should take new directions under the influence of these new basic conceptions of mental functioning. Problems of relations between psychological functioning and brain functioning take on quite a new light in view of the new knowledge regarding intellectual abilities. Problems of intellectual development and of intellectual decline need recasting in terms of all the special forms of abilities. In applied fields where intelligence assessment is routinely needed, no longer will a single score be sufficient, not even two scores, where a richer description of individuals is desirable and useful. No longer can it be assumed that an IQ measures all aspects of intelligence.

The technology of education, especially, stands to gain very much from an application of SI theory and SI concepts. Philosophy of education can now become much more pointed and much more elaborated. Curriculum development should be carried out with much better guidelines. Teaching and examination methods and procedures can be worked out with considerably more sophistication regarding what and how different aspects of intellectual functioning are being cultivated. These and the other areas of implications from SI theory have been elaborated upon elsewhere (Guilford, 1967).

THREE
THE GOAL OF FACTORIAL INVARIANCE

This chapter and the next will deal with more technical matters, some devoted mainly to factor analysis as a scientific method, and others to particular techniques that were employed in the research program of the Aptitudes Research Project. Because of the crucial features of indeterminacy in applying factor analysis, involving communalities, the number of factors to be extracted, and how rotations should be done, it is necessary to defend the particular choices of techniques applied in the investigations by the ARP. Owing in part to the uncertainties just implied, the findings from factor analysis and other multivariate procedures have not received the general credence and acceptance that in some instances they have deserved.

This chapter will discuss problems of invariance of factors and their relations to tests, and invariance of psychological interpretations. Note that an important logical distinction must be made between invariances of mathematical factors that are found by computation from data and psychological factors that follow from interpretation of those factors. The two are, of course, operationally connected. Both kinds of invariance have been major concerns of the authors and of others who made contributions to the ARP investigations, placing much greater value on psychological invariance. Ways were found to achieve the latter, but it is desirable to bring out the various issues connected with the general subject of factor invariance.

FACTORIAL INVARIANCE AS SCIENTIFIC REPRODUCIBILITY

A requisite of empirical, scientific method, in conjunction with relatively objective observation and more or less clearly defined enumeration and measurement, is replicability. Any scientist's procedures and findings should be capable of imitation or adaptation so that the observed results or their necessary implications are replicated within a predetermined margin of error.

In the traditional bivariate experimental design, where all independent variables are held constant but one, which is systematically varied, and concomitant variations of the dependent variable are observed, exact or approximate replicability of procedure and results is relatively straightforward. Standard statistical tests are available to determine, within set confidence intervals, whether the results have indeed been replicated. Variations in sampled populations and in the methods of control and measurement, however, introduce some uncertainties into rigorous tests of the degree of replication of results.

The avenue through which we can determine the likelihood of experimental results arising from chance, and hence reach conclusions regarding replicability, generally derives from knowledge of the standard errors of the statistics that summarize the results. Because the standard errors of most of the parametric statistics commonly used by bivariate experimentalists can be estimated, those investigators can rather routinely evaluate the results of their experiments; indeed, the experienced experimenter can intentionally design his experiment so as to yield information appropriate to the most powerful statistical test of his results. The same strategy also holds in many applications of the multivariate experimental methods. Where the investigator does not go beyond his observed statistics, partitioning his data as he wishes, he can evaluate their significance and reach conclusions that can be considered reasonable.

When the investigator goes beyond his observed statistics, however, things are not so easy. Factor-analytic operations fall into this category, and consequently suffer from its limitations. Although the factor analysis begins with replicable, objectively observable data and obtains replicable, descriptive statistics (correlation coefficients, covariance terms, etc.), the analyst proceeds at least one step further to derive other descriptive statistics from his observed statistics.

Now the standard errors of statistics derived from statistics are *theoretically* determinable. But this determination is complicated by the variety of ways one can lose degrees of freedom so important in determining statistical significance. And as the variety of ways of losing degrees of freedom increases, so do the varieties of sampling distributions of the derived statistics and their confidence intervals. When the factor analyst is interested in the significance of a factor loading derived from his observed statistics, he has to consider the number of subjects from which the loading was derived, the number of factors extracted, and the proportions of variance (communalities) of the measurements that are accounted for by those factors. To complicate the situation even more, rarely is the factor analyst interested in particular factor loadings; rather, he is interested in constellations of loadings, which represent factors and tests.

As may be gathered from the preceding paragraph, the demonstration of replicated factor-analytic results is most difficult to accomplish in a rigorous manner. In fact, such a demonstration has not yet been achieved in a completely convincing manner. This unique and challenging situation has given rise to a great deal of thinking, with some attempts to measure factor replicability, which is known as "factorial invariance."

APPROACHES TO THE ACHIEVEMENT OF INVARIANCE

The notion that psychological factors can be consistently identified over several studies arises only when we consider factors as unitary functional constructs in nature that underlie some types of behavior and are relatively uninvolved in other types. If a demonstrated factor is regarded as nothing more than a sample-specific description of empirical variables or measures determined by their covariations, the need for the concept is voided. This view also regards measures as having no necessary generality within the dimensionality of human behavior. It is probable that no factor analyst holds this point of view, for generalization is very likely to be prominent among his goals. Investigators may be interested only in reducing the dimensionality of a realm of behavior, but they may also be interested in generalizing from the measures employed to a universe of ideal measures or in generalizing from the sample of subjects to the universe of subjects in an effort to characterize all humans within a single frame of reference.

The Role of Simple Structure

Heretofore, many factor analysts have assumed that the best route to the invariance of factors is by way of rotating factor axes to simple structure. A simple-structure solution is recognized as being only one of an infinite number of possible solutions, but it is generally thought to be a unique solution. The simple-structure criterion for a rotated factor matrix demands that each factor be represented by a small cluster of measures that reflect, almost solely, the same underlying dimension, and that no other measures reflect the same dimension appreciably. But there is actually no guarantee, only much consensus, that the demonstrated dimensions are unique over measures or over populations. But consensus on this point is by no means unanimous (see Butler, 1969).

Although it is true that the principal factors are less stable over replications of the same experiment (Cliff & Hamburger, 1967) and are less invariant in that sense than factors rotated to some sort of simple structure, it is still possible for a simple-structure solution to fall short of uncovering invariant, unitary dimensions. This is particularly likely to happen in the case of exploratory studies where no hypotheses are held regarding the nature, number, and degree of independence of the factors. If many measures are dimensionally complex, the simple-structure factors derived from them will also be complex, if the simple-structure criterion can be satisfied at all. The natures of the principal factors are completely dependent upon the composition of the battery of measures from which they were derived, but simple-structure factors also share that dependence to a large extent. They do not transcend the limits of the samples of subjects or of measures (Guilford & Zimmerman, 1963).

Without apparently worrying very much about whether or not applications of simple-structure criteria maximize the psychological invariance of their factors, some psychologists have contrived a number of analytical solutions that, according to various mathematical criteria, maximize the degree of simple structure in a factor matrix. Although it is true that the analytical-rotational solutions do generally yield simplicity of factor structure, they are often found not to yield invariant findings over different studies (Guilford & Hoepfner, 1969). Factor invariance over different studies, however, is the kind of replication upon which a body of scientific knowledge is built.

The inability to demonstrate adequately that certain rotational procedures could guarantee some degree of meaningful factorial invariance has led some psychologists into investigations of the varieties of factorial invariance and how they might be measured. Determining the degrees of factorial invariance in many cases has lessened the confidence that many investigators had given with little reservation to the value of mathematically prescribed rotational solutions.

TYPES OF FACTORIAL INVARIANCE

Approaches to the problem are as varied as the conditions under which factors are determined. As emphasized earlier, invariance can be of a phenomenal (numerical or configurational) or of a theoretical (meaningful or psychological) type. In addition, we may be concerned with invariance of factors over time, over individuals, or over measurement devices. Table 3.1 represents some of the more common variations along the parameters of measures and populations.

Each cell of Table 3.1 is uniquely defined by the conjunction of categories on the two parameters, and each represents a distinct type of factorial invariance that has practical meaning for psychologists. Digrams composed of the initial letters of the variations in measurements and populations, respectively, are indicated in their respective cells.

Invariance with Same Measures and Same Population

Studies of the FF type are concerned with replicating factors in various samples from the same population with the same measures. If the term "population" is

Table 3.1 Matrix of Six Common Types of Factorial Invariance

	Populations	
Measurements	*Fixed*	*Different*
Fixed	FF	FD
Partly fixed	PF	PD
Different	DF	DD

defined at an intermediate level of generality, such studies can be seen to embrace factor analyses for separate sex or age groups or split-sample cross-validations. In the most restricted case, the FF type of invariance involves replicating factors with the same battery of tests and the same subjects, but sampled on different occasions. In this case, the FF type pertains to the amount of stability of factors as characteristics of conjunctions of measures and subjects. In addition to the relevance of the FF type to the reliability problem, variations of its design are of interest to investigators studying changes, e.g., in the development of children (Osborne, Anderson, & Bashaw, 1967); in intellectual strategy over episodes of learning (Dunham, Guilford, & Hoepfner, 1968; Games, 1962); in aptitude involvements in psychomotor performances during practice (Fleishman, 1966; Tucker, 1967); or in the dynamic structure of personality over the course of therapy (Boe, Gocka, & Kogan, 1966).

Invariance with Same Measures but Different Populations

Investigations of the FD type are concerned with the stability of factors over populations, with no necessary concern as to the generality or breadth of meaning of each factor. Illustrative examples of attempts to establish this type of invariance include the cross-cultural factor analyses of Guthrie (1963) and of Vandenberg (1967). Analyses at different age levels is a more common example, where the same battery of tests can be used.

Invariance with Partial Change in Measures

The second row in Table 3.1 provides for two types of invariance where measures utilized to represent the factors are partly the same over analyses and partly different. Replacing, adding, or subtracting measures in different analyses has several advantages. First, the investigator can add new measures that he believes might represent certain factors better. Second, he can, of course, explore new factors and determine whether or not they are distinct from already known factors. Third, he need not be saddled with the errors of prior analyses; he can thus capitalize upon what was learned previously. The retaining of some previously analyzed tests together should help ensure that certain factors will be replicated, and their possible relations to new tests can be determined.

The advantages of the partly fixed set of measures will accrue whether the same or different populations are employed. The difference between the PF and PD types of invariance is parallel to the difference between the FF and FD types. Utilization of marker tests to represent reference factors when new factorial domains are investigated provides common examples of the PF and PD designs. These designs fall into the class of replication that Lykken (1968) calls "operational"; we are interested in whether similar conditions and procedures will yield similar results.

Invariance with Entirely Different Measures

Factorial invariance of the DF type also belongs to the class of operational replication, in part. In this case, different measures are employed in the same population in an attempt to isolate dimensions that are still congruent across two nonoverlapping sets of measures. Multitrait, multimethod designs (Campbell & Fiske, 1959) are essentially of this variety, although they were not intended particularly for invariance studies.

The most stringent test of the general validity of findings is called "constructive replication" by Lykken (1968). In the DD type of design, all duplication of measures and of population is avoided. If we can be satisfied that factors obtained from such disparate sources are the "same," we are then able to conclude that such factors have considerable generality within broad populations of measures and of subjects. Attempts to align the cross-sectional findings of intellectual abilities over widely differing age groups illustrate a study of the DD type (Stott & Ball, 1963).

INDICES OF FACTORIAL INVARIANCE

In spite of the fact that so very little is known regarding sampling errors and sampling distributions of factor loadings, singly or in sets or configurations, a number of methods have been proposed for assessment of the degrees of matchings of factors. Some of these give attention to particular loadings, some to profiles of loadings for factors, and others to larger configurations of loadings.

Numerical Invariance and Configurational Invariance

The most compelling family of invariance indices are those reflecting numerical invariance. Two factors that exhibit numerical invariance have corresponding factor loadings that are identical within the limits of sampling error. If the estimates of factor-loading standard errors provided by Cliff and Hamburger (1967) are accurate, indices of numerical invariance could be formulated, and the obtained between-factor-loading differences could be evaluated with respect to sampling distributions. It should be noted that strict numerical invariance is possible only under the condition of the most restricted FF design, where samples and measures are the same. In the PF design, a loose sort of numerical invariance could be measured by considering only measures in common to both studies, although this procedure might call for a vector-normalizing or other vector-equating device.

It is unfortunate that the factorial-invariance designs that have more general interest for investigators do not allow the use of numerical indices. In these cases we must be satisfied with some kind of correlational index, at best. Such indices reflect the similarity of configuration or pattern of factor-vector pairs and are the best type of indicator when factor loadings can be expected to vary for reasons other than chance fluctuations. If changes in population affect the sizes of factor loadings in proportion to the resultant changes in the variances of the measures, then the vector configurations could still indicate invariance.

In cases where no measures are in common to pairs of factors in question (in DF or DD types of designs), there are no corresponding loadings to be paired for comparison or for correlation, and matching of factors for similarity must be based entirely upon subjective impressions or upon some form of indirect comparison involving an external criterion. We may regard such attempts at determining factorial invariance as belonging to the family of psychological invariance, for which there are no numerical indices.

Indices of invariance can be computed in a number of ways, yielding as many different values. Leyden (1953) has listed six factor-matching criteria that give rise to various indices. Since each index is appropriate to one or a few invariance situations, we shall consider each type in terms of the most powerful indices appropriate to it.

Type FF: Same Measures, Same Population   Two indices assess invariance for the FF case. A *coefficient of pattern similarity*, with an attendant chi-square evaluation, indicates the profile similarity in factor loadings for factor pairs. The coefficient is based upon the observed differences in pairs of corresponding factor loadings and is compared with the expected differences expressed in terms of standard errors. A second index, appropriate when one sample supplies both factor matrices, is a kind of coefficient of congruence, for which factor scores for matched pairs of factors are intercorrelated. The necessary variations in this coefficient are due to the fact that it confounds changes in factor loadings (sampling errors) with subject changes (factor instability). Whereas one would usually determine each of the pairs of vectors of factor scores from its appropriate factor matrix, sampling errors in the factor matrix reduce the size of the intercorrelations. Pinneau and Newhouse (1964) have suggested that only one factor matrix be used in computing the factor scores, so that their intercorrelations reflect only factor-score reliability or subject invariance.[1]

Type FD: Same Measures, Different Populations   A factor-score intercorrelation over a pair of factors, one from each population, for the FD case is termed the *coefficient of invariance*. It reflects both the angle in a population common-factor space through which one would need to rotate a factor for it to coincide with another, and also the difference between the two, at their coincidental location, in the configuration of their loadings. If one computes two sets of factor scores for each population, its own set and a set based upon the factor analysis of the other population, and if he then combines the two populations and intercorrelates the factor scores, the off-diagonal, other-factor-set intercorrelation indicates the extent to which the two factors from different studies show common variance. If the factors are orthogonal within each factor solution, the extent to which the variance of a given factor is common to the total variance of the other study can be obtained by summing the squared intercorrelations for that factor with all other-study factors.

Matching factors on the basis of a matrix of invariance coefficients yields pairs of factors that have some degree of invariance, but not necessarily a maximum degree. Degree of invariance can be maximized by matching a factor from one matrix with one or more factors from the other matrix, but the lack of restriction of a one-to-one matching in this case compromises the intuitive notion of what factorial invariance should be. An alternative solution that fits better with the notion of invariance involves rotating the two sets of orthogonal factors to maximum similarity through either an analytic (Meredith, 1964; Cliff, 1966) or a nonanalytic procedure, so that the coefficient of invariance becomes a *coefficient of similarity* and can be seen as a canonical correlation. Although the coefficient of similarity does not directly answer the question of how invariant the factors are, but rather how similar they can be made to be through

---

[1] For methods of deriving factor scores, see Chapter 4.

a bootstrapping operation, it nonetheless indicates the type of factorial invariance for which psychologists are striving in theory integration.

Because these correlational varieties of indices are relatively insensitive to differences in numerical values of factor loadings, they reflect configural invariance. Pinneau and Newhouse (1964) have suggested the interclass correlation as an appropriate measure of numerical invariance. Less sophisticated measures of configural invariance include Tucker's *phi* (1958), a cross-product index of factor similarity; intercorrelations between sets of factor loadings, which are also insensitive to numerical levels of loadings; intercorrelations between sets of squared factor loadings, which are insensitive to algebraic signs of loadings; and salient-variable similarity indices, which do not presume any interval-scale property of the loadings.

Type PF: Some Measures the Same, Same Population The PF type of invariance implies that factors remain invariant when measured by different batteries of tests involving those factors. Indices of the similarity of factors, when each factor is defined by a few measures in common with the other factor, must depend upon the common measures. Tucker's inter-battery method of factor analysis was developed to yield indices appropriate to answer questions concerning invariance under the PF type of situation when the same sample supplies both factor matrices (Tucker, 1958). As a first step, two factor matrices composed of factors common to both test batteries are obtained by factoring the intercorrelations between tests across batteries. The factor extraction must, of course, proceed without communality estimates, which would nonetheless be necessary to transform the two sets of data for parallelism (Gibson, 1960), and must yield a minimum number of battery-common factors. The two battery-common factor matrices may be rotated independently. Factor scores can then be estimated from each battery. The correlations between corresponding factor scores are interpreted as factor-reliability coefficients, indicating indirectly that the factors transcend the batteries from which they were operationally determined.

Although the inter-battery method enables one to determine the PF type of invariance, it also prevents one from finding factors that are not common to the two batteries. Although this situation can be remedied by an additional analysis within each battery, there may be considerable difficulty in reconciling the inter- and intra-battery findings.

Type PD: Some Measures the Same, Different Populations An index of invariance under the PD condition could yield, at best, only a hint as to the invariance of relevant factors. Presuming that factors could be matched in some way in the two populations, factor intercorrelations or profile-similarity indices could be computed for the common measures only. Of course, such indices might well ignore the major differences of factor pairs. It is here, where the very essence of factorial invariance takes on great theoretical importance, that indices are not available. This situation holds for the DF and DD conditions also. Although it is not unreasonable to decry as little more than a professional illusion the belief among psychologists that they can match factors by intuition of the identity of meanings, this approach is at present the only way in which the body of psychological knowledge can grow.

Intuitive Matchings of Psychologically Meaningful Factors How does a psychologist "intuit" his factors and match them to others? Associating the mathematical vectors with meaningful psychological constructs depends primarily upon the measures highly correlated with the vectors. The common characteristics of measures and what they appear to require the subject to do in the way of mental exercise are taken to be signs of a factor's meaning. The investigator is also interested in those measures that do not correlate much with the vector, those in the hyperplane of the vector. Consideration of the contrasting natures of factor measures and hyperplanar measures aids in deciding on the nature of the factor. Beyond these well-known rules for interpretation, each psychologist undoubtedly develops his own ancillary "tricks of the trade" for discerning factor characteristics.

In an exploratory factor-analytic study, the factors are named in the manner just described. The sole external criterion for interpretation would involve the investigator's implicit hypotheses and his knowledge of findings within the same area of investigation. If the study is in part replicative of previous factor-analytic studies, the investigator may rely on the additional criterion of historical consistency. Factors resembling those found earlier are commonly identified in a historically consistent manner. The degree of factorial invariance in this case is completely dependent upon the accuracy of the intuition of the earlier investigator. Thus, factors named on a historical basis generally earn more respectability (see French, 1951; French, Ekstrom, & Price, 1963), but there is some risk that both investigators may have missed the mark.

When a factor analysis is carried out deliberately to confirm previous findings, hypotheses based upon previous findings, or a theory or model that predicts a dimension, the identification of the factor depends once again upon the investigator's intuition, but also upon the validity of the hypothesis or model. Since in most cases the hypothesis or model is developed from a synthesis of many previous, interrelated findings, it is reasonable that such psychological factors should be accorded a higher status as invariant, meaningful constructs.

HANDLING OF THE INVARIANCE PROBLEM BY THE ARP

Early in its investigations, the ARP depended very much upon available historical consensus concerning previously reported factors. The major summary of psychological factors prepared by French (1951) attempted to align factors found by different investigators, utilizing the intuitive type of index of invariance, the only one available. French used the intuitions of the original investigators as well as his own. Proper qualifications were frequently mentioned, as should be expected in such a situation. The French summary was available to the ARP in its initial efforts, as well as the original reports of analyses, mostly by Thurstone and his students and the A.A.F.'s aviation psychologists' reports of analyses, as mentioned in the preceding chapters. Although looking for verifications of factors reported earlier, the ARP was alert to discrepancies that called for reinterpretations and reexaminations.

Some of the abilities hypothesized to comprise the SI model have histories to be found in sources such as French's summary. The SI model has accounted for most early historical factors in two ways. Some newly obtained factors were represented by much the same sets of tests as for the traditional ones. Some other test sets for traditional factors that did not fit into the SI model have been broken up into two or more less extensive sets by ARP research, indicating less general psychological factors that do fit into the model. Instances of both kinds are mentioned in the preceding chapters, and they will be treated in greater detail in the chapters to follow.

The majority of the analyses in the ARP program were in the PF category, with partial changes in test batteries but with two fixed populations—young, male adults in military service and senior high school students. Other minor population changes involved several ninth-grade groups and one sixth-grade sample. There were some instances of the DF design, also some of the PD and even DD designs. Consequently, most of the numerical indices of invariance could not reasonably be applied. Of the very few instances of the FD type in which one or two of the indices could be justified, their uses led to unimpressive results.

With the goal of maximizing invariance of psychological factors through rotations to congruence, the use of any applicable index of invariance would smack of a self-fulfilling prophecy. The next chapter will relate how, with the most favorable selection of measures, at least after the SI model became available, and with rotations of axes guided by theoretical considerations, identifications of hypothesized abilities were forthcoming in 93 percent of the attempts to demonstrate them. This compares with a "batting average" of only 32 percent, when selection of measures was just as favorable but rotations were made toward a mathematically described criterion of simple structure. In the latter approach, not only were the SI abilities mostly missed but there was very little invariance of psychological factors of any kind over 31 analyses. General impressions of the levels of psychological invariance achieved in the 31 analyses by theory-oriented analyses can be gained by inspection of the major tables of factor loadings in Chapters 5 through 9.

FOUR
METHODS OF ANALYSIS

The invariant SI abilities with which this book is largely concerned are not in the same category as new factorial dimensions reported from exploratory analyses. Although many of the aptitude factors to be discussed are original confirmations of experimental hypotheses, particularly from the more recent analyses, those from reanalyses of earlier studies are often products of a clear "bootstrapping" operation. In the latter case, the circularity of events is like this: Results of early exploratory analyses, which started with systematic but not fully intercoordinated hypotheses, gave rise logically to the SI model, which was then utilized not only as the basis for all further hypotheses, but also as the criterion of what should have been found in the early studies.

Although this iterative procedure does not follow orthodox experimental method, it is a way in which major models or theories can be indirectly tested. The question was asked: Can the refined model account for previous findings as well as predict new ones? The choice of previous data to use in the post hoc validations was not difficult to make. The data from previous research of the

Aptitudes Research Project not only were readily available, but were more than moderately relevant to the hypotheses to be tested. A more crucial test, and by far more complex to carry out, of systematically validating the SI model against other factor-analytic data in the literature had to be delayed.

The aim of this chapter is to outline, step by step, the analytical procedures employed, to defend their use, and to present some of the methodological consequences of special interest. Since the methods of development of score variables (test instruments and scoring procedures) are described in the original sources, and are quite orthodox, the account of methods here will begin with the

Table 4.1   Tests Combined into Composite Variates, Listed by Reports

Report Number	Test Description
8	Numerical Operations test, parts I and II
9	Syllogisms I and Syllogisms II
12	Outlining, parts I and II
17	Word Listing I and Word Listing II Controlled Associations IIIa, IIIb, IIIc, IIId, and IIIe Thing Listing I, Thing Listing II, and Thing Listing III Two-word Combinations–First Letters, and Four-word Combinations–First Letters
18	Apparatus test, drastic scoring and minor scoring Cartoons, parts I and II Seeing Problems, parts I and II Verbal Analogies I, parts I and II Verbal Classification, parts I and II Vocabulary Completion, parts I and II
27	Alternate Uses, parts I and II Consequences (obvious), parts A and B Consequences (remote), parts A and B Expressional Fluency, parts A and B Plot Titles (clever), parts I and II Plot Titles (nonclever), parts I and II Seeing Problems, parts A and B Utility Test, parts I and II
32	Commonsense Judgment I and Commonsense Judgment II Pertinent Questions, parts I and II Possible Jobs, parts I and II Similarities, parts I and II Verbal Analogies I, parts I and II Verbal Classification, parts I and II

problems of variable selection and intercorrelation and will continue with the procedures for factor extraction, axis rotation, and factor interpretation. Incidental multivariate procedures of regression of criterion variables on factor scores, computation of factor scores, and projection of variables into a predetermined factor space will conclude the technical discussions.

PREPARATION OF THE EARLIER DATA FOR REANALYSES

All the analyses to be reported are based upon correlation coefficients given in the original research reports (see Appendix A for the list). This choice was partly for the reason that some of the raw-score data were no longer retrievable and partly because checking of the correlations in cases where the basic information was available showed uniform accuracy.

It was decided early that not all the variables analyzed in the early studies should be included in the reanalyses. Some analyzed variables were inappropriate for finding common factors of any sort, or for finding factors representing intellectual abilities. Such variables were either omitted or combined with other variables, as reported in Tables 4.1 and 4.2

In some early studies, limitations in testing times or special features in experimental designs for certain analyses led to the inclusion of pairs or small sets of tests of greater similarity than should ordinarily be tolerated in factor analyses. Sometimes the same tests were systematically varied in order to test special hypotheses concerning the nature of certain abilities and how they could best be measured. In other cases, particularly when the tests were administered to younger populations, part scores were independently introduced in the analyses, in order to cover the largest number of factors in limited time. In both cases, there was high probability that components of specific variances would distort common-factor loadings for the factors directly concerned and perhaps exert indirect distortions, or bring out specific components as additional common factors. Many of these effects were recognized and pointed out in the earlier reports. The desire was to avoid them in the reanalyses. To this end, both authors inspected each battery of tests before an analysis was initiated, arriving independently at decisions as to which variables should be combined and which omitted.

Since raw scores were not utilized, the combining of variables was accomplished by calculating new correlation coefficients that would reflect the correlational patterns of unweighted sums of composites. The formula used for this procedure was

$$r_{cs} = \frac{\sum_{i=1}^{n} r_{ci}\sigma_i}{\sqrt{\sum_{i=1}^{n} \sigma_i^2 + 2\sum_{i=1}^{n} r_{ij}\sigma_i\sigma_j}} \qquad (4.1)$$

where r_{ci} = correlation between an outside variable (c) and a component (i) of the new composite

σ_i = standard deviation of component (i)

r_{ij} = correlation between each pair of components, where $i > j$ (See Guilford, 1965, p. 427.)

The variables combined and the reports pertaining to them are listed in Table 4.1.

As mentioned earlier, some tests were deleted from the analyses before those analyses were started. This was done on the basis of information derived from the original analyses and from knowledge of the nature of SI abilities. The most frequent reason for a deletion was that the test would not have aided in the definition of intellectual-ability factors. All variables designed to reflect specific learned skills, biographical information, psychomotor skills, basic perceptual processes, measurements of achievement, performance ratings, and composites of tests were commonly eliminated.

Among the remaining test variables, all representing intellectual abilities, further deletions were made of tests that were judged to be too complex factorially to help define uniquely any dimension. Had such complex tests remained in the reanalyses, they would have had large communalities, sharing some common-factor variances with many different tests. A consequence might be too much influence on the locations of factor axes in wrong places. Another consequence might be significant loadings on several factors, thus minimizing the clean appearance of an otherwise simple-structure matrix.

Other tests were eliminated because they were known to be weak measures of their leading factors and were the sole representatives of those factors in their particular studies. Had such a variable remained in an analysis, the result would be, at best, a very weak singlet that could not be named. At worst, by virtue of some chance-inflated correlation, it could have helped to generate the appearance of an uninterpretable doublet, or it could have gone significantly along with the tests for some other factor. Either of the latter outcomes would have reduced the degree of invariance to be found. All the deleted variables, the reports in which they appeared, and reasons for deletion are listed in Table 4.2.

APPLICATION OF UNIFORM ANALYTICAL PROCEDURES

Factor Extractions

All 31 correlation matrices[1] were submitted to the BMDO3M factor-analytic program for principal-factor[2] extractions.[3] For the initial extraction, the squared multiple correlation (SMC) for each variable, with all other variables serving as predictors, was inserted into the major diagonal to serve as a tentative communality estimate for that variable. Since the SMC is a lower-bound estimate of

---

[1] Test names, correlation matrices, principal-factor matrices, rotated factor matrices, and varimax-rotated factor matrices for all 31 studies may be requested from Hoepfner.

[2] The "principal-factor" solution is the same as that discussed by Harman (1960, p. 109). Most recent books on factor analysis explicate the principal-factor or principal-components extraction procedures.

[3] Computerized analyses were done at Health Science Computing Facility, at the University of California at Los Angeles, and the Computer Sciences Laboratory, at the University of Southern California.

Table 4.2 Test Deleted, Their Reports, and Reasons for Deletion

Report Number	Factor-analyzed Variable	Reasons for Deletion
6	Dial and Table Reading	Complex measure
	Mechanical Information	Would have formed a weak singlet, representing CFT alone
	Coordinate Reading	Specific achievement measure
	Practical Judgment	Factorially complex
	Numerical Operations I	Factorially complex
	Instrument Comprehension	Specific achievement measure
	Biographical Data Blank–Bombardier	Weak aptitude measure
	Biographical Data Blank–Pilot	Weak aptitude measure
	General Information	Factorially complex
	Two-hand Pursuit test	Psychomotor measure
	Rotary Pursuit test	Psychomotor measure
	Finger Dexterity test	Psychomotor measure
	Rudder Control test	Psychomotor measure
8	Circle-Square I	Factorially complex
	Circle-Square II	Factorially complex
9	Practical Estimation	Factorially complex
	Figure Estimation I	Might have formed a weak singlet, representing EFR alone
	Figure Estimation II	Too perceptual, not intellective
	Ratio Estimation	Too perceptual
	Age	Nonintellective
	Education	Nonintellective
12	Awareness of Variables	Might have formed a weak singlet, representing EMC alone
	Ranking of Variables	Dependent upon subjective standards
	Mechanical Principles	Might have formed a weak singlet, representing CFT alone
13	Aptitude–Quantitative I	Factorially complex
	Aptitude–Quantitative II	Factorially complex
	Biographical Interest	Nonintellective
	Mathematics Achievement	Complex achievement measure
	Mechanics of Expression	Complex achievement measure
	Algebra and Plane Trigonometry Grade	Complex achievement measure
	Analytic Geometry and Calculus Grade	Complex achievement measure
	Celestial Navigation Grade	Complex achievement measure

Table 4.2 *(Continued)*

Report Number	Factor-analyzed Variable	Reasons for Deletion
	Communications Grade	Complex achievement measure
	Engineering Drawing and Descriptive Geometry Grade	Complex achievement measure
	English Composition and Speech Grade	Complex achievement measure
	Foundations of the Modern World Grade	Complex achievement measure
	Geography Grade	Complex achievement measure
	Nautical Astronomy Grade	Complex achievement measure
	Physics I and II Grade	Complex achievement measure
17	Two-word Combinations	Factorially complex
	Four-word Combinations	Factorially complex
	Word Synthesis Rating	Factorially complex
18	Group Indicator	Nonintellective
	Random Variable	Nonintellective, introduced solely for methodological reasons
27	Predicaments	Factorially complex
	Language Factors MA	Factorially complex
	Problems	Factorially complex
33	Motivation Ratings	Nonintellective
	Sex	Would have formed a weak singlet
	Experience	Nonintellective
	Administrator	Nonintellective

communality, fewer factors were expected to be extracted on the initial run, which proved to be so in all cases. The number of real factors (those associated with positive eigenvalues) extracted, on the other hand, exceeded the number of factors hypothesized on the basis of the SI model. Adopting the hypothesized number of factors as the number to be rotated, new communalities were computed, based on this number. The new communality estimates replaced the diagonal entries, and new principal factors were extracted. This iteration procedure was continued until no communality estimate changed more than .05. Actually, most estimates changed not at all from one iteration cycle to the next.

Estimation of communalities is directly related to the problem of when to stop extracting factors, or how many psychological factors there are in the data. A review of the many proposed criteria for the stopping of factorization leaves one bewildered. For each proposed criterion there are at least two criticisms pointing out peculiar shortcomings or potential dangers in its use. It is interesting that all the proposed cutoff criteria look for decision-guiding information within the data themselves, and never, in the name of scientific objectivity, look elsewhere for such criteria. When one considers, however, that the major criticisms of each criterion center upon the limitations and the problems of extrapolations from the sample data, it would appear that some external criterion, as objective as possible, should be preferred.

Table 4.3 Characteristics of the Hypothesized Number of Factors

Report Number	Number of Factors Hypothesized	Number of Variables	Ratio of Variables to Factors	Proportion of Common Variance Accounted for by the Hypothesized Factors	Eigenvalue of the Last Hypothesized Factor	Number of Real Factors Extracted
3	22	34	1.55	.995	.070	25
6	23	39	1.70	.981	.166	29
8	23	50	2.17	.949	.242	35
9	19	42	2.21	.932	.379	30
12	19	48	2.53	.943	.242	33
13	16	24	1.50	.998	.069	18
14	8	17	2.13	.946	.228	12
16A	17	28	1.65	.998	.053	19
16B	13	26	2.00	.978	.156	18
16C	12	26	2.17	.968	.190	18
17	13	30	2.31	.960	.206	20
18	12	32	2.67	.909	.327	23
21	11	21	1.82	.974	.199	16
22	15	34	2.27	.946	.274	24
23	14	30	2.14	.967	.173	21
26	13	32	2.46	.933	.289	20
27	13	21	1.62	.986	.067	16
29	13	29	2.23	.948	.245	20
31A	14	28	2.00	.971	.207	20
31B	14	28	2.00	.966	.209	20
32	13	36	2.77	.934	.279	24
33	18	50	2.78	.937	.328	32
34	19	48	2.53	.928	.334	33
35	25	59	2.36	.954	.253	41
37	16	50	3.13	.933	.352	32
38	19	51	2.68	.940	.315	33
39	16	44	2.75	.940	.352	29
40	25	74	2.96	.908	.458	48
41	17	47	2.76	.917	.389	31
42	15	42	2.80	.916	.389	27
43	18	52	2.89	.930	.375	34

The SI model served as the basis for just such a criterion for the reanalyses, as it had served for the more recent original analyses. The authors independently hypothesized the number of factors (even the special nature of each one) that could be extracted in each analysis and could be interpreted by placement within the model. Agreement was nearly perfect; disagreements were discussed and final decisions were reached before extractions were begun. Table 4.3 lists the number of factors hypothesized for each of the 31 correlation matrices, the number of variables in each case, the ratio of variables to factors, the proportion of total common-factor variance accounted for by the hypothesized factors, the size of the eigenvalue for the last-extracted factor, and the number of real factors (with positive eigenvalues) extracted, not all of which were rotated, of course.

Inspection of Table 4.3 reveals several characteristics of the analyses and some interesting, although not unexpected, findings. Going down the fourth column, with reports ordered chronologically, one sees a strong trend for the ratio of tests to factors to increase. This trend is due to the fact that later studies (Report 26 and succeeding reports) were designed to test a particular number of SI factors, and singlets were almost never planned, whereas in earlier studies when SI abilities were unknown, many SI abilities were represented by only one test each, and singlets were common. All the early singlets were later supported by finding that their tests represented SI abilities.

The entries of the fifth column of Table 4.3 indicate that, most frequently, the hypothesized factors accounted for 90 to 95 percent of the variance in the test batteries. Where such a proportion approaches 100 (analyses 3, 13, and 16A), we may expect the largest number of singlet factors, and the greatest likelihood of overextraction, with some inclusion of specific variances in the adopted common-factor space. The relation between over- and underextraction and the size of last eigenvalue (sixth column of Table 4.3) is inverse, as expected. The studies with the smaller last eigenvalues are more likely to involve overextraction. The fact that most of the last eigenvalues are in the range .20 to .40 argues well for the premise that overextractions, if they occurred, were not frequent. The last column of Table 4.3 strengthens this argument, for in all cases at least two additional real factors were extracted.

Other criteria for determining the number of factors to be retained were not ignored. Several were tried in order to see whether any one of them might agree with the number indicated by SI hypotheses. The numbers of factors that should have been retained under several criteria are listed in Table 4.4. Of the three criteria more successfully applied to the analyses, Guttman's weaker, lower-bound estimate (1954) consistently underestimates the number of factors (see Tucker, Koopman, & Linn, 1967). The rule of extracting 95 percent of the variance, as suggested by Cattell (1966), and the criterion of stopping extractions when the eigenvalues dip below .30 both seem to yield estimates of rank that are of similar order of magnitude as that indicated by the number of hypothesized SI abilities. An attempt was made to apply Cattell's "scree" test (1966) to the data, but as Cureton (1968) found, this method gave ambiguous results. There was frequently no scree (unusual dip) in the eigenvalues plot after the second factor. It is the contention of the authors that the best guide to

METHODS OF ANALYSIS 51

estimation of the number of factors, whenever possible, is to design the factor-analytic study so well that each expected factor is well represented by tests, and to retain that many factors to test the hypotheses permissively (Guilford, 1961).

Table 4.4 Numbers of Factors Retained under Various Criteria of Retention

Report Number	Number of Factors Hypothesized	Extractions with Communality Estimates		Extractions with Unities in Diagonal
		Number Having Eigenvalues $\geqslant .30$	Number Accounting for 95% of Common Variance	Number Having Eigenvalues $\geqslant 1.00$
3	22	12	15	8
6	23	15	19	10
8	23	20	23	13
9	19	21	20	13
12	19	17	20	12
13	16	10	11	8
14	8	6	8	4
16A	17	10	10	6
16B	13	9	10	6
16C	12	10	10	6
17	13	11	12	7
18	12	12	14	10
21	11	9	10	4
22	15	14	15	10
23	14	10	12	5
26	13	12	14	8
27	13	7	9	6
29	13	10	13	8
31A	14	11	12	7
31B	14	10	12	7
32	13	12	14	8
33	18	18	19	10
34	19	20	21	14
35	25	23	24	14
37	16	18	18	12
38	19	19	20	11
39	16	17	16	9
40	25	31	30	22
41	17	18	20	13
42	15	17	17	9
43	18	19	21	12

Factor Rotations

The 31 principal-factor matrices, each composed of the hypothesized number of factors expected on the basis of SI theory, were rotated orthogonally to a least-square fit to their respective hypothesized-factor target matrices. The initial target matrix for each study was an ideal one, each variable being targeted only on its expected factor. Each row of the initial target matrix had only one nonzero loading, equal to the square root of the communality, which is the test's vector length, assigned to the factor for which the test was hypothesized. The ideal matrices were provided with no residual factors to serve as catchalls, and the targeted factors were marked by two or more tests, except where strong singlets were expected.

In the orthogonal, least-square, targeted solution, the need is to determine an orthogonal-transformation matrix which, when premultiplied by the principal-factor matrix, will yield the best estimate, in the least-squares sense, of the target matrix. The best estimate of the target is defined as that matrix whose rows are maximally collinear with those of the target. The goal is then to find the transformation matrix that will make the sum of products of corresponding factor loadings from target and estimator (rotated matrix) a maximum.

To state that we wish to maximize the sum of products of the corresponding row elements of target and estimator (to achieve a least-squares fit), when the elements of the estimator are the corresponding sums of products of the empirical (principal-factors) factor matrix premultiplied by the unknown transformation matrix, is to state that we wish to maximize the products of the sum of elements of the target, postmultiplied by the sum of the corresponding elements of the product of the unknown transformation matrix and the empirical factor matrix.

Maximizing the sum of products of the corresponding factor loadings from target and estimator is equivalent to maximizing the traces of the target postmultiplied by the product of the unknown transformation matrix, transposed, and the transpose of the empirical factor matrix, since the sum of products of corresponding elements from the two matrices is the trace of the product of the matrices to which they are equivalent.

Since the unknown orthogonal transformation matrix can be represented as the product of two other transformation matrices, one with orthogonal columns and the second with orthogonal rows, the problem is redefined to determine those two transformation matrices that will maximize the trace discussed in the preceding paragraph. This trace can be maximized using the Eckart-Young theorem so that the transformation matrix sought is equivalent to the product of eigenvectors of various products of the empirical factor matrix and the target, and their transposes.

In terms of a matrix-algebra flow diagram, the rotational solution (fully outlined by Cliff, 1966) follows.

Let F = the empirical factor matrix (of principal factors)
A = the target matrix (conforming to simple structure, positive manifold, and hypotheses)
$\hat{A}$ = least-square estimate of the target matrix
T = unknown transformation of F to $\hat{A}$

The computational procedure is as follows:

$$A'F = B \tag{4.2}$$
$$BB' = C \tag{4.3}$$

Compute eigenroots and eigenvectors of the symmetric matrix C. Let D be the r by r matrix whose columns are the eigenvectors of C; then

$$B'D = E \tag{4.4}$$
$$T = \text{normalized E} \tag{4.5}$$
$$FT = \hat{A} \tag{4.6}$$

Unfortunately, the solution produced by these steps does not always approximate the target matrix very well, in spite of the least-square fit. The rotated matrix frequently exhibits gross discrepancies from the target matrix. Such discrepancies imply that, from an empirical point of view, the target is unrealistic and in some respects impossible. Certain discrepant loadings in the initial rotated matrix are examined to determine whether tests might have been mistargeted due to faulty hypotheses, or whether they might be factorially complex and not univocal, as targeted. When tests do not load on their respective targeted factors, but on other ones instead, their loadings in future targets are either retained much as planned or switched to the favored factor, or variances are divided between targeted and favored factors, depending upon the conviction with which the original hypotheses were held. In such ways, each subsequent least-square solution applied to the principal factors is adjusted to yield to the realities forced upon the solution by the original correlation matrix. Correlation coefficients are often very stubborn facts.

One of the minor disadvantages of the targeted-rotation solution (common to all least-square solutions) is that the strong factors tend to get stronger and the weak ones weaker.[4] Frequently, target matrices after the first are given small negative loadings in places to suppress the drawing of variables toward strong factors. Small positive loadings are also introduced in places to help shore up weak factors. Additional pressures in the target matrices take the form of small negative loadings where tests have unreasonable significant loadings (greater than .30), and small positive loadings where tests have unacceptable negative loadings that cannot be accounted for on the basis of negative intercorrelations. After 4 to 11 such iterations, the rotated matrices have commonly exhibited considerable simple structure, positive manifold, and most important of all, psychological meaningfulness.

Human limitations in foreseeing the results of whole-matrix, orthogonal rotations preclude the possibility that the rotational solution is completely satisfactory. Therefore, slight graphic adjustments (sine-cosine transformations of two factors at a time) are made after continuation of the computer rotations does not improve the factor picture. These adjustments always maintain positive manifold and simple structure and increase psychological meaningfulness. How invariant the aptitude factors, thus located, prove to be over different populations of persons and tests will be revealed by results given in the next five chapters.

---

[4] Where "stronger" means represented by a large number of tests.

SOME FEATURES OF RESULTS OF THE ANALYSES

The reanalyses of the older data, and also the new analyses of more recent data by the procedures described, resulted in the confirmation of 98 of the 120 abilities predicted by the SI model. Table 4.5 lists, in trigram form, all the demonstrated abilities (uppercase letters) and undemonstrated abilities (lowercase letters). It can readily be seen that the major areas of undemonstrated but predicted abilities are for behavioral memory, behavioral convergent production, and behavioral evaluation, where systematic studies have not been made. There is every reason to believe that the remaining 22 abilities could be demonstrated through systematic research along the lines of completed investigations.

In addition to this statement of the numbers of abilities that have been demonstrated, there are results that bear on methodological issues to report. One of these questions concerns the number of different factor-pair separations achieved in the analyses. Clearly, if, for example, the factor for CMR were shown to be independent of 4 other factors only, we should have less confidence in the demonstration of its separateness than if its independence from 40 other factors had been achieved.

If maximizing the number of factor-pair differentiations were the goal, one should have to investigate 7,140 $[n(n-1)/2]$ possible separations among the 120 hypothesized factors, or 4,753 separations among the 98 factors for the demonstrated abilities. Reference to the various ARP studies shows that ensuring a maximum number of demonstrated separations took a poor second place to the goal of separating new factors from all known factors that might be related to the tests designed for them. What happened historically, intentionally, is that many factor pairs were separated many times, because both members of pairs were important reference factors in the exploration of new aptitude areas. The systematic program of analyses proceeded on a cautious, logically planned route, rather than a wide-ranging, broad-sampling one. Nonetheless, there was interest in knowing how many different factor pairs had been successfully separated. Of the 4,753 possible empirical separations, 1,821, or 38.3 percent, have been accomplished, each one or more times.

In the context of separations of factors, the perennial issue of orthogonal versus oblique rotations arises. As an empirical basis for justification of orthogonal rotations, Guilford (1964) pointed out that 17 percent of all coefficients of correlation among tests of intellectual abilities in 23 earlier ARP studies were within the interval from −.10 to +.10. Extending that study to include all analyses represented in this volume gave 18 percent (8,674 of 48,140 coefficients). Extending the hypothesized zero correlations to include all those in the confidence interval of 95 percent gave a percentage above the 24 found in the earlier study. The conditions are therefore considered good for determining orthogonal simple structure.

Earlier, Guilford and Hoepfner (1969) made a comparative study of the effectiveness of targeted versus varimax rotations applied to the earlier studies, in terms of satisfaction of the criteria of positive manifold, simple structure, and interpretability of factors. It was found that better positive manifold could be achieved by targeted rotations, for varimax rotations yielded some intolerable negative loadings after rotation. With respect to simple structure, the two methods seemed to be just about on a par, with a slight edge in favor of varimax rotations. But in terms of interpretability of factors in terms of SI abilities, the targeted method gave vastly superior results. Leaving all singlet factors out of account, only 32 percent of the varimax factors could be identified as representing SI abilities, whereas 93 percent of the targeted factors could be so identified, in 26 analyses combined.

Table 4.5 SI Factors That Have Been Demonstrated (Uppercase Trigrams) and Those That Have Not Been Demonstrated (Lowercase Trigrams)

Operation Categories	Content Categories				Number Known
	Figural	*Symbolic*	*Semantic*	*Behavioral*	
Cognition	CFU	CSU	CMU	CBU	
	CFC	CSC	CMC	CBC	
	CFR	CSR	CMR	CBR	
	CFS	CSS	CMS	CBS	24
	CFT	CST	CMT	CBT	
	CFI	CSI	CMI	CBI	
Memory	MFU	MSU	MMU	mbu	
	MFC	MSC	MMC	mbc	
	MFR	MSR	MMR	mbr	
	MFS	MSS	MMS	mbs	18
	MFT	MST	MMT	mbt	
	MFI	MSI	MMI	mbi	
Divergent production	DFU	DSU	DMU	DBU	
	DFC	DSC	DMC	DBC	
	dfr	DSR	DMR	DBR	
	DFS	DSS	DMS	DBS	23
	DFT	DST	DMT	DBT	
	DFI	DSI	DMI	DBI	
Convergent production	nfu	NSU	NMU	nbu	
	NFC	NSC	NMC	nbc	
	NFR	NSR	NMR	nbr	
	nfs	NSS	NMS	nbs	15
	NFT	NST	NMT	nbt	
	NFI	NSI	NMI	nbi	
Evaluation	EFU	ESU	EMU	ebu	
	EFC	ESC	EMC	ebc	
	EFR	ESR	EMR	ebr	
	EFS	ESS	EMS	ebs	18
	EFT	EST	EMT	ebt	
	EFI	ESI	EMI	ebi	
Number known	27	29	30	12	98

Table 4.6   Frequencies and Percentages of Correlation Coefficients and Factor Loadings

	Frequencies			Percentages		
Intervals	Correlation Coefficients	Targeted Factor Loadings	Varimax Factor Loadings	Correlation Coefficients	Targeted Factor Loadings	Varimax Factor Loadings
+.96−1.00						
+.91−+.95						
+.86−+.90						
+.81−+.85		3	6		.015	.029
+.76−+.80	6	8	22	.012	.039	.108
+.71−+.75	18	21	51	.037	.103	.250
+.66−+.70	44	52	83	.091	.255	.407
+.61−+.65	114	90	119	.237	.442	.584
+.56−+.60	286	135	135	.594	.662	.662
+.51−+.55	702	181	125	1.458	.888	.613
+.46−+.50	1,378	206	141	2.862	1.011	.692
+.41−+.45	2,482	234	147	5.156	1.148	.721
+.36−+.40	3,892	228	152	8.084	1.119	.746
+.31−+.35	5,028	272	294	10.444	1.335	1.443
+.26−+.30	6,322	1,003	434	13.132	4.922	2.130
+.21−+.25	6,610	1,442	738	13.730	7.076	3.621
+.16−+.20	6,490	2,351	1,357	13.481	11.536	6.659
+.11−+.15	5,566	3,002	2,203	11.562	14.731	10.810
+.06−+.10	3,912	3,534	3,099	8.126	17.341	15.207
+.01−+.05	2,576	3,113	3,667	5.351	15.275	17.994
.00	406	531	749	.843	2.606	3.675
−.01−−.05	1,262	2,060	2,856	2.621	10.108	14.014
−.06−−.10	518	1,146	1,718	1.076	5.623	8.430
−.11−−.15	258	489	987	.536	2.400	4.843
−.16−−.20	152	202	536	.316	.991	2.630
−.21−−.25	66	56	268	.137	.275	1.315
−.26−−.30	28	16	131	.058	.079	.643
−.31−−.35	18	0	96	.037	.000	.471
−.36−−.40	2	0	44	.004	.000	.216
−.41−−.45	2	0	44	.004	.000	.216
−.46−−.50	2	1	32	.004	.005	.157
−.51−−.55		1	34		.005	.167
−.56−−.60			33			.162

Table 4.6 *(Continued)*

Intervals	Frequencies			Percentages		
	Correlation Coefficients	Targeted Factor Loadings	Varimax Factor Loadings	Correlation Coefficients	Targeted Factor Loadings	Varimax Factor Loadings
-.61--.65			28			.137
-.66--.70			23			.113
-.71--.75			15			.074
-.76--.80			11			.054
-.81--.85			1			.005
-.86--.90						
-.91--.95						
-.96-1.00						
Total	48,140	20,379	20,379	99.993	99.990	99.998

The data in Table 4.6 enable us to make some additional comparisons that bear indirectly on these issues. For a positive manifold, one should not ordinarily expect to find loadings below the level of -.10. But reference to the distribution of correlation coefficients in Table 4.6 shows that nearly 5 percent of them were negative, four of them even more negative than -.40. Some negative factor loadings stronger than -.10 may therefore well be tolerated. We can compare the two distributions for targeted and varimax rotations with respect to frequencies of negative loadings. Before the frequency distribution for varimax loadings was prepared, all rotated factors were reflected where necessary to make the bulk of the loadings positive for each factor. In the two distributions of factor loadings, we find that the percentages of loadings below -.10 were approximately 4.7 for the targeted rotations and 10.8 for the varimax rotations. The percentages below -.20 were about 1.3 and 3.4, respectively. It appears that although both rotation methods call for some price in terms of unusually low negative loadings to pay for other desired features in the results, the varimax shows much more of this weakness.

As Butler (1969) correctly points out, a number of different rotational solutions for the same data can qualify for the description of simple structure. There are no generally accepted criteria as to optimal simple structure. One of the important features of simple structure, however, is the proportion of hyperplanar factor loadings. Defining such loadings as being in the interval from -.10 to +.10, we can compare the two distributions in Table 4.6 as to frequencies of hyperplanar loadings. Approximately 28 percent of the targeted-solution loadings satisfy this definition, as compared with 35 percent of the varimax-solution loadings. Another desired feature of simple structure is simplicity or uniqueness of tests, i.e., each test should have the smallest possible number of significant loadings (.30 or higher), preferably only one. In the earlier study referred to above (Guilford & Hoepfner, 1969), for 12 selected tests that had been analyzed numbers of times, the average numbers of significant loadings per test were slightly lower on the average for the targeted solutions. The very great superiority with respect to interpretability of factors in targeted rotations was pointed out earlier.

ADDITIONAL MULTIVARIATE TECHNIQUES

In the course of the ARP search for SI factors, the factorial constructs have been utilized in various ways in validation studies. In this last section of Chapter 4, procedures of multiple prediction, factor-matrix extension, and estimation of factor scores will be briefly described.

Multiple Prediction

Predictive-validation studies were carried out in research communicated in Reports 31 and 41, among others. Test scores and various estimations of factor scores were utilized to predict criteria of achievement of various kinds. Both validation studies utilized a standard stepwise multiple-regression procedure (BMD06M, of Dixon, 1965). This procedure selects as the first variable in the prediction equation the one with the highest correlation with the criterion, and each succeeding variable is selected for the size of its partial correlation with the criterion, holding constant the prior prediction composite. At each step of the procedure, an F test is applied to the increase in the multiple correlation coefficient, from which one can determine the point of no more significant increases, where the addition of predictors is terminated.

Factor-matrix Extensions

In Report 39 (and tangentially in other reports) the relationships between aptitudes and measures of learning were studied by extending rotated factor matrices to include criterion variables. In this way, the factor components of the criterion variables can be determined, without letting those factorially complex variables contribute to, and probably interfere with, the factor analysis of the predictor variables. The extension procedure developed by Dwyer (1937) and Mosier (1938) was employed. In matrix notation, estimated projected factor loadings are computed by the formula

$$V = R'F' (FF')^{-1} \tag{4.7}$$

where V = the matrix of estimated factor loadings of the t variables on the m rotated factors

R = the intercorrelation matrix of the t variables with the n variables in the original factor analysis

F = the matrix of rotated factor loadings of m rotated factors and n analyzed variables

The result of applying this procedure is to add rows to the rotated factor matrix, the loadings being determined by the intercorrelations of the new variables with the factored variables. No probability statements can be made concerning the extended-matrix coefficients, but the relative sizes of those coefficients and their systematic relations with other variables often lend logical support to their interpretations.

Factor Scores

Two kinds of factor scores were utilized in making predictions, as in Reports 31 and 41. There are two important advantages for using factor scores in making multiple predictions, one theoretical and the other statistical. Correlations between aptitude tests and a criterion tell us little that is generalizable unless we can relate the test variables to some more stable and enduring variable—one, it is hoped, that is embedded in sound theory. SI aptitude factors supply such variables, and the obtained factor-score correlations with a criterion are generalizable, indicating the importance of each factorial ability to performance on the criterion. One practical consequence is that other tests measuring the same factor can be substituted with some confidence, for example. The statistical advantage is that there are always fewer factors than tests, hence fewer multiple predictors and less loss of degrees of freedom. As compared with the method of factor-matrix extension for finding factor loadings, the use of factor scores permits statistical evaluations of results, where the former method does not.

In Report 31, factor scores were estimated by the simple operation of summing standard scores for the tests uniquely selected to represent each factorial ability. Such rough approximations to factor scores have the disadvantage that the representative tests are usually not free from variances from other factors. With no suppression feature for counteracting these secondary contributions, such factor scores are likely to be correlated positively, in spite of the fact that the factors that they represent are uncorrelated. The intercorrelations among factor scores used in the study of Report 31 ranged as high as .50.

In the study of Report 41, factor scores were obtained by a method suggested by Bartlett (1937), a least-square, complete estimation method that provides for minimizing secondary variances. It does require the weighted combinations of large numbers of tests such as would have been factor-analyzed together. Basically, the method takes into consideration not only the loading of each test on the factor concerned, but also its amount of unique variance in the determination of the weight applied to that test in the formation of the equation for a factor score. Harris (1967) and MacDonald and Burr (1967) show that Bartlett's estimation method has the following favorable characteristics: (1) The method yields scores with high correlations with their respective true factor scores; (2) the scores are univocal in that they have zero correlations with noncorresponding true factor scores; and (3) the scores are unbiased estimates of the corresponding true factor scores.

The factor scores were obtained from a computer program that followed the algorithm implied by the equation

$$F = (A'U^{-2}A)^{-1} A'U^{-2}Z' \qquad (4.8)$$

where A = the n by p common-factor pattern matrix
U^{-2} = the n by n diagonal matrix of the reciprocals of the unique variances
Z = the matrix of standard scores for individuals

The multiple correlation of each factor with the n test scores can be determined from the original formula given by Bartlett:

$$R_p = \sqrt{1 - \frac{|J_{pp}|}{|J|}} \tag{4.9}$$

where $|J|$ = the determinant of the matrix formed from $(A'U^{-2}A)$
$|J_{pp}|$ = the cofactor of the element in row and column p of the J matrix

For factor scores computed by the ARP by this method, such coefficients, which are loadings of the factor scores on their respective factors, ranged from the mid .50s to the low .90s.

SUMMARY

This chapter has given brief accounts of the computational procedures employed in factor analyses in the more recent studies and in reanalyses in the earlier studies conducted in the Aptitudes Research Project program, also certain procedures for multivariate predictions of criteria and maximizing the use of information regarding structure-of-intellect abilities.

After extractions of the number of principal factors in accordance with the number of SI abilities hypothesized to be represented, rotations were made iteratively toward targeted factor matrices initially constructed in accordance with the hypothesized factor structure. The dominant goal was to achieve the maximum degree of invariance, a goal that was discussed in the preceding chapter.

Incidental procedures used in connection with multiple predictions of criteria of learning and academic achievement were also described, including methods of estimating factor loadings for variables not included in the factor analyses and for estimating factor scores for individuals. Some evaluative comments were offered for most of the multivariate procedures discussed.

FIVE

ABILITIES IN REASONING AND PROBLEM SOLVING

This chapter and the next three will present accounts of factor analyses within initially selected areas of intellectual functioning. The heuristic categories, within which the earlier studies are grouped, were chosen before the structure-of-intellect theory was developed. The categories for later studies reflect the emergence of that general theory. It will be seen that some of the traditional concepts have had to be replaced as new systematic considerations came into the picture and that a few of them have gained support.

Within each chapter, the various factor-analytic studies will be treated in chronological order. In accounting for each study, attention will be given to the hypotheses that were investigated and to tests that were designed for each purpose. Further information regarding the nature of all tests will be found in Appendix B, where sample items are given, with tests listed in alphabetical order for ready reference. Further information about each study will be concerned with the important things learned from the original factor analysis, where it differs from the reanalysis, with the latter's targeted rotations of axes. All numerical data will be from the latter source. A summary of the factors and factor loadings for tests is given in a single table in each chapter. It turns out that the great majority of the abilities that emerged from the analyses treated in this chapter are in the cognition and convergent-production operation categories.

THE REASONING–A ANALYSIS[1]

Hypotheses concerning Reasoning Abilities

The major source of information basic to hypothesized reasoning abilities included the first large factor analysis by L. L. Thurstone (1938) and a number of analyses performed in the Army Air Force Aviation Psychology Research Program in the early 1940s (Guilford & Lacey, 1947).

Thurstone's analysis had indicated three possible reasoning abilities— induction, deduction, and an ability that he characterized as "thinking under restrictive conditions," which was marked prominently by a test composed of arithmetical-reasoning problems. He hesitated to accept the latter as a reasoning ability. It appeared that he was not expecting more than the two reasoning abilities, which fit the time-honored concepts of "induction" and "deduction."

The Air Force findings led to the conclusion that there are three reasoning abilities, denoted as "Reasoning I," "Reasoning II," and "Reasoning III." Reasoning I was marked consistently by arithmetical-reasoning tests and was called "general reasoning," since a number of other tests, varying widely in nature, were also commonly loaded on it. Reasoning II was conspicuously marked by a figure-analogies test, suggesting that the factor is concerned with seeing relations. Identification of this factor with Thurstone's induction factor was considered doubtful. Thurstone defined his induction factor as the ability to "find a rule or principle for each item in the test" (1938, p. 86). Finding a rule or principle might subsume seeing a relation, but either concept in his definition seems more complex than that of "relation." Furthermore, among Thurstone's leading tests on the factor were Number Series and Figure Classification, in which the rule or principle is a system in the one case and a class idea in the other. A possible link lies in another of his tests, Pattern Analogies, which is a figure-analogies test and which was also loaded on his induction factor. From present-day hindsight, it appears that Thurstone's first-found induction factor was a confounding of at least three SI abilities—cognition of symbolic systems (CSS), indicated by his number-series test, cognition of figural classes (CFC), indicated by his figure-classification test, and cognition of figural relations (CFR), indicated by his Pattern Analogies.

The Air Force Reasoning III factor was marked by two tests that are of special interest here. One was called "Spatial Reasoning" and the other was "Decoding." The former requires the discovery of a principle that applies to the placement of the letters X and Y in series of dashes. The latter requires the deciphering of a code by which letters in words are associated with flags. In

---

[1] For each study to which reference is made in this and the immediately following chapters, citations will be given to particular Aptitudes Research Project reports by number, as listed in Appendix A. For the Reasoning-A study, see Reports 1 and 3. See also Green, Guilford, Christensen, and Comrey (1953).

either case a symbolic system must be discovered, which implies ability CSS. From these results it appears that Reasoning III is closer to Thurstone's induction factor, as he defined it, then is Reasoning II. On one occasion a figure-classification test was found on the A.A.F. factor. This fact weighed heavily in hypothesis formation in the first reasoning analysis by the Aptitudes Research Project, the Reasoning-A study.

The Air Force results showed nothing that might be related to Thurstone's deduction factor, but the latter served as the basis for a fourth expected primary ability in the first ARP reasoning analysis. Four expected reasoning abilities (or kinds of abilities), then, were listed as follows:[2]

Reasoning I
  a. Manipulating symbols
  b. Solving problems
  c. Defining problems
  d. Testing hypotheses
  e. Organizing sequences of related steps
Reasoning II
  a. Seeing rules or principles (Thurstone's induction)
  b. Seeing systems
  c. Seeing trends
  d. Seeing relations
  e. Seeing identity of relations
  f. Analyzing forms
Reasoning III
  a. Seeing common elements or properties
  b. Classifying (in general)
  c. Classifying forms
  d. Educing correlates
Reasoning IV
  a. Drawing inferences (deductions)
  b. Syllogistic reasoning

Hypotheses for Reasoning I In accounting for the alternative hypotheses listed under each type of reasoning, beginning with Reasoning I, it is appropriate to quote from the early reports (Report 1), with minor editorial changes.

> Because of the very general involvement of the A.A.F. Reasoning I in many different kinds of tests, this factor might be a general ability to manipulate symbolic material. This would make Reasoning I a general thinking factor, since thinking is characterized by the use of symbols. A somewhat more restrictive hypothesis assumes that Reasoning I is a general ability to solve problems. Not all thinking is problem solving. If it can be shown that this factor is coextensive with tests that do pose problems, this second hypothesis would be supported. A still more restrictive hypothesis is that Reasoning I is the ability to define, formulate, or structure given

---
[2]It should be noted that hypotheses I, II, and III here depart somewhat from strict parallels with the three A.A.F. reasoning abilities.

problems. This is an essential step in all arithmetic-reasoning items. The examinee must grasp the set of variables and numerical values, and he must realize their interrelationships and their contributions to the finding of a solution.

A fourth conception of the factor is that it is an ability to test hypotheses. The previous conception—defining the problem—is often a matter of forming hypotheses. Several false starts are commonly made before the correct nature of the problem is grasped. The more quickly such errors can be eliminated, the better the performance. Having correctly conceived the problem and having rejected wrong hypotheses, something more remains to be done. There must be a sequence of steps organized in order to arrive at the answer. A fifth hypothesis concerning Reasoning I is accordingly that it is the ability to organize such a sequence of steps. Any one of the last three hypotheses could be supported if it turns out that tests featuring the kind of operation implied have higher loadings on Reasoning I than has arithmetic reasoning. [Report 1, p. 3]

Hypotheses for Reasoning II   The favored hypothesis for Reasoning II in the preceding list was that it coincides essentially with Thurstone's definition of induction—the ability to see rules and principles. It was thought, however, that "rules" and "principles" permit several interpretations and can be of different kinds, for which alternatives are listed. Hypotheses IIb, c, and d interpret those concepts as systems, trends, and relations, respectively. Hypothesis IIe, seeing identity of relations, goes beyond seeing a relation, as such. Hypothesis IIf, analyzing forms, reflects the fact that a Gottschaldt-figures test, in which examinees (Es) have to see simple figures that are concealed in more complex ones, had shown some relations to the A.A.F. Reasoning II factor. It was recognized that the task in that test is quite different from an act of induction.

Hypotheses for Reasoning III   The hypotheses under Reasoning III reflect the expectation that some kind of ability, or abilities, would be found in classification tests, or tests involving the seeing of class ideas. It might be a general ability for forming classes, as represented by hypothesis IIIb, or a general ability to see common elements in exemplars of a class, as in IIIa. There might be a limited ability of either kind for dealing with figures or forms, as suggested by the relationships already found between figure-classification tests and some of the reasoning tests. In connection with hypothesis IIId, it was recognized that in analogies tests, especially if they are of a completion type, Es not only have to perform the first act of seeing a relation between two things but must also think of a fourth member of the analogy. Hindsight suggests that this hypothesis belongs better under Reasoning II, since it deals with relations rather than classes.

An Issue for Reasoning IV   The two-way distinction under Reasoning IV merely raises the question of whether Thurstone's deduction ability is a general one, going beyond formal, syllogistic reasoning, or whether it is restricted to the latter. Thurstone's results tended to favor the broader view, but he had no clearly inference-drawing tests other than in syllogistic form in his test battery.

Tests Designed for the Hypotheses

One or more tests were designed for each of the 11 special hypotheses, which meant that several kinds of outcome could have occurred. There could have been one comprehensive factor that had all or most of the tests designed for the hypotheses in any of the four major groups loaded significantly on it. Today this kind of outcome would not be expected, except in the case of Reasoning IV. In other cases, tests differ in content, some being figural, some symbolic, and some semantic. We can now also see that they differ with respect to kind of product. At the time the first reasoning study was being planned, however, the inclination was to follow the expectation from Gestalt psychology that content does not matter—that whatever the kind of mental act, the same ability would apply in spite of difference in kind of information. The investigators were at that time also unaware of distinctions as to products of information.

At the other extreme, the kind of outcome could have been a different factor for every one of the 11 hypotheses, provided there were a minimum of two good, representative tests for each hypothesis. Between the two extremes there could have been from 5 to 10 factors. We shall see later just how many SI abilities were represented. The actual outcome in the first analysis was in the direction of SI abilities, with small groups of tests determining factors that were in line with some of the hypotheses, and only in case IV was there a single factor for a major hypothesis. Let us see first how each hypothesis was represented by tests.

Tests for Reasoning I For hypothesis Ia, a number of tests using purely symbolic items were constructed, the symbols being numbers or letters. Three tests had the title "Number and Operations Changes," distinguished as I, II, and III.[3] Form I of this test told E which arithmetical-operation signs were to be interchanged, e.g., the signs $-$ and $\times$. Then five alternative, potential equations were given with E to say which one would be a correct statement, applying the given interchange. In form II of this test, E is given a potential equation that is incorrect and five stated alternative interchanges of sign, one of which, if applied, would make a correct equation. In form III, E is first given a single statement that could be a correct equation after an interchange of two signs or two numbers. He has to discover what the change must be. Then he is given five alternative inequalities, one of which could become an equation if the same interchange as he has discovered is applied.

The fourth purely symbolic test was entitled "Symbol Manipulation," in line with the hypothesis being tested. The task requires E to note first some stated definitions of symbols, then a symbolic statement of a certain relationship from which other relations can be deduced. Other stated relationships are then

---

[3]For sample items for tests mentioned in the chapters, see the alphabetical list of tests in Appendix B.

given, with E to say which are true and which false in view of the given statement. For example, given the statement x S y (S being defined as "smaller than"), is it true or false that

x E y (E being defined as "equal to")

y S x

x NG y (NG being defined as "not greater than")

No special tests were designed for hypothesis Ib, which anticipated a general problem-solving ability. The arithmetical-reasoning test called "Problem Solving" was the clearest example. It is difficult to say which other tests best qualify for this category. Many of them do so in their own ways. That is, their items may be regarded as problems. The second clearest example is Ship Destination, which is actually a kind of arithmetical-reasoning test in which the complexity of the problems can be varied systematically. To support hypothesis Ib, many of the other tests would have to come out loaded along with these two tests on the same factor.

Hypothesis Ic puts the emphasis upon only one stage in solving problems, the relatively early stage of seeing the problem's structure. The test most clearly designed for this hypothesis—Essential Operations—is composed of statements much like those in the presentation of an arithmetical problem. Each item asks a question, then lists five alternative facts, four of which are essential to solving the problem and one of which is not. E is to show that he understands the problem by pointing out the irrelevant fact. He needs no further steps; no computation is needed. If this test were to come out strongly along with the two just mentioned, and only those two, the result would suggest that the step of comprehending the problem is a critical one for measuring the ability represented by those two tests.

For hypothesis Id, testing hypotheses, a test called "Secret Writing" was designed. It calls upon E to decipher a code that associates digits and letters. Much trial-and-error behavior is almost inevitable in performing on this test. Each "trial" has its own hypothesis, and most hypotheses have to be rejected.

Organizing sequences of operations (hypothesis Ie) had no good test representing it. Problem Solving and Ship Destination involve such a step, but what was needed was a test limited to that step. It can be said that tests calling for the ordering of actions were given a good tryout in a later analysis of planning (see Chapter 6) and that they helped to bring out a unique "ordering" ability. That ability is quite distinct from that of general reasoning and is unrelated to its tests.

Tests for Reasoning II   Hypotheses under Reasoning II generally involve some kind of inductive activity, for, from given examples, E is supposed to see or to discover some kind of rule or principle, in the form of a relation, a trend, or a system. A test (Circle Reasoning) that illustrates hypothesis IIa (seeing rules or principles) presents in each item a sequence, from left to right, of dashes and small circles, with one of the circles blackened. Which circle is blackened in each of the first rows is determined by a rule, e.g., the second circle in the row, the first circle after the first dash, and so on. *E* is to show that he has grasped the rule by marking the appropriate circle in the fifth row.

For hypothesis IIb, seeing systems, the Letter Triangle test is a good illustration. Each item is a pattern of single letters, with one letter at the apex and four letters along the base line, the letters forming an alphabetical sequence that is different in each item, as in the following set:

```
              d    ___
         b    e    ___
    a    c    f    ?___
```

What letter should appear in the place of the question mark? Five alternative answers are given.

Hypothesis IIc, seeing trends, was suggested by the fact that in some unpublished results in the A.A.F. research, a Figure Matrix test was found related to the factor on which a figure-analogies test commonly appeared. In each item of the figure-matrix test there are places for nine figures in a matrix of three rows and three columns. In each row the same trend occurs, e.g., the object increases in number, and in each column another kind of trend occurs, e.g., the figure becomes darker. Some of the appropriate figures are shown in the item, and some cells are left blank. One blank cell has a question mark in it, and below the matrix five alternatives are potential figures for replacing the question mark. The trends are quite short, but long enough for *E* to determine their directions.

Several tests were promising representatives of the seeing-relations hypothesis (IId). Verbal Analogies I was constructed for this purpose. Although it was realized that there may be two different abilities involved in analogies tests, this test was designed to emphasize the *seeing* of relations rather than the fulfillment of relationships, or in Spearman's terminology, it emphasized "eduction of relations" rather than "eduction of correlates." This emphasis was attempted by making the relation relatively difficult to see and by supplying the multiple-choice answers. One item reads

athlete : scholar : : hand :   ?

Answers: A. seclusion   B. write   C. study   D. book   E. brain

The test Word Matrix involves presentations of some interrelations, as in

| ground | street | automobile |
| air | route | ?___ |

Answers: A. airplane   B. bird   C. kite   D. balloon   E. cloud

Because of the complexity involved in this test, it is perhaps better qualified as a measure of cognition of systems.

No special test was designed for hypothesis IIe. From the vantage point of present knowledge, this hypothesis is stated as if it pertains to *evaluation* of relations, where identity is the criterion to be satisfied. The inclusion of the one test called "Hidden Figures," which uses Gottschaldt figures, was to determine whether such a test would again be found related to the same kind of reasoning factor as in the A.A.F. research, as mentioned earlier.

Tests for Reasoning III Three hypotheses under Reasoning III pertain to classes, for which classifying tests were designed. IIIa pertains to seeing common elements or properties. Figure Matching illustrates an emphasis upon this kind of activity. Given in each item a certain figure, E is to select from among five other figures the one that has the most properties in common with it.

The classifying (in general) idea of hypothesis IIIb would be supported if all the varied tests, some figural and some verbal, went together on the same factor. IIIc would be supported if the figural-classifying tests determined a factor of their own. The Figure Matching test just described is one example. Figure Classification is a matching test in which each given object is to be matched with a set of three (among alternative sets) with which it has at least one property in common.

In a Figure Exclusion test, a set of five figures is given, one of which does not belong to the class; E is to say which it is. There was a parallel Word Classification test with items like

    A. horse   B. cow   C. man   D. flower   E. dog

There was no other verbal classification test, so it was not possible in the first analysis to see whether two classification abilities would be indicated, one figural and one verbal, but it could be determined whether the verbal test would go with the figural ones on the same factor.

For the unique hypothesis for educing correlates, several tests qualified. There was a test Verbal Analogies II, in which the relation between the first pair of words is rather easy to see but there is some doubt as to which alternative completion is correct. There was a test Figure Analogies Completion, in which E has to supply correct correlates; alternatives are not given. In another figure-analogies test, called "Prescribed Relations," E is given the first figure and is told what its relation or relations are to the second figure. He is to find that figure among the alternatives. A test called "Correlate Completion" was a kind of analogies-completion test, using words. Sometimes the relation was a matter of spelling, as in

    rat tar   tin nit   reed _____

with two sample relationships being given. In other items the relations were meaningful, as in

    fish swim   man walk   bird _____

The mixed content (symbolic and semantic) in this test was later recognized, but there was little or no concern about content in the first study. Certain results from the first analysis did demonstrate the importance of such a distinction.

Tests for Reasoning IV Three tests were used to throw a little light on deduction. Only a question of generality was at stake, as indicated earlier. Two syllogistic tests were included. One was Thurstone's False Premises, in which E

simply states whether the conclusion is true or false. The premises are nonsensical, such as "All fish are clowns." In the test Syllogisms the statements are realistic, and four alternative conclusions are given. The informal test Inferences gives only one premise of a factual nature, with five alternative conclusions, one being deducible, the others not.

The Original Analysis

The techniques of analysis employed by the ARP have been mentioned in preceding chapters. The kinds of subjects utilized in the analyses primarily concerned in this chapter are reported in Table 5.1. Only results and conclusions remain to be discussed here. For the original analysis of the first reasoning study, emphasis will be upon positive findings that had some historical significance.

In this analysis 13 axes were rotated, of which 12 were interpreted psychologically. Of these, 7 were dependent mainly upon tests designed as reasoning tests, and 5 were regarded as nonreasoning, reference factors, which are of little interest to us here. From the standpoint of present knowledge, the outcomes were far from satisfactory, for 22 SI abilities were apparently represented in the test battery, and they could not all be accounted for by rotating only 13. Actually, if later inspection was valid, as many as 14 of the SI abilities

Table 5.1 Populations and Samples for Analyses Pertaining to Reasoning Abilities and Problem Solving*

Report Number	Brief Title of the Analysis	N	Population
3	Reasoning A	139	A.F. cadets
		144	Officer candidates
6	Reasoning B	395	A.F. cadets
		343	Student officers
14	General Reasoning	170	Coast Guard cadets
16	Reasoning, Creativity, and Evaluation	411	A.F. cadets (two groups)
		219	Naval air cadets
22	Problem Solving	219	Naval air cadets and student officers
23	Symbolic Abilities	240	Naval air cadets and student officers
40	Figural Cognition and Evaluation	188	Students of architecture

*Age range was approximately 18 to 25 years. Education level was generally from high school graduation to two years of college.

were represented strongly by only one test each. When such single representatives are present in an analyzed battery, they tend to go hither and yon, wherever their correlations with other tests will permit, and their placements on factors probably represent chance contributions to the coefficients of correlation, as well as minor genuine relationships to those other factors. At any rate, their presence in factor lists lends confusion as to the precise nature of the abilities more strongly represented. Some of the seven reasoning factors determined largely by reasoning tests in this analysis have been persistently recognized in later analyses, and they were probably not so very far from SI counterparts.

Fate of the Hypotheses Having presented hypotheses regarding factors to be expected, in earlier discussion, let us note briefly the fate of those hypotheses. Much fuller information can be found in Report 3. The hypotheses listed earlier will be mentioned roughly in turn.

Ia—MANIPULATING SYMBOLS No *general* factor of this kind was found. A limited one was found, however, represented by the three Number and Operations Changes tests, together with Symbol Manipulation. The factor was called "symbol substitution," in recognition of the three similar tests just mentioned, in which substitution of symbols was the common feature. This feature did not apply to Symbol Manipulation. Later on, this test helped identify the SI ability for evaluation of symbolic relations (ESR). Very simple equations, as in this test, are apparently symbolic relations, and the same may be said of the equations in all the Number and Operations Changes test forms. In all these tests, E has to judge whether given symbolic statements are correct, given circumstantial information.

Ib—SOLVING PROBLEMS (IN GENERAL) No factor involving problem-solving tests was sufficiently general to support this hypothesis. The tests Problem Solving and Ship Destination did go together, as expected, but the number of tests going with them on this factor was very limited. The fact that an arithmetical-reasoning test led the list required the label of "general reasoning," in line with A.A.F.-research tradition.

Ic—DEFINING PROBLEMS The one good test to represent this hypothesis was Essential Operations, which went with the two last-mentioned tests on general reasoning, but not strongly enough for us to say that the factor is an ability to structure problems. Better tests for this hypothesis were constructed in later analyses.

Id—TESTING HYPOTHESES The clearest tests for this hypothesis did not determine a factor of their own, but went with the inference and syllogism tests on a factor called "logical reasoning." This ability was identified later with the SI ability for evaluation of semantic implications (EMI). After all, testing a hypothesis is evaluating it, the hypothesis itself being an implication from the given information.

Ie—ORGANIZING SEQUENCES OF STEPS No special tests for this idea were in the battery. It is now recognized that ordering a sequence of steps is a convergent-production activity, and the sequence itself is a system. Therefore, we should look for tests measuring SI abilities NFS, NSS, and NMS, depending upon the content. The last two abilities just mentioned were later demonstrated by the use of tests that call for ordering.

Tests designed for Reasoning II determined three factors. Circle Reasoning and Letter Triangle, which were proposed earlier as representatives of hypotheses IIa and IIb, respectively, went together to determine largely a factor labeled "eduction of conceptual patterns."[4] The term "conceptual" marked the fact that no figural tests were involved. No distinction had been made at that time between symbolic and semantic content. This factor has often recurred, marked by these same two tests, and the ability has been identified more definitely as cognition of symbolic systems (CSS).

IIc—SEEING TRENDS   The only indication regarding the possible fate of trend tests was that they would probably go with the relations tests, as the Figure Matrix test did. Subsequent experience has supported this conclusion, where trends provide a sequence of elements such that the relation is the same between neighboring elements, e.g., the relation "greater than" or "comes after."

IId—SEEING RELATIONS   Here we find that there were two factors. One was led by Figure Matrix and was interpreted as "eduction of figural relations," owing to the fact that its five leading tests had figural content. This factor foreshadowed the SI ability for cognition of figural relations (CFR), for which Figure Matrix continued to serve as a marker. The other factor was called "eduction of conceptual relations," and it was marked by Verbal Analogies I and Word Matrix, particularly. It foreshadowed the SI ability for cognition of semantic relations (CMR). The parallel between these two factors was one of the findings that led to the expectation of other differentiations in terms of content, and eventually the use of the morphological type of model for the structure of intellect, as explained in Chapter 2. These two factors and others of similar kind are proof that thinking abilities *do not* transcend content boundaries but are materially, if not entirely, restricted within those boundaries.

IIe—SEEING IDENTITY OF RELATIONS   Without enough tests to make possible the separation of a single factor of this kind, one was not seriously expected. But this kind of ability was later demonstrated in the area of evaluation abilities where relations are involved. Deciding whether or not two given relations are identical is a matter of evaluation.

IIf—ANALYZING FORMS   The only test representing this hypothesis was Hidden Figures, which did not have enough help to determine a separate factor. Instead, it went on a factor called "eduction of correlates," without making much sense in that relationship. It was learned much later that it is a relatively strong test for the SI ability for convergent production of figural transformations (NFT). It has consequently been concluded that finding a simple figure

---

[4]The term "eduction" was borrowed from Spearman. The factor name could have been "*seeing* conceptual patterns."

embedded within a more complex one is not so much a form of analysis as it is a reorganizing of line patterns in the complex figure to make the simple figure. Reorganization is one form of transformation.

Three hypotheses under Reasoning III called for one or more abilities pertaining to seeing common properties of things or seeing classes. IIIb called for a general ability to see classes, and IIIc for seeing classes of forms or figures. Actually, no clear classes abilities or classifying abilities were found in the Reasoning-A analysis. The tests devoted to classes scattered in different directions in the original analysis. The truth of the matter is that there were too many different classes abilities represented for the number of tests available to bring them out by analysis. In later analyses, Figural Classification and Figure Exclusion have helped locate SI ability CFC, but they usually need the aid of another CFC test to do this. The test Word Classification alone represented SI ability CMC, not sufficient, by ordinary techniques of rotation, to locate a factor.

IIId—EDUCTION OF CORRELATES   A factor that looked good for such an ability was brought out in the analysis. But subsequent enlightenment forces us to suspect that this factor was a confounding of SI abilities NSR and NMR, possibly with some NFR also, for tests having among them three kinds of content were loaded together on the factor. The test called "Correlate Completion" itself had both symbolic and semantic items, it may be recalled. And Figure Analogies Completion, a lone representative for NFR, also came out on the factor. Generating a unique correlate that is called for by each item in these tests is a matter of convergent production. Thus, the expectation that an analogies test would represent two different abilities, depending upon the emphasis, whether on *seeing* the relation or on *completing* the relationship by giving the correlate, was fulfilled. Although designed for the correlate-completion hypothesis, Verbal Analogies II went instead on other factors. The multiple-choice form of this test evidently defeated its purpose, where the completion form of Figure Analogies Completion succeeded.

The answer to hypotheses IVa and IVb was in favor of a single factor, not two, on which all three intended tests went together, syllogistic and informal. It was concluded, however, that the ability is not deductive in nature, for deduction implies *drawing* conclusions, whereas all three tests give E the answer, albeit among distracting answers. It was believed that a truly deductive test would require E to supply the answer—to draw his own conclusion, right or wrong. This thinking places any deductive ability in the convergent-production category. If E is given potential conclusions (right and wrong) to decide among them, he is evaluating. Since conclusions are implications, he is evaluating implications, and the factor named "logical reasoning" in the original analysis was most likely nearest to SI ability EMI. The parallel *deduction* ability NMI was later demonstrated by other kinds of tests, including a syllogism test in completion form.

Reasoning as a Concept   Although the analysis in the first reasoning study left much to be desired, the results were sufficient to arouse some real misgivings regarding the usefulness of "reasoning" as a technical or systematic concept. It is difficult to say which of the tests are actually reasoning measures and which of the factors are reasoning abilities. We are thus left without those possible empirical bases for delimiting the term. We are not helped very much by saying that only factors that involve induction or deduction belong in the reasoning category. Guilford (1960) has suggested that we recognize several kinds of induction, all in the cognition category of the SI model, including the products of classes, relations, systems, and implications, for all kinds of content. This would mean 16 kinds of inductive ability. He also suggested that we recognize two kinds of deduction (for each kind of content), both in the convergent-production category, involving relations and implications. This would mean eight kinds of deduction. But with the more precisely defined concepts provided by SI theory, the usefulness of the concepts of "induction" and "deduction" now seem to be of limited value, and they can be profitably replaced by the SI concepts.

The Analysis with Targeted Rotations

As hinted earlier, later inspection of the tests in the first reasoning battery suggested that 22 SI abilities were represented, many of them by one test each. Accordingly, after new extractions of principal components, the first 22 were selected for rotation of axes. The solution yielded the significant ($\geqslant .30$) factor loadings that may be seen in Table 5.2, grouped by factors.[5]

It must not be supposed that aiming axes at single tests "discovers" factors. One would not ordinarily accept a singlet as a demonstration that any factorial ability exists. But taking care of a test that represents substantially only its own factorial ability by giving it an orthogonal axis prevents that test from confusing the factorial picture elsewhere in the solution.[6] Examination of the nonsinglet factors for analysis 3 in Table 5.2 will show that they are very clear-cut, with only two to five tests reasonably loaded on each one.

From Table 5.2 it can also be seen how well the factorial abilities found in the targeted rotations in the first analysis were replicated in later analyses, and how certain tests show much invariance in relation to those abilities. Where a certain test does not appear on a factor in one or more analyses, most likely the test was absent from the battery. Certain tests that became favorites as markers do appear repeatedly.

We shall now give brief attention to the nature of the nonsinglet factors. Figure Exclusion and Figure Classification came together in this analysis to represent CFC, as they were expected to help determine a classification factor in the original analysis but did not. Circle Reasoning and Letter Triangle determine a factor, as before, that is now recognized as CSS. Along with them is Secret Writing, which was targeted not for CSS but rather for NSI (as indicated in Table 5.2). It is reasonable that there should be some CSS variance in this test, for E has to see or cognize the code and its application in each item as a pattern or structure.

---

[5]Table 5.2 includes significant loadings, not only from the targeted analyses of special interest in this chapter but also from analyses by the ARP having information to contribute regarding factors in the cognition and convergent-production categories, in which most of the abilities that may be regarded under the heading "reasoning" appear.

[6]In Table 5.2, loadings for tests on singlet factors are indicated by the superscript "s." Although one should not expect those loadings to be accurate, it will be noted that they are very much in line with parallel values found on nonsinglet factors.

Table 5.2 Tests Loaded Significantly on Factors Representing Cognition and Convergent-production Abilities in 24 Analyses[a]

Factor Test	3	6	8	9	12	13	14	16A	16B	16C	21	22	23	31A	31B	32	33	34	35	38	39	40	41	43
CFU																								
Close-Ups[b]	—	—	—	—	—	—	—	—	—	—	—	—	—	—	—	—	—	—	—	—	—	63	—	—
Hidden Print	—	—	—	—	—	—	—	—	—	—	—	—	—	—	—	—	—	—	—	—	—	56	—	—
Figure Completion	—	—	—	—	—	—	—	—	—	—	—	—	—	—	—	—	—	—	—	—	—	56	—	—
Street Gestalt Completion	—	—	49	—	—	—	—	—	—	—	—	—	—	—	—	—	—	43	—	—	—	—	—	—
Mutilated Words	—	—	44	—	—	—	—	—	—	—	—	—	—	—	—	—	—	49	—	—	—	41	—	—
CFC																								
Figure Classification	41	64	—	50	—	—	—	—	42	—	—	—	—	—	—	—	—	—	43	—	47	52	—	53
Picture Classification	—	—	—	50	—	—	53s	47	—	—	—	—	—	—	—	—	—	—	50	—	—	—	—	—
Figural Class Inclusion	43	—	—	—	—	—	—	—	—	—	—	—	—	—	—	—	—	—	—	—	46	36	—	53
Figural Exclusion	—	38	—	—	—	—	—	—	—	—	—	—	—	—	—	—	—	—	—	—	44	—	—	—
Figural-Hierarchical Grouping (NFC)	—	—	—	—	—	—	—	—	—	—	—	—	—	—	—	—	—	—	—	—	42	—	—	—
Multiple Figural Similarities (DFC)	—	—	—	—	—	—	—	—	—	—	—	—	—	—	—	—	—	—	—	35	—	—	—	—
Limited Words (DSI)	—	—	—	—	—	—	—	—	—	—	—	—	—	—	—	—	—	—	30	—	—	—	—	—
CFR																								
Spatial Comprehension	—	—	—	—	—	—	—	—	—	—	—	—	—	—	—	—	—	—	—	—	—	58	—	—
DAT Abstract Reasoning	—	—	—	—	—	—	—	—	—	—	—	—	—	—	—	—	—	73	—	—	—	—	—	—
Figure Matrix	51s	—	—	—	—	—	—	48	61	—	—	—	—	—	—	—	—	35	—	—	—	31	—	55
Figure Analogies	—	55s	—	—	—	—	—	55	58	—	—	—	—	—	—	—	—	—	—	—	—	31	—	39
Perceptual Relations	—	—	—	—	—	—	45	37	—	—	—	—	—	—	—	—	—	—	—	—	—	—	—	—
Naming	—	—	—	—	—	—	—	—	—	—	—	—	—	—	—	—	—	—	—	—	—	—	—	—

Figure Series	—	—	—	—	—	—	—	—	—	—	—	—	—	—	—	—	—	—	—	—	—	38	—	—
Necessary Facts (CMS)	—	—	—	—	—	—	—	—	—	—	—	—	—	—	—	—	—	—	—	—	—	35	—	—
Hidden Figures (NFT)	—	—	—	41^s	—	—	—	—	—	—	—	—	—	—	—	—	33	—	—	—	—	—	—	—
CFS																								
Space Positioning	63^s	—	—	—	—	—	—	—	—	—	—	—	—	—	—	—	—	—	—	—	—	69	—	—
Space Orientation	—	—	—	—	—	—	—	—	—	—	—	—	—	—	—	—	—	—	—	—	—	—	—	—
Spatial Orientation	—	—	—	—	—	—	—	—	—	—	—	—	—	—	—	—	—	—	—	—	—	39	—	—
Spatial Visualization (CFT)	—	—	—	—	—	—	—	—	—	—	—	—	—	—	—	—	—	—	—	—	—	31	—	—
CFT																								
Aptitude–Spatial (C.G.)^c	70^s	53	57	55	—	68^s	—	—	—	—	—	—	—	—	—	—	—	—	—	—	—	—	—	—
Punched Holes	—	81	61	55	—	—	—	—	—	—	—	—	—	—	—	—	—	—	—	—	—	—	—	—
Mechanical Principles	—	—	—	—	—	—	—	—	—	—	—	—	—	—	—	—	—	—	—	—	—	—	—	—
Block Rotation	—	—	—	—	—	—	—	—	—	—	—	—	—	—	—	—	—	—	—	—	—	66	—	59
Spatial Visualization	—	—	—	—	—	—	—	—	—	—	—	—	—	—	—	—	—	—	—	—	—	51	—	—
Paper Folding	—	—	—	—	—	—	—	—	—	—	—	—	—	—	—	—	—	—	—	—	—	49	—	44
Block Visualization	—	—	—	—	—	—	—	—	—	—	—	—	—	—	—	—	—	—	—	—	—	41	—	—
Match Problems II (DFT)	—	—	—	—	—	—	—	—	—	—	—	—	—	—	—	—	—	—	—	—	—	52	—	—
Space Positioning (CFS)	—	—	—	—	—	—	—	—	—	—	—	—	—	—	—	—	—	—	—	—	—	41	—	—
Blocks (CFS)	—	—	—	—	—	—	—	—	—	—	—	—	—	—	—	—	—	—	—	—	—	37	—	—
Figure Matrix (CFR)	—	—	—	—	—	—	—	—	—	—	—	—	—	—	—	—	—	—	—	—	—	36	—	—
Problem Solving (CMS)	—	—	—	—	—	—	—	—	—	—	—	—	—	—	—	—	—	—	—	—	—	36	—	—
CFI																								
Circle Continuation	—	—	—	—	—	—	—	—	—	—	—	—	—	—	—	—	—	—	—	—	—	71	—	—
Line Continuation	—	—	—	—	—	—	—	—	—	—	—	—	—	—	—	—	—	—	—	—	—	49	—	—
Blocks (CFS)	—	—	—	—	—	—	—	—	—	—	—	—	—	—	—	—	—	—	—	—	—	33	—	—

Table 5.2 *(Continued)*

Factor / Test	3	6	8	9	12	13	14	16A	16B	16C	21	22	23	31A	31B	32	33	34	35	38	39	40	41	43
CSU																								
Disemvowelled Words	—	—	—	—	—	—	—	—	—	—	—	—	—	—	—	—	—	—	—	—	—	—	—	—
Correct Spelling	—	—	—	—	—	—	—	—	—	—	—	—	61	—	—	—	55	—	—	56	—	—	52	—
Omelet Test	—	—	—	—	—	—	—	—	—	—	—	—	—	—	—	—	47	—	58s	62	—	—	51	—
Four-Letter Words	—	—	—	—	—	—	—	—	—	—	—	—	62	—	—	—	—	—	—	—	—	—	—	—
Disarranged Words	—	—	47s	—	—	—	—	—	—	—	—	—	—	—	—	—	—	—	—	—	—	—	—	—
Word Combinations	—	—	—	—	—	—	—	—	—	—	—	—	55	—	—	—	32	—	—	—	—	—	—	—
Alterations	—	—	—	—	—	—	—	—	—	—	—	—	31	—	—	—	—	—	—	—	—	—	—	—
Memory for Misspelling I (MST)	—	—	—	—	—	—	—	—	—	—	—	—	—	—	—	—	—	—	—	58	—	—	—	—
Word Transformations (NST)	—	—	—	—	—	—	—	—	—	—	—	—	42	—	—	—	35	—	—	—	—	—	—	—
Sound Grouping (ESC)	—	—	—	—	—	—	—	—	—	—	—	—	—	—	—	—	30	—	—	—	—	—	—	—
CSC																								
Number Group Naming	—	—	—	—	—	—	—	—	—	—	—	—	73	—	—	—	47	—	—	63	53	—	—	—
Number Classification	—	—	—	—	—	—	—	—	—	—	—	—	66	—	—	—	43	—	—	39	53	—	—	—
Number Relations	—	—	—	—	—	—	—	—	—	—	—	—	45	—	—	—	—	—	—	—	—	—	—	—
Letter Classification	—	—	—	—	—	—	—	—	—	—	—	—	—	—	—	—	—	—	—	43	—	—	—	—
Number Grouping	—	—	—	—	—	—	—	—	—	—	—	—	—	—	—	—	31	—	—	—	—	—	—	—
Best Number Pairs (ESC)	—	—	—	—	—	—	—	—	—	—	—	—	—	—	—	—	54	—	—	—	—	—	—	—
Sign Changes II (ESR)	—	—	—	—	—	—	—	—	—	—	—	—	—	—	—	—	35	—	—	—	—	—	—	—
Number Series Corrections (CSS)	—	—	—	—	—	—	—	—	—	—	—	33	—	—	—	—	—	—	—	—	—	—	—	—
Memory for Word-Number Relations (MSR)	—	—	—	—	—	—	—	—	—	—	—	—	—	—	—	—	—	—	—	33	—	—	—	—
Best Number Class (ESC)	—	—	—	—	—	—	—	—	—	—	—	—	—	—	—	—	32	—	—	—	—	—	—	—

Test																				
Multiple Grouping of Nonsense Words (DSC)	—	—	—	—	—	—	—	—	—	—	—	—	—	—	—	—	—	—	—	—
CSR																				
Seeing Trends II	—	—	—	—	—	39s	32s	—	—	—	40	46	35	—	46	—	53	31	—	—
Word Relations	—	—	—	—	—	—	—	—	—	—	42	54	45	—	31	—	41	44	—	—
Letter Analogies	—	—	—	—	—	—	—	—	—	—	31	—	—	—	—	—	—	—	—	—
Word Groups (CSC)	—	—	—	—	—	—	—	—	—	—	44	—	—	—	—	—	—	—	—	—
Number Combinations (DSS)	—	—	—	—	—	—	—	—	—	—	—	—	—	—	—	—	35	—	—	—
Figure Classification (CFC)	—	—	—	—	—	—	—	—	—	—	—	—	—	—	—	—	35	—	—	—
Jumbled Words (EST)	—	—	—	—	—	—	—	—	—	—	—	—	—	—	35	—	—	—	—	—
Word Choice (ESC)	—	—	—	—	—	—	—	—	—	—	—	—	—	—	31	—	—	—	—	—
Number Rules (DSR)	—	—	—	—	—	—	—	—	—	—	—	—	—	—	—	—	30	—	—	—
CSS																				
Rules	—	—	—	—	65	—	—	—	—	—	—	—	—	—	—	—	—	—	—	—
Letter Series	—	48	—	—	—	57	—	—	—	—	—	52	59	—	—	—	39	40	—	—
Number Series	—	—	31	—	—	57	—	—	—	—	—	—	—	—	—	—	—	—	—	—
Letter Triangle	49	—	—	—	—	50	—	—	—	—	44	47	44	—	39	—	—	40	—	—
Circle Reasoning	67	31	—	—	32	45	—	—	—	—	30	—	—	—	30	—	—	57	—	—
Number Series Correction	—	—	—	—	—	—	—	—	—	—	42	—	—	—	—	—	—	—	—	—
Code Analysis	—	—	—	42s	—	—	—	—	—	—	—	—	—	—	—	—	—	—	—	—
Secret Writing (NSI)	35	—	—	—	41	—	—	—	—	—	—	—	—	—	—	—	—	—	—	—
Correlate Completion II (NSR)	—	—	—	—	—	—	—	—	—	—	—	—	—	—	—	—	—	—	—	—
Similar Pairs (ESR)	—	—	—	—	—	—	—	—	—	38	—	31	—	—	—	—	—	—	—	—
Sentence Order (NMS)	—	—	—	—	—	—	—	—	—	—	—	—	—	—	36	—	—	—	—	—
Verbal Relations Naming (NMR)	—	—	—	—	32	—	—	—	—	—	—	—	34	—	—	—	—	—	—	—

Table 5.2 *(Continued)*

Factor Test	3	6	8	9	12	13	14	16A	16B	16C	21	22	23	31A	31B	32	33	34	35	38	39	40	41	43
CST																								
Finding Letter Transformations	—	—	—	—	—	—	—	—	—	—	—	—	—	—	—	—	—	—	—	—	—	58	—	—
Seeing Letter Changes	—	—	—	—	—	—	—	—	—	—	—	—	—	—	—	—	—	—	—	—	—	48	—	—
Reading Backwards	—	—	—	—	—	—	—	—	—	—	—	—	—	—	—	—	—	—	—	—	—	48	—	—
Reading Confused Words	—	—	—	—	—	—	—	—	—	—	—	—	—	—	—	—	—	—	—	—	—	45	—	—
Seeing Puzzle Meanings (CMT)	—	—	—	—	—	—	—	—	—	—	—	—	—	—	—	—	—	—	—	—	—	32	—	—
CSI																								
Word Patterns	—	—	—	—	37s	—	—	—	—	—	—	—	50	34	39	—	42	—	51	—	—	—	—	—
Symbol Grouping	—	—	—	—	—	47s	—	—	—	—	—	—	47	44	37	—	33	—	33	—	—	—	—	—
S Test	—	—	—	—	—	—	—	—	—	—	—	—	—	—	—	—	41	—	—	—	—	—	—	—
Similar Number Relations Cross-Out (MSR)	—	—	—	—	—	—	—	—	—	—	—	—	—	—	—	—	—	—	36	—	—	—	—	—
Word Choice (ESC)	—	—	—	—	—	—	—	—	—	—	—	—	—	—	—	—	32	—	—	—	—	—	—	—
CMU																								
Verbal Comprehension	51s	66	56	61	78s	—	76	67	—	—	57	64s	50	52s	—	—	67	—	72	50	62	68	58	—
SCAT Verbal	—	—	—	—	—	—	—	—	—	—	—	—	—	—	—	—	—	79	—	—	66	—	—	—
CAT Vocabulary	—	—	—	—	—	—	—	—	—	—	—	—	—	—	—	—	—	67	—	—	—	—	—	—
Word Completion	—	—	—	—	—	—	—	—	—	—	—	—	—	—	—	—	—	67	—	—	—	—	—	—
Vocabulary Completion	—	—	—	—	59	—	—	—	—	47	—	55	—	—	—	—	—	64	—	—	62	64	—	—
Reading Comprehension[d]	—	48	—	71	76	57	63	—	—	—	—	—	—	64	69	—	—	—	—	—	—	—	—	—
PSAT Verbal	—	—	—	—	—	—	—	—	—	—	—	—	—	—	—	—	72	—	—	—	—	—	—	—
Henmon-Nelson Vocabulary	—	—	—	—	—	—	—	—	—	—	—	—	—	—	—	—	—	70	—	—	—	—	—	—

Test	Values
CTMM Language MA	—
Word Substitution	—
ITED Verbal	56
Sentence Synthesis	—
Verbal Opposites (C.G.)	48
Story Titles	—
Transitions (coherence)	43
Synonyms	—
Sentence Order (NMS)	38, 39, 42, 49
Concept Grouping (NMC)	45
Multiple Analogies (DMR)	41
Word Linkage (CMR)	38
Sound Grouping (ESC)	—
Word Classification (CMC)	36
CAT Arithmetical Reasoning (CMS)	37
Seeing Deficiencies (CMI)	35
Seeing Trends II (CSR)	35
Inventive Verbal Relations (NMR)	35
Matched Verbal Relations (EMR)	30, 35
Verbal Analogies (C.G.) (CMR)	33
Inference Test (EMI)	34
Sentensense (EMU)	32, 32
Correct Letter Order (ESS)	—
Associational Fluency (DMR)	30
DAT Numerical Ability (MSI)	30

79

Table 5.2 (Continued)

Factor Test	3	6	8	9	12	13	14	16A	16B	16C	21	22	23	31A	31B	32	33	34	35	38	39	40	41	43
CMC																								
Word Classification	35s	53s	—	38	—	—	57	51	—	—	—	—	—	—	—	—	—	—	—	38	—	—	—	—
Verbal Classification	—	—	—	48	—	—	37	43	—	—	51	—	—	—	—	51	—	56s	—	35	—	—	—	—
Facts and Opinions	—	—	—	53	—	—	—	—	—	—	—	—	—	—	—	—	—	—	—	—	—	—	—	—
Sentence Pairs	—	—	—	—	—	—	—	—	—	—	—	—	—	—	—	—	—	—	—	—	—	—	—	—
Logical Classification	—	—	—	49	—	—	—	—	—	—	—	51	—	—	—	—	—	—	—	—	—	—	—	—
Critical Evaluation	—	—	—	49	—	—	—	—	—	—	—	—	—	—	—	—	—	—	—	—	—	—	—	—
Object Naming (shifts)	—	—	—	—	—	—	—	—	—	—	—	—	45	—	—	—	—	—	—	—	—	—	—	—
Sentence Classification	—	—	—	44	—	—	—	—	—	—	—	—	—	—	—	—	—	—	—	44	—	—	—	—
Titles	—	—	—	44	—	—	—	—	—	—	—	—	—	—	—	—	—	—	—	—	—	—	—	—
Word-Group Naming	—	—	—	—	—	—	—	40	—	—	—	—	—	—	—	—	—	—	—	—	—	—	—	—
Best Word Pairs	—	—	—	—	—	—	—	—	—	—	—	—	—	—	—	—	—	—	—	—	—	—	—	—
Group Classification (NMC)	—	—	—	—	—	—	—	—	—	—	—	—	—	—	30	—	—	—	—	41	—	—	—	—
Classified Information (MMC)	—	—	—	—	—	—	—	—	—	—	—	—	—	—	—	—	—	—	—	—	—	—	—	—
Word Extensions (EMI)	—	—	—	—	—	—	—	—	—	—	—	—	—	—	30	—	—	—	—	33	—	—	—	—
CMR																								
Verbal Analogies (C.G.)	—	—	—	—	—	66	—	—	—	—	—	—	—	—	—	—	—	—	—	—	—	—	—	—
Identical Verbal Relations	—	59	—	—	—	—	—	—	—	—	—	—	—	—	—	—	—	—	—	—	—	—	—	—
Verbal Analogies I	57	34	—	50	—	—	—	—	—	—	—	56s	—	—	—	—	37	32	—	—	—	—	—	—
Word Matrix Test	—	49	—	—	—	53	—	—	—	—	—	—	—	—	—	—	—	55	—	—	—	—	—	—
Verbal Opposites (CG)	—	—	—	—	—	—	—	—	—	—	—	—	—	—	—	—	—	—	—	—	—	—	—	—
Word Matrix	51	—	—	—	—	—	—	—	—	—	—	—	—	—	—	—	—	—	—	—	—	—	—	—
Verbal Analogies II	52	45	—	—	—	—	—	—	—	—	—	—	—	—	—	—	—	—	—	—	—	—	—	—

Variable																										
Verbal Analogies Completion	—	—	—	—	—	—	—	—	49	—	49	39	—	—	—	—	—	—	—	—	—	—	—	—	—	—
Sensitivity to Order	—	—	—	—	—	—	47	—	—	—	—	—	—	—	—	—	—	—	—	—	—	—	—	—	—	—
Word Linkage	—	—	—	—	—	—	—	—	—	—	—	—	—	—	—	—	48s	45s	—	—	—	—	—	—	—	—
Verbal Relations Naming	—	—	—	—	—	—	—	—	—	42	—	—	—	—	—	—	—	—	—	—	—	—	—	—	—	—
Inventive Verbal Relations	—	—	—	—	—	—	—	—	—	41	—	—	—	—	—	—	—	—	—	—	—	—	—	—	—	—
Matrix Order	—	—	—	—	—	—	—	—	—	39	—	—	—	—	—	—	—	—	—	—	—	—	—	—	—	—
Reading Comprehension (CMU)	—	—	—	—	—	—	—	42	—	—	—	—	—	—	—	—	—	—	—	—	—	—	—	—	—	—
Figure Analogies (CFR)	—	—	—	—	—	—	—	—	—	—	—	35	—	—	—	—	—	—	—	—	—	—	—	—	—	—
Correlate Completion (NSR)	33	32	—	—	—	—	—	—	—	—	—	—	—	—	—	—	—	—	—	—	—	—	—	—	—	—
Verbal Comprehension (CMU)	—	—	—	—	—	—	—	—	—	—	—	32	—	—	—	—	—	—	—	—	—	—	—	—	—	—
Reflections (CBI)	—	—	—	—	—	—	—	—	—	—	—	—	—	—	—	—	—	—	—	—	31	—	—	—	—	—
Best Word Class (EMC)	—	—	—	—	—	—	—	—	—	—	—	—	—	—	—	31	—	—	—	—	—	—	—	—	—	—
CMS																										
Problem Solving	61	—	—	—	—	—	—	—	—	—	—	—	42	—	—	—	—	—	—	—	—	—	60	74	—	—
Ship Destination	49	39	52	47	46	—	74	53s	—	—	—	—	—	50s	49s	—	48	44	59	—	42	—	43	—	—	—
ITED Quantitative	—	—	—	—	—	—	—	—	—	—	—	—	—	—	—	—	—	61	56	—	61	—	—	—	—	—
Necessary Facts	—	—	—	—	—	—	58	—	—	—	—	—	—	—	—	—	—	—	—	—	—	—	—	32	—	—
CAT Arithmetic Reasoning	—	—	—	—	—	—	—	—	—	—	—	—	—	—	—	—	—	—	56	—	—	—	—	—	—	—
Arithmetic Reasoning (A.A.F.)[e]	—	41	47	57	33	—	—	—	—	—	—	—	—	—	—	—	—	—	—	—	—	—	—	—	—	—
Essential Operations	40	48	—	—	40	—	35	—	—	—	—	—	—	—	—	—	—	—	—	—	—	—	—	—	—	—
Necessary Arithmetic Operations	—	—	—	—	—	—	45	—	—	—	—	—	—	—	—	—	—	—	—	—	—	—	—	—	—	—
Word Matrices	—	—	45	—	—	—	—	—	—	—	—	—	—	—	—	—	—	—	—	—	—	—	—	—	—	—
Practical Judgment	—	—	49	41	—	—	—	—	—	—	—	—	—	—	—	—	—	—	—	—	—	—	—	—	—	—
Reading Comprehension	44	—	—	—	—	—	—	—	—	—	—	—	—	—	—	—	—	—	—	—	—	—	—	—	—	—
Circle-Square-Triangle	—	—	—	—	—	—	41	—	—	—	—	—	—	—	—	—	—	—	—	—	—	—	—	—	—	—
Interpretations	—	—	—	39	—	—	—	—	—	—	—	—	—	—	—	—	—	—	—	—	—	—	—	—	—	—

Table 5.2 (Continued)

Factor Test	3	6	8	9	12	13	14	16A	16B	16C	21	22	23	31A	31B	32	33	34	35	38	39	40	41	43
CMS																								
Balances	—	—	—	—	—	—	38	—	—	—	—	—	—	—	—	—	—	—	—	—	—	—	—	—
CAT Vocabulary (CMU)	—	—	—	—	—	—	—	—	—	—	—	—	—	—	—	40	—	—	—	—	—	—	—	—
Seeing Problems (CMI)	—	—	—	—	—	—	—	—	—	—	31	—	—	—	—	—	—	—	—	—	—	—	—	—
Figure Matrix Test (CFR)	—	—	—	—	—	—	—	—	—	—	—	—	—	—	—	—	—	35	—	—	—	—	—	—
Competitive Planning (EFI)	—	—	—	—	—	—	—	—	—	—	34	—	—	—	—	—	—	—	—	—	—	—	—	—
Mechanical Principles (A.A.F.) (CFT)	—	—	33	—	—	—	—	—	—	—	—	—	—	—	—	—	—	—	—	—	—	—	—	—
CMT																								
Cartoons	—	—	—	—	—	—	—	62	65s	—	—	—	—	—	—	—	—	—	—	—	39	—	—	—
Social Institutions (indirect)	—	52	—	—	—	—	—	—	—	—	—	—	—	—	—	—	—	—	—	—	—	—	—	—
Social Institutions	—	—	—	—	—	45s	—	47	59	—	—	—	—	—	—	—	—	—	—	—	—	—	51	—
Seeing Different Meanings	—	—	—	—	—	—	—	—	—	49	—	—	—	—	—	—	—	—	—	—	—	—	—	—
Social Situations	—	—	—	—	—	—	—	—	—	—	—	—	—	—	—	—	—	—	—	—	—	—	—	—
Daffinitions	—	—	—	—	—	—	—	—	—	—	—	—	—	—	—	—	—	—	—	—	—	—	—	—
Similarities	—	—	—	—	—	—	—	40	39	—	—	—	—	—	45s	—	—	—	—	43	—	—	—	—
Verbal Picture Translations	—	—	—	—	—	—	—	—	—	—	—	—	—	—	—	—	—	—	—	—	—	40	—	—
Implied Uses	—	36	—	—	—	—	—	—	—	—	—	—	—	—	—	—	—	—	—	—	—	—	—	—
Seeing Puzzle Meanings	—	—	—	—	—	—	—	—	—	—	—	—	—	—	—	—	—	—	—	—	—	36	—	—
Remembering Puns (MMT)	—	—	—	—	—	—	—	—	—	—	—	—	—	—	—	—	—	—	—	—	—	40	—	—
Alternate Uses (DMC)	—	—	—	—	—	—	—	—	—	34	—	—	—	—	—	—	—	—	—	—	—	—	—	—
Multiple Word Extractions (DST)	—	—	—	—	—	—	—	—	—	—	—	—	—	—	—	—	—	—	—	—	—	—	32	—

CMI

Test																											
Pertinent Questions	—	—	—	66	—	—	—	—	—	—	—	—	—	—	—	—	—	—	—	—	—	—	—	—	—	—	—
Apparatus Test	—	—	—	—	70	68	—	—	—	—	48	67	45	—	—	66	38	—	46	—	—	—	—	—	—	—	—
Alternative Methods	—	—	—	—	—	55	—	—	—	—	61	54	—	—	—	—	—	—	—	—	—	—	—	—	—	—	—
Seeing Problems	—	—	—	—	—	—	—	—	—	—	63	30	58	—	—	51	—	—	55	42	—	—	—	—	—	—	—
Social Institutions (direct)	—	—	—	73	—	—	—	—	—	—	—	—	—	—	—	—	—	—	—	—	—	—	—	—	—	—	—
Effects Test	—	—	—	—	—	61	—	—	—	—	—	—	—	—	—	—	—	—	—	—	—	—	—	—	—	—	—
Transitions (logical aspects)	—	—	—	—	—	—	—	—	—	—	—	—	60	—	—	—	—	—	—	—	—	—	—	—	—	—	—
Contingenceis	—	—	—	—	52	—	—	—	—	—	—	—	45	—	—	—	—	—	—	—	—	—	—	—	—	—	—
Seeing Deficiencies	—	—	—	—	44	—	—	—	—	—	43	53	—	—	—	—	—	—	—	—	—	—	—	—	—	—	—
Predicaments	—	—	—	—	—	—	—	—	—	—	—	—	47	—	—	—	—	—	—	—	—	—	—	—	—	—	—
Social Institutions	—	—	—	—	44	—	—	—	—	—	48	36	—	—	—	—	—	—	—	—	—	—	—	—	—	—	—
Verifications	—	—	—	—	44	—	—	—	—	—	—	37	—	—	—	37	—	—	—	—	—	—	—	—	—	—	—
Similarities	—	—	—	—	—	41	—	—	—	—	37	—	—	—	—	—	—	—	—	34	—	—	—	—	—	—	—
Alternate Uses (DMC)	—	—	—	—	—	41	—	—	—	—	—	—	—	—	—	—	—	—	—	—	—	—	—	—	—	—	—
Planning Skills II (DMI)	—	—	—	—	40	—	—	—	—	—	—	—	—	—	—	—	—	—	—	—	—	—	—	—	—	—	—
Ship Destination (CMS)	—	—	—	—	—	—	—	—	—	—	—	38	—	—	—	—	—	—	—	—	—	—	—	—	—	—	—
Planning Elaboration (DMI)	—	—	—	—	37	—	—	—	—	—	—	—	—	—	—	—	—	—	—	—	—	—	—	—	—	—	—
Consequences (obvious) (DMU)	—	—	—	—	—	—	—	—	—	—	—	—	—	—	—	—	—	—	37	—	—	—	—	—	—	—	—
Consequences (remote) (DMT)	—	—	—	—	—	—	—	—	—	—	36	—	—	—	—	—	—	—	—	—	—	—	—	—	—	—	—
Controlled Association II (DMR)	—	—	—	—	33	—	—	—	—	—	34	—	—	—	—	—	—	—	—	—	—	—	—	—	—	—	—
Cartoons (CMT)	—	—	—	—	—	—	—	—	—	—	—	34	—	—	—	—	—	—	—	—	—	—	—	—	—	—	—
Possible Jobs (DMI)	—	—	—	—	—	—	—	—	—	—	—	—	—	—	—	—	—	—	—	32	—	—	—	—	—	—	—
Unusual Methods (DMT)	—	—	—	—	30	—	—	—	—	—	—	—	—	—	—	—	—	—	—	—	—	—	—	—	—	—	—

Table 5.2 *(Continued)*

Factor Test	3	6	8	9	12	13	14	16A	16B	16C	21	22	23	31A	31B	32	33	34	35	38	39	40	41	43
NFC																								
Figure Concept Grouping	—	—	—	—	—	—	—	—	—	—	—	—	—	—	—	—	—	—	—	—	—	—	—	—
Figure-Hierarchical Grouping	—	—	—	—	—	—	—	—	—	—	—	—	—	—	—	—	—	—	—	—	—	—	—	—
Figure Grouping	—	—	—	—	—	—	—	—	—	—	—	—	—	—	—	—	—	—	—	—	50	—	—	—
Figure Exclusion (CFC)	—	—	—	—	—	—	—	—	—	—	—	—	—	—	—	—	—	—	—	41	—	32	—	38
NFR																								
Figure Analogies Completion	43s	45s	—	45s	—	—	59	—	—	—	—	—	—	—	—	—	—	—	—	—	—	—	—	—
Completion of Figural Changes	—	—	—	—	—	44	—	—	—	—	—	—	—	—	—	—	—	—	—	—	—	—	—	—
NFT																								
Internally Consistent Figures	—	—	—	—	—	—	—	—	—	—	—	—	—	—	—	—	—	—	—	—	—	—	—	—
Penetration of Camouflage	—	—	57	—	—	—	—	—	—	—	—	—	—	—	—	—	—	—	—	—	—	—	—	47
Hidden Figures	47s	51s	—	—	—	—	—	—	—	—	—	—	—	—	—	—	—	39s	—	—	63	39	31	52
Street Gestalt Completion (CFU)	—	—	34	—	—	—	—	—	—	—	—	—	—	—	—	—	—	—	—	—	31	—	—	37
NFI																								
Planning Air Maneuvers	—	—	—	—	—	—	—	—	—	—	—	—	—	—	—	—	—	—	—	—	—	—	—	—
Pattern Arrangement	—	—	—	—	—	—	—	—	—	—	—	—	—	—	—	—	—	—	—	—	53	—	—	—
Match Problems II (DFT)	—	—	—	—	—	—	—	—	—	—	—	—	—	—	—	—	—	—	—	—	44	—	31	—

	1	2	3	4	5	6	7	8	9	10	11	12	13	14	15	16	17	18	19	20	21
NSC																					
Letter Grouping	—	—	—	—	—	—	—	—	—	—	—	—	—	—	61	—	—	—	—	—	—
Word Groups	—	—	—	—	—	—	—	—	—	—	—	—	—	—	—	—	—	—	—	—	—
Restricted Figure Classification	—	—	—	—	—	—	—	—	—	—	—	—	—	—	47	—	—	—	—	—	—
Seeing Trends II	—	—	—	—	—	—	—	—	—	—	37	—	—	—	30	—	—	—	—	—	—
Letter Concept Grouping	—	—	—	—	—	—	—	—	—	—	—	—	—	—	—	—	—	—	—	—	—
Letter Group Exclusion (CSC)	—	—	—	—	—	—	—	—	—	—	—	—	—	—	41	—	—	—	—	—	—
NSR																					
Correlate Completion II	41^s	—	—	—	68	—	41^s	47	—	—	—	—	—	50	53	—	—	—	—	—	—
Correlate Completion	53^s	—	37^{,s}	—	62	—	—	35	—	—	—	—	—	—	—	—	—	—	—	—	—
Vocabulary Completion	—	—	—	—	—	—	—	—	—	—	—	—	—	—	—	—	—	—	—	—	—
Letter-Number	—	—	—	—	—	—	—	—	—	—	—	—	—	51	58	—	—	—	—	—	—
Word Changes (NSS)	—	—	—	—	—	—	—	—	—	—	—	—	—	—	36	—	—	—	—	—	—
Number Rules (DSR)	—	—	—	—	—	—	—	—	—	—	—	—	—	—	33	—	—	—	—	—	—
Word Relations (CSR)	—	—	—	—	—	—	—	—	—	—	—	—	—	—	31	—	—	—	—	—	—
NSS																					
Word Changes	—	—	—	—	—	—	—	—	—	—	—	—	70	68	56^s	—	56	—	—	—	—
Operations Sequences	—	—	—	—	—	—	—	—	—	—	—	—	53	44	—	—	30	—	—	—	—
Number-Group Naming	—	—	—	—	—	—	—	—	—	—	—	—	—	—	34	—	38	—	—	—	—
Limited Sums	—	—	—	—	—	—	—	—	—	—	—	—	—	—	38	—	—	—	—	—	—
Word Relations (CSR)	—	—	—	—	—	—	—	—	—	—	—	—	—	—	—	—	—	—	—	—	—
Letter Triangle (CSS)	—	—	—	—	—	—	—	—	—	—	—	—	—	—	37	—	—	—	—	—	—
Number Relations (MSI)	—	—	—	—	—	—	—	—	—	—	—	—	—	—	36	—	—	—	—	—	—
Series Relations (ESS)	—	—	—	—	—	—	—	—	—	—	—	—	—	—	—	—	31	—	—	—	—

Table 5.2 (Continued)

Factor / Test	3	6	8	9	12	13	14	16A	16B	16C	21	22	23	31A	31B	32	33	34	35	38	39	40	41	43
NST																								
Camouflaged Words	—	—	—	—	—	—	—	—	—	—	—	—	46	47	45	—	62	—	—	—	—	—	35	—
Limited Word Revision	—	—	—	—	—	—	—	—	—	—	—	—	—	—	—	—	—	—	—	—	—	—	48	—
Word Transformations	—	—	54	—	—	—	—	—	—	—	—	—	—	—	—	—	—	—	—	—	—	—	—	—
Sentence Gestalt I (right)	—	—	62	—	—	—	—	—	—	—	—	—	51	46	38	—	43	—	—	—	—	—	—	—
Form Reasoning (CSS)	—	—	—	—	—	—	—	—	—	—	—	—	—	—	33	—	—	—	—	—	—	—	—	—
Four Letter Words	—	—	—	—	—	—	—	—	—	—	—	—	43	—	—	—	—	—	—	—	—	—	—	—
Efficient Word Transformations	—	—	—	—	—	—	—	—	—	—	—	—	—	—	—	—	—	—	—	—	—	—	—	—
Best Number Class (ESC)	—	—	—	—	—	—	—	—	—	—	—	—	—	—	—	—	—	—	—	—	—	—	37	—
Word-Pair Revisions (DSI)	—	—	—	—	—	—	—	—	—	—	—	—	—	—	—	—	31	—	—	—	—	—	33	—
NSI																								
Form Reasoning	60	45	—	—	—	—	57	—	—	—	—	—	—	—	45	—	59	—	—	—	—	—	—	—
Sign Changes	—	—	—	—	48s	56s	72	—	—	—	—	—	—	66	59	—	30	—	—	—	—	—	—	—
Form Reasoning II	—	—	—	—	—	66s	—	—	—	—	—	—	—	—	—	—	—	—	—	—	—	—	—	—
Number and Operations Changes II	—	47	—	—	—	—	—	—	—	—	—	—	—	—	—	—	—	—	—	—	—	—	—	—
Secret Writing	41	—	—	—	—	—	—	—	—	—	—	—	—	—	—	—	—	—	—	—	—	—	—	—
Number and Operations Changes I	—	40	—	—	—	—	—	—	—	—	—	—	—	—	—	—	—	—	—	—	—	—	—	—
Numerical Operations (MSI)	—	—	—	—	—	—	—	—	—	—	—	—	—	32	36	—	—	—	—	—	—	—	—	—
NMU																								
Word-Group Naming	—	53	—	—	—	—	44	56	—	—	—	—	—	—	—	—	—	—	—	45	—	—	—	—
Verbal Relations Completion	—	—	—	—	56s	—	—	—	—	—	—	—	—	—	—	—	—	—	—	—	—	—	—	—

Variable																								
Naming Meaningful Trends	—	—	—	—	—	—	—	—	—	—	—	—	—	63s	—	—	—	—	—	—	—	—	—	—
Picture-Group Naming	—	—	—	—	—	—	—	—	—	—	—	—	—	—	42	38	—	—	—	36	35	—	40	—
Verbal-Relations Naming	—	—	—	—	—	—	—	—	—	—	—	—	—	—	—	40	—	—	40s	—	—	—	—	—
Paired Similarities	—	—	—	—	—	—	—	—	—	—	—	—	—	—	—	—	37s	—	—	—	—	—	—	—
Perceptual Relations Naming	—	—	—	—	—	—	—	—	—	—	—	—	—	—	—	—	—	—	—	—	—	—	—	—
Naming	—	—	—	—	—	—	—	—	—	—	—	—	—	—	32	—	—	—	—	—	—	—	—	—
Naming Trends	—	33	—	—	—	—	—	—	—	—	—	—	—	—	—	—	—	—	—	—	—	—	—	—
NMC																								
Figure Concepts (uncommon)	—	—	—	—	—	—	—	—	—	—	—	—	—	—	—	—	—	—	57	—	—	—	—	—
Word Grouping	—	—	—	—	—	—	—	—	—	—	—	—	—	—	—	—	—	—	50	—	—	42	—	—
Group Classification	—	—	—	—	—	—	—	—	—	—	—	—	—	—	—	—	—	—	—	—	—	43	—	—
Concept Grouping	—	—	—	—	—	—	—	—	—	—	—	—	—	—	—	—	—	—	—	—	—	37	—	—
Largest Class	—	—	—	—	—	—	—	—	—	—	—	—	—	—	—	—	—	—	—	—	—	34	—	—
Verbal Classification (CMC)	—	—	—	—	—	—	—	—	—	—	—	—	—	—	—	—	—	—	—	—	—	36	—	—
NMR																								
Inventive Verbal Relations	—	—	—	—	—	—	—	50	63	—	—	—	—	—	—	—	—	—	—	—	—	—	—	—
Associations III	—	—	65	—	—	—	—	—	32	43	—	—	—	—	—	—	—	—	—	—	—	—	—	—
Associations IV	—	—	52	—	—	—	—	—	44	46	—	—	—	—	—	—	—	—	—	—	—	—	—	—
Verbal Relations Naming	—	—	—	—	43	—	—	—	—	—	—	—	—	—	—	—	—	—	—	—	—	—	—	—
Verbal Analogies Completion	—	—	41	—	—	—	—	—	40	—	—	—	—	—	—	—	—	—	—	—	—	—	—	—
Vocabulary Completion	—	—	—	—	—	—	—	—	37	—	—	—	—	—	—	—	—	—	—	—	—	—	—	—
Associations I	—	34	—	—	—	—	—	—	—	—	—	—	—	—	—	—	—	—	—	—	—	—	—	—
Picture-Group Naming	—	—	—	—	—	—	—	—	33	—	—	—	—	—	—	—	—	—	—	—	—	—	—	—
Associations II	—	30	—	—	—	—	—	—	—	—	—	—	—	—	—	—	—	—	—	—	—	—	—	—

Table 5.2 *(Continued)*

Factor / Test	3	6	8	9	12	13	14	16A	16B	16C	21	22	23	31A	31B	32	33	34	35	38	39	40	41	43
NMS																								
Sentence Order	—	48s	—	—	—	—	—	—	—	—	—	—	—	58	32	—	—	—	—	—	—	—	—	—
Picture Arrangement	—	—	—	—	50	—	—	—	—	—	—	—	43	39	41	—	—	72s	—	—	—	—	—	47
Ordering I	—	—	—	—	—	—	—	—	—	—	—	—	51	—	—	—	—	—	—	—	—	—	—	—
Word Matrices	—	—	—	—	45	—	—	—	—	—	—	—	—	—	—	—	—	—	—	—	—	—	—	—
Outlining	—	—	—	—	—	59s	—	—	—	—	—	—	—	—	—	—	—	—	—	—	—	—	—	—
Procedure Applications	—	—	—	—	36	—	—	—	—	—	—	—	—	—	—	—	—	—	—	—	—	—	—	—
Matrix Order	—	—	—	—	32	—	—	—	—	—	—	—	—	—	—	—	—	—	—	—	—	—	—	—
Temporal Ordering	—	—	—	—	30	—	—	—	—	—	—	—	—	—	—	—	—	—	—	—	—	—	—	—
Seeing Deficiencies (CMI)	—	—	—	—	37	—	—	—	—	—	—	—	—	—	—	—	—	—	—	—	—	—	—	32
NMT																								
New Uses	—	—	—	—	—	—	—	—	—	—	—	—	—	—	—	—	—	—	—	—	—	—	57	—
Gestalt Transformations	—	—	47	45	—	—	—	—	38	—	38	—	—	—	—	—	—	—	—	—	—	—	—	—
Object Synthesis	—	—	41	62	—	—	—	—	50	—	—	—	—	—	—	—	—	—	—	—	—	—	51	—
Picture Gestalt	—	—	46	—	—	—	—	—	—	—	—	—	—	—	—	41	—	—	—	—	—	—	—	—
Predicaments	—	—	—	—	—	—	—	—	—	—	—	34	—	—	—	—	—	—	—	—	—	—	—	—
Alternate Uses (DMC)	—	—	—	—	—	—	—	—	—	—	—	—	—	—	—	—	—	—	—	—	—	—	—	36

NMI																		
Syllogisms III	—	—	—	—	—	—	—	—	—	—	—	—	—	—	—	—	—	—
Common Needs	—	—	—	—	—	—	—	—	—	68	—	—	—	—	—	45	—	—
Sequential Association	—	—	—	—	—	—	—	—	—	—	—	—	—	—	—	43	—	—
Missing Links	—	—	—	—	—	—	—	—	—	—	—	—	—	—	—	40	—	—
Attribute Listing II	—	—	—	—	—	—	—	—	—	—	—	—	—	—	—	—	31	—
Syllogisms I and 2 (EMI)	—	—	—	—	—	—	—	—	—	31	—	—	—	—	—	—	—	—

[a]Decimal points omitted.
[b]Tests were targeted in rotations toward the factors under which they appear except those followed by trigram symbols for other factors.
[c]C.G. indicates a Coast Guard Aptitude test.
[d]Three forms: A.A.F. (analyses 3–12), C.G. (analysis 13), and Iowa–ITED (analyses 31A and B).
[e]A.A.F. indicates an Army Air Force test.
[s]A loading on a singlet factor.

The tests involving word relations all get together to determine CMR in this solution, as they did not in the original one. They took along with them the Inference Test for a minor loading, in spite of the fact it was not targeted to go along on CMR, which may mean that seeing semantic relations is, after all, somehow a component in that test.

The picture of general reasoning (CMS) is much sharper than before, with only the three stronger tests loaded on it. Essential Operations still lags in third place, which does not add much confidence to the idea that general reasoning is a matter of seeing semantically the structure of problems. But there is stronger evidence to come later that general reasoning is CMS and that structuring problems and other things semantically is its main feature.

Factor NSI appears in the Reasoning-A study only with targeted rotations. Form Reasoning had led the tests for the rotated but uninterpreted factor in the original analysis. Secret Writing was targeted for this SI ability, the ability to produce symbolic implications convergently. This targeting is reasonable because each conceived hypothesis about a code is such an implication. *E*s who can more often be right quickly in their convergently produced implications do better in the test.

Factor ESR needs no comment except to note that the symbol tests that were on the symbol-substitution factor originally are more clearly segregated in the results in Table 5.2. Although the syllogism and inferences tests went together in the original analysis to determine what was called "logical reasoning," in the targeted rotation False Premises, one of the syllogistic tests, needed separation from the other two and got it by going on EMR, as some syllogistic tests do, while some divide their allegiance between EMI and EMR. In such tests, evidently, *relations* are evaluated. The pair of tests loaded on EMI in Table 5.2 show that formal and informal inference-judging tests do hang together on a factor.

THE REASONING-B ANALYSIS

Hypotheses

The study called "Reasoning B" was planned and largely executed before the results from Reasoning A were known.[7] There was accordingly no good basis for revising the hypotheses regarding factorial abilities to be expected, and the hypotheses discussed earlier still served as guides to this investigation. The results of a reasoning analysis by Adkins and Lyerly (1951) had become available, however. It did not call for any revisions of hypotheses, but three of its tests seemed to offer the opportunity to represent some of the hypotheses where representation had been weak.

Two other new tests were introduced also to bolster weak places in the battery. Of the 34 tests of the Reasoning-A battery, 27 were used in the new analysis, plus the five new ones. Some tests were regarded as dispensable, in view of the fact that the Air Force classification battery, which the aviation students had taken as a matter of routine, contained a few tests that could be substituted.

---

[7]See Report 6. See also Guilford, Green, Christensen, Hertzka, and Kettner (1954).

Twenty-two tests in the A.F. battery were included in the analysis because members of the A.F. Personnel and Training Laboratory were interested in determining what reasoning abilities might be represented by some of its tests.

New Tests

The new test Sentence Order was thought to be a good representative for hypothesis Ie (organizing a sequence of steps). Each item of that test presents three sentences, each stating one of three related events; for example,

   _____ She bought some food.
   _____ She cooked dinner.
   _____ She drove to the market.

E is to say what the correct order of the events should be by writing the digits 1, 2, and 3 in the blanks.

A test Seeing Trends was developed to give information concerning hypothesis IIc (seeing trends). In each item a sequence of figures, numbers, letters, or words is presented, each representing a trend of some kind. E is to state what trend he sees in the sequence. The use of the three kinds of content in the same test illustrates again the expectation that factor abilities would transcend content categories, a belief that still applied in the planning of the Reasoning-B study. Had the results from Reasoning-A been known, there should have been some segregation of items differing in content.

The new test Identical Verbal Relations was added to represent hypothesis IIe (seeing identity of relations). This is a form of analogies test in which a pair of related words is given and each of the alternative answers is a different pair of words, one pair having the same relation as the first.

In order to add another test calling for recognition of class ideas, Word-Group Naming was added to the battery. Each item presents five common words that have one or more properties in common. E is to name the class idea in order to show that he sees the class. This test could represent both hypotheses IIIa and IIIb.

Possibly representing hypothesis IVa was the new test Absurdities. In each item of this test one or two sentences are given. Some items "make sense" and some do not, with E to say which it is in each case. The supposed relevance of this test for hypothesis IVa arose from its underlying similarity to tests involving informal judgments of the soundness of inferences or deductions.

The Original Analysis

As in the Reasoning-A analysis, from the standpoint of present knowledge, the results with graphic rotations left much to be desired, with respect to factors from the reasoning tests, at least. Those factors are of first concern here. The U.S.A.F. battery tests yielded the usual factors, of which only general reasoning is of interest to us here. This factor was led by Arithmetic Reasoning and Ship Destination, with Essential Operations near the bottom of the list, which included six other tests. The presence of most of these other tests can be attributed to the fact that there were still 12 tests in the battery, each representing only one SI ability. Sixteen factors were rotated, but 23 SI abilities should be expected.

In addition to general reasoning, five other factors that had been identified in Reasoning A appeared to be replicated in Reasoning B. They were

Eduction of perceptual relations
Eduction of conceptual relations
Eduction of patterns
Eduction of correlates
Logical reasoning

Although the stronger marker tests were much the same in the two analyses, other tests on each of these factors did not show as much invariance in their affiliations with factors. There was just a hint of an SI ability in a new factor on which the test Figure Classification was the strongest. Figure Exclusion did not go significantly with it on this factor, as it has gone on CFC in a more recent analysis (Report 39).

The Targeted Solution

In the targeted rotations for Reasoning B, those Air Force tests that offered little prospect of having anything in common with ARP tests were omitted, which left seven of them to help determine factors representing intellectual abilities. Giving each of the 23 expected SI abilities a positive target in rotations of 23 axes yielded the results seen in Table 5.2. Again, by accounting for all the SI abilities by targeting single tests for 12 of the 23 factors, the picture emerges with considerable clarity and also with much agreement with the targeted solution for Reasoning A. In spite of the changes in composition of the test battery, there was much invariance of factors and of their relations to tests.

Figure Classification and Figure Exclusion did come out together, as before, to determine a CFC factor. Mechanical Principles, an Air Force test, helped Punched Holes determine CFT, or visualization. In this mechanical test, pictured devices, some with cogwheels, are presented, with E to say in which direction one part will go if another part goes in a specified direction. In Punched Holes, the folding of a sheet of paper is shown in a line drawing, and a hole of a certain shape is cut out at a certain place. E is to show by means of a line drawing how the paper would look after unfolding, with properly shaped holes in the right places.

The tests Letter Triangle and Circle Reasoning again determined CSS, without the help of Secret Writing, which had been omitted in Reasoning B. Word Classification was still alone to represent CMC, in spite of the addition of the Word-Group Naming test, which was thought to be another semantic-classification test. But the fact that E had to name the class idea put this test on what was first called the "naming factor." That factor has been identified as the SI ability for convergent production of semantic units (NMU). Another naming test (Naming Trends) also went on NMU rather than on CMR, which had been its expected factor. The new test Identical Verbal Relations went so strongly on seeing semantic relations (CMR) that it seems not to call for any other factor to account for it. Thus, hypothesis IIe does not call for a separate relations ability; its feature applies to CMR.

The general-reasoning factor, CMS, had Essential Operations leading the list in the Reasoning-B analysis, supporting the idea that understanding problem structures is the key concept regarding this ability. Finding that the Air Force Reading Comprehension test goes with the three regular tests for CMS suggests that the ability pertains to the cognition of structures other than problems, as well. Reading Comprehension's primary relationship was to CMU, verbal comprehension, or knowledge of word meanings. Reading Comprehension can very well logically require the understanding of thought patterns also; hence its relation to CMS.

Cases of lack of invariance of these results with those from Reasoning A occurred with the Number and Operations Changes tests. Two such tests in this analysis went with Form Reasoning to help determine NSI, which involves drawing deductions with symbolic information, while deserting Symbol Manipulations on ESR. The appearance of the Number and Operations Changes tests on ESR was given some rationalization earlier. Their appearance on NSI can also be rationalized. E has to produce a number of symbolic conclusions (implications) from given symbolic information, as he solves the items in these tests. It may be that in further analyses these tests would be found related to both NSI and ESR. They were not analyzed in later studies, but a similar test, Sign Changes, has consistently gone on NSI in later analyses (see Table 5.2). In this test, E is told what signs are interchanged, then he solves some simple equations using those changes.

For the factor representing EMI, the Inference Test and the Syllogisms test again came out as a doublet. Thurstone's False Premises had been omitted, being regarded as superfluous, since it can be regarded as a second form of Syllogisms. The new test Absurdities had been put in the battery instead, as another type of "logical-reasoning" test. But in the light of later experiences with evaluation factors, Absurdities was targeted for SI ability EMU. The reason was that a very similar test, Sentensense, in which each item is a single sentence with two main ideas in it, to be judged on whether the two ideas are consistent, had been a substantial supporter of a factor identified as EMU (Report 32; also Hoepfner, Nihira, & Guilford, 1966). The reason that it pertains to evaluation of units rather than implications is probably because one idea is not deduced from or implied by the other; hence no implication is being evaluated. Thus, Absurdities was easily separated from the two EMI tests, but representing a singlet in the targeted solution, its factor was not identifiable with assurance in this analysis.

THE STUDY OF GENERAL REASONING

Hypotheses concerning General Reasoning

It may be recalled that prior to the initial studies of reasoning abilities, five alternative hypotheses had been proposed for the factor of general reasoning:

    a. Manipulating symbols
    b. Solving problems
    c. Defining problems
    d. Testing hypotheses
    e. Organizing sequences of related steps

Two definite factors were found in addition to that of general reasoning, to account for a and e, thus eliminating those two hypotheses. Hypothesis d had not been accounted for in a similar manner, so it was thought to have some further claim to life. Final decision could not be reached as to whether b or c is a better description of the general-reasoning ability. The analysis that focused attention on general reasoning was initiated with revisions of hypotheses b and d, giving them somewhat better differentiating features and better representation in terms of tests.[8]

In the order of their supposed likelihood, the most likely first, the three new hypotheses were as follows:

A. DEFINING PROBLEMS   New thinking in connection with this hypothesis recognized at least three steps: (1) determining what information is needed for a solution; (2) deciding which information is relevant; and (3) determining what operations are required for reaching a solution. Such specifications are more readily translated into test ideas.

B. HANDLING COMPLICATED PROCEDURES   This idea recognized complexity as a feature of tests involving general reasoning; the amount of ability required is proportional to the degree of complexity of the problem that can be solved.

C. TRIAL-AND-ERROR MANIPULATION   This hypothesis emphasizes the searching behavior that goes into the solving of problems of certain kinds. The tests designed for this hypothesis may be described as inductive, in view of the fact that the examinee discovers thought patterns through exploratory analysis.

Tests for the Hypotheses

For hypothesis A(1), Necessary Facts presents in each item all the needed facts except one when it asks the question to be answered. E is to supply the missing fact. A sample problem reads

A rectangular water tank is being built. It is 5 feet high and 9 feet long. How many cubic feet will it hold?

For hypothesis A(2), Essential Operations is a multiple-choice test that presents an extra, irrelevant fact in each item. Having been employed in the two earlier analyses, Essential Operations was described earlier.

For hypothesis A(3), the new test Necessary Arithmetic Operations was designed. A problem is completely stated, with E to select the correct answer from among five alternative pairs of proposed arithmetical operations; e.g.,

- A. Add and multiply
- B. Multiply and divide
- C. Subtract and divide
- D. Add and subtract
- E. Divide and add

Four tests were designed for hypothesis B. Ship Destination, which was described earlier, was included because its items vary from simple to complex;

---

[8] See Report 14; also Guilford, Kettner, & Christensen (1956).

from few to many variables. Form Reasoning II was a revision of the Form Reasoning test used earlier. The revised form presents more complicated problems. The Balances test presents in each item a balance with two prescribed weights of unequal values, one on each pan. From a given list of other weights, E is to select two that will bring about balance. The Circle-Square-Triangle test is a complicated one, associating each geometric form with a prescribed object, in each item, and presenting the forms in alternative order of inscription.

As mentioned earlier, the tests for hypothesis C were inductive, calling for the discovery of rules or patterns, where there are a number of plausible alternatives involved. The test Rules presents three sets of three figures each, with a statement that a certain figure was chosen from each set according to a rule. E is to discover the rule. Secret Writing was used earlier. It involves discovering a code that associates letters with digits systematically. Sign Changes II is a revision of Number and Operations Changes I. In it, only sign changes are used, and the equations are only a bit more complicated.

In order to provide continuity with previous analyses, Problem Solving, an arithmetical-reasoning test, was included in the battery. Also included was a Coast Guard test known as "Aptitude—Quantitative, Part I." This test includes two kinds of items, one being of the arithmetical-reasoning type and the other of the number-series-completion type. From present knowledge, this test should represent both CMS and CSS, which should have been expected to complicate things a bit in the factor analysis. Adding further uncertainty was another Coast Guard variable entitled "Mathematical Achievement," which covered secondary school mathematics, with an emphasis upon problem solving involving some ingenuity rather than knowledge of mathematical concepts.

The Original Analysis

Three factors came out very much in line with hypotheses A, B, and C, respectively. On the factor recognized as general reasoning, Ship Destination led, and Necessary Arithmetic Operations and Necessary Facts were significantly loaded, as was Aptitude—Quantitative, Part I. Two of the three tests especially included for the factor were on it. The third, Essential Operations, which had gone rather weakly on general reasoning before, went on the factor called "logical reasoning" instead, but not very strongly. Problem Solving did not go with Ship Destination, as it had gone twice before, but divided its major variance components with logical reasoning and a factor interpreted as "mathematical achievement" instead. Problem Solving correlated higher with the two mathematical Coast Guard tests than it did with most of those in the list for general reasoning; hence its destination in this analysis was not unexpected, once the correlations were known. Although Ship Destination had been allocated to the hypothesis for handling complicated procedures, the fact that it had gone on factors recognized as general reasoning before helped determine the choice of interpretation given its factor in this study. It did have a significant secondary loading on the factor named "handling complicated procedures," to be discussed next.

Three of the four tests designed for handling complicated procedures came out together on a factor, the list being led by Form Reasoning II and having Ship

Destination and Balances on it significantly. Only the test Circle-Square-Triangle was missing. It went instead very weakly on the factor for visualization. Sign Changes II, which had been designed for hypothesis C (trial-and-error manipulation), came in this list. The conjunction of this test with Form Reasoning II leading on this factor would nowadays suggest the factor for convergent production of symbolic implications (NSI), for both involve deductive operations involving symbols.

The factor named for hypothesis C had two of the designed tests leading on it—Rules and Secret Writing. The third test (Form Reasoning II) had its primary relationships with the preceding factor, as just related. The conjunction of the two leading tests now suggests SI ability CSS, for both involve seeing symbolic patterns or principles.

One of the major conclusions from this study is that more than ever the evidence pointed toward hypothesis A: that general reasoning is the ability to conceive of structures, of which an arithmetical problem is a good example, if that structure is sufficiently complex. Simpler structures might be relations or implications. Tests designed to show what information is needed or relevant and what pattern of numerical operations is needed helped determine that factor in this analysis. Another major conclusion is that the two other major hypotheses of this study were still too indefinite to suggest particular operations and products such as are needed to determine tests that bring out factors representing SI abilities. In structuring problems, level of complexity could still be a relevant feature, and the presence of Ship Destination prominently on the general-reasoning factor here and elsewhere supports that idea. If there is trial-and-error manipulation involved, possibly some divergent-production ability or abilities may come into play. No such tests were in the battery for testing this hypothesis.

The Targeted Solution

In the targeted solution, all except one of the Coast Guard tests were eliminated. The chances are that in general they are factorially complex and would therefore not help clear up the factor structure, to say the least. The difficulty expected from two of them was mentioned earlier. The Coast Guard test that remained in this solution was Reading Comprehension, with the prospect of helping segregate the factor for CMU. This it did, as can be seen in Table 5.2.

It will also be seen that a better CSS factor was located, with the conjunction of Secret Writing and Circle Reasoning on it, as in previous analyses, but with Rules still leading on the factor earlier identified as trial-and-error manipulation. The CMS factor corresponds to the one identified as general reasoning before, but with Essential Operations also significantly loaded. Added tests on the factor were Circle-Square-Triangle and Balances. Problem solving again refused to go with these tests, and not having the mathematics-achievement tests to go with it, found itself on a singlet factor in this analysis. Its correlations with the CMS tests in this study were evidently too low.

There is little more to be said about the targeted solution, except to point out the interesting fact that Necessary Arithmetic Operations, which requires no actual number operations, went on MSI with the Numerical Operations test, which does require them. This may mean that in Necessary Arithmetic Operations many *E*s succeed in selecting the right pair of operations by trying out some of the given alternative pairs. The presence of Reading Comprehension on EMI in spite of the fact that it was not so targeted must mean that some testing of deductions by *E* is involved. Experience has shown that reading-comprehension tests can be slanted in various ways factorially, depending upon the test writer's inclinations, explicit or implicit.

STUDIES OF REASONING, CREATIVITY, AND EVALUATION ABILITIES[9]

After two analyses devoted to reasoning abilities (Reasoning A and Reasoning B), one analysis being concentrated on creative-thinking abilities (Reports 4 and 8) and another on evaluation abilities (Reports 7 and 9), it seemed desirable to investigate several abilities from each category together in the same analysis. A major purpose was to determine whether abilities found in each of these categories are distinct from abilities found in the others or whether possibly some pairs of abilities might actually prove to be the same. Further opportunities were afforded, also, to attempt to answer some questions remaining concerning certain factors found within each domain. In this chapter we are concerned with the reasoning abilities involved in that study.

In the earlier studies, altogether 31 factors had been found. Eleven of these factors were outside the three domains of interest in this investigation. Of the remaining 20, 11 were selected for further investigation. Some of the 20 factors were omitted because they were to be investigated more intensively in later studies that were planned. Others were omitted because they had been too weak to be interpreted with any degree of confidence. The reasoning factors to be studied in this analysis were

   Eduction of perceptual relations
   Eduction of conceptual relations
   Eduction of conceptual patterns
   Eduction of correlates
   Symbol manipulation

General reasoning and logical reasoning were included without any new hypotheses or tests being designed for them.

Hypotheses for Five Reasoning Abilities

In accordance with earlier practice, alternative hypotheses were adopted for each of the five reasoning abilities, with the hope of finding just how broad each factor is, i.e., whether it is so broad as to embrace the properties of all the hypotheses for that factor or so narrow as to satisfy only one or two of them. As in the earlier studies, it was thought possible for tests designed for one subhypothesis to determine a new, separate factor.

A number of other questions and issues of a general nature also arose. One of these issues was concerned with the definition of "reasoning." The first three

---

[9]See Reports 11 and 16; also Kettner, Guilford, & Christensen (1959).

factors in the list given above seemed to come in the area of induction or inductive reasoning. It was suggested that they might better be called "discovery" abilities, since all were involved with the discovery of relationships, simple or complex, among given objects or words (Report 11). The factor for eduction of correlates has to do with the fulfillment of relationships. The factor for symbol manipulation found in the Reasoning-B study involved operating with relations between symbols. Since relations are involved in all these factors, it was thought that "reasoning" could be redefined as "relational thinking." This is as near as the investigators came to providing an operational definition for "reasoning." General reasoning would fit this definition in that the ability is concerned with structures of interrelationships. Logical reasoning would fit the definition in that statements of a syllogism, formal or informal, are interrelated.

Another issue arose concerning verbalizing abilities. In prior studies, evidence was obtained concerning the discovery factors by asking E to show that he had discovered the relation or pattern. It was thought that more direct and more dependable evidence could be obtained by simply asking E to name or describe the relation or pattern. Assuming that the act of naming or describing is so easy that there would be no variance contributed to test scores by reason of individual differences in that aspect of the performance, the variance in the discovery factors might thus be enhanced, and their tests might be univocal for their respective discovery factors. On the other hand, if the naming or describing act introduces appreciable unique variance into the scores, there should be a new common factor or factors.

Several possible outcomes were thought possible in the way of naming ability. There could be three naming abilities, one for each of the three discovery abilities concerned. There could be two naming abilities, one for perceptual tasks and one for verbal tasks. Or there could be only one naming ability, the nature of the task's content being irrelevant. Adding to the considerations of this issue were some findings of Adkins and Lyerly (1951). They found a factor designated as "perception of abstract similarities," which was represented by two verbal-classification tests, and a factor they called "concept formation," which was defined as an ability to formulate verbal concepts. The leading tests representing the latter factor were Word-Group Naming and Picture-Group Naming. This factor would suggest a naming ability common to both perceptual and conceptual tasks, but it pertained to the naming of classes rather than the naming of relations and patterns. This raised the further question: Is there an ability in common to naming classes, relations, and patterns?

The Hypotheses and Subhypotheses The major and minor hypotheses for this study are first listed and then very briefly discussed.

    I. Eduction of perceptual relations
       a. Seeing perceptual relations
       b. Seeing perceptual similarities

    II. Eduction of conceptual relations
       a. Seeing conceptual relations
       b. Seeing conceptual similarities

III. Eduction of conceptual patterns
   a. Seeing conceptual patterns
   b. Seeing rules or principles
   c. Seeing trends
IV. Eduction of correlates
   a. Finding something to fit a given perceptual relation
   b. Finding something to fit a given conceptual relation
V. Symbol manipulation
   a. Symbol manipulation
   b. Symbol substitution
VI. Verbalizing ability
   a. Naming perceptual relations
   b. Naming conceptual relations
   c. Naming classes
   d. Stating rules or principles
   e. Describing trends.

It will be noted that under I and II the two alternatives in either case pertain to relations and similarities. The reason for this is that in earlier analyses tests dealing with similarities often came out on factors interpreted as dealing with relations. If findings of such a conjunction were to continue, they could be rationalized by saying that similarity is a kind of relation. But the original hypotheses in Reasoning A made a definite place for an ability or abilities for seeing classes, and Reasoning B had an uninterpreted factor led by a test designed for a factor for seeing similarities. Thus, the possibility for class-discovery abilities was not ruled out. In hypotheses I and II the replicated separation of a perceptual or figural ability from a conceptual one was clearly recognized. Some relation-seeing tests involving symbolic material were added to the battery to see whether they would go on the factor of eduction of conceptual relations. The distinction between symbolic and semantic (verbal) abilities had not yet been seriously considered as a possibility.

Under hypothesis III appear alternatives in line with three earlier subhypotheses. Although the one ability that had been demonstrated in this area (in one analysis only) was interpreted in terms of seeing patterns, it was thought to be desirable again to make possible a separation of tests representing rules, principles, or trends to determine additional factors.

Eduction of correlates had been found in both prior reasoning analyses and also in an analysis of evaluation abilities (Reports 7 and 9). Figural, symbolic, and meaningful-verbal tests were found loaded on it, as was a leading test containing both symbolic and semantic items. In the new analysis, the two latter kinds of items were separated, and generally better representation of different kinds of content was otherwise provided, to see whether there would be two factors (perceptual and conceptual, respectively) instead of one. The tests were all of the completion format, which accounts for the type of wording for the two subhypotheses.

With similar lists of tests to which Symbol Manipulation belonged in common, a factor called "symbol substitution" was found in Reasoning A, and one called "symbolic manipulation" was found in Reasoning B. In this study, better representation of tests was provided for both ideas, in the hope of determining whether there might be two factors rather than one.

Hypothesis VI was introduced, not with the expectation of finding an additional reasoning ability, but to take care of the expectation that there would be one or more abilities involving naming or describing classes, relations, rules, principles, or trends. There could be as many as five such abilities, as indicated by the list given under VI, or there could be none. There had been none before, but there had been insufficient tests in any previous analysis to give such a factor a chance to appear.

Hypotheses concerning the creative-thinking abilities and evaluation abilities involved in the study under discussion will be presented in the following chapters, where they have more precedent and greater relevance. Results from all tests that were analyzed together are presented in Table 5.2 if they fall within the cognition and convergent-production categories.

The Three Analyses

Of the 62 tests used in this study, 32 were thought to represent the five reasoning abilities of special interest, with from 2 to 6 representing each subhypothesis (see Reports 11 and 16). Eight of the tests represented hypotheses under VI, but only c and e in that group had more than one representative, so that something less than six verbalizing factors could normally be expected. There were six reference factors, with their marker tests, to account for possible secondary variances in reasoning tests.

Three separate analyses were performed, denoted as 16A, 16B, and 16C. The reason for three was that the entire battery would have required 12 hours of testing time, more than could be obtained for a single group of subjects. Three overlapping 8 hour batteries were accordingly administered and analyzed. From this arrangement, most expected factors could appear in only two of the three analyses, and some possibly in only one.

The results from these three analyses represented, to that time, the most comprehensive advance in terms of information about abilities, and they made possible the first material steps toward the general structure-of-intellect theory. For the first time some clear distinctions were found between symbolic abilities and both figural and semantic abilities. For the first time, more than one ability pertaining to classes were clearly differentiated from abilities pertaining to relations.

Let us consider briefly the results in relation to the hypotheses. Hypothesis Ia was confirmed, with Figure Analogies and Figure Matrix prominently together in two analyses. For hypothesis Ib, a new factor for perceptual classification was found in one analysis, with Picture Classification, Figure Classification, and Picture-group Naming, and only these three tests, together on it.

Hypothesis IIa was abundantly confirmed, in that two factors of the kind expected came out of the analysis. That is, one called "eduction of conceptual relations" appeared in two analyses (A and B), with Verbal Analogies I and Verbal Analogies Completion leading on it. A factor named "eduction of structural relations" came out strongly in analysis B, with Correlate Completion II and Seeing Trends II strongly on it. Although it had not been anticipated that the former would involve much variance in *seeing* symbolic relations, it evidently does so. Seeing Trends II presents items of the type

> anger   bacteria   camel   dead   excite

with E to name the relation involved, which is an advance by one letter in alphabetical order for the initial letters of the words. Such an item is like one which presents a succession of the same relation in neighboring pairs of words. Correlate Completion II has been described previously. The most significant aspect of finding these two abilities is the differentiation of two parallel "conceptual" variables, one now recognized as semantic and the other as symbolic.

Although a liberal number of tests should have been encouraging for the finding of more than one factor in the area of major hypothesis III, only one was found. The trend tests continued to represent relations abilities, and no discrimination could be found between the factorial nature of tests for seeing patterns and those for seeing rules or principles. Circle Reasoning and Letter Triangle led the list of tests on a factor called "eduction of conceptual patterns." The new tests Letter Series and Number Series went along with them. A very simple example of a letter-series test item is E F E F E ___ ___ ," with the examinee to add the next two letters. An example of a number series test item is "15 18 21 24 27 30 ___ " for which E is to state the rule; in this case, "+3." It will be noted that all four of these tests are composed of symbolic material, from which came the later identification as SI ability CSS.

For hypothesis IV, again, one factor was recognized as being sufficient, with Correlate Completion II and Figure Analogies Completion heading the list. These tests are symbolic in the first case and figural in the second. The remainder of the list of tests on this factor also included both figural and symbolic tests, from which we should now conclude that the factor was a confounding of NFR and NSR. There was some indication of a parallel factor for NMR, although it was not so recognized. Two tests had been designed for this kind of conceptual-completion ability—namely, Verbal Analogies Completion and Inventive Verbal Relations. In the latter, E is to give a word to complete a relationship, being given a word and the relation to be fulfilled. The two tests helped determine another factor, but there were additional tests along with them that do not all help identify the factor as NMR, being somewhat heterogeneous in their properties.

The tests designed in connection with hypothesis V separated to determine two factors, both appearing in analysis 16A, so that we may conclude that they are distinct. The factor called "symbol manipulation" was determined primarily by Symbol Manipulation II and Sign Changes II. Symbol Manipulation II is more complicated than the earlier form by the same name. Each item, after the given statement, contains two statements preceding a block of items:

If x E y and y NE z (if x equals y, and y is not equal to z) then

1. x NE z and y E x

2. x S z and x L z (x is smaller than z, and x is larger than z)

Multiple-choice answers are of the type

A. Both parts are true. B. One part is true, the other indeterminate.

Sign Changes II gives incorrect equations such as 1 + 2 = 4 x 1, with E to say what sign change would make the equation true, with multiple-choice answers. In both cases, it turns out that the multiple-choice format helps make these tests evaluative in nature and their factor is now identified as SI ability ESR.

The factor called "symbol substitution" in the earliest analysis was determined primarily by Sign Changes and Form Reasoning, which are now recognized as determiners for factor NSI. The completion format for Sign Changes, especially, helps put the factor in the convergent-production category. Both the factors just discussed are obviously symbolic as to content category.

Hypothesis VI pertained to tests requiring E to name or describe relations, classes, and trends. There were eight such tests, and the major question was the number of verbalizing abilities to expect. The answer was rather clear. In each of two analyses there was only one naming factor, with four of the naming tests on it. A fifth test was not originally designed for this hypothesis but helped determine it in one analysis. It was Object Synthesis, in which E is to name an object that can be made of two other objects. The verbalizing tests that did not go on the naming factor separated in different directions, some of those directions being reasonable, some not. At any rate, they did not hang together to determine a second naming ability. The factor that did emerge was called "naming abstractions," in view of the fact that both classes and relations were being named in four of the tests and ignoring the fact that objects were being named in the fifth test (Object Synthesis). All three kinds of content were represented in the tests. The major inference should be that it does not matter what is named, class or relation, figural, symbolic, or semantic as to content; the same semantic ability is concerned. A factor for SI ability NMU was later recognized, and the one found in these analyses was probably close to it in common-factor space.

The Targeted Analyses

As previously, the results from the targeted solution are to be found in Table 5.2. All the SI abilities for which there were reasonable indications in the original analysis were identified more clearly and definitively in the targeted solution. But, as usual in the earlier analyses, where many SI abilities were represented each by one test only, there were many singlet factors. This situation is somewhat ameliorated by the fact that, where there was a singlet in one of the three analyses, there were one or more corresponding nonsinglets in one or both of the other two analyses. In 6 of all 24 factors brought out by targeted rotations, only singlets represented them. Four of these are in the evaluation area; only two are in the reasoning area.

Only a few of the special highlights of the targeted solution will be mentioned. Two factors were found by the latter procedure that were missed by the original solution. One was cognition of symbolic classes (CSC), found in two analyses. The definitive tests were Letter Grouping and Word Groups. Letter Grouping is a classification test of the "exclusion" type. E is given four letter groups, each composed of four letters, and is to say which group does not belong to the class; for example,

    AABC   ACAD   ACFH   AACG

Word Groups is a class-naming test. In it, E is given four words, such as

    read   retire   rearming   restless

which all begin with "re," and E is to report this fact.

The other new factor has been identified as representing ability EMC, an ability that was recognized in three analyses. This ability belongs in the evaluation category, and a discussion of it will be found in Chapter 7.

A noteworthy clarification of factors occurred in the eduction-of-correlates area. Where the original solution gave what was noted previously as a confounding of NFR and NSR, a separation of the two was effected in the targeted solution. A factor for ability NMR that was detected in two analyses of the original solutions was found also in the third analysis by the targeted method. Other differences in the two solutions pertain to creative and evaluative abilities, which will be treated in the next two chapters.

ANALYSIS OF ABILITIES IN PROBLEM SOLVING

The placing of the analysis of abilities expected to play roles in problem solving among studies of reasoning abilities has the support of a traditional association of the two.[10] It turned out that at least half of the factorial abilities involved in the study were relational in character and were inductive or deductive. Two new deductive abilities were demonstrated for the first time, thus adding empirical justification for including the problem-solving study in this chapter.

    A Problem-solving Model

Although the way was left open for the discovery of a unique problem-solving ability, as was true from the beginning of the analyses devoted to reasoning abilities, the initial belief in this study was that problem solving is a complex affair, involving a number of unique abilities, depending upon the nature of the problem. In spite of this belief, problem solving, in whatever connection, was thought operationally to possess a characteristic overall pattern, involving certain sequences of events.

A number of such patterns or models have been suggested for problem-solving episodes, beginning with John Dewey (1910). Considering all these earlier suggestions, the model adopted as the starting point for this investigation included five steps, phases, or aspects: preparation, analysis, production, verification, and reapplication.

The preparation phase is the one in which the problem arises and is recognized as being a problem. In this phase, enough information may be available to alert the solver concerning the general nature of the problem and its degree of urgency. There is just the beginning of understanding as to the nature

---

[10]See Report 22; also Merrifield, Guilford, Christensen, & Frick (1962).

of the problem, which is carried to a much more complete status in the phase of analysis.

By virtue of analysis, the solver becomes better oriented, with conceptions of the situation as it exists and of the goal situation that would exist if the problem were solved. He has situation-based data and goal-based data. He needs somehow to bridge the gap between the two.

In the production phase, alternative solutions are generated, designed to bridge the gap between the problem situation and the goal situation. The generation of solutions is conducted under the influence of a search model that is set up in accordance with the understanding of the nature of the problem and the goal to be achieved.

In the verification phase, solutions are considered in comparison with the search model, and some or all are rejected. Rejection often leads to backtracking, which involves the phase of reapplication. The backtracking may involve the generation of new solutions from the same search model, or possibly a new search model, or even a revision of the understanding of the problem.

The structure-of-intellect theory and model were not yet available during the initial planning of the study of problem solving abilities. It became clear later that the analysis phase of the problem-solving model involves cognition abilities; the production phase involves divergent and convergent production; and the verification phase involves evaluation. The problem-solving model served the purpose of suggesting abilities in these four operation categories.

Hypothesized Problem-solving Abilities

In hypothesizing abilities on the basis of the problem-solving model, emphasis was placed upon the production phase, and special attention was given to operations of thinking forward from the conceived problem situation and thinking backward from the conceived goal situation. Six hypothesized abilities were thus generated, four pertaining to thinking forward from the problem situation and two pertaining to thinking backward from the goal situation. After each hypothesis was adopted and new tests were developed (or old ones adapted) for the testing of that hypothesis, consideration was given to what already known factorial ability might be heavily involved, and the known factor was later given an SI designation. The six hypotheses and the kinds of information associated with them, as just indicated, will be presented next.

I. The Ability to Think Rapidly of Several Attributes or Characteristics of a Given Object

TESTS

Attribute Listing I E lists attributes of a given object, e.g., "chewing gum," such as "is made from chicle," "comes wrapped in paper," "sticks to furniture," etc.

Differences E lists ways in which two objects differ; e.g., given "apple and banana," he could say "round versus long," "hard versus soft," "thin peel versus thick peel," etc.

Similarities E gives as many as six ways in which two objects are alike; e.g., given "apple and orange," he might say "sweet," "have seeds," "grow on trees," etc.

The previously known abilities that were thought to have possible relationships to these tests (denoted later in SI terms) were divergent production of semantic units (DMU) and divergent production involving relations (DMR). The marker tests that were included in the battery to test these ideas were Ideational Fluency and Associational Fluency, respectively.

II. The Ability to Classify Objects or Ideas

TESTS

Sentence Pairs From two short lists of sentences, E is to match sentences such that the two of a pair have similar meaning.

Word Grouping Given a list of 12 familiar words, E is to group them in four mutually exclusive sets.

The SI ability thought most likely to be involved is cognition of semantic classes (CMC), for which the marker test was Verbal Classification. In this test, E is given a list of words and is to put each word in one of two classes that are represented by two sets of words or to say that it fits neither class.

III. The Ability to Find Different Relations between Attributes of an Object or Situation

TESTS

Figure Concepts (uncommon) From a collection of line drawings of common objects, E is to find sets of two each, the members having something in common. In scoring this test, pairs were weighted in proportion to their degree of uncommonness, determined statistically, a score designed to emphasize credit for remote connections. This system also weights level of abstraction.

Paired Similarities Given pairs of verbalized concepts, E is to state one way in which the two are similar; e.g., "quarter-fifth"; "nickel-quarter"; "quarter-inning"; etc.

Sequential Associations Given four common words, E is to arrange their order so that each is naturally associated with the next in sequence. A sample item reads

    pen   pig   read   write

    ___   ___   ___   ___

Writing the digits 1 to 4 on the blanks, in this item E should give the order 2, 1, 4, 3 to achieve the best associative sequence.

The relevant SI abilities were thought to be cognition of semantic relations (CMR) and convergent production of semantic relations (NMR). They were represented by the marker tests Verbal Analogies I and Vocabulary Completion, respectively.

IV. The Ability to Think of Alternative Outcomes of a Given Situation

TESTS

Multiple Grouping   Given a list of common words, E is to group and regroup them in various meaningful ways.

Object Synthesis III E is to list as many as five things that could be made using both of two given objects; e.g., given "nail and cane," he could list "spear," "hook," "cross," etc.

The generation of alternatives required by both of these tests immediately suggests divergent production. The most obvious SI ability suggested by Multiple Grouping is divergent production of semantic classes (DMC). Two DMC marker tests were included in the battery—Brick Uses (shifts) and Object Naming (shifts). In both tests the multiple responses are scored in terms of the number of times E changes classes.

At the time this study was being organized, distinctions between products were not well recognized, so two other abilities, DMU and DMT, were also suspect; DMT especially for the test Object Synthesis III, in which the simple objects take on different functions as they are used in different, more complex objects. Taking on different functions means transformation. The DMT marker test included was Cartoons, in which, given a cartoon, E is to write an appropriate "punch line" for it. It was previously thought to represent DMT (Report 17). Because the original Object Synthesis test had previously helped determine factor NMT, ability NMT was tolerated in this connection for Object Synthesis III, in spite of allowing as many as five alternative answers. The marker test for NMT was Gestalt Transformation, which asks which object could be adapted to some unusual purpose, with multiple-choice answers being given to E.

V. The Ability to List Attributes of the Specified Goal or Desired Situation

TESTS

Apparatus Test (drastic changes); Apparatus Test (minor changes)   These "tests" were actually two scores derived from the responses to the Apparatus test. The latter asks E to state two things that are wrong or deficient about each of a number of common appliances, such as a telephone or a refrigerator. The "desirable goal" is a better appliance, in the context of this study, and each thing wrong pertains to some attribute of the object. The two scores, discriminating between drastic and minor changes, were expected possibly to indicate different abilities.

Attribute Listing II E lists the necessary attributes of an object needed to serve a given purpose; e.g., for "driving a long nail into a hard post" he might say "object can be held in the hand"; "it is harder than the nail"; "it has a flat striking surface"; etc.

An Apparatus Test had previously helped prominently to determine a factor called "sensitivity to problems." The first placement of this ability in the SI model was in the cell evaluation of semantic implications (EMI), with the thought that the objects were being evaluated and found wanting. A marker test for the supposed EMI ability was accordingly chosen, namely, Seeing Problems, which asks E to state what difficulties could arise in using common objects, such as a candle. It was thought that the "drastic changes" score for the Apparatus Test might call for some originality; hence DMT might be involved. Its marker test, Cartoons, has already been mentioned.

VI. The Ability to Educe Logically Sufficient Antecedents to a Specified Situation   The produced solutions in connection with the problem-solving model are realistically prior to the goal situation in time, and hence can be regarded as antecedents. Four tests were designed dealing with seeing antecedents to events.

TESTS

Common Needs   This test requires E to pair off objects from two short lists for the reason that both members of a pair require a similar operation before they can be used. For example, a banana and a book of matches require an uncovering act, a stamp and a mailbox presuppose the writing of a letter, and so on.

Contingencies   A situation is described and various circumstances that prevail; e.g., "Sally and Jane go berry picking." Certain objects that might possibly come into use are named; e.g., "ointment," "safety pin," and "cane." E is to state what occasions might call each object into use; e.g., "insect bites," "torn dresses," "wild animal," respectively.

Episodes E is to write two explanations for a specified action. One example of an action is a man sitting reading a magazine. He suddenly closes the magazine and strides out of the room. Possible explanations are that his wife has called him to dinner or he suddenly realizes that he is late for an appointment.

Possibilities E is to name as many as four alternative objects that could be used to perform a specified task.

It was recognized that all these tests in their various ways call for implied answers, and that probably cognition is the operation. Hence SI ability CMI was indicated, for which the marker test was Pertinent Questions. In this test E is to ask several questions that occur to him in connection with a proposed action, such as setting up a new hamburger stand in a chosen location. The four new experimental tests involve seeing antecedents, whereas Pertinent Questions involves seeing consequences, but it was suspected that both kinds of activity would entail the cognition of semantic implications.

A Possible Problem-solving Factor With the possibility that a unique problem-solving-ability factor might exist, four variables were put in the battery, based on three tests, one of which was scored in two ways. These tests were designed in accordance with the problem-solving model that was basic to the study, and each emphasized filling a gap between the initial situation and the final or goal situation. With the thought that such tasks represent the pattern of problem-solving tasks in general, there was also the opportunity to find whether known abilities could account for some of the variances in individual differences in those relatively complex activities.

TESTS

Missing Links E produces three words to complete a chain of associations between two given words; e.g.,

     red _____ _____ _____ beer

E might fill the gap by giving the words "sunset," "weather," and "cold" in the three blanks in the order given.

Predicaments Each item in Predicaments presents a practical problem. A sample describes the arrival of a group of friends at a picnic, where they find that they have a solid piece of cheese and no knife for slicing. E is to select from alternative available objects two that might be adapted to solving the problem. With the alternatives "harmonica, matches, thermos bottle, and guitar," he should select "thermos bottle" and "guitar," parts of which could be adapted in whole or in part to making thin slices of cheese.

Transitions This test presents the beginning and ending for each of a number of short stories, with E to fill the gap with events that he believes to be consistent with what went before and what comes after. The "logical" score is based upon the number of elements that he gives among those that should be accounted for. The "coherence" score for a story is a scorer's rating of E's discourse for degree of coherence.

Some Reference Factors and Their Tests In addition to some of the already mentioned, expected and known factorial abilities that might be relevant in these problem-solving tests, three other SI abilities were thought to be possibly related. These abilities and their marker tests were

    Cognition of semantic units (CMU), with the test Verbal Comprehension, a multiple-choice vocabulary test
    Cognition of semantic system (CMS), with the test Ship Destination
    Evaluation of semantic relations (EMR), with the test Logical Reasoning

For some time it was thought that the multiple-choice tests in syllogistic and near-syllogistic form were measures of EMR, but it was later demonstrated that they are usually more heavily loaded on EMI (Report 32).

It has probably been noticed that all the SI abilities thought to be possibly relevant are in the semantic category. This restriction was intentional. By the time this study was planned, the three-category content distinctions were recognized. In order to keep this analysis of reasonable size, it was decided to remain within the one content category. Generalization of conclusions to other content categories may not be taken for granted, but the parallel nature of abilities in the content categories lent some hope for expecting that such generalizations would be reasonable.

The Original Analysis

Fourteen factors were extracted and rotated, of which 12 could be given psychological interpretation. No unique factor common to the four problem-solving variables was evident. All factors could be identified as SI abilities, and the problem-solving test variables were significantly loaded on several of them, not exclusively on any one. There were five cognition abilities represented— CMU, CMC, CMR, CMS, and CMI; three divergent-production abilities—DMU, DMR, and DMT; three convergent-production abilities—NMC, NMR, and NMI; and supposedly one evaluation ability—EMI (known at that time as "sensitivity to problems" and treated in the next chapter). Of the 12 interpreted factors, two were reported for the first time—NMC and NMI. If we may say that the cognition abilities are inductive and the convergent-production abilities are deductive, then eight of the abilities accounted for were in the area of reasoning. By this time, however, the concept of "reasoning" was rapidly losing significance with the ARP.

The Targeted Analysis

By hindsight, 15 SI abilities were thought to be represented, and 15 factors were extracted and rotated. The results identified the same 12 abilities as before, with three others added—CMT, DMC, and NMT. The most noteworthy difference between the two solutions was that the tests for factors CMI and EMI in the original analysis were brought together on a single CMI factor in the targeted analysis. This change reflected the finding in the interim that the factor thought to be "sensitivity to problems" and identified with SI ability EMI is, after all, CMI. A related noteworthy finding was the relatively large number of tests on factor CMI, including one of the problem-solving variables—Transitions (logical aspects) (see Table 5.2). The reason for this is the emphasis on "filling a gap" in the problem-solving model. What goes into the gap is implied by what is on either side of it, i.e., the problem situation and the goal situation. Another problem-solving test—Missing Links—went strongly on factor NMI. Thus, seeing implications and producing (deducing) implications are prominent activities in solving such problems.

The other problem-solving variables had their major affiliations elsewhere. Predicaments loaded significantly, but to a small extent, on the factor for NMT. The similarity of the task in this test to that in Gestalt Transformations is obvious. Both require using an object or part of an object to perform some new and unusual function. The variable Transitions (coherence aspects) went most strongly on CMU. This result might be a function of the kind of scoring used, which was a rating on each story completion given by the scorer, who may have used apparent verbal comprehension as the chief criterion, perhaps unwittingly so. Other relationships of the problem-solving scores to some of the factors may be seen in Table 5.3.

Fate of the Hypotheses We next note briefly what happened to the six hypotheses regarding the components of problem solving, as shown by the targeted solution. The first hypothesis, on thinking of attributes of objects, failed to achieve coherent support. The test Attribute Listing I had no significant loading on any factor, and its communality was only .16 in this test battery. Its reliability was only .25, so it has little possibility in its present form of having relations to any common factors. The test Differences, in which each item entails listing differences seen between two given objects, proved to be a fair measure of ideational fluency (DMU). The test Similarities, which called for listing common attributes of pairs of objects, however, went most strongly on the factor for DMR, with a trace of DMC. A similarity appears to be a relation, where a difference is not; thus the two tests reflect different abilities.

The hypothesis about ability to see classes produced two tests that did, in fact, pertain to classes, but Sentence Pairs came out strongly on CMC, whereas Word Grouping came out strongly on NMC. The first of these tests called merely for matching sentences for similarity of meaning, so cognition was sufficient. The second test required a partitioning of a set of word meanings into mutually exclusive classes; hence production is involved. The same kind of separation of classes tests was found later to be more general (Report 39).

The tests for the hypothesis about finding relationships also went in different directions. Figure Concepts (uncommon) helped determine the factor for NMC. This result suggests that the task is one of partitioning the 20 pictured objects by twos. Had there been many reclassifications, using each object more than once, there should have been some DMC variance. The latter factor was

Table 5.3 Loading of the Four Problem-solving Variables on Their Strongest Factorial Components*

Test Variables	Factors							
	CMU	CMC	CMT	CMI	DMU	DMR	NMT	NMI
Missing Links	.17	.13	.17	.16	.30	.22	−.04	.40
Predicaments	.07	.20	−.04	.47	.08	.11	.34	.07
Transitions (coherence)	.43	.18	.24	.28	.28	−.06	−.09	.12
Transitions (logical aspects)	.01	.07	.21	.60	.13	.05	.12	.00

*A factor was included here if there was a loading of .20 or greater on any of the four variables.

available in the analysis. The test Paired Similarities went on a factor identified as NMU, the naming ability that received so much attention in analyses 16A, B, and C, reported just previously. It is essentially a class-naming test. Sequential Associations helped determine factor NMI, a deductive ability. The four words are to be rearranged so that each word is reasonably associated to the next. E must produce a series in which each word naturally implies the next.

Thinking of alternative outcomes, the fourth hypothesis, suggests divergent production, as mentioned earlier. The suspected SI factors DMC and DMT did materialize in the two intended tests in the targeted analysis.

Attribute Listing II was the most natural representative of hypothesis V, since it involved a listing of attributes of a goal situation. The attributes to be listed are for an object that is needed to serve a certain purpose. The task calls for implications, and ability NMI was the test's strongest affiliation, but only minimally, at that. Its communality was .39, and with a reliability of only .41, its common-factor components seem to be entirely accounted for in this analysis.

In the targeted analysis, the two scores for the Apparatus Test were combined, as had been the procedure for all analyses prior to this study, and it helped determine its characteristic factor CMI rather than EMI. This point was discussed earlier. Where there were two scores—drastic and minor—in the original analysis, the score based on drastic changes went with DMT, and the score for minor changes went with CMI. Drastic changes are unusual and thus are likely to involve transformations. Two responses are called for in every item; hence some divergent production. With the two scores combined, with the variance for minor changes outweighing that for drastic ones, CMI won out at the expense of DMT.

Hypothesis VI pertained to eduction of "logically sufficient antecedents" to situations. This expression suggests implications, and two of the four tests came out in that category, Contingencies for CMI and Common Needs for NMI. Episodes had no significant loadings, but it should be a promising type of test for ability DMI, especially if more than two alternative answers are called for. Possibilities came out on DMT in the targeted analysis. Each item calls for as many as four objects that can be used to perform a given function. Multiple answers involve divergent production, and with more than one or two responses to an item, E undoubtedly becomes involved in some unusual uses and transformations; hence ability DMT.

General Conclusions

The general upshot of the findings in this investigation of problem solving is that that phenomenon appears to be even more complicated than before. The model of problem solving employed involves more than the production phase on which this study was more or less concentrated. Even within the production phase, quite a number of abilities were found to be relevant to hypotheses. There was also some restriction in emphasis upon "gap-filling" problems; there are other types of problems. On the negative side, it appears that there is no unique problem-solving ability, and that the functions implied by the SI model can go a long way in accounting for different aspects of problem solving. Actually, almost any test can be regarded as a problem-solving task of its own kind. Those aimed at the differentiation of particular unique abilities often succeed in excluding most other abilities from affecting individual differences in scores, while letting one of them make the dominant contribution to variance among scores.

THE STUDY OF SYMBOLIC ABILITIES
Of the series of analytical studies treated in this chapter, the one devoted to symbolic abilities was the first to be planned on the basis of structure-of-intellect theory. The reason for including a report of that study here is that more than half of the abilities involved come in the inductive (cognition) and deductive (convergent-production) categories.[11] Many of them pertain to classes, relations, and systems, which were the products of information involved in tests of reasoning abilities in previous studies.

When it became realized that there is a content category of symbolic information, psychologically distinct from figural and semantic, it was also apparent that relatively less was known about that area of abilities. Hence, the study under discussion was initiated primarily to make up for that deficit. It was also the first major attempt to determine whether abilities hypothesized from the SI model could be demonstrated by factor analysis. The predictive value of the SI model could thus be tested. Altogether the model calls for 30 symbolic abilities, differing as to kind of operation and as to kind of product. Only 11 such abilities had been previously recognized. In order to keep the study within practical limits, hypothetical abilities were selected from the cognition and convergent-production categories only.

Hypothesized Abilities and Their Tests
Five symbolic abilities in the two operation categories just indicated were under investigation for the first time by the ARP–CSU, CSC, CSI, NSU, and NSS. Two others–CSR and NST–were studied for the sake of confirmation, for they had been found previously in one analysis only. New tests were used for all seven of these abilities. They are briefly characterized as follows.

CSU—Cognition of Symbolic Units

TESTS

Alterations   For each given, familiar word, E indicates whether or not another word can be made simply by reversing the order of any two adjacent letters; e.g.,

    SUE   BRAKE   TIME   LOIN

Disemvowelled words   Familiar words are given for recognition, with all the vowels left blank; e.g.,

    m ___ g ___ c   d ___ ct ___ r   s ___ rpr ___ s ___ .

Four-Letter Words   Words are to be recognized and circled within lines of mixed letters; e.g.,

    A M G E W I N D Y E T K C Q R O C K W Z L U R E M V

---

[11]See Report 23; also Guilford, Merrifield, Christensen, & Frick (1961).

Omelet Test   *E* is to rearrange four letters to make a familiar word; e.g., the four letters "P A N L."

CSC—Cognition of Symbolic Classes

TESTS

Letter Grouping   Four groups of four letters each are given. Three belong to a class—for example, because each group contains two A's, as in

    CAYA   LRAA   TGAQ   AKAW

E is to point out the nonmember.

Number Classification   *E* is to say which of five numbers belongs in the same class with each set of three numbers, such as "44 77 22" or "45 10 85," where the correct alternatives are "66" and "40," respectively.

Number Relations   *E* is to recognize a pair of numbers that does not belong to the set of number pairs because it does not possess the same relation. In the pairs 1–5, 2–6, 5–8, and 3–7, the third (5–8) does not belong because the common relation is "four less than." Here is an example of the fact that, if the test is successful for CSC, there can be a class of relations. In other tests it is commonly classes of units of information.

CSR—Cognition of Symbolic Relations

TESTS

Letter Analogies   By analogy to the tests Figure Analogies and Verbal Analogies is a test composed of single letters. A sample item reads "mo fh j ___," with the alternative answers "k, l, u, i, p."

Seeing Trends II   This trend test was described and illustrated earlier in this chapter.

Word Relations   Another analogies test uses words that are related by certain spelling characteristics. It is like Correlate Completion II, except that alternative answers are given, as in

    on   no   top   pot   part   _____
    A. art   B. pat   C. rapt   D. tart   E. trap

CSI—Cognition of Symbolic Implications

TESTS

Limited Sums   *E* is to combine digits from a given list in such ways as to arrive at specified totals, using addition only. For example, he might be asked to make totals of 7 or 9, given the digits 1, 2, 3, 4, 4, using each one only as often as it appears in the list.

Symbol Grouping E is given a set of scrambled symbols such as "$X-OX-X$" and is told to rearrange them by moving one or more adjacent symbols so as to get all X's first, dashes next, and O's last, in as few moves as possible.

Word Patterns E arranges a number of short words in a kind of crossword-puzzle pattern so as to write as few letters as possible.

NSU—Convergent Production of Symbolic Units

TESTS

Number–group naming E states how the three numbers of each set are alike. For example, he is to say that the numbers 35 110 75 are "divisible by 5."

Word groups E states the common property of each set of four words, where that property is a feature of spelling; e.g.,

      maim   test   gang   label

These two tests were used to test the possibility that if the thing to be named or described is a symbolic property, the ability would be NSU. To take care of the alternative possibility that a convergently produced name or description is in the semantic category and the ability is NMU, regardless of its source, a marker test for the factor for NMU was put into the battery.

NSS—Convergent Production of Symbolic Systems

TESTS

Operations Sequence   The kind of system that worked for the parallel ability NMS requires E to arrange actions or events in temporal order, so tests of this type were developed for NSS, where the events deal with letters or numbers. The problem in each item is to start with a given number and to arrive at another given number, applying in proper sequence three given operations. For example, starting with the number 6 and arriving at the number 18, what is the appropriate order for the operations $+3, \div 2$, and $\times 3$?

Word Changes   An analogous test with words gives a starting word and an end word, with four other words needed to go from the first to the last word, changing one and only one letter at a time. A sample item gives SET and CRY as initial and final words, respectively. The intervening words are DAY SAT DRY SAY, but not in that order.

NST—Convergent Production of Symbolic Transformations

TESTS   A factor that appeared suggestive for SI ability NST had been found in one previous analysis (Report 18). Only one clearly reasonable test appeared on the factor, but it led the list. The test was Camouflaged Words. Each item is a meaningful statement in which there is concealed the name of a sport or a game. E is to make that name by breaking down given words and forming a new one, usually from the end of one word and the beginning of the next, as in the sentence, "He could not reach essential conclusions." Other tests were added in this investigation.

Word Combinations   This test confines the same operation to pairs of words.

> Given the words: 1. bridge, 2. beam, 3. open.
> Which of these words provide endings? A. duress, B. zero, C. pledge, D. need, E. none of these.
> Answers: 1—D (gene); 2—C (ample); 3—A (endure).

Word Transformations   Used in the first analysis of creative thinking (Reports 4 and 8), this test presents phrases, e.g., THE RED OLIVE, the letters of which are to be regrouped without changing their order to form new words; e.g., in this case, THERE DO LIVE.

The Original and Targeted Analyses

The two analyses agreed well enough, with differences in certain details only, so they can be discussed together. On the positive side, of the expected new factors, both solutions found CSU, CSC, and NSS. Both confirmed factors CSR and NST, which needed additional support. Both failed to find a factor common to the two tests designed for NSU. In the original analysis those two tests went with Picture-Group Naming on a factor marked by the latter test for NMU. In the targeted analysis, Number-Group Naming led the list for CSC, which would indicate that the cognition of classes dominated the variance for that test. Word Groups, however, went on NSC, which is reasonable, for it is a classification test of the exclusion type, which requires E to form two classes, one class having only one member. But it also went on CSR, for which there is no obvious reason.

General Conclusions

By way of general conclusions, we may say that the SI model was quite successful in pointing to previously unknown abilities that could be demonstrated, and that reconfirmed factors consistently claim their SI placements. We can say that symbolic abilities are separable from semantic abilities, since factors for CMU, CMS, and NMS were distinct from their parallel mates CSU, CSS, and NSS, respectively, in this study. As a third conclusion it looks as if, to find a factor for the SI-hypothesized ability NSU, we shall need tests that require the actual production of symbolic units. Such a test might well have much in common with crossword puzzles. It is possible that although the thing produced must be a certain combination and sequence of letters, the specifications could be either symbolic or semantic, or both.

AN ANALYSIS OF FIGURAL-COGNITION AND FIGURAL-CONVERGENT-PRODUCTION ABILITIES

A study (Report 40) that was aimed primarily at figural-evaluation abilities quite late in the series reported in this volume also gave considerable attention to the six figural-cognition abilities. These six abilities were included primarily to determine whether evaluation tests had controlled cognition variances successfully. But it was also realized that the six had never previously been analyzed together in the same study, and here was an opportunity to differentiate them from one another and to verify their placements in the SI model. There were also opportunities to check on their differentiations from three parallel figural-divergent-production abilities, two convergent-production abilities, and one memory ability, all figural. New tests were developed also in order to examine certain hypotheses regarding the best kinds of tests to represent the figural-cognition abilities. There were attempts to settle certain special issues in connection with some of the factor tests.

The Visual-Figural-Cognition Abilities and Their Tests

Most attention here will be given to the new tests; for sample items the reader is referred to Appendix B. Formerly analyzed tests in the figural-cognition category are also illustrated in the same place.

Cognition of Figural Units (CFU) Tests dating back to Thurstone's analysis of perception (Thurstone, 1944) helped determine for him a factor that he called "perceptual speed," which was subsequently known as "closure" and in the ARP research was eventually known as "CFU." His Mutilated Words test was used in the analysis under discussion for the sake of continuity. A new form of his Hidden Digits test was constructed and given the new name "Hidden Print," since it contained both digits and letters as figures. Each letter or digit is formed by a pattern of dots, sprinkled within and about which is a collection of randomly distributed dots to make recognition difficult.

A new test called "Figure Completion" is a new form of the Street Gestalt Completion test, in which pictures of familiar objects are printed in fragmented form, with E to name each object. Another new test for CFU is called "Close-ups," for the reason that each item is a photograph of some familiar object, or part of an object, taken at very close range. Again, E is to name the object, e.g., a keyhole or a part of a pineapple.

It was hoped that two general questions about CFU tests would be answered in the new analysis. One was on how much emphasis should be placed upon assumed acts of "closure." All tests in this short list clearly require closure in the sense of filling gaps in objects in order to cognize them as units, with the exception of Close-Ups, in which lines and surfaces are not fragmented. If the latter test were to go strongly on the same factor as the other tests, we could conclude that closure is not an essential feature for tests of CFU.

There is the second question of whether closure against distractions, as represented by the test Hidden Print, is a necessary condition for measuring CFU. Some earlier writers had emphasized this distraction feature for tests of closure. If Hidden Print were to be absent from the list of tests for CFU in the analysis, the result would suggest that distracting information is not a necessary condition. It had already been shown a number of times that tests requiring closure without distractions are well qualified for CFU.

Cognition of Figural Classes (CFC) Only two marker tests were included to determine the factor for this ability. They were Figure Classification and Figural-Class Inclusion. The former is in a short matching format and the latter in a multiple-choice format (see Report 39 for information on previous performances).

Cognition of Figural Relations (CFR) An incidental issue was recognized in connection with tests for CFR. Some of the previously used tests for CFR present relations between pairs of figures that could also be cognized as changes or transformations, e.g., a rotation of a figure over a certain number of degrees. This fact can be coupled with outcomes of analyses in which some tests are found loaded on both CFR and CFT. Test revisions were aimed at ridding previously used tests of CFR from this kind of confusion.

Previously useful tests for CFR have been Figure Analogies and Figure Matrix, which have been encountered earlier in this chapter. A new test, Figure Series, is an adapted form of R. B. Cattell's Series. In the new form, a somewhat complex figure or set of figures is shown with a progressive change in three steps. E is to select from five alternatives the figure that should be the fourth in the given series. As in all exact-trend tests, the relation of each object to the next in the series is the same.

Cognition of Figural Systems (CFS) An issue arising in connection with tests for CFS also involves tests for CFT. In the past, it has seemed that successful tests for CFS have involved systems that include the viewer; his body provides the frame of reference for the perceived systems. Such tests will be called "body-centered." The tests successful for CFT, on the other hand, have involved systems apparently free from the viewer's frame of reference We may call them "figure-centered" systems. There was interest in seeing whether both kinds of systems would be suitable in tests for either CFS or CFT.

Two traditional, body-centered tests in the new analysis were Spatial Orientation, an abridged form of the Guilford-Zimmerman Aptitude Survey, Part V, and Space Positioning, a new form of Clark Wilson's Spatial Orientation test (see Reports 1 and 3).

Spatial Comprehension was a new test. It gives verbal descriptions of arrangements of objects in a certain location, such as a room, emphasizing positions in relation to one another. The effect is probably to get E's body out of the system.

The new test, Blocks, is an adaptation of Thurstone's Block Counting test. Pictured in each item is a neat pile of brick-shaped blocks. The problem for E is to count the number of blocks that touch each block that is marked with a letter. It was hypothesized that the pile of ordered blocks is a figure-centered system and that E shows his appreciation of the arrangement of blocks in the process of counting the touching blocks.

Cognition of Figural Transformations (CFT) A test known to be successful for CFT is Spatial Visualization, which is Part VI of the Guilford-Zimmerman Aptitude Survey, used in abridged form in this analysis. It is thought to be primarily of the figure-centered type, but it has a secondary loading on EFS, which may mean that it is not entirely free from some body centering.

Block Rotation is an adaptation of a common, usually unpublished, type of test. E is shown first a block of somewhat complex form and then five alternative views, one of which represents the first block after rotation. The test can be considered at least partially body-centered, depending upon E's strategy.

Block Visualization describes entirely verbally how a rectangular block of wood of a certain size is painted in different colors on its surfaces, then cut into small, cubical blocks. E is to say how many cubes have sides of certain colors or color combinations. It was thought that the verbal presentation would help rid the test of body-centered aspects.

Paper Folding shows a sketch of a sheet of paper being folded in certain ways, then a hole of a certain shape being cut at a certain location. Five alternative answers show the unfolded paper with possible creases and holes, with one of them having creases and holes in the right places and of the right shapes. Paper Folding should be primarily a figure-centered test.

Cognition of Figural Implications (CFI) In connection with CFI, a serious question arose about the previous identifications of the A.A.F.'s foresight factor and the ARP's equivalent "perceptual-foresight" factor with CFI. The marker tests for CFI typically present pathways from starting points to goals, as in Route Planning (a maze-tracing test) and Planning a Circuit (an electrical-circuit-tracing test). Now a figural implication should be an extrapolation from given lines to lines not given, whereas in these two tests there is nothing to be extrapolated; complete lines are given. Rather, there is a task of comparing given implications and deciding which one is satisfactory. This seems instead to satisfy the definition of "evaluation"; hence in the analysis in question, these two tests were hypothesized for EFI.

Two new tests were developed for CFI, in each of which extrapolation of lines by E is necessary. Circle Continuations gives in each item a part of a circle and five alternative lettered points. E is to say through which point the circle would pass if it were completed. The other new test for CFI was Line Continuations. A single line is shown up to the point of crossing two parallel, straight lines or two "parallel" curved lines, at an acute angle. Four short lines are shown as potential continuations of the line on the other side of the parallel lines, one of the four being correct. In both new tests there is a gap to be filled as an extrapolation, or we can say that one of the continuations is correctly implied by the given information.

The analysis was not confined to these two tests for CFI, as things turned out. This was fortunate, because the two tests are so similar. One difference is the Poggendorf illusion in the second one and no apparent illusion in the first. A third A.A.F. test had been selected to go with the two, namely, Competitive Planning. This test had previously helped determine a factor along with the other two planning tests—Route Planning and Planning a Circuit. But it differs in that E has to see an extrapolation, when he completes squares in that test. Not all the information is given. E is to play the game of completing squares for two contestants so as to complete as many squares as he can for both. Some starting lines are given, but E has to write in the implied lines—implied by what is given at each move and by the rules of the game. It can be said here that Competitive Planning stayed with the other two planning tests, together with new tests for EFI, so all three are best regarded as evaluation tests. A third test, Blocks, went with the two line-continuation tests reasonably to help determine a new factor for CFI. This finding will be discussed later.

Convergent-Production Factors and Their Tests

Convergent Production of Figural Transformations (NFT) In scattered studies done by the ARP, factors had been found, usually represented by tests in which E has to produce a reorganization or to revise the use of certain lines in order to see a hidden figure. The most characteristic tests have been the A.A.F. instrument, Penetration of Camouflage, and Hidden Figures, which uses the Gottschaldt figures. The former is a hidden-faces test. In the latter, one of five simple figures may be found embedded in each more complex figure. Those two tests were used as markers for NFT in the figural analysis of Report 40. The earliest evidence of such an ability was from Thurstone's analysis of perception, in which he found a factor interpreted as "flexibility of closure" (Thurstone, 1944).

The ARP factor was again identified as NFT in the analysis of Report 40, but leading the list of tests much more strongly was a new test, Internally Consistent Figures. Each item presents a somewhat complex line drawing composed of joining planes, with E to say whether or not the internal arrangements are mutually consistent. As long as E sees each figure as a two-dimensional affair, there is no inconsistency in any of them. When he makes three-dimensional representations out of the figures, half of them are normal; the planes join as they should. But the other half are impossible because the planes could not join in the manner shown, as in a real object. The test had been designed for EFS, to show individual differences in detecting inconsistencies in complex figures. The test's loading on EFS was insignificant, but the loading on NFT was .63. This result was interpreted to mean that the main problem for E is to produce a transformation from a two-dimensional view to a three-dimensional view, after which the detection of inconsistencies is so easy that there is little or no EFS variance in the scores, as indicated by the loading of .08 on that factor.

Convergent Production of Figural Implications (NFI) The discovery of this ability as a factor is an example of serendipity. Two tests, each designed for some other ability, correlated with one another in a way that determined a new factor as well as any pair of tests can do so for the first time.

Planning Air Maneuvers presents a pair of capital leters that E is to imagine that he is producing by skywriting in his airplane. The starting point for the plane is given, also the end point, and E is shown the smallest turn he can make with his plane. The task is definitely figural. It is a matter of production, for E is to construct a path from start to finish. The task is convergent, for E is to produce the most efficient path under the given conditions. Enough information is given to lead to that solution. This test had been included as a marker for DFT, on which it had gone more than once before, without having any other NFI test to take it onto its more reasonable factor. It had correlated with Match Problems II to the extent of .26 to .38 in seven analyses, suggesting that it did involve some DFT variance. With some changes in scoring procedure in the evaluation analysis, it correlated only .22 with Match Problems II.

120   THE ANALYSIS OF INTELLIGENCE

The other test strongly on NFI was Pattern Arrangement. This is a quite complex test, involving the joining and overlapping of simple patterns of adjoining squares and triangles to make more complex, specified patterns. E is to try to reach the most efficient solution, using as little total space as possible. As in Planning Air Maneuvers, the given figural information and the rules imply one, and only one, most efficient solution. Otherwise, the two tests are quite different.

Results from Targeted Rotations

Only targeted rotations were made, in this late study by the ARP. The solution resulted in considerable new information, some of which has already been mentioned in discussing the tests. One reason for the great gain in information was that so many new tests were developed for the special purposes of obtaining answers to particular questions and issues. The fact that old tests for a factor came out together with new ones that followed SI definitions confirmed the previous placement of each factor in the SI model.

Details concerning factor loadings of the figural-cognition and figural-convergent-production tests on their respective factors may be seen in Table 5.2. For the most part, tests designed for certain SI abilities were univocal for their factors. A few major discrepancies will be noted.

The Blocks test refused to go on the factor for CFS, but probably not because it is a figure-centered test rather than a body-centered test. Its strongest loading was on evaluation of figural implications (EFI), and another significant loading was on CFI; two implications abilities. The implication aspect is easily rationalized. The blocks that E counts are mostly hidden by the blocks in front, among which are the lettered ones. The points of contact of the touching blocks are almost entirely hidden and must be inferred from visible information—hence the involvement with implications. E has to infer touching blocks in order to count them, and judging from the amount of weight shown for EFI, he must do considerable checking of his implications in order to arrive at a correct count. The third significant loading for Blocks was on CFT, which suggests that E's impressions of the pile of blocks undergo some transformations as he attempts to count partially hidden blocks.

A marked failure in a hypothesis was that Spatial Comprehension went strongly on CFR and univocally so, not on CFS. Presenting to E piecemeal the descriptions of the relative locations of objects with respect to one another apparently requires that E see only relations, not the entire system. It thus happens that the two figure-centered tests (Spatial Comprehension and Blocks) designed for CFS refused to go on CFS. The body-centered tests went together, as usual, on CFS. This supports the earlier conclusion that the characteristic test items for CFS are body-centered. It is probably best, however, to leave the issue open, with some future possibility that a figure-centered test can be found relevant for SI ability CFS.

All the tests designed for CFT went significantly on that factor, plus a number of other tests of no special concern to us here. Thus, if some of the CFT tests are actually body-centered, it can be concluded that that type of test is adequate for CFT. There could be some body-centering in the tests Spatial

Visualization and Block Rotation. But to the extent that they have this property, there might be some loading on the factor for CFS. This was true (and often has been true) of the former; it was not true of the latter.

The unusual number of tests with secondary loadings on CFT deserves only the comment that ability CFT seems to be a kind of general-purpose ability, where individuals resort to visual thinking, with manipulations. The test battery for the analysis under discussion was administered to students of architecture. It is plausible to suggest that, more often than is normal, regardless of the context in which the problem arises, figural or not, students of architecture adopt a strategy that resorts to visual thinking. Visual thinking probably commonly involves ability CFT.

GENERAL SUMMARY

It is of interest to see what the general outcomes have been from investigations of reasoning and problem-solving abilities. These investigations grew out of Thurstone's reporting an induction ability and a deduction ability, from his first PMA analysis, and the Army Air Force psychologists' distinctions among three reasoning abilities, none of which clearly agreed with Thurstone's inductive and deductive interpretations. There was some resemblance between the A.A.F.'s Reasoning II and Thurstone's induction, but the A.A.F.'s studies did not actually employ tests of a deductive nature, thus to throw any new light on Thurstone's deduction factor.

The course of the investigations by the ARP can be characterized as successive discoveries that abilities can be differentiated in terms of kinds of information involved—differences in substance or content and differences in form or product. For some time it was assumed that operations of reasoning are the same regardless of the kind of content. But very early a differentiation between perceived or figural information and verbal or semantic information was observed. It was not until later that the third category of symbolic content was seen as differentiated from the two other kinds.

Along the way, it was also realized that there are a number of inductive abilities and also deductive abilities, and that they are logically associated with the cognition and convergent-production operation categories, respectively, when those concepts were generated in connection with the structure-of-intellect theory and model.

At one point it was realized that there are separate abilities for dealing with classes and relations, which opened the way for further distinctions in terms of products. Systems were recognized as complex products, first in connection with the erstwhile factor known as "general reasoning," then with the repeated finding of abilities concerned with seeing patterns, of perceptual, conceptual, and symbolic composition, for factors later identified with abilities CFS, CMS, and CSS, respectively, in the SI model. Units, implications and transformations were recognized later.

With two or three exceptions, the abilities coming under the original heuristic label "reasoning" turned out to be in the cognition and convergent-production operation categories. It was suggested that conceptions and interpretations derived from the structure of intellect be substituted for the traditional concepts of "induction," "deduction," and "reasoning," since the new concepts are firmly based on empirical referents.

The listing of the abilities that became known in the two operation categories in question (plus the behavioral-cognition abilities treated in Chapter 9) shows that all 24 expected cognition abilities have been demonstrated, and also 15 of the 24 convergent-production abilities. Missing from the latter group are factors NFU, NFS, NSU and the six hypothesized ones pertaining to behavioral information. None of these nine abilities had been investigated by the ARP at the time this was written.

SIX

ABILITIES IN CREATIVE THINKING AND PLANNING

Of all the investigations in any area by the ARP, those aimed at creative abilities have been rewarded with the most novel results, have been given most attention, and have had the most consequences in the form of stimulating thinking and research by others. Before these studies, psychologists in general had maintained a conception of intelligence and biases in intelligence testing that almost entirely excluded creative aspects. Correction of those traditional views and practices was long overdue.

    The studies under the label "creative" covered a larger range of ages among experimental subjects than was true for other areas. Of the nine analyses to be given special attention in this chapter, five were done at the young-adult level, one at the senior high school level, two at the ninth-grade level, and one at the sixth-grade level. Six of the nine can be described as attacking the area in a general sense, one other study put the spotlight on fluency, another on flexibility, and still another on transformation abilities. The one investigation of planning abilities fits into the creative area because planning has innovative aspects.

Table 6.1 Populations and Samples for Analyses Pertaining Primarily to Creative-thinking and Planning Abilities*

Report Number	Brief Title of the Analysis	N	Population
8	Creative-thinking Abilities	301	A.F. air cadets
		109	A.F. student officers
12	Planning Abilities	364	A.F. air cadets
17	Fluency Abilities	221	Naval air cadets
18	Flexibility Abilities	208	A.F. air cadets
26	Creative Abilities at the Ninth-grade Level	204	Ninth-grade students
27	Creative Abilities at the Sixth-grade Level	403	Sixth-grade students
29	Figural- and Symbolic-divergent-production Abilities	238	Naval air cadets
35	Figural-, Symbolic-, and Semantic-divergent-production Abilities	205	Ninth-grade students
41	Transformation Abilities	187	Senior high school students

*All service-associated subjects were exclusively male, while school groups were mixed as to sex membership.

A tenth study, on behavioral divergent production, is treated in a later chapter on behavioral abilities. An eleventh was part of a study of semantic-memory abilities. Table 6.1 presents some details concerning the nine investigations contributing exclusively to this chapter, including information on the kinds of populations and numbers of cases in the samples.

THE FIRST STUDY OF CREATIVE-THINKING ABILITIES[1]
Hypotheses and Their Sources

There had been very little precedent for a study of component abilities most relevant for creative production, for no systematic, comprehensive factor analysis had been done specifically in that direction. The kind of information available was derivable from only a few incidental findings. Garnett (1919b) had found a factor for "cleverness" in an analysis of ratings. Hargreaves (1927) had found factors that he identified as "fluency" and "originality" in an analysis of tests. L. L. Thurstone (1938) had found his "word fluency," and Fruchter (1948) had added a factor for "associational fluency" from a new analysis of part of Thurstone's data. Carroll (1941) and C. W. Taylor (1947) independently reported a factor that could be called "expressional fluency," in their analyses of verbal-expressive behavior.

[1] See Reports 4 and 8; also Wilson, Guilford, Christensen, & Lewis (1954).

On the other hand, the literature was well supplied with numerous anecdotal and speculative accounts of creative episodes, mostly derived from productive geniuses of recognized creative talent. From this source and from the limited factor-analytic information, Guilford and his students in successive semesters of seminars attempted to draw up a list of probable abilities and other traits that might be demonstrable by factorial analysis as basic dimensions of individual differences and that are logically relevant to creative thinking.

The first study in this area by the ARP began with a list of eight prospective abilities, or unique kinds of abilities. The initial effort rested on two assumptions. One was that whatever qualities distinguished creative geniuses have, they are held to some degree by others in the general population; there is continuity between the status of geniuses with respect to these qualities and the status of nongeniuses. People are not in two widely separated groups in these respects. The other assumption is that the nature of the psychological functions involved in creative thinking can be discovered from a study of how individuals differ in unique ways, and hence by factor analysis. These assumptions made it logically possible to investigate creative qualities without resort to the study of geniuses only.

The Hypotheses   The following major hypotheses will be discussed in turn:

    I. Sensitivity to problems
   II. Fluency
  III. Flexibility
  IV. Originality
   V. Analysis
  VI. Synthesis
 VII. Redefinition
VIII. Penetration

I. SENSITIVITY TO PROBLEMS   It was supposed that many creative people are especially sensitive to the existence of problems. This quality might show itself in a number of ways. It might be in the form of awareness of needs for change or for new devices or methods, or the awareness of defects and deficiencies in things as they are known to exist. The idea was tolerated that the trait may be a general perceptual sensitivity, which enables an individual to become quickly aware of the odd, the unusual, and apparent inconsistencies. Such a disposition would offer the individual numerous problems to solve. Without problems, the individual has little opportunity for showing creative qualities. The relations between creativity and problem solving have been treated at great length by Guilford (1967).

The tests designed for this hypothesis were of three kinds, each kind representing what might be considered a subhypothesis, although some kinds were represented by only one test each. The latter circumstances would not permit testing whether a separate ability corresponds to each subhypothesis. Three tests were in the category "seeing defects, needs, and deficiencies." Common Situations asks the examinee (E) to say what difficulties might be encountered in a well-known activity, such as washing one's car at home. The

Apparatus Test asks E to state two things that he sees lacking in a common device, such as a telephone or a refrigerator. To explore the same supposed ability in another area of common experience, the test Social Institutions was developed. In each item E has to say what he sees as a deficiency in social institutions such as divorce or the sales tax.

Only one test—Unusual Details— was designed for the idea that we should expect a broader ability to see the odd and the unusual. This test presents pictorially some familiar objects in situations. There are some missing parts and some inconsistencies in each picture.

For a still broader view of sensitivity to problems, for the subhypothesis for seeing what needs to be done, the F Test was designed. The only instruction given was for E to "do something with each item," having to see what to do himself. Every item is of a different kind, and any reasonable or relevant act or solution to it is acceptable. In pretesting, there were instances of frustration on the part of some Es, for they had not encountered such an unstructured task in the form of a test before; hence the "F" in the title of the test.

II. FLUENCY Fluency tests call for multiple answers to the same given information, in limited time. Two variables were thought to be important in connection with the test conditions. One is the amount of restriction imposed upon E with respect to the category within which his responses are to fall. The category could be simple or complex; there could be a little constraint imposed upon E's output or a great deal. The number of specifications for the category could be one or more than one. For example, we could ask E to name all the things that are edible, or we could limit him to all things edible, soft, and white. The other variable is the probable potential supply of responses. Even with the same degree of restriction imposed by the instruction, some items could be on topics about which most Es know many things and other items on topics about which they generally know very little. It would be very desirable, of course, if all Es in a population had equal memory stores with respect to the class specified.

The test Controlled Associations presents E with stimulus words that are commonly known and that have a number of potential synonyms. The form of the test used in this investigation offered E 12 lines for synonym responses to each given word; hence there was relatively little restriction but also relatively limited potential. Two other tests with simple restrictions but with somewhat larger potential were Number Associations and Brick Uses. In Number Associations E is given a particular number to which he is to present some associated ideas. For example, the number 4 could suggest "quarter," "quadruplets," "four horsemen," "quadrilateral," "foursome," and so on. The potential number of uses for a common brick is also rather large. Where a single item like this has a time limit, time becomes another source of restriction. The test writer's problem is to find the optimal degree of restriction of each kind.

Examples of tests with complex restrictions are Plot Titles and Impossibilities. In the first case, in suggesting different titles for a given short-story plot, E has to stay within the bounds of relevance and appropriateness. The story itself provides limits. The single source also tends to reduce the potential for the item. To name things that are impossible calls for a review of ways in which the suggested idea *could* be possible. The limits thus vary from one possible answer to another, but the basis of restriction is rarely simple.

III. FLEXIBILITY   The term "flexibility" suggests as many as three different meanings in the context of intellectual performances, and more particularly, in terms of tests that could be expected to indicate flexibility. Three tests were aimed at flexibility in the form of adaptability to changing instructions. One was Sign Changes, in which two sign changes are given; e.g., E is to substitute $\times$ for $-$ and $-$ for $+$ in solving equations with two combinations of two numbers each. New sign substitutions are given after each small block of items. Circle Square I and Circle Square II have two potential answers for each item; either a square circumscribing a circle or a circle circumscribing a square. Each item mentions two objects, one of which has corners and can therefore be readily associated with a square, and the other of which has a rounded contour and can therefore be readily associated with a circle. In Circle Square I, E is told to put the harder object on the outside and then is given a list of pairs of objects, e.g., "marshmallows, soap box." "Soap box" being harder, E should mark the answer with the square on the outside. In Circle Square II, E's adaptability is more obviously tested by changing the instruction with every item; e.g., "Put the one that is smoked on the outside" and "Make the more informative the inside one."

Another interpretation of flexibility was described as "freedom from inertia of thought." For this hypothesized ability, one test was Match Problems. In each item, E is presented with a number of adjacent squares, whose sides are formed with matches. He is told to remove a specified number of matches, leaving a specified number of complete squares. Another test was Implied Uses, in which E is to give a list of alternative meanings for the same given word. For the word "take," he might say "to take in marriage," "to take for a ride," "to take food," or "to take notes," and so on. Readiness to shift meaning is a common kind of flexible action.

A third interpretation comes under the descriptive category "spontaneous shift of set." To obtain a score for this kind of trait, the Brick Uses test, which is also scored for fluency by simply counting the total number of relevant answers, is also scored in terms of the number of *categories* of uses that E exhibits. Every shift from one category to another is taken to indicate a spontaneous shift of set. At various times the flexibility score has been the total number of categories of uses and the number of shifts of category. The two are very highly correlated, of course. Only when Es shift back to a category previously dropped would there be an additional point in the "shift" score that is not counted in the "number of categories" score. Later scoring practice has favored the shift score, for it slightly increases variances, and every shift can be defended as a flexible act.

IV. ORIGINALITY   Of all the qualities associated with creativity, originality is probably the most commonly recognized. Before we can do anything about testing to determine how original individuals are, however, it is necessary to find meanings of the term that lend themselves to operational dealings with the concept. Three such interpretations provided subhypotheses. One is that an original act is rare in the population to which the individual belongs; its probability of occurrence is very low. Three tests were constructed on the basis of this hypothesis.

Quick Responses is a free-association form of test, using 50 stimulus words from the Kent-Rosanoff list. In group testing, each stimulus word is given orally, and E is given 5 seconds in which to write his response. A popularity or frequency index was determined for every word in a sample of about 400 young men. The index gave each response a weight inversely proportional to its frequency. An individual's score on the test is the sum of the weights for his response.

Two other kinds of tests were developed following the same principle. In Number Associations, a scoring procedure weighting every response according to its frequency in the population was also used, in order to obtain an individual's score for originality interpreted as "uncommonness of response." Figure Concepts presents line drawings of 20 different, familiar objects, from which E is to form small classes of two members each. The uncommonness with which each class was formed by the sample of Es again provided the basis for giving weighted scores.

Another operational conception of originality was in terms of remote associations, assuming that the more original person can see more tenuous and less obvious connections between things and between ideas. Two similar association tests were designed for this hypothesis and one that is not so clearly associational. Associations I presents a pair of stimulus words, with E to give a single word association with both. Given the two words "Indian" and "money," a response word that connects the two is "nickel," but "copper" or "wampum" would be acceptable. It was thought that the restriction of satisfying two associative connections would force E to produce more unusual or less well-associated responses.

Associations II represents an attempt to put the same kind of test into multiple-choice form. Five alternative initial letters for possible responses are given. For example, for the two stimulus words "pole" and "mail," the alternatives could be "g, l, p, s, w," among which "p," for "post," would be correct. Hindsight suggests that the new feature might well introduce some variance in abilities DSU or NSU, or both. Both are concerned with the production of words beginning with a given letter. We shall see that, like multiple-choice tests in general, Associations II failed to indicate degrees of originality or of other divergent-production abilities.

The test Unusual Uses (later known as "Alternate Uses") gives E a commonly known object and its conventional use, to which he is to add a number of uncommon uses for the object. Told that a newspaper is ordinarily used for reading, E might say it could also be used to "swat flies," "wrap garbage," "line shelves," "protect one from the rain," and so on. It was thought that the uses are associated with the given object, but relatively weakly. We shall see later that this test helped much more to support an ability other than originality.

The third feature or sign of originality was "cleverness of responses." There is no rigorous or fully objective index known for cleverness, but it is a commonly noted quality, and degrees of cleverness can be judged by experienced observers. A single test that was to help identify originality as a distinct trait was Plot Titles. Given briefly the facts of a short story, E is to suggest as many appropriate titles for the story as he can in the time allowed. Scorers developed criteria for discriminating between titles that should be regarded as clever and those that are nonclever. The number of "nonclever" responses is used as a score for fluency and the number of "clever" responses as a score for originality.

V. ANALYSIS   It was thought that the more creative person is a better analyzer of experiences than most. With greater facility he can break things down into their natural components. Two issues arose in connection with this hypothesis. First, is analysis of perceived material so much like the analysis of conceived material that one and the same ability would apply to both? The other issue had to do with the level of complexity at which analysis takes place. Does the same ability apply to the analysis of complicated and simple wholes? These questions guided the construction of tests in this area.

The test Figure Analysis involves an analysis of a conglomerate of lines into familiar objects. Analysis is not easy, for two or more objects share lines in common. This task was regarded as a perceptual analysis of perceived objects. The test Figure Concepts, mentioned earlier, was considered to be a matter of conceptual analysis of conceived objects. The same test (Figure Concepts) that was scored for originality, as indicated before, was also scored in terms of number of acceptable classes reported. It was assumed that, to be able to form a class, E has to abstract properties of the objects, and this is an analytical process.

Two other tests were entirely verbal. Sentence Analysis asks E to list all the facts and assumptions that are implied in each given sentence. Paragraph Analysis asks for the same kind of activity for a given paragraph. These two tests were aimed at the simple-complex variable in analysis, referring to an issue mentioned previously. It would take more than the four tests just described to determine whether there might be as many as four analytical abilities involved, but at least there should have been some basis for determining whether there is a unitary analytical ability at all, and if so, which of the four tests are most strongly related to it.

VI. SYNTHESIS   In connection with synthesizing activity, there were four subhypotheses, and a much better than usual representation by seven tests was provided to determine whether there is one underlying ability or more than one. The general conception of a synthesizing ability was that it is concerned with organizing parts into wholes. The question of whether such an ability would transcend both figural and conceptual material arose here as before. Two of the tests were strictly figural, and four were strictly verbal. There was some belief that Thurstone's factor that he called "perceptual speed," which was later regarded as a "closure" ability, is a matter of figural synthesis, as his two prominent tests suggest (Thurstone, 1944). One was the Street Gestalt Completion test, which presents fragmented, familiar objects in silhouette form for recognition, and the other was Mutilated Words, which blocks out parts of letters in words that are to be recognized (see Appendix B for sample items of both tests). Both tests were used in the analysis under discussion, to see whether they would uniquely determine an ability for production of perceived objects by synthetic acts, or "closure," to use Gestalt terminology, as Thurstone did.

Another subhypothesis dealt with a possible ability to produce conceptual objects by combining simple objects. Object Synthesis presents the names of familiar objects, e.g., "pliers and shoestring," from which E is to suggest another object that is made up of the two. He might suggest "pendulum" "plumb bob," or "something to demonstrate centrifugal force," for example. Concept Synthesis presents the names of two objects which are not to be integrated but in conjunction are supposed to suggest a single idea to E. For example, "cloth" given with "wound" would be expected to suggest "a bandage."

A third hypothesis under synthesis conceived of an ability for the production of logical or meaningful order. For this idea, the tests Word Matrices and Sentence Synthesis were designed. Each word matrix was designed to have three rows and three columns, with a blank space provided at each intersection. Three of nine words intended to make up each matrix appear in their appropriate cells. The other six words are listed, and E is to place them so as to produce a logical arrangement throughout the matrix. In Sentence Synthesis, the words of a sentence are given in scrambled order, with E to put them in the correct order.

The fourth subhypothesis was that the production of classes out of given sets of objects might be regarded as a synthetic act. No special tests were developed for this idea, but there was some thought that the test Figure Concepts, which has been mentioned twice before, might represent this kind of synthesis. If it went on any synthesis factor, the conclusion would be that that factor is broad enough to include the act of producing class groups. If it did not appear on a synthesis factor, the idea that it represents a special synthetic ability could not be rejected, however. There seemed to be a sufficient number of synthetic tests to determine at least one synthetic ability if one exists. There were possibilities of finding as many as three represented by at least two tests each.

VII. REDEFINITION   Gestalt psychologists had made a great deal of the theory that mental structures, or "Gestalten," are often reorganized, and this is a form of learning. Sometimes the term "redefinition" was used, as when an organism revises the way in which he uses an object. It was decided that much creative effort involves such revisions of what is known in order to make it useful in solving problems.

Here again, the suspicion that such an ability does not transcend kind of information had its effects on test construction. One subhypothesis considered a possible perceptual-reorganization ability. The more obvious test for this idea was Penetration of Camouflage, borrowed from the A.A.F. wartime testing activity. It involves a hidden-faces task. Sentence Gestalt consists of two paragraphs in which the words have all been run together, all letters being capitals. E is to draw a vertical line between successive pairs of words so as to make meaningful prose. It would be recognized at this time that this task is a symbolic one, probably involving mostly cognition of symbolic units (CSU), except where a word perceived at first has to be broken down to make two different words, in which case the ability for convergent production of symbolic transformations (NST) would be involved.

A second hypothesis under redefinition was for shift of function. The tests for this idea pertain to change of use of familiar objects or of their parts. Gestalt Transformations asks this kind of question

> Which of these five objects could best be adapted to starting a fire?
> A. cabbage, B. fountain pen, C. pocket watch, D. cookie, E. bowling ball.

The keyed answer is C (pocket watch), for the face cover could be removed and used as a condensing lens. Picture Gestalt is similar except that each problem presents a photograph of a room, e.g., a kitchen, with numerous familiar objects showing, followed by a list of uses to each of which something (to be named by E) in the picture could be adapted.

A single test represented a third idea described as "moving a part from one whole to another." Word Transformation presents in each item a phrase, such as THE RED OLIVE, with E to regroup the letters to make a new phrase, THERE DO LIVE.

VIII. PENETRATION   The hypothesis that the more creative person can penetrate further into his experiences, seeing more of things than is on the surface, came as an afterthought. It was derived from observations that certain tests seemed to have potential for differentiating individuals with respect to such a quality. For example, in the Social Institutions test, which was first designed for the hypothesis for sensitivity to problems, preliminary testing showed that some responses were rather direct and obvious implications while others showed further penetration into the matter. In scoring this test, then, a score for responses indicating things rather obviously wrong was used for the sensitivity-to-problems hypothesis, and a score for remote responses was used for the penetration hypothesis. The other test designed for this hypothesis was Consequences, which asks E to list the outcomes for hypothetical events affecting human beings, such as everyone suddenly going blind. This test was also scored in two ways, one for number of obvious consequences and the other for the number of remote consequences.

In deciding which score variable to factor-analyze, it was necessary to consider those tests which were scored in two ways, to see that there were no obvious signs of experimental interdependence. For Plot Titles, Consequences, and Social Institutions, two scores were used in the analysis because in each case the correlation of the two scores was near zero. In the instance of Brick Uses, the fluency and flexibility scores correlated only .23, so both were used. In the cases of Figure Concepts and Number Associations only the "uncommon" scores were used because there were signs of intolerable experimental dependence. Two scores were used from Sentence Gestalt, one for number of correct separations of words and the other for number of omissions, in spite of a correlation of $-.35$ between them. Six score variables were added from the Air Force classification battery, which the Es had taken at about the same time as the Project's creative-thinking battery. They were used as marker tests to help determine some previously known factors that might show up in more than one of the creative-thinking tests.

Results

Fate of the Hypotheses for Analyzing and Synthesizing Abilities As in the preceding chapter, only factorial results reflecting upon the hypothesized abilities will be mentioned, and then not in great detail. To mention the most striking negative results first, there were no factors that could be regarded as either analytical or synthetical abilities. There should have been more than ample opportunity for at least one synthetic ability to appear, since there were supposedly seven synthetic-activity tests in the analysis. Incidentally, this is another striking example showing that one does not always get out of a factor analysis what one puts into it, a point under discussion in Chapter 2.

There was one factor on which two tests selected for their potential for demonstrating a figural-perceptual synthesis appeared moderately—Street Gestalt Completion test and Mutilated Words—but these two had previously defined a factor for Thurstone that he identified as "perceptual speed." The idea that "closure" may be regarded as a kind of synthesis had been entertained, but the two closure tests seem to involve something else. This "something else" was later recognized when the factor marked by those tests was located in the SI model for the ability for cognition of visual-figural units (CFU-V). Units are distinguished by being closed off from their surroundings, so to speak, but this suggests analysis, not synthesis. The most telling argument against the existence of unitary analyzing and synthesizing abilities is the fact that tests designed for each of those two hypothesized abilities went off in different directions in the factor analysis, except for the two closure tests, which hung together. There are many analytical acts, but their kinds are along the lines of abilities better defined in other ways. The same general statement applies to synthesis.

Fluency Abilities More than one fluency ability was expected, and three were found. One appeared equivalent to Thurstone's word fluency and another equivalent to the associational-fluency factor as found by Fruchter (1948) and Zimmerman (1953) in reanalyzing Thurstone's 1938 data. Word fluency is now identified with the SI ability for divergent production of symbolic units (DSU) and associational fluency with divergent production of semantic relations (DMR). The third fluency factor in this group was named "ideational fluency," which was heavily supported by Plot Titles (nonclever), Consequences (obvious), and Brick Uses (fluency), along with three other tests, two of them quite reasonably—Common Situations and Impossibilities. Ideational fluency is now known as the SI ability for "divergent production of semantic units" (DMU).

Flexibility Factors Two flexibility factors were found, one recognized as "spontaneous flexibility" and the other as "adaptive flexibility." The former came largely as expected from Brick Uses (shifts) and similar tests—Unusual Uses, for example, which also involves shifting from class to class without instruction to do so and probably without E's awareness that he is doing so. Adaptive flexibility had a corresponding hypothesis, but it was represented in the results of the analysis by only one test designed for it—Sign Changes—and by another test, Match Problems, which was designed for the hypothesis for freedom from inertia of thought. The two kinds of flexibility are now known as "divergent production of semantic classes" (DMC) and "divergent production of figural transformations" (DFT), respectively.

Originality A factor identified as originality was well represented by a number of tests designed for all three subhypotheses. Plot Titles (clever) represented the cleverness hypothesis; Quick Responses and Figure Concepts (uncommon) represented the uncommonness-of-response hypothesis; and Unusual Uses represented the remote-association hypothesis, as did Consequences (remote), which had been designed for another purpose. Thus, the three conceptual and operational approaches to assessment of originality indicated only one originality factor. In later analyses, there were additional opportunities to demonstrate more than one originality factor, but coherence of tests designed to reflect the three principles has consistently been maintained. This outcome is a refutation of the assertion that is sometimes made that if tests for a factor are sufficiently varied, they will subdivide and indicate two or more abilities of lesser scope. The originality factor was later identified with the SI ability for divergent production of semantic transformations (DMT). Even in the first analysis, it appeared only in connection with verbal tests.

A Redefinition Factor A single redefinition factor was recognized in two of the verbal tests designed for it—Gestalt Transformation and Picture Gestalt. These tests were helped by Object Synthesis, which was designed for a synthesis ability that did not appear. Of the three tests that did not appear on the redefinition factor, one was figural (Penetration of Camouflage) and the other two were symbolic in content. The two symbolic ones probably represent two different abilities and hence gave no sign of a common factor in this analysis. Since the redefinition factor pertained to conceptual information, and since there were keyed right answers, it has been identified with convergent production of semantic transformations (NMT) in the SI model.

Sensitivity to Problems A sensitivity-to-problems ability was indicated strongly in the analysis by just two tests—Social Institutions (direct-implications score) and the Apparatus Test. The two of them were designed for the subhypothesis for seeing defects, needs, or deficiencies, and hence the factor was easy to define. The F test did not help, probably not because it is so unstructured or general but because it is symbolic in content. The failure of other tests to help determine factors where they had been expected can be attributed to the same principle; they lacked kinds of information (content or product) or operation in common with the tests that did succeed. As we shall see later, the sensitivity-to-problems factor was eventually identified with the SI ability for cognition of semantic implications (CMI). Naturally, a problem is *implied* by the object or institution. Starting with the given idea, E thinks beyond it to possible weaknesses that he is told to look for.

Penetration The second score from Social Institutions, the one for penetrating responses, strongly helped produce another doublet factor, along with the total score from the Apparatus test. Some of the responses to the latter could evidently also qualify as remote or penetrating. Later thinking placed the

Table 6.2 Factors and Their Tests with Significant Loadings, in the Category of Divergent Production*

Factor / Test	8	12	13	16C	17	18	21	22	26	27	29	34	35	37	39	40	41	42
DFU																		
Make a Figure Test	—	—	—	—	—	—	—	—	—	—	55	—	61	—	—	46	—	—
Sketches	—	—	—	—	—	—	—	—	—	—	45	—	52	—	—	34	—	—
Dot Systems	—	—	—	—	—	—	—	—	—	—	40	—	52	—	—	—	—	—
Make a Mark	—	—	—	—	—	—	—	—	—	—	51	—	46	—	—	—	—	—
Designs (DFS)	—	—	—	—	—	—	—	—	—	—	—	—	37	—	—	—	—	—
Monograms (DFS)	—	—	—	—	—	—	—	—	—	—	36	—	36	—	—	34	—	—
Making Objects (DFS)	—	—	—	—	—	—	—	—	—	—	33	—	—	—	—	—	—	—
Figure Production (DFI)	—	—	—	—	—	—	—	—	—	—	—	—	—	—	—	33	—	—
DFC																		
Alternate Letter Groups	—	—	—	—	—	—	—	—	—	—	—	—	50	—	57	—	—	—
Figural Similarities	—	—	—	—	—	—	—	—	—	—	36	—	46	—	—	—	—	—
Multiple Grouping of Figures	—	—	—	—	—	—	—	—	—	—	—	—	—	—	40	—	—	—
Multiple Figural Similarities	—	—	—	—	—	—	—	—	—	—	—	—	—	—	35	—	—	—
Varied Figural Classes	—	—	—	—	—	—	—	—	—	—	30	—	31	—	—	—	—	—
DFS																		
Designs	—	—	—	—	—	—	—	—	—	—	54	—	52	—	—	63	—	—
Monograms	—	—	—	—	—	—	—	—	—	—	58	—	54	—	—	52	—	—
Making Objects	—	—	—	—	—	—	—	—	—	49[s]	53	—	50	—	—	—	—	—
Make a Figure Test (DFU)	—	—	—	—	—	—	—	—	—	—	30	—	41	—	—	38	—	—
Figure Production (DFI)	—	—	—	—	—	—	—	—	—	—	—	—	41	—	—	—	—	—
Sketches (DFU)	—	—	—	—	—	—	—	—	—	—	35	—	—	—	—	—	—	—

DFT

Match Problems	55ˢ	60	59ˢ	—	—	—	—	—	—	—	—	—	—	—	—	—
Match Problems II	—	53	—	—	—	—	41	—	—	—	—	—	—	—	—	—
Match Problems III	—	—	—	—	—	—	—	46	—	—	60	—	63	—	—	—
Match Problems IV	—	—	—	—	—	—	—	—	—	—	49	—	63	—	—	—
Match Problems V	—	51	—	—	—	—	—	—	51	33ˢ	—	—	65	—	—	—
Planning Air Maneuvers	—	—	—	—	—	—	54	41	55	—	—	—	52	—	—	—
Squares	—	—	—	—	—	—	42	—	—	—	—	—	—	—	—	—
Dot Systems (DFU)	—	—	—	—	—	—	—	—	—	35	—	—	—	—	—	—
Symbol Elaboration (DSI)	—	—	—	—	—	—	—	—	—	33	—	—	—	—	—	—

DFI

Decorations	—	—	—	—	—	—	—	—	65	—	—	—	58	—	37	—
Figure Production	—	36	—	—	—	—	—	—	47	—	—	—	52	—	59	—
Production of Figural Effects	—	—	—	—	—	—	—	—	49	—	—	—	44	—	—	—
Making Objects (DFS)	—	—	—	—	—	—	—	—	—	—	—	—	34	—	—	—
Effects (CMI)	—	36	—	—	—	—	—	—	—	—	—	—	—	—	—	—
Unusual Methods (DMT)	—	34	—	—	—	—	—	—	—	—	—	—	—	—	—	—
Sketches (DFU)	—	—	—	—	—	—	—	—	—	—	—	—	—	—	31	—
Alternate Signs (DMT)	—	—	—	—	—	—	—	—	—	—	—	—	—	—	31	—

DSU

Word Fluency	—	—	—	—	70	—	—	—	49	—	—	—	58	—	—	—
Rhymes	—	—	—	—	65	—	—	—	—	—	—	—	—	66	—	—
Suffixes	—	—	—	—	69	—	—	—	64	—	—	—	54	62	—	—
Syllables	—	—	—	—	—	—	—	44ˢ	—	—	—	—	—	—	—	—

Table 6.2 *(Continued)*

Factor / Test	8	12	13	16C	17	18	21	22	26	27	29	34	35	37	39	40	41	42
DSC																		
Multiple Grouping of Nonsense Words	—	—	—	—	—	—	—	—	—	—	—	—	—	—	51	—	—	—
Multiple Letter Similarities	—	—	—	—	—	—	—	—	—	—	34	—	51	—	37	—	—	—
Name Grouping	—	—	—	—	—	—	—	—	—	—	50	—	36	—	39	—	—	—
Number Grouping	—	—	—	—	—	—	—	—	—	—	33	—	—	—	—	—	—	—
Alternate Letter Groups (DFC)	—	—	—	—	—	—	—	—	—	—	31	—	—	—	—	—	—	—
DSR																		
Number Rules	—	—	—	—	—	—	—	—	—	—	59	—	48	—	—	—	—	—
Alternate Additions	—	—	—	—	—	—	—	—	—	—	40	—	62	—	—	—	—	—
Number Combinations	—	—	—	—	—	—	—	—	—	—	—	—	32	—	—	—	—	—
Number Grouping (DSC)	—	—	—	—	—	—	—	—	—	—	32	—	57	—	—	—	—	—
Word Relations (CSR)	—	—	—	—	—	—	—	—	—	—	32	—	37	—	—	—	—	—
Multiple Analogies (DMR)	—	—	—	—	—	—	—	—	—	—	—	—	31	—	—	—	—	—
Numerical Operations (MSI)	—	—	—	—	—	—	—	—	—	—	—	—	31	—	—	—	—	—
Alternate Letter Groups (DSC)	—	—	—	—	—	—	—	—	—	—	—	—	30	—	—	—	—	—
Symbol Elaboration (DSI)	—	—	—	—	—	—	—	—	—	—	—	—	30	—	—	—	—	—
DSS																		
Make a Code	—	—	—	—	—	—	—	—	55[s]	—	—	—	56	—	—	—	—	—
Match Problems II (DFT)	—	—	—	—	—	—	—	—	—	—	—	—	48	—	—	—	—	—
Multiple Grouping (DMC)	—	—	—	—	—	—	—	—	—	—	—	—	32	—	—	—	—	—

DST													
Multiple Letter Changes	—	—	—	—	—	—	—	—	—	—	—	48	—
Multiple Word Extractions	—	—	—	—	—	—	—	—	—	—	—	48	—
Hidden-Word Production	—	—	—	—	—	—	—	—	—	—	—	47	—
Seeing Letter Changes (CST)	—	—	—	—	—	—	—	—	—	—	—	39	—
DSI													
Word-Pair Revisions	—	—	—	—	—	—	—	—	—	—	—	67	—
Limited Words	—	—	—	—	—	—	—	—	60	—	—	—	—
Symbol Elaboration	—	—	—	—	—	—	45^s	—	49	—	—	—	—
Hidden-Word Production	—	—	—	—	—	—	—	—	—	—	—	41	—
Number Rules (DSR)	—	—	—	—	—	—	—	—	33	—	—	—	—
Reading Backwards (CST)	—	—	—	—	—	—	—	—	—	—	—	35	—
DMU													
Plot Titles (nonclever)	65	45	57	58	46	46	73	—	60	59	—	76	53	70	—	—
Consequences (obvious)	66	43	—	60	—	65	54	—	57	71	—	41	62	44	50	—
Brick Uses (fluency)	63	—	65	—	58	48	—	—	—	—	—	—	—	—	—	—
Utility Test (fluency)	—	—	—	—	—	—	—	—	50	—	—	—	61	64	—	—
Common Situations	66	—	—	—	—	—	—	—	—	—	—	—	—	—	—	—
Ideational Fluency	—	—	—	—	41	—	—	54	53	—	—	—	47	52	48	—
Impossibilities	51	—	—	—	—	—	47	—	—	—	—	—	—	—	—	—
Differences	—	—	—	—	—	—	—	47	—	—	—	—	—	—	—	—
Descriptive Completion	—	—	—	—	43	—	—	—	—	—	—	—	—	—	—	—
Alternate Headlines (arrangement)	—	—	—	—	43	—	—	—	—	—	—	—	—	—	—	—
Sentence Analysis	31	—	—	—	—	—	—	—	—	—	—	—	—	—	—	—
Planning Elaboration II (DMI)	—	—	—	—	—	—	—	—	—	—	—	—	30	44	—	—

Table 6.2 (Continued)

Factor / Test	8	12	13	16C	17	18	21	22	26	27	29	34	35	37	39	40	41	42
DMU																		
Alternate Signs (DMT)	—	—	—	—	—	—	—	—	40	—	—	—	—	—	—	—	—	—
Word Listing 0 (DSU)	—	—	—	—	36	—	—	—	—	—	—	—	—	—	—	—	—	—
Consequences (remote) (DMT)	—	—	—	—	—	33	—	—	—	—	—	—	—	—	—	—	—	—
Brick Uses (shifts) (DMC)	—	—	—	—	32	—	—	—	—	—	—	—	—	—	—	—	—	—
Word Arrangement (DMS)	—	—	—	—	32	—	—	—	—	—	—	—	—	—	—	—	—	—
Social Institutions (CMI)	—	—	—	—	—	—	32	32	—	—	—	—	—	—	—	—	—	—
Similarities (DMR)	—	—	—	—	—	—	—	32	—	—	—	—	—	—	—	—	—	—
Multiple Grouping (DMC)	—	—	—	—	—	—	—	—	32	—	—	—	—	—	—	—	—	—
Missing Links (NMI)	—	—	—	—	—	—	—	30	—	—	—	—	—	—	—	—	—	—
DMC																		
Brick Uses (shifts)	55	—	—	—	54	69	61	49	—	—	—	—	55	—	—	—	—	—
Utility Test (shifts)	—	—	—	—	—	—	—	—	52	31	—	—	53	52	73	—	—	—
Alternate Uses	54	—	—	—	—	47	59	—	40	42	—	—	53	50	46	—	47	—
Multiple Grouping	—	—	—	—	—	—	—	46	45	—	—	—	46	—	57	—	33	—
Object Naming (cluster)	—	—	—	—	—	56	—	—	—	—	—	—	—	—	—	—	—	—
Object Synthesis (DMT)	—	—	—	—	—	35	—	—	—	—	—	—	—	—	—	—	—	—
Consequences (remote) (DMT)	—	—	—	—	—	—	—	—	39	—	—	—	31	—	—	—	—	—
Brick Uses (fluency) (DMU)	—	—	—	—	36	37	—	—	—	—	—	—	—	—	—	—	—	—
Associational Fluency (DMR)	—	—	—	—	—	—	—	—	37	—	—	—	—	—	—	—	—	—
Seeing Problems (CMI)	—	—	—	—	—	—	—	—	—	35	—	—	—	—	—	—	—	—
Alternate Signs (DMT)	—	—	—	—	—	—	—	—	—	—	—	—	33	—	—	—	—	—
Similarities (DMR)	—	—	—	—	—	—	—	32	—	—	—	—	—	—	—	—	—	—
Possible Jobs (DMI)	—	—	—	—	—	—	—	—	—	32	—	—	—	—	—	—	—	—

DMR																					
Associational Fluency	51	—	67	—	63	57	—	—	53	—	41	51	—	—	56	31	—	—	—	—	—
Controlled Associations II	—	45	—	—	68	—	—	—	—	—	—	34	—	—	—	44	—	—	—	—	—
Simile Insertions	—	—	—	—	—	51	—	—	—	—	39	—	—	—	56	—	—	—	—	—	—
Multiple Analogies	—	—	—	—	—	—	—	—	—	—	55	—	—	—	41	—	—	—	—	—	—
Associations IV	—	—	—	53	38	—	—	—	—	—	—	—	—	—	—	—	—	—	—	—	—
Number Associations (uncommon)	51	—	—	—	—	—	—	—	—	—	—	—	—	—	—	—	—	—	—	—	—
Similarities	—	—	—	—	30	—	—	53^s	40	—	—	—	—	—	—	—	—	—	—	—	—
Practical Judgment	—	41	—	—	—	—	—	—	—	—	—	—	—	—	—	—	—	—	—	—	—
Associations III	—	—	—	—	36	—	—	—	—	—	—	—	—	—	—	—	—	—	—	—	—
Simile Completion	—	—	—	—	—	36	—	—	—	—	—	—	—	—	—	—	—	—	—	—	—
Attribute Listing I	—	—	—	—	—	—	—	—	34	—	—	—	—	—	—	—	—	—	—	—	—
Verbal Comprehension (CMU)	—	—	—	—	—	—	—	—	—	—	—	—	—	—	40	—	—	—	—	—	—
Expressional Fluency (DMS)	—	—	—	—	—	—	—	—	—	—	39	—	—	—	—	—	—	—	—	—	—
Vocabulary Completion (CMU)	—	—	—	—	33	—	—	—	—	—	—	—	—	—	—	—	—	—	—	—	—
Alternate Uses (DMC)	—	—	—	—	32	—	—	—	33	—	—	—	—	—	—	—	—	—	—	—	—
DMS																					
Expressional Fluency	—	—	—	—	—	60	—	—	—	—	40	48^s	—	—	49	—	—	—	—	—	—
Simile Interpretations	—	—	—	—	—	57	—	—	—	—	48	—	—	—	42	56^s	—	—	—	—	—
Word Arrangement	—	—	—	—	—	59	—	—	—	—	—	—	—	—	—	—	—	—	—	—	—
Word Synthesis (words)	—	—	—	—	—	54	—	—	—	—	—	—	—	—	43	—	—	—	—	—	—
Alternate Headlines (words)	—	—	—	—	—	37	—	—	—	—	—	—	—	—	—	—	—	—	—	—	—
Descriptive Completion	—	—	—	—	—	30	—	—	—	—	—	—	—	—	—	—	—	—	—	—	—
Ideational Fluency (DMU)	—	—	—	—	—	—	—	—	—	—	—	—	—	—	43	—	—	—	—	—	—
Word Fluency (DSU)	—	—	—	—	—	—	—	—	—	—	—	—	—	—	35	—	—	—	—	—	—

Table 6.2 *(Continued)*

Factor Test	8	12	13	16C	17	18	21	22	26	27	29	34	35	37	39	40	41	42
DMS																		
Plot Titles (clever) (DMT)	—	—	—	—	33	—	—	—	—	—	—	—	—	—	—	—	—	—
Associational Fluency (DMR)	—	—	—	—	—	—	—	—	—	—	—	—	31	—	—	—	—	—
Simile Insertions (DMR)	—	—	—	—	32	—	—	—	—	—	—	—	—	—	—	—	—	—
DMT																		
Plot Titles (clever)	58	43	54	47	48[s]	51	33	—	46	45	—	43	57	62	—	55	35	—
Consequences (remote)	48	35	—	55	—	46	62	—	36	44	—	70	—	42	—	—	56	—
Symbol Production	—	54	—	—	—	—	—	—	—	—	—	—	—	—	—	—	—	—
Possibilities	—	—	—	—	—	—	—	47	—	—	—	—	—	—	—	—	—	—
Chain Association (cluster)	—	—	—	—	—	47	—	—	—	—	—	—	—	—	—	—	—	—
Alternate Signs	—	—	—	—	—	—	—	—	44	—	—	—	47	—	—	31	—	—
Object Synthesis III	—	—	—	—	—	—	—	42	—	—	—	—	—	—	—	—	—	—
Quick Responses	41	—	—	—	—	—	—	—	—	—	—	—	—	—	—	—	—	—
Unusual Methods	—	39	—	—	—	—	—	—	—	—	—	—	—	—	—	—	—	—
Object Synthesis (NMT)	—	—	—	34	—	53	—	—	—	—	—	—	—	—	—	—	—	—
Utility Test (shifts) (DMC)	—	—	—	—	—	—	—	—	46	—	—	—	—	—	—	—	—	—
Plot Titles (nonclever) (DMU)	—	—	—	—	—	46	—	—	—	—	—	—	—	—	—	—	—	—
Alternate Uses (shifts) (DMC)	—	—	39	37	—	37	—	—	—	—	—	—	—	—	—	—	—	—
Whoppers	—	—	—	—	—	—	—	—	—	—	—	—	—	—	—	—	36	—
Brick Uses (fluency) (DMU)	—	—	30	—	—	41	—	—	—	—	—	—	—	—	—	—	—	—
Naming Meaningful Trends (NMU)	—	37	—	—	—	—	—	—	—	—	—	—	—	—	—	—	—	—
Pertinent Questions (CMI)	—	—	—	—	—	—	—	—	—	—	—	—	—	—	—	—	34	—

	1	2	3	4	5	6	7	8	9	10	11	12	13	14	15
Seeing Problems (CMI)	—	—	—	—	—	—	—	—	—	—	—	—	—	—	—
Seeing Different Meanings (CMT)	—	—	—	33	—	—	—	—	—	—	—	—	33	—	—
Associational Fluency (DMR)	—	—	—	32	—	—	—	—	—	—	—	—	—	—	—
Simile Interpretations (DMS)	—	—	—	—	—	—	31	—	—	31	—	—	—	—	—
Apparatus Test (CMI)	—	—	—	—	—	—	31	—	—	—	—	—	—	—	—
DMI															
Possible Jobs	—	45	—	—	—	50	35	—	35	58	—	—	56	—	—
Planning Elaboration	—	45	53	—	—	—	54	—	—	—	—	—	43	—	—
Planning Skills II	—	50	51	—	—	—	—	—	—	—	—	—	—	—	—
Planning Elaboration II	—	—	—	—	—	43	—	—	45	45	—	—	—	—	—
Planning Skills	—	40	—	—	—	—	—	—	—	—	—	—	—	—	—
Ideational Fluency (DMU)	—	—	—	—	—	—	—	—	36	—	—	—	—	—	—
Seeing Problems (CMI)	—	—	—	—	—	33	—	—	—	—	—	—	—	—	—
Simile Interpretations (DMS)	—	—	—	—	—	—	—	—	31	—	—	—	—	—	—
Plot Titles (clever) (DMT)	—	—	—	—	—	—	—	—	30	—	—	—	—	—	—

*Decimal points omitted.
sLoading on a singlet factor.

penetration factor with the SI ability for cognition of semantic transformations (CMT), and subsequent experience has supported that placement, although good confirming evidence had to wait for a number of years.

Relation to Creative Thinking The major theoretical upshot of this first creative-thinking analysis was the later recognition of the divergent-production category of abilities, an entirely new concept. In general, the demonstration of a category of divergent-production abilities as a significant basis for creative thinking and creative production was an important step forward. Finding the abilities in itself was not sufficient to lead to the conclusion that secrets of creative processes had been found, but other work has linked those abilities to what is commonly recognized as creative output, according to information assembled by Guilford (1967, chap. 6).

The Targeted Solution

In preparation for the new analysis of the creative-thinking battery, it was realized that probably 23 SI abilities were actually represented, some of them by one test each, so all were targeted for in the rotation of axes, and a very reasonable-looking solution was found. The same divergent-production abilities stood out as before, except for DSU. What was thought originally to be Thurstone's word-fluency factor (SI ability DSU) actually had no good DSU test to determine that factor. The tests that had gone together in the first analysis went in different directions in the targeted solution, such as toward CSU and NST, which did not appear as factors in the original analysis. They were not known at that time. As Table 6.2 shows, the divergent-production factors had lists of tests, each much more restricted than in the original analysis. Agreement with later analyses was also much improved. The tests that had been designed for hypothesized analyzing and synthesizing abilities went more reasonably on factors for abilities outside the divergent-production category.

THE ANALYSIS OF ABILITIES IN PLANNING

There was little precedent for replicated factors that had been proposed for planning abilities. The Air Force research (Guilford & Lacey, 1947) had reported such factors on two occasions, but the resemblance between the two factors was not very close. The last comment also applies to possible planning factors reported by Guilford, Fruchter, and Zimmerman (1952) and by Adkins and Lyerly (1951). The ARP therefore believed that a fresh, comprehensive start was in order.[2]

In the typical case, planning involves productions of arrangements of things—objects, tasks, operations, and sometimes people. Although there are productive activities involved, there must also be appreciations of situations and their requirements. Approaching the problem of planning in this general way, six major hypotheses were generated, under each of which at least two alternatives

---

[2] See Reports 10 and 12; also Berger, Guilford, & Christensen (1957).

were envisaged. The list will be given first, for it is quite systematic. Some elaboration will then be given, with descriptions of tests designed to fit the various alternatives.

The List of Hypotheses

I. Orientation
   a. Sensitivity to order: seeing an order or trend in a somewhat confused situation
   b. Recognition of variables: awareness of the pertinent variables operating in the situation or descriptions of it

II. Prediction
   a. Extrapolation: seeing the effect of a spatial or temporal extension of a present trend
   b. Foresight: relating what is given to what lies ahead

III. Elaboration
   a. Specification: giving essential details
   b. Production of alternative methods: finding different arrangements for an adequate situation
   c. Symbolization: producing adequate representations for ideas

IV. Ordering
   a. Temporal ordering: arranging steps in a time sequence
   b. Hierarchical ordering: arranging subject matter according to classes and subclasses

V. Ingenuity
   a. Inventing new methods: generating new or uncommon procedures
   b. New applications: adapting known methods to new situations

VI. Evaluation
   a. Importance of variables: deciding upon the relative importance of variables
   b. Seeing deficiencies: detecting shortcomings of a proposed procedure

Tests for the Hypotheses

As is often the case, the meaning of a hypothesis is much more definite and richer in connotations from consideration of the kinds of tests that are designed to represent it. In general, inspection of the list of six major hypotheses suggests how much planning activity resembles the general model for problem solving that was presented in the preceding chapter. There is a need to survey and to become oriented to the situation within which the need for planning arises. The first two hypotheses suggest what are now recognized as cognitive abilities. The next three involve productive-thinking activities, which is the main reason for treating the study in this chapter. And the last hypothesis is on evaluation. From the present perspective, it happens that planning, when broadly considered, offers special consideration in cognition, production, and evaluation.

I. Orientation The kind of plan produced or adopted depends upon the manner in which the planner orients himself to the situation, i.e., in terms of the order or disorder he sees in a mass of information, and variables he recognizes as operating in the situation. He must see some kind of order; hence tests were designed for ability to perceive order. Matrix Order is in this category. A list of words is arranged in three rows and three columns. In a row or column, or in one of the diagonals of the matrix, the words form meaningful sequences. Each sequence is meaningful in only one direction or it could be meaningful in either direction. E draws lines with arrowheads to indicate meaningful sequences and their directions (see Appendix B).

In Sensitivity to Order, each item contains five words. In half the items the words are in correct order and in the other half they are not, one word being out of place. E indicates what he thinks are correct orders by writing plus signs. In other items he circles each word out of order and puts a check mark where he thinks it should be.

The Seeing Trends test of this study is of the same kind as that mentioned early in the preceding chapter, except that only semantic information is involved, and in each item a small deviation from a fully correct order is introduced. It was believed that such deviations are more realistic of everyday trends that one encounters.

Orientation to a planning problem was also thought to involve awareness of variables to be dealt with in the situation. Can the planner recognize those variables? The test Pertinent Questions presents E with a number of proposed situations, in each of which there are conflicting conditions, and about which he needs further information. A sample item reads:

> A student who has just graduated from college is offered positions in two different parts of the country. What four questions have to be considered in making a choice?

Each response was expected to involve a different aspect of the question.

Awareness of Variables is a multiple-choice test developed by the Human Resources Research Laboratories at Bolling A.F.B. The stem of each item states a practical, personal problem. Each alternative answer offers a pair of alternatives representing a different aspect of the problem. E is to choose the two most important considerations. The element of "importance" now suggests that the test may be in the evaluation category.

II. Prediction A planner must constantly be concerned with possible future outcomes of each aspect of his plan and of the plan as a whole. This involves prediction, viewed as extrapolation from given information, or "foresight," to use a more common term. To test for ability to extrapolate in the purely visual-perceptual area, the Series test from R. B. Cattell's culture-free tests was used. This test presents a progressive change in a pictured object, with E to select from five alternatives the figure that shows what the next step should be.

In the semantic area, the test Effects was designed. A sample item reads

> There have been more girls born in the last five years than boys. What effects will this have 20 years from now (in addition to the obvious fact that there will be more women than men)?

Lines for four different responses are provided for *E*. The resemblance of this test to Consequences, which was described in connection with the previous study, will be noted. Consequences was also used in the planning battery. The differences are that the most obvious effect is stated in the item of the Effects test, and *E* is limited to four responses. In scoring both, a distinction is made between obvious and remote responses.

Two foresight tests used figural information, both adapted from the A.A.F. sources. Competitive Planning asks *E* in each item to plan moves for both opponents in playing the game of completing squares, starting with a design of unfinished squares. Route Planning is a maze-tracing test. *E* is to say through which point (among alternatives) each route must go, beginning at a corner of the square maze and arriving at the center goal box. Porteus has long maintained that maze tests are measures of foresight, in his opinion a very important aspect of intelligence.

A symbolic foresight test was called "Symbol Grouping." In a sample item is given

$$0 - - X \; X \; O \; X$$

E is to show how he would move one or more adjacent symbols so as to achieve an order in which all *X*s appear first, all dashes second, and all *O*s third, from left to right, and to do this in the most efficient manner. The smaller the number of moves *E* makes, the better his score for the item.

A semantic test of foresight was called "Contingencies." Described already in Chapter 5, it involves foreseeing what possible condition or event might require the use of each specified object.

III. Elaboration If a plan is to work effectively, no critical details should be overlooked. Can the planner supply all the minor steps or essentials? In order to see how well *E* can think of all specifics, and do so in a planning context, the test Planning Skills II was designed. Planning Skills I was used in the Planning battery as a kind of criterion instrument. It had been designed by Irving Lorge for assessing "decision making" in a military situation. A problem is rather fully stated regarding a morale situation on a military base, with *E* to present a complete plan for coping with the situation. Planning Skills II is a variation, in which one aspect of the situation is emphasized, calling for more detailed planning. This test, then, was to provide a "specification" score. A slightly different specification test presents *E* with the outlines of a total plan, to which he is to add detailed steps to implement the application of the plan. This test was given the name "Planning Elaboration."

A different kind of elaboration test, Figure Production, has no immediate planning implication. *E* is presented in each item with a simple line figure, such as an ellipse, to which he is to add other lines to make a familiar object. His score is the number of different additions he voluntarily gives. For example, he might make of the ellipse a teacup, or he might make a tin can with a pictorial label on it.

For elaboration in the form of methods for carrying out a task, two other kinds of tests were designed. Alternate Methods describes a task that may be carried out in different ways. *E* is to suggest as many ways as he can. An example of a task is:

> A house located near a stream is on fire. Twenty men, each carrying a bucket, arrive to help put out the fire. The house is about 20 yards from the stream. In how many ways could one organize this bucket brigade to deal with the fire?

A figural test for the same purpose is Match Problems II, a variant of the Match Problems test described in connection with the first creative-thinking analysis. In this version of the test, problems were chosen that could be solved in different ways, and *E* is given in each item four identical patterns of squares or triangles on which to show as many as four different solutions.

Two tests were introduced to determine whether there is a possible unique ability to symbolize. This is a different conception than the symbol-manipulation hypothesis of the preceding chapter. In this case, *E* must translate semantic ideas into visual-figural representations. In the test Symbol Production, *E* may be given the short sentence "Ring the bell," with the instruction to offer in line drawings a symbol to represent "ring" and one to represent "bell." The symbols are not to be real objects, but may resemble or suggest objects in some way. The other test, Line Drawing, was adapted from a much earlier test developed by Guilford and Guilford (1931) for assessing aptitude for students in art design. To each given adjective, *E* is to produce a single line that he thinks best represents it. Scoring in the new use of the test is based upon the extent to which the line given by *E* conforms to the most popular rendition in terms of form, direction, and type of line.

IV. Ordering A plan must have an order of some kind, and the planner has the task of producing that order. Two kinds of order were represented by tests in this study, temporal ordering and hierarchical ordering. Planning a sequence of operations or steps is somewhat like programming for a computer, where a fixed sequence of steps must be provided. A test called "Temporal Ordering" presents in scrambled order the steps or systems that are needed to accomplish a practical goal, such as changing a flat tire, with *E* to think of the correct order. He is then quizzed in items to determine to what degree he arrived at that order.

A Picture Arrangement test was borrowed from the Adkins and Lyerly (1951) battery. It shows the four parts of a cartoon strip, with *E* to put them in the correct order in accordance with the story being told by the pictures. Another test from the same source is Sentence Order. Each of three short sentences states an event in a series, but not in the correct temporal order. *E* is to establish that order.

In an Outlining I test, seven or more statements are given, each statement having its level of generality and its possible subordinate and supraordinate relations to other given statements. *E* is given blanks arranged in hierarchical fashion and is to locate each statement in its appropriate blank. Outlining II is of the same kind, with different subject matter to be organized hierarchically. The scoring is in terms of proper level of generality for a statement and proper relations to other statements.

A fourth ordering test comes in neither of the two categories just mentioned. Its category might be called "morophological ordering," for it is in the form of cross-classifications. The Word Matrices test is the same as the one described under the first creative-thinking analysis. It requires E to organize a list of nine given words in a 3 by 3 matrix, meaningfully and logically.

V. Ingenuity   "Ingenuity" is a close synonym for "cleverness," which was found to be related to originality in the previous study reported in this chapter. Two new tests were developed for this hypothesis, in which ingenuity pertains to new methods. Unusual Methods involves problems that are ordinarily handled in ways that are familiar to everyone, but E is told to suggest two different and unusual ways of dealing with each problem. One problem is to "relieve the boredom and fatigue of doing steady work in a business or industry," and E is told of the conventional ways of dealing with the problem. He is to suggest others.

The other test, Verifications, describes in each problem a physical or biological phenomenon in nontechnical terms. For example, E is told that the inside of a large gas flame is not as hot as the outside, and he is asked to suggest two ways in which this phenomenon could be demonstrated.

One test represents ingenuity in relation to new applications of known methods. Procedure Applications describes to E a method that is used to accomplish a certain result. In one problem E is given a description of the chemical method of successive crystallization, used to remove impurities. E is to suggest how the same principle can be applied elsewhere; for example, removing soap by successive rinsing of clothes.

VI. Evaluation   One place in planning activity at which evaluation is probably involved is at the stage of orientation, or "sizing up the situation." At this stage one of the processes hypothesized was recognition of variables. Two tests were used in this study to test the subhypothesis of an ability to evaluate the importance of variables.

The test Essential Operations, previously mentioned in connection with the early investigations of reasoning abilities, asks E to say which of five variables is irrelevant to understanding or structuring a problem. Such a decision can be viewed as a matter of evaluating variables. The other test, Ranking Variables, calls for relative judgments rather than absolute judgments of variables. In each item a problem is given in which some decision has to be made, and a number of facts are given that would be of help in making a decision. E's task is to rank all the facts in order of relative importance in helping reach a decision. The item content of this test is the same as for the test Awareness of Variables, mentioned under the subhypothesis for awareness of variables. Ranking variables is a more demanding evaluation task.

The evaluative subhypothesis denoted as "seeing deficiencies" is reminiscent of the hypothesis for sensitivity to problems encountered in the previous study. A new test called "Seeing Deficiencies" was constructed, with problems pertaining to plans for work activities, as when a growing city faces the pressing needs to improve both its streets and its sewer system. What is wrong with the idea of doing the street-improvement job first? E is required to give only one response to each item.

Reference Factors and Their Marker Tests

In a number of places in the review of hypotheses and tests under the banner "planning" it was noted that certain hypotheses and tests bore resemblance to those in connection with studies of reasoning, creative thinking, and evaluation. It was important, therefore, to have certain of the factors from those areas represented by marker tests, in order to see whether already known factors accounted for any of those in common to new tests.

In order to find possible links between new planning abilities and the two factors reported from the Air Force research, two A.A.F. tests that more faithfully represented the factors of that type were included in the planning study reported here. Planning Air Maneuvers assumes that E is a skywriting pilot who must plan on paper how to write two adjacent capital letters by flying the shortest possible path. The starting and finishing positions of the airplane are pictured in orientation with the two large capital letters. E is shown the sharpest turn the plane can make, and he is to tell in which direction his plane should be flying along each stroke of each capital letter. The other A.A.F. planning test was Planning a Circuit, which involves electrical circuits through a meter from five possible power sources. Five potential circuits are pictured, only one of which would function.

Because of the similarity of planning to problem solving and because of the already strong conviction that the general-reasoning factor is the dominant one for structuring problems, it was suspected that at least some of the orientation tests would be found on the general-reasoning factor. Ship Destination and Arithmetic Reasoning were included as marker tests for general reasoning, to identify that factor.

Because of the recognized relevance of evaluation in connection with planning, two evaluation tests were included as market tests—Logical Reasoning (a multiple-choice syllogism test) and the Inference Test (a multiple-choice, informal deduction test). Because it was recognized that ingenuity shares much with creative thinking, several divergent-production tests were included to see whether the new tests designed for ingenuity would, after all, be divergent-production tests. Plot Titles and Consequences, with their two scores each, both represented ideational fluency and originality. Controlled Associations II was a sole representative for associational fluency, and Match Problems was the representative of adaptive flexibility, along with Sign Changes, which had gone with it on that factor previously. There were some other marker tests for still other abilities, but they do not concern us particularly here.

The Original Analysis

The first analysis involved 52 test variables, of which five were obtained from the Air Force classification battery. Seventeen factors were extracted and rotated, of which 14 were interpreted psychologically.

As could have been predicted on the basis of present information, many of the new tests found their strongest affiliations on already known factors. Some new abilities were demonstrated, however. Two of the new abilities were labeled "perceptual foresight" and "conceptual foresight." The tests supporting the former were much in line with those determining the A.A.F. factor for planning, including Competitive Planning, Planning a Circuit, and Route Planning, which led the list. Conceptual foresight was supported by tests expected from the general hypothesis for prediction, including Effects, Contingencies, and Consequences (remote). But the strongest test was Pertinent Questions, which had been designed for a hypothesized ability for awareness of variables. The emergence of these two foresight factors added to the growing recognition of two different contents—figural and semantic. They added another parallel pair of abilities, thus pointing to the kind of model for all intellectual abilities. In the SI model, they were for some time identified as CFI and CMI.

There was support for two other major hypotheses in the finding of an elaboration ability and an ordering ability. On the elaboration factor were the tests Planning Elaboration and Planning Skills II. The appearance of Figure Production on the same factor, although it was developed as an elaboration test, aroused some curiosity because of its figural nature. But it was the only figural-elaboration test, and it was found in later analyses that a figural-elaboration factor could be readily separated from the semantic-elaboration factor when additional figural-elaboration tests were in the battery with that test.

The tests designed for ingenuity did not call for a new factor. Symbol Production led the list for the factor known as "originality" in the first creative-thinking analysis, but Verifications and New Applications did not go along. This separation of the ingenuity tests helped later to interpret originality in terms of the product of transformation, of SI theory. It was realized that in order to produce line symbols for a word, E has to effect some modifications of meaning. This feature does not seem to apply to Verifications and New Applications.

The Targeted Solution

Nineteen factors were expected from application of SI theory, so 19 were extracted and rotated. Five of the rotated factors were singlets (with one test significantly loaded on each one), because the abilities involved were represented sufficiently strongly by only one test each. Eleven of the factors were clarified as SI Abilities, with two or three tests significantly loaded on each one.

Three factors had 5, 7, and 10 tests with significant loadings, those for DMT, NMS, and CMI, respectively. DMT (originality) gained by having three

Table 6.3 Loadings of the Two Planning Skills Tests on Their Strongest Factorial Components*

	Factors			
Test Variables	CMI	DFI	DMT	DMI
Planning Skills	.17	.19	.28	.40
Planning Skills II	.40	.21	.04	.50

*Factors were included if either test had a loading of .20 or greater.

new tests designed for ingenuity in symbolization and for extrapolation loaded on it, the tests being Symbol Production, Unusual Methods, and Consequences (remote).

The several ordering tests helped together to produce one ordering factor, for SI ability NMS. Five of the seven tests were ordering tests, and even a sixth test, Seeing Deficiencies, had an ordering aspect to it. The two matrix tests on this factor indicate that the ability is not confined to production of temporal order. CMI was most richly supported by its 10 tests, all except one of which logically involve the seeing of implications of a meaningful nature. See Table 6.2 for details.

The Factorial Composition of the "Criterion" Planning Tests It was stated earlier that a planning task was adapted as a kind of criterion—Lorge's Planning Skills test. We may also regard the modified version, Planning Skills II, as a more special criterion. With these two variables in the analysis, we have a chance to see what factors of this study were significantly loaded in those tasks. Table 6.3 extracts the pertinent information from Table 6.2. We see that abilities involving implications have the strongest relationships to variances in the two tasks, especially the cognition of implications and divergent production of implications. The stronger loadings for the semantic abilities than for the figural are natural, in view of the semantic nature of the tasks. The possible traces of figural implications (for the ability later thought to be CFI) might reflect spatial arrangements that entered into the planning in a small way, as imaged by the planners. Differences between the two planning tests can possibly be attributed to the change in task. Planning Skills calls for the production of broad steps, whereas Planning Skills II calls for more detailed planning for some aspects of larger plans. In such a manner the factor-analytic approach can give us some notions as to what more complex tasks require in terms of human intellectual resources. Knowing a criterion variable in terms of factor composition suggests immediately what factors should be emphasized in selection and classification batteries that are to be tried experimentally.

A STUDY OF VERBAL FLUENCY

The study described in Report 17 concentrated on fluency factors.[3] The study is unique for its systematic variations of a number of test conditions, internal and external, and in quantitative as well as qualitative ways, in order to determine optimal conditions for measurement of each ability. Only after something is already known regarding the most invariant tests for a factor can such variations be profitably introduced. This kind of effort for fluency factors proved to be very fruitful.

Variations, Hypotheses, and Tests

By the time this study was initiated, over the years there had been about 10 analyses involving one or more of the four recognized fluency factors. At the same time, it was yet too early to have the advantage of structure-of-intellect conceptions to help guide the planning of the investigation.

---

[3] See Report 17; also Christensen & Guilford (1963).

One striking feature of the results from earlier analyses was the fact that a test that came out on one of the fluency factors in one analysis might come out on another fluency factor in another analysis. There was less crossover of tests, for word fluency (for SI ability DSU) with the other three—ideational fluency (DMU), associational fluency (DMR), and expressional fluency (DMS)—than there was among the last three, for the latter have in common the same kind of content, differing from that for DSU. But a general effect on the ARP investigators was to tolerate the idea that some tests might be thrown in the direction of one or another factor, depending upon minor changes in testing conditions, such as amount and kind of restrictions upon responses, the time limits, and so on. These were the kinds of variables that were altered systematically.

Temporal Period of Production When an examinee lists multiple, alternative responses to a given item in a divergent-production test, he characteristically produces responses at a diminishing rate. Since his responses come from his memory store, this means that he produces the most available responses first, working toward the least available. It is reasonable to ask whether his ability to produce more available responses is the same as that to produce less available ones. It was hypothesized that ideational fluency is better indicated early in the work period, and since later responses tend to be less common, they may be a better indicator of originality.

The same hypothesis could be tested for almost any divergent-production ability, but in order to leave time for studying the effects of other variations, the hypothesis was examined only in connection with associational fluency and its test, Controlled Associations. The hypothesis should be modified to say that the associational-fluency factor, which is ordinarily best indicated by the total score in this test, is optimally measured by responses given neither early nor late in the working period. Controlled Associations asks E to write alternative synonyms for given words. The number of synonyms given in limited time is the score. The 5-minute time ordinarily given for each item was broken down as follows:

Controlled Associations IIIa: the first $\frac{1}{2}$ minute
Controlled Associations IIIc: the second $\frac{1}{2}$ minute plus the second minute
Controlled Associations IIId: the third minute
Controlled Associations IIIe: fourth and fifth minutes

A score was derived from each work period.

Restriction of Class Ideational fluency had been found consistently involved in "thing-listing" tests, but sometimes these tests also appeared to be related to associational fluency. Thing listing is a matter of naming objects that belong in a specified class, such as in response to the instruction "Name things that are round," which would mean a near minimum of restriction. More constraint is introduced by saying "Name things that are round and soft." Still more constraint would be added by saying "Name things that are round, soft, and white." It was hypothesized that a low-level condition of restraint would favor measurement of ideational fluency, and a high-level condition would measure relatively more the factor of associational fluency. Three thing-listing tests of the types just illustrated were used:

Thing Listing I: low restriction
Thing Listing II: medium restriction
Thing Listing III: high restriction

The same kind of variation was applied to tests for word fluency. The level of restraint was varied in terms of the number of prescribed letters to be used in the words of a list, in four tests:

Word Listing 0: no letter specified
Word Listing I: one letter specified, e.g., each word contains an S
Word Listing II: two letters specified, e.g., each word contains E and M
Word Listing III: three letters specified, e.g., S, T, and B

It was hypothesized that the lower the restraint level, the more variance there would be in ideational fluency and the less in word fluency. It is thus seen that, in general, ideational fluency was believed at that time to be a feature of easy word-recall tasks. The distinction between symbolic and semantic information attached to words had not yet been realized.

Number of Connected Words The favored interpretation of the expressional-fluency factor was that it involves the production of connected discourses. Word fluency and associational fluency involve the production of single words, but those abilities sometimes show up in relation to expressional-fluency tests. Accordingly, one hypothesis was that the more words to be produced in organized speech, the more expressional fluency is involved. The fewer words in each response, the more the test should involve the other two kinds of fluency. Three tests can be considered as tasks for testing this hypothesis. One involves production of single words unrelated to anything in particular; one involves two-word sentences; and the third involves four-word sentences. The tests were

Word Listing 0
Two-word Combinations
Four-word Combinations

The same hypothesis was tested by a second triad of tests in which letter restrictions were imposed. The tests were

Word Listing I
Two-word Combinations: initial letters given
Four-word Combinations: initial letters given

It may be recalled that Word Listing 0 had no letter requirement and that Word Listing I specified that each response must contain a given letter.

Number of Connected Sentences The question was raised whether expressional fluency is better measured by asking E to write several coherently connected sentences or by simply asking for disconnected sentences, as in the tests just described. Two tests represented this variation. Word Synthesis (related sentences) presents E with 10 words to be used in writing connected sentences in a paragraph. The score is a rating of the paragraph for coherence. Word Arrangement gives E four words to be used in each of several different sentences, not connected.

Rearrangement versus Substitution of Words One hypothesis concerning tests of expressional fluency was that the ability would be well measured by tests requiring E to express the same organized idea in many different ways. Such expressions could be varied either by rearrangement of the same words or by substituting other words. Which, if either, should be more effective? Two tests, one of each kind, were designed: Alternate Headlines (rearrangement), and Alternate Headlines (word substitutions). In either case, E was given a headline to be restated in several different ways; e.g.,

MAN DROWNS IN VAIN EFFORT TO SAVE FIANCÉE

No instruction was given regarding rearrangement or substitution of words. The two scores emphasized the two tendencies, respectively. There was some expectation that word substitution would introduce some associational fluency, whereas word rearrangement would be restricted more to expressional fluency. This expectation followed from the fact that giving synonyms is a task that involves associational fluency.

Synonymous versus Nonsynonymous Associations Tests having loadings on associational fluency have not all involved giving synonyms. In fact, there was some suspicion that tests calling for production of synonyms by association might go more toward the verbal-comprehension factor, whereas giving other kinds of associative responses might be better for the associational-fluency ability. Two tests, one involving synonyms and one not, were constructed in order to test this hypothesis. Associations III presents two words, with E to give a word that is a synonym to both, but for different reasons. For example, the item

    nonsense _____ bed

calls for the word "bunk" as a synonym to either of them. Association IV gives items like

    jewelry _____ bell

with the instruction not to give a synonym. The common response here is "ring."

Simile Completion and Simile Interpretation Tests calling for some kind of completion of similes in alternative ways had previously shown relations to factors called "expressional fluency" as well as to associational fluency and ideational fluency. Some variations were introduced in three similes tests in order to learn more about their factorial functions. The three kinds were

    Simile Insertion, an item of which reads

        The kitten's paws were as _____ as velvet.

    Simile Completion, an item of which reads

        The kitten's paws were as smooth as _____ .

    Simile Interpretation, an item of which reads

        The kitten's paws were like velvet, _____ .

In the first of the three, alternative attributes (adjectives) must be produced. In the second, alternative objects (nouns) are to be given. In the third, alternative explanatory statements are called for. It was hypothesized that the third would be more closely related to expressional fluency because not single words but organized discourses must be generated. The first two were expected to be more related to ideational and associational fluency, with expressional fluency possibly entering into the one that calls for production of attributes.

The Original Analysis

The first analysis involved 41 test variables, from which 13 factors were extracted and 12 were rotated and given interpretation. Since there were two factors for which two or more forms of the same test were used in the analysis, and two tests that were each scored in two different ways, there was real danger that specific variance in each case might augment common-factor variance. But in three cases specific factors were accounted for as orthogonal dimensions, and in the fourth case they seemed to have no effect other than possibly slight inflations of common-factor loadings.

This study had as its goal determinations of some effects of different test conditions upon relations of tests to known fluency factors. It did not attempt to demonstrate any new abilities, and none was found. In assessing the outcome, therefore, we shall be concerned with answers to the questions posed by the hypotheses stated earlier. Answers to the questions depend upon comparisons of factor loadings as to size under the different conditions. But factor loadings are not directly comparable where communalities of tests and reliabilities differ. Comparability could have been achieved by a process of "correction for uniqueness," which takes into account the tests' communalities. But because communalities depend upon the special combinations of tests that appear in an analyzed battery, the investigators made corrections for reliabilities only. Reliabilities are not dependent upon what other tests are present or absent.

Temporal Period of Production   In connection with the Controlled Associations test the hypothesis was that there should be more variance from ideational fluency (IF) in the earliest moments of work on an item of the test, that originality (O) should increase in importance for the later moments, and that associational fluency (AF) should be strongest during the middle of the work period on the item.

The results showed that in the four work periods that were scored, IF had rather consistent loadings of .24 to .34 (corrected for unreliability), with no indication of a trend. Factor O (originality) had smaller loadings, −.01 to 20, with no systematic trend. The AF loadings did have a slight tendency toward higher loadings for the middle period (.52 and .47 versus .45 and .38, for the two middle versus the first and fourth periods). The useful information in this result is that the first three minutes of work on items in Associational Fluency give about equally strong indicators of AF, and that the last two minutes of testing time for items are of slightly less value. It would be well, then, to allow only three minutes per item and use the extra time, if need be, for additional items. There is apparently little danger of getting into originality variance, nor will IF variance be significant (in terms of uncorrected factor loadings). We do not know how much of this conclusion can be applied to other tests of AF and tests of other fluency factors.

Restriction of Class In connection with thing-listing tests, in which E is to list names of objects to fit given class specifications, the degree of restriction was controlled in terms of the number of attributes specified for the class in each item, as mentioned earlier. For low, moderate, and high restrictions, one, two, and three attributes, respectively, were given. One check on the effectiveness of these conditions is to compare means per item in the three levels. They were 8.2, 4.6, and 1.4, respectively.

It was expected that lower restriction would favor variance in IF and higher restriction would favor variance in AF. The results show that there was little variance in AF at any level of restriction, and that the variance in IF is maximal at a moderate level, with corrected loadings of .33, .72, and .55 at low, moderate, and high levels, respectively. The differences are so decisive that a test with two restrictive attributes seems the best condition for an IF test of the thing-listing type. A general conclusion from the fate of these tests and those of Controlled Association is that the type of test is a much more important determiner of which factor is measured than is a variation in either working time or amount of restriction.

It should be noted that one, two, or three restricting class specifications cannot be of uniform value for all classes. The memory pool for a class with two or more specified properties may sometimes be larger than that for some other class with only one specification. The number of named attributes is therefore only a rough guide.

Effects of restriction of a different kind were studied in connection with word-fluency or word-listing tests. Degree of restriction was varied in terms of the number of letter requirements, from none at all to three. In this case, the control of class size is better than in the case of the thing-listing tests for IF. The hypothesis suggested was that the greater the restriction, the larger the variance would be in word fluency (WF); and the lower the restriction, the greater the variance in IF. This hypothesis does not take into account the difference in content—symbolic versus semantic, a distinction not realized at the time.

The results showed that with no restriction there was only slight variance in factor WF (a loading of .22, corrected), but that the other three levels of restriction yielded about the same level of loading (.72, .73, and .65 for one-, two-, and three-letter specifications, respectively). The reason the test with no restriction failed to measure WF is that no class was specified, as in the instruction "List words containing the letter F." The tests with restrictions had zero loadings on factor IF, and the test with no restrictions had a loading of only .25 (corrected). It seems to be clearly demonstrated, therefore, that IF is not involved in any genuine word-fluency test. The lack of relevance for degree of restriction up to three specified letters must mean that, even in the most restrictive condition employed, the potential pool of words was reasonably large.

Although not related to any hypothesis, the relations of some of the word-listing tests to two nonfluency factors are of interest. Verbal Comprehension had a zero loading in the test without any restrictions, .24 in the test with a one-letter specification, and .47 and .59 in those with two and three letters of restriction, respectively. This suggests that a test of WF should be limited to one specified letter; otherwise much verbal comprehension comes in. This is reasonable. With little restriction, E has a large pool of familiar words upon which to draw, but with two or three letters specified, the pool shrinks in size, and he could make a high score only by getting into words that are less familiar and thus less available to him. A large vocabulary is apparently a help in such tests. In E's memory pool, the symbolic and semantic aspects of words would thus appear to be retained together. In the practice of testing for DSU, the advantage of a large vocabulary might be offset somewhat by adopting a shorter time limit for each item and adding more items. In selecting the specified letter for a class, even when it is only one, the test maker should take into account the probable size of pool of familiar words in the specified class. Results such as those cited here demonstrate how even a small change of a certain kind in test conditions can bring about material changes in factor composition of tests.

Number of Connected Words Tests of this hypothesis were made by comparing the loadings of tests requiring the listing of single words versus two connected words versus four connected words, the last two cases in the form of sentences. Two such explorations of hypotheses were possible, one with three tests, none of which has one specified letter for each word, and the other with three parallel tests in which a single-letter specification was given for each word. By hypotheses, it was expected that the larger the number of words to be given in each response, even in the range from one to four words, the greater the expressional-fluency (EF) loading; the smaller the number of words per response, the greater the loadings for IF and WF should be.

The hypothesis with regard to EF was supported in both cases, but more definitely in the case requiring a specified letter for each word. The (corrected) loadings for EF with no letter specifications were .29, .55, and .41 for one-, two-, and four-word responses, respectively. With a letter specification for each word, the corresponding EF loadings were .16, .50, and .76. Without producing connected discourse at all, no significant loadings occurred on factor EF. The interpretation of EF as the ability to produce connected discourse was therefore clearly supported. In neither case were any loadings on factor IF significant for tests with any number of words. The same was true for factor WF, when no letter specifications were given. When there was a letter specification, however, WF had a corrected loading of .72 in Word Listing I (one word to be given, with a one-letter specification) and a loading of .41 in the test Two-Word Combinations (first letter given). Thus, in part, the latter test, although with a loading of .50 for EF, is nearly as strong for WF. In Four-Word Combinations (first letter given), the loading of WF was only .28, even with correction, whereas its loading on EF was .76. Thus, as the sentence to be given becomes longer, WF is less important, and EF is more important. Giving E initial letters in EF tests can make them in part WF tests, but not materially when there are as many as four words to each response. Then, organizing the sentence becomes sufficiently important to obscure the need for WF or to benefit from its help.

Number of Connected Sentences The issue in this particular hypothesis testing was whether organizing a number of sentences in a coherent sequence would be a better indicator of factor EF than would producing a number of unconnected sentences. In the first case, the test Word Synthesis (words) asks E to use 10 given words in writing several sentences, and his work is rated for degree of coherence shown. In the second case, the Word Arrangement, E uses four words in each of several unconnected sentences. The latter proved to be a good measure of EF, with a (corrected) loading of .61, while the former failed as a measure of EF, with a loading of only .25. In interpreting EF, therefore, emphasis should be on the sentence, not on the paragraph. This finding stands as yet without verification.

Rearrangement versus Substitution The Alternative Headlines test was scored in two ways in order to determine which would yield a better score for factor EF It was expected that the "substitution" score, based on the number of times E makes substitutions in the given headlines, would measure AF relatively more, and that the "rearrangement" score would measure EF relatively more. The results did not bear out these expectations. The loadings for the rearrangement score were zero for either factor. This score had no significant loadings on any factor in the analysis. The substitution score had loadings near minimal significance on both AF and EF factors. Substitutions would be in the form of synonyms, and giving a variety of synonyms is the best-known kind of task for AF tests. The lack of relation of the rearrangement score to EF suggests that it is necessary for E to frame his own organized thought in a good test of expressional fluency. This idea is consistent with the placement of EF in the cell for SI ability DMS. A better multiple-rearrangement test in which E is instructed to give alternative headlines only by rearrangement of the given words might measure ability DMT or DST, depending upon whether the rearrangement of words is more semantic or symbolic.

Synonymous versus Nonsynonymous Associations Two highly restrictive association tests were given, in which E is to give a single word in response to two stimulus words so that the response is associated in its own way with each of the stimulus words. It was thought that the test that requires the response to be a synonym of each stimulus word would be significantly loaded with the factor of verbal comprehension (VC), while the other test would be more loaded on AF. It turned out that Associations III and Associations IV behaved factorially in much the same way. Both had significant loadings of about .4 on VC, indicating that a large vocabulary can be moderately helpful in both. Both had zero loadings on associational fluency, but their highest loadings were on another factor identified as semantic "correlate completion," which was mentioned in the preceding chapter. It is now known that these association tests are mostly in the convergent-production category, not the divergent-production category as fluency tests are. They measure most strongly SI ability NMR, whereas factor AF is for ability DMR. Fluency cannot ordinarily be measured by means of a test with single-response items.

Simile Completion and Simile Interpretation Under this heading two issues were raised earlier. One has to do with one-word responses versus multiple-word responses. The other, when responses are single words, is concerned with completions in the form of adjectives, for attributes, versus those in the form of nouns, for objects. The multiple-response condition, as in Simile Interpretations, was expected to go in the direction of factor EF, and the single-word responses in the direction of either IF or AF, or both. The results were that Simile Completion (giving nouns) was not significantly related to any of these three abilities. Simile Insertions (giving adjectives) was moderately related to AF but not even significantly to the other two factors. There is a similarity between Simile Insertions and Controlled Associations, in that both require the production of adjectives o° similar meaning (the relation is similarity); hence the SI location should be DMR for the ability. It may be that with nouns there is limited potential for similarity, or for other kinds of relations that would apply in a DMR test, so that Simile Completion has little chance of affiliation for the AF factor. The test went instead on the originality factor. Since the latter is identified as DMT, in giving noun responses in Simile Completion, E must have to indulge in some changes in meanings.

Simile Interpretations was strongly related to EF, but not significantly related to the other two factors. This test fulfills the connected-discourse requirement of good EF tests. In fact, short sentences must be composed in order to make a statement of interpretation. Thus, with only three contrasting tests we learn a number of things regarding three fluency factors.

General Conclusions In general, we see from this analysis that variations in test conditions can often make material differences in the factor compositions of tests. In the one case (Controlled Associations), in which scores came from different time segments of work on an item, there is a law of diminishing returns in terms of measurement of the primary factor (AF). The originality factor did not enter the tests' factorial composition in later moments of work, even though the later responses may have been less common. On the other hand, the results suggest that a strict time limit is important for testing fluency abilities; a test with unlimited time not only would probably be a waste of time but would lower factor loadings in fluency factors, perhaps to zero. The longer Es work on a single item, the more the number of responses should approach the total potential, and verbal-fluency tests should become measures of size of vocabulary, and hence ability CMU. This would also mean that the "uncommon" responses are not necessarily indicators of originality. This conclusion gains support from earlier analyses. In the analysis of the first section of this chapter, of three tests scored with weighting for uncommoness of responses, only Quick Responses was significantly loaded on DMT in the targeted solution, and even this test failed to go with DMT in analysis 16C, to be mentioned later. The score for Alternate Uses commonly has a minimally significant loading on DMT in different analyses. Its items call for unusual uses, but the uses are by no means so very uncommon in the population. The probable secret for the DMT variance in Alternate Uses is the reconstruction of objects involved, and hence the production of transformations. In general, some uncommon responses may involve transformations, and some may not. Thus, unusualness per se is not a safe indicator of originality when defined as ability DMT.

The condition of restriction is important, but not exactly in the way originally supposed. First, it was found that at least some restriction is necessary for good measurement of any kind of fluency. The general expectation that lowering restrictions in almost any kind of fluency test would increase probability of ideational-fluency variance was not vindicated. The kind of test items is a much more important condition. But too much restriction is likely to reduce either word-fluency or ideational-fluency variance and to send the tests in scattered directions in the case of thing-listing (IF) tests. The latter are optimal for IF when the level of restriction is moderately low.

Moderate levels of another variable were found to be optimal also for tests of expressional fluency. The production of single-word responses, and even of two-word responses, is not adequate for measuring EF, nor is the production of a sequence of related sentences. Short sentences of standard length—for example, of four words each—appear to be about optimal, all things considered. Conditions also appear to be a little better when initial letters of words are specified. Shorter sentences and sentences without specified letters tended to send a test toward either word fluency or writing speed, or both, as the dominant sources of variance in total scores.

The Targeted Solution

For the targeted solution, the major interest shifted from effects of changing test conditions to determining whether the factors obtained and their relations to tests showed invariance with results from other analyses. Different forms of the same test, such as Word Listing and Thing Listing, and scores from successive time intervals of work on Controlled Associations were combined to give only one score in each case.

Thirteen factors were extracted and rotated. All were interpreted in line with SI theory except that there were two singlet factors. The fluency factors—DSU, DMU, and DMS—were well represented, as they should have been in view of the liberal number of fluency tests included. From Table 6.2 it can be seen that DSU is clear-cut, being represented by only three strong variables—Word Fluency (a combination of valid word-listing tests), Suffixes, and Rhymes. DMR was also clear-cut, being represented by Associational Fluency (a composite of the valid parts of Controlled Associations), Simile Insertion, and Simile Completion. The latter is the test calling for noun responses. Its loading had been only .09 in the original analysis, but reached a significant .36 in the targeted analysis.

Among the leading tests on DMU were familiar ones—Brick Uses (fluency), Plot Titles (nonclever), and Ideational Fluency (a composite of thing-listing tests with moderate restrictions). Alternate Headlines (rearrangement score) went on DMU, where it had had a zero loading in the original solution. This is not easy to rationalize, in that class specifications are not obvious in items of this test. It could be said, however, that the class is given by the expression "headlines that are rearrangements of the given one." Word Listing 0, which had no stated restrictions of any kind, and consequently had been expected to show some relation to DMU, had a loading of .36 on that factor in the targeted solution and one of .23 in the original analysis. Perhaps this means that E tends to generate his own meaningful class or classes, to which he names members, as a tactic in taking this test. Evidence for this is seen in the clustering of responses apparently within classes. The principal loading was .55 on writing speed in the original analysis and .51 in the targeted analysis. Its freedom from externally imposed restraints evidently permitted words to come to E more rapidly than he could write them, for the most part.

On factor DMS, the leading, familiar tests were Expressional Fluency [essentially the same as Four-Word Combinations (first letter)] and Simile Interpretations. Other tests are reasonably loaded on DMS, including Word Arrangement and Alternate Headlines (words), which had gone at least in the direction of DMS in the original analysis. Word Synthesis (words), which involves writing connected sentences that are to contain 10 given words, went strongly on DMS. In the original solution it had gone with Word Synthesis (rating for coherence) on a specific factor because those two variables were derived from the same test, with an intercorrelation of .56. In the targeted analysis the rating-for-coherence score was omitted.

About the only general conclusion to be drawn from the targeted solution, and this conclusion applies to most, if not all studies, is that when factors are better represented by tests, there is more invariance from one analysis to another.

A STUDY OF INTELLECTUAL FLEXIBILITY

The investigation of flexibility[4] was a direct consequence of the finding of two different flexibility factors in the first creativity analysis, which was treated first in this chapter. Like the two preceding analyses, it was initiated without benefit of structure-of-intellect theory, but its findings made some contributions toward the development of that theory. Its main objective was to learn more about the abilities called "spontaneous flexibility" and "adaptive flexibility," to delineate their properties more clearly, and to examine their possible relations to traits of rigidity.

It was hypothesized that there are two or more dimensions of rigidity, as there are of flexibility, even in the limited realm of thinking, and that traits of flexibility are at opposite poles from those of rigidity. It was also believed that forms of rigidity-flexibility in the realm of thinking are distinct from forms of rigidity in the areas of psychomotor, perceptual, and attitudinal aspects of behavior, although this idea was not tested. Expected least of all was a single flexibility-rigidity trait that pervades all areas of behavior, for there was already the evidence for two such dimensions in the area of thinking alone.

Hypotheses and Tests

The thinking behind the choice of tests and the construction of new tests for this analysis were in terms of two kinds of flexibility and two hypothetical kinds of rigidity that are as nearly opposite to them as could be reasonably conceived. Opposite to "spontaneous flexibility" was thought to be "perseveration," a kind of inertia. Opposite to "adaptive flexibility" was believed to be "persistence." The four concepts were defined as follows:

> *Spontaneous flexibility*: The ability to introduce diversity into ideas generated in a relatively unstructured situation
> *Perseveration*: The tendency of thinking behavior, once operating, to run its temporal course until exhaustion or disruption from some disturbing influence

---

[4] See Report 18; also Frick, Guilford, Christensen, & Merrifield (1959).

Adaptive flexibility: The ability to change set in order to meet requirements imposed by changing conditions

Persistence: The insistence, with continuing motivation, upon pursuing one line of approach to a problem in the face of altered conditions

With two or more tests representing each of these concepts, several different outcomes were possible. There could be two (logically) bipolar factors, four unipolar factors, or two unipolar, flexibility factors, the tests for perseveration and persistence going off in different directions. There were other possible outcomes, more or less regular, but not seriously considered.

Spontaneous Flexibility   Two slightly different definitions of this concept led to two different sets of tests. One conception regarded it as the ability to shift mental set freely, making it possible to get away from the more obvious and the more trite responses. The test Riddles (clever) asks E to give answers to riddles, but only the clever ones are counted toward the score. An example shows E what it meant by "clever." If the question is "What city is preferred by actors?" the obvious answer might be "Hollywood"; it is realistic. But the answer "publi*city*" is regarded as clever and would be counted toward the score.

In Rhyming Definitions, a phrase is given for which E is to supply a two-word definition with rhyming words. A pretty girl can be defined as a "slick chick," and a baby's finger can be defined as a "midget digit." In the two tests just mentioned, single answers are called for, not multiple responses as in divergent-production tests, in which spontaneous flexibility had previously been found. But it was thought that getting away from "the more obvious and more trite" responses, even in giving one response, would be sufficient to represent the ability in question. The concept of "divergent production" had not yet become current.

The second definition of "spontaneous flexibility" emphasizes the divergent-production idea. It regards spontaneous flexibility as the ability to react to a relatively unstructured situation in divergent channels or directions. Brick Uses (shifts) provides the prototype of this conception. New tests included to represent this subhypothesis were Impossibilities (used in the first creativity analysis) and Twenty Questions. In a sample item of Twenty Questions, E is told that the object to be guessed is a vegetable. He is to ask as many as 20 questions, each of which can be answered by "yes" or "no," and the answers should yield information useful in guessing the object. It was believed that both of these tests require considerable search for ideas, with flexibility.

Perseveration   One conception of "perseveration" was inertia in thinking; a tendency to let thinking run its course. Brick Uses (shifts) was put in this category because the individual with considerable perseverative tendency keeps naming uses in the same category until he has exhausted it. A similar new test was Object Naming, in which E is told merely to list a number of objects. It was scored in terms of the degree of clustering of responses, that is, runs of objects in the same class.

The other conception of "perseveration" was with regard to themes, as shown in a tendency to elaborate upon the same theme versus changing to new themes. Chain Associations and Syllables were two new tests for this idea of "perseveration." In Chain Associations, E lists words, each one to be associated to the one preceding it. In Syllables, E is to list two-syllable, nonsense words of his own invention. Both tests are scored for the tendency to avoid runs. A run in Chain Associations would be a series of closely related words, thus grouped under a "theme." A run in the Syllables test would be a series of consecutive words within which only minor changes in letters are made.

Adaptive Flexibility The first of three subhypotheses emphasized the ability to restructure problems. For this purpose, tests contained problems that require insights, with shifts of meaning. This is particularly true of Insight Problems and Puzzles. A sample problem from the first of these tests reads

> A man went out to hunt a bear one day. He left his camp and hiked due south for 10 miles, then due west for 10 miles, where he killed a bear. He went back to camp, a distance of exactly 10 miles. What color was the bear? Why?
> Answer: White, a polar bear; only at the North Pole would the distances described be possible.

The Puzzles test presents problems also requiring drastic shifts of interpretation. Planning Air Maneuvers was previously found together with Match Problems II on the factor identified as "adaptive flexibility" in the planning analysis. Both are figural in content. There was interest in knowing whether the new verbal tests would go along with them on the same factor. There was growing suspicion that this kind of result would not occur.

The second conception of "adaptive flexibility" in this study was an ability to solve a problem in several ways. Match Problems II was included under this principle. A new test called "Squares" is of the same type. In a checkerboard pattern with six rows and six columns, E is to locate a specified number of Xs in squares so that no two are in the same row, column, or diagonal, and to do this in more than one way.

The third conception emphasizes deserting associative connections just used and adopting some new ones in their places. Tests representing this subhypothesis were Circle Squares II, which has been described earlier, and Circle-Square-Triangle. The same geometric objects must be associated with different named objects in the various items, E keeping the associations free from confusions.

Persistence Three meanings of "persistence" were bases for still other tests. One meaning was the continued, maladaptive use of learned procedures. For this hypothesis the famous Luchins (1953) Water Jars test was brought into use in a form adapted to group testing. An important reason for using this test was to see whether the kind of rigidity it was supposed to measure is aligned with adaptive flexibility. The test presents first a series of five problems, each calling for a statement of the operations by which a person could fill a large jar with a specified capacity *W*, having at his disposal three smaller jars of capacities *X*, *Y*, and *Z*. Every one of the five problems can be solved by means of the same pattern of operations, by the same formula. The sixth and other problems following can be solved either by using the same formula or by simpler and shorter methods. Will *E* continue to use the less efficient, formula method?

Another reason for using the Water Jars test was to determine its factor composition, since it had been so widely used as a measure of rigidity. There was some expectation that it would measure general reasoning and logical evaluation as well as, or in place of, adaptive flexibility. After all, the items are like arithmetical-reasoning problems.

The second subhypothesis under "persistence" emphasizes continued operation of habitual meanings. Two previously employed tests were adapted for use under this hypothesis. One was Sign Changes, and the other was Object Synthesis. These tests have been described earlier.

The third idea was that persistence is resistance to restructuring. In testing for this conceived trait, three former tests were adapted and one new one was constructed. Hidden Figures, Penetration of Camouflage, and Figure Analysis all involve seeing familiar figures concealed in more obvious figures. Camouflaged Words requires *E* to see new words formed by combining the end of one word with the beginning of the next in a sentence. In this particular test, *E* is told to look for the name of a sport or a game in each sentence; e.g.

> I did not know that he was ailing. (sailing)
> He took a Mongol for his bride. (golf)

From the fact that Camouflaged Words is a symbolic task, as became realized later, it should not have been expected to go along with the three figural tests, even though the tasks are similar otherwise. The three tests could determine a figural-flexibility factor, but one test alone could not determine a symbolic-flexibility factor. Such a separation was effected in later analyses.

The Original Analysis

The most general and somewhat decisive result was that no new factors were needed to account for either the perseveration or the persistence tests. The rigidity tests generally went along with flexibility tests on various factors. Of six tests for spontaneous flexibility, three went significantly on that factor, known as "DMC" in the SI model. Of the four tests for perseveration, two went with those three to help define DMC. Of the seven tests for adaptive flexibility, four went on that factor, which is for SI ability DFT. From the standpoint of present knowledge, the factor identified as DFT in the original solution was a confounding of DFT with NFT. Of the seven tests designed for persistence, only two went on DFT, but only three of the seven were figural, the others being symbolic or semantic in content. Lack of appropriate kind of content can be given as the reason for most of the failures of the flexibility and rigidity tests going on factors DMC and DFT, spontaneous and adaptive flexibility, respectively.

Another interesting generality in the results was a tendency for tests designed for the four major hypotheses to go on factors that involve transformations—NFT, NST, and DMT as well as DFT. By the time the factors were interpreted, structure-of-intellect categories had become known, and two new transformation factors were recognized—NFT and NST—DFT and DMT having been identified earlier for adaptive flexibility and originality, respectively. Thus new kinds of flexibility were recognized, and the flexibility and rigidity tests helped in reaching the conclusion that transformation-production abilities, convergent as well as divergent, are traits of flexibility.

Factorial Nature of the Water Jars Test This analysis gave a rather clear answer concerning the factorial composition of the goup form of the Water Jars test. Its major variances were found to be from general reasoning, with a loading of .42, and logical evaluation, with a loading of .45, much as had been predicted. There were only insignificant loadings on either of the two flexibility factors under investigation or for any transformation abilities (Frick & Guilford, 1957). The widespread use of this test as a measure of rigidity received no validation support whatever from this analysis. The targeted solution, to be mentioned next, gave a CMS loading of .69 and a loading for EMI that failed to reach significance.

The Targeted Solution

Targeting was extended to the additional factors of CMI for the Twenty Questions test, DSU for the Syllables test, and NFT for several figural tests of the hidden-figures type. The new factor NST had been suggested by the original analysis, but being the only representative of its factor, Camouflaged Words came out as a singlet. Twenty Questions also came out as a singlet, for lack of support from other tests for its factor. The findings from the later analysis do not call for additional conclusions. The loadings may be seen in Table 6.2.

CREATIVE ABILITIES AT THE NINTH-GRADE LEVEL

In all the studies mentioned thus far in this chapter, the experimental subjects or examinees were young, male adults. With the finding of a number of divergent-production (DP) abilities that could be replicated in different analyses and that seemed to be quite relevant logically to creative thinking, questions arose as to whether the same factorial structure in this area would be found with younger groups and with females as well as males. It was expected that the tests of fluency, flexibility, and elaboration that had been successful in determining the factors in young adults could also be used with ninth-grade students. Thus, examinees at that age and educational level were sought as subjects.[5]

By the time this investigation was being planned, the SI theory had been developed sufficiently to serve as a guide in constituting a test battery. The new SI conceptions for the various abilities suggested that better tests could be constructed for some of the DP factors. At least there was room for tests better fitting the threefold specifications for abilities in the SI model. Thus, a few new tests were developed for analysis along with the more faithful markers from earlier analyses.

Besides the major objectives of determining the structure of divergent-production abilities at the younger age level, and for females as well as males, there was secondary interest in the factor structure for individuals of high IQ as

---

[5] See Report 26.

compared with those of moderate IQ. Since IQs were available for most of the students, it was possible to determine possible relations between divergent-production abilities and IQ. With the SI theory available, it was realized that most of the already known divergent-production abilities were in the semantic category. Exceptions were adaptive flexibility (DFT), word fluency (DSU), and expressional fluency (then identified with ability DSS). It was decided to explore further into the figural and symbolic categories as natural next steps, but not extensively in this particular analysis because the number of factors would be so large as to take the battery beyond available testing time.

There was one SI-hypothesized ability in the figural area, however, that received special attention, namely, DFI. It may be remembered that in the planning study a test that appeared to be figural, Figure Production, went with the semantic planning tests to determine a factor then called simply "elaboration." From SI theory, Figure Production should go with other figural tests on a figural factor parallel to a semantic factor DMI, not on DMI. This hypothesis was tested by constructing two new tests for DFI and one new test for DMI, to see whether two separate divergent-production-of-implications factors would appear.

The case of DSS also called for attention. The first placement of the expressional-fluency factor in the SI model was in the cell for DSS. The reasoning was that a sentence is an organized grammatical structure, and structural aspects of speech are in the realm of symbolic information. The finding in the fluency study to the effect that expressional fluency seemed to involve the expression of a semantically organized construct, a relatively complex idea, had been ignored in assigning this factor to DSS. The appropriate tactic was to develop two new tests that should surely represent DSS and to analyze them along with two good tests of expressional fluency.

Expected Factors and Their Tests

With SI abilities furnishing hypotheses for factors, it is only necessary to list them, to comment only on incidental matters connected with them, and to mention the tests used to mark them. Where tests are new, they will be briefly described. We shall begin with the semantic abilities.

Ideational Fluency (DMU) Three marker tests for DMU from previous studies were Consequences (obvious), Ideational Fluency (like Think Listing I of the fluency analysis), and Plot Titles (nonclever). A partially new instrument was the Utility Test, which includes Brick Uses as its first part and a parallel item calling for uses of an ordinary wooden pencil as its second part. As in Brick Uses, a simple count of the number of uses given is the DMU score.

Spontaneous Flexibility (DMC) Two marker tests were Alternate Uses (formerly Unusual Uses) and the Utility Test (shifts), in which the DMC score is the number of times E changes category of uses. Multiple Grouping was a new test designed to confirm the placement of spontaneous flexibility in the DMC cell of the SI model. Given the names of seven common objects, E is to classify and reclassify them in a number of ways. There is a much more obvious reclassifying task in this test than in the other two.

Associational Fluency (DMR) Two previously used tests were Associational Fluency I (formerly Controlled Associations) and Simile Insertions. The new test, Multiple Analogies, was constructed so as to possess more clearly the SI properties of DMR. Analogies tests had almost always been found to represent relations abilities in either cognitive or productive operation categories. Divergent production calls for multiple responses, so pairs of words were chosen, each of which has several possible relations. The pair of words FATHER–DAUGHTER has the relations of parent–child, old–young, male–female, tall–short, and possibly others. One could ask E to provide such word pairs as his multiple responses, but to make the test somewhat easier for the younger subjects, first members of such pairs were provided, with E to give the correlates. Giving correlates had been found sufficient in measurement of the ability for correlate completion (NSR), for example.

Originality (DMT) Two dependable tests were used as markers for DMT–Consequences (remote) and Plot Titles (clever). The third test, Alternate Signs, was a thoroughly revised Symbol Production, similar to that test only in principle. In it, E is to produce several different pictorial symbols to represent each given single word, e.g., "weight," and drawings of real objects are acceptable.

Semantic Elaboration (DMI) As stated earlier, it was suspected that the previously obtained elaboration factor was a confounding of DMI and DFI. Two tests for the planning analysis were used intact–Planning Elaboration II and Figure Production, a possible figural test. Possible Jobs was newly designed to emphasize multiple, semantic implications. E is given a line drawing of an object such as an electric light bulb and is to suggest different jobs, occupations, or groups of people for which the object could stand as a symbol. For a light bulb he might say, "electrician," "electrical manufacturer," "missionary," "teacher," "bright student," and so on. Although the stimulus is figural, the thing implied is semantic.

Adaptive Flexibility (DFT) The marker tests for DFT were two, carried over from earlier studies–Match Problems II and Planning Air Maneuvers. Match Problems V was a type somewhat different from Match Problems II, in that it specifies only the number of matches to be removed, not also the number of squares to remain. This variation offers more alternatives and was consequently thought to be easier for the younger subjects.

Figural Elaboration (DFI) The new figural-divergent-production factor expected in this study was for SI ability DFI. For this hypothesized factor, two new tests were designed. Decorations presents E with outline drawings of familiar objects, such as articles of furniture and of clothing. E is to add decorative lines to these outlined objects, and since the same object is presented twice, he has more room for multiple responses. Production of Figural Effects presents E with very simple lines of different kinds. To each of them he is to add other lines so as to make more complex figures, the latter *not* to be realistic objects. In Figure Production E *is* to produce realistic objects, which could possibly have accounted for the test's semantic affiliation with DMI in the earlier analysis. In the new analysis, Figure Production had an opportunity to go on DFI only, or on both DFI and DMI. It was not expected to go solely on DMI again.

Word Fluency (DSU) DSU marker tests were Suffixes and Word Fluency, the latter being like Word Listing I of the fluency study.

Possible Expressional Fluency (DSS) Although the two clearly semantic tests might determine a new factor DMS, they are listed here along with two new ones. The semantic tests were Expressional Fluency [like Four-word Combinations (first letters) of the fluency study], and Simile Interpretations. The new tests that followed the SI properties of a DSS ability were Make a Code and Number Combinations. The former asks E to invent simple, alternative codes, using letters and digits, in symbolic systems. Number Combinations asks E to make a number of equations, given a few numbers and rules. It was thought that an equation could be a symbolic system.

The Original Analysis

In the original study at the ninth-grade level four different analyses were carried out. This was possible because the battery of 35 tests was administered to about 700 students in one junior high school and to about 200 in another. One analysis, symbolized by "T," was based on the total of the second sample, which contained members of both sexes and had a wide range of IQ. The larger sample was subdivided to form groups of about 200 each, one composed of boys only (B) and the other of girls only (G). In both these groups, the IQ ranges were restricted to from 95 to 119. The fourth analysis was based on data for students whose IQs were all 120 and above and was known as "analysis H." This group was drawn from both high schools, so there were a few cases of overlap of subjects in analyses T and H.

For the groups T and H, the variable of sex membership was put into the battery for analysis. There were no marked sex differences, except for the interesting finding that girls tended to excel in tests of fluency and boys to excel in tests of flexibility. Some differences between means were statistically significant, and some were not. Some test scores from the school records were added to the test variables in order to help mark factors for CMU and numerical facility.

The Factors Supported We shall take up the obtained factors in the same order in which they were mentioned earlier. All the expected factors received at least some support.

DMU was supported fully in that three of its tests came together on factors in all four analyses, and the fourth test, the Utility Test, came out with them in all but analysis H (high IQ). Two tests for DMC came out together on a factor in each analysis. The new test, Multiple Grouping, came out on the same factor only in analysis T; thus, its reclassification feature did not give much support to assigning spontaneous flexibility to SI ability DMC. Better support with this test has been obtained in later studies.

The two marker tests for DMR consistently helped determine this factor in all four analyses. The new test, Multiple Analogies, which was pointed more definitely at the SI definition of this factor, failed to help determine it except in analysis H. In every group its highest loading was on CMU, which suggests a problem with vocabulary for the subjects in this test. A different format for multiple analogies and more care in selecting words might make a successful DMR test.

A clear DMS factor was found, distinct from a weaker DSS. That is, the two verbal tests went on one factor, and the two symbolic tests went elsewhere. In every analysis, Expressional Fluency and Simile Interpretations helped determine DMS. They were alone in doing so in analyses B and G, but had other tests with them in analyses T and H.

Factor DMT was supported by Plot Titles (clever) in all four analyses and by Alternative Signs in three. Consequences (remote) failed to appear significantly on DMT, except for sample B (boys). This failure was an exceptional finding, for even in a sixth-grade sample, this test variable had a significant relation to DMT (Report 27).

There was a distinct separation of two elaboration factors, for DMI and DFI, with Planning Elaboration II appearing for DMI in three cases and the new test, Possible Jobs, also appearing for it in three cases. In all four analyses Figure Production went with the two new figural tests to determine the new factor for DFI, and not at all on the factor for DMI, as in the planning study.

For DSU, the two marker tests, and only the two in three analyses, performed as expected. The finding of a new DSS, distinct from DMS, was mentioned earlier. With only two tests possibly to represent it, there could be some doubt of finding a DSS dimension. The factor did not appear in the G (girls) analysis, and the two tests came out together as the entire support for DSS only in the analysis for boys. At any rate, these two tests refused to go with well-recognized expressional-fluency tests. Additional tests designed for DSS are needed to find further evidence to support the factor.

DFT was strongly supported, all three tests designed for it coming out together. One to three additional tests came on the factor also to some extent in three of the analyses.

Some General Conclusions   On the whole, there is much evidence that the same divergent-production factors found in adult, male populations can also be demonstrated for ninth-grade populations. Most of the tests that had marked those factors for the adults also usually marked them for the younger population. The same factors are usually found for both sexes, so that very similar factor structures apply to both. The only marked differences in this study was the appearance of DSS in the boys' analysis and not in the girls'. It did appear in a mixed sample.

Although it might have been expected that the factor structure would be clearer in analyses B, G, and H, as compared with analysis T, owing to the restriction in ranges of IQ in the three groups other than T, such does not appear to be the case. The average number of tests per factor was 4.0 for group T, 3.1 for group B, 3.7 for group G, and 3.6 for group H. A gifted group confined to one sex might have exhibited a sharper picture, as indicated by fewer tests per factor. It must be remembered, too, that restriction on range of IQ does not mean a great deal with regard to restriction on DP abilities, since the correlations between IQ and DP tests tend to be low.

The Targeted Solution
Since there were so many similarities in the factor structures in the four different original analyses, only one of the sets of data was used in the targeted analysis, that for group H. Fourteen factors were extracted and rotated, including the two nonintellectual factors of sex and writing speed. Only one intellectual factor was a singlet, and that was for what was thought to be DSS, for which only the test Make a Code functioned to give a significant loading.

As may be seen in Table 6.2, most of the factors were confined to their intended tests. Some of the tests that failed generally to go on their expected factors in the original analysis did better. Multiple Grouping had not gone on the factor for DMC in sample H before, but it did in this analysis. Multiple Analogies, which had gone on the factor for DMR with only minimal significance before, went to the head of the list for group H in this solution. Consequences (remote), which went for DMT only for group B before, went for DMT in the targeted analysis. The new test, Possible Jobs, which had not gone on DMI as intended for groups T and H in the orignal analysis, went strongly for DMI in the targeted solution, although it still had some relation to CMI, as in the original analysis. CMI was poorly marked by only one of its characteristic tests—Seeing Problems—and was possibly not optimally located in this solution If it was, there is indication that Possible Jobs has cognition variance as well as DP variance, and Seeing Problems has DP variance as well as cognition variance, at least for the ninth-grade sample.

CREATIVE ABILITIES AT THE SIXTH-GRADE LEVEL

The possibility of investigating whether the divergent-production abilities could be found differentiated at the sixth-grade level arose when a graduate student in education, Elnora Schmadel, proposed relating measures of divergent production to academic achievement. In a cooperative effort, about 400 students became available for testing with a 4-hour battery.[6]

Selection of Tests
Selection of the factors to be investigated was based upon previous experiences at higher age levels: factors for abilities regarded as most relevant for creative thinking and factors most replicated. The list then included the six semantic-divergent-production abilities, sensitivity to problems, and adaptive flexibility. Two tests were selected for each of the expected factors, except for sensitivity to problems and expressional fluency, for which there was only one test each. The list of tests follows:

Ideational fluency (DMU):
Plot Titles (nonclever)
Consequences (obvious)

---

[6] See Report 27.

Spontaneous flexibility (DMC):
  Alternate Uses
  Utility Test (shifts)

Associational fluency (DMR):
  Associational Fluency
  Simile Insertions

Expressional fluency (DMS):
  Expressional Fluency

Originality (DMT):
  Plot Titles (clever)
  Consequences (remote)

Elaboration (DMI):
  Planning Elaboration
  Possible Jobs

Sensitivity to problems (CMI):[7]
  Seeing Problems

Adaptive flexibility (DFT):
  Match Problems V
  Making Objects

In adapting the adult test forms to the younger group, with ages mostly at ten to eleven years, some minor changes were made, especially in the instructions. Test titles were usually changed, in order to make them more appealing to children. Time allowances were made a little more liberal for some of the tests, since there is so much writing to be done by Es. A Marking Speed test and the variable of sex membership were inserted in the battery to locate those possible sources of variance.

Making Objects was a new test thought to be favorable for DFT. In it E is presented with several simple geometric figures that he is to combine and recombine in different ways in order to construct specified objects, such as a table lamp, a face, or a doll. It was thought that each new use of a figure means a transformation. We shall see that in no study has that test gone on DFT; it has gone on DFS. Considering the list of factors and their representative tests given above, this means that there was a third factor (DFT) that was left represented by only one test; also a fourth, counting Making Objects as being for DFS.

The Original Analysis

With many abilities poorly represented, the original analysis may still be said to have distinguished four DP factors—DMU, DMC, DMR, and DMT. They were distinguished from one another and also from factors represented by parts of an IQ test, which supported factors probably correctly identified for abilities CMU, CMR, and numerical facility.

---

[7] At the time this study was planned it was believed that the factor for sensitivity to problems belonged in the SI place for EMI.

The Targeted Solution

Reference to Table 6.2 will show that five of the semantic-DP abilities are supported by doublet factors, much as should have been expected. The general conclusion is that insofar as the factors had support from tests, they were differentiated in much the same manner as in older groups of subjects. An unexpected result was that the tests Seeing Problems and Possible Jobs showed significant relations with the factor of DMC. This could mean that these younger Es gain in numbers of responses in those tests, in part, by shifting class categories. Were the intended factors better determined (CMI and DMI), this deviation might not have occurred.

FIGURAL- AND SYMBOLIC-DIVERGENT-PRODUCTION ABILITIES

At the time this study was initiated,[8] the structure of intellect was fully utilized in hypothesizing what new abilities should be expected. Eight DP abilities had been demonstrated, six of them semantic and one each in the figural and symbolic categories (DFT and DSU). The SI model implies as many as 10 more DP abilities, outside the behavioral area. During the early course of the study, two additional DP factors had become known, as reported in connection with the ninth-grade study. DFI was clearly indicated, and there was some evidence for DSS. Consequently these two factors could be set aside. During the course of test construction it became evident that tests designed for DFR and DST were not very promising. That left six SI abilities to be investigated for the first time in this study, namely, DFU, DFC, DFS, DSC, DSR, and DSI.

Thus, the major objective of this study was to determine whether the SI theory could predict undemonstrated abilities. The choice of the DP area for this purpose was determined by the growing interest in creative-thinking abilities to account fully for creative potential for the visual arts, and symbolic-DP abilities to help account for creativity in mathematics. There was a minor objective, in connection with factor DFT, which had been demonstrated more than once before, but whose placement in the SI model was in some question, and better tests were desired for it. DFT was therefore added to the list of six. As it became evident that both a sample of naval aviators and a ninth-grade sample would be available, an additional objective was to determine the similarity in factor structure that would occur when the age and education differed but the test battery was the same. Would the same factors appear, and would their relations to tests be comparable?

The DP Factors and Their Tests

With the SI model as the source of hypothetical abilities, there were two ways in which the model was used in deriving ideas for new tests. One was to keep within the guidelines of the three parameter values for each ability. The other was to take advantage of known successful tests in parallel positions in the model. Examples will be illustrated in some of the tests now to be described.

---

[8] See Report 29.

DFU Tests The tests developed for DFU included Make a Mark, Sketches, and Make a Figure test (fluency). Successful DMU tests have given E some class specifications for which he is to provide a list of class members, such as naming things that are white and soft. Make a Mark instructs E to draw in each of a number of outlined squares that are provided a simple open figure in one item and a simple closed figure in another, for example. In Sketches, we may say that the class specification is presented in figural form. For example, in each of a number of squares, given an ellipse, E is to make objects containing an ellipse.

Make a Figure presents in each item a set of simple lines, e.g., two short curves and a short straight line, with E to make a number of units, each of which combines these elements in different ways. It was realized that making arrangements of elements might take the test in the direction of DFS also, which did prove to be the case in the analysis. The "(fluency)" attached to the title of this test means that the count of acceptable units produced is the score for ability DFU. A count of the number of times E shifts from one class to another, as in the parallel test, Brick Uses, was intended to be a score for DFC.

DFC Tests Four score variables were made available for DFC, from these sources: Make a Figure Test (shifts), Alternate Letter Groups, Figural Similarities, and Varied Figural Classes. The first test variable was just mentioned in discussion of DFU tests. It turned out that decisions as to when shifts in kinds of figures occur are very difficult to make, with the result that the score had no contribution to make toward any factor. It is possible that Es did very little thinking in terms of classes in this test.

Alternate Letter Groups presents E with a set of eight capital letters in simple line drawings. E is to group three or more as a class, by virtue of their common figural properties, such as "all straight lines," "contain parallel lines," "have rounded tops," and so on. He is to reclassify letters from the given group in as many different ways as he can.

Figural Similarities was constructed on the basis of the same principle— multiple grouping or reclassifying activity, as in the parallel test for DMC, Multiple Grouping. Whereas in the latter and in Alternate Letter Groups E is to state which units are to be grouped, in Figural Similarities an effort was made to use a multiple-choice format, in the following manner. Each of six figures was given a letter symbol, with letters A to F. All possible triads were formed and presented as possible genuine class groups, with E to respond by answering "yes," "?," or "no." This form of the test was chosen in order to determine whether a test with multiple-choice format could measure a DP ability. From the standpoint of present knowledge, this test might well be a measure of EFC, unless some of the classes are difficult to see, in which case some CFC variance would enter as a component.

DFS Tests The three tests proposed for DFS were Designs, Dot Systems, and Monograms. The conception of DFS calls for tasks in which E must organize the same elements in different ways in order to produce different organized wholes. In Designs, E is given a number of line elements, such as a straight line, a dot, a semicircle, and an angle, from which, by combining them in different ways, he can make various patterns such as are seen in wallpaper, dress goods, or linoleum.

In Dot Systems, E is given a layout of dots in four rows and four columns (with the last row of two dots only). In each solution, he is to arrange the letter T to appear twice, each letter fitting four dots. The arrangements are to be varied in different ways.

In Monograms, the elements given are three capital letters, assumed to be the initials of a person's name. The three are to be arranged in alternative patterns, each of which might represent a different monogram.

DFT Tests From the first studies of creative-thinking abilities, some form of the Match Problems test had helped define the factor for adaptive flexibility, later recognized as DFT. The first form of the test did not call for multiple solutions to each item. As the concept of "divergent production" became known, this feature became puzzling, for DP tests have always otherwise called for multiple solutions. It seemed possible that multiple figural transformations could occur during the single solution, in trial-and-error behavior.

In the earliest form of the Match Problems test, however, two items required some drastic departures from the ordinary solution. One kind of departure was in the form of making one of the remaining squares four times as large as the rest. Another left overlapping squares. It could have been that these items (two out of ten) accounted in large part for the involvement with DFT. Match Problems III was constructed so as to capitalize upon problems which offer such drastic departures from the conventional solutions. Like Match Problems II, it calls for multiple solutions also, some of them orthodox.

There was also a question of simplifying Match Problems for use with younger groups. Simplification was achieved in one way in Match Problems IV, which specifies the number of squares to be left but not the number of matches to be removed. It calls for multiple solutions, as in Match Problems II. In contrast with Match Problems IV in one respect, Match Problems V specifies the number of matches to be removed but not the number of squares to be left.

Making Objects had been designed for ability DFT, but refused to go with Match Problems II, as related in the preceding section. The new hypothesis for it was SI ability DFS. This new study gave it two opportunities to go with other tests designed for DFS in the two analyses, one for adults and one for a ninth-grade sample.

DSC Tests Two of the tests for DSC followed the multiple-grouping principle. They were Name Grouping and Number Grouping. An example of a smaller problem for Name Grouping presents a list of names

1. Gertrude
2. Bill
3. Alex
4. Carrie
5. Belle
6. Don

E is to indicate the classes he forms on the basis of spelling properties of the names.

An item in Number Grouping might present the numbers 2, 3, 4, 5, 17, 23, and 36; from which groups can be formed, e.g., multiples of 3, odd numbers, or prime numbers.

Varied Symbols gives a set of three nonsense words, such as PEQ, TMU, and EXF. Five other alternative nonsense words are also presented for potential grouping, each in turn, with all three, the four making a class. All classes are to be for different common properties.

DSR Tests Construction of tests for DSR posed some special difficulties. One important consideration was that although the parallel tests for CSR present related symbols, with *E* to show that he is aware of the nature of the relations, the parallel tests for production abilities seemed to require operating with correlates. In tests for the convergent-production abilities, NSR and NMR, analogies-completion tests and correlate-completion tests had been more natural. The same was true in tests for DMR. Associational Fluency gives one unit and the relation of similarity, with *E* to produce multiple correlates.

But analogies-completion and correlate-completion tests for DSR seemed out of the question, since symbols lack the connotative meanings so common with words. Fortunately, it is possible to ask for alternative relations, and the tests constructed for DSR were of this type. The three tests were Alternate Additions, Letter Group Relations, and Number Rules. The two number tests were possible because numbers can be so easily connected by the relations "less than," "equal to," and "greater than, " or by the fundamental operations. Each operation sign stands for a relation.

Alternate Additions presents several simple numbers with the instruction to combine them, by addition only, in different ways to achieve a specified sum. For example, the digits 1, 2, 3, and 4 can be summed in different ways to equal the total of 7. In another numerical test, Number Rules, *E* is given a starting number, e.g., 2, and is told to arrive at another specified number, e.g., 6, by operating with other numbers in ways that are needed. *E* is to do this in different ways in order to emphasize divergent production. Thus, *E* himself introduces the varied relationships of numbers.

Letter Group Relations is of a different kind. It asks *E* to state whether or not a given triad of letters, such as "ABC," presents internal relations which can possibly be found in a list of other triads, such as "MNO," "TEO," "BRJ," and "IGH." "MNO" and "RTW" can be accepted as showing the same relations, i.e., alphabetical order, although the letters are not adjacent in the alphabet in "RTW."

DSI Tests For DSI, only two tests were provided, both accepting the requirement of the SI theory that this ability pertains to production of varied implications from the same given information. Symbol Elaboration presents two very simple equations having at least one term in common. What other equations are implied by or can be deduced from this information? If the given equations are $Z = A + D$ and $B - C = D$, *E* could derive the equations $D = Z - A$, $B - C = Z - A$, and so on.

Limited Words is an anagrams task of a special kind. From a given pair of short words, E is to produce other pairs of words, using exactly the same letters. Thus, the pair SHIRT-BEAN could become "hairs-bent" or "bears-thin." The one combination of letters implies others. The numbers of alternatives in items of this test are limited, however.

The Original Analysis

The first major finding to report regarding the analyses in the two populations is that the seven divergent-production abilities under special investigation could be identified with factors in the ninth-grade data but not in the young-adult data, in which six were identified, with DFC missing. In only two of these cases can it be said that the factors were "overdetermined," i.e., for factors DFU and DFS, where as many as three tests in each case helped determine each of those factors. In four other cases two tests designed for each factor were prominent in determining it, at least in one of the two populations. The similarity of lists of tests determining the same factor in the two populations was only fairly good. It was clear that, although there were indications of the factors expected, more than three tests should have been designed for each factor.

A few special findings are worthy of note. The tests that came out on factors DFU and DFS quite often had significant loadings on both those factors. Only one test for DFU (Sketches) was significantly loaded on DFU and not on DFS, for both populations, but this was true also for Make a Mark in the analysis for adults. Only Making Objects had a significant loading on DFS and not on DFU, and that only for the adolescent population. In view of the fact that some of the units produced involve making arrangement of elements, and such units become a little complex, and the fact that some systems could be taken as units, this kind of intermingling of tests for two factors is understandable. This interpretation is preferred to the one that some factor analysts would prefer, that the two factors are really oblique. But just how oblique they would appear to be would depend upon which tests of the two factors happen to be analyzed together.

Confirming earlier suspicions, Making Objects went decisively on DMS in both analyses. The assembling of the same elements to form different wholes is a matter of producing systems, even when each element is a very familiar object and more or less loses its identity in the new whole. Considering a comparison of Making Objects with other tests of DFT or NST, we find a clue to account for the misfire. Those other tests involve *breaking down* old structures in making new ones. This does not happen to the given objects in the test Making Objects; they are used as they are given. In tests of NST, letter sequences in old words are extracted and regrouped to form new words. In match-problems tests, E destroys one pattern of squares in order to achieve some new specified kind of pattern.

Another invalid prediction was with regard to the Dot Systems test. Designed for DMS, it went very weakly on DFT only for the adults but a little more strongly on DFU for the adolescents. Apparently the arrangement of two copies of the same capital letter, such as T in a pattern of dots, is not constructing much of a system. If we accept the result for the younger group, it is a matter of varied placement of a letter or of choosing its position. This might suggest that a unique placement is a figural unit. The adults' loading on DFT for this test would call for some effort to rationalize the involvement of figural transformation, if the loading were higher.

As for the match-problems tests used in this analysis, in both populations the new test Match Problems III proved to be a strong measure of DFT, stronger than Match Problems IV, in both populations. This could mean that specifying both the number of matches to be removed and the number of squares to be left is a better condition than just one specification, at least when the one specification is the number of squares to be left. But we shall see in the next study of this chapter that this kind of result does not always happen.

Not having any semantic-DP tests in the battery, we cannot be sure that the newly demonstrated abilities are distinct from their parallel semantic abilities. The next study will have the answers to this question. That there is discrimination between the seven DP factors investigated and corresponding cognition abilities is indicated by the fact that four cognition factors were found in the analysis, being marked by one or two tests each. They were CFC, CSU, CSR, and CMU. This indicates not only the separation between cognition and DP abilities, but also that the cognition problems were kept at a low level of difficulty in DP tests. In other words, cognition was controlled.

The Targeted Solution

Since the data for the adolescent population were to figure in the targeted analysis to be reported in the next section, a targeted solution in this study was confined to the data from the adults. The results are in Table 6.2. Of the seven DP factors of special interest here, only one was represented by a singlet. This was DSI, for which only two tests had been included, one of which failed. This test was Limited Words, which went on DSI for the adolescents in the original solution, but elsewhere for the adults. There was one doublet factor, DFC, where such a factor had been entirely missed in the original analysis. Alternate Letter Groups failed here, where it had gone on the DFC factor for the adolescents in the original solution.

FIGURAL-, SYMBOLIC-, AND SEMANTIC-DP ABILITIES[8]

It happened that the ninth-grade group that took the tests for the study just preceding, in January, 1960, was the same as group T in the larger ninth-grade study, which had taken the battery including the semantic-DP tests in December, 1959. The time lapse was so short that a single analysis of the combined test batteries seemed justified. This provided the opportunity for distinguishing semantic-DP abilities from those in figural and symbolic areas. Twenty-three aptitude factors were hypothesized in the 57 tests. Only a targeted solution was obtained for this large analytical problem, with results to be seen under the label 35 in Table 6.2.

The most important finding of this joint analysis was that the six semantic-DP factors could be very clearly separated from the five figural and five

---

[8] See Report 35; also Guilford & Hoepfner (1966).

symbolic factors of the same operation category. Thus, all the DP abilities in the SI model that have been investigated have been supported with evidence. The extensiveness of the evidence can be put in the following manner. One factor (DFT) was supported by five tests; two were supported by four tests each; seven by three tests; five by two tests; and only one, DSS, by a single test. Of the five supported by only two tests each, three have had stronger support in other analyses. Factor DSU, for example, was represented by only two tests in this analysis.

Some of the more special findings are of interest. There was clearer segregation of tests for DFU and DFS in this analysis in that, of six tests loaded significantly on DFU, two were DFS tests, and of five tests loaded on DFS, only two were DFU tests. Among tests for DFT, Match Problems III, IV, and V proved to be about equally strong. This suggests that forms IV and V, which specify only one condition (number of squares to be left and number of matches to be removed, respectively) are indicators of DFT as strong as form III, which specifies both. They were stronger than Match Problems II, which also has the two specifications. The possibility that loadings for the match-problems tests were somewhat inflated by virtue of specific overlaps suggests some need for caution in making these comparisons.

The verification of so many DP factors and their abilities in the three content areas provided encouragement to proceed with investigation of the same kinds of abilities in the behavioral category. That study is reported in a later chapter on behavioral abilities. In general, as elsewhere, the separation of parallel abilities that differ only in content seems easier than separations of those differing in operation only. Most difficult of all are separations between factors differing only in products. The failure of tests to go on their expected factors, more often than not, appears to be due to lack of experimental control of how examinees tackle the items. Their strategies and tactics undoubtedly have significant bearings upon the kind of product that is important. In spite of the fact that Es could make translations from one content category to another, either such tactics are not effective or the choice of content to utilize differs too much from person to person. Such problems are grist for future investigations.

A STUDY OF TRANSFORMATION ABILITIES

As experience accumulated, the relative importance of the transformation abilities for creative thinking grew materially. The recognized abilities in the transformation layer of the SI model were demonstrated incidentally in studies aimed at other categories, never in a study aimed especially at that product category. The analysis reported in this section put the spotlight on transformation abilities.[9]

According to theory, there are 20 transformation abilities to be expected, of which 13 had previously been identified. Of the seven unknowns, two were under investigation simultaneously in other studies—MFT in a figural-memory study and DBT in a behavioral-divergent-production study. Three others are in the general behavioral content category, namely, MBT, NBT, and EBT, which it

---

[9] See Report 41.

was thought best to leave for study within those three operation categories. This elimination process left only two transformation abilities to be investigated for the first time, CST and DST. A number of those already demonstrated needed additional support and more univocal tests. There were also some issues that remained to be resolved. From all these considerations, 10 transformation abilities were selected for study. They are confined to the symbolic and semantic content categories, but they represent all five operation categories. A second objective of the study was to determine possible roles of transformation abilities in school learning.

To help resolve some issues, six SI abilities outside the transformation category were brought into the analysis. Usually, it was a matter of ensuring that tests for certain transformation abilities were so constructed as to be clear of variances reflecting other abilities.

The Factors and Their Tests

Cognition of Symbolic Transformations (CST) With tests for cognition of transformations, including CST, we are interested in knowing whether or not E is aware that changes of certain kinds have occurred. He can show evidence of this by matching one presented change with another, each change being transposable; by describing the change; or by answering questions that he could not answer without knowing the nature of the change. In printed tests, all we can show are static views, a before-and-after status in the item of information.

In Finding Letter Transformations, E is given a word spelled correctly and also incorrectly, and he is asked to say what change in certain letters has occurred in going from the one spelling to the other. Common changes are omissions, additions, substitutions, and transpositions. Acceptable descriptions may be worded in any way that is understandable.

Reading Backwards presents E with simple statements that are printed backwards, with words in reverse order, also letters within words. E shows his grasping of the transformations by making an appropriate response, as to the statement "nezod a ni selppa ynam woH."

Reading Confused Words makes use of spoonerisms or "bloopers" in speaking, e.g., the words "redboom," "static aires," and "pots of wower," which E should take to be "bedroom," "attic stairs," and "watts of power," respectively.

Seeing Letter Changes is in a short matching format. In each very short word there is usually a change in one or two letters. E is to show that he notices what the change is in one pair of words by finding it reproduced in another pair. For example, if he sees a pair "cad-cod," he should match it with the pair "set-sit." Only the middle vowel has been replaced. To keep the product from becoming a relation, there is no systematic connection between before and after vowels in the pair of transformed words. If E sees the pair "aye-yea," he should match it with the pair "tan-ant."

Cognition of Semantic Transformations (CMT) "Similarities" was the name of the test that had been thought to help determine rather dependably the factor for CMT in a number of previous analyses. In it, E is to tell a number of ways in which two objects are alike, e.g., an apple and an orange. The rationale was that each time E finds a new attribute in common to the objects, he is altering his definitions of them. But this test also had significant loadings on DMC, which involves jumping from class to class. In Similarities, E is also shifting from class to class. In order to avoid the unwanted DMC component, a new test presents only *one* object or word at a time, with E to state its different meanings. For the word "scale," E might say "balance for weighing, fish scales, consecutive musical notes, to scale a wall." Thus, E would achieve redefinitions without placing the same semantic unit with another in different classes. This test was called "Seeing Different Meanings."

Another test that had helped to mark CMT was Cartoons. For each cartoon presented, E is to give a suggestion for a "punch line." Such expressions are usually clever or humorous, and thus involve something in the way of transformations seen in meanings conveyed by the cartoon.

Another new test was Seeing Puzzle Meanings, in which E is presented with a rebuslike puzzle, which he is to translate into a meaningful expression or sentence. The given information includes figural and symbolic content, so there were recognized dangers of involving CFT and CST as well as CMT. The fact that the transforms are to be semantic, however, contributed to the expectation that the test would be primarily for CMT.

In Verbal-Picture Transformations, unusual verbal descriptions are given to common objects, e.g., "a piece of furniture copying notes," which should be seen as "writing desk," and "a lawn that jumps about," which should be seen as "grasshopper." Such a test might be getting close to convergent production, but that possibility could be tested, since ability NMT was represented in the analysis.

Memory for Symbolic Transformations (MST) Having cognized certain changes in literal or numerical material, E remembers some of those transformations, which are fixated to the extent that they are available for at least a short time interval. A recognition or recall test can provide the evidence. Memory for Hidden Transformations presents short sentences on the study page, in each of which a short word is embedded, such as

We walked through the gate among the flowers.

The embedded word, "team," is underlined. On the test page E later sees another sentence:

She came to tea Monday.

He is to say whether or not the underlined transform is hidden in the same manner as the one he saw on the study page. Obviously, here, it is not.

Memory for Misspellings presents on the study page a list of very familiar words misspelled phonetically so that they are easily recognized for the words intended, e.g., "boan" and "kettl." On the test page E is given the list of words correctly spelled and is to write each word as it was seen misspelled on the study page, thus showing that he remembers the transformation.

Memory for Word Transformations presents on the study page some groups of consecutive letters, each group representing two words strung together. When divided by a slanted line in one place, there is one pair of meaningful words, and when divided at another place, another pair of words appears. The way of dividing the set of letters is the transformation. The groups of letters are repeated on the test page, sometimes divided in the same way as on the study page and sometimes not. For example, the group BIND/ARE on the study page may also appear as BIND/ARE on the test page, but EARN/ICE and EAR/NICE are not the same. E is to say which are the same and which not.

Memory for Semantic Transformations (MMT) For this ability, E must first cognize meaningful shifts as represented by words and then show that he remembers the shifts later. Double Meanings presents E with a pair of sentences each containing the same literal word but with different meanings, as in

> She carried the food in a paper bag.
> The hunter went out to bag a deer.

The word with the two different meanings is underlined. On the test page, pairs of sentences are also presented with underlined words, one in each sentence. Sometimes the underlined words are synonyms of the word with the double meaning on the study page, and sometimes not. For the pair just cited, the test sentences read

> John took his lunch in a paper sack.
> Mother wants to obtain a new chair.

In these sentences the underlined words are synonyms of "bag," for different reasons. In other test items the underlined words would not be synonyms of two words spelled alike on the study page.

In the test Homonyms, E studies a pair of sentences in which two words such as "right" and "write" appear, as in

> You are on the right road.
> I must go home and write a letter.

On the test page, E studies a multiple-choice item pertaining to these homonyms. The stem of the item is a synonym for one of the words, namely, CORRECT; one of the four alternative answers is a word that is a synonym of the other word, i.e., a synonym for "write."

Remembering Puns presents on the study page sentences each of which contains a pun, the pun word underlined; e.g., "The bird-loving bartender was arrested and charged with contributing to the delinquency of a mynah." On the test page, given the word MYNAH, E is expected to supply the word "minor," thus showing that he remembers the transformation in meaning attached to the same (auditory) symbol.

Divergent Production of Symbolic Transformations (DST) Tests for DST should emphasize the production of alternative changes, starting from the same information. Hidden Word Production asks for different ways of embedding a word in sentences or phrases. If the word to be hidden is EVERY, for example, E might write

> Give very few prizes.
> He taught Eve rye-bread baking.
> She will ever yearn for him.

Multiple Letter Changes gives E a relatively short word, such as RATER, which is to be used to make a number of other words just by substituting two letters only. E might give the words "river," "paver," "Rover," "radar," "cuter," and "vaner."

In Multiple Word Extractions, E is given a pair of polysyllabic words, each broken up into its natural syllables, such as

      man i fes to   ne o pla ton ism

Without being permitted to use any complete syllable as a word, E might respond with the words "an," "if," "fest," "stone," "ton," "tone," "one," "Plato," "Toni," and "is." The best syllables for measuring DST should be those that can be usefully broken up in a number of ways, as in the productions just given: "stone," "tone," "ton," and "one."

Divergent Production of Semantic Transformations (DMT) The novel approach to DMT in this study was in a new test called "Whoppers." E is given a described situation, such as an auto show, and is to imagine what a compulsive liar might report having seen after visiting the place, such as "fur hubcaps," "glass cushions," and "knitted tires." It was hoped that this test might be successful for DMT, because it is very much easier to score than Plot Titles (clever) or Consequences (remote), the most common markers for DMT.

Convergent Production of Symbolic Transformations (NST) The previously successful test Camouflaged Words was used as a marker for NST, with two new tests added. Efficient Word Transformations gives E a set of four short words, which are to be overlapped by virtue of the fact that the final letters of one word are identical with the beginning letters of another. If four given words are

      ENTER   LOOP   OPEN   POLO

the most efficient overlapping, in terms of the minimum number of letters that need to be written, gives

      POLOOPENTER

The result does not have to be a real word.

Limited Word Revisions calls for the rearrangement of the letters in given words so as to produce other words. The given words are so chosen and rules are so given as to limit the kind of rearranging that can be done and to ensure that there is only one right answer in each case. The words TALE, GAPE, and ELBOW can become "late," "page," and "below," respectively.

Convergent Production of Semantic Transformations (NMT) Successful tests for this ability in the past have followed the principle of requiring E to say which of alternative objects could best be used to serve some unusual purpose, such as using a wire from a coat hanger to tie a package, as in Gestalt Transformations, or a combination of two named objects to serve some new purpose, as in Object Synthesis. No tests of these types had previously been strongly loaded on NMT, but they rarely failed to help determine it. There was a suspicion that the tests would do better for measuring the factor if the object to be employed in some new manner were a part of a whole that had to be broken down, e.g., the string from a guitar to be used for slicing cheese.

The New Uses test was a revision of Picture Gestalt, both of which present a photograph of a room from a home, followed by a list of 10 needs or uses to be served by parts of objects selected from the picture. Object Synthesis was also revised, with the aim of more surely requiring transformations.

Daffynitions was written in order to see whether a test not using objects could be successful for NMT. In this test, words have to be redefined and used in a quite different way than usual. For the word "dessert," E might be expected to write something like "Dessertainly is delicious." For the word "decide," E should write something like "Deside of de barn is red." E is not limited to the possibility of only one right answer, as in a completely convergent test, but he is very much restricted. He has to maintain the sound of the given word in making his response.

Evaluation of Symbolic Transformations (EST) EST was represented in this analysis by two tests that were formerly at least moderately successful. Decoding requires E to say which of two words can be more easily decoded, in view of the nature of a simple coding from letters to digits, which has been explained to him. Jumbled Words asks E to say whether one given word is a correct anagram of another, exactly the same letters being used but in different order.

Judging Mathematical Expressions, a mathematical task, was a new one for EST. At the top of each test page an algebraic expression is given, and below it are 15 other expressions. Some of them are exact transforms of the given model, and some are not, and E is to say which it is in each case. For example, if the given expression is $2(a - b)/4(a + b)$, is $(a - b)/(2a + 2b)$ a correct transform, derivable from it?

Evaluation of Semantic Transformations (EMT) It was not at all certain that the factor for this ability had been properly demonstrated before (Hoepfner et al., 1966). One test, Useful Changes, had gone on a factor as a singlet, but it was not certain that the factor was for EMT. Useful Changes gives in each item a function to be served, e.g., "slicing cheese," with three suggested objects, all of which could be adapted, some with better success than others. With the three alternatives being "guitar, plate, paperclip," "guitar" is the keyed answer, for a wire from the guitar would make the best cutting edge.

In such an item, E still has to produce a transformation; hence one might expect some NMT to occur, perhaps even to dominate the measurements by the test. A new test was devised that should avoid this possibility. Judging Object Adaptations names the object to be used in the unusual way, e.g., a telephone, with three alternative uses. E is to say which use is most unusual, ingenious, or clever. The three uses given for the telephone might be

A. get help in an emergency, B. pound a nail, C. keep a dog near a tree.

C is keyed, since more in the way of transformation is entailed with the telephone cord used as a leash.

The third test for EMT got away from the uses of objects. Punch Line Comparisons presents E with a cartoon and below it a number of pairs of possible punch lines. In each pair, one of the punch lines involves more of a transformation than the other. E is asked to choose in each case the one that is more "humorous, unexpected, or clever."

The Reference Factors and Marker Tests With so many symbolic and semantic tests in the battery, there was some concern that abilities CSU and CMU might make contributions to total-score variances here and there, so those two abilities were represented as a check on this point. CMI was represented because of a number of instances in earlier analyses in which tests had significant loadings on both CMI and CMT. Efforts were made to keep the two groups of tests from crossing over in this analysis.

MSI is the memory ability that is a strong component in numerical-operations tests. With some number tests in the battery, it was important to segregate variance from this ability, where this might be necessary.

Divergent production of symbolic implications (DSI) had never been strongly represented by tests, and there had been some suspicion that some of its tests might involve SI ability DST, which was being studied for the first time in this analysis. Symbol Elaboration was used unchanged as a marker for DSI, but Limited Words was revised, and a new name was applied—"Word Pair Revisions." Given two short words, such as HIS and NOT, E is to derive from exactly the same letters several other word pairs, e.g., SIN HOT, HIS TON, and THIS NO. The new test in this list was Multiple Symbolic Implications, in which E is told to produce several different combinations of three numbers each, in order to achieve another given number. For example, in how many ways could E sum three numbers to give 12, or multiply three numbers to give 60?

As to the reference factor DMC, it was stated earlier that an older CMT test, Similarities, kept sharing its variance with the factor for DMC. Marker tests for DMC were therefore included to check on the question of whether the new test, Seeing Different Meanings, would be free of DMC variance.

Results of the Targeted Analysis

Factor loadings for tests on cognition and convergent-production factors found in this study will be seen in Table 5.2. Those for divergent-production factors appear in Table 6.2; for memory factors in Table 8.2; and for evaluation factors in Table 7.2. Here some comments will be made concerning things learned from the results of the analysis. Some of the tests did not perform exactly as expected, but there is something to be learned from such miscarriages.

The Cognition Factors The factor for CSU came out more sharply than usual, with no significant loadings on it from any tests not designed for it. We may conclude that other tests had been so constructed as to control CSU variance.

The new factor CST was demonstrated very strongly by the four tests made for it, with Finding Letter Transformations leading on it. Reading Confused Words was also univocal for CST. Reading Backwards had a secondary loading on DSI, which may mean that E could grasp certain backward words quickly, then get the others by implications, trying one implication after another, however, in a divergent, search activity. Seeing Letter Changes had secondary loadings on both DST and MMT. The DST component suggests that Es often resorted to producing alternative hypotheses, one after the other, concerning what transformation had taken place or could be matched. The involvement with MMT is not easily explained. Only the test Seeing Puzzle Meanings, which was intended for CMT, had a "foreign" loading on CST. This rebuslike test, as stated in its description, presents much information in literal form, and some CST variance should not have come as a complete surprise. But the role of CST should mean that E has to see some transformations in the letter and number material before translation into semantic content.

Only one non-CMU test had a loading for the CMU factor. That test was Remembering Puns, which had shown that same component once before. It is apparent that cognizing the puns on the study page of that test is somewhat dependent upon word knowledge. Perhaps Es of lower vocabulary levels do not have all the connotative aspects of meanings of the words involved in the puns.

The four tests meant for CMT helped determine that factor, with the aid of three others. Two tests, Verbal-Picture Translation and Cartoons, were univocal, and the latter result links the factor with those formerly identified with CMT. Daffynitions was designed for NMT, but instead went univocally on CMT, a decisive departure from hypothesis. Evidently the transformations are there to be seen in Daffynitions; E does not have to produce them. If E were given the word and had to write the "daffynitions," he would have to do some productive work, but the factor might then be for DMT, especially if multiple answers were called for. Remembering Puns had a secondary loading on CMT, as it had on CMU. There was more than vocabulary difficulty, apparently. If E cannot see the transformations in that test, of course he cannot remember them. Another possibility is that E can use his CMT ability to advantage in taking the recall test in Remembering Puns. He could possibly see puns in that test that he had not seen on the study page or had seen but forgotten.

CMI was clearly determined by two univocal tests—the Apparatus Test and Seeing Problems. Pertinent Questions had a small secondary loading on DMT, but there was no confusion between CMI and CMT tests, a finding that had been a disturber of fit to theory in earlier analyses. The remaining confusion is for CMI tests and DMT tests. The DMT test, Consequences (remote), had a small secondary loading on CMI, not a new finding.

The Memory Factors The three memory factors were clearly separated from one another. MST had its three intended tests all to itself, and only those three. MMT had two univocal tests in Homonyms and Double Meanings, but Remembering Puns was complex, as mentioned earlier in discussions of CMU and CMT. MSI monopolized its two markers, including Numerical Operations, with none of the other number tests showing significant relations to the factor.

The Divergent-production Factors The three DST tests brought out this new factor clearly, two of its tests being univocal. Multiple Word Extractions had a minimal secondary loading on CMT, for no apparent reason. A secondary loading for this test on the parallel CST would have been understandable.

No overlapping of tests for DST and DSI appeared as had been feared. But one marker for DSI, Symbol Elaboration, took off and landed on the factor for EST instead. The reason probably was that another algebraic test, Judging

Mathematical Expressions, correlated sufficiently with Symbol Elaboration, due to some common relationship to a variable of mathematical sophistication, to pull it toward EST. It did not correlate strongly enough with the other DSI tests in this analysis to keep it on DSI.

The revised test for DSI, Word-Pair Revisions, was very strong on DSI, but had a secondary loading on NST. Transformations were natural aspects of this test, as its title suggests, and the fact that there were so few possible alternative transforms probably put it in the convergent-production category; hence the involvement of NST rather than DST. The new test, Multiple Symbolic Implications (producing a numerical value in different ways by alternative combinations of numbers), was univocal for DSI.

The factor for DMC appeared, with no CMT tests on it. Similarities, which had shown some connection with it in the past, was not in the analysis, but the new test that took its place, Seeing Different Meanings, stayed clear of it, as expected.

The new test, Whoppers, designed for DMT did go on its intended factor, but not strongly. The reason may be that in the successful DMT tests alternative responses must be produced by revisions in *the same given information*, whereas in Whoppers the alternative responses are given in connection with a given situation or location. Each response can be a transformation of something different, not of the same thing.

The Convergent-production Factors   A new and better test for NST came out for NST, replacing Camouflaged Words, the favorite for some time. The new leader for NST was Limited Word Revisions. The other new test, Efficient Word Transformations, was univocal, but was no stronger than Camouflaged Words.

Newly revised tests looked very good for NMT, all being univocal. New Uses, a new form of Picture Gestalt, led the list. Object Synthesis was a strong one for the ability. Useful Changes, formerly designed for EMT, and still hypothesized for it in this study, made the switch to NMT. It evidently requires too much convergent production and too little evaluation. The singlet factor that it represented in an earlier analysis was evidently not EMT.

The Evaluation Factors   Indicated by its two marker tests a factor for EST came out as before. The new test, Judging Mathematical Expressions, came out strongly on the factor. This suggests that, more generally, different kinds of algebraic tests might help determine a number of symbolic factors, in populations having at least a first course in algebra. It would be best practice to use only one algebra test in an analysis, however, lest the variable of mathematical sophistication introduce extra contributions to community among the algebra tests. A number of algebra tests, each limited to a uniform kind of problem, as in Judging Mathematical Expressions, could be put into a factorial frame of reference derived from nonalgebraic tests, however, by extension of a factor structure. This kind of operation was described in Chapter 4, and applications of it will be noted in Chapter 10.

The factor identified with EMT in this analysis could very well be entirely a new one; neither of the tests on it had been used before, and Useful Changes, which was thought to represent EMT in an earlier analysis, went on NMT instead. Punch-Line Comparisons and Judging Object Adaptations were univocal on the factor now recognized as EMT.

Summary for Transformation Abilities

The study of 10 of the 20 transformation abilities of the SI model led to a number of gains. Seven of the 10 were given stronger support with new and revised tests. Three turned out to be newly demonstrated factors those for CST, DST, and EMT. The latter was based entirely on new tests designed for that ability in this study.[10]

In all five operation categories, transformation abilities involving symbolic and semantic content were clearly separated. There was a minimum of overlapping of tests in common to transformation factors. What overlapping occurred usually involved a different product as well as a different operation.

The relation of transformation abilities to learning in an academic setting was a second objective of the study just discussed. There were some definite relationships, showing the roles of transformations in learning, but the report of this aspect of the study is reserved for Chapter 10.

SUMMARY ON CREATIVE-THINKING AND PLANNING ABILITIES

The exploratory studies on creative and planning abilities began with ad hoc hypotheses regarding the kinds of abilities to be expected, derived mainly from logical considerations of the kinds of thinking in which creative producers and planners have to engage in order to be successful. The studies eventuated in two whole intersecting classes of abilities, which find their places in the SI theory of intelligence. Let us review the early hypotheses briefly and note the kinds of abilities to which they led.

Hypotheses regarding Creative Thinking Only two of the eight original hypotheses about creative thinking failed to yield distinct coherent abilities represented by factors, namely, for the hypothesized abilities for analysis and synthesis. Factor analysis did not slice the intellect in such a fashion. These concepts have therefore little general referential utility in accounting for intellectual activity.

Of the remaining six hypotheses for creative-thinking abilities, two led to cognition abilities. Sensitivity to problems is a matter of seeing implications from given information. The given information more readily suggests something beyond itself for some individuals than for others. Although tests designed for this hypothesis most often turned out to represent the ability for cognition of semantic implications (CMI), it is good reasoning by analogy to think that the parallel abilities, CFI, CSI, and CBI, have similar values in their own content domains. Although not everything implied by experience is a problem, problems are included among things implied.

The other hypothesis leading to cognition abilities was that for penetration, whose tests determined a factor eventually identified as cognition of

---

[10]Mooney (1954) had announced earlier a factor that resembles the one for CST in this study, but it was probably confounded with factors for other SI abilities.

semantic transformations (CMT). The penetrating person sees more aspects of a given experience, and he is able to do so because he sees transformations readily. By analogy, again, the parallel abilities CFT, CST, and CBT should serve similar roles.

The hypothesis for fluency led to three kinds of abilities concerned with the facility for generating information based upon that which the individual has in his memory store. The well-known act of recall is involved, but it is not simply reenactment of remembered associations, for much generated information is in response to cues with which it was not connected in learning. Much of it comes by way of "transfer recall." There are three kinds of fluency because there are three different products of information involved—units, relations and systems. Coupled with four kinds of content, there are 12 fluency abilities almost all of which have been demonstrated.

From the hypothesis for flexibility, two kinds of this type of ability have been distinguished, in terms of two products of information—classes and transformations. Flexibility with regard to classes means lack of rigidity of class membership for items of information. Items of information are often retrieved from memory storage with class cues as the instigating information. Readiness to switch class cues can broaden significantly the chances for retrieval of needed information, except where a very small class happens to be the correct one. If the cue class is the wrong one, freedom to change class would be necessary. The same kind of flexibility applies in all four content categories, so there are four such abilities—DFC, DSC, DMC, and DBC.

The other kind of flexibility pertains to transformations. It is sometimes true that there is no information in the memory store that exactly fills the requirements, in which case it is well to be ready to make changes with the chance that, with alterations, the retrieved information will be adequate. There are also four such abilities within the divergent-production operation category, including DFT, DST, DMT, and DBT. But this kind of ability, concerned with transformations, goes well beyond the divergent-production category, as we saw in considering all the transformation abilities in the last section, to the extent of 20 in all. Studies relating divergent-production and transformation abilities to age showed that differentiation of abilities in these areas is the same at the ninth-grade level as at the adult level and that many of the same differentiations have occurred at the sixth-grade level.

Hypotheses regarding Planning Two of the hypotheses regarding planning abilities, orientation and prediction, led to certain cognition abilities. Orientation has to do mainly with systems, and prediction has to do with implications. The area of cognition has four systems abilities and four implications abilities. It was noted above that the latter also serve roles in being sensitive to problems.

The planning hypotheses for ingenuity and elaboration led to divergent-production abilities. "Ingenuity" means essentially the same as "originality," which became associated with SI ability DMT. The set of four transformation abilities in the divergent-production category can actually lay claim to those popular descriptions "ingenuity" and "originality." "Elaboration" means suggesting added details to something already produced. What is added is implied by what is already there. There are four such divergent-production abilities—DFI, DSI, DMI, and DBI.

The hypothesis for evaluation could be interpreted with sufficient breadth to include all 24 evaluation abilities of the SI model. This generous treatment of the hypothesis can be justified, for any information that is cognized or produced, in any content or form (product), is subject to evaluation.

Thus, we see that although the study of creative thinking and planning led most directly to the divergent-production category and to the transformations product, abilities in other operational and informational categories can and probably do play their essential roles in creative thinking and planning, for both can be regarded as species of problem solving, which, considered in all its contexts, may depend upon almost any intellectual abilities as well as upon any kind of stored information.

SEVEN
EVALUATION ABILITIES

The major impetus for initiating analytical studies of evaluation abilities by the Aptitudes Research Project was the fact that the Air Force investigators had found a number of times a factor interpreted as "judgment," without their achieving a very clear conception of the nature of the ability it represented (Guilford & Lacey, 1947). The first ARP analysis[1] was conducted well before the structure-of-intellect theory was conceived. Three analyses were performed after that event, as related in Reports 32, 33, and 40.

THE FIRST ANALYSIS OF EVALUATION

The A.A.F. judgment factor had been found most often in relation to tests called "Practical Judgment" and tests having to do with estimations of commonly experienced objects and events, involving variables of size, distance, and velocity (verbally described, not perceived). Items in Practical Judgment tests

---

[1] See Reports 7 and 9; also Hertzka, Guilford, Christensen, & Berger (1954).

presented types of everyday problems such as a soldier might encounter, with alternative solutions offered, one of which the examinee was to select as wisest. Loadings on the "judgment" factor were usually minimally significant for both kinds of tests, and there were also loadings as high on the factor of mechanical knowledge and a factor identified as "planning."

In initiating the first ARP study in this area, it was decided to use the term "evaluation," in order to reduce ambiguity somewhat. For example, one use of the term "judgment" has applied it to the area of psychophysics. Another use has been in connection with problem solving. Initial consideration of evaluation abilities envisaged a large range of performances, however, from the evaluation of conclusions as in syllogistic reasoning to the detection of errors in pictures of objects and situations. Further reduction in ambiguity awaited the results of analytical studies.

Hypotheses of Evaluative Abilities

The formation of hypotheses took into consideration the various kinds of criteria involved. Evaluations can be made in terms of logical requirements, as in formal logic and in informal, verbal thinking, or in terms of practical feasibility as dictated by experience or social custom. Consideration was also given to the distinction between perceptual and conceptual problems, which had proved to be significant in analyses in other areas. It was thought that the ability for judging pictorial information might be different from that for judging thoughts initiated by verbal information. A distinction between speed and power was also taken into account, particularly since Thurstone (1944) had reported a factor identified as "speed of judgment." The organization of hypotheses proceeded accordingly along the lines just drawn—formal versus informal, perceptual versus conceptual, and speed versus power. Not all these categories were combined systematically with all others, but opportunities were provided for finding abilities differing together in these respects. Certain combinations were emphasized, as shown in the following outline of the hypotheses:

I. Conceptual evaluation in terms of logical necessity
   A. Formal logic; validity of syllogistic conclusions
   B. Discrimination of verbal (conceptual) materials
   C. Relevance of information; adequacy of generalizations

Table 7.1 Populations and Samples for Analyses Pertaining to Evaluation Abilities

Report Number	Brief Title of the Analysis	N	Population
9	Evaluative abilities	332	A.F. air cadets
		75	A.F. student officers
32	Semantic-evaluation abilities	202	Eleventh-grade students
33	Symbolic-evaluation abilities	226	Twelfth-grade students
40	Figural-evaluation abilities	188	Students of architecture

II. Conceptual evaluation in terms of practical feasibility, experience, or social custom
   A. Appraisal of common situations; utilization of common objects; selection of means for attaining goals or meeting emergencies
   B. Estimation of (conceived) sizes, weights, or speeds of common objects
   C. Appraisal of adequacy of behavior in social situations
III. Perceptual evaluation in terms of logical necessity and experience
   A. In classification of perceptual material
   B. In detection of errors in pictures of common objects and situations
IV. Speed of evaluation
   A. In simple perceptual tasks
   B. In simple conceptual tasks

Tests for the Hypotheses

Syllogistic Tests   For the hypothesis involving formal logic, a number of syllogism tests and inference tests were selected or devised. Both multiple-choice and completion forms were utilized. In the former, the number of premises given in each item varied from one to four in different tests. The number of alternative conclusions varied from two (a true-false form) to three. A sample item from Syllogisms I reads

> All soldiers are men.
> Some citizens are soldiers.
> Therefore, some citizens are men. (True or false?)

A sample item from Syllogisms II reads

> All Americans are English-speaking.
> No Eskimos are English-speaking.
> Therefore:
>   A. No Eskimos are Americans.
>   B. Some Eskimos are Americans.
>   C. No English-speakers are Eskimos.

A sample item from Syllogisms III reads

> All living things breathe.
> All insects are living things.
> Therefore: _____

The Logical Reasoning test form in this analysis presented in each item two to four premises and a single conclusion to be judged as true or false.

Inference Tests   Inference tests are quasi-syllogistic. The number of premises may be only one, as in the Inference test, from which a sample item reads

> Most of the trees in the forest are green. (It follows that:)
>   A. There are no yellow trees in the forest.
>   B. There are some yellow trees in the forest.

C. Some of the trees in the forest are green.
D. Green trees are the tallest in the forest.
E. Pine trees are green.

A sample item from Inferences II reads

No parachutes are available for passengers of commercial aircraft but life jackets are usually available on passenger ships.
Conclusion: _____

A number of different conclusions would reasonably be acceptable for an item such as this.

Classification Tests   The seven tests designed for the hypothesis for discrimination of verbal (conceptual) material turned out to be involved with classes in one way or another. They involved discriminating items of information by putting them in specified, appropriate, alternative classes. Sentence Evaluation asks E to say whether each given sentence in a short paragraph is (A) a fact, (B) a possibility, or (C) a name of something. Sample sentences are

1. The natives of New Zealand have wooden houses which meet the requirements for a cool climate.
2. The Rarotongen word "vari" means "mud."
3. The gods informed the people of Tahiti of the disaster.

Facts and Opinions asks for the identification of each sentence in two categories: fact and opinion. Sample sentences are

1. In 1939 there were two world's fairs held in the United States.
2. The Democratic party has done more for this country than the Republican party has.

Critical Evaluation asks E to say whether each statement is based primarily on emotion or prejudice versus reason and thought. Sample sentences are

1. All the people who drink hard liquor should have their driver's licenses taken away.
2. The police should revoke the licenses of those people who drive while drunk.

Titles contains items that might be responses to a Plot Titles test, such as was described in the previous chapter. The scorer of such a test must decide whether each suggested title is clever or nonclever. The aim was to make an evaluation test that required the same kind of task of E. In Titles, after reading a short plot, such as the fable of the fox and the grapes, E is to say which of each pair of suggested titles is more clever. Sample items are

1. A. "The Fox Goes Hungry"
   B. "The Philosophical Fox"
2. A. "The Frustrated Fox"
   B. "The Fox Griped about Grapes"

Logical Classification consists of statements containing "ought." *E* is to classify those statements in five categories, as they pertain to (A) custom, (B) completeness, (C) safety, (D) utility, and (E) welfare, respectively. The sentence "You ought not to cross the street against the red light," would, of course, be classified in the category of "safety."

Verbal Classification, originated by L. L. Thurstone (1938), presents in each item four words representing one class, e.g., domestic animals, and four words representing another class, e.g., articles of furniture. Eight other given words are to be classified with the one class or the other, or with neither (see Appendix B). This differs from the other classification tests in that the classes are not named; *E* must first see what the classes are. Having done that, he assigns each of the eight words to one of the classes or he reports that it belongs to neither.

Word Classification is of the "exclusion" type; that is, four words are given, e.g., the names of objects, with *E* to say which one does not belong to the class represented by the other three. For example,

A. horse   B. snake   C. man   D. flower

Hindsight tells us that semantic classes are the items of information that are crucial in all these tests. Cognition is usually involved, and sometimes convergent production. Three of the tests that were analyzed in the study of classes abilities (Report 39) did, indeed, show significant variances from CMC–they were Sentence Evaluation (renamed in that study as "Sentence Classification"), Verbal Classification, and Word Classification. Verbal Classification had a significant loading on NMC, also, probably because the act of partitioning items of information into classes is more prominent in that test and is a feature of NMC tests in general.

Tests of Judgment of Relevance and Adequacy   Five tests appeared under the hypothesis for relevance of information; adequacy of generalization. Interpretations presents *E* with a short paragraph of expository reading material. Instead of multiple-choice items as in a reading-comprehension test, a series of statements follows the paragraph, with *E* to say whether each one is (A) correct, (B) incorrect, or (C) no decision is possible in view of the information given.

Generalizations gives in each item a general statement followed by other statements whose contents either (A) support or (B) do not support the general one.

Word Selection presents items of the following type:

A *book* always has   A. words   B. pages   C. pictures   D. a story

In such an item an act of evaluation seems inevitable. Every alternative answer could be correct but only B (pages) is a denotative property of a book.

In Evaluation of Comparisons, each item is made up of two words representing objects that are to be compared, such as the two games

X–basketball
Y–football

Which one of the three following statements is the most justified comparison?

A. X requires more teamwork than Y.
B. X draws larger crowds than Y.
C. X has fewer men on a team than Y.

It will be seen that there must be some additional experiential basis for making a decision in this item.

It was recognized that some of the tests in this list have resemblance to an ordinary reading-comprehension test, which raised the question of whether that kind of test, particularly in multiple-choice form, would have some evaluation variance. So Reading Comprehension, a test routinely administered in the A.A.F. aircrew classification battery, was included for the hypothesis under discussion. In fact, it was wondered whether multiple-choice tests of the alternative-answer form might not generally show some evaluation variance. That particular question came up for special study in the analysis of Report 32.

Tests of Goal Attainment and Judgment The rather complex hypothesis denoted as IIA earlier was represented by five tests. Embracing at least three ideas, the five tests could possibly give rise to more than one factor. The hypothesis reads "appraisal of common situations; utilization of common objects; selection of means for attaining goals or meeting emergencies."

Absurdities contains items similar to some in the Binet scales. For each statement that is given, E is to say whether it (A) makes sense or (B) is absurd. Sample statements are

1. Mrs. Smith has had no children, and I understand the same was true of her mother.
2. While the businessman was eating his lunch, he was interrupted by a long-distance telephone call.
3. I have three brothers—Paul, Ernest, and myself.

Object Synthesis pertains to the second part of the hypothesis statement, having to do with utilization of an object. Each item gives the names of two common objects, and E is to write the name of an object that he could make from the two. Had the distinction between production abilities and evaluation abilities been realized at the time this test was proposed as a measure of evaluation, it would have been reserved for the analysis of production abilities, as it had been used in the first study of creative-thinking abilities. Object Synthesis II looked much better as an evaluation test, however. After giving the two objects to be combined, the test also gives four possible composites, with E to say which would probably function best; e.g.,

Given: lace curtain   wire coat hanger
to make: A. a bandage   B. a Christmas wrapping   C. a mop   D. a butterfly net

The keyed answer is D. The requirement for a judgment seems obvious.

Gestalt Transformations had been used originally in the analysis of creative-thinking abilities, along with Object Synthesis, and the two had helped determine the "redefinition factor" later identified with convergent production of semantic transformations (NMT). Because of its multiple-choice format and its resemblance to Object Synthesis II, it was used as a possible evaluation test.

The A.A.F. test Practical Judgment was adopted for use in connection with the hypothesis under discussion. The items of that test also call for the choice of objects—in this case, to use in solving practical problems.

Since an estimation test had helped determine the A.A.F's judgment factor, such a test was used in this study. It asked practical questions, such as

> Using a shovel, with which material could you fill a box most quickly?   A. Soft dirt   B. loose sand   C. loose gravel   D. sand and gravel mixed?   (Keyed answer: A.)

One test had to suffice for the act of appraisal of adequacy of behavior in social situations. In each item of Social Situations, a common type of situation is described, and four alternative actions are suggested, one to be selected as best under the circumstances. A sample item reads

> You are on a weekend trip with a group of friends. Most of them would prefer to spend the day hunting, but you would prefer to go fishing. You should
> A. go hunting with them.
> B. tell them to go hunting while you go fishing
> C. try to convince them that they will have a better time fishing
> D. offer to toss a coin to decide whether the whole group goes hunting or fishing

Judgment of Figural Information   As might be expected from the hypothesis for classification of perceptual material, the tests designed for it involve figural information, one auditory and four visual in nature. The Sound Grouping test, from Thurstone's PMA battery, is a classification test in the exclusion form. A sample item reads

> A. comb   B. foam   C. home   D. come

Which one should be excluded because it does not sound like the rest? This test has appeared in a number of ARP analyses, but it has never had other CFC or NFC tests with auditory information with which it could go, as parallel tests have done for parallel factors. In analytical results, it has floated around, usually with small loadings, with exceptions to be noted later.

Figure Classification is the same as that designed for use in the reasoning analyses. It contains short sets of matching items. Figure Matching had also been used in one or more of the reasoning analyses. Each item calls for the best match for a given figure, to be found among five alternative figures.

One new test designed for the first evaluation analysis was known as "Symbolic Judgment." In each item a word or phrase is given and is followed by four alternative symbols that might reasonably stand for the given information. A sample item reads

> Given: ARC   A. a   B. +   C. 0   D. C

Generally, each alternative has some claim to reasonableness. It is a question of which one comes nearest to representing the given thing to be symbolized.

Another new test was Picture Classification. Like Figure Classification, this test is in a matching format. For example, a beaker is to be matched with a set of three other kinds of containers—teapot, pail, and quart jar. A hat with a feather on it is to be matched with three other objects that contain feathers—pillow, bird, and badminton shuttlecock.

For the hypothesis for detection of errors in pictures of common objects or situations, there was only one test—Unusual Details. It is the type of exercise that asks "What is wrong with this picture?" The test contains 16 sketches of common situations, with two unusual or incongruous features in each of them. E is to find these discrepancies and to state what they are.

Tests of Speed of Judgment Two similar tests were written for the hypothesis for speed of judgment, when the information is conceptual or semantic. Word Checking I presents sets of four names of objects, with E to find in each set the one that is man-made, as in the list

    A. valley   B. mountain   C. highway   D. river

Word Checking II is the same except that there are two specifications for the class to which the object belongs; e.g., it is "not growing and smaller than a football." One set of objects is

    A. frog   B. pebble   C. lake   D. fisherman

For a possible factor of speed of judgment with visual-figural material, two tests were used—Figure Estimation and the Ratio Estimation test, the latter being a contemporary experimental test designed by A.A.F. psychologists. Items in Figure Estimation ask E to select that figure among four that has either the largest area, the longest total length, or the largest number of dots, in three kinds of items, respectively. In Ratio Estimation, E is given pairs of straight lines, the shorter being always on the left. He is to say what percent the shorter line is of the longer one. The kind of judgment is thus very different from that in any other evaluation test. It comes closer to types found in psychophysical observations, and was interesting on that account. All the tests in this group are very easy, and speed is an important condition.

Some Reference Factors One or two marker tests were added to the battery to represent each of seven previously known abilities believed not to belong in the evaluation category but thought to be possibly represented as common factors in some of the new tests. The list of abilities included verbal comprehension (CMU), general reasoning (CMS), correlate completion (probably a composite of NFR, NSR, and NMR), ideational fluency (DMU), associational fluency (DMR), and perceptual speed (later identified with EFU).

The Original Analysis

In an exploratory analysis in virgin territory, as in the case of this study, it was difficult to predict how many factors to expect from the tests included. There were 10 subhypotheses, which might have been a basis for expecting 10 evaluation abilities. There were altogether 36 tests to represent these subhypotheses, but the latter were not represented evenly; some were underrepresented to the extent of only one test each. Ten evaluation factors were therefore not expected.

To mention the reference factors first, it can be said that six of the seven were located and identified. The test Associational Fluency, which had the sole responsibility for locating its factor for DMR, went along with 10 new tests on another factor.

Of the factors that could be interpreted as forms of evaluation, the one called "logical evaluation" stood out most strongly; it was best represented by a number of syllogistic and inference tests. Of the six tests of these two kinds, only Inferences II (a completion form) did not go along. Syllogisms III is also in completion form and did go along. The main difference between the two tests is that the former gives only one premise, opening the way for more than one right answer, versus two premises requiring one right answer in the latter.

Three other factors were thought to be in the evaluation category. One was called "perceptual evaluation," being marked by the Ratio Estimation test, Figure Estimation (but only Part I, with comparisons of areas), and Sound Grouping. A factor called "experiential evaluation" was marked primarily by Unusual Details and Object Synthesis. The third was thought to be "speed of evaluation," determined primarily by the two Word Checking tests and the Ratio Estimation test. Because the Word Checking tests were so similar, had they been alone on a factor, one could pass it off as a specific, or a new common factor combined with a specific.

Three of the many classification tests went off together to mark a factor identified as "verbal classification." There was no parallel factor for "perceptual classification." A redefinition factor, marked in part by Gestalt Transformation and Object Synthesis, was not entirely unexpected. A block of verbal tests held together to determine a factor that very likely represented a composite of abilities. The targeted rotations broke up that group into more reasonable, smaller clusters.

The Targeted Solution

The pertinent results (for evaluation factors) of the targeted rotations appear in Table 7.2. It was recognized that logically 19 SI abilities were represented in the battery of 47 tests, and that, since a number of abilities were represented by one test each, there would be some singlet factors. With 19 factor axes rotated, there were seven singlets, which, of course, cannot be identified with confidence. For example, Sound Grouping had been targeted for ESC (where it had gone in the original analysis of symbolic-evaluation abilities, as seen in Report 33). But the singlet factor on which it appeared could be an auditory CFC, or something else. Figure Matching was thought to represent EFC, but this would need verification in a new analysis with other tests of EFC present. The analysis of figural-evaluation abilities (Report 40) provided the opportunity, as will be seen later in this chapter. Symbolic Judgment was thought to represent ESI in the targeted analysis, but it has not been analyzed with other ESI tests, as a check on that hypothesis.

Table 7.2 Factors and Their Tests with Significant Loadings, in the Category of Evaluation*

Factor / Test	3	6	8	9	12	14	16A	16B	32	33	40	41
EFU												
Perceptual Speed	71	60	67	—	—	—	—	—	—	—	—	—
Spatial Orientation I (A.A.F.)†	—	72	61	49	—	—	—	—	—	69	—	—
Identical Forms	61	—	—	—	—	—	—	—	—	63	48	—
Speed of Identification (A.A.F.)	—	62	—	—	—	—	—	—	—	—	—	—
Judgment of Size	—	—	—	—	—	—	—	—	—	—	60	—
Spatial Orientation II (A.A.F.)	—	53	—	57	—	—	—	—	—	—	—	—
Judging Figural Combinations	—	—	—	—	—	—	—	—	—	—	43	—
Derivations (ESU)	—	—	—	—	—	—	—	—	—	31	—	—
EFC												
Figure Matching	46s	46s	—	58s	—	—	41s	36s	—	—	49	—
Best Figural Class	—	—	—	—	—	—	—	—	—	—	51	—
Judging Specified Figures	—	—	—	—	—	—	—	—	—	—	40	—
Best Figure Pairs	—	—	—	—	—	—	—	—	—	—	37	—
Best Figural Class Separation	—	—	—	—	—	—	—	—	—	—	32	—
EFR												
Prescribed Relations	46s	52s	—	—	—	—	49s	—	—	—	43	—
Correct Figural Trends	—	—	—	—	—	—	—	—	—	—	46	—
Perceptual Relations Judgment	—	—	—	—	—	—	—	—	—	—	36	—
Identical Figural Relations	—	—	—	—	—	—	—	—	—	—	34	—
Angle Estimation	—	—	—	—	—	—	—	—	—	—	31	—
Figural Analogies (CFR)††	—	—	—	—	—	—	—	—	—	—	30	—

EFS								
Judging Figural Balance	—	—	—	—	—	—	—	43
Closest Spatial Series	—	—	—	—	—	—	—	40
Best Map Placement	—	—	—	—	—	—	—	32
EFT								
Least Movement	—	—	—	—	—	—	—	47
Judging Rearrangements	—	—	—	—	—	—	—	36
EFI								
Essential Maze Routes	—	—	58	—	—	—	—	51
Most Effective Path	—	—	52	—	—	—	—	48
Competitive Planning	—	—	—	—	—	—	—	43
Judging Figural Elaboration	—	—	—	—	—	—	—	36
Poster Judgment	—	—	—	—	—	—	—	34
Best Move Selection	—	—	—	—	—	—	—	31
Blocks (CFS)	—	—	—	—	—	—	—	41
ESU								
Symbol Identities	—	—	—	—	—	—	—	62
Letter "U"	—	—	—	—	—	—	—	56
Derivations	—	—	—	—	—	—	—	34
Sign Changes (NSI)	—	—	—	—	—	—	—	32
ESC								
Best Number Class	—	—	—	—	55s	—	—	50
Sound Grouping	53s	55s	—	—	—	—	—	41
Sign Changes II	—	—	—	43s	—	—	—	43

Table 7.2 (*Continued*)

Factor Test	3	6	8	9	12	14	16A	16B	32	33	40	41
ESC												
Word Choice	—	—	—	—	—	—	—	—	—	31	—	—
Number-Group Naming (CSC)	—	—	—	—	—	—	—	—	—	35	—	—
Symbol Manipulation (ESR)	—	—	—	—	—	—	—	—	—	31	—	—
ESR												
Number and Operations Changes I	54	—	—	—	—	—	—	—	—	—	—	—
Number and Operations Changes II	55	—	—	—	—	—	—	—	—	—	—	—
Number and Operations Changes III	54	—	—	—	—	—	—	—	—	—	—	—
Symbol Manipulation	38	53^s	52^s	—	47^s	—	—	—	—	59	—	—
Symbol Manipulation II	—	—	—	—	—	45^s	46^s	—	—	—	—	—
Related Words I	—	—	—	—	—	—	—	—	—	43	—	—
Similar Pairs	—	—	—	—	—	—	—	—	—	35	—	—
ESS												
Way-Out Numbers	—	—	—	—	—	—	—	—	—	57	—	—
Series Relations	—	—	—	—	—	—	—	—	—	48	—	—
Correct Letter Orders	—	—	—	—	—	—	—	—	—	43	—	—
Correct Number Series	—	—	—	—	—	—	—	—	—	31	—	—
Symbol Reasoning	—	—	—	—	—	—	—	—	—	41	—	—
Best Number Class (ESC)	—	—	—	—	—	—	—	—	—	32	—	—
Word Changes (NSS)	—	—	—	—	—	—	—	—	—	32	—	—
ITED Verbal (CMU)	—	—	—	—	—	—	—	—	—	31	—	—

	1	2	3	4	5	6	7	8	9
EST									
Jumbled Words	—	—	—	—	—	—	—	48	54
Judging Mathematical Expressions	—	—	—	—	—	—	—	—	48
Decoding	—	—	—	—	—	—	—	37	40
Typing Errors	—	—	—	—	—	—	—	30	—
Symbol Elaboration (DSI)	—	—	—	—	—	—	—	—	34
Number Grouping (DSC)	—	—	—	—	—	—	—	34	—
Word Relations (CSR)	—	—	—	—	—	—	—	30	—
ESI									
Best Letter Set	—	—	—	—	—	—	—	53	—
Symbolic Judgment	—	—	56s	—	—	—	—	—	—
Abbreviations	—	—	—	—	—	—	—	47	—
Letter Problems	—	—	—	—	—	—	—	38	—
EMU									
Word Checking II	—	—	75	—	—	—	—	—	—
Word Checking I	—	—	72	—	—	—	—	—	—
Double Descriptions	—	42s	—	—	—	—	66	—	—
Absurdities	—	—	45	—	—	—	—	—	—
Product Choice	—	—	—	—	—	—	—	43	—
Sentensense	—	—	—	—	—	—	—	40	—
Generalizations	—	—	30	—	—	—	—	—	—
EMC									
Best Word Class	—	—	—	—	—	—	—	61	—
Class Name Selection	—	—	—	—	—	42	—	50	—
Remote Verbal Similarities	35s	49s	—	—	—	—	—	—	—

Table 7.2 *(Continued)*

Factor / Test	3	6	8	9	12	14	16A	16B	32	33	40	41
EMC												
Critical Evaluation	—	—	—	—	—	—	44s	40	—	—	—	—
Important Facts	—	—	—	—	—	—	—	—	38	—	—	—
Complete Thoughts (EMI)	—	—	—	—	—	—	—	—	37	—	—	—
EMR												
Verbal Analogies III	—	—	—	—	—	—	—	—	58	—	—	—
Matched Verbal Relations	—	—	—	—	—	—	—	—	50	—	—	—
False Premises	50s	—	—	—	—	—	—	—	—	—	—	—
Best Trend Name	—	—	—	—	—	—	—	—	47	—	—	—
Syllogisms I and II	—	—	—	45	—	—	—	—	—	—	—	—
Evaluation of Comparisons	—	—	—	35	—	—	—	—	—	—	—	—
Verbal Analogies I (CMR)	—	—	—	—	—	—	—	—	41	—	—	—
Logical Reasoning (EMI)	—	—	—	50	—	—	—	—	35	—	—	—
Word Extensions (EMI)	—	—	—	—	—	—	—	—	35	—	—	—
Verbal Classification (CMC)	—	—	—	34	—	—	—	—	—	—	—	—
EMS												
Word Systems	—	—	—	—	—	—	—	—	55	—	—	—
Unusual Details	—	—	44	60	—	—	—	—	—	—	—	—
Unlikely Things	—	—	—	—	—	—	—	—	55	—	—	—
Social Situations	—	—	—	46	—	—	—	—	—	—	—	—
Paragraph Analysis	—	—	40	—	—	—	—	—	—	—	—	—

	C1	C2	C3	C4	C5	C6	C7	C8	C9	C10	C11	C12	C13	C14	C15	C16	C17
EMT																	
Punch-Line Comparisons	—	—	—	—	—	—	—	—	—	—	—	—	—	—	—	47	—
Judging Object Adaptations	—	—	—	—	—	—	—	—	—	—	—	—	—	—	—	45	—
EMI																	
Word Selection	—	—	—	68	—	—	—	—	—	—	—	55	—	—	—	—	—
Sentence Selection	—	—	—	—	—	—	—	—	—	—	—	54	—	—	—	—	—
Complete Thoughts	—	—	—	36	—	—	—	—	—	—	—	46	—	—	—	—	—
Logical Reasoning	—	—	—	36	60	37	—	—	—	—	—	36	—	—	—	—	—
Syllogism Test	51	46	—	—	—	—	45	32	—	—	—	—	—	—	—	—	—
Inference Test	49	47	51s	—	—	—	40	—	—	—	—	36	—	—	—	—	—
Syllogisms I and II	—	—	—	—	—	—	—	—	—	—	—	36	—	—	—	—	—
Word Extension	—	—	—	—	—	—	—	—	—	—	—	—	—	—	—	—	—
Commonsense Judgment I	—	—	—	31	—	—	—	—	—	—	—	35	—	—	—	—	—
Inferences II	—	—	—	48	—	—	—	—	—	—	—	—	—	—	—	—	—
Logical Classification (CMC)	—	—	—	—	—	—	—	—	—	—	—	37	—	—	—	—	—
Synonyms (CMU)	—	—	—	34	—	—	—	—	—	—	—	—	—	—	—	—	—
Evaluation of Comparisons (EMR)	—	—	—	34	—	—	—	—	—	—	—	—	—	—	—	—	—
Syllogisms III (NMI)	—	—	—	—	—	—	—	—	—	—	—	—	—	—	—	—	—
Reading Comprehension (CMU)	—	—	—	—	—	34	—	—	—	—	—	—	—	—	—	—	—

*Decimal points omitted.
†An Army Air Force test.
§Loading on a singlet factor.
††Test targeted in rotation for the factor indicated by the trigram.

In addition to a factor for SI ability EFU (perceptual speed), which was strongly determined by two A.A.F. tests as on a number of occasions before, four evaluation abilities involving semantic information were thought to be identified in the targeted solution. The two word-checking tests, which were thought to lead on a speed-of-judgment factor in the original solution, were found to lead very strongly (probably with some inflation in the loadings) on a factor identified with EMU. Actually, when the study for the analysis of semantic-evaluation abilities was being planned, Word Checking II became the model for a test called "Double Descriptions," which seemed to fit the SI definition for EMU. The presence of Absurdities moderately on the same factor is consistent with the finding later in the semantic-evaluation analysis that the similar test Sentensense was also loaded on EMU. Both tests involve inconsistencies within single sentences.

The tests Unusual Details ("What's wrong with this picture?") and Social Situations kept together in the targeted rotations, both more strongly, without being accompanied by Object Synthesis and Word Checking I, which had added false notes to the picture of a factor for EMS in the original analysis. There is some possibility, however, that Social Situations will be found later to have some behavioral-evaluation variance, probably in relation to SI ability EBS.

Several interesting things happened with the syllogism and inference tests. One tactical change in carrying out the targeted solution was to combine Syllogisms I with Syllogisms II to give a new test variable Syllogisms I-II. The reason for this union was the marked similarity of these two tests, one being a two-choice test and the other a three-choice test. Syllogisms III is in completion form, and for that reason it was reasonable to expect that, since E has to draw his own conclusion, there might be much NMI variance. With Syllogisms III given its own target factor, it took Syllogisms I-II along with it, with sufficient loading to conclude that there was some NMI variance in that combination also. Although no conclusions must be stated in the latter test, many Es may actually draw their own conclusions first and then look for them among the given alternatives. Why Logical Reasoning, with its four alternative conclusions, did not also share some relation to the NMI factor, then, needs to be explained.

Syllogisms I-II and Logical Reasoning led in determining a factor identified as EMR. This result can be rationalized on the ground that both premises and conclusions in syllogisms state relations. The thing to be judged is consistency between relations of premises and conclusion. The presence of Evaluation of Comparisons on the same EMR factor helps very much to identify that SI ability. The things compared bear some relation to one another, such as "more teamwork than," "bigger crowds than," and "less men than," as in the sample item given earlier.

But these same two syllogism tests helped moderately also to determine the factor identified with EMI, where they had gone more strongly in the original solution. Conclusions are implications from premises; hence EMI is a more logical expectation for syllogism tests than is EMR. The two inferences tests, which are informal deduction tests, both went on EMI but not on EMR. The completion form in Inferences II might have been expected somewhat on the factor for NMI, but it did not make a significant appearance there. The completion form of test in Syllogisms III did show a small degree of relation to EMI, suggesting that, to some extent, Es reach right answers only after some evaluation and perhaps rejection of wrong conclusions that occur to them in that test.

It should be noted that the test Word Selection, which led the list of tests for EMI in this solution, is quite different from syllogism and inference tests, yet fulfills the description of a task of evaluating semantic implications. When we say that X always has a Y, we are also saying X implies Y. X also implies other things as well, among the alternative answers in this test, but not as strongly, or with logical necessity.

SEMANTIC-EVALUATION ABILITIES

The analysis of semantic-evaluation abilities[2] was the first to be done with a systematic selection of a block of six evaluation abilities from the SI model. Among the six abilities, the operation and content categories were held constant, the abilities of primary interest differing only in terms of the kind of product involved. The abilities selected for special study were EMU, EMC, EMR, EMS, EMT, and EMI. Earlier analyses, including the one first directed at evaluation abilities, were thought to have found (1) a factor of logical evaluation, which was tentatively accepted as a candidate for SI ability EMR, (2) a factor of experiential evaluation, which held some promise of being for EMS, and (3) a factor of sensitivity to problems, which was connected logically with the EMI cell of the SI model, after that system was developed (Guilford, 1959b). The support for the last of these three placements was the argument that seeing that something is wrong with common objects or institutions is an act of evaluation; the things under consideration are assigned some negative value, so to speak. Thus, an important issue in the semantic-evaluation analysis was this identification of sensitivity to problems with EMI.

Although some of the tests that had brought out these three semantic abilities previously were used again, in order to maintain continuity between the earlier studies and this one, there was considerable new test development, aimed at the kinds of abilities defined by the six positions in the SI model. As indicated in Chapter 2, the model was used in two ways in generating ideas for new tests—following the three-fold specification of a particular cell, and constructing parallel tests for parallel abilities.

In applying the latter heuristic to tests for ability EMU, for example, tests for parallel abilities CMU, DMU, and NMU were examined. The best-known measure for CMU is a multiple-choice vocabulary test, in which the correct alternative is a synonym of the word to be defined, and the others are not. The corresponding idea for a measure of EMU was to make *all* the alternative answers synonyms, one of which comes closest in meaning to the stem word. Two tests of this kind were designed for EMU. It was thought to be important to keep the stem word and the alternative answers as familiar as possible to all Es, lest the test also measure CMU.

---

[2] See Report 32; also Hoepfner, Nihara, & Guilford (1966).

A good test for DMU gives in each problem two class specifications, e.g., "round and hard," with E to list objects having both those properties. In an EMU test, E can be given the class specifications and also a list of possible answers, some of which meet the stated requirements and some of which do not. This principle was also applied in a test for EMU. It had been applied in Word Checking II of the first evaluation analysis.

Hypotheses and Their Tests

Evaluation of Semantic Units (EMU)   The test Double Descriptions was based on the principle just mentioned. It was put into multiple-choice format, however, with items of the type:

> Which object most completely satisfies the description of being both round and hard?   A. gold   B. phonograph record   C. steel   D. coin

Both B and D would qualify, but D is better (harder).

Synonyms and Word Substitution were designed according to the similarity to vocabulary tests, as mentioned above. The difference between these two tests is that in Word Substitution the stem word is presented in a sentence, with E to indicate which word is the best substitute for the underlined word, whereas in Synonyms it is presented by itself. Sample items, the first one for Word Substitutions, are

> Given sentence: He was a good doctor, but alcohol was his <u>ruin</u>.   A. plague   B. undoing   C. fate   D. punishment

> Given word: LAMP (is most like)   A. torch   B. wand   C. candle   D. lantern

Evaluation of Semantic Classes (EMC)   Although, operationally, a class is a collection of things that belong together by reason of one or more attributes that they have in common, it is the class idea or attribute complex that is the product to be evaluated in some way. Testing can get at this ability more or less directly in different ways, as results have indicated.

Best Word Class asks E to choose the class name that best describes a given set of words or objects. One sample item asks for the best of four class names offered for a given object; e.g.,

> PALM is in the class of   A. plant   B. tree   C. flower   D. leaf

In Best Word Pairs, sets of two words each are given, with E to say which pair forms the best class, in terms of the number and importance of the shared properties. A sample item reads

> Given pairs: A. mare–hen   B. sow–mare   C. hen–sow

Class Name Selection asks E to say which alternative name is most precise for a set of four words or objects, as in

> Given words: cat   cow   mule   mare
> Given class names: A. farm animals   B. four-legged animals   C. domestic animals

Evaluation of Semantic Relations (EMR)   Since the repeatedly found factor of logical evaluation had been assigned to the SI cell of EMR, its consistent marker test Logical Reasoning was included. The most recent form of that syllogistic test presents two premises and four alternative conclusions, only one of which is correct. The alternative conclusions are somewhat inviting, and would sometimes be given in a completion form of item with the same premises. Other tests for EMR were designed more clearly in line with SI properties. This step was taken in part to determine whether Logical Reasoning would remain on EMR or would go entirely with EMI tests.

In other operation categories, particularly cognition, items involving trends had proved to be measures of abilities dealing with relations. A trend of objects arranged in order of size involves a repeated relation of "larger than." Best Trend Name asks E to select the name that best describes the trend in each item. A sample item reads.

    Given words: horse   push cart   bicycle   automobile
    Trend names: A. speed   B. time   C. size

The danger that this test would measure CMR as well as EMR was surely reduced by giving E the alternative names. Still, if there were some cognition difficulty in spite of this help, some CMR variance might be evident in the results.

In each item of Matched Verbal Relations, E selects the pair of words that represents the relation most similar to that in a given standard pair of words; e.g.,

    Standard pair: BIRD–SONG
    A. fish–water   B. man–letter   C. pianist–piano   D. horse–ranch
    Answer: B (man produces a letter as a bird produces a song).

Analogies tests had been found suitable in connection with relations in other operation categories, so a special form of analogies, other than the one just mentioned, was designed for evaluation of relations. It was called "Verbal Analogies III." Verbal Analogies I had been designed for CMR, and Verbal Analogies II for NMR. In Verbal Analogies III, the relation between the first two words of the item is quite easy to cognize. Each of the alternative answers from which to select the best fourth word of the analogy bears a well-recognized relation to the third word, but one comes nearest to being the same as between the first two words; e.g.,

    Given words: TRAFFIC : SIGNAL as RIVER : ____?____
    A. bank   B. dam   C. canal   D. sand bags
    Answer: B (a dam regulates the flow of a river as a signal regulates the flow of traffic).

In an item of Word Linkage, E chooses from alternatives the word that is related to both of two given words but in different ways, as in

    Given pair: JEWELRY–BELL
    Alternatives: A. ornament   B. jingle   C. ring

It should be noted that this test differs from the others in that a particular relation is not to be judged for suitability or accuracy. It is a matter of satisfying two different relations, neither of which is given. We shall see that this feature made quite a difference in the ability measured by this test.

Evaluation of Semantic Systems (EMS) In considering kinds of systems and what it is about a system that calls for evaluation, we can well quote from Report 32:

> Systems are organized or structured aggregates of information, or complexes of interrelated parts. In the case of NMS, a parallel ability in the area of convergent production, the semantic systems have been conceived as organized, ordered, or interrelated series of events, as illustrated by Picture Arrangement, Sentence Order, and Temporal Ordering. The tests that define CMS, a parallel cognitive factor, deal with reasoning problems, as in arithmetical reasoning. Such tests commonly emphasize the ability to understand the structures of problems, including the goal to be attained. The essential character of the CMS factor seems to involve the handling, manipulation, and keeping track of different aspects of a problem in relation to one another. Present knowledge concerning the CMS and NMS factors seem to suggest the diversity of characteristics of semantic systems. It seems that the semantic system can be a sentence—a complex of relationships among ideas, an organized thought—a sequence of events, or a common situation. For this reason, the tests developed for the EMS factor sampled a variety of problem items that could be expected to involve semantic systems. [p. 8]

In Complete Thoughts E decides whether or not each statement is a complete sentence. English teachers note that inability to do this correctly is a common weakness among students. The statement "The parrot with his bright feathers" is, of course, not a complete sentence, while "Light breaks in secret places" is.

Still another EMS-designed test using the sentence as the kind of system was called "Sentensense." Like the test Absurdities of the first evaluation analysis, each sentence does or does not contain an internal inconsistency. The sentence, "Johnny, who is seven, went to Europe with his mother ten years ago," has an obvious inconsistency. We shall see that both these sentence tests failed to go with the other EMS tests, giving rise to some interesting speculations.

A test using a problem as a system was called "Important Facts." Given a problem situation, E is to judge which one of the four given facts is most important in dealing with the situation, and which fact is least important. A sample problem is

> Given problem: You are to sing in an opera and must decide which costume to wear.
>
> Given facts:
> A. The opera is named *A Dutch Maiden*.
> B. The scenery is green and blue.
> C. The spotlights will be blue.
> D. The theater will be small.

Unlikely Things is a revision of Unusual Details, which was thought to represent EMS in the first analysis. The change was from a completion to a multiple-choice format. The earlier form asks "What is wrong with this picture?" and the later form presents four potential errors or discrepancies, two to be chosen as being most important.

Where Unlikely Things uses a situation as a system, Word Systems uses a 3 by 3 matrix composed of words, in which rows and columns involve classes and relations. In each item, three such matrices are given, each with one or more errors (inconsistencies). E is to find the one with the most and worst errors and the one with the fewest errors.

Evaluation of Semantic Transformations (EMT)   From Report 32 we read:

> A transformation is defined as a change. In the semantic area, this usually means a change in interpretation or use of various objects, ideas, concepts, and other verbally meaningful materials. . . .The tests that have defined the NMT factor—Gestalt Transformation, Object Synthesis, and Picture Gestalt—require E to produce answers that involve changes in uses or interpretations of common objects. Plot Titles, one of the tests that has defined the DMT factor, requires E to interpret a given story in different ways in order to write a number of clever titles. [p. 8]

These considerations suggested new tests for EMT.

Product Choice is similar to Object Synthesis. In it, E selects one of the given alternative objects that could best serve a stated purpose, having been made by combining two specified objects.

Story Titles (formerly just "Titles") asks E to say which of suggested story titles related to a given story is best in terms of relevance to the story and provision of a new view or interpretation of the story. Examples of items were given earlier, in connection with the fable of the fox and the grapes.

Useful Changes is parallel to the NMT test Gestalt Transformation. Instead of giving alternative objects, only one of which could readily serve the unusual purpose, this EMT-designed test gives objects all of which could serve the purpose, one better than the others, as in

> Which object could best be used to slice cheese?
> A. guitar   B. plate   C. paper clip

The guitar could supply a thin wire, which would make the best cutting edge.

Evaluation of Semantic Implications (EMI)   In order to test the hypothesis that the factor of sensitivity to problems had been appropriately placed as SI ability EMI, two marker tests for that factor were included. They were the Apparatus Test and Seeing Problems. The first calls for two things seen wrong with a common appliance, whereas the latter asks for as many as five problems that might arise in the use of each given object.

Other tests were chosen for EMI because they fit the SI specifications for that ability. In a new test, Sentence Selection, E is to choose from alternatives the one statement that is true in view of the given information. A sample item reads

> Given statement: In the mid-Pacific on Buna-Buna, the game of ticky-ticky is played outdoors.
> Alternatives:
> A. People in Buna-Buna like to play games.
> B. Ticky-ticky is a difficult game to play.
> C. There is an island called Buna-Buna.

It will be seen that this test is actually a form of inference test. For that reason, it might have an affiliation for the test Logical Reasoning and hence go at least partly on factor EMR, or both could go on factor EMI.

Two tests thought to represent commonsense judgment were included in the list for EMI. In the analysis of planning abilities, mentioned in the previous chapter, two tests went along with the A.A.F. test Practical Judgment, and others, to determine a factor recognized as judgment. One was Seeing Deficiencies, in which E is to give reasons why a proposed plan is faulty. The new form of this test to be used for EMI was called "Commonsense Judgment I." It offers five alternative deficiencies, with E to select the two most serious ones. The other test, Commonsense Judgment II, was a revision of the test Verifications, also used in the planning study. In that connection, E is to suggest ways of demonstrating the truth of given facts about natural phenomena. As a test for EMI, Commonsense Judgment II asks for the choice of the best two methods among five that are given. It was thought that both tests involve implications.

Reference Factors and Their Tests Reference factors were selected mostly from the cognition category, with the expectation that there would be more difficulty in distinguishing evaluation abilities from cognition abilities and with the expectation that cognition variances would not be successfully controlled in all evaluation tests. All six of the semantic-cognition abilities were represented, but with minimal numbers of tests. As for the other operation categories, marker tests were included for NMT, because two tests designed for EMT were so similar to tests for NMT. A marker test for DMI was included because the Apparatus Test and Seeing Problems used for EMI call for the production of alternative implications, and there had been some difficulty in separating factors for DMI and EMI (the latter then thought to be sensitivity to problems) in an earlier analysis (Report 26).

The Original Analysis

The first solution to the analysis demonstrated all the semantic-evaluation factors except for EMT. The leading tests for EMU were Double Descriptions, which was designed for EMU, and Sentensense, which was designed for EMS. It had been designed for EMS with the thought that a sentence is a semantic system; it is an organized thought of some complexity. In rationalizing the appearance of Sentensense on EMU, we can say that Es took the sentences as units or the two parts of the sentences as units. Sometimes the two parts are consistent with one another, sometimes not.

The other two tests with some relation to EMU were Product Choice and Useful Changes, both of which involve judgments of objects as units. They had both been designed for EMT, but it is apparent that in those tests it is not the transformations, as such, that must be judged; it is results of transformations in the first case and the objects involved in the transformations in the second.

The failure of the two word-substitution tests to come out on the factor for EMU and their going instead on the factor for CMU is a striking result. Word Substitutions, which calls for substitution for a word given in a sentence, was more strongly loaded on CMU than was Synonyms. The finding of these tests related to CMU adds something to the conception of CMU and its tests. Heretofore it had been known that mere familiarity with words, as in reading vocabulary, could be sufficient to indicate an individual's status on verbal comprehension. We now have evidence that items requiring more precise discriminations in word meaning also assess the ability for verbal comprehension.

The factor for EMC was determined by a number of tests, led by Class Name Selection and Best Word Class. The third test designed for EMC, Best Word Pairs, went significantly on CMC rather than on EMC. One reason must have been that too many Es have difficulty in seeing the class ideas. Another may be that when Es were instructed to select the best class, they were given no clear criterion of "best." In this result, and in others, it is clear that in a good evaluation test E must have a definite criterion. There are other needed conditions, which will be discussed later.

Of the four tests designed for EMR, three led the list for its factor, including Verbal Analogies III, Best Trend Name, and Matched Verbal Relations. The fourth test, Word Linkage, was found to be the strong leader on the parallel factor for CMR. Seeing the relations involved was apparently the important contributor to differences in scores on this test.

The weak, even insignificant, loading for Logical Reasoning on this factor was thought to be a rather decisive call for changing the SI identification of the former logical-evaluation factor. Logical Reasoning went strongly on EMI in this solution, but it divided its variance about equally between EMR and EMI in the later targeted solution.

Of the hypothesized tests for EMS, two can be said to have determined a factor, Unlikely Things strongly and Word Systems weakly. The other three failed to join them. We have already seen that Sentensense went to the factor for EMU, for apparently sufficient reasons. Important Facts went on the factor for EMC, for insufficient reasons. It asks E to select the most and least important facts to consider in solving a practical problem. It may be that in using a problem as the kind of system in an EMS test, the entire problem structure must be judged, not single facts pertaining to it. Complete Thoughts went on the factor for EMI, suggesting that in doing that test E is judging implications. Deciding whether or not a statement is a complete sentence may mean that the subject of a sentence implies the predicate, and vice versa, and in this test it is a matter of deciding whether the implied part is present or absent.

One of the more important and decisive results of this analysis was that the two tests for sensitivity to problems parted from the tests especially designed for EMI. They went, instead, with the marker test for CMI—Pertinent Questions.

The conclusion is that being sensitive to a problem is a matter of *cognizing* implications, not evaluating them. In the total economy of problem solving, this broadens somewhat the role of cognition and narrows somewhat the role of evaluation. Reference to the TOTE (test-operate-test-exit) model of behavior proposed by Miller, Galanter, and Pribram (1960) suggests that the initial T is a different kind of process than the second T (and later T's). They had treated all T's as if they were the same kind of activities, whereas the finding under discussion suggests that they may be of different kinds.

The best tests for EMI proved to be Sentence Selection, an inference test, and Logical Reasoning. Word Extension came out with more than a minimal loading as some degree of verification of the expectation. The presence of Complete Thoughts, which was just mentioned, had not been expected, but its being on EMI has been rationalized.

Five of the semantic-cognition abilities were accounted for in the analysis, so it is possible to say that, in general, those five semantic-evaluation abilities were successfully separated from the semantic-cognition abilities. There proved to be much involvement of cognition variance in evaluation tests, but this was confined to a few tests. Experience gained in this analysis was valuable later in constructing evaluation tests free of cognition variance.

The Targeted Solution

In general, the targeted solution changed the picture very little from that described above, except to separate sets of tests a little more sharply, with higher loadings where tests belonged and lower ones where they did not belong, according to theory. A few details will be mentioned.

Logical Reasoning, which had gone significantly on EMI only in the original solution, divided its variance between EMR and EMI in the targeted analysis, more in line with earlier results. Word Extension divided its variance between those two factors in both solutions. There have been other instances in which tests tend to involve both relations and implications as products. This uncertainty may be because a relation is often the basis for having an implication; the coming of one of the related items instigates the other term. Implications do come for other reasons, hence it should be possible to compose implications tests that bear no significant affiliation to relations factors. This possibility was demonstrated by the tests Sentence Selection and Complete Thoughts.

There were actually two targeted analyses: one before the results from the transformation study (see Report 41 or Chapter 6) became known and the other after that information was available. In the first targeted solution, with Useful Changes pointed at an extra factor (for EMT) allowed for it, that test came out as a strong singlet. In the transformation study, Useful Changes went with other tests on a factor for NMT. In the second targeted analysis in this study, with Useful Changes targeted for NMT and with no extra factor rotated for EMT, this test fitted well with the NMT group. It was thus eventually concluded that an EMT factor had not been demonstrated in the semantic-evaluation study.

SYMBOLIC-EVALUATION ABILITIES

The investigation of the six symbolic-evaluation abilities[3] implied by the SI model was initiated before the results from the corresponding study of semantic-evaluation abilities had become known. Consequently, most of the problems of test writing were the same, and so were the strategies employed.

A new issue became evident, however, calling for overt attention. In the developing conceptions of "evaluation" as an operation, two major views emerged. One conceived of evaluation as sensitivity to errors, where the latter term was defined broadly so as to include defects, deficiencies, and inconsistencies. This view had been recognized in planning the semantic study, before it was known that sensitivity to problems belongs under cognition rather than evaluation. In operational terms, the view of sensitivity to errors suggested the use of tests calling for absolute judgments: decisions that things are all right or not all right. Decisions are of the yes-no type.

In the other view, gradations of "goodness" of information are emphasized. When items of information fall short or deviate from a standard, some may deviate more than others. This "estimation" view calls for relative judgments—for example, saying which of several items of information deviate most from a given standard, and possibly, also, which deviates least. Actually, both views can be brought logically under the same definition of "evaluation." The definition adopted for the study states that evaluation is a matter of decision concerning criterion satisfaction. Accordingly, more attention was paid to kinds of criteria in this investigation than formerly, and a variety of criteria was introduced.

Another source of variation among tests came from the recognition that symbols can be in the form of letters, numbers, syllables, and words. The way was left open for specialization of factors in two or more ways according to kind of symbol. Combining kind of symbol with kind of criterion and the distinction between absolute and relative judgments could have led to a large number of tests, where there are three or more for each possible factor. The total number of tests had to be kept reasonably small, but by sampling procedures it was possible to have different combinations of conditions represented somewhere among the six SI abilities. Of the 25 tests designed for the six factors, 13 were classified in the "sensitivity" category and 12 in the "estimation" category. Six tests featured number symbols; seven utilized letter symbols; nine utilized words; and three used combinations of letters and numbers. There were three instances in which two or more tests with the same kind of symbols appeared in the list for the same SI hypothesis.

Hypotheses and Tests

Evaluation of Symbolic Units (ESU)   The five tests for ESU showed considerable variety. Correct Spelling represented the sensitivity view, with words as the symbolic units. The test is composed of 60 of the most commonly misspelled English words, half of them with errors and half without, with E to say "yes" or "no."

---
[3] See Report 33; also Hoepfner, Nihira, & Guilford (1966).

Anagram tests have been found to represent SI ability CSU. By analogy, the test Derivations gives a relatively long word, e.g., GENERALIZATIONS, followed by a list of short words, half of which can be derived using letters from the long word, and half of which cannot. E is to say which are properly derived. It is interesting to note that, because it is an anagrams test, it was first intended for EST, since transformations (rearrangements of letters) are involved. But pretesting results showed the test's affiliation for ESU tests. As in some EMT-designed tests in the semantic study, it proves to be the end product, the unit, that is evaluated, not the transformation.

Symbol Identities was designed by analogy to successful tests of what was believed to be the parallel ability EFU. In such tests, E is to say whether or not two given pictured figures are identical. Symbol Identities presents items like

    748102 −−−−−− 749102
    tmipoty −−−−−− timpoty
    L. R. Cowan −−−−−− L. R. Cowan

E writes S for "same" and D for "different" in the blank spaces. This kind of test has enjoyed popularity as part of clerical-aptitude scales.

By analogy to Double Descriptions, a test designed for EMU and previously described, the test Letter "U" was designed. A long list of words is given, of which about half contain that letter and half do not. The principle is that a class specification is given, with E to say whether or not each given unit satisfies that specification.

Familiar Letter Combinations was introduced to explore another kind of criterion, that of familiarity. The items are three-letter syllables that more or less commonly appear in words, and E is to say which of each pair of syllables appears more often in ordinary English print. The frequencies with which the syllables ordinarily occur are known from counts made by Underwood and Schultz (1960). Syllables of widely different frequency levels are paired to make the test of more appropriate level of difficulty. It will be noted that relative judgments are called for.

Evaluation of Symbolic Classes (ESC) Four experimental tests were designed for this hypothesized ability, three of which were entirely new. Best Number Class provides four defined classes—EVEN MULTIPLES, ODD MULTIPLES, SQUARES, and PRIMES—to which the values from 1 to 4, respectively, are arbitrarily assigned. E is to put each of a list of given numbers into the class that will earn the most points, which means that any number is likely to be classifiable in more than one group. For example, the number 100 is an even multiple and it is also a square. It should be classified as a square in order to earn more points.

Another number test used for ESC was Best Number Pairs. E's task is to choose the one pair of numbers that makes the best class, from a set of three pairs. The order of classes, from best to poorest, is specified as "squares, multiples, odd-or-evens," and a fourth category is "no property in common." Given the three number pairs

    A. 6–4   B. 4–9   C. 9–6

E should choose pair B, since the numbers are perfect squares.

The test Word Choice asks E to select the one of three alternative words that goes best with a set of three that form a class by reason of spelling properties. If the set is

    school   fleet   doomsday

the rather obvious common feature is the repetition of a letter. Which of the following words best fulfills the same feature?

    A. delete   B. relate   C. expect

None has an immediate repetition of any letter. All have repeated e's, but A has a second repetition, which makes it the keyed answer.

For the fourth test for ESC, Thurstone's test Sound Grouping was adapted. This exclusion-type classification test has already been described. E is to point out the one word among four that does not sound like the three class members. There was some chance that this test deals primarily with auditory-figural information rather than the visual-symbolic information that should be used for tests of ESC, but that risk was taken.

Evaluation of Symbolic Relations (ESR). The relations between words or numbers in tests of ESR pertain to spelling and numerical properties. Similar Pairs asks E to say whether two pairs of words possess the same internal relations, for example in the pairs

    1. kire–lire   fora–gora   (yes)
    2. brake–rake   freed–reed   (yes)
    3. moan–noam   toes–seot   (no)

Related Words I is a multiple-choice test of a similar nature. Which of the following three pairs of words possesses most nearly the same internal relation as the given standard pair?

    Given: GRAND–RAN
    A. country–cot   B. respite–sit   C. loving–log

In no pair is the relation exactly the same, but pair B comes closest. Thus, Related Words I is an estimation test, with relative judgments required, where Similar Pairs calls for absolute judgments.

Two tests used in earlier analyses were thought to have some promise for ESR. Both had been designed as symbolic-reasoning tests. Sign Changes II presents an unbalanced numerical expression, such as $3 + 1 = 6 \times 2$. The expression can be made into a correct equation by adopting a change in an operation sign. With alternative sign changes offered to E, the task could be a matter of evaluation: an act of accepting or rejecting each alternative. For the inequality just given, the alternatives are

    A. Instead of + you −
    B. Instead of + you ×
    C. Instead of × you −
    D. Both A and C

The other test, Symbol Manipulation, was encountered a number of times in Chapter 5, where a sample item was given. In a general sense, this is a syllogism test in which premises and conclusions are statements of equality and inequality. One premise is given, then several possible conclusions follow, each of which E is to judge as being true or false. The fact that verbally stated syllogism tests had shown repeated relationship to an ability identified tentatively with EMR supported the choice of this test for ESR.

Evaluation of Symbolic Systems (ESS) A system of symbols is some kind of organized pattern, with meaningful internal relations. Systems can be compared with one another for identity or similarity, or a single system can be examined for internal consistency.

Best Letter Set asks E to say which of three letter combinations is most like a given standard set; e.g.,

Given standard: EKN
Alternatives: A. JFI   B. PAQ   C. EBT

Set C is the keyed answer because, like the standard set, it begins with a vowel.

Number series and letter series are examples of symbolic systems, for each series incorporates a principle or two. In an evaluation test, E is not to discover the principle, for that would be true of a cognition test. He is given a statement of the rule of organization and asked to say whether each given series does or does not follow the rule.

In Correct Letter Orders, one given rule reads "Alternate letters in the alphabet (skipping one)." A few letter series are then given for judgment, such as

1. M O Q S U W   (yes)
2. P R S U W Y   (no)

In Correct Number Series, a rule is also stated, e.g., "Alternately add 1 and multiply by 3." Does the rule apply to the following series?

1. 2 3 9 10 30 31   (yes)
2. 4 5 15 16 49 50   (no)

Series Relations is also a kind of number-series test. E is given a series of three numbers, in which each number is related to the one preceding it in much the same way, but not exactly the same. Given the series $\underline{17}$ 9 2, which of the following alternatives comes nearest to describing that relation or principle?

A. -8   B. ÷2   C. -7

E is also told that the underlined element in the series is a fixed value; hence answer A is considered correct in this item. It would produce other numbers closest to those given.

In the test Way-Out Numbers, E is given a list of four ordered numbers and is told to choose either the first or the last in the list, whichever he considers to be farther from the other three numbers. For example, if the list is

31 36 45 47
A   B

answer A is correct. The instructions call for a quick, intuitive type of judgment, and speed is an important condition in this test.

Evaluation of Symbolic Transformations (EST) The three tests designed for EST considered a symbolic transformation to be either a change from one kind of symbol to another, as in decoding information, or a change in a symbol to meet certain requirements.

The test Decoding involves a very simple mapping of letters into the numbers 1 to 5, which leaves many ambiguities in the picture. A sample code and sample items will be found in Appendix B. Items in the test present two words each, with E to say which word could be more easily decoded if each were presented in the numerical-code form. A third alternative answer is the case of two words being equally easy to decode.

Jumbled Words uses anagrams for items. That is, a short word, such as START, is given, and also given are five alternative words:

    1. stare   2. stars   3. tarts

Only 3 could be made correctly using all the letters of START and only those letters.

In Typing Errors, E is given an incorrectly typed word. With a picture of a typewriter keyboard before him, E is to select from alternative real words which one is probably the one intended by the typist, i.e., contains the most likely typing error, the keyboard being arranged as it is. A variable of typewriting experience was correlated with scores from this test to determine whether it had any bearing on success in the test. The correlation was near zero.

Evaluation of Symbolic Implications (ESI) An implied item of information naturally follows some other item of information. Words can be implied by virtue of their spelling characteristics, and hence can be used in ESI tests. Abbreviations presents E with a shortened spelling of a common word and three alternative complete words, one of which is most reasonably implied by the abbreviation. A sample item reads

    crnt   A. crescent   B. coronation   C. current

Letter Problems was designed in parallel with a successful NSI test, Form Reasoning. In the latter, E is first told that certain geometric-figure symbol pairs are equivalent to other single symbols. Substituting the symbols for symbol pairs in given equations, E solves each equation. In the evaluation test Letter Problems, letters are used instead of geometric forms, and E does not solve each equation but decides whether the equation (A) can be easily solved, (B) can be solved with difficulty (as by transpositions), or (C) is impossible to solve. For example, in a set of "definitions," among other things, E is informed that $TZ = U$ and that $UU = T$. Given the problem TZU, he should say that it is easily solved, for combining the two definitions, TZU should equal T. For some problems, such as UVW, no definition is available for the combination UV, and hence the problem cannot be solved.

Symbol Reasoning involves statements of equality and inequality, composed of symbols. Alternative statements are to be judged as to whether they can be correctly inferred from given statements. An example is

Given: $2x < 3y < 2z$

which of the following statements are true, false, or uncertain?

1. $2x = 2z$ (false)
2. $y < z$ (true)
3. $x = y$ (uncertain)

This test clearly involves quantitative *relations* and might therefore be expected to have some affiliation for ESR. It also resembles the semantic test Logical Reasoning, which divides its major variance between EMR and EMI. Symbol Reasoning might accordingly be expected to share variance with ESI and ESR.

The S Test was included in this analysis as a possible contender for membership in the ESI list, but without much expectation that it would go with ESI tests. A similar test (F Test) had been designed for the hypothesis for sensitivity to problems in the first analysis of creative abilities. A sample item for the F Test might be "G H I J," with which E is to do anything that occurs to him. The original theory was that he generates his own problem, but hindsight suggests that what he adds is his implication. The test did not go on the same factor with the Apparatus Test and Social Institutions, which did determine a sensitivity-to-problems factor. It was later realized that the reason for the lack of relation of the F test to that factor is its symbolic composition; almost all items were in the symbolic category. But because the sensitivity-to-problems factor had been allocated to the EMI ability, there was some possibility that the S Test would go on the factor for ESI. It was still not known that sensitivity to problems actually refers to CMI rather than EMI. But the possibility that the S Test would go with tests for CSI prompted the inclusion of marker tests for the CSI factor, to see in which direction that test would go.

The Original Analysis

First, it is to be noted that the analysis brought out evidence for all six of the symbolic-evaluation abilities as distinct from one another and from the five parallel cognition abilities that were represented in the analysis. There were also separations from one memory ability (MSI), one divergent-production ability (DSC), three convergent-production abilities (NSS, NST, and NSI), and one other evaluation ability (EFU). The separation of ESU from EFU is especially noteworthy, because the two had been confounded so often in earlier analyses by other investigators.

The leading tests for ESU proved to be Symbol Identities and Letter "U." The former is parallel to the best tests for EFU, and the latter follows the principle for a good test for EMU (Double Descriptions). Derivations was minimally successful for ESU, but it was just about as strong for ESR, for no discernible reason. Its relative failure for ESU may be attributed to a lack of a definite criterion for evaluation, such as the criteria applying to the two more successful tests, identity in the one case and class membership in the other. The same reason could account for the complete failure of Familiar Letter Combinations, but not in the case of Correct Spelling. The latter proved to be a fairly good test for CSU; it is a cognition test rather than an evaluation test. In this case, sensitivity to errors does not seem to mean evaluation. We also learn that CSU (visual) manifests itself in awareness of fully correct spelling as well as recognition of words, as such, from minimal cues, as in the test Disemvoweled Words.

The four tests designed for ESC all came out together to help determine such a factor, but so many tests not designed for ESC also appeared on the factor that the picture of the ability represented was somewhat blurred. In fact, the list of tests was led by a test (Sign Changes II) that had been designed for ESR. The role of classes in this test is not clear.

Three of the ESR-designed tests determined the interpretation of that factor, with one ESU test added to the list. The failing test, Sign Changes II, went on ESC, as already mentioned. The intruder was Derivations, which called for decisions as to whether each given short word could have been produced as an anagram from letters in the long word. The relation of this test to ESR may have been due to the part-whole relation existing (or not existing) between each short word and the long word.

Four of the five tests designed for ESS came out together to define such a factor. Series Relations, a kind of number-series test, was the leader, followed by Way-Out Numbers. The other series tests—Correct Letter Orders and Correct Letter Series—were only moderately successful. In these two tests the rules or principles of the series are given verbally, and E has the task of comparing given series with his conception of those rules. The test that failed—Best Letter Set—is rather different, E having to say which of three sets of three letters each is most like a given set of three. Perhaps the rules were too simple, as they must be, in limited trigrams. The test might have gone logically on ESC, but it went strongly on ESI, for no apparent reason.

The three tests for EST, and only those three, came together on the same factor, which must have been for EST. Jumbled Words is the one that would logically appear best for EST, and it led the list, with no significant secondary loading. Decoding had almost as strong a loading on ESC as on EST. Typing Errors barely made the list, but it was univocal for EST.

Three of four tests tentatively allotted to the hypothesis for ESI were loaded on a factor, with an ESS-designed test (Best Letter Set) leading the list. There had been some expectation that the S Test, designed for a possible sensitivity to symbolic problems, would go with the ESI tests. The alternative expectation was that it would go with the CSI marker tests. It did the latter. Of the successful ESI tests, Abbreviations proved to be the strongest for that factor, and it was univocal. The judging of inferences in the other two successful tests proved to be in the direction of ESI, but it is apparent that they should be improved for the purpose. The relation of Symbol Reasoning to ESR that had been tentatively expected did not materialize.

The Targeted Solution

The Targeted approach made so little change in the final results that there is little need for discussion. Numerical results appear in Table 7.2. One improvement in the case of the factor for ESC was a reduction in the number of non-ESC tests in the list from seven to three, which clarified the empirical picture of that factor somewhat. The picture for ESS was made a little less clear, however, by virtue of adding another logically irrelevant test (ITED Verbal) to its list.

General Discussion

Besides demonstrating the separability of the six hypothesized symbolic-evaluation abilities from one another and from parallel abilities in cognition and other operation categories, this study revealed something more about the nature of evaluation and how best to measure it. It may be recalled that several issues were incidentally investigated in this analysis.

Both sensitivity and estimation tests, with their absolute and relative judgments, respectively, were effective in measuring the same evaluation abilities. On the whole, tests requiring absolute judgments gave factor loadings that averaged a bit higher than those requiring relative judgments. On the whole, tests requiring absolute judgments tend to be simpler, and as elsewhere, simpler tests also seem likely to be more nearly univocal for their particular factors.

There was a general question concerning the kinds of criteria for judgment in evaluation tests. It appears that results are better where criteria are logical and are more explicit—for example, with judgments of identity, class membership, and consistency. More vague criteria, such as probability of appearance of selected syllables in English text, were not adequate. Conditions appear to be best when there are definite models for comparison, as in perceived information, although in some cases comparison with remembered or conceived models was sufficient. Because of the emphasis upon logical types of criteria, it seems unlikely that either aesthetic or ethical judgments will be found within the operation category of evaluation as now conceived. The limitation to comparing and judging in terms of logical criteria sets more definite boundaries to the major category concept.

As in other contexts—e.g., cognition or memory—number, letter, and word tests (where it is spelling characteristics of words that matter) are apparently equally suitable for the measurement of symbolic abilities.

FIGURAL-EVALUATION ABILITIES

With the full benefit of experiences gained in three prior analyses in the same area, it was easier to construct a definition that more clearly delineated the meaning of evaluation as an SI concept (see Report 40). Improvement in the definition was obviously necessary, for in the two previous analyses there were too many tests designed for evaluation that also proved to have variances from cognition abilities. There were also too many tests that, although they were evaluative and in the right content category, were partly or wholly for the wrong product. The improved definition reads: Evaluation is the "process of *comparing information, in terms of known specifications,* with a *given standard* of information, on the basis of *logical criteria* such as identity and consistency" (Report 40, p. 7). The important aspect of this definition is the shift of emphasis from decision making, which is a more complex activity (Guilford, 1969), to comparison of two or more items of information. The definition also calls for full specifications of the bases for comparison and of the criteria to be satisfied.

In each new test developed for an evaluation ability, an attempt was made to take into account all parts of this definition. The logical rigor implied by the definition led even more strongly to the conclusion that in judging figural items of information, aesthetic criteria probably would not be sufficiently objective. To test this conclusion empirically, three tests that leave some room for subjective standards were included, to see whether they would be significantly related to any evaluative abilities. They will be described along with the other new tests.

Hypotheses and Tests

Evaluation of Figural Units (EFU) A long history, as factorial studies go, lies behind the factor that was eventually identified with EFU, and before that identification was known as "perceptual speed." In his first classic analysis, Thurstone (1938) found a factor that he simply called "perceptual ability," in spite of the fact that some nonfigural tests were loaded significantly on it. One of its strongly definitive tests was Identical Forms. In that test, E is to say which figures match exactly.

Thurstone and others gave further attention to this factor, finding new tests loaded on it, but still with such a liberal number of nonfigural tests that the factor they found can now be regarded as some kind of composite of EFU, ESU, and EMU (e.g., in the studies by Coombs, 1941, and by Bechtoldt, 1947). The Air Force research (Guilford & Lacey, 1947), however, found that a factor such as Thurstone's Identical Forms helped to identify was more and more confined to figural tests. It was called "perceptual speed" because, in the typical tests of it, E makes very easy comparisons of objects for identity, in comparing airplanes, aerial photographs, and maps, in highly speeded tests.

In planning the analysis of figural-evaluation abilities, the ARP raised the question as to whether speed is a necessary feature of EFU and EFU tests. Could tests involving more difficult matchings and allowing more time also be used to represent the same ability? Accordingly, two new tests were constructed for EFU, with moderate working time in one and liberal time in the other. The question was also raised whether a criterion of identity is the only one that can be utilized. Two other tests observed another kind of criterion—membership in specified classes.

In tests involving the identity criterion, matchings are usually made among figures all of identical size; the variables to be considered in matching are shape and internal details. Could judgments of identity with respect to size also be used in a successful test for EFU? In Judgment of Size, matchings are made for size only. In each item a simple, standard, outline figure is presented, surrounded by four others, differing in size only, except one. The differences in size are so small that liberal time could be allowed; it is not a speed test.

It will be noted that Judgment of Size presents a task with essentially psychophysical judgments. It should be added that two other tests tried out in preliminary testing also involved psychophysical judgments, and that they failed to show promise for EFU. One involved judgments of line length, and the other involved judgments of numerosity of small objects in rectangular frames. Reliabilities were very low, as were the correlations with known tests of EFU. Thus, it cannot be assumed that all kinds of psychophysical judgments would involve the common-factor ability EFU. We shall see later that a test involving judgments of angles was moderately successful for EFR.

One test utilizing the criterion of class membership was Judging Specified Figures, which was developed by analogy to Double Descriptions, a successful test for EMU. The principle for both tests is to present one or two class properties and to ask whether given potential exemplars of the prescribed class fulfill the requirement. In Judging Specified Figures, the description might read: "The object contains at least one square and one dotted line." A number of different figures follow, with E to say whether each object belongs in the class.

Judging Figural Combinations can be said to be of the same type, the difference being that the specifications are given pictorially instead of verbally. It asks E to compare sets of small figures, the sets differing in composition. The figures within sets differ in size or in shape. E is to decide whether the two sets contain the same figures, in the same shapes and sizes; positions within sets may differ. This test was moderately speeded.

To maintain continuity with earlier studies involving perceptual-speed factors, Thurstone's Identical Forms test was included as a marker in the analysis.

Evaluation of Figural Classes (EFC)   Best Figural Class is analogous to Best Number Class, which was successful for ESC in the symbolic study. Each of four classes is defined and given an arbitrary weight, from 1 to 4 points. Each item is a figure to be placed in the appropriate class that wins the greatest number of points.

Best Figure Pairs is an analog of the semantic test Best Word Pairs. E must say which of three given pairs makes the best class, where "best" is determined by a rank ordering of the class property defining each class. Unlike Best Word Pairs, however, in Best Figure Pairs there is no alternative "none of these." That feature was thought to be one reason for a stronger loading on CMC than on EMC in the earlier analysis.

Best Figure Class Separation requires E to select the pair of figural properties, illustrated for him, that would provide the best basis for forming two classes out of the given figures. The classification must be complete. It was expected that E would have to compare two or more possible *ways* of classifying the figures.

Figure Matching had been originally designed as a nonverbal reasoning test. It had been analyzed a number of times in ARP history, without its going on any one factor consistently. It was later thought that this was due to its having no other EFC test in any analysis heretofore and that it might go on EFC in the analysis under discussion. In each item the test presents a key figure and five alternative figures, with E to say which alternative is the most like the key figure. Essentially, the task is to form classes of two figures each. Because the instruction to say which figure is most similar to another is not completely rigorous (some room is left for personal choice as to which attributes or variables are most important), there was some doubt about the expectation of the test's going strongly on the factor for EFC, as originally thought. A step toward clearer specification was the change in instruction asking E to say which alternative has the most properties in common with the key figure. He could at least count the common attributes, if he recognized all of them.

Evaluation of Figural Relations (EFR)   Quite a variety of tests, six in all, were analyzed for the hypothesis of an EFR ability. Angle Estimation has some resemblance to an exercise in psychophysical judgment. It requires E to compare angles, each formed by two short, straight lines, and to say which given alternative is closest to the standard in angular separation. The hypothesis was that an angle is one form of relation of one line to another.

In earlier tests involving relations, successful use had been made of trends of some kind. In Perceptual-Relations Judgment, trends in simple objects such as lines, triangles, and the like are used. Imagine a series of five vertical straight lines decreasing in length from left to right, but not all by equal ratios. With the lines designated as A to E, four pairs of ratios (relations) are formed as if they were in items in analogies form, e.g.,

$$A : B = B : C = C : D = D : E$$

when the ratios are equal. The examinee is to say which analogies are correct. He is comparing relations with respect to identity.

Correct Figural Trends also makes use of progressive series as the title implies, but the figures are complex, and the relations are not simple ratios. The nature of the trend is described verbally to E, so he has little or no cognition problem. One trend is described as follows: "The closed figure becomes more open and the open figure becomes more closed at each step." The problem is to decide whether both changes are equivalent at all steps, in a series of five figures.

Prescribed Relations is another test which had been used much earlier as a potential measure of nonverbal reasoning, but which had not settled on any one factor previously. E is presented with a standard figure and a description of changes to be made in that figure. Alternative figures are given, one of which is the end result of the changes. The relations are the changes. Although changes are ordinarily regarded as transformations, the task in this test was thought to emphasize "before" and "after" conditions that are conceived as being related in certain ways.

Nearest Figural Relations is one of the three subjective-judgment tests mentioned earlier, analyzed with the prediction that it would go weakly on EFR, if at all. E is asked to select from four alternative pairs of figures the one pair that has a relation most like that of a standard pair. The subjective aspect enters because no alternative pair has exactly the same relation as the given pair, and E is given no specifications as to what variables are important in the comparison process. The criterion of identity does not apply, nor does any other well-defined criterion.

Identical Figural Relations does apply a criterion, namely that of identity. E is to say whether or not pairs of figures have the same relation as a key pair (the standard). This test is analogous to Similar Pairs, which was partially successful for representing ESR.

Evaluation of Figural Systems (EFS) Judging Figural Balance asks E to say which of three types of balance a sketch of a two-dimensional arrangement of objects and lines represents. Without rigorous definitions of balance, such a task would probably be in the category of aesthetic impression, with subjective aspects. The three types of balance were designated as "symmetrical," "informal," and "complete." (See Appendix B for definitions and samples of these types.) E is to say of each item which of the three types is best represented. It was recognized that because of this test's resemblance to Best Figural Classes there was some possibility of its involving EFC instead of, or in addition to, EFS. The results removed this doubt.

Best Map Placement presents a medieval map of a city locale, with small squares cut out. Alternative squares, some taken from the same locations within the map and some not, are to be matched to the vacant spots. The criterion for best placement is consistency with surrounding features in the map.

Internally Consistent Figures presents potentially three-dimensional sketches composed of interconnected planes. E has to perceive the figures as three-dimensional before he can answer the question of whether each one is organized as a three-dimensional arrangement of planes should be. Half of them are impossible solid objects. The test fits logically the definition of evaluation, with a criterion of internal consistency, but as we shall see, it went widely astray in the analysis.

Closest Spatial Series presents in each item four photographic views of scenes that include buildings, as on a campus. Each series comprises successive scenes a viewer might see in walking down a street or in a circle around the buildings as a group. E's problem is to say whether the difference between views 1 and 2 is greater or less than that between 3 and 4. The test is an analog of Way-Out Numbers, which was satisfactory for the parallel ability ESS.

Similar Orientations is like the preceding test in that photographs are taken of the same scene from different directions. It differs in that the scene is of a collection of wooden blocks of different shapes, spaced in an arrangement on a table, and only two views are taken. E's task is also different. He is given three other such pairs of views, and he is asked to say whether the change in direction from which the view is taken is the same in each of the three as in the single, standard view.

The last two tests utilize spatial systems in which the viewer is a part of the system, whereas the other tests utilize systems without the viewer as a part. The occasion for this type of variation was that in the cognition category of figural abilities, factors for CFS and CFT have often been distinguished by the fact that CFS tests include the viewer in the systems, whereas CFT tests do not.

Evaluation of Figural Transformations (EFT) Different types of changes were incorporated in potential tests for this ability. Changes were utilized in both two- and three-dimensional figural objects, for the reason that in the cognition area it had been noted that two-dimensional changes are usually successfully used in relations-ability tests, whereas three-dimensional changes are characteristic of successful transformation-abilities tests. There was also some interest in possible differences in figure-centered systems versus viewer-centered systems, as mentioned under the EFS factor.

Judging Rearrangements presents mostly figures of two-dimensional objects with changes in rearrangements of parts. It uses figure-centered systems. E's task is to say whether the allegedly rearranged figure is a possible transform of the given figure. The test is an analog of Jumbled Words, in which one word of a pair represents a rearrangement of the letters in another word or it does not.

Artistic Interpretations was prepared as one of the three tests with incomplete specifications of the task. A sketch of a familiar object is shown as the standard, e.g., an umbrella of a certain style. E is to say which of four alternative umbrellas represents the least change in style. Since a change is to be evaluated, the test should go on EFT, if on any figural-evaluation factor. It was expected to have a low, even insignificant, loading on CFT.

Least Movement involves rotations of a solid object in three-dimensional space. The object is a photographed flatiron. A starting position of the iron is shown, with three alternative views, each in a different orientation. Which alternative shows the least change of orientation is the question for E. The spatial system probably does not include the viewer in most cases.

Evaluation of Figural Implications (EFI) A special problem was involved in selecting tests for EFI. The problem arose from the suspicion that what had been regarded as the factor for CFI, or formerly "perceptual foresight," should have been identified with EFI instead. Two of the marker tests, especially, involving planning of routes with all potential pathways shown explicitly, leaving nothing to be supplied in the way of implied lines by E, require judgments of alternative pathways, and hence evaluation. The two tests were Route Planning, a maze-tracing test, and Planning a Circuit, renamed "Essential Maze Routes" and "Most Effective Path," respectively. The third successful test for what was thought to be CFI had been Competitive Planning, in which E plays the game for two competitors in completing incomplete squares so as to maximize the scores for both players. Since E has to complete the squares to show the "moves" implied at different steps, it was thought that this test would stay on the factor for CFI. Results showed, however, that it stayed with the other two, and all three went on a new factor for EFI. The factor was identified with EFI by the presence of three new tests more clearly designed for that ability.

Of these three tests, Best Move Selection was designed to force E to compare implications. Each item presents a pattern of a very few squares. E is given four game pieces, each with its own characteristic moves, according to given rules. E is asked which piece could be used to move from square to square so as to cover the pattern most efficiently.

Judging Figural Elaborations presents in each item a starting line or two, plus some symbols showing how additions could be made. Five complete geometric figures are given for use in connection with all items. Symbols indicate the midpoint of a line, an intersection point, and where a single line might be added. Given this kind of information, E is to say which complete geometric figure, if any, could be produced, elaborating it according to the code and the rules.

Poster Judgment is quite a different kind of test. In each problem E is to say which letter styles could be used to fit a given printed phrase into a limited rectangular poster space. It was thought that E has to compare the implications of the size and spacing of letters in a certain style with implications from the phrase and the allowable space.

The Targeted-Rotation Analysis   At the date of this study, only targeted solutions were applied. The numerical results are given in Table 7.2 for evaluation factors. In general, the differentiation of the new evaluation factors from the six figural-cognition factors and from one another was exceptionally successful. There was a large proportion of evaluation tests that were univocal for their own factors, and almost no other tests had loadings on the new factors.

There were two noteworthy failures of tests designed for certain evaluation abilities but going fully on other factors, however. Judging Specified Figures, designed for EFU, went instead on EFC. The test had its figural and evaluative features, but the product was different from that expected. This switch was not entirely surprising, for it was recognized that classes play a role in the test's items. We are left with a question, however, as to why Judging Figural Combinations did not also go on EFC; it went where intended, on EFU. The most obvious difference between these two tests is the verbal specification of classes in the former and the figural specification of classes in the latter. It might be natural for verbal specifications to work for Double Descriptions as a test for EMU, and not for EFU. On the other hand, verbal specifications worked in the case of the test Letter "U," as a measure of ESU, also a nonverbal variable.

Another, more marked, loss of a test intended for a certain figural-evaluation ability was the case of Internally Consistent Figures, which went outside the evaluation category to land on NFT. Evidently, the crucial problem lies in E's transforming a two-dimensional view into a three-dimensional view in each item of this test. Once this is done, it is easy to judge internal consistency. Seen as a two-dimensional figure, every item is internally consistent.

The only noteworthy instance of a nonevaluative-designed test going strongly on an evaluation factor was the test called "Blocks." In this test an organized stack of brick-shaped blocks is presented. Some blocks can be almost fully seen, but others are exposed to view only in part, perhaps only one end. For each lettered block, E is to say how many blocks are touching it. Blocks had been designed as a figure-centered systems test for cognition ability CFS. Its strongest loading (.41) was for EFI, with smaller, but significant loadings on CFT and CFI. With two implications abilities involved in it, we look to see how and why this is so. It must be because the touching blocks that are counted have to be largely inferred from what can be seen. Most of the points of contact are out of sight. Not only must E see the implications, but because of the EFI variance, it appears to be even more important to make a check on what he infers. In other words, he evaluates his implications.

The Tests with Subjective Aspects   Of the three tests involving some subjective components in the acts of comparison, two just missed having significant loadings on their most likely evaluation factors, but those loadings were their highest on any factors. Nearest Figural Relations was constructed like an EFR test. E

has merely the loose instruction to find a pair of figures that has a relation most like that in the standard pair. The loading on EFR was .29.

Designed for EFT, Artistic Interpretations had a loading of .28 for that factor, its highest in the analysis. E's problem in this test is to select the alternative sketch of an object that shows the least change in style from the standard sketch of the same object. It may be noted that this task is similar to that in the test Least Movement, in which E is to say which alternative shows the least movement. This test was quite successful. In Least Movement, the kind of change is specified—a rotation or successive rotations of the same object. In Artistic Interpretations, the change or changes are in form and in style, and in one part of the object or in some other; thus it is left to E to decide which differences to use and how they should be weighted.

The third "subjective" test was Figure Matching, with the question in each item: "Which alternative figure has the most properties in common with the standard figure?" The "most properties in common" takes a step in the direction of a defined basis of comparison, which may help account for the test's loading of .39 on EFC. Another contributor to the success of this test, where failure could have been expected, is that it had been item-analyzed twice in preparation for the analysis, with items replaced or revised to increase internal consistency.

Tests with Psychophysical Judgments Of three tests that may be said to involve psychophysical-type judgments, one led the list for its factor but the other two were minimally significantly loaded. Judgment of Size was the highly successful test, on the factor for EFU. Angle Estimation had the marginal loading of .31 on the CFR factor, and Perceptual-Relations Judgment was only a bit stronger for the same factor. It was mentioned earlier that, in pretesting, two other tests involving psychophysical judgments were unpromising. It may be that tests involving simpler psychophysical judgments would be better measures of abilities in the general perceptual category than in the intellectual category. There has been a replicated factor for line length, for example, represented by tests asking for judgments of "greater than," "equal to," and "less than," for linear distances and extents (Guilford & Lacey, 1947). It would be interesting to see whether judgment categories of "equal" and "not equal" would make a difference in the ability involved. The answer to such questions might be one clue to the placing of one line to be drawn between perception and intellect.

GENERAL CONCLUDING REMARKS

The bit of factorial history in this chapter pertaining to evaluation abilities represents a trend in definition of an operation category and illustrates how important it is to have a precise conception of the category concept. Beginning with the commonsense concept of "judgment," which has numerous connotations, the substitution of a more definable term "evaluation" helped some, but not a great deal. Step by step, in three successive analyses, it became clear what had to be done in the way of controlling the examinee's operations in tests, both by means of clear and full instructions and by designing items that control E's strategy in the right directions. Even a slight loosening of the structuring of the task is sometimes sufficient to reduce the loading on an evaluation factor, even to the point of insignificance. The definition reached during the last analysis appears to be adequate: Evaluation is the process of comparing items of information, in terms of known specifications, on the basis of logical criteria such as identity and consistency.

With 18 of the 24 evaluation abilities demonstrated by means of test construction and factor analysis, there remain the six hypothesized behavioral-evaluation abilities to be investigated. Having demonstrated that the six SI products apply in the areas of behavioral cognition and behavioral divergent production, investigators should expect that those products will also apply in the operation category of behavioral evaluation. The need for rigorous specifications in tests for measuring evaluation abilities in the other content areas should be expected also with behavioral-cognition abilities. This requirement suggests the question of the relations of evaluation to ethical or moral judgments. The existence of such judgments cannot be denied. There is the further question of whether kinds of moral or ethical logic exist or can be developed. This is not to say that in daily activities behavioral-evaluation judgments have no bearing on conduct, for they do have a bearing on behavior, and conduct is behavior. But the information processing of intellectual function aims at what is, not at what ought to be. The latter aim belongs to the realm of ethics.

EIGHT
MEMORY ABILITIES

As in the case of evaluation abilities, the area of memory abilities constitutes a single structure-of-intellect operation category. As for all operational categories, the memory category calls for 24 distinguishable abilities. As in the later analyses by the ARP, within an operational category the strategy was to work on abilities for a single content category at a time, investigating, in turn, semantic-, symbolic-, and visual-figural-memory abilities. This choice seemed desirable because experience showed that abilities differing in product categories only are the most difficult to distinguish by factor analysis.

There was some concern for demonstration of distinctions between memory abilities and parallel cognition abilities on the one hand, and between memory abilities and parallel divergent-production abilities on the other, so parallel abilities in those two operation categories were represented in the memory analyses, with appropriate marker tests. Cognition tests are largely *recognition* tasks, taking "recognition" in a broad sense, for cognition depends very much upon the memory store. Divergent-production tests are largely *recall* tasks, for the information produced comes mostly from the memory store.[1]

At this point it is important to distinguish clearly between memory as an operation and the memory store. The latter depends upon all past cognitions and on how well their aftereffects have been retained. Individual differences in the extents of memory stores, however, depend upon the range of opportunities and actual exposures to information as well as upon retentiveness. Individual differences in divergent-production performances in tests reflect in part the extensiveness of information in the memory store (Guilford & Hoepfner, 1966), but in addition, there are individual differences in efficiency in retrieval of information, which are more important contributors to differences in divergent-production performance.

Operationally, tests of memory abilities are different from tests of cognition in that they attempt to ensure a high degree of equivalence of exposure of individuals to certain information. The information is so chosen that it can be assumed that all *E*s have approximately equal degrees of cognition of the material exposed. The test for retention of this information should then reflect most fully only individual differences in retentivity for that information. Recognition and recall tests do about equally well as measures of retentivity under the conditions of memory tests. Neither should reflect differences in exposure to the information, as is the case with cognition and divergent-production tests.

ANALYSIS OF SEMANTIC-MEMORY ABILITIES[2]

Before the ARP investigation of semantic-memory abilities there had been some indications of one or two abilities that fit that category. H. P. Kelley (1964) had found evidence (about 10 years earlier than that date) of an ability that could be identified as MMU and another that had features of SI ability MMS, but also with some indications that the factor represented some confounding with MMI. Christal (1958) had also found evidence for factors that were candidates for SI abilities MMS and MMI.

In addition to testing the hypotheses regarding the separability of the six semantic-memory abilities as factors, this analysis gave attention to some secondary issues, two of which are relevant in this account. The modern distinction between short-term and long-term memory had to be recognized. There is no universal agreement among specialists on the subject as to the dividing line in retention time between short- and long-term memory. The prevailing conception seems to limit short-term memory to 1 or 2 seconds after stimulation. For permanent or semipermanent retention there seems to be needed a time, measured in minutes, at least, during which consolidation or fixation takes place. The retention interval in the tests of the semantic-memory analysis used in this

---

[1] Convergent production also depends upon the memory store, but not so extensively as divergent production. In convergent production, the given information provides restrictions that funnel search toward particular items of information. This places less of a premium upon wealth of stored information and upon productiveness of recall.

[2] See Report 37; also Brown, Guilford, & Hoepfner (1968).

study varied from a few seconds (the time required to turn a page of the test booklet and to get to work on the test page) to 2 minutes (the total working time usually given for each test page). The abilities most obviously investigated were therefore concerned with very short, long-term memory, unless we accept the idea of an intermediate-term memory. It is likely that there is a high correlation between such memory and longer-term memory, for if items of information are not retained for the first 2 minutes, they are not likely to be retained in the postfixation period. On the basis of this study, however, we cannot say whether there are other memory abilities that apply beyond the fixation time. Perhaps it is best to regard the abilities represented in the usual factor-analytic investigation as learning abilities, where the learning is of the type described as memorizing.

In order to determine whether both recognition and recall tests of retention indicate the same abilities, both kinds of tests were commonly introduced as measures of each hypothesized ability to see whether they would hang together or would separate into two groups for the hypothesized kind of memory ability. French (1951), for one, had predicted that there would be two factors, or two kinds of factors, for the two kinds of retention tests, respectively.

The Hypothesized Memory Abilities and Their Tests

Memory for Semantic Units (MMU) Semantic units, in common parlance, are meanings, ideas, or thoughts in the form of particular wholes. The stimulation for semantic cognitions in tests is ordinarily through visual or auditory channels, in the form of pictures of real objects or events or printed words in the one case, and spoken words in the other. This circumstance creates some problems for the writing of semantic-memory tests. For any of the memory abilities represented in this study, it is important that what E cognizes and also remembers is in semantic form. We do not want him to succeed in any items by virtue of cognizing and remembering figural or symbolic aspects of what is presented. If printed words are presented and E shows that he recognizes or recalls those same words, did he do so perhaps by visualizing the appearance of each word or by remembering its literal composition?

Some controls for the figural and symbolic aspects of the presented items of information are therefore necessary. One device that was expected to accomplish this control was to present on the retention-test page synonyms or short definitions for the words E observes on the study page. For example, the test Memory for Word Meanings lists for study such words as KNIFE and WINTER, and E is to recognize the definitions "Used to cut" and "A season of the year" on the test page.

There was an opportunity to see what would happen when conditions were otherwise, for two tests assessed retention of the same words given again on the test page. One was a recognition test and the other a recall test. It was remembered that subjects in memory experiments seem to find semantic or meaningful memory easier than nonsemantic memory, and that when given a choice they are likely to favor the meaningful mode, sometimes translating figural or symbolic information into semantic form.

One test, Picture Memory, presents objects in pictorial form and asks for a written list of names of the objects in the retention test. This kind of retention test would not preclude E's use of visual-figural aids, but again, it was expected that semantic memory would be favored by most Es.

Although this study did not attempt to test the hypothesis that there are incidental-memory abilities distinct from intentional-memory abilities, the test for MMU called "Test Name Recall" is in the incidental-memory category. After Es had taken the usual six or seven tests in a certain test booklet, the names of the tests were presented in a pair-comparison arrangement in order to test specifically their retention for order and thus for ability MMS. Then Es were tested immediately for MMU by being asked to write the list of test titles with which they had just been working, in another incidental-memory test.

Memory for Semantic Classes (MMC) MMC is concerned with remembering class ideas or concepts. In designing tests for MMC, the strategy was to present small sets of exemplars, each set for an easily recognized class, easily recognized so as to minimize possible variance for the parallel ability CMC. On the test page the class presented for recognition is represented by a new set of exemplars. In this manner an effort was made to control for memory of particulars as a possible aid in remembering classes. The class idea should be easily recognized also in the new set of exemplars. Classified Information is based upon the principles just described. For example, on the study page E might find the set SILK WOOL NYLON, and the class idea is to be recognized on the test page in the set RAYON COTTON FELT. A set on the test page not representing any class on the study page might be SNOW ICE SLEET. A similar recognition test that embodies the same principles in pictorial form is Picture Class Memory (see Appendix B for a sample item).

An MMC test of a different character, Remembering Classes, asks E to recognize classes he has noted on the study page by selecting appropriate names for them on the test page. Another test for MMC, known as "Concept Recall," asks E to name one more class member for each of the classes he remembers from the study page. In Learned Information (classes), E reads a short essay and then is given a recall test in which he attempts to reproduce the ideas given in the essay. The score is the number of elements E gives grouped under more general concepts represented in the essay.

Memory for Semantic Relations (MMR) In the preparation of tests for MMR, the same principle of transposability was applied as in the case of MMC tests, in order to control for memory for units. In Memory for Word Relations, on the study page E finds pairs of words, with a different relation in each pair, e.g., ALLEY–HIGHWAY. On the test page E is given one of these words and along with it four alternative pairs, one of which contains the same relation as appeared with that word, e.g., "highway," with the alternative pairs

    A. lion–kitten   B. creek–river   C. boat–river   D. track–train

Alternative B is the correct answer.

In Remembered Relations, each sentence given on the study page involves a relation, e.g.,

Tar is darker than cement.

the relation being "darker than." On the test page is a corresponding multiple-choice item. The statement of fact is given, with the relation part left blank. Sometimes the relation is reversed in direction, e.g.,

Cement is _____ than tar.

with the alternative completions

A. harder   B. lighter   C. more useful   D. none of these

The relations given as alternatives could all be true, or in some cases, "none of these" could apply.

Analogies tests have been favorites where relations are concerned. In Recalled Analogies, the study page presents a number of incomplete analogies, such as

Native : tourist ∷ resident : ___?___

It is presumed that the relation is cognized by all, or almost all, Es and that the analogy can be easily completed. A recall test is given in which each item gives only the third word of the analogy, with E to provide by recall the appropriate completion. For the analogy in question, the item reads "Resident : _____." E should have to remember the relation in order to complete the analogy appropriately.

The fourth MMR test was Memory for Definitions, based on the thought that a word and its definition are connected as by a relation. On the study page E is given pairs, each composed of a word and a particular definition of that word, e.g., SKIM—a kind of milk. A corresponding item on the test page has four proposed definitions for SKIM, all of them being correct (for anyone who has not studied the pair), e.g.,

SKIM—   A. remove   B. a liquid   C. read rapidly   D. pass over

The correct definition is not worded exactly the same as on the study page, in order to control for MMU variance.

Memory for Semantic Systems (MMS)   In operation categories other than memory, the linear order of a set of units has been a usable form of system, although it is not the only kind that has been used. Some tests designed for MMS use the order of ideas in sentences or paragraphs as the kind of system. In Learned Information (systems), which utilizes an essay-reproduction test also scored for classes, as described earlier, the systems score represents the extent to which the key concepts are treated in the given order in E's reproduced essay.

In Memory for Facts, sentences are read to E, regarding which he is later asked questions. It is expected that the better E remembers the order of words in the sentences, the better he can answer the questions. In Sentence Memory, E listens to sentences varying in length, to each of which he attempts to give a correct repetition immediately. It is therefore a kind of semantic-memory-span test.

Memory for Test Order gives E a pair-comparison test for the titles of six or seven tests just completed in a test booklet. The pair-comparison format was preferred to having E attempt to write all the titles in correct order, for this task also depends upon memory for units. It was preferred to a rearrangement format, in which E would be given all the titles in scrambled order, to put them in correct order, for this entails some difficult scoring problems.

Memory for Semantic Transformations (MMT) The source of common semantic transformations was sought in such events as double meanings, puns, homonyms, and redefinitions. Double Meanings is a two-choice, recognition test in which E studies pairs of short sentences. Both sentences contain the same word, underlined to call attention to it. The meaning of the word is different in the two contexts, as in the sentences

> She brought some groceries home in a bag.
> The hunter planned to go out and bag a deer.

On the test page, E is to select pairs of definitions or synonyms that represent pairs of underlined words he has seen. For example, among the given pairs

> a letter—a beverage   name—summons   sack—obtain

the third pair accounts for the word meanings in the two sentences given above.

Homonyms is a four-choice, recognition test in which Es study pairs of sentences containing words that are the same in sound only; e.g.,

> There is a hole in the wall.
> He ate the whole pie.

A meaning corresponding to one of the words in the homonym pair is given in an item on the test page, with four potential companion meanings. For the pair in the two sentences just given, the test item is

> ENTIRE—   A. nut   B. ship   C. hollow space   D. operation

Remembering Puns is a structured-recall test. The "structured" qualification means that a cue word is given on the test page, whereas in a "free-recall" test no specific cues are given. On the study page of Remembering Puns, single sentences are given, each containing a pun word, which is underlined. A sample sentence reads

> The bird-loving bartender was arrested for contributing to the delinquency of a mynah.

On the test page, the corresponding recall item is

> MYNAH— _____

Puns are appreciated as sources of humor, where individuals understand them, and this kind of understanding means ability CMT. Production of puns depends upon ability DMT, as shown in analyses stressing divergent-production abilities. Many responses to the items in the Plot Titles test, described in Chapter 6, are scored as "clever" because they involve puns.

Other instances of redefinition or shifts of meaning, especially if rather sudden, can be the source of humor, as in connection with riddles. Another MMT test is Unusual Answers, which uses riddles. The purpose of the items in this test is to determine whether E can remember the point of the riddle after he has been given a clever answer to it. On the study page are riddles, with the answers; e.g.,

What can never be beaten?   Answer: A broken drum.

The corresponding item on the test page asks

What is special about a broken drum? _____

The Substitutions test makes use of another kind of redefinition, with respect to the use of objects. On the study page each statement gives an unusual use for a common object; e.g.,

A gummed label may be used as a bandage.
A cigarette filter may be used as a pin cushion.
A mop may be used as a wig.

On the test page is a matching test, with a list of objects from the study page in scrambled order to be matched with a list of uses (paraphrased) that also appeared on the study page.

Memory for Semantic Implications (MMI)   Of the traditional methods for dealing with verbal memory, that of paired associates most obviously involves memory for implications. Learning words in pairs and then being tested for the strength of "associations" between the members of pairs describes the subject's task. The use of meaningful words should put the task in the semantic category; the use of nonsense syllables should put the task in the symbolic category. Although the learning of connections between members of pairs is an obvious part of the task, there has been a growing suspicion that the learning also involves increasing familiarity with the units (see Asch & Lindner, 1963, for example).

Familiarity with pair members means involvement with MMU. To test this hypothesis, one of the MMI tests in this study was in the form of the traditional paired-associates experiment. After E has studied his pairs, the test page presents the first member of each pair, with E to write the second member. The important difference between the traditional method and the one in Paired Associates Recall is that, in the former, exposures are pair by pair, with exact timing for each pair. In the latter, E is free to control his own timing of the exposure to pairs and their order of observation. In both, a structured-recall test presents the first member (A) of a pair, with the subject to respond with the second member (B). The number of correct B responses is the score.

In order to control for ability MMU, another test, Related Alternatives, employs a multiple-choice format, and the alternative implication to be chosen is an obvious one. On the study page, family names are paired with occupations; e.g., SMITH—bricklayer. On the test page, the corresponding item is

SMITH—   A. piano   B. microphone   C. brick   D. typewriter

The alternatives are not names of occupations, not even the correct one, "bricklayer," in order to control for memory for units, either semantic or symbolic. It should also be noted that the first member of each pair is actually a symbolic unit, a family name. But the unit to be remembered as the B member is a semantic unit, for which a meaningful object is provided to show recognition. It was hypothesized that the content area of the second member would determine the content area of the ability involved. There was no opportunity to see whether this test would be loaded on a factor for MSI, however; there was only the opportunity to see whether it would measure MMI.

A test that calls for structured recall of an implication, but not in the traditional manner, is called "Books and Authors." On the study page a family name of an author is paired with the title of a book he is supposed to have written. The book title clearly implies an occupation, e.g., "Brooks: *Pictures I Have Painted.*" On the test page E is to give the name of the occupation corresponding to the author's name. The corresponding test item for the pair just given is "Brooks: _____ ," to which is expected the reply "painter" or "artist."

In order to achieve a still different kind of MMI test, Descriptions was designed. In this test E is to see the most obvious implication to two given words, e.g., LACE—PERFUME, for which he is expected to think "feminine," or something in that area. On the test page, the pair of nouns is not repeated as a cue. Instead, a list of adjectives is presented for yes-no discriminations, half of which are expected implications that E should recognize, if his learning exercise has been successful. If E did not achieve the most likely implication in studying the pairs of words, the given adjectives in the retention test are expected to be close to what he did infer, so as to serve as a test of his retention.

Hypothesized Reference Factors and Their Tests

The reference factors were all semantic, outside the memory category. The four other operation categories were represented by at least one SI ability each. Cognition had two abilities—CMU and CMS; convergent production and evaluation had one ability each—NMS and EMC; and divergent production had a full set of the six semantic abilities. The decision to include these six was largely in deference to the high school personnel where the test battery was administered, because of special interest in gaining information regarding creative potential of the students. But since so many of the memory tests were in free-recall format

Table 8.1   Populations and Samples for Analyses of Memory Abilities

Report Number	Brief Title of the Analysis	N	Population
37	Semantic-memory abilities	175	Eleventh-grade students
38	Symbolic-memory abilities	266	Tenth-grade students
43	Visual-figural-memory abilities	202	Grades 9 through 12

(no cues given), it was important to see how much relation there might be with the "recall" types of tests used for divergent-production abilities. The main differences between the two types of recall tests are that in memory tests there is restriction to selected items of information, to which all *E*s have presumably had equivalent, recent exposure, whereas in divergent-production tests all relevant items of information in *E*s' memory stores are eligible for recall, and exposures were uncontrolled and not recent.

For descriptions of the abilities and their common tests in the nonmemory categories, the reader is referred to the pertinent earlier chapters—Chapter 5 for abilities CMU, CMS, and NMS; Chapter 6 for the six divergent-production abilities; and Chapter 7 for EMC. Table 6.2 reports loadings for the tests for the divergent-production abilities, obtained in the semantic-memory analysis.

Results from Targeted Rotations[3]

The original and targeted rotational solutions were so nearly identical that only the results from the latter need be treated here. Only the results for the memory factors and tests will be mentioned, except to say that the 10 nonmemory abilities were well supported as expected, except for the singlet representing DMS.

Only the more general features of the results need discussion. Details concerning significant factor loadings may be seen in Table 8.2. The main hypothesis that the six semantic-memory abilities, defined in terms of SI properties, could be differentiated was clearly supported, with at least one univocal test for each ability. "Univocal" means no significant loadings ($\geqslant$.30) on other factors. Of the 28 tests designed for the memory abilities, only 5 failed to show significant loadings on their intended factors and of them, 3 were loaded significantly on other memory factors.

Differentiation of the memory abilities from the 10 nonmemory abilities was excellent. Only one nonmemory test showed some significant memory variance. That test was Sentence Order, in which *E* puts three given sentences, which state three related events that have a natural order, into correct order. It may be that some short-term memory is actually involved in this test. Its significant memory loading was on the factor for MMS, which is parallel to NMS, for which the test was a marker.

Three memory tests had strong loadings on verbal comprehension (CMU). Sentence Memory, which was designed for MMS, went exclusively on CMU, with a loading of .59. Memory for Facts, which was also designed for MMS, had its highest loading of .40 on CMU and divided its other affiliations about equally between MMU and MMS. Memory for Definitions designed for MMU, had its only significant loading of .34 on CMU. In these cases the results indicate individual differences in understanding or cognition of the semantic conceptions in those tests. A requisite for a good memory test is that all *E*s shall have essentially full comprehension of the studied information. These three miscarriages can be reasonably attributed to inadequate test construction that did not ensure ease of comprehension.

---

[3]For information on the subjects in the three memory analyses, see Table 8.1.

A less successful aspect of the study was the fact that 18 of the memory tests had second significant loadings on memory factors for which they were not intended. The most clear-cut lists of tests were for abilities MMU, MMR, and MMS, with two, one, and one significant loadings for tests designed for other memory abilities coming out on those three factors, respectively. The other three memory factors had more unexpected memory tests loaded on them. In some cases these discrepancies could be rationalized; in others they could not. The shortcomings in test construction could probably be corrected in replicated studies.

Table 8.2 Factors and Their Tests with Significant Loadings in the Category of Memory Abilities*

Factor / Test	37	38	39	40	41	43
MFU						
Figure Recognition	—	—	—	—	—	57
Remembering Faces	—	—	—	—	—	52
Figural Letter Recognition	—	—	—	—	—	46
Object Recognition	—	—	—	—	—	36
Recognition of Figural Classes (MFC)†	—	—	—	—	—	44
Remembering Hand-Object Pairs (MFI)	—	—	—	—	—	40
MFC						
Figural Class Recall	—	—	—	—	—	58
Figure Recall	—	—	—	—	—	51
Memory for Figural Classes	—	—	—	—	—	34
Recognition of Figural Classes	—	—	—	—	—	33
Object Class Memory	—	—	—	—	—	32
Figural Relations Recall (MFR)	—	—	—	—	—	40
Memory for Hidden Figures (MFT)	—	—	—	—	—	34
MFR						
Matrix Trend Recall	—	—	—	—	—	75
Memory for Figural Analogies	—	—	—	—	—	46
Figural Relations recall	—	—	—	—	—	38
Remembering Figural Trends	—	—	—	—	—	33
Figural Subtraction Recall (MFT)	—	—	—	—	—	36
MFS						
System-Shape Recognition	—	—	—	60	—	46
Monogram Recall	—	—	—	50	—	48
Orientation Memory	—	—	—	56	—	43
Remembering Object Orientation	—	—	—	45	—	43
Visualization Memory (MFT)	—	—	—	—	—	39

Table 8.2 *(Continued)*

Factor	Test	37	38	39	40	41	43
MFT							
	Front-View Recognition	–	–	–	–	–	59
	Remembering Spatial Changes	–	–	–	–	–	47
	Visualization Memory	–	–	–	–	–	44
	Memory for Hidden Figures	–	–	–	–	–	43
	Figural Subtraction Recall	–	–	–	–	–	32
	Figural Relations Recall (MFR)	–	–	–	–	–	39
	Memory for Figural Analogies (MFR)	–	–	–	–	–	35
	Monogram Recall (MFS)	–	–	–	–	–	33
MFI							
	Paired Figure Recall	–	–	–	–	–	48
	Remembering Flag-Letter Pairs	–	–	–	–	–	47
	Face-Shield Matching	–	–	–	–	–	42
	Remembering Hand-Object Pairs	–	–	–	–	–	33
	Books and Authors (MMI)	–	–	–	–	–	41
	Number-Letter Association (MSI)	–	–	–	–	–	36
MSU							
	Memory for Listed Nonsense Words	–	56	–	–	–	58
	Memory for Digital Units	–	46	–	–	–	–
	Recall of Nonsense Words	–	40	–	–	–	48
	Related-Number Association	–	32	–	–	–	–
	Recalled Words (MMU)	–	–	–	–	–	36
	Number-Letter Association (MSI)	–	–	–	–	–	35
	Memory for Nonsense Word Classes (MSC)	–	34	–	–	–	–
	Memory for Name and Word Classes (MSC)	–	32	–	–	–	–
MSC							
	Memory for Word Classes	–	–	63	–	–	–
	Memory for Nonsense Word Classes	–	38	82	–	–	–
	Memory for Number Classes–Recall	–	45	–	–	–	–
	Memory for Name and Word Classes	–	41	–	–	–	–
MSR							
	Memory for Name Relations	–	57	–	–	–	–
	Memory for Letter Series	–	42	–	–	–	–
	Similar Word Changes Cross-Out	–	41	–	–	–	–
	Memory for Word-Number Relations	–	32	–	–	–	–
	Related Number Association (MSU)	–	36	–	–	–	–

Table 8.2 *(Continued)*

Factor / Test	37	38	39	40	41	43
MSS						
Memory for Order of Listed Numbers	—	50	—	—	—	—
Memory for Word-Number Relations	—	44	—	—	—	—
Consonant, Digit, and Nonsense Word Span	—	42	—	—	—	—
Memory for Nonsense Word Order	—	40	—	—	—	—
Memory for Transpositions	—	34	—	—	—	—
MST						
Memory for Misspelling	—	43	—	—	67	—
Memory for Word Transformations	—	41	—	—	63	—
Memory for Hidden Transformations	—	42	—	—	54	—
MSI						
Number-Letter Association	—	60	—	—	49	36
Symbols and Letters, Digits and Symbols	—	42	—	—	—	—
Numerical Operations	—	35	—	—	50	—
Remembering Symbol Codes	—	—	—	—	—	35
Recall of Nonsense Words (MSU)	—	40	—	—	—	—
Symbol Comparison and Number Order (ESU)	—	40	—	—	—	—
Remembering Object Orientation (MFS)	—	—	—	—	—	38
MMU						
Test Name Recall	51	—	—	—	—	—
Memory for Meanings	—	—	—	—	—	50
Picture Memory	49	—	—	—	—	43
Recalled Words	46	—	—	—	—	—
Word Recognition	42	—	—	—	—	—
Remembering Symbol Codes (MSI)	—	—	—	—	—	43
Memory for Facts (MMS)	37	—	—	—	—	—
Substitutions (MMT)	34	—	—	—	—	—
Paired Associates Recall (MMI)	—	—	—	—	—	34
Memory for Listed Nonsense Words (MSU)	—	—	—	—	—	33
MMC						
Classified Information	48	—	40	—	—	—
Picture Class Memory	40	—	40	—	—	—
Learned Information–Classes	37	—	—	—	—	—
Concept Recall	33	—	—	—	—	—
Double Meanings (MMT)	38	—	—	—	—	—
Memory for Word Meanings (MMU)	34	—	—	—	—	—
Memory for Word Relations (MMR)	33	—	—	—	—	—

Table 8.2 *(Continued)*

Factor	Test	37	38	39	40	41	43
MMR							
	Remembered Relations	51	—	—	—	—	—
	Descriptions	45	—	—	—	—	—
	Memory for Word Relations	44	—	—	—	—	—
	Outcomes	39	—	—	—	—	—
	Recalled Analogies	39	—	—	—	—	—
	Classified Information (MMC)	30	—	—	—	—	—
MMS							
	Learned Information–Systems	51	—	—	—	—	—
	Memory for Test Order	47	—	—	—	—	—
	Memory for Facts	36	—	—	—	—	—
	Sentence Memory	30	—	—	—	—	—
	Sentence Order (NMS)	37	—	—	—	—	—
	Unusual Answers (MMT)	36	—	—	—	—	—
	Test Name Recall (MMU)	35	—	—	—	—	—
	Descriptions (MMR)	31	—	—	—	—	—
	Learned Information–Classes (MMC)	31	—	—	—	—	—
MMT							
	Unusual Answers	55	—	—	—	—	—
	Homonyms	36	—	—	—	—	52
	Double Meanings	49	—	—	—	—	36
	Remembering Puns	42	—	—	—	—	40
	Substitutions	38	—	—	—	—	—
	Learned Information–Classes (MMC)	38	—	—	—	—	—
	Memory for Word Meanings (MMU)	36	—	—	—	—	—
	Memory for Test Order (MMS)	36	—	—	—	—	—
	Concept Recall (MMC)	35	—	—	—	—	—
	Seeing Letter Changes (CST)	—	—	—	—	35	—
	Outcomes (MMR)	33	—	—	—	—	—
MMI							
	Related Alternatives	59	—	—	—	—	49
	Books and Authors	56	—	—	—	—	60
	Paired Associates Recall	58	—	—	—	—	44
	Classified Information (MMC)	32	—	—	—	—	—
	Memory for Figural Classes (MFC)	—	—	—	—	—	32

*Decimal points omitted.
†Factor for which test was targeted in rotation of axes.

SYMBOLIC-MEMORY ABILITIES[4]

Some Issues Regarding Previously Known Factors

The major objective of the symbolic-memory analysis, as for the semantic-memory analysis, was to determine whether the six abilities of this kind could be empirically distinguished from one another and from parallel nonmemory abilities. But there were also some questions raised in this particular area by previous factor-analytic research. Some attempt was made to resolve these issues, as another objective.

The Number Factors In his extensive review of factors, French (1951) reported three supposedly primary abilities that have direct relevance for this area. Most well-known of these is the number or numerical-facility factor, which French regarded as being one of the most firmly established. Two fairly recent studies first raised some questions about this well-accepted factor (Davis, 1956; de Mille, 1962). In both cases, a numerical-operations test was analyzed in a battery that also contained tests from the Wechsler scales, and other tests. In three analyses, the number test helped determine a factor along with Wechsler's Digit Symbol test. Since the latter has been regarded as a memory test, with some reason, it can be concluded that the factors in these three analyses were for the SI ability for memory for symbolic implications (MSI). One could not reasonably claim that the Digit Symbol test, a substitution task, is a number-factor test. No numerical operations are involved. If the MSI interpretation is correct, it is interesting that the numerical-operations test involves some well-practiced implications of long standing, whereas the Digit Symbol test involves mostly short-term memory. In a subsequent analysis (Guilford, Hoepfner, & Petersen, 1965), a numerical-operations test shared its common-factor variance between abilities MSI and NSI (convergent production of symbolic implications). Both involve implications, and both relationships are reasonable. The evidence for a numerical-operations test's relations to MSI has been regarded as weak, however, because in previous analyses there had been no more than one memory test to suggest that the factor was for MSI. There have also been doubts expressed concerning whether the Digit Symbol test actually involves memory (Luchins & Luchins, 1953). In the analysis reported here, therefore, other potential MSI tests were included in the battery in addition to one of the digit-symbol type.

Another important consideration is that, in almost all analyses showing a numerical-facility factor, two or more numerical-operation tests were included. This could mean that the numerical-facility factors obtained were confoundings of MSI with specific numerical-operations variance. In the new analysis, only one numerical-operations test was included along with tests designed for MSI.

Memory-span Factors A number of analyses had previously reported memory-span factors. In early treatments of the SI model, a memory-span ability was placed in the cell for memory for symbolic units (MSU), with the argument that the set of digits or letters in sequence that E reports correctly is a symbolic unit. He grasps and remembers it as a whole. There was some suspicion, however, that

[4] See Report 38.

there was much specificity about the reported memory-span factors, for they were commonly found from memory-span tests only, with items varying only from digits to letters. The overwhelming experience of the ARP research is that digits and letters may be used almost interchangeably in tests for the same abilities. Another variation that might not be sufficient to avoid the charge of specificity had been from visual to auditory presentation of digits and letters. In this instance, visual and auditory inputs may also be interchangeable conditions. Thus, all such traditional memory-span tests could be regarded as alternative forms of the same psychological task. Although a common factor is thus easily obtained, it might be a confounding of a specific with a common factor. In the analysis under discussion, there was only one memory-span test in the battery, along with new tests designed for MSU.

Another hypothesis that developed about the SI placement of memory-span factors, to the extent that they represented a common factor, was that they belonged in the cell for memory for symbolic systems (MSS). In memory-span tests, E must report the elements *in their correct order,* and order is a common kind of system. With other MSS tests in the battery, a decision could possibly be reached as to whether a single memory-span test would go on the factor for MSU or on that for MSS, or possibly on both.

Rote-memory Factors   Still another traditional type of factor needed clarification. It had been called "rote memory" by Thurstone, and a similar factor was called "associative memory" in the Air Force research (Guilford & Lacey, 1947) and in French's review (1951). The tests for such a factor were typically in the traditional paired-associates format. But examination of the various batteries from which rote-memory factors were reported showed that the kind of information to be memorized had been varied. The paired units were sometimes, perhaps most often, symbolic, sometimes semantic, and sometimes figural, and there were instances of mixed content within pairs. There was considerable doubt, therefore, whether all the "rote-memory" factors reported actually represented one and the same ability. On the basis of SI theory, we should not expect them to do so.

The early placement of rote memory was in the SI cell for MSR, a symbolic ability, because the term "rote" implies lack of meaning, and because most often, as already stated, most tests for the factors had been symbolic. The reason for the "R" aspect of the placement was the supposition that E uses relations that he can see between members of pairs of symbols as an aid in remembering connections between them. On second thought, however, in the case of the usual symbolic pairs there is limited basis for seeing useful relations. The fact that the members of pairs are matched in an arbitrary manner suggests that implications rather than relations are probably emphasized in cognition and learning. Implications characteristically arise by virtue of circumstantial connections between things. By reason of certain favorable conditions, such as contiguity and repetition, implications grow in strength. The expectation in the new analysis, then, was that tests of the paired-associates type would have the factor MSI in common, for "rote" material. But it was also expected that tests in formats other than paired associates could be found related to the same factor. It has already been stated that a numerical-operations test and a digit-symbol test had previously gone on a factor identified as MSI and should be expected to do so in a new analysis.

The Hypothesized Abilities and Their Tests
Memory for Symbolic Units (MSU) Several alternative conceptions of MSU and the kinds of tests that would be most pertinent led to the construction of an unusual variety of tests for this hypothesis. After preliminary evidence as to their intercorrelations was obtained, five tests were retained for analysis, including the memory-span test, still tentatively hypothesized for MSU.

Memory for Listed Nonsense Words requires the study of a list of nonsense syllables, followed by a recognition test that presents the syllables mixed with as many new ones. Recall of Nonsense Words requires memorizing syllables, followed by a free-recall listing of the same syllables in any order. Memory for Digital Units presents a set of two-digit numbers orally, the set being recited five times with changed order each time. This is followed by a recognition test. In Nonsense Word Cross-Out, E reads a rather long list of nonsense syllables. Some of the syllables are repeated, and E is to cross out such repeated syllables as he comes to them. The test is highly speeded so as to discourage E from looking back for checking purposes.

The use of nonsense syllables in MSU tests should control for semantic memory, except as E uses implied meanings of his own production. The use of two orally presented tests and three visually presented tests could possibly determine whether there is an auditory MSU ability distinct from a visual MSU, a differentiation based only on the circumstance of visual versus auditory input. It would require symbols that are unpronounceable for the visual-input tests, and sound symbols that have no corresponding conventional visual counterparts for the auditory-input tests, to demonstrate whether there are genuinely separate visual-symbolic- and auditory-symbolic-memory abilities, however. The use of three recognition tests and two recall tests could possibly determine whether there are separate recognition and recall abilities where symbolic units are concerned. Although it would take more tests than were included for MSU to test adequately for effects of these two variations, if all four kinds came out on the same factor, the indication would be negative in both instances.

A very different kind of test for MSU (and also for MSS) was Symbol Comparison and Number Order, originally designed as two different tests.[5] Each item of the first part requires E to compare a set of symbols on the front of a sheet of paper with a corresponding set on the back of the sheet. Turning the page by E is expected to allow enough time to make the test at least in part a memory test. Symbol Comparison uses symbol sets like 6669A and Z,397, whereas Memory for Number Order, the other part of the test, uses five-digit numbers and only the order of the digits may change from the front to the back. Because of the requirement of memory for order in this part of the test, it was hypothesized that the total-test score might have a loading on MSS as well as a loading on MSU. The two tests were combined because of their unusually high

---

[5]Adapted with permission from a test developed by Psychological Services, Inc., Los Angeles, Calif.

intercorrelation. It turned out, however, that this relation was due more to a nonmemory ability in common—ESU, a result that will be cited later.

Memory for Symbolic Classes (MSC) Symbolic classes can be formed from names or other words or from nonsense syllables that have spelling features in common, or from numbers with numerical properties in common. It was found in preliminary explorations (Tenopyr, 1966) that a test composed of name sets and a test of word sets correlated very high, so they were combined in a test called "Memory for Name and Word Classes." On the study page E reads sets of names, such as IRIS IRENE IRVING, in which the common feature is rather obvious. On the recognition-test page E should remember the class sufficiently to accept "Ira" as a member of a class that he saw represented but to reject "Ida," which is not a member. On the study page of another part of the test E reads the set of words PAN RAN CAN, and on the test page he is to recognize that "fan" belongs to an observed class, whereas "fun" does not. It should be noted that no names of classes and no specific words from the study page are given on the test page. Thus, presumably it is the transposable class idea that must be remembered.

Memory for Nonsense Word Classes presents on the study page some sets of three syllables each, such as GUZ GAZ GYZ. The retention test differs from that in the preceding test in that recognition of an appropriate new class member is to be made in a multiple-choice item. The item corresponding to the class just given reads

    1. GIS   2. GOZ   3. LOZ   4. MIZ

Memory for Number Classes—Recall requires memorizing and free recall of class ideas involving numbers only, identifying them by verbal descriptions. Examples of number sets are 5, 10, 25; 307, 602, 704; and 621, 821, 521. The class concepts not only are obvious but can be easily verbalized, which might suggest some involvement with MMC. This possibility could not be tested because of lack of MMC tests in the analysis. This test differs from the others in the group for MSC in that it uses numbers and requires recall in the form of class names or descriptions. The easy naming of the classes was expected to avoid variance from the factor for NMU, the naming ability. A similar test for CSC has avoided that ability.

Memory for Symbolic Relations (MSR) A relation is a definable connection between two items of information, usually units; in the present context, symbolic units. Such relations can readily be found between members of selected pairs of words, syllables, or numbers.

Memory for Name Relations presents full names of three persons; in each case a certain relation can be seen between spelling of the given name and the surname, e.g., Sam Martin, Tom McTavish, and Pam Merton, in which it is seen that the last letter of the first name is identical with the first letter of the second. On the test page the corresponding multiple-choice item reads

    Tim: A. Thompson   B. Traver   C. Mensch   D. Tolman

Note that the names have been changed but the stem name and the correct alternative surname (C) replicate the relation that was presumably observed on the study page. The terminal letters of the first and second names are identical with those on the study page, in order to tie the relation on the test page with a particular one on the study page.

Memory for Numerical Relations presents on the study page two pairs of numbers, with the same relation involved in the two pairs, e.g., 4–9 and 12–17. In the retention test, E is to describe as many relations as he can remember from those observed, in an essentially free-recall test. To the illustrative relation E could write "five more than" in one of the common blanks provided:

The second is _____ the first.

In Memory for Word-Number Relations we have an example of a test in which both words and numbers are used, with words expected to be seen as related to numbers. The study page might give the pairs "dead–285, read–785." The corresponding multiple-choice test item would say

    lead–   A. 382   B. 984   C. 486   D. 685

There is some degree of transposition involved, thus controlling for memory for particular units of information. The tenuous kinds of relations, however, ran the risk of involving MSI as well as or instead of MSR.

Similar Number Relations Cross-Out is like a cross-out test mentioned earlier (Nonsense-word Cross-out, designed for MSU). In a long list of paired numbers, as E reads the pairs, he is to cross out every one that has a relation that he has seen earlier in the list. In this test, also, the relation is transposed. E's who remember the relations better and who therefore need not look backward in the list should do better in this speeded test.

A similar test, called "Similar Word Changes Cross-Out," presents a page of word pairs. In each pair a simple change has been made in the spelling of the first word to obtain the second. The "change" in each pair was expected to be cognized as a relation rather than a transformation. The same kind of change, in new words, appears later on the page, with E to cross it out if he remembers it. For example, if he saw the pair "brink–brine," and later came across "sink–sine," he should cross out the latter. If he saw "nit–tin" early in the list, he should cross out "rat–tar" appearing later.

Memory for Symbolic Systems (MSS) The hypothesis for MSS supposes that a structure observed in complex symbolic information—for example, in an algebraic expression or equation—can be and is often remembered as a system. In all the MSS tests but one, order of elements is the kind of system utilized. To the extent that order is important in memory-span tests, span tests belong in this category. Preliminary work (Tenopyr, 1966) showed that memory-span tests tended to go with the new MSS tests. In order to have only one span test, to avoid involvement with a span-test specific, a single representative span test was made up of a combination of tests using consonants, digits, and syllables. It was called "Consonant, Digit, and Nonsense-word Span." Both visual and auditory presentations of the short series of elements were employed, with E to write the elements immediately after exposure in the order of presentation. The combination of the span tests was justified statistically by the fact that their intercorrelations were in the vicinity of their reliability coefficients.

Memory for Nonsense Word Order presents in each part a list of nonsense syllables that are to be memorized in the given order. The length of list (15 syllables) is well beyond the normal memory span. The retention test is in a pair-comparison format, giving pairs of syllables, with E to say which came before the other in the studied list. Thus, E's memory for order only was presumed to be tested.

Memory for Transpositions gives tape-recorded, oral presentations of two paired series of four digits each, which are immediately repeated by the examiner. In the second presentation of the two series there is a possible transposition of two digits, sometimes in the first series, sometimes in the second series, and sometimes in neither. E is to say which of these three alternatives applies.

An MSS test not using order as the kind of system was Memory for Letter Series. On the test page are given series like the following:

z   zz   zzz   zzzz   zzzzz
xxxxxxxx   xxxx   xxxxxx   xx   xxxx

The retention test is in multiple-choice form, with four alternatives. In it, the same letter is used in connection with the same rule or principle as on the study page. That is, there would be an item with four alternative series using the letter z, one of which is identical in principle with that on the study page. But, although following the same principle, the series might begin with a different element, e.g., three z's rather than one.

Memory for Symbolic Transformations (MST)   Several kinds of transformations were utilized in tests designed for MST. The changes involve shifts in position of the decimal point in a number test, misspellings in a word test, regroupings of letters to make new words out of old ones, and anagrams, in each of four tests, respectively.

Memory for Decimal Point Shifts presents a movement of decimal point, such as 8.163 changed to 81.63, in one pair. In the test-page item, the same combination of digits is again given in paired form, with a shift in decimal point. E is to say whether the *shift* is or is not the same as he saw on the study page. Hindsight suggests that since the shift is merely a change of position of a marker element, the transformation may be primarily figural rather than symbolic.

Memory for Misspelling presents for learning a list of common words, each misspelled but supposedly recognizable as the word intended, e.g., the given words "boan" and "ketl." On the test page each intended word is presented correctly spelled, with E to write its misspelled form to show that he has seen and remembered the transformation.

In Memory for Hidden Transformations, the study-page material gives sentences in which hidden words are embedded, the words being marked, as in the sentence "The for<u>k ind</u>icates the direction." Another sentence reads "The fat <u>opera</u> singer danced." On the test page are new sentences with the same words embedded, but in half the cases the formation of the new words from the old ones involves the same transformation, and in half the cases it does not. In the sentence "The cat opened the door" the transformation is the same, but in the sentence "It puts him back in debt" the transformation is not the same. E is to answer with "same" or "different," accordingly.

The test Memory for Word Transformations presents on the study page a sequence of letters that is divided into two words by means of a slash mark, e.g., BIND/ARE and EARN/ICE. On the test page the same letter sequences are divided the same way in half the items and not the same way in the other items. The division EAR/NICE would not be the same, but BIND/ARE is the same. In every case, two divisions yielding two words are possible. The divisions giving real words make this test different from Memory for Decimal Point Shifts; otherwise it is a change or no change of position of a shilling mark versus that of a decimal point.

Memory for Symbolic Implications (MSI) It may be remembered that there was expectation that a single test of numerical operations in an analysis would show significant relation to the hypothesized factor for MSI, given other MSI tests in the analysis. Accordingly, a composite numerical-operations test, involving all four basic operations, was utilized. In Tenopyr's preliminary analysis (Tenopyr, 1966) the four tests had been included separately. They generated a strong number factor, which can be regarded as primarily a numerical-computation specific, and only one of them (for addition) had a significant loading on the factor for MSI, and that loading was small. The four number tests intercorrelated .61 to .79, which justified combining them in the later analysis in a single experimental variable, which was expected to load significantly on MSI, with no number factor evident.

Number-Letter Association is in the typical paired-associates format. Each pair is composed of a two-digit number followed by a letter. In the structured-recall test, the numbers are given in scrambled order, with E to write the letter corresponding to each number. There was some expectation that the use of a single implied letter would tend to avoid relation of this test to MSU, since it ordinarily takes more than one letter to form a symbolic unit—a syllable, for example.

The Related Number Association Test is also a paired-associates affair on the study page, presenting number pairs such as 7–10 and 3–6. The retention test is in four-choice form, however. Because the second number of a pair bears some observable relation to the first, it was realized that there was reason for this test's going on MSR. There was interest, however, in gaining some idea of the dividing line between MSR and MSI tests.

Two tests resembling Wechsler's Digit Symbol instrument were designed, one called "Symbols and Letters" and the other "Digits and Symbols." E writes letters associated with symbols, as paired off in a visible code in the first case, and symbols to go with digits in the second case. In such tests, it is expected that E will learn and remember the associations (implications) so that he becomes free from the need to look at the code, thereby gaining speed and a good score. The two tests correlated so high that they were used in combination as one variable in the factor analysis.

Other Abilities and Their Tests

Five of the symbolic-cognition abilities were represented by two or more tests each, excepting only SI ability CST, which had not been demonstrated as yet by the ARP.

The high school personnel at the place where the test battery was administered asked that a number of behavioral-cognition tests be included in order to obtain information for their own use. Advantage was taken of this interest to replicate in large part the earlier analysis in this area (see Report 34, and Chapter 9 of this volume). This step precluded the inclusion of any symbolic factors in the production categories. But such abilities had been liberally sampled in the semantic-memory analysis, to provide indirect evidence that might apply in the symbolic area as well.

One symbolic-evaluation factor was included in the analysis, for special reasons. This factor was for ability ESU, which was expected to be involved materially in the tests of the digit-symbol type. In such tests, E undoubtedly does much checking, referring back to the code as he writes his answers, at least before he feels sufficient confidence in his memory of the appropriate substitutions. There was even more expectation that ESU would be involved in the test Symbol Comparison and Number Order, which asks E to compare series of digits or letters for identity on front and back of the same sheet. ESU's leading test, Symbol Identities, asks for comparison of such pairs on the same side, no page turning being necessary.

Results with Targeted Rotations

By the time the statistical analysis of symbolic-memory abilities was being carried out, only targeted rotations were used; hence there is only one solution to report. In general, the solution demonstrated the distinctness of the six expected memory abilities, distinct from one another, from the five symbolic-cognition abilities, the five behavioral-cognition abilities, and the one evaluation ability. Of six tests that did not perform as expected, two had no significant loadings on any of the factors. Those two were Memory for Numerical Relations, which had very nearly significant loadings on three cognition factors, for CSC, CSR, and CSI. This suggests difficulty in seeing the relations between numbers, such as those involved in the test. The second of the two tests was Memory for Decimal Point Shifts, which was just generally weak on all factors. In describing this test earlier, some doubts were expressed. The salient ability in this test might be either CFS or MFT, or both, rather than MST, since it involves visual cognition of location and memory for changes in location.

There were six instances in which memory tests had significant loadings on cognition factors, which would indicate difficulties with cognition in those tests. Memory for Misspelling, intended for MST, went instead very strongly on CSU. We can infer that the Es definitely had difficulty in seeing what real word each misspelled counterpart actually stands for. It is noteworthy that another test, Correct Spelling, also loads quite high on CSU. In this test, half the words are spelled correctly and half incorrectly. A later revision of Memory for Misspelling, aimed at correcting the cognition difficulty, yielded a strong relation to MST and an insignificant one to CSU (see Report 41). The loading for the revised test on MST may be seen in Table 8.2.

Some of the other miscarriages for tests can also be rationalized. Two memory tests went on the evaluation factor ESU, a result that was forecast. Symbol Comparison and Number Order had been expected to divide its main variances between factors for MSU and MSS, but it showed almost no relation to those two factors. The other memory test going significantly on ESU was Symbols and Letters, Digits and Symbols, which went on ESU even as strongly as on its intended factor for MSI. The hypothesis that E's comparisons of his substituted symbols with code elements in this test would involve ESU was vindicated. The appearance of Number Operations on ESU, along with others that involve speed, suggests that the obtained ESU factor in this analysis might be somewhat confounded with a speed variable or a motivational variable of some kind. It does not seem likely that doing numerical operations would involve ESU.

There were only four instances in which a memory test for a certain product came out significantly on a memory factor for some other product. In this respect, the analysis was more clear-cut than that for semantic abilities, indicating that test control for products was better achieved in this analysis. Two tests for MSC—Memory for Nonsense Word Classes and Memory for Name and Word Classes—had secondary loadings on MSU, with their primary loadings on MSC. These results suggest that memory for units representing the classes on the study page was of some help, and that control of MSU by using transpositions of classes was not entirely successful. The appearance on MSR of Related Number Associations, designed for MSI, was not a surprise. Its insignificant loading (.17) on MSI suggests that, where relations can be seen in a paired-associates type of test, they will be utilized in memorizing the pairs of elements. Tests for MSI should therefore steer clear of relations, where possible. The appearance of the same test slightly on MSU suggests that remembering the numbers, as such, was of some assistance.

VISUAL-FIGURAL-MEMORY ABILITIES

Only two previous investigations, both outside the ARP, had good claim to having demonstrated SI visual-figural-memory abilities. The Air Force research had yielded a visual-memory factor (Guilford & Lacey, 1947), which probably justified recognizing it as representing SI ability MFS, but it is not certain that it does not also represent MFU. The tests for it emphasized memory for objects and their arrangements within maps of given areas. In a major study directed toward visual-memory abilities, Christal (1958) found an ability for remembering locations of objects on printed pages. This ability could also be identified as SI ability MFS. Another factor that was most strongly represented by tests of memory for colors might have qualified for ability MFU, had there also been stronger evidence of tests of memory for figures and objects on the same factor. It might have represented largely a special color-memory ability, perceptual rather than intellectual.

Hypothesized Abilities and Their Tests

The pattern for the investigation of the six visual-figural-memory abilities in the SI model had been fairly well prefabricated by experiences in studies of the parallel semantic and symbolic abilities. The usual strategies in test development were employed. The selection of other abilities to be represented by reference factors will be related later.

As in the other two memory areas, consideration was given to the need for using both recall and recognition tests for each of the six abilities under special investigation. The use of recall tests was more limited, however, because in the figural category, they require that E sketch his answers. Because Es differ considerably in drawing skills, they could not be asked to sketch more than very simple objects. It turned out that there was only one recall test for each of the six abilities, except in one case where there were two. This circumstance would not make possible the determination of separate recall and recognition factors except in the one instance, but it would make possible the conclusion as to whether the single recall tests show involvement with the same abilities as the recognition tests.

Memory for Figural Units (MFU) In Figure-Letter Recognition, E studies a page of scattered letters, all different, and each letter in a different style of print. In each multiple-choice item on the test page, every letter represented on the study page is given in four different styles, only one of which is identical with the style studied.

On the study page of Figure Recall, E examines 10 relatively simple geometric-type shapes. He is to try to reproduce them on the test page. No weight whatever is given to sketching excellence. E has only to show that he remembers the nature of each figure.

In Figure Recognition, E studies more complex geometric figures. On the test page the same figures are mixed randomly with an equal number of new ones, with E to say whether or not he has studied each one.

A popular instance illustrating figural memory is remembering faces of people. In Remembering Faces, the study page presents sketched faces of 10 different people, 5 of each sex. They are also otherwise easily discriminated. On the test page, the 10 faces are mixed with as many more new faces, in a yes-no recognition test.

In Object Recognition, the study page contains sketches of 15 familiar objects, e.g., a necktie, a screwdriver, or eye glasses, each in a certain style. On the test page is a four-choice item for every object, in four different styles.

Memory for Figural Classes (MFC) In figural classes the common features are in the form of figural properties or elements. In each MFC test, E is to cognize the common figural ideas from sets of three figures each. Cognition is made very easy in order to minimize cognition variance—in this particular case, variance from CFC. E should not fail an item for failure to see the class concept.

Figural Class Recall presents sets of three figures each on the study page, with common elements such as a dot, a right angle, or a broken line. On the test page, regardless of the forms of the studied figures, E is given an answer space in which to show that he remembers one of the classes he has noted on the study page. Each answer space is in the form of an outline of a circle or square, the outline being formed of widely spaced dots. E is to put within each answer space the common element of a class on the study page.

In Memory for Figural Classes, having studied sets of three figures each, E is given twice as many single figures on the test page, half of which belong in classes of the study page.

On the study page of Object Class Memory, the sets are of three familiar objects each. The objects are grouped, not because of any common realistic property, but because of similarity of shape—e.g., oval objects, elongated objects, or objects with similar projections. A yes-no recognition test is then given, including single objects that may or may not satisfy class-membership requirements with groups on the study page.

Recognition of Figural Classes is like each of the two tests just mentioned in some respects. The main differences are in the kinds of figures and kinds of common attributes.

Memory for Figural Relations (MFR) The one recall test for MFR (Figural Relations Recall) presents 12 pairs of triangles of equal size and shape, differing in terms of internal lines in such a way that it may be said that the second is related to the first in some recognizable fashion. In the retention test, E is given the first member of each pair, and he is to sketch the second member. It was realized that E can look upon the difference between the two members of a pair as a change from one to the other, and hence as a transformation. The results lent some foundation to this concern.

Memory for Figural Analogies presents for study 10 pairs of related figures. The retention test presents the same relation transposed to two new figures, with two misleading answers in a multiple-choice format.

Matrix Trend Recall presents a 4 by 4 matrix for study, in each cell of which is an appropriate kind of figure. A certain relation applies in all rows and another in all columns. Having understood the relations, and seeing a starting figure in one cell on the test page, E is expected to say what kinds of figures should go in the marked cells. Below the test matrix are 20 figures, each with a number, with E to show which figure should go in which cell by writing its number in the cell.

Remembering Figural Trends presents 10 five-step trends on the study page. E is to recognize those same trends in new series of figures on the test page. Where trends are dressed in terms of squares on the study page, they are in circles on the test page, making use of the transposability of relations.

Memory for Figural Systems (MFS) Figural systems used in SI tests have commonly been in the form of arrangements of lines or objects. In Monogram Recall, each study page shows five different arrangements of three given capital letters to form monograms. On the test page E is given the same three letters, and he is told to arrange them in the same five ways, sketching those arrangements.

In Orientation Memory, E is to memorize the arrangement of 10 quite different houses or other buildings shown in a section of a street map. Given the same 10 buildings on the test page, each labeled with a number, he is to write numbers in locations in a new copy of the map.

Remembering Object Orientation presents sketches of familiar objects in five rows and three columns on the study page, with E told to remember the relative positions of the objects. Given selected pairs of these objects on the test page, E selects one of eight arrows that tells the direction the second figure has from the first, as arranged on the study page. The analysis later showed that to some extent the use of the directional arrows took on the nature of symbols, the test having some variance from MSI.

System-Shape Recognition presents on the study page nine odd-shaped objects, elongated, simple, and curvaceous. On the test page, each item presents three such figures arranged in a small rectangle. E is to decide whether the combination and arrangement are the same as for three corresponding figures seen on the study page.

Memory for Figural Transformations (MFT) One kind of figural transformation used in a test is a subtraction of a given part from a relatively complex figure. Figural Subtraction Recall shows E how a part is removed, leaving a given remainder. On the test page, E makes a similar kind of subtraction in a new complex figure, which is drawn in dotted lines, showing the remainder by sketching it.

Front-View Recognition asks E to imagine a rotation in a pictured three-dimensional object so that he would be looking at it from directly in front. The test page gives correct and incorrect front views and asks for recognition of the front views E should have imagined.

On the study page of Memory for Hidden Figures, E is shown by means of drawings how a simple figure has been concealed in a larger, more complex figure. On the test page, the more complex figure is shown completely in dotted lines, with E to find and pencil in the hidden figure.

Two other tests deal with orientations of objects in space. Visualization Memory utilizes odd-shaped blocks as objects, sketched in two dimensions. The study page shows a particular turn, and the test page shows for recognition a transpose of the same turn in a new object. Remembering Spatial Changes is a similar test, but it uses realistic objects, such as a chair or a camera.

Memory for Figural Implications (MFI) Memory-for-implications abilities call for learning tasks of the paired-associates type, which sets the pattern for most MFI tests. The memorizing task is always of this type, but the retention test is usually a recognition task, to avoid E's need to remember the units of the presented material, as such. A structured-recall test of the traditional type invites memory-for-units variance.

The matching retention tests for MFI included three forms. Face-Shield Matching calls for memorizing connections between family shields and faces. Remembering Flag-Letter Pairs presents a flag of a certain type paired with a letter of a certain style in each pair. Remembering Hand-Object Pairs presents a hand in different positions paired with familiar objects, each of a certain style.

In the one recall test (Paired Figure Recall), the traditional paired-associates task was utilized in the retention test also. E is given the first member of the pair and is to sketch the second member in response to it.

Reference Factors and Marker Tests As in the earlier memory analyses, some concern was shown about possible cognition-ability variances, in spite of efforts to control for those sources. Marker tests were included for abilities CFC, CFR, and CFT, to sample three parallel abilities.

Not much had been done previously to determine whether memory abilities for one kind of content are readily separable from those for other kinds of content. Tests representing MSU and MMU were therefore included, so that three memory-for-units abilities were in the same analysis. Likewise, there were tests for MSI and MMI as well as for the experimental ones for MFI.

It had been found previously that there was little danger of the confounding of parallel memory factors with either divergent- or convergent-production factors, but tests representing DFU, NFT, and NMS were included, more to check on certain figural-memory tests than to investigate the separability of the operation categories involved.

Results from the Targeted Solution

From the factor loadings given in Table 8.2, some of the following conclusions can be seen. Of the 27 MFX tests, 26 were loaded significantly on their intended factors. This is a higher percentage than in the two previous memory analyses. Only Figure Recall, designed for MFU, went on MFC instead. It was suggested (Report 43) that a common habit of aiding memory by classifying units of information may have been widely used in this test, and remembering the classes provided cues for recall of units. In this test the units were very easily classified.

Of the 26 tests having significant loadings on their expected factors, however, 5 had higher loadings on figural-memory factors other than those intended. Some of these miscarriages could be rationalized. Recognition of Figural Classes, intended for MFC, was loaded .44 on MFU versus .33 on MFC. It was suggested that, in this particular test, the common element of each class was so easily cognized as a figural unit that it was often in that way that a class idea was remembered.

Remembering Hand-Object Pairs was written for MFI, but it loaded .40 on MFU and .33 on MFI. The trouble was likely caused by the fact that the hand positions of the first members of pairs were so difficult to discriminate in recall that much of the difficulty in the retention test depended upon memory for the units, as such. Thus, in MXI tests, there can be units variance because of need for remembering first members of pairs as well as second members. The latter need has also been demonstrated.

There were instances of miscarriage in which MFR and MFT tests were involved. Figural Subtraction Recall, an MFT test, went a bit more strongly on MFR, and an MFR test, Figural-relations Recall, went about equally on MFT. The difficulty with ensuring that Es will cognize relations as relations, and transformations as transformations, in presenting figural material has been commented upon in other places (Report 40). A third test showed some of the same confusion: namely, Memory for Figural Analogies, another MFR test that went secondarily on MFT.

In spite of these five instances of misdirection, plus six others in which there were secondary, significant loadings for MFT tests (two on nonfigural factors), there were 16 instances of univocal tests for the figural-memory factors, a sufficient number for acceptance of the conclusion that the six abilities were demonstrated as being distinct. Hindsight tells how some of the tests could be improved so as to reduce misdirections.

The inclusion of four other memory abilities, two symbolic and two semantic, parallel to two figural-memory abilities, showed much more crossing of content lines than had been anticipated and indicates the need for further analyses in which such outcomes have opportunities to occur. The crossovers are definitely not all in the direction of semantic memory, as one might expect. For example, although Books and Authors had a loading of .60 on its intended factor for MMI, it had a loading of .41 on MFI. This suggests that there may have been much imagined visual content memorized and functioning in the retention test. Such a translation of content did not occur in the cases of two other MMI tests.

Another instance involved the test Recalled Words. When analyzed with semantic-memory tests only (Report 37), it had a significant loading on MMU. In this analysis it went on MSU to the extent of a loading of .36, but insignificantly on MMU. This suggests a preference for memory for the literal construction of the words rather than the meanings they carry, in this test in the MFX analysis.

Translations in the other direction, i.e., toward semantic content, apparently did occur in three instances, two of them toward factor MMU. One of these was the case of an MSU test, Memory for Listed Nonsense Words, which went secondarily on MMU, the two loadings being .58 and .33, respectively. A new test for MSI, Remembering Symbol Codes, went on MMU to the extent of .43, with a loading of .35 on its intended factor. Wherever a semantic-memory component shows up in a nonsemantic-memory test, the ready explanation is that Es commonly semanticize the information as a matter of habit in an attempt to remember it more surely. That this principle does not always apply was shown in earlier examples.

SUMMARY AND CONCLUSIONS

The demonstration of the 18 SI memory abilities in three analyses leaves only the 6 hypothesized behavioral-memory abilities unaccounted for. Successes thus far lend every encouragement to expect that those six abilities can be demonstrated. The six parallel cognition abilities and the six divergent-production abilities with behavioral content indicate indirectly that what is cognized is probably remembered in the same forms, and it is retrieved in the same forms. Learning and retention are the connecting links.

Experience with memory tests, when analyzed with nonmemory tests, indicates that there need be little danger of involving the former with nonmemory abilities. The greatest danger was realized early, that of keeping cognition-ability variance out of memory tests. This involvement was found to be easily controlled by reduction of the difficulty level for cognition to a point at which there can be few failures in the learning parts of the tests. In spite of the fact that recall tests of retention involve retrieval of information from storage, which is also true of production tests, divergent or convergent, there is almost no confusion of tests in either direction. It was pointed out that the conditions for memory and production tests are very different. There is also the possibility that the locus or mechanism for shorter-term storage, as in memory tests, and long-term storage are not the same. Very little has been done by way of testing the differentiation between tests of memory and of evaluation. The two operations are so different that little overlap among tests should be expected. No overlap has appeared in the few opportunities that have been offered.

As compared with other operation categories, the memory area seems to exhibit more than usual difficulty in keeping tests for one product from showing relations to other product categories. It is true that this kind of deviation in factorial directions of tests is encountered elsewhere, but it seems most troublesome in the memory area. The limited instances in which memory tests for different contents have been analyzed together also show deviations as to that parameter of the SI model. Prevention of deviations of any kind calls for experimental controls of the strategies and tactics that examinees are likely to apply to items of the test. Such controls can be applied in the instructions, in the choice of format, in the ways in which items are written, and in the setting of time limits for work on the tests. Refinements of controls may require experimental testing and analysis before acceptable conditions are achieved. The problem of control is more serious in memory tests, partly because of their two-stage character. Too many options may be left to examinees in the study-and-learning part as well as in the retention-test part. Controls need to be applied at both stages. Laboratory techniques are always available, but this approach entails individual testing, impractical until computerized test administration on a mass basis becomes a reality.

Although recall and recognition tests of retention commonly went together on the same factors, experience during rotations of axes showed some difficulty in keeping the two types of tests together in some instances. A sufficient number of factors was not permitted in the extraction and rotation solutions to allow the two kinds of tests to separate, even if they were inclined to do so. What can be said is that the two kinds of tests for an SI factor have much in common, enough to keep them on the same factor. But there is need for special investigation of this problem, if more refined answers are to be obtained.

In general, some of the memory factors found preceding the ARP analyses in that area have been shown to be wide of the mark as representatives of SI abilities or even as "primary" abilities. The rote-memory factor apparently stood for three SI abilities—MFI, MSI, and MMI—in various degrees and in different combinations, sometimes involving memory for units as well as for implications. Memory-span factors were largely specific to that kind of test, but the SI ability that they most commonly represented was MSS. Visual-memory factors previously reported were probably for MFS or MFU, or were confoundings of the two. Not previously suspected of having any connection with memory abilities, the various numerical factors reported have been largely numerical-specific but in part involved with memory ability MSI. Without the background use of SI theory, none of these clarifications of memory abilities could have been so readily brought about.

NINE
BEHAVIORAL ABILITIES

This chapter differs from the preceding ones by being devoted to a particular content area rather than to an operation category. The first chapter regarding the finding of intellectual abilities as factors (Chapter 5), although devoted to the preliminary categories of reasoning and problem-solving abilities, turned out to be a treatment primarily of cognition and convergent-production abilities. Chapter 6 was aimed toward what were conceived to be creative-thinking and planning abilities, and it turned out to be primarily on divergent-production abilities. Chapters 7 and 8 were primarily about evaluation and memory abilities, respectively, coinciding with two of the operation categories by the same names in the structure of intellect. Two major analyses were best reserved for the category of behavioral abilities because of their very novel, common character, their roles in social intelligence.

SOCIAL INTELLIGENCE
The two analyses in question may be said to have broken the ice in the important area of social intelligence. Problems of understanding the behavior of

people in face-to-face contacts, of "empathy," of "person perception," and of "social sensitivity," and problems of influencing or managing the behavior of others have been recognized for a long time, but little systematic work has been done on basic understanding of those phenomena. E. L. Thorndike (1920) had pointed out that there is an aspect of personality that can be called "social intelligence," distinct from what he also recognized as "concrete" and "abstract" intelligences. His "concrete" intelligence conforms very well to the SI content area of figural information, but his "abstract" intelligence could apply to either the symbolic or semantic content categories, or both. However that may be, the suggestion that social intelligence could be accounted for as a fourth category of information (Guilford, 1958) made possible new empirical approaches to social-intelligence problems. It carries the implication that there are 30 abilities involved in social intelligence, as specified by SI theory, 6 abilities for dealing with different products of information within each of the 5 operation categories. The behavioral abilities dealt with in this chapter are in the cognition and divergent-production operation categories, abilities in the former having been demonstrated in three analyses and those in the latter having been investigated in only one.

BEHAVIORAL-COGNITION ABILITIES

Since cognition is basic to all other operations, it was decided to enter the field of behavioral abilities by determining whether or not six such abilities could be differentiated from one another and from abilities that should be parallel in other content areas.[1] The human organism obtains most of the input that leads to information regarding the behavior of other people through what he can see or hear and from what they say or do not say. The cues about their attention, perception, thinking, feelings, emotions, and intentions come indirectly through figural and symbolic intermediaries. This fact makes possible the presentation of material in figural and verbal form and therefore in printed tests. The examinee can also let us know what behavioral information he has achieved by responding in speech symbols. Tests were accordingly developed, presenting items in figural form, auditory as well as visual, and also in printed-word form. There was much concern, however, in the use of both verbal presentations and verbal responses, lest the test turn out to be strongly loaded with semantic content. Consequently, pictorial material was very much favored, and also nonverbal responses, such as choices among pictorial items of information.

Hypotheses and Tests

There were the two customary major strategies in developing tests for each of the hypothesized abilities expected. The most obvious starting point was the definition of the ability itself, in terms of its location in the SI model. For example, for the hypothesized ability for the cognition of behavioral relations (CBR), one would think first of what behavioral relations there can be. The relation of opposition seems to be applicable because in behavior there are opposite attitudes, feelings, and intentions. The test designed to determine

---

[1] See Report 34.

whether *E* can see where opposites occur was in the form of stick figures. Given a stick-figure representation of a person who is rested and active, which of three other stick figures represents the person who is tired and inactive? If one figure represents optimism, which of three others indicates pessimism? The restriction to one relation was somewhat of a risk, but the test went along with other relations tests in the analysis.

The other major source of test ideas was the observed nature of successful tests for parallel SI abilities. A test for CBU was developed by imitation of a test for CMU, for example. A good measure for CMU is a multiple-choice vocabulary test. The parallel CBU test presents the photograph of a face with a certain expression—for example, for a state of annoyance. Four alternative faces are given from which the answer is to be chosen, one of the four showing annoyance in a somewhat different manner. In order to help prevent figural similarity from giving away the right answer, the stem face is of one sex and the alternative faces are of the other.

Two kinds of expressive stimuli have just been mentioned, stick figures in the one case and photographs in the other. Other stimulus materials were in the form of line drawings, not only of faces but also of hands, arms, feet, torso with arms, and of the whole body in different postures. Other sketches presented two people, or parts of people, showing possible behavioral relations between them, such as friendliness, animosity, dominance of one over the other, and so on. More complex stimuli were in the form of cartoon strips or photographs of three people in social situations. Auditory presentations were from tape recordings of voices with different vocal expressions, in either simple exclamations or short verbal statements.

Motion-picture stimuli would undoubtedly have extended greatly the range of possibilities, but this type of test material was rejected for several reasons. Pictured actions of persons that last for an appreciable length of time are in danger of changing and therefore of giving ambiguous impressions. Some good controls could probably be applied by using animated films. But the main reasons for not trying motion-picture material were the prohibitive cost and the inordinate time required to produce satisfactory items. The decision was to see how far one could go with printed and tape-recorded material, which later appeared to have been a wise one.

Some effort was made to utilize tests of different kinds for each hypothesized ability, i.e., photographs, words, sounds, line drawings, and cartoons, in order to avoid possible specific overlap between tests of a factor due to common test material. Photographs were used for five of the expected factors, verbal material for all six, sound for three, line drawings for four, and cartoons for five. Sometimes two of the media were used in combination. Sometimes the same medium was used in both presentation and response; sometimes two different media were used.

Cognition of Behavioral Units (CBU) Four tests were designed for the cognition of units. The test called "Faces" has already been described. It is in multiple-choice format, calling for matching two faces for similarity of mental state portrayed. Unlike many erstwhile studies of facial expression, no verbalization on the part of E is at all necessary. This feature should presumably reduce danger of semantic involvement in the task. The photographs were obtained from the Marjorie Lightfoot and Frois-Wittman series (Hulin & Katz, 1935; Schlosberg, 1952; Levy & Schlosberg, 1960), which have been used in a number of experimental studies. At first, the test items were so designed that the matching faces had similar Schlosberg scale values. But such matchings proved to be entirely too easy. More subtle matchings were therefore prepared, in order to achieve a good test-score distribution. For samples of pictorial items, the reader is referred to Appendix B.

The test Expressions is an analog for Faces, using line drawings for different body parts and for whole-body postures as items. The alternative-answer figures in the four-choice items represent body parts different from those of the stem figures.

In Inflections, E chooses the one of four sketched facial expressions that represents the same feeling as a tape-recorded vocal expression. The vocal expressions were applied to six words and phrases, e.g., "yes," "mother," "I did it," "well," "really," and "that's good." Each of these terms was stated with inflections such as could be found in five different social situations. Three different actors were employed to utter the words and phrases in a variety of ways. From this material the test items were selected. In each item the same recorded sound was reproduced so that E heard it four times in succession, to permit him to compare the sound with each of the four alternative faces in turn. Half the recorded voices and their corresponding faces were male, and half were female. E's task was to decide which face goes naturally with each vocal expression.

In Questions II, E is to say which of four given questions is most likely the one that might have provoked the photographed facial expression. The photographs were adapted from a collection of faces prepared by Halsman (1949), whose subject was the very expressive actor Fernandel. This test was first designed for ability CBI, with the thought that the awareness of the cause of a given effect would be cognition of an implication. But preliminary testing showed that the test was inclined to go with CBU tests rather than CBI tests, so with some rewriting aimed more at CBU, the experimental test Questions became Questions II. When E chooses the most appropriate questions to account for the facial expressions, he is telling us that he is interpreting the face correctly, and he does this without the need for verbalizing his interpretation.

Cognition of Behavioral Classes (CBC) Classes of behavioral items of information can be indicated by *sets* of expressive stimuli. In order to avoid involvement in semantic class ideas, however, it seemed necessary to form sets of representative expressions whose class ideas are not easily verbalized. Different forms of tests that had been found successful for cognition of classes in other content areas were utilized. These forms have been denoted as "inclusion" tests, in which E puts an item of information in its appropriate given class; "exclusion" tests, in which E finds one of four or five items of information that does not belong in the class with the rest; and "naming" tests, in which E verbalizes the class idea. The latter runs the double risk for going on the factor for CMC, if that dimension is represented by other CMC tests in the analysis, or on the factor for NMU, the naming factor.

After much experimental effort, four CBC tests remained for use in the analysis. Expression Grouping is of the "inclusion" type. E selects one of four alternative expressions that goes with a set of three that define a class. The expressions are in line drawings, representing various parts of the body or in some instances almost the whole body, in mixed fashion.

In Picture Exclusion, E selects one of four given expressions that does not belong in the class defined by the other three. In each set of four there are two photographs of face-and-shoulder views, mixed more or less randomly as to sex. One photograph was of hands only, and one of the whole body, with face masked out. In the latter case, the pictures were of drama students (male and female) with athletic figures, dressed in tights, posed in different postures.

In Odd Strip Out, an exclusion-type test, the class representatives, or exemplars, are in the form of systems. It had been learned previously that classes of systems can be recognized by examinees. Each system in the test is represented by a comic strip featuring the character Ferd'nand. Three strips are presented in each item. In two of them Ferd'nand reacts in a certain way, and in the third he reacts differently. E is to identify the strip that does not belong because the behavior is different. For example, in two of three strips in one of the items, Ferd'nand acts in a way showing that he is oblivious to or he disregards the feelings of others; in the third strip he does not.[2]

The test Sound Meaning presents expressive vocalizations, such as sighs, laughs, screams, and whistles, uttered by a male and a female who were not actors. An item of the test is composed of a set of three such tape-recorded sounds. E indicates his cognition of the class by choosing one of four descriptive words. Very broad classes of feelings or emotions are represented. For example, one item includes the three sounds: heavy breathing, a startled laugh, and a whimper. The alternative answers are "weary," "startled," "depressed," and "fearful." The words of a set are far apart in semantic meaning and are commonly understood; thus discriminations of word meaning should be excluded and so should ability CMU. E does not have to produce the names, so ability NMU should be excluded. Each alternative answer may name the class of one or two of the sounds, but only one names the class applying to all three.

Cognition of Behavioral Relations (CBR) When one thinks of a behavioral or social relation, a connection between a dyad of interacting people is likely to come to mind. Two CBR tests involve dyadic relationships. One of these, called "Social Relations," is based upon the profile, or near-profile, figures previously used by Cline (1956). Faces that have their own expressive values when viewed alone, such as wary, surprised, or dejected, take on different qualities when seen vis-à-vis another face with another expression. Each item of Social Relations is

---

[2] A very useful feature of the Ferd'nand cartoons (authored by Mik and copyrighted by United Feature Syndicate) is that the action in each strip is in pantomime, and the significance of the action is heavily psychological. These cartoons served well in several of the tests in this study.

composed of two such faces vis-à-vis. With them are three statements such as a person might be saying to another, or such as one might be thinking in the presence of the other. The face of the person who is said to be thinking or saying one of the three comments is indicated by an arrow. The three statements might be

    A. "I don't agree with you."
    B. "What a bore."
    C. "Who does he think he is?"

All these could possibly apply to the marked face, when one considers that one person's expression. But considering the expression of the two in combination, only one statement is highly reasonable. The alternative statements had been derived by giving the pairs of faces to a group of examinees in a preliminary test that was in completion form, the Es writing comments for the marked face.

In Silhouette Relations, each item is composed of a pair of silhouette figures of a male and a female, with head and shoulders showing, facing one another. These figures were adapted from Knapp (1963). The position and posture of one of these figures by itself would convey little in the way of behavioral meaning. By putting the two vis-à-vis, they both take on meaning in a dyadic relationship. Variations in relation are introduced by raising or lowering either figure or by tilting it toward or away from the other. E is to give his judgment of the mental state of one of the figures by saying which of three photographed faces applies. In half the test the faces are of females and in the other half males, with E to indicate how the female (male) feels.

The correct answer requires taking into account both persons. The relation involved is difficult to verbalize, and Es often remark about how unsure they are about their answers. Yet the scores range above the chance level, indicating that they are cognizing much of what is presented.

In cognition of relations in other informational content, it has been found that analogies tests are quite functional. It was natural that an analogies test should be tried for CBR. It was called "Cartoon Analogies," although cartoons are not actually involved; expressions are. As in a typical analogies test, a fourth term (an expression) is to be found that is related to the third term as the second is related to the first. Presenting E with alternative answers should minimize the hypothetical convergent-production ability NBR and maximize the expected cognition ability CBR. Producing behavioral relations that would be conceived abstractly, as analogies tests require, is not an easy task; the number of relations that can be utilized seems rather limited, such as cause-and-effect, action-and-reaction, and opposition. For example, in one item the two pairs show in each case a threatening expression to which a protective expression is matched, as an instance of a cause-and-effect relation.

Stick Figure Opposites confines itself even to a single relation, as it was described earlier. There had been a precedent for one-relation test in Inventive Opposites, in which E is to produce two words meaning the opposite, or nearly the opposite, to a given word. That test has gone on a semantic-relations factor along with tests utilizing varieties of relations (see Report 17). In the four tests designed for CBR, then, some involved relations between persons and some relations between mental states.

Cognition of Behavioral Systems (CBS)   For the purposes of test construction, a behavioral system was conceived either as a temporal sequence of events in which human interactions are the important links between events or as a conception of a cross-sectional view of a situation, also involving human interactions. Both kinds of system proved to be useful in CBS tests. Two or more persons are involved in each item. If only two, there is something more than a relation between the two; a third person may be implied.

In Missing Cartoons, each item is based upon a complete cartoon strip featuring Ferd'nand. One of the four sections of the strip is left blank. Four alternative scenes are presented, with E to select the one that makes the most sense in terms of interactions of the persons concerned. It will be recalled that these cartoons are in pantomime. All four alternative answers make sense semantically, but one makes best sense psychologically. The blank appears in any one of the four panels of the cartoon strip.

Missing Pictures is an analog to Missing Cartoons, in photographic form. Scenes of interpersonal actions in sequences of four each were planned, staged, and photographed. The characters in the scenes were posed mostly by ordinary college students, without dramatic experience, but the director of the scenes and of the socially pregnant events had had experience in directing television shows.

Facial Situations involves photographs of the faces of two persons, using a Lightfoot (female) face paired with a Frois-Wittman (male) face in each item. Sometimes the faces are turned in the same direction, sometimes not. Other persons are often implied by alternative statements that were designed to explain the situation and to serve as alternative answers. For example, in an item in which the girl looks happily maternal and the man looks proud, the alternative statements are

1. He was told that the child looks like him.
2. They have accepted the invitation.
3. He got the promotion.

Cognition of Behavioral Transformations (CBT)   In cognition of transformations, one must be aware that a change of some kind is taking place or has taken place, and one must also comprehend the nature of that change. Five tests were designed for ability CBT.

Cartoon Exchange is like Missing Cartoons, up to a point. A cartoon strip involving Ferd'nand is shown with one panel marked by an arrow instead of missing. Below the cartoon strip are four alternative candidates for substitution for the marked panel, one to be selected so as to change the nature of the story most markedly. In a rather typical item in Cartoon Exchange, Ferd'nand notices a pretty girl and he uses the small hoop with which he has been playing as a means of getting acquainted with her. Three of the four alternative substitutes would not change Ferd'nand's intention. The fourth panel would change the story to the effect that he sees an old friend and goes over to talk with her.

Picture Exchange is parallel to Cartoon Exchange, with photographed scenes in four-part stories. Four alternative scenes are offered as substitutes for the marked scene in the series that tells the story. One of them would change the story most.

There was another "exchange" test of a different type, known as "Expression Exchange." First, in each item is given a face with a certain sketched expression. Second, beside is another line drawing, of hands, arms, or body, in an expression consistent with that for the face. For example, the two expressions in one item indicate that something is repulsive. Three alternative faces are given, from which E is to choose one that, if substituted for the first face, would change the significance of the second expression most. It must go naturally with the second expression, but for a different reason.

Social Translations is a quite different kind of test. Its items are entirely verbal, but they carry behavioral significance. In each item, E chooses one of three pairs of people between whom a given statement has a different intentional meaning. The setting within which the statement is made can affect its psychological significance to a great extent. If a parent says "I don't think so" to a child, it probably has little implication of emotion. But if a student says "I don't think so" to a teacher, it can mean disbelief and a challenge.

Who Said It? is a still different kind of test. The pictorial materials are photographed pictures of babies' faces, each showing a strong expression. When a statement such as would be characteristic of an adult is attributed to a baby, as shown in a book by Bannister (1950), it is often humorous because a transformation is involved. Attributing adult emotions and sophistication to an infant is a transformation. In each test item a statement is given, e.g., "Another martini? Oh, I really don't think I should." One of the four babies pictured with the statement has some appearance of being under the influence, for some other reason, naturally.

Cognition of Behavioral Implications (CBI)   An implication is suggested by given information, as in predicting a future event from a present one. In Cartoon Implications a single panel from a Ferd'nand cartoon is given in each item. E is to report what he thinks happened just before or what happens next, with the belief that either an antecedent or a consequent that one thinks of is an implication from a present event. E is to choose one of four verbal statements that specifies an antecedent or consequent to the given situation. E has to size up the situation, and this led the test definitely astray.

Cartoon Predictions uses only consequents as things implied by the present event. The single cartoon panel and the alternative views presented as possible implications in each item were drawn by a novice cartoonist. Making behavioral predictions is, of course, a most common activity in daily life. Does the SI ability to see behavioral implications largely account for success in such activity?

In the course of ARP investigations, an ability first recognized as sensitivity to problems eventually became identified with SI ability CMI, which is the neighboring parallel to CBI. A test that should indicate how readily E can see behavioral problems should have promise for CBI. A psychotherapist often has to sense the real feeling or intention of his patient and its significance, "reading between the lines" of what the patient says. The items in the test Reflections were accordingly selected from statements such as patients make to their counselors. E is to choose from alternatives what the patient's verbal statement most likely means. A given statement might be: "I'm just wondering how I'll act; I mean how things will turn out." The three alternative implications read

1. She's looking forward to it.
2. She's worried about it.
3. She's interested in how things will turn out.

Answer 2 was keyed as correct. During pretesting, this test proved to be much too difficult. In order to supply more cues for E to use in the items, the patient's statement is read to Es by means of a tape recording as they read it, with voiced expressions consistent with the statement and its correct implication. This procedure gave a much better score distribution.

Some Reference Factors In order to determine whether the new behavioral tests were successful in minimizing semantic abilities, marker tests for five of the semantic-cognition abilities were put into the battery, i.e., for all except CMT, for which the avilable tests were of uncertain factorial content at the time. Tests of two figural-cognition abilities, CFU and CFR, were included to represent that content category, since so many behavioral tests depended upon figural cues.

With the thought that in adapting to the novel behavioral tests E might sometimes benefit by having high status on semantic and figural fluency and flexibility abilities, marker tests for ideational fluency (DMU), semantic adaptive flexibility (DMT), and flexibility in seeing figures (NFT) were included. With the thought that naming expressions might help some individuals, in spite of the fact that item construction studiously avoided this activity, marker tests for NMU, the naming ability, were included. With the remote possibility that the liberal number of cartoon tests might tend to generate a "cartoon" factor, attributable to that special kind of material, an additional cartoon test was included, entitled "Picture Arrangement." Each item is a cartoon strip with the four panels in scrambled order, with E to report what the correct order should be. The test is a marker for convergent production of semantic systems (NMS). A companion marker test for ordering stated events (Sentence Order) was included to help mark that factor. Other marker tests are listed in Report 34, along with further reasons for representing certain reference factors.

Table 9.1 Samples of Subjects for Analyses Devoted Primarily to Behavioral Abilities

Report Number	Brief Title of Analysis	N	Population
34	Behavioral cognition	236	Eleventh-grade students
42	Behavioral divergent production	192	Students in grades 10 through 12

Table 9.2 Significant Factor Loadings for Tests on Behavioral-cognition and Behavioral-divergent-production Factors*

Factor / Test		Analysis	
	34	38	42
CBU			
Stick Figure Expressions	–	–	50
Faces	37	–	51
Expressions	35	–	47
Questions II	40	–	
Inflections	37	–	–
Missing Cartoons (CBS)	37	–	
CBC			
Expression Grouping	61	43	–
Picture Exclusion	38	54	–
Cartoon Predictions (CBI)	–	48	–
Expressions (CBU)	33	–	–
CBR			
Silhouette Relations	36	40	48
Social Relations	43	33	41
Cartoon Analogies	35	–	–
Stick Figure Opposites	33	–	–
Expression Grouping (CBC)	–	40	–
CBS			
Missing Cartoons	53	52	64
Missing Pictures	60	43	57
Odd Strip Out	52	–	–
Facial Situations	32	–	–
Cartoon Implications (CBI)	42	–	–
CBT			
Social Translations	54	38	–
Picture Exchange	44	43	–
Expression Exchange	42	–	–
Cartoon Exchange	36	–	–
Odd Strip Out (CBS)	32	–	–
CBI			
Cartoon Predictions	53	–	–
Reflections	40	39	–
Cartoon Implications	31	–	–
Missing Cartoons (CBS)	33	–	
DBU			
Alternative Picture Meanings	–	–	67
Expressing Mixed Emotions	–	–	55

Table 9.2 *(Continued)*

Factor	Test	Analysis 34	38	42
	Multiple Emotional Expressions	–	–	52
	Creating Social Relations (DBR)	–	–	36
	Suggested Feelings and Actions (DBI)	–	–	36
	Alternate Line Meanings (DBT)	–	–	32
DBC				
	Multiple Behavioral Grouping	–	–	60
	Alternate Expressional Groups	–	–	43
	Alternate Face Groupings	–	–	30
DBR				
	Alternate Facial Relations	–	–	65
	Multiple Expression Changes	–	–	63
	Varied Emotional Relations	–	–	58
	Forming Alternative Faces	–	–	48
	Creating Social Relations	–	–	37
	Alternate Face Groupings (DBC)	–	–	42
	Alternate Line Meanings (DBT)	–	–	31
DBS				
	Writing Behavioral Stories	–	–	52
	Creating Social Situations	–	–	43
DBT				
	Multiple Cartoon Fill-Ins	–	–	49
	Multiple Story Plots	–	–	43
	Alternate Cartoon Completions	–	–	42
	Consequences (remote) (DMT)	–	–	36
	Consequences (obvious) (DMU)	–	–	31
DBI				
	Multiple Social Problems	–	–	53
	Behavioral Elaboration	–	–	38
	Suggested Feelings and Actions	–	–	36
	Alternate Social Solutions	–	–	32
	Multiple Emotional Expressions (DBU)	–	–	43
	Alternate Cartoon Completions (DBT)	–	–	40
	Plot Titles (clever) (DMT)	–	–	39
	Creating Social Situations (DBS)	–	–	35
	Plot Titles (nonclever) (DMU)	–	–	33
	Multiple Story Plots (DMS)	–	–	33

*Decimal points omitted.

Testing Conditions

A few requirements were adopted for the selection of a sample of subjects for testing with the behavioral-cognition battery. Since the expressive materials pertain to a middle-class, Caucasian population, scores from minority-group examinees were not used in the analysis. As a further control on semantic-ability differences, only subjects with IQs ranging from near average upward were used. A group of 52 gifted students was added at the request of the school in which the tests were administered. The mean IQ was 117.7 on the Henmon-Nelson scale. The Es had a mean chronological age of 16.7 years, which should mean sufficient sophistication to understand the social situations presented in the tests. For other information, see Table 9.1.

The Targeted Solution

The targeted rotations gave a solution that represented a very good fit to theory (see Table 9.2 for details of factor loadings on the behavioral-cognition factors). Of the 23 behavioral-cognition tests, 20 went significantly on their intended factors, and three did not. Only one test, Reflections, which was designed for CBI, had a significant loading on a nonbehavioral factor, and that was for CMR. There is no obvious reason for this unexpected affiliation, for CMR is not parallel to CBI, and a role for semantic relations is not clear.

On the whole, the very clear-cut segregation of behavioral abilities and tests from those in other content categories was a resounding vindication of adopting the fourth kind of information in SI theory. Even the varimax rotations, which came as a byproduct of the factor-extraction program used, threw behavioral tests together and apart from other kinds of tests. But it failed to separate the six behavioral-cognition factors satisfactorily from one another.

Some of the reasons for this failure appear in results from the targeted solution, where six behavioral tests went on behavioral factors for which they were not intended, four of them in a secondary manner and two in a substitutive manner. Examination of these tests usually suggests reasonable explanations. Odd Strip Out, which was first designed for CBC, requires the classification of *systems*. The systems have to be cognized before the classes can become evident, and the system-cognition step was apparently sufficiently difficult to reflect individual differences in CBS. Thus, the test loaded .52 on CBS and not significantly on CBC, so it was eventually targeted for CBS in rotations.

Cartoon Implications was designed for CBI, but its highest loading of .42 was on CBS, and it loaded only .31 on CBI. Seeing the situational system in the cartoon picture is necessary before the correct implication can be seen; hence the strong relation of the test to CBS.

Missing Cartoons was highest for its intended factor for CBS, but it had two secondary significant loadings, one on CBU and one on CBI. The first of these two loadings indicates that seeing units of information (individual mental dispositions) is of some help in seeing total situations. The loading on CBI might mean that the picture to supply the missing one is implied by the one or more immediately preceding. The preceding picture is pointed to as the most probable instigator of the implication here, because elsewhere it has been found that implications almost always run in the forward direction. Instances of that principle in this study were the failures of Questions and of Cartoon Implications to show strong relations to CBI, for which they had been originally written.

Of the 24 tests not designed for behavioral abilities, none went significantly on behavioral-cognition factors. This finding is another empirical reason for believing in the need for logical segregation of behavioral abilities as a separate category.

BEHAVIORAL DIVERGENT PRODUCTION

The second major study in the area of behavioral information or social intelligence was on divergent-production (DP) abilities.[3] The success of the study of cognition abilities was more than sufficient encouragement to test the hypotheses of abilities in another operation category. Because of the relevance of divergent-production abilities for creative thinking, and owing to the importance of the latter type of activity, these abilities were the next to be investigated. Behavioral-cognition functions serve to keep us aware of what behavior is going on and enable us to interpret it. The parallel divergent-production abilities should be important for coping with other individuals in face-to-face encounters and elsewhere.

Both kinds of abilities provide significant contributions to solving interpersonal problems. The cognition abilities, as in other content areas, should enable the person to detect problems and to analyze them. The divergent-production abilities should generate from the memory store the information that is needed toward solutions. The forms in which the items of behavioral information were originally cognized and stored, and the forms in which they are retrieved for use in problem solving, should be the same six products as found elsewhere in intellectual processing.

Tests for the Six Hypothesized Abilities

Much was learned in the analysis of cognition abilities that could be applied to advantage in the new study, but there were some new problems that had to be faced. The earlier investigation had demonstrated that word symbols can be quite generally used to stand for behavioral information as they always have been used to stand for semantic information. It is not necessary, then, to avoid verbal tests, provided the words clearly represent behavioral content. If used expressively, words convey behavioral information rather directly. In divergent-production tests, however, items must be in completion form, and we should like the examinee's answers to reflect behavioral content. If E does not reflect behavioral information, and if only statements implying such information are accepted in scoring a test, E has wasted his time, and he obtains a low score that may not represent his status for the behavioral ability.

Ensuring behavioral content in E's responses to items was promoted by a procedure applied in the test instructions. In presenting a few alternative answers to a sample item, the test writer pointed out some unacceptable answers, some

---

[3] See Report 42.

unacceptable because, although semantically realistic, they are void of behavioral content. This step was in addition to stressing the need for answers that refer to thoughts, feelings, or intentions of persons mentioned in the test item.

Another problem pertains to scoring E's answers. The scorers need to be very much aware of the usage of words by the particular population that takes the tests, and aware of nuances of behavioral meanings that are shared in that population. The latter kind of sensitivity is also important when it becomes necessary to decide whether an E gives duplicate responses. The selected scoring assistants were required first to score high on behavioral-cognition tests.

It would have been possible to ask E to give alternative line drawings as answers to test items, but this idea was rejected. Drawing skills are quite varied; sketching is time-consuming, where speed counts; and many Es would probably not accept sketching as a way of responding. Asking E for vocal expressions and expressions produced in the face or other body parts would confine investigators to individual testing, which is out of the question for a large test battery given to a very large sample for factor analysis. Four such tests, two with facial expressions and two with vocal expressions from E, were tried out in a small sample for two of the hypothesized DBX abilities, along with printed tests for the same abilities, just to gain information on the utility of such responses. The tests with expressive responses did not prove to assess the same abilities as did the printed tests, nor did the two kinds of expressive tests measure the same ability (see Report 42).

Divergent Production of Behavioral Units (DBU) As for all six of the DBX hypotheses (where "X" stands for each product in turn), all tests had to be entirely new, for none existed. As in other areas, although most responses must be verbal statements, the information presented to E is varied, sometimes in pictorial form and sometimes verbal.

Looking at successful tests for the parallel ability, DMU, we find that a good form presents E with two specifications of a class, naming its common properties, and asks him to list things that belong in the class In Chapter 6 it was related that investigators have found that two specified properties is the optimal number, better than either one or three. Expressing Mixed Emotions is that kind of test. For example, it might ask what a person would say if he were vexed and amused. Listed replies might be

> "Well, you pulled a good one, didn't you?"
> "That's funny, but don't do it again."
> "Ouch; ha, ha."

Following the same principle, but giving only one class property, is the test Multiple Emotional Expressions. For example, E may be asked to give several statements that a person might utter if he were angry.

In Alternate Social Meanings the class specification is given not by naming some mental state but by describing some overt behavior. A sample item reads

> "If one person winks at another what could he be thinking or feeling?"

Possible answers might be
"He doesn't know what we know."
"I'm trying to lead him on."
"You're cute."

Alternative Picture Meanings specifies the class of responses by representing a particular expression in a line drawing. E is to list statements that the person might be making or thoughts and feelings that he might be experiencing. A picture of a face with a hand astride the nose, with thumb and forefinger holding eyes closed appears in a sample item. To this picture E might respond

"I can't study any more tonight."
"I wish you hadn't told me."
"Let me see; if $x = a^2$ ..."

As these sample responses suggest, this kind of problem invites E to go from class to class rather than remain in a single narrow class, from which one might expect some DMC variance. The responses are in a broad class—the mental states going with the particular picture.

Divergent Production of Behavioral Classes (DBC) Abilities parallel to DBC, i.e., DFC, DSC, and DMC, pertain to ready shifting from one class to another in giving information, which is a kind of flexibility first qualified as "spontaneous." A DXC ability can be assessed by a test that calls for producing a number of alternative classes, given the same things to be classified. Readiness to reclassify the same things is the critical aspect of such a test.

Among the tests designed for DBC, the items to be classified in alternative ways are in the form of verbal comments indicating emotional states, photographs of faces in different expressions, and line drawings. The items to be reclassified need to be behaviorally ambiguous, but not too ambiguous. In selecting the items, ambiguity was determined by presenting each item to a number of observers who were asked to name the mental state represented. An item was adopted if it had two or more names attached to it. But items with four or more meanings attributed to it were discarded as being too general. Another requirement was that the selected items could not be readily classified on some other content basis, figural in the case of pictures and semantic in the case of statements.

In Alternate Expressional Groups, sets of eight line drawings are given, involving the face, hands, feet, or whole body. From each set, E is to form as many class groups as he can, each having at least three expressions in it, and each group representing a different class. He does not need to explain his basis for the group.

Alternate Face Groupings is the same kind of test as Alternate Expressional Groups except that the elements to be grouped are photographs of faces, again eight to a set. Some sets are all of one sex, and some are mixed as to sex.

Multiple Behavioral Grouping presents sets of eight statements, each very brief and emotionally loaded. E is to form as many classes as he can, regrouping the items in different ways. In the following sample problem, six statements are given:

1. You get out of here
2. Are you sure
3. What a bore
4. How could you do such a thing
5. Didn't you listen to me
6. I wonder what time it is

One group here could be a combination of 1, 3, and 4, indicating a negative attitude, even rejection. Another possible group is 2, 4, and 5, indicating a common questioning state of mind. It will be noted that all punctuation marks were omitted, in order to confine the cues to what is said.

Divergent Production of Behavioral Relations (DBR) In the study of behavioral-cognition abilities (Report 34), it was found that some successful relations tests dealt with relations between pairs of individuals who are showing certain expressions. They are interacting, and the expression of one derives its meaning in part from the expression of the other. One might be reprimanding the other; one might be trying to persuade the other; or one might be thinking the other is a bore but be politely listening. Such connections are behavioral relations, as the earlier results indicate. One successful relations test dealt not with connections between pairs of people, but with pairs of expressions that could have been from the same person.

In each problem of the DBR test, Alternate Facial Relations, eight photographed faces are given, each with its unique expression. The faces are all of the same person, one male and one female in two problems, and of two persons, male and female, in the third. With each set of photographs a statement is given, which E may apply to any selected face, and to others in turn. The statement might be "Wait; that's not what I really meant." E is to choose different pairs of faces so that the first is making the statement to the other. If he chooses faces B and D, B is making the statement to D; if he chooses G and B, G is making the statement to B. In each choice, the comment has a different behavioral significance or meaning, depending upon the two expressions.

Forming Alternate Faces employs a novel technique. E can form a sketched face by combining a given upper half with a selected lower half. On each page of the test, 12 lower halves are presented, each with a different expression of mouth, lower nostrils, and chin. A slip of paper that can be detached from the test booklet contains upper halves of three faces, including eyes and brow in different expressions. E is to choose different combinations to complete different faces, each of which he thinks fits a situation that is described. For example, if he is told that "Ted has just received some bad news," E then finds as many combinations (full faces) as he can that go reasonably with that situation.

This test was originally written for DBU, with the thought that E is forming alternative units. In pretesting experiments, however, it insisted on correlating with DBR tests rather than DBU tests; hence the change in hypothesis. In rationalizing DBR for this test one might point out that the prescribed situations imply another person who is in relation to Ted. One statement reads "Ted has just been scolded by his teacher for being late," and another reads "Ted has just received a ticket for speeding." An implied second person is not always clear, however, as in the statement "Ted has just seen an accident," and another, "Ted has just found out that his wallet has been stolen." Another hypothesis for DBR as a component of the test might emphasize the relation between upper and lower parts of the faces that E produces.

Varied Emotional Relations presents in each problem nine sketches, each with its own expression. Most expressions are in faces, but a few are in hands, arms, and torso, or combinations of these parts. E is to deal with the same relation throughout the test—cause and effect. That is, he is to select pairs of expressions such that one expression, and the behavior that goes with it, in one of a pair of persons is the cause of behavior and its expression in the other person. In a sample item with three faces, one is a man who is whistling. Another is the face of a girl showing a coy expression. They could be paired in a common cause-and-effect affair. The third face is of a girl with upturned nose. She could be the "effect" member of another pair, snubbing his advance. The two girls could form a pair if E thinks of the coy girl telling the rejecting girl some unpleasant gossip.

A DBR test that calls for verbal responses instead of pairing pictured expressions is Creating Social Relations. Two people are shown in line drawings, with expressions that can suggest different relations between them. A sample item shows a woman from the waist up, with arm raised and finger pointing forward. The other person is a man, showing face and shoulders, with eyes raised toward the ceiling. E is to suggest alternative things the man is saying or thinking in this situation. He might write

"I couldn't help it."
"Will you ever stop talking?"
"I'll let you have the first round."

Divergent Production of Behavioral Systems (DBS)   A good example of a very complex behavioral system would be a psychological novel. On a much smaller scale, the production of short-story plots should also deal with DBS, provided interpersonal feelings and attitudes form critical connecting links in the pattern of the plot. This kind of task was used in more than one test for DBS.

In Creating Social Situations, the emotional states of three people are described, e.g., a fearful woman, an angry man, and a surprised child. E is to account for these dispositions by combining them into a short episode. The characters are to be reacting to one another rather than to anything or anyone outside of the group. With the three characters just mentioned, E might say that the child has brought home an unsatisfactory report card and is surprised at his father's violent reaction. The mother is afraid for the child's safety.

Writing Behavioral Stories is very much like the Thematic Apperception Test in its task and its mode of administration. E is presented with a pictured scene that shows three interacting persons, e.g., a young man and two young ladies, in different postures and expressions. *E* is asked, "How do the people feel or what are they thinking and why?" He is then to write a number of different stories. The number of different systems he can produce is his score.

Multiple Cartoon Fill-Ins presents the first and last panels of a three-part cartoon strip, with two or three persons involved in each scene. *E* is to tell verbally what happened between the two scenes in order to make different, complete stories. The cartoons are entirely in pantomime, which provides degrees of ambiguity for varied stories. In a sample problem, the first picture shows the man, Ferd'nand, sitting in a waiting room of a doctor or dentist. The nurse is motioning to another man to come to the inner office. In the last picture, Ferd'nand is under an office desk and the nurse is looking for him. *E* might write statements like the following to provide different completions:

> Ferd'nand thinks his ring rolled under the desk and he has gone after it.
> He has heard the other man yell with pain and is hiding.
> He is being playful with the nurse.

Divergent Production of Behavioral Transformations (DBT) The changes in any area of information can be a modification of a unit or system, and perhaps of any other kind of product. A change in interpretation of a particular expression would be a transformation of a behavioral unit. A change in a story plot would be a transformation of a system. The latter kind of change seemed easiest to put into test form.

Alternate Cartoon Completions presents in each problem two consecutive events in a cartoon strip, without a concluding frame. *E* is to suggest alternative conclusions so as to change the nature of the story each time. In the sample item, Ferd'nand is dressed as a scoutmaster and two Boy Scouts are helping an old lady across the screet. The boys then offer to help a pretty young woman across the street, but Ferd'nand holds up a prohibiting hand. What will the concluding episode be like? *E* is to give alternative completions, changing the nature of the story with respect to the feelings, thoughts, and attitudes of the participants. *E* might say

> He'll ask if the boys are bothering her.
> He'll try to make a date with her.
> The girl will say "Dad, where did you get those shorts?"

Multiple Expression Changes is also concerned with a succession of events. Three steps are stated, such as

1. A man trips a lady who is walking by.
2. She falls, and the man apologizes to her.
3. The lady then becomes angry.

From a page of 15 men's faces, each with a different expression, *E* is to select sets of three to go with the three stated events. In tripping the lady, the man might be surprised, amused, or sorry. When he apologizes to her, he might be either genuinely sorry, placating, or perfunctory. As she shows anger, he might show surprise, amusement, or vexation. It was expected that the changes in sets of reactions that E has to produce would provide measurement of the hypothesized ability DBT. We shall see that something went awry.

Alternate Line Meanings is a quite different kind of test. Its designing took into account the fact that some transformations are redefinitions, and in this test E is asked to produce some redefinitions. The given stimuli are simple lines with different forms, slants, and widths or degrees of heaviness. From somewhat ancient history (Guilford & Guilford, 1931) it was known that simple lines can be used to express human feelings and emotions in ways that were interpretable by many observers. This connection was utilized in the test Alternate Line Meanings. Given a light, slight, horizontal wave, most observers are likely to say that it represents gentle motion, tranquility, or relaxation. Given a heavy, zig-zag line sloping upward to the right, many observers agree that it indicates power or anger. In the test adapting such connections to an attempted assessment of DBT, E is to give as many different behavioral interpretations of each line as he can. By giving new meanings to replace others, it is assumed that E is producing transformations. Since he is restricted to psychological dispositions, he is redefining behavioral units.

In Multiple Story Plots, E is thought to be changing systems. In each problem, E is given verbally the beginning of a story plot; e.g.,

> Two sisters, A and B, are romantically interested in the same young man. One day he comes to their house unexpectedly.

E is to take the story from there, and to make each completion different. E might give such completions as

> A tells C that B does not want to see him. Instead of discouraging him, this makes C all the more interested in B.
> A and B praise each other to C, who becomes more confused than ever about which one he likes better.

The difference between this test and a systems test for DBS is a subtle one. It remained to be seen whether it would show relation to DBS.

Divergent Production of Behavioral Implications (DBI) The difference between seeing implications as in ability CBI and producing implications as in the case of DBI is a small but important one. It is true that some tests, for semantic implications, for example, show relations in both directions, cognition and divergent production. The difference seems to be in how far afield E must go in order to suggest implied information. The first one or two implied responses may simply mean seeing implications that are already available in the memory store, connected in memory with the given information. In divergent production, at least, there is some degree of inventiveness in most produced responses, some *transfer* recall.

The test Suggested Feelings and Actions is perhaps the clearest example of what DBI means. That is, it satisfies clearly the definition for that ability. This test presents to E a description of a situation and asks him to suggest a number of different feelings that the situation might be expected to arouse and along with each feeling some action that might be expected. The giving of implied actions runs a chance of getting over toward semantic ability DMT, however.

In other content areas, the DXI abilities are often referred to as "elaborative." Elaborations are extra additions to what is already there, and they are suggested as implications from that source. One test for DBI was named in "Behavioral Elaborations," Each part of this test asks E to say what a person would be likely to do if another person in his presence does something referring to him. For example, it asks the question

If a person A winks at person B, what will B do?

E is to offer a number of suggested actions, such as

Become embarassed, and blush.
Pretend he did not see the wink.
Wink back.

It is expected that the multiple responses that E gives will rapidly get beyond his most ready implications, and hence beyond cognition.

The test Multiple Social Problems is in the category known as "sensitivity to problems." In order to provide E with well-known problem situations, each one asks a question like

What personal problems can a BROTHER and SISTER have with each other?

Other questions pair other members of the family, also a boy and his girl friend. Each problem is implied by known aspirations, interactions, conflicts, and other kinds of events involving two people of familiar status and relationship.

In Alternate Social Solutions, E is to suggest solutions to problems, each alternative solution being implied by the problem and its interpretation. The problems are social ones, involving interacting persons. E does not have to choose any one solution or defend any of them; he is to indulge in free output of behavioral ideas. In a sample problem, E is to imagine that he is on a weekend trip with others. The others all want to go hunting, but E prefers to go fishing. What different tactics or solutions can E think of? He might suggest

Flip a coin to decide the matter.
Promise to go hunting tomorrow if they go fishing today.
Let the majority vote decide the matter.

Reference Factors and Their Tests

Abilities outside the DBX list were to be represented by reference factors and their tests. Three of them were CBX abilities (CBU, CBR, and CBS) and four were DMX abilities (DMU, DMC, DMT, and DMI). Tests were added for CMU, which served to represent verbal IQ. There was special interest in relating the new abilities to IQ. Results from the CBX tests are reported in Table 9.2, and those from the DMX tests in Table 6.2.

Results of the Targeted Rotations

The major hypothesis regarding six distinct abilities for divergent production of behavioral information was amply supported. Six such abilities were represented by orthogonal factors, with 19 of the 22 tests designed for those abilities appearing loaded significantly on the factors for which they were intended. In only two instances were loadings higher on other factors in the list of six.

Multiple Expression Changes was designed for DBT but went instead on DBR. After the fact, it does indeed appear that the items of this test, each involving two persons, call for producing successions of relations between the two. The change in the pattern of the story could have been lost because of E's analytical attention to particular events in the story.

Multiple Cartoon Fill-Ins was designed for DBS but came out on DBT. The successful tests for DBS require E to invent his own story framework, a behavioral system. In Multiple Cartoon Fill-Ins E has only to complete a story, the framework of which is largely already given by the first and final cartoon panels of a cartoon strip. He changes only one event in the sequence of events; hence the emphasis is upon transformation.

The six DBX abilities are essentially unrelated to the traditional verbal IQ, as indicated by the fact that their tests had no significant loadings on the factor for CMU, the dominant component of verbal-IQ tests. They are also distinct from behavioral-cognition abilities, as shown by the fact that no CBX tests were significantly loaded on DBX factors and no DBX tests were significantly loaded on CBX factors, of which three were represented.

The DBX abilities are distinct from semantic-divergent-production abilities, in spite of the fact that two DBX tests had significant loadings on DMX factors and four DMX score variables had significant loadings on two DBX factors. These strayings of tests can be logically accounted for. For example, the two scores from Plot Titles (clever and nonclever, for DMT and DMU, respectively) had second loadings, both on DBI. Consideration of the stories given in Plot Titles shows that behavioral information is involved. The stories are about interactions of persons. Titles should, of course, reflect this content. The story titles are implied by the stories; thus behavioral implications are being produced in multiple responses. In another example of straying tests, the two scores from Consequences (obvious and remote, primarily for DMU and DMT, respectively) had second loadings on DBT. Examinations of the items in Consequences show that some of those items pertain to behavioral matters, such as social changes. Involving changes in ways of living, the responses might well reflect behavioral transformations. And changing ways of living apparently involve transformations, whether each one is remote or obvious, as suggested by the DBT variances in both scores.

CURRENT STATUS OF KNOWLEDGE OF SOCIAL INTELLIGENCE

With the successful demonstrations of the six behavioral-cognition and six behavioral-divergent-production abilities, there is considerable encouragement to make similar investigations of behavioral abilities in the other three operation areas—memory, convergent production, and evaluation. Of the 22 abilities of the SI model that have as yet not been demonstrated, 18 are behavioral. The production of behavioral-memory tests would seem to offer no novel problems. The comparison and judging of items of behavioral information according to logical criteria would seem to be quite possible to represent by means of evaluation tests. Logic-tight deductive operations with behavioral information in the form of convergent-production activities seem at first to be rather challenging. The area of life where such activities may be exercised is that of legal matters, in the reaching of conclusions regarding responsibility and guilt. Such a reference makes more plausible the idea of investigating behavioral-convergent-production abilities.

The intellectualizing of a large part of behavior concerned with understanding and dealing with people does not promise full knowledge of the economy of social behavior, but it should make this aspect of living more meaningful and lead to new technologies. Limitations should also be recognized. Having understanding of the behavior of others and being able to generate varied ideas in solving interpersonal problems still leaves us with the need for habits and skills for putting behavioral ideas into effect. For the latter step, Guilford has hypothesized a family of executive functions, which also means a family of executive abilities and skills (see Report 42; also Guilford, 1967). But the same limitation applies in other content areas as well, when overt outcomes are called for; behavioral information is not unique in this respect.

TEN

SOME EXTRA-INTELLECTUAL-APTITUDE RELATIONSHIPS

The contents of this chapter are somewhat heterogeneous, but they are concerned with only two general problems. One concerns the validation of factor-test scores for the prediction of academic or academic-type criteria of achievement. Answers to such problems also provide some information concerning the general relevance or construct validity of the intellectual-aptitude concepts. The other general problem concerns possible relationships between intellectual-aptitude traits and nonaptitude personality traits—traits of temperament and motivation. The latter problem has more general interest in view of psychoanalytically inspired theory to the effect that intellectual abilities develop as a consequence of other innate personality dispositions (Hayes, 1962).

Some of the validation studies employed course grades as criteria (Reports 13, 15, and 31); one used ratings of achievement, also (Report 15); one used systematically designed achievement examinations (Report 31); and two used measures of amount learned in particular learning tasks (Reports 39 and 41). Another validation study employed ratings of expected performance in military assignments (Report 21). Still another used both global and analytical ratings by teachers of creative aspects of children's performances in school (Report 28). In one study, professional people estimated the degree of relevance of described factorial abilities for success in their work (Report 25). Two studies dealt with correlations between factorial-ability scores and assessments of nonaptitude traits, with either inventory scores or ratings by observers as criteria (Reports 20 and 28).

Factor analyses were made of intellectual-ability-test scores in five of the studies (Reports 13, 21, 31, 39, and 41). The samples of examinees that were involved are described briefly in Table 10.1. The factor loadings resulting from the analyses have been presented for the most part in various factor-loading listings in the preceding chapters. One purpose for each factor analysis was to determine whether the tests represented their factors within the populations involved. In some cases a second objective was to push forward the exploration of the structure of intellect in new directions (Reports 39 and 41). In other cases there was the desire to obtain factor scores to replace test scores.

PREDICTIONS OF TEACHERS' RATINGS OF CREATIVITY

An aspect of one investigation by the ARP is considered to be in the category of a construct validation, involving correlations of factor-test scores with ratings by teachers (Report 28). This study was done with children at the seventh-grade level, and was confined to semantic-divergent-production abilities, all six of which were believed to be represented by tests. Another aspect of the investigation pertained to relations of divergent-production abilities to nonaptitude scores and ratings, on which something will be reported later in this chapter.

The Abilities and Their Tests

The six semantic-divergent-production abilities were represented by one test each, with the exceptions of DMU and DMT, for which there were two scores each. The abilities and their tests are listed in Table 10.2, with the most common

Table 10.1 Populations and Samples for Analyses involved in Studies with Validation Objectives

Report Number	Brief Title of the Analysis	N	Population
13	Coast Guard validation	178	Coast Guard cadets
15	Validity in higher mathematics	146	Advanced mathematics students
21	Marine officer validation	204	Marine officers
27	Construct validity for DP tests	443	Seventh-grade students
31	Ninth-grade-mathematics validation	428	Ninth-grade students
39	Abilities in concept learning	177	Grades 11 and 12
41	Transformation abilities	197	Gifted students, grades 10 through 12

name of the test as it was originally written for adults given first and the name of the children's form second. The children's forms contained the same items, but the instruction pages had been rewritten in order to adapt the tests better to the sixth-grade level (see Report 27). The subjects for this validation study were the same as had been utilized in the analysis of divergent-production abilities, as reported in the same reference. Eight of the tests were administered again a year later, near the beginning of the school year, to seventh graders. It is not known how well tests repeated a year later still represented their SI abilities for a factor analysis could not be repeated with a greatly curtailed battery.

The Rating Variables

Teachers were asked to rate each student on 13 different defined traits, six of them being somewhat in line with SI abilities and the remaining ones designed for nonaptitude traits, which are irrelevant here. The two kinds were mixed in the rating system, and the teacher was asked to rate all the students in her room on each trait before going on to the next. A 3-inch vertical-graphic scale was provided, with a definition of the trait, usually with some elaboration. The aptitude traits included:

Creativity: "The ability, interest, and personality needed to produce many different inventive and original ideas, as well as the ability to shift from one task to another." (This was obviously an attempt to obtain a global assessment of a composite of abilities entering into creative performance.)

Recognition of implications: "The degree to which the student can recognize many relevant details of a situation or action." (This variable might pertain to ability CMI or possibly DMI.)

Spontaneous flexibility: "The degree to which the student typically shifts his mode of response or method of approach to a problem."

Adaptive flexibility: "The degree to which the student can shift from one method of approach to another, when the shift is made necessary because the original method *does not work*."

Table 10.2 Abilities and the Tests That Represented Them in the Construct-validity Study at the Seventh-grade Level

SI Ability	Common Title	Title for Children
DMU_1	Plot Titles (nonclever)	Names for Stories (nonclever)
DMU_2	Consequences (obvious)	What Would Happen (obvious)
DMC	Alternate Uses	Different Uses
DMR	Associational Fluency	Similar Words
DMS	Expressional Fluency	Four Word Sentences
DMT_1	Plot Titles (clever)	Names for Stories (clever)
DMT_2	Consequences (remote)	What Would Happen (remote)
DMI	Planning Elaboration	Make a Plan

Originality: "The degree to which the student can produce clever, unusual, or 'inventive' ideas."

Fluency: "The degree to which the student can produce *many* ideas."

It can be noted how the definitions deviate from those that have been given after full recognition of each ability's location in the SI model was achieved. The last two variables may be associated with abilities DMT and DMU, respectively, but the two traits of flexibility seem too similar, and both probably miss their marks, which should presumably have been DMC and DFT, respectively.

In spite of detailed training of the raters, the intercorrelations of the ratings of the six aptitude variables listed above were of about the same order of magnitude as the reliability coefficients. The raters were the homeroom teachers of the students and the nonhomeroom teachers, who saw less of the students but saw them in their classes. The estimates of reliability were obtained from correlations between ratings given in the fall and again in the spring. Ratings for boys were kept separate from those for girls. Also, ratings from homeroom teachers were kept separate from those from other teachers. For the six apti-

Table 10.3 Correlations of Divergent-production-test Scores and CTMM IQ with Ratings of Creativity by Teachers and with IQ*

Predictor	Homeroom Teacher Rating		Nonhomeroom Teaching Rating		CTMM IQ	
	Boys	Girls	Boys	Girls	Boys	Girls
DMU_1	.04	−.03	−.03	−.04	−.12	−.15
DMU_2	.21	.25	.03	.23	.12	.22
DMC	.29	.40	.06	.33	.30	.46
DMR	.33	.41	.23	.24	.35	.44
DMS	.23	.31	.21	.19	.42	.30
DMT_1	.31	.42	.12	.23	.31	.44
DMT_2	.21	.26	.20	.26	.28	.31
DMI	.31	.40	.07	.29	.25	.37
IQ	.38	.48	.30	.46	1.00	1.00
DPC	.47	.53	.32	.41	−	−
AC + TC	.56	.61	.40	.54	−	−
$(AC + TC)_c$	.50	.56	.29	.48	−	−

*The last three rows contain multiple correlations, for composites with optimal weights for predictors. The first eight rows are for single-test representatives of divergent-production abilities. Code to predictors: DMU_1—Plot Titles (nonclever); DMU_2—Consequences (obvious); DMC—Alternate Uses; DMR—Associational Fluency; DMS—Expressional Fluency; DMT_1—Plot Titles (clever); DMT_2—Consequences (remote); DMI—Planning Elaboration; DPC—divergent-production composite; AC—an aptitude composite, including DPC plus IQ; AC + TC—aptitude composite plus trait composite; $(AC + TC)_c$—same as AC + TC with multiple Rs corrected for number of predictors. CTMM—California Test of Mental Maturity.

tude-rating variables, the median reliability estimates ranged from .61 to .74, with a mean of .67. The median intercorrelations of the six aptitude-rating variables ranged from .58 to .73 in the same four groups, also with a mean of .67. It is clear that there was very little discrimination among the rating variables. We should expect correlations of these criterion variables with predictor variables to be just about the same for all predictors within the universe of the abilities concerned.

Intercorrelations between Predictors and Criterion Variables

Since the rating-criterion variables are more or less interchangeable, only the correlations between the global variable of "creativity" will be considered here, with selected correlations reported in Table 10.3. The predictor variables are indicated by symbols, which are explained below the table. In addition to the eight divergent-production tests, representing the six semantic-divergent-production abilities, the CTMM IQ, which was obtained from the school records, and certain composite predictors are included. The sample sizes were 227 for the boys and 216 for the girls, so that coefficients of .13 and .18 may be considered significantly different from zero at the .05 and .01 levels, respectively. For the composite predictors, the coefficients are multiple Rs and the contributing predictors were differentially weighted in multiple-regression equations.

Some generalizations seem permissible, arising from the data in Table 10.3. With the exception of one of the tests for DMU (Plot Titles—nonclever), all tests correlated significantly with the criterion when ratings were obtained from homeroom teachers. There were four additional exceptions when ratings were obtained from the nonhomeroom teachers. On the whole, the ratings for "creativity" appear to be related to all the divergent-production predictors except for DMU, for which the outcome was in doubt, since one test for DMU (Consequences—obvious) did show relations in three cases out of four, but one test did not. In this particular group of subjects, the two tests that usually represent DMU were apparently factorially different.

In general, predictions of the rating criterion were slightly higher for girls than for boys, and slightly higher for homeroom raters than nonhomeroom raters. Some of the validity coefficients for single tests were of the same order of magnitude as for IQ. With one exception in the four groups, the DP aptitude composite (DPC) correlated slightly higher with the criterion than did IQ. The coefficients in the last two columns present correlations between the tests and IQ, showing that there was apparently some basis for teachers to rate students on creativity in the direction of their IQs. Correlations between teachers' ratings of the six aptitude traits and IQ are of a similar order of magnitude—from .30 to .40.

The failure of the teachers to discriminate among the rating variables can be excused to some extent by the fact that the tests representing the factors also intercorrelate positively up to .51 for the boys, with a median of .28, and up to .55 for the girls, with a median of .40. Correlations among such tests ranged somewhat lower when the same subjects were given the much larger battery for factor analysis in the preceding year (Report 27.) There is no known basis for blaming the higher intercorrelations upon the condition of retesting.

PREDICTIONS OF GRADES IN THE U.S. COAST GUARD ACADEMY
The Predictors

The original factor analysis (Report 13)[1] was based upon a battery that included 20 ARP marker tests, 9 score variables from the Academy's aptitude battery, and grades in 9 of the Academy's courses. The intercorrelations of many of the grade variables were so high that two strong uninterpretable achievement factors emerged, to confuse the picture. With the coming of the SI model, it was realized that a number of SI abilities were underrepresented. A reanalysis that included rotations toward SI-ability targets was based upon a smaller battery that included only 4 of the Academy's aptitude-score variables in addition to the 20 ARP tests. The result was in the form of 16 SI factors, 7 of which were singlets. The best tests representing these abilities are the predictors for the report in this chapter.

The tests for some of the various factors are named in Table 10.4. Only nine factors are represented there, for no factor was listed if none of its tests had at least one significant correlation with a course grade. With an N of 110 (the number for whom data were complete), an r of .20 is significant at the .05 level, and one of .25 is significant at the .01 level. The numbers of significant rs for the two levels of significance well exceed the numbers to be expected from chance. The factors whose tests had no significant correlations with grades were for abilities CSI, CMI, CMT, DMI, NSI, NMR, and NMS. The only striking aspect of this list is that all four abilities involving implications appear to be unrelated to grades in all 10 courses. This suggests that grading in these courses did not rest upon data that show what the students could do by way of seeing or producing implications. Abilities involving relations or transformations seem to have some significant correlations with grades (see Table 10.4). Of the nine abilities in the significant category, two involve relations and three involve transformations. Two appear to involve units, but this conclusion will be modified later.

Visualization (CFT) appears to be involved in three of the course grades most strongly for Engineering Drawing and Descriptive Geometry (r = .41), where one should most expect it. Its minor variance in Physics grades is understandable, but its minor appearance in Foundations of the Modern World, a course in history, is not, unless there was much graphic conceptualizing connected with the course and its examinations.

Of the two tests most strongly loaded on CMU, Vocabulary Completion had no significant correlations, while Reading Comprehension had seven. It is surprising that word knowledge was not a rather consistent source of variance in a number of courses, as it so often is. Furthermore, the strongest component of a reading-comprehension test is usually CMU. From the disparate predictive performance of these two CMU tests, it must be concluded that it is some other factorial component in Reading Comprehension that makes the difference. The next strongest component of a reading-comprehension test is commonly the factor for CMS. If that is true in this case, it would appear that the Academy's courses and examinations emphasized less the learning of isolated concepts (units) and more the understanding of organizing rules or principles (systems).

---

[1] See also Kettner, Guilford, & Christensen (1959).

Table 10.4 Correlations between Selected Factor Tests and Grades in Courses at the U.S. Coast Guard Academy*

Factor	Tests	Algebra and Plane Geometry	Analytical Geometry	Celestial Navigation	Communications	Engineering Drawing and Descriptive Geometry	English Composition and Speech	Foundations of the Modern World	Geography	Nautical Astronomy	Physics I and II
CFT	Aptitude–Spatial	12	11	-05	00	41‡	04	-24†	-10	-03	20†
CMU	Vocabulary Completion	-06	-02	11	11	07	15	05	01	19	06
CMU+	Reading Comprehension	19	23‡	22†	-01	04	34‡	33‡	26‡	21†	21‡
CMR	Aptitude–Verbal Analogies	08	01	06	01	-05	28‡	15	10	17	04
CMR	Aptitude–Verbal Opposites	11	09	13	08	-01	40‡	19	10	18	09
DFT	Match Problems	-09	15	22†	16	22†	14	09	04	18	23‡
DMU	Brick Uses (fluency)	00	01	00	11	04	25‡	21†	14	-05	-03
DMU	Plot Titles (nonclever)	16	11	07	16	03	12	13	12	03	12
DMC	Alternative Uses	-02	-06	04	09	00	06	21†	17	-01	06
DMR	Associational Fluency	-05	00	-01	04	03	26‡	31‡	23‡	00	04
DMT	Plot Titles (clever)	00	15	18	13	13	22†	30‡	20†	16	11
NSR	Correlate Completion II	18	08	23‡	05	08	26‡	-05	-06	06	08
NSR+	Correlate Completion	12	11	21†	08	08	18	11	08	20†	14
NMU	Verbal-relations Completion	12	10	09	-07	-04	24†	14	11	25‡	16
NMR	Associations IV	-04	-03	16	08	00	14	32‡	16	10	03

*Decimal points omitted.
†Significant at the .05 level.
‡Significant at the .01 level.

Ability CMR has significant correlations only with English Composition and Speech, both tests telling the same story in this respect. There were near-significant correlations for Nautical Astronomy and Foundations of the Modern World. Although the low correlations generally throughout, even when significant, do not promise much in the way of prediction of grades from single tests, they do suggest some genuine factorial components in the grades and some hope of practically useful *multiple* predictions, where two or more factors show significant relations with the same grade variable. Multiple correlations were not computed in this investigation. One of the objectives was to look for relevant factors that might have been missed in the Academy's aptitude battery.

Match Problems, representing ability DFT, a figural ability, had three significant correlations in courses where they might have been expected—Celestial Navigation, Engineering Drawing and Descriptive Geometry, and Physics. In writing their examinations, it must have paid the students to produce figural transformations, such as movements and shifts in patterns, and also to try out different alternative solutions to problems.

The two tests representing ideational fluency (DMU) did not agree very well as to correlations with grades. Brick Uses (fluency) had two significant correlations, with English Composition and Speech and Foundations of the Modern World, whereas Plot Titles (nonclever) did not. Of all the courses that involving writing and speech would seem to offer the greatest opportunities for divergent production, a creative activity. Opportunities in a course in history should depend upon the manner in which it is taught and the kind of examinations.

Of the two tests for DMR and NMR, Associational Fluency was significantly related to English Composition and Speech as well as to the history course, confirming the hypothesis of roles for divergent-production activity in those two courses, with some involvement also in Geography. The other test, Associations IV, shows some relation to only one of these courses—Foundations of the Modern World. This test's lower correlations with grades suggests a smaller role for a convergent-production ability as compared with a parallel divergent ability.

Another divergent-production ability—originality (DMT)—showed significant relations with the same three courses as for Associational Fluency, for its one strong test of Plot Titles (clever). Its much weaker test, Alternate Uses, had one significant correlation, and that was the history course. Thus, it can be hypothesized that of all the courses, that pertaining to history provided the most opportunity for divergent thinking and may have rewarded that kind of thinking. It could have been a problem-oriented course.

Two tests for NSR, which were very similar in nature, had relatively high correlations with two courses—Celestial Navigation and English—with the second test showing some relation also to Nautical Astronomy. It is of interest that, by reference to navigation, at least, two of these courses had similar content. Correlate Completion II was composed only of symbolic items, whereas Correlate Completion contained semantic items also. This difference could provide some basis for expecting differences in those tests' correlations with grades.

The one test for NMU, Verbal-relations Completion, had significant correlations with two courses, English and Nautical Astronomy. The results associated with abilities NSR, NMU, and NMR indicate that convergent production was of some small consequence in three of the courses. Convergent production abilities must have been important in mathematics courses, but such abilities were not well represented by tests, so this possibility could not be well tested.

Looking at Table 10.4 from the standpoint of its columns, which show the abilities that have some relevance for certain courses, we see that grades in the English course were most predictable, with seven abilities possibly contributing to variances in the grades. A multiple R could be of substantial size for that course. Next most predictable were grades in Foundations of the Modern World, with five abilities involved. Least predictable would be grades in Algebra and Plane Geometry and Communications. This strongly suggests that SI abilities outside the list of 16 represented in this study should be investigated in those connections, for the grades must have had some degree of reliability, and much of the true variance must be in the intellectual domain.

As to the general satisfaction with predictions from the Academy's aptitude battery, the four tests represented in Table 10.4 (including Reading Comprehension) all show at least one significant correlation with course grades. About as much can be said for the other four aptitude tests not represented here (the ninth test being a nonaptitude measure). Three of the other four were heavily weighted with mathematical items and consequently cover some courses that were poorly covered by the four tests of Table 10.4. It is very unlikely that any of the aptitude tests represented the four divergent-production abilities of Table 10.4; hence, for some courses, there could be significant gains in prediction by adding to the battery some tests from that category of abilities. Whether the convergent-production factors for NSR, NMU, and NMR are represented in the Academy's battery is an open question.

On the whole, it can be seen that the various courses at the Academy, at the time this study was made, were factorially complex and were related to quite different patterns of SI abilities. The prospect for a high degree of prediction of grades in each of the courses would be greatest when the right combination of properly weighted scores is used. Much space was devoted to the account of the validity coefficients and to speculations about the courses, in order to lend support to this general principle. How the predicted grades should be combined in order to obtain an overall prediction of academic success in the Coast Guard Academy is another problem, but not very difficult to solve in a practical manner.

A quite different achievement criterion for the Academy cadets came from a summer cruise in which they took part. The "cruise rating" was obviously quite complex. First, it was a combination of an "adaptability" score and a "preference" score. The former was a composite of five rating variables that emphasized conformance to military and professional customs and rules. The latter was based upon how much each man's superiors (officers and upperclassmen) would like to have him in their command. In spite of the emphasis upon conformity, in the factor analysis, the only significant loading was .32 on ideational fluency. This would suggest that the man's exhibition of imagination contributed to impressions he made on superiors, even though they may have rated conformity.

PREDICTING ACHIEVEMENT IN HIGHER-MATHEMATICS COURSES
The second academic-validation study was confined entirely to mathematics courses at the upper-division and graduate levels in three institutions of higher learning in the Los Angeles area (Report 15).[2] Most of the criterion variables were indicators of achievement in different levels of calculus.

The Subjects
Altogether, 148 subjects were involved, most of whom were volunteers; hence motivation could be considered to be generally dependable. It was determined that as a group the volunteer subjects did not differ significantly in relevant respects, such as college-entrance scores, from those who did not take part in the experiment. The numbers coming from the three institutions were 56, 22, and 70. Thirty-two were enrolled for mathematics majors, 16 for physics majors, and 100 for engineering curricula.

The Abilities and Their Tests
This study was initiated in the early days of the ARP history, when only a small number of factors of intelligence had been found. Five of the selected SI abilities included were previously known, and four were new. Selection of the abilities to be included was made in consultations with teachers of the mathematics courses involved, except that they could not see relevance for the factor for numerical facility (now recognized as representing a combination of MSI and NSI) in their advanced courses. Had abilities MSI and NSI been explained to them, their decisions might have been very different. Ability CMU was also given low status by the instructors, but it is such a dominant component of academic-aptitude tests that the investigator was interested in seeing how much it might be related to learning in higher mathematics.

The selected abilities and their tests were:

Spatial orientation (CFS): Spatial Orientation (Part V of the Guilford-Zimmerman Aptitude Survey, or GZAS)
Spatial visualization (CFT): Spatial Visualization (Part VI of the GZAS)
Seeing symbolic patterns (CSS): Circle Reasoning
Verbal comprehension (CMU): Vocabulary
General reasoning (CMS): Ship Destination
Numerical facility (MSI-NSI): Numerical Operations (Part III of the GZAS)
Adaptive flexibility (DFT): Match Problems
Originality (DMT): Plot Titles (clever)
Logical evaluation (EMI-EMR): Syllogisms I

In scoring the tests, attention was given to signs of malingering on the part of these higher-level students. Only in the Vocabulary and Numerical Operations

---
[2] See also Hills (1957).

Table 10.5 Predictive-validity Coefficients Relating SI-ability Tests to Criteria of Achievement in Higher-mathematics Courses

Institution	Curriculum	Criterion	N	CFS, Spatial Orientation	CFT, Spatial Visualization	CSS, Circle Reasoning	CMU, Vocabulary	CMS, Ship Destination	MSI-NSI, Numerical Operations	DFT, Match Problems	DMT, Plot Titles	EMI-EMR, Syllogisms I
A	P & E[a]	Grades in calculus I[b]	33–40	.26	.34[d]	.11	.28	.00	.27	.39[d]	−.07	.14
A	P & E	Grades in calculus II	34–41	.38[d]	.31[d]	.14	.05	.07	.18	.54[e]	−.14	.04
A	P	Grades in adv. cal.	11–12	.17	.44	.38	.03	−.05	.27	.56	−.46	.42
C	E	Grades in calculus	55	.24	.14	−.19	−.03	−.09	.19	−.08	−.02	.25
B	M	MGPA	19–21	.02	.28	.17	—[c]	−.09	—	.05	−.10	.38
C	E	Achievement test	71	.26[d]	.06	−.04	.17	.20	.03	−.10	.06	.39[e]
A	P	Ratings	13–16	.22	.34	.05	−.26	−.16	.11	.68[e]	−.33	.20
A	E	Ratings	20–22	.35	.16	.23	.11	.23	.39	.33	−.20	.14
B	M	Ratings	17–19	.68[e]	.36	.20	—	.29	—	.30	.20	.72[e]

[a] P—physics major; E—engineering curriculum; M—mathematics major.
[b] First year of calculus.
[c] Test scores not used because of signs of malingering.
[d] Significant at .05 level.
[e] Significant at .01 level.

tests, in two small groups, were signs of malingering sufficient to reject the results for use in the study.

The Criteria

The criteria of achievement were of three kinds—grades, proficiency examinations, and ratings given by instructors. Some grade criteria were restricted to first-year calculus, second-year calculus, and advanced calculus, while others were averages of grades in selected higher-mathematics courses (denoted by MGPA in Table 10.5). Ratings were obtained in smaller classes, usually at the graduate level. Physics and engineering students were rated on their ability to handle the mathematics in connection with their fields of work. Mathematics majors were rated on their promise for completing graduate work satisfactorily and for research in mathematics. The proficiency examination at one engineering school covered analytical geometry, calculus, and use of the slide rule.

Indications of Validity

Since the aptitude tests were administered usually in the same year in which the criterion information was obtained, both concurrent and predictive validity coefficients were involved. In the resulting coefficients reported here (Table 10.5), data from the three institutions were kept separate, as were data from different kinds of criteria. In two exceptional instances data from physics and engineering students were combined, because the former group was quite small.

After the SI theory was generated, hindsight showed that the greater possibilities for predicting achievement in mathematics beyond arithmetic should be found among tests for symbolic abilities, as the next study to be discussed will show. Only two tests in the study under discussion were in the symbolic category. This generalization still stands, even after noting in Table 10.5 that those two tests had no significant correlations. The nonrelevance of the MSI-NSI combination had been predicted by the mathematics instructors.

It may or may not be significant that the higher coefficients in Table 10.5 appear in connection with groups of engineering students, apart from the fact of larger samples in those groups. The complete lack of relevance for CSS is somewhat of a surprise, probably to mathematicians as well as to psychologists. Grasping or comprehending mathematical expressions must be important. One possible reason for no significant correlations for Circle Reasoning may be that this test was much too easy for these mathematics students. It can also be said that its loading for CSS has sometimes been low, even in groups with little mathematical sophistication. A more difficult test for CSS might show that this ability is, indeed, relevant for students in higher mathematics.

The two well-known spatial abilities show relevance in two or more groups. This finding seems to be somewhat dependent upon the institution and the kind of criterion, but this point needs further investigation. The third visual-figural test, Match Problems, shows even stronger degrees of validity, but this is restricted to one institution. It is interesting that although this test, which indicates a type of flexibility with respect to visual patterns, has some signs of validity, the corresponding semantic ability, DMT, seems entirely irrelevant, with even an excess of negative coefficients. If the latter finding is at all meaningful, it suggests that being flexible with respect to semantic information is more of a handicap than an asset in learning higher mathematics. We have no information with respect to the value of being flexible in dealing with symbolic information, for no test represented DST. This ability should be of great importance for being fluent and flexible in producing symbolic mathematical ideas.

It was no surprise to find that a test for CMU alone showed no relevance in any group, since the verbal score in academic-aptitude tests is not noted for predictive power in mathematics courses. It was somewhat surprising, however, to find that the CMS test, Ship Destination, had no significant validity coefficients. It does relate strongly to arithmetical-achievement tests that are composed of verbally stated problems. It may be that students in higher mathematics do not think in semantic terms, that they think only in figural and symbolic terms. In the algebra study to be reported next, it was found that CMS was losing out in relative importance in high school algebra, as compared with its relevance in higher arithmetic.

The one test in the evaluation category, Syllogisms I, showed strong and significant relations in two groups, one of engineers and one of mathematics students; and in one group with an achievement-test criterion and in another with a rating criterion. Representing both EMI and EMR, the test deals with semantic information. This suggests that, although students of higher mathematics may conceive of their problems in symbolic terms, as suggested above, they may resort to semantic thinking in evaluating results of their manipulations. We should also obtain information about the relevance of abilities ESR and ESI, and of abilities EFR and EFI, to make the exploration complete in terms of this portion of the SI model.

Some General Inferences

A positive suggestion from the data in Table 10.5 is that, somewhat commonly, among the SI abilities that are assets in achievement in higher mathematics are CFS, CFT, DFT, and either EMI or EMR, or both. The possibility for CSS as a relevant function should not be entirely rejected, in spite of the poor showing for that component as represented by Circle Reasoning. The drastic difference in coefficients in connection with different institutions and different criteria indicate that we cannot generalize very much from one situation to another, and that validation studies are needed in each situation. Furthermore, a much greater variety of abilities should be taken into account, particularly those pertaining to symbolic products of information. It may yet be possible to find quite high multiple-correlation indices of predictive validity in higher-mathematics courses.

VALIDATION OF SI ABILITIES IN NINTH-GRADE MATHEMATICS
Objectives of the Study

The major purpose of this study[3] was to determine the relationships of a number of the SI abilities that had been demonstrated by 1960 to achievement in ninth-grade algebra, and to determine how effective multivariate predictions of achievement could be. It was recognized that one of the greatest advantages

---
[3] See Report 31; also Guilford, Hoepfner, & Petersen (1965).

of using factor abilities in a multiple-regression equation is the broad coverage that this procedure provides in terms of psychological variables usually involved in a factorially complex criterion. Another advantage lies in the minimal correlations among components of the prediction equations, thus permitting maximal or near maximal multiple correlations for the number of predictors. Furthermore, there is much to be said for the rational basis provided by knowledge of relevant abilities in terms of a frame of reference like the SI model. The operations of the investigation serve as a pattern of the kind of validation study to be recommended, as far as it goes.

Conditions at the high school at which the experimental subjects were found provided the basis for some minor objectives. The school's curriculum provided four levels of mathematical instruction at the ninth-grade level, two levels of general mathematics and two of algebra. The lowest group of students in terms of general aptitude took a course known as "Basic Mathematics," which dealt with advanced arithmetic, equations, and a few algebraic concepts. The second-level course was called "Non-College Algebra," which went a bit further into elementary algebra. The lower algebra course was called simply "Regular Algebra," and the higher one was "Accelerated Algebra," which extended into the intermediate algebra. The validation study became a fourfold one, offering the possibilities of finding how the pattern of relevant abilities might change from one course to the other and how the abilities important for success in algebra may differ from those relevant for arithmetic. Since the school had the problem of guiding students into one course or another, it was decided to see whether measures of abilities would possibly discriminate between successful algebra students and successful general-mathematics students. This called for a discriminant-function analysis.

Another circumstance was that the school had administered three standard aptitude-test instruments to the students: the California Test of Mental Maturity (CTMM), the Differential Aptitude Test (DAT), and the Iowa Test of Basic Skills (Iowa), either at the end of the eighth year or at the beginning of the ninth. Since these tests sometimes serve as predictors of success in courses, including mathematics, there was the opportunity to observe how well such tests served the purpose as compared with composites of SI-ability scores.

Choice of the SI Abilities

Because it was highly impractical to include tests of all the known SI abilities (owing to limitations in testing time), in a kind of "shotgun" approach, there had to be considerable selection of abilities and their tests. Reports of four earlier investigations were studied for possibly relevant information (Weber, 1953; Kline, 1956; Werdelin, 1958; and Canisia, 1962). Although it was possible that among them these investigators collectively brought as many as 26 SI abilities into their studies, as indicated in their factor analyses, they did not find much evidence for validity for abilities other than the customary ones that dominate general academic-aptitude tests—CMU and CMS. The major source of selection for this study, then, was the knowledge of the nature of the SI abilities themselves, and their apparent logical relevance for mathematics at the levels under investigation.

First, it seemed that the most relevant content area is symbolic, since operations with numbers and letters are obvious in mathematics. This should be more true of algebra than of arithmetic. Of the product categories in the SI model, units and classes seemed most dispensable,[4] where choices had to be made. But relations, systems, transformations, and implications all seemed relevant, relations and implications being perhaps most relevant at the levels of mathematics investigated. All five of the operations categories seemed to be relevant. But within the complete set of 20 remaining symbolic abilities considered (five operations times four products), only 11 had been demonstrated and had factor tests available to measure them.

Of the 11 abilities, 8 were regarded as being of first importance: CSS, CSI, MSI, DSR, NSR, NSS, NST, and NSI. Two others for which there had been previous factor analyses—CSR and DSI—were also included, although evidence concerning how to test for them had been rather weak. At the time the mathematics-validation study was under way, tests were being developed for an analysis of symbolic-evaluation abilities, among which some tests appeared promising and their probable abilities seemed relevant: ESR, ESS, EST, and ESI. Tests for these abilities were brought into use late in the investigation. Some of them were later analyzed in other studies. Two nonsymbolic abilities chosen for attention were CMU and CMS, because they appear to be dominant components of academic-aptitude tests.

Since a number of the abilities involved had been demonstrated only at young-adult levels, it was regarded necessary to determine whether those abilities could be demonstrated at the ninth-grade level and whether all tests represented their expected factors adequately. This thinking called for new factor analyses for the tests used in this study. Analyses were applied to all the tests except the few new symbolic-evaluation tests just mentioned.

The Tests and Their Expected Factors

Since the tests are the referents for the SI abilities given attention in this study, brief descriptions are in order. More information on most of them will be found in Appendix B, with illustrative items. The tests are listed here in alphabetical order, and following each test name is the trigram for its expected factor. A single sentence may serve to characterize each test sufficiently for the reader's purposes here. It tells what the examinee must do in each test.

Factor Tests to Be Analyzed   Twenty-five tests for selected SI abilities were to be in the analysis:

1. Alternate Additions (DSR)—Show in different ways how numbers in a given set may be related (by numerical operations) in order to give a specified total value.
2. Best Trend Name (EMR)—Choose the word that best describes the order of four given words, the order involving a variable such as time.

---

[4] The "new" mathematics had not yet been introduced at this high school. The classes abilities should have some relevance in that connection.

3. Camouflaged Words (NST)—Find concealed within a meaningful sentence a group of consecutive letters that, in the given order, spells the name of a sport or game.
4. Circle Reasoning (CSS)—Discover the common principle by which one circle is blackened in each of four rows of mixed circles and dashes.
5. Correlate Completion II (NSR)—Supply a word that bears the same relation to the single word as the relation between words in two given pairs, the relation being based upon letter combinations rather than meanings of the words.
6. Form Reasoning (NSI)—From a table of equations involving geometric forms as symbols, solve some other equations involving the same forms.
7. Letter-Number (NSI)—Find the relations between letters and digits, and use each relation to find the number that corresponds to a new letter.
8. Letter Series (NSR)—Find the rule of order in a series of letters, then fill in a blank space with the letters that would fit the rule.
9. Letter Triangle (CSS)—With letters arranged systematically within a triangular pattern, which letter should appear in a marked, vacant place?
10. Matched Verbal Relations (EMR)—Choose one of four pairs of words that has the same relation as that of the given pair.
11. Necessary Facts (CMS)—Determine what information is needed to attain solutions for given arithmetical problems in which needed facts are missing.
12. Number Rules (DSR)—Starting with a given number, arrive in several different ways at a second given number, applying a single arithmetical operation at each step.
13. Numerical Operations (Guilford-Zimmerman Aptitude Survey, Part III) (MSI)—Apply simple indicated operations to numbers.
14. Picture Arrangement (NMS)—Given the four pictures from a cartoon strip in scrambled order, arrange them in correct temporal sequence.
15. Right Order Test (NSS)—Starting with one given number, do three given numerical operations in the right order to obtain a second specified number.
16. Seeing Trends II (CSR)—Describe a trend in a series of words, where a certain letter relation determines the trend.
17. Sentence Order (NMS)—Arrange three given sentences in a sensible sequence of events.
18. Ship Destination (CMS)—State how many miles a ship travels from one point to another, considering such variables as distance, direction, wind, current, and starting position.
19. Sign Changes (NSI)—Solve simple arithmetical equations, in which the operation signs are to be changed according to rules.
20. Symbol Grouping (CSI)—Rearrange scrambled symbols in a specified systematic order as efficiently as possible.

21. Word Changes (NSS)—Given a set of words, one designated as first and one as last, arrange the remaining words in proper sequence so that only one letter is changed in going from one to the next.
22. Word Linkage (EMR)—Choose from a list of three words the one that is related to the given words by virtue of two different meanings.
23. Word Patterns (CSI)—Arrange a list of short words efficiently in a kind of crossword-puzzle design.
24. Word Relations (CSR)—Recognize the same (spelling) relation between words in each of two pairs, then complete a third pair using the same relation.
25. Word Transformations (NST)—Regroup the letters of words in a phrase so as to make another phrase.

Parts of Standard Tests   Parts of some of the standard tests already administered to the subjects offered promise of representing certain SI abilities. Advantage was taken of this fact in adapting three of the following tests (26, 28, and 32) for this purpose (dominant SI abilities hypothesized are in parentheses):

26. CTMM Language MA (CMU)
27. CTMM Non-Language MA (MSI and CMU)
28. Iowa Reading Comprehension—Test R (CMU)
29. Iowa Arithmetic Concepts—Test A-1 (CMU and MSI)
30. Iowa Arithmetic Problem Solving—Test A-2 (MSI and CMS)
31. DAT—Verbal Reasoning (CMU, CMR, and NMR)
32. DAT Numerical Ability (MSI)
33. DAT Abstract Reasoning (CFR)
34. DAT Clerical Speed and Accuracy (ESU)

SI Tests Not Analyzed in This Study   Tests designed mostly for certain symbolic-evaluation abilities were:

38. Abbreviations (ESI)—Choose the word that the given unusual abbreviation most likely implies.
39. Condensations (EST)—Choose the better of the two shorthand alternatives, the choice being based on the unique meaning of the shorthand.
40. Letter-Number Scales (ESS)—Given the numerical values of two letters of the alphabet, estimate the numerical value of a third letter, from three alternatives, none of which may be exactly correct.
41. Limited Words (DSI)—Given two words, make up additional pairs of words using all the letters in the given pair rearranged, and no others.
42. Most Similar Sets (ESS)—Choose which of two letter-number sets is most like the given set.
43. Number Combinations (DSS)—Write several different equations using only the given numbers and given operations signs.
44. Sign Changes II (ESR)—Decide which sign changes are necessary to make a numerical expression into an equation.

The Criteria

Course grades earned in the four courses were used as one kind of criterion variable, but most dependence was placed on two specially prepared achievement tests, one for the general-mathematics courses and one for the algebra courses. The items of the achievement tests were selected so as to cover the specific objectives of the courses, as indicated by the teachers.

Procedures

Test Administration The 25 tests to be factor-analyzed were administered to approximately 600 students in the early fall of 1961. A small battery including tests 38 through 44 was administered in May, 1962, not long before the criterion tests were given.

The Factor Analysis The factor analysis included SI tests 1 through 25 and tests 26, 28, and 32 from the standard-scale lists, the latter in order to help identify abilities CMU and MSI. Two analyses were carried out, one for the general-mathematics groups combined and one for the algebra groups combined. Both sexes were included, after it had been determined that analyses in the two sex groups separately showed no notable sex differences in factor structure. The two groups for analysis by mathematics levels numbered 211 and 217, respectively. In each analysis, principal components were extracted and subjected to varimax rotations, followed by graphic rotations in order to improve fits to SI theory.

In addition to the objective verifying that the tests would function in measurement as had been expected, the intention was to obtain factor scores from the tests in order to reduce the number of predictor variables and to avoid linear restraints in multiple-regression analysis. Factor scores were obtained by the simplest of methods, by summing standard scores for tests loaded strongly on each factor. This procedure does not ensure minimal intercorrelations of factor scores, even though no test appeared in more than one composite for the same mathematics group. The maximum correlation between any pair of factor scores was .50. Tests representing the factors differed somewhat for the two mathematics groups, but there was at least one test in common to scores for the same factor in the two cases.

Multiple-regression Solutions Multiple-regression equations and multiple R's were computed for 56 different predictive equations, with the appropriate criterion as the dependent variable within each of the four course groups. The N's ranged from 73 to 101 in the four groups. Combinations from the independent variables (the predictors) included 13 factor scores, the 7 special SI-test scores (tests 38 to 44), 2 CTMM scores, 3 Iowa scores, and 4 selected DAT scores, and also a combination of all 9 standard-academic-aptitude scores.

In order to determine whether the SI-factor scores would add significantly to multiple predictions obtainable from the academic-aptitude scores alone, multiple regressions were constructed including the 13 factor scores and each of the three sets of academic-aptitude tests in turn, with F tests made to determine significance of increases in multiple R in each case.

A second set of multiple-regression treatments applied a stepwise computing program, which starts with the best single predictor, then adds the next best joint predictor in turn at each step, with an F test to determine whether the gain in prediction is significant. The process of adding predictors was stopped just before an F significant at the .10 level was exceeded. In this treatment, the two groups of predictors (20 SI variables and 9 academic predictors) were combined separately, with separate equations. Although the scores from academic predictors are usually combined by simple addition in academic practice, a more fair comparison with respect to potential for prediction is made by applying optimal weighting to those variables as well as to the SI variables. No cross-validations for the regression equations were made, because subdivisions of the samples would be too small relative to the number of predictors.

Table 10.6   Correlations of Factor-test Scores with Scores in Two Mathematical-achievement tests[1]

Factor	Test	Correlations with Scores	
		For General Mathematics	For Algebra
CSR	Word Relations	.32	.13
CSR	Seeing Trends II	.36	.20
CSS	Letter Series	.32	.30
CSS	Letter Triangle	.23	.18
CSI	Word Patterns	.27	.12
CSI	Symbol Grouping	.24	.31
CMU	CTMM Language MA	.42	.16
CMU	Iowa Reading Comprehension	.32	.18
CMS	Ship Destination	.27	.45
CMS	Necessary Facts	.35	.11
MSI-NSI	Numerical Operations (GZAS)	.39	.06
MSI+	DAT Numerical Ability	.63	.11
DSR	Alternate Additions	.40	.11
DSR	Number Rules	.43	.21
NSR	Correlate Completion II	.42	.33
NSR	Letter-Number	.12	.20
NSS	Word Changes	.20	.30
NST	Camouflaged Words	.23	.12
NST	Word Transformations	.31	.23
NSI	Sign Changes	.43	.10
NMS	Sentence Order	.29	.09
NMS	Picture Arrangement	.30	.08
EMR	Matched Verbal Relations	.29	.30
EMR	Best Trend Name	.29	.00

[*]Coefficients of .14 and .18 are significant at the .05 and .01 levels, respectively.

Discriminant Analysis In order to determine whether weighted combinations of tests could be used effectively to discriminate between successful general-mathematics students and successful algebra students, a discriminant-function analysis was applied. In this connection, the standard aptitude tests were not included, because they had been used in part to help sort the students into the various courses. "Successful" students in either case were those who made achievement-test scores above the median in the general-mathematics and algebra criterion tests, respectively. Original SI-test scores were used rather than factor scores, because the latter were standard scores (standardized within mathematics groups); hence the means would have been equated for the two groups to be discriminated. Thus, 25 SI-test scores were used in one discriminant analysis and 7 in the other.

Results

Correlations of SI Tests with the Criteria Evidence of predictive validity, such as we have seen in the studies previously mentioned, is offered in Table 10.6. Tests to represent their factors were selected because they did so in both mathematics groups in new targeted factor rotations of axes toward SI theory. Of the 24 correlations with the general-mathematics criterion, all but one were significant at the .01 level, and of their correlations with the algebra criterion, 12 were similarly significant. As we shall see from other evidence, predictability of the algebra criterion was much better for the Accelerated Algebra group than for the Regular Algebra group, a difference that is concealed by the data in Table 10.6, and a circumstance that reduces the correlations generally in the second column. Predictions of the general-mathematics criterion were about equally

Table 10.7 Loadings and Percentages of Variance Attributable to Factors in the Criterion-test Scores

Ability	General Mathematics		Algebra	
	Loading	Variance	Loading	Variance
CSR	.20	4	.04	0
CSS	.08	1	.25	6
CSI	.07	0	.18	3
CMU	.22	5	.09	1
CMR	−.21	4	−.12	1
CMS	.14	2	.14	2
MSI	.35	12	−.10	1
DSR	.40	16	−.02	0
NSR	.13	2	.08	1
NSS	−.02	0	.18	3
NST	.08	1	.17	3
NSI	.24	6	.26	7
NMS	.15	2	−.10	1
EMR	.30	9	.10	1
Total variance,%		64		30

good in the two general-mathematics groups and were also better than predictions of the algebra criterion in the case of the Regular Algebra group.

Differences in validity coefficients are the most striking thing about the two columns in the table. For at least 15 of the 24 tests, the coefficient is distinctly higher for the general-mathematics groups. The abilities involved are CSR, CMU, MSI, DSR, NST, NSI, and NMS. In no case is the correlation consistently and distinctly higher for the algebra group. The most important implication is the great factorial complexity of either criterion and therefore the potentiality for good multiple-regression predictions.

Factor Loadings of the Criterion Variables A clearer picture of the importance of each SI ability in the criterion-score variable can be seen in terms of their factor loadings, which are presented in Table 10.7. The two criteria were not analyzed with the tests, but after the rotated factor matrix was obtained from the analysis of the tests, a vector for each criterion variable was located within the reference frame of the factors. This step was possible from the knowledge of the correlations of the criterion variables with the tests, by a procedure described in Chapter 4.

It will first be noted that the loadings in Table 10.7 are definitely smaller than the correlations with the tests of the factors seen in Table 10.6. The reason is that the correlation between a test and a criterion is not limited to the product of the two factor loadings, those for the factor that the test most represents. A criterion-test correlation is a sum of products of all corresponding loadings of the two variables on all the factors taken into account.

As should be expected, there are much stronger loadings for the general-mathematics criterion. In the order of contribution, the variance of the general-mathematics score can be accounted for by factors representing DSR, MSI, EMR, NSI, CMU, CMR, and CSR, with a negative loading for CMR. The percentage of variance accounted for is 64 (the communality being .64). For the algebra criterion the ranking of the abilities for importance is in the order: NSI,

Table 10.8 Multiple Correlations for Predictions of Mathematical-achievement Scores from Weighted Combinations of Standard Tests and of Factor Tests*

Prediction Composite	Mathematical Course			
	Basic Mathematics	Non-College Algebra	Regular Algebra	Accelerated Algebra
9 standard tests	.60	.53	.22	.74
2 CTMM scores	.34	.40	.18	.37
3 Iowa tests	.53	.31	.20	.62
4 DAT tests	.57	.53	.24	.70
7 factor tests	.42	.56	.27	.51
13 factor scores	.46	.45	.39	.75
20 factor predictors	.48	.54	.38	.74

*The multiple Rs are unbiased, i.e., corrected for shrinkage.

CSS, then equally, CSI, NSS, and NST. All are symbolic abilities, where for general mathematics three are semantic. The combined contributions to total-score variance of the algebra test was only 30 percent. This low showing is attributable to the low predictability of the criterion in the Regular Algebra group.

Multiple Correlations Table 10.8 summarizes the most relevant data in answer to the question of goodness of multiple predictions, in comparisons of standard-test predictors versus SI-score predictors. Of the three standard-test composites, that for the four DAT tests is most highly predictive and that for the CTMM scores is generally least predictive. The standard-test composites did generally better than the SI-score composites in predicting achievement in general mathematics, whereas the SI variables did somewhat better in predicting achievement in algebra, more so in Regular Algebra. All R coefficients were corrected for shrinkage, to represent better the expected population values.

Improvement in Prediction from Factor Scores Multiple correlations were obtained with the 13 SI-factor scores added to the standard-test scores in multiple predictions of the appropriate criterion within each of the four course groups. The results are given in Table 10.9. This treatment was applied for each of the three standard instruments separately.

It will be noted that there are distinct gains in the R coefficients, with differences that become significant in all cases involving algebra courses. The general inference is that each source, standard test and SI score, contributes some component variance not represented in the other, at least in the prediction of algebra achievement.

Table 10.9   Increases in Multiple Correlations (R) from Adding 13 Factor Scores to Each of 3 Standard Composites from Academic-aptitude Tests, and F Ratios for Testing Significance of Increases*

Predictor	Basic Mathematics		Non-College Algebra		Regular Algebra		Accelerated Algebra	
	R	F	R	F	R	F	R	F
CTMM (2 scores)	.35		.41		.21		.38	
CTMM + 13 scores	.59	1.58	.59	1.60	.54	2.25†	.80	6.06‡
Iowa (3 scores)	.55		.34		.24		.63	
Iowa + 13 scores	.65	1.05	.58	1.94†	.54	2.10†	.82	3.23‡
DAT (4 scores)	.59		.55		.29		.72	
DAT + 13 scores	.64	0.46	.59	0.48	.55	2.07†	.85	3.36‡

*Multiple Rs not unbiased.
†Significant at the .05 level.
‡Significant at the .01 level.

Factor Contributions to Multiple Prediction   The relative importance of predictor variables is best seen by comparing their beta coefficients, for these values reflect what each of the predictors contributes when others are taken into account. Although a few of the standard-test scores may come close to representing unique abilities—for example, the DAT Abstract Reasoning probably features CFR, and DAT Clerical Speed and Accuracy comes close to ESU—others appear not so univocal for factorial abilities. When put together in a regression equation, some factorial components of certain tests are somewhat suppressed by scores representing the same components in other tests, sometimes to the extent of having negative beta weights. Some of the same effects can occur with factor scores, where those variables are not completely univocal for their respective factors.

Let us consider the score variables having statistically significant beta coefficients in the application of the stepwise multiple-regression analysis mentioned earlier. Such regression equations were derived for the nine standard-test predictors on the one hand and the 20 factor representatives on the other, for each of the four mathematics courses. The listing of the significant predictors in

Table 10.10   Predictors Contributing Significantly (F at the .10 Level) in Multiple-regression Equations, with Multiple-correlation Coefficients, for Weighted Composites of Standard Aptitude Tests and of Factor Tests and Factor Composites

	Predictors				
	Standard-aptitude-test Scores		Factor Tests and Composite Factor Scores		
Course	Test	R	Variable	R	N
Basic Mathematics	DAT Numerical Ability	.59	MSI	.59	77
	Iowa Reading Comprehension		DSI		
			NMS		
Non-College Algebra	DAT Numerical Ability	.49	ESR	.62	95
	DAT Abstract Reasoning		NSR		
			(ESS)*		
			MSI		
			EMR		
Regular Algebra	DAT Numerical Ability	.29	DSR	.45	101
	CTMM Non-Language MA		MSI		
Accelerated Algebra	Iowa Reading Comprehension	.76	NSR	.78	73
	DAT Numerical Ability		EMR		
	DAT Clerical Speed and Accuracy		DSR		
	DAT Abstract Reasoning		NSS		
			(ESS)		

*Factor symbols in parentheses indicate that the test was designed for the factor but it has not been factor-analyzed.

the order of their appearance in the equations is presented in Table 10.10, with the multiple Rs associated with the equations.

First to be noted is that the DAT Numerical Ability test appeared significantly in all four equations that included only the standard tests, and it appeared as the leading predictor in all courses except Accelerated Algebra. Whether these results can be attributed to that test's MSI component only or whether some other factorial component or components of that test helped, we do not know, for the test has not been analyzed. Other numerical-operations tests also show variance contributed by ability NSI, for example. Although the factor score for MSI appeared significantly in three of the four equations composed of factor-variable predictors (see Table 10.10), it headed the list for Basic Mathematics only. It did not appear at all in the list for Accelerated Algebra. This is a more reasonable finding. The inference is that the DAT Numerical Ability represents some unknown contributor in addition to MSI.

The Iowa Reading Comprehension test was a significant contributor to predictions in two courses, Basic Mathematics and Accelerated Algebra, curiously, since they are the two most disparate courses. Although the leading component of this test may have been CMU, there is no confirmation that this is the source of validity, for no univocal CMU variable appears in any of the four factor-variable equations represented in Table 10.10.

The appearance of the DAT Abstract Reasoning in two of the lists of valid standard predictors indicates that ability CFR is relevant in two courses: Non-College Algebra and Accelerated Algebra. It might have appeared in the list for Regular Algebra also, had the criterion been as predictable in that course as in the others. CFR's relevance in algebra courses could be attributed to the use of graphic representation in cartesian coordinates in those courses, in contrast to Basic Mathematics.

Examination of the factor variables that make significant contributions shows that 9 of the 20 represented in this study appear at least once in the list. MSI appears three times, and four others (DSR, NSS, ESS, and EMR) appear two times each. Of the five cognition abilities, none appears in the list for any of the four courses. Only one memory ability was represented in the study, so nothing can be said about the contributions from the memory category. But the two production categories (divergent and convergent) and the evaluation category are fairly well represented. The relevant abilities are not confined to those concerning symbolic content, for two of four semantic abilities were relevant and there was one figural ability (CFR) indicated by a DAT test. Seven of eleven abilities involving relations or systems were relevant, where abilities for other product categories did less well. Except for implications, however, the product categories were very poorly represented in this investigation.

The Discriminant Analysis As indicated earlier, the discriminant analysis was confined to the SI-factor tests. One analysis was made using the 25 tests that were factor-analyzed, and the other involved the 7 tests that were not analyzed. Tests of the following factors showed the greatest contributions to the first discriminant function, with proportions of .03 or greater: NSS, DSR, CMS, and NST, in decreasing order of importance. With 102 successful algebra students to be discriminated from 105 successful general-mathematics students, there were only 12 misclassifications in each group. A phi coefficient of correlation for the derived 2 by 2 contingency table was .77.

For the function including the seven unanalyzed tests, the strongest contributors to discrimination were believed to be for abilities DSI, ESS, and DSS. Only the ESS test was not later analyzed; the factor contributions of the other two tests have been confirmed by analysis. With the second discriminant equation applied, there were only nine students misplaced in each group, with a phi coefficient of .83. It can be said that, considering the two discriminant analyses, the tests for abilities probably not represented in standard tests, except for CMS, provide excellent bases for classifying students in algebra versus general-mathematics courses, with about 90 percent accuracy. Although there was some overlap between the list of significantly predictive variables *within* course groups and that of more strongly discriminating variables *between* course groups in the discriminant analysis, there were some differences, such that the same combination of predictors could not serve both purposes optimally.

Discussion and Conclusions

This study illustrates how a multiple-predictor battery can be developed for a high degree of success in the prediction of factorially complex criterion variables, including course-achievement criteria. Furthermore, it shows how the operations can proceed with knowledge of the underlying aptitude variables involved, so that generalized conclusions may be drawn, with both theoretical and practical consequences. The study could serve as a model for the investigation of any particular course of instruction. It is recommended, however, that where possible a cross-validation procedure should be applied, in order to achieve greater generalizability of conclusions and applications. It is also suggested that all possibly relevant SI abilities be included in a study, where this can be done.

More specifically, it was found that

1. Batteries of factor scores were better predictors of achievement than any of three standard-test combinations, especially in the prediction of achievement in algebra.
2. Adding scores for certain factors to components of standard aptitude tests gave increased prediction of achievement, significantly so in the algebra courses.
3. Combinations of factor-test scores discriminated between successful (above-median) algebra students and successful general-mathematics students with an accuracy of about 90 percent.
4. With only predictors that contributed significantly to multiple predictions, some 12 different SI abilities were found to be relevant. Other abilities not represented in the study may later be added to the list. Cognition abilities seem relatively less important, while evaluation abilities seem most promising, along with divergent- and convergent-production abilities. Memory abilities were mostly ignored in this investigation.
5. Some abilities seem relevant for both prediction of achievement within course groups and discriminating between them, while other abilities seem relevant for only one of these purposes.

THE ROLE OF SI ABILITIES IN CONCEPT LEARNING

A large proportion of the time and energy devoted to teaching and learning is given to the acquisition of new concepts on the part of the learner. Recognizing this fact, one validation study by the ARP was devoted in part to a more analytical consideration of SI abilities in relation to the learning of a certain kind of concept.[5] The criteria to be predicted were learning-task scores obtained by a group of subjects (S) in the course of discovering and retaining concepts.

A concept is a mental construct, of which there are different kinds, identifiable as products of information. A concept may be a unit, with its combination of attributes; a class, with its set of common properties belonging to a collection of objects or events; or a system, with its unique organization. Whatever its ultimate form, a concept is learned as a class idea, which means that the SI abilities pertaining to classes should logically have first claim to relevance in concept learning.

The Concept-learning Tasks

Three concept-learning tasks were devised, similar in most respects but differing in the kind of information involved—figural, symbolic, and semantic. In each task, S was presented singly, in mixed sequence, 24 exemplars of each of four concepts. In the figural-concept task, for example, there were four different concepts to be discovered. The exemplars for concept A all included intersecting lines; those for concept B, right angles; for C, dotted lines; and for D, parallel lines. In a "teaching book," on one page an exemplar was presented. S gave his guess as to the particular concept by responding with one of the four letters, A to D, encircling one of them. On the next page, the exemplar was repeated along with the letter label that S should have given, so he had immediate feedback information as to success or failure and as to the correct answer. On the same page, a new exemplar was presented, to which S was to give a letter response, and so on, through 96 pages. S was told to turn the page at a signal given every five seconds and to write a letter, even if he thought it were only a guess. The teaching-book mode of the experiment was to meet the requirement of group testing, where approximately 200 Ss were involved.

The other two concept-learning tasks were of the same format. The exemplars for the symbolic concepts were sets of four letters each, e.g., EJMC, with S to discover the principle or class property. The four class ideas were (A) the set contains a repeated letter, e.g., MVHV; (B) each exemplar contains the letter "A"; (C) the set begins with a vowel; and (D) the four letters are in alphabetical order, although not consecutive.

Each semantic exemplar presented four common words, one of which represented the common property for its class; e.g., the words "smile, garden, chief, storm." The four class ideas were (A) kinds of leaders (the set just given belongs to this concept); (B) names of parts, e.g., "wheel"; (C) names of sounds made by animals, e.g., "growl"; and (D) names of foods.

---

[5] See Report 39; also Dunham, Guilford, & Hoepfner (1968).

Tests and Their Abilities
Since class ideas play such obviously prominent roles in the three learning tasks, abilities involving classes were given highest priorities in the selection of potential predictors. In the SI model there are 20 such abilities. Since no learning task represented behavioral information, five abilities of the 20 could be eliminated from the study. Because of the need to keep the test battery within realistic time limits, the abilities for evaluation of classes were relinquished. This reduced the list of class abilities to 12—for 3 kinds of information times 4 kinds of operation. One additional ability had to be omitted for lack of available, analyzed tests for it—memory for figural classes (MFC).

Some of the class abilities to be included had not been demonstrated before, and there were also some new tests prepared for class abilities that had been previously demonstrated, so a factor analysis was needed to verify the appropriate functioning of these new tests, as well as to demonstrate new class abilities. The analysis was needed for a more important reason, and that was to establish a factor structure as an operation independent of the analysis of the test scores. By an extension procedure the learning scores were then to be located as vectors within the preestablished factor structure. The decision for this approach was in recognition of the fact that the learning scores were likely to be factorially complex and therefore of little help in locating the factor axes. In fact, they could have been considerably confusing. Methods were available for extending a factor structure to include additional experimental variables when their correlations with the analyzed variables are known (see Chapter 4).

For the purposes of factor analysis, it was thought necessary to include four abilities not concerned with classes, with marker tests for those factors. The abilities concerned were CMU, CMS, DSU, and NMU. It was thought possible that these abilities could be represented to some degree in the class tests and would need to be accounted for. A secondary reason for including reference factors for CMU and CMS is that they have so often dominated academic-aptitude tests. Would they also play demonstrable roles in restricted tasks of concept learning?

Tests for the Class Abilities In order to give this study some referential basis, one or two tests designed for each ability are listed, with minimal description here. Further descriptions can be found in Appendix B. We begin with tests of cognition of classes:

> Figure Classification (CFC)—(E is to) Choose the exemplar that goes with each class set of three others, in a short matching format.
> Figural Class Inclusion (CFC)—Choose one of five alternative figures that belongs with a class of two, in a multiple-choice format.
> Letter Classification (CSC)—Choose the set of four letters, e.g., LSUG, that belongs in each class, which is represented by three such letter sets, in a short matching format.
> Number Classification (CSC)—Select one of five numbers that belongs in each set of three numbers each, in a short matching format.

Verbal Classification (CMC)—Assign each of several words to one of two classes (each represented by five exemplars) or to neither.

Sentence Classification (CMC)—Say whether each sentence conveys (A) fact, (B) possibility, or (C) name.

Memory for Nonsense Word Classes (MSC)—Choose from a set of four alternative nonsense syllables on the test page one that belongs in a class represented by three other syllables seen previously on a study page.

Classified Information (MMC)—Say whether each set of three meaningful words on the test page represents the same class as another set of words seen previously on the study page.

Alternate Letter Groups (DFC)—Given a number of capital letters, classify and reclassify them in various ways as to figural properties.

Multiple Figural Similarities (DFC)—Given three complex figures that can be conceived as representing different classes, select alternative single figures in turn to be grouped with them, each for a different reason.

Name Grouping (DSC)—Given a number of persons' first names, classify and reclassify them in various ways according to letter content.

Multiple Letter Similarities (DSC)—Given 3 four-letter sets that can be conceived as representing different class ideas, group with them one of several given letter sets, one at a time, each for a different reason.

Multiple Grouping (DMC)—Given the names of several objects, form alternative subsets of three or four each, reclassifying the same object in different ways.

Utility Test (DMC)—List different uses for a common brick (or pencil), the list being scored in terms of the number of changes in class use.

Figure Grouping (NFC)—Given a set of 12 figures, group them in four mutually exclusive classes, using all the figures.

Figure-Concept Grouping (NFC)—Given a target figure and a list of other figures, group figures from the list with the target figures, each group having its own common attribute.

Letter Grouping (NSC)—Given 12 nonsense syllables, classify them into four mutually exclusive groups, using all syllables.

Word Grouping (NMC)—Given 12 meaningful words, classify them into four mutually exclusive groups, using all the words.

Concept Grouping (NMC)—Given a target word and a list of other words, group selected words from the list with the target word, each group based upon a different attribute of the target word.

Marker Tests for Reference Factors The marker tests used for the reference factors are generally more familiar. For CMU they were Verbal Comprehension and Word Completion—multiple-choice and completion vocabulary tests, respectively. For CMS they were Problem Solving (arithmetical- reasoning problems) and Ship Destination. For DSU they were Word Fluency and Suffixes. For NMU they were Figure-Group Naming, Word-Group Naming, and Naming Meaningful Trends (formerly known as "Seeing Trends").

The Learning Scores and Their Uses

Three different kinds of learning scores were used with the concept-learning tasks. A "stage" score measured each individual's performance in terms of number of correct responses, on each one of the tasks at 12 different short intervals of time within the total learning period that included 96 trials. Each stage score was therefore based upon eight successive trials. "Mastery" scores were obtained for each concept in each task by determining at which trial S was considered to have mastered the concept, as indicated by a run of correct responses in the trials following. The "concept-verbalization" score for each task was based upon the number of concepts, out of four, that S could define or describe at the end of the learning exercise.

Each learning score was related to the common factors by extending the reference frame to include that variable. With the use of the stage scores, it was possible to determine whether there were any systematic changes or trends in loadings on a certain factor as a function of practice and learning. In accordance with the results of Fleishman (1966) and his associates, we might expect to find that some abilities would be relatively more important early in the learning episode and decrease systematically in importance, whereas others might be less important early and increase in importance. Still others might have their maximal loadings at some intermediate positions in the learning sequence. For example, divergent-production abilities might be more important early, where there is generation of alternative hypotheses, whereas convergent-production abilities might be more important later when experience leads to one right response in each trial. It should be expected that the content category for each task, figural, symbolic, or semantic, would determine the content category of the more important abilities at any stage of learning.

The mastery score is one commonly used in the experimental laboratory, and it tells us about the rate at which Ss complete the learning of any particular task or part of a task. It does not make possible the analytical relating of extent of learning to each factor as the stage score does. The concept-verbalization score also indicates an overall efficiency in learning a task. It should tell much the same story as the mastery score, except that the naming aspect is an additional feature. This aspect might be expected to introduce some variance in ability NMU, the naming ability.

Factorial Relations to Learning Scores
Factor Loadings of the Stage Scores   Complete tabulation of the loadings of the 12 stage scores for each of the three tasks may be seen in Report 39. Here we shall note only some of the more salient findings.

In interpreting factor loadings obtained by the procedure described for learning scores of any kind, it should be kept in mind that there is likely to be a bias downward in values. Thus, finding a nonchance factor loading for a factor can be taken as evidence of a role for that factor, but finding no loading is not evidence of absence of a role for the factor. According to the same principle, nonzero factor loadings can be underestimates of the degrees to which certain abilities or functions operate in the learning task. Factor loadings should not be overestimates of those roles except for the intervention of chance.

Difficulty levels of the tasks are involved in this phenomenon. Near the beginning of learning on a task, where scores of performance are largely a matter of chance, there is little reliability and little opportunity for any factor role to show itself. Near the end of learning, if most Ss have achieved perfect scores, reliable variance is again near zero and factor loadings cannot be far from zero. In the tasks of this investigation, the scores started with means of about 4.0, where a chance score would be 2.0, and terminal scores had means of about 7.0, where 8.0 was a perfect score. Thus, it may be assumed that there was much room for variations and the detection of factorial components. These qualifications apply most strongly to the stage scores; they apply in a less direct way to the other two kinds of scores.

Returning to the results, first to be noted is that the factor loadings of all learning scores are rather small. Very few are above the limit of significance for interpretability that is usually applied to factor loadings (.30). There is no way to compute the standard error of factor loadings, but Cliff and Pennell (1967) have shown by Monte Carlo methods that the sampling errors in factor loadings are somewhat comparable with those for coefficients of correlation. With the sample of 177 students in this study, we might say with some degree of assurance that a loading as high as .20 should be given attention.

The great majority of the loadings were on the positive side, in accordance with the generally positive correlations between the test scores and the learning scores. Those values ranged up to .40 for the figural-concept task, to .35 for the symbolic task, and to .48 for the semantic task. The communalities for the figural task ranged from .11 to .39 in the 12 score variables; for the symbolic task, .10 to .31; and for the semantic task, .12 to .48. The reliability levels for the learning scores (as estimated by correlations between neighboring stage scores) were somewhat higher than these values, indicating that some of the common-factor variances that could be accounted for were not accounted for in terms of the 15 aptitude factors of the experiment. The extra "true" variance may have represented some intellectual abilities not covered in this study.

Another general statement that can be made is that the factor loadings for a task with a certain informational content were not always higher on factors having the same kind of content. The figural task definitely had higher loadings on CFC than on CSC and CMC, but in the divergent-production area it had its highest loadings on DSC, and in the convergent-production area its loadings were about the same on NFC, NSC, and NMC. In the production areas, the symbolic task had its highest loadings on DSC and NSC, but in the memory area, its loadings ran definitely higher on MMC than on MSC. The latter result looks as if the Ss generally tended to translate the information regarding symbolic classes into semantic form and to remember it in that "language." Although it would seem natural for Ss to remember concepts in verbalized (semantic) form, as we often find in the experimental laboratory, for that kind of memory appears to do best, we find that for the semantic task, the Ss appeared to depend as heavily upon ability MSC as upon MMC for an aid to learning the concepts. It is possible that resourceful Ss use more than one "language" as an aid to memory. Dependence upon abilities DFC and DSC also appeared to be greater than on DMC. The kind of learning strategy that would do this can only be surmised. In the case of convergent-production abilities, learning in the semantic task was most dependent upon NMC late in the learning episode (trials 5 to 12) but more upon NSC in early trials (2 to 4).

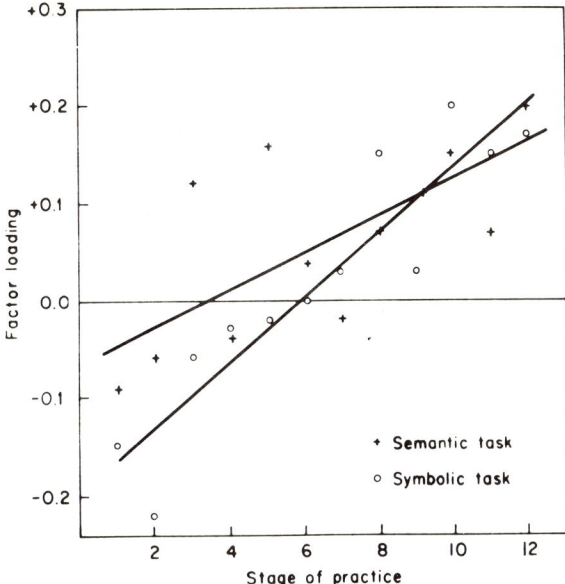

FIGURE 10.1   Factor loadings in stage scores as a function of amount of practice, for factors CSC and CMC in symbolic and semantic tasks.

Trends in Factor Loadings with Learning   Inspection of the lists of loadings shows what appear to be systematic changes as functions of trials. Two of the most interesting ones are presented in Fig. 10.1. The points represent exactly the factor loadings, for the CSC factor as a function of trials in the symbolic task, and for the CMC factor as a function of trials in the semantic task. Loadings on CFC as a function of trials in the figural task (not shown) started near zero, then jumped to a plateau of about .17 in trials 6 to 12. The trends in the CSC and CMC loadings in Fig. 10.1 are essentially linear, and straight lines fit their respective sets of points with Pearson rs of .73 and .93.

What need explaining are the systematic extensions of loadings below zero in the early trials. A negative loading should mean that the more of the ability a person has, the more poorly he tends to do in the task. This relationship can be rationalized by saying that with high CSC or CMC ability, in each case, S is too ready to see possible erroneous concepts. Those who are less ready to see possible concepts guess more at random, which would lead to zero factor loadings. In later trials, the ability is a help for everybody to see the correct concepts, and loadings become increasingly positive. If the learning exercise were carried to the point at which all Ss knew all four concepts, the loadings would again become zero. But that level was not achieved; the final mean score was below the perfect score of 8 even at the last trial, which left room for variance in learning scores.

The loadings of stage scores on the divergent-production factors are close to uniform size throughout the learning period. Those for the figural task on DFC had a mean of .05, and those for the semantic task on DMC had a mean of .09, both essentially zero. In those two tasks it would seem that essentially no divergent production of classes was of any consequence. This is understandable with respect to the figural task, since the variety of possible class ideas in that task is very limited. The loadings for the symbolic task on DSC had a mean of .18, which indicates a generally positive relationship. In the symbolic task the potential number of class ideas is probably much greater than for the figural task. It is not so easy to make a statement regarding the possible number of alternative class ideas for the semantic task, but it is probably small compared to that for the symbolic class.

The loadings of the stage scores in relation to factors NFC, NSC, and NMC, respectively, generally started low and worked irregularly upward, but only for the semantic task in relation to NMC did the loadings clearly exceed .20 in as many as six trials. The hypothesis suggested earlier to the effect that divergent production would be more important early and convergent production later was thus supported in the second respect but not in the first. The relations of NSC loadings to stage scores for the symbolic task were near zero for the very early trials and rather uniformly high thereafter.

The trends with respect to the memory factors, MSC and MMC, were of special interest because of the relatively high loadings in that operation area. Figure 10.2 shows the trends for the symbolic- and semantic-task scores both on the semantic factor MMC, as functions of learning trials. The symbolic-task scores had only low loadings on the corresponding memory ability, MSC. The probable translation of class ideas into semantic form for memory purposes was mentioned earlier. The curves were derived by applying a process of running averages to the successive points, iteratively. The nonlinear correlations were .88 and .86, for the symbolic and semantic tasks, respectively. It will be observed that the curve for the semantic task is systematically higher, as it should be, although the differences are small.

The stage scores for the figural task had their highest loadings, not on MMC, as might have been expected, but on MSC. For trials 5 through 11, all loadings were .10 and above. This result suggests that the Ss somehow used labels to represent figural-class ideas, remembering them in the form of labels; perhaps they used the labels A, B, C, and D, but also perhaps some labels of their own inventions.

Factors in the Mastery Scores The mastery scores indicate rate of learning over the entire practice period; hence they convey less detailed information than do the stage scores. Some information of another kind, however, is gained by the fact that there is a separate score for each concept, and some of the concepts are easier to learn than others. The latter fact might lead us to expect some differences in factor structure as a function of difficulty. Any concept that is much too easy or much too difficult to learn might yield little variance and hence small factor loadings, as the means come close to the lower limit of zero or the upper limit of 24.

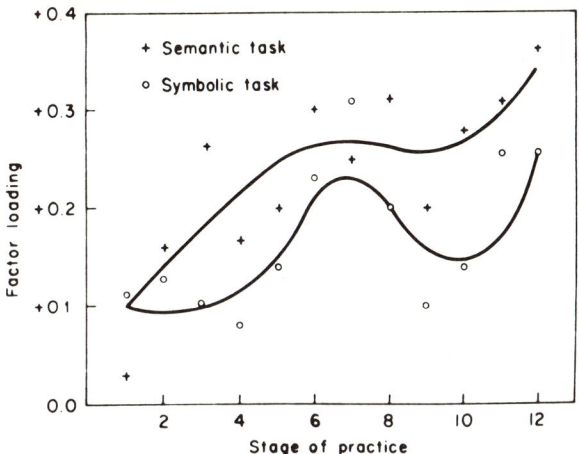

FIGURE 10.2 Trends in factor loadings on factor MMC for symbolic and semantic tasks as functions of amount of practice.

The factor loadings for the 12 mastery scores tended to be smaller than those for the stage scores, but the highest loadings tend to be on the same factors for the same tasks. For the four figural concepts the loadings on CFC ranged from .13 to .23, with a mean of .18. The loadings for the same concepts on MSC ranged from .18 to .27, however, with a mean of .21. Loadings for the same concepts were lower on factors DFC and NFC.

For the symbolic concepts, there were loadings of consistently noteworthy size only on factor DSC, in agreement with the generally higher loadings of the stage scores from the same task on DSC. On MMC, two of these concepts had loadings above .20, but two had zero loadings, which is in only partial agreement. Loadings for the four semantic concepts were higher on two factors on which stage-score loadings were also generally higher. On MMC the loadings ranged from .13 to .25, with a mean of .18. On NMC the loadings ranged from .24 to .33, with a mean of .28. There was no apparent relation of factor loadings to difficulty level of the concepts, at least within each set of four concepts of the same kind. The highest of the four loadings could apparently apply to any of the concepts, from the easiest to the most difficult. A more searching and systematic study of this point might show some kind of relationship.

Factors in the Concept-verbalization Scores There were only three verbalization scores, one for each task. Loadings of these scores tended to be a bit higher than for the other kinds of scores, and they tended to support better the findings with respect to stage scores than did the mastery scores. One prior expectation was that variance in an additional factor, NMU, might be found, owing to the requirement for S to name or describe each concept at the end of practice. The answer to this hypothesis was quite decisive; the three loadings on NMU were positive but very small, averaging .11. It is probable that offering S

the option "to describe" did not require of him a great deal of convergence; he could show that he knew each concept by giving a rough statement.

The three tasks had significant loadings (≥.20) on their respective cognition factors, CFC, CSC, and CMC, as should be expected, generally with lower loadings on other cognition factors, except that the semantic task had a higher loading on CSC than did the CSC task (.28 versus .23), if so small a difference is at all dependable. The semantic task's loading on CMC was a striking .41, but the figural task had a similar loading on CMC of .40, higher than its loading of .20 on CFC. The hypothesis that Ss verbalized their figural concepts as they went along seems supported, but curiously, the figural task's loading on MMC was only .09. If the Ss translated their figural concepts into semantic form, it would appear that they did not remember them so much in that form. The results from the stage scores suggest that Ss were likely to remember some kind of labels for their figural concepts, but also that they did some remembering in semantic form. On this point the two kinds of scores seem to disagree.

That the semantic concepts were remembered in semantic form is indicated by a loading of .36 for the verbalization score on MMC. But the expectation that the same kind of score for the symbolic task would be loaded strongly on MMC was not fulfilled, for the loading was only .10.

As found for stage scores, the only significant role for a divergent-production factor was for DSC in the case of the symbolic task, with a loading of .32. For the convergent-production abilities, the only significant loading was for the semantic task on NMC, in agreement with results from the other two kinds of scores.

Roles of the Four Reference Factors   The reference factors included those for abilities CMU and CMS, the favorite academic-aptitude abilities. Is the learning of concepts such as were involved in the tasks of this study related to those abilities? Among the stage scores, CMU had only two significant loadings out of 36 for the three tasks combined, and these loadings were for the semantic task. Among the 12 mastery scores, there were also two significant loadings of .26 for two of the semantic concepts, the other two loadings being .15 and .04. Among the three verbalization scores there was a significant .23 for the semantic task. Thus, knowledge of words does seem to provide some source of aid or limitation in the learning of semantic concepts.

CMS is an ability to see organizations. It had four significant, positive loadings in later trials in the symbolic task. This suggests that seeing semantic systems in the four-letter sets could be of some help. CMS had significant loadings for two of the figural concepts and one of the symbolic concepts when mastery scores were used, and a loading of .20 for the figural task when the verbalization score was used. There was apparently no organizing problem in the semantic task with which ability CMS could be of any help.

Reference factor DSU had two stray loadings of .20 and .23 among the 36 stage scores, probably without any indication of relevance. It had only small loadings among the 12 mastery scores and also the three verbalization scores. The fourth reference factor, NMU, was expected to have significant loadings only for the verbalization scores, and their failure to appear has already been mentioned. Loadings were generally small for the other two kinds of scores, as should be expected.

Some Generalizations

A number of comments should be made by way of summary and by way of implications from the findings. Most general is the affirmation of the promising qualities of the procedure of analyzing learning scores, particularly the operation of putting vectors representing those scores into a preestablished reference frame that is determined by good, representative SI-factor tests, where the aptitude dimensions to be expected are in the intellectual domain. In applying this approach, we also see the importance of having a range of difficulty in components of the task and of ending the practice short of perfect scores for all Ss. The fact that the selected abilities to be related to the learning scores fell short of accounting for all the reliable variances of the learning scores indicates the need for covering a liberal number of possibly relevant abilities. Such tasks and their learning scores are likely to be quite complex factorially.

The fact that the loadings in the learning scores were so generally small should not occasion much doubt that several of the abilities were relevant. The sizes of the correlations between factor-test scores and learning scores should in themselves serve as proofs that there are variables in common to the two sets of measures. It does not take a factor analysis to justify this general conclusion. Another bit of evidence is in the form of clear trends in factor loadings for learning scores as functions of practice, even when the loadings were very low, and in two cases crossed the zero level. Trends, if genuine, imply system, and system means regularity, not randomness, in events.

Relevance of the Class Abilities   The hunch that class abilities would be found relevant seems to have been vindicated. Although there were only four abilities not involving classes, their relations to the learning scores were generally weaker. It was expected that abilities CFC, CSC, and CMC would be especially relevant, since, whatever else S does, he must necessarily recognize the class ideas. The learning scores tended to be related to these factors, but they were even more strongly related to others. The negative relationships of the earliest stage scores from the symbolic and semantic tasks to CSC and CMC, respectively, kept the means of these loadings very low. Although there is a possibility that the general downward bias was operating in this event, nowhere else was a trend into the negative region evident. Hence, these negative loadings can be given credence.

The two memory factors showed more consistently positive influence on task scores than did most factors, although there was no opportunity to verify this for the factor MFC. MMC showed relatively strong relations (up to 10 percent) with the semantic task, but also with the symbolic task. It is possible that inclusion of some of the other, nonclass, memory abilities would have added to the list of relevant factors, for units of information had to be remembered as well as classes, and also systems (in the case of the four-letter words in the symbolic task). The factor CMS showed some tendency of role playing in the symbolic task. Memory for symbolic implications might be involved in all the tasks, for S had to learn to associate each concept with a letter, which is like an implications-memory kind of test item.

From another important point of view, it is not surprising that memory abilities should show significant roles in the tasks, for there is much in common operationally between these tasks and tests of memory abilities. In the latter, too, there must be learning, and there is a test of status of individuals after learning to indicate how much information has been retained from the exposure.

Observable effects of divergent production were small and uncertain, and without observable continuous trends for the figural and semantic tasks. There were indications of contributions up to 9 percent in the symbolic task, which more obviously provides opportunities for divergent production. The expectation that divergent production would be more important early in learning and convergent production late in learning was not borne out, except that NMC came out strongly late in the semantic task. That task was the most difficult one, with mean stage scores still below 6.0 in trials 8 through 12.

The Translation between Contents Mention was made of instances in which a task with one kind of SI content had unexpectedly as high or higher loadings on factors of other content. This shift did not always show a preference for processing information in semantic form, and it sometimes went systematically in the reverse direction as well. This kind of result is in contrast to the behavior of tests that are especially designed for factor analysis of SI abilities in certain content categories. Such tests very rarely cross content lines. The difference must be attributable to the better control of the processing of information in the SI tests. In a task less well controlled, as in the concept-learning exercises, it would appear that S has preferences and that sufficient proportions of the Ss have similar preferences among contents differing from that for the kind of information presented in the task.

Complexity of Learning Task Those who have analyzed learning scores in a task usually find that several factors are involved; the tasks are factorially complex. They may involve all the SI operation categories, more than one kind of product, and even more than one kind of content, as just discussed. From this point of view, the activity in the concept-learning task resembles problem solving, as described in the structure-of-intellect problem-solving (SIPS) model (Guilford, 1967). The pattern of abilities involved depends upon strategies and tactics introduced by the problem solvers. Ss are usually not told in detail how they are to go about solving their problem. Even if they were, they would probably deviate from the prescribed programming in significant numbers.

Relationships among Different Learning Scores It was pointed out that, on the whole, the factors playing the strongest roles for one kind of score were also those most important in the other two kinds of scores. This result should be reassuring to those who deal with concept-learning problems in the laboratory and who may wonder whether one kind of score represents the same aspects of performance as another. But one should not generalize very far from this one indication of similar factorial content for different scores, nor should one take for granted that different scores are interchangeable. Note the failure of the verbalization score to indicate the role of the naming ability, NMU. The process of putting learning scores within a factorial reference frame is the only known method by which one can determine what the score variables have in common. The intercorrelations of those scores would tell about how much variance there is in common, but they would not tell us the reasons. A further informative and evaluative step would be to look into the kinds of strategies that the Ss applied to the learning tasks.

ROLES OF TRANSFORMATION ABILITIES IN SCHOOL LEARNING

The study of relations of transformation abilities to school learning was conducted in connection with a major factor analysis involving 10 transformation abilities, as the classes abilities had been investigated in connection with concept learning in the study described in the preceding section. The factor analysis was reviewed in Chapter 6, with descriptions of tests, so it is unnecessary to provide that information here. The criterion measure was a very general and representative one. Since an overwhelming proportion of learning events in school involve reading and fixing in memory information derived from books, a Studying and Remembering test was designed to provide the criterion measure.

Hypotheses regarding Transformations in Learning

A theoretical reason for expecting transformation abilities to have some relation to learning came from the insistence of Gestalt psychologists that much learning is a matter of redefinition of what one already knows. Redefinition is one kind of transformation, as indicated by the fact that some tests that have been found to represent transformation abilities clearly involve redefinitions. For example, representative tests for ability NMT call for redefinition of objects in revising the use or function of the object. Before the SI model was developed, the same ability was referred to as "redefinition" ability, and the tests for it were based upon Gestalt theory. One of its better tests was named "Gestalt Transformation." It was realized later that there are relevant kinds of transformations other than redefinition.

A source of empirical support for the hypothesis has been in the form of some significant correlations reported between tests of transformation abilities and measures of school achievement (Cline, Richards, & Abe, 1962; Getzels & Jackson, 1962). Incidental information of this kind can also be cited in validation studies discussed earlier in this chapter. In a very recent study of reading achievement, Kluever (1968) found that tests for MST and MMT were strongly discriminating between groups of good and poor readers and correlated with reading achievement within groups. The validation aspect of the study under consideration here thus seemed to have promising precedents. Further, a broader sampling of transformation abilities was involved than in any previous investigation of its kind.

The Criterion Test

The Studying and Remembering test was composed of three parts. Each began with an essay of about 400 words on some timely subject, believed to be interesting to high school students. The topics were on the use of drugs, the importance of proteins in one's diet, and the nature of the stock market. By a preliminary trial it was determined that students who had read these special selections did much better in a multiple-choice test on their contents than did a group who had not read them. A 10-item, 4-choice test followed the reading of each essay, to which the Es could no longer refer. The three parts were given on different days, but a single, total score was obtained.

Multivariate Prediction of the Criterion Score

In determining the relative values of the various abilities for contribution to prediction of the criterion measure, the Studying and Remembering score, Bartlett's (1937) procedure for deriving factor scores from the test scores was employed. This procedure minimizes the intercorrelations of the factor scores. A stepwise multiple-regression analysis was performed in order to establish the order of importance of the factor scores in a weighted composite.

The best single predictor was the score for ability CMU, as could have been predicted. The student's repository of semantic concepts is almost everywhere involved in academic learning. Right behind the CMU predictor, with its beta weight of .40, was the one for ability MMT, with a beta of .32, and following that came the score for CMT, with a beta of .22. These results indicate the importance of *seeing* revisions of conceptions as one reads new material, and what is probably more important, of *remembering* these revisions. It may be supposed that as the student reads, each revision has a bit of "shock value," which favors remembering the revision and hence remembering the new idea, as shown in the multiple-choice test. This hypothesis should not preclude the occurrence of additional revisions as the student takes the retention test, with CMT again involved.

To continue the list of significant contributors to prediction, we find other transformation abilities concerned. The stepwise method provides an F test for the significance of each increment to prediction. Seven predictors were included in the equation before the increments failed to reach significance at the .05 level. The fourth predictor, after those for CMU, MMT, and CMT, was for DST, with a beta of .20. The symbolic aspect of this ability could have arisen from the fact that two of the reading essays contained numerical facts. The multiple-choice items may have involved some facility in producing revisions in supposedly already known numerical facts. The fifth predictor was for EST, the parallel evaluation ability. This result would support the hypothesis just given for DST. E could be doing some problem solving concerning numerical data, with alternative conclusions and a testing of those conclusions, and hence DST and EST. The sixth ability significantly involved was for DMC, a facility for shifting from one semantic class to another. Perhaps as the student reads, he puts things in their appropriate classes, and as he reads further he has to shift to new classes. The seventh ability was for convergent production of semantic transformations (NMT). This result suggests that E has to make some revisions in taking the multiple-choice test, revisions that are forced upon him by what he knows, in order to reach the right answer.

Five of the seven abilities just mentioned are in the transformation category, but of course, 10 of the 16 abilities in the investigation were also in the same category. The multiple correlation, with seven predictors, was .58. It is possible that abilities not included in this study could be found to make additional significant contributions to prediction. The correlations of the score for CMU with the learning criterion was .40, which seems to be near the level attained by present academic-aptitude tests, which probably lack any components for memory or for transformations. The score composite of this study also lacked any predictors involving abilities such as CMS, memory abilities other than MST and MMT, and such implications abilities as NMI and EMI. Other kinds of tests for assessment of residues of the study exercise might involve additional abilities.

IMPORTANCE OF SI ABILITIES AS VIEWED BY CREATIVE INDIVIDUALS

One investigation by the ARP was regarded not as a validation study but as a kind of exploration that might precede a predictive-validity study (Report 25). If one wanted to determine which abilities are relevant in the successful performance of research scientists, for example, he would not want to take up considerable working time of those persons by administering to them a lengthy battery of tests. Even if he could narrow the list by logical selection among the SI abilities, the number of tests might still be considerable. It was thought that a better and more restricted list of abilities to be covered could be effected by asking scientists themselves how important they thought different intellectual abilities are to them in carrying out their work. Incidentally, this foreshadows a new kind of job-analysis technique, using the SI concepts as a frame of reference.

Procedures

The approach to obtaining the opinions of scientists and others from whom one should expect creative performances of some degree of significance was to ask individuals in these groups to rate described SI abilities as to relative importance in their work. A personal interview was held with each individual before he was asked to make the ratings. Each of 28 SI abilities was defined as it seemed best at the time of study, and a specific example of an activity that should be heavily dependent upon that ability was also presented. Examples of definitions and activities are:

> "CMI: To anticipate needs or consequences of a given situation. Example: An administrator considering a proposed change in a payroll form in terms of probable consequences."
>
> "NMT: To shift the functions of an object, or part of an object, and to use it in a new way. Example: Putting a cake of dry ice under a heavy machine so that it sinks into place as the ice evaporates."

The Sample of Abilities The source of selection of abilities to be rated was limited to the 46 SI abilities that had been demonstrated at the time. The ARP personnel reduced that number by agreeing that 18 probably had little chance of being rated as relevant. Within the 28 remaining abilities, the selection was neither random nor systematic; not random because of the bias in favor of abilities believed to have some relevance; not systematic because the 46 known abilities sampled the SI model very unevenly. The heaviest representation was for the cognition and divergent-production (operation categories) with only one ability representing the memory category. The three content categories (omitting the behavioral area) were rather evenly represented. All six product categories were represented, those of relations and transformations being somewhat favored.

The Subjects The major results were obtained from two professional groups. One was composed of 35 research personnel, including physical scientists, engineers, and engineering psychologists. All were recognized by their peers as being outstanding. They worked in various parts of the country. The 50 nonresearch personnel included specialists in education, training, personnel work, and military affairs.

The Rating System The rating task involved the use of cards, on each of which was the definition of one SI ability and the example that went with it. The SI code for the ability was not mentioned. The Ss were told to sort the cards in seven piles, ranked as to importance of the abilities in their work. They were to end up with from three to five in each pile, thus forcing the distribution toward rectangular form and enhancing discriminations. The piles were given numerical values from 1 to 7, which were used to find means and standard deviations, for rough comparisons.

Results

The means of the ratings of abilities ranged from 2.0 to 6.4, which is an indirect indication of considerable agreement among raters. The stability of the means is indicated by standard errors usually near .25 of a scale unit. The rank-order correlation between means of the research and nonresearch groups was .87. In spite of general high agreement, however, there were some noteworthy differences for particular abilities.

The highest-ranking mean rating given by the research group was for SI ability DFT. Transformation abilities in general had high mean ratings for this group. Of the seven transformation abilities, five appear among the eight highest-ranking abilities. Following DFT, in order, these abilities were CMT, NST, NMT, and NFT. CFT was rated in twelfth place and DMT in eighteenth place. Except for the fact that DFT led all abilities, convergent-production abilities tended to be rated higher than divergent-production abilities.

For the nonresearch group, divergent-production abilities did relatively better, especially DMC, which was ranked number 3 (against 14.5 for the research group), and DMU, which was ranked number 6 (against 19 for the research group). DMT was ranked unexpectedly low by both groups (18 by the research group and 15 by the nonresearch group). Engineers, as a special group, ranked DMU in tenth place, DMC in eighth place, and DMI in ninth place (seventeenth place for the research group).

The high regard of the research scientists for transformation abilities should have been expected and probably indicates a recognized need for flexibility. The higher value placed on convergent production than on divergent production was not expected. It should be noted, however, that the convergent-production abilities rated were those dealing with flexibility. It may be that because scientists are looking for "right" answers, they overlook the amount of divergent production that takes place and is actually an aid on the way to right answers. To make a really fair comparison of divergent and convergent abilities, it would be necessary to match them for content and product categories. There were three such abilities that could be matched—DMR versus NMR, DFT versus NFT, and DMT versus NMT. For these matched comparisons, the two groups of raters had the same higher-than-average regard for the three convergent abilities and just about average regard for the three divergent abilities.

One important consideration should be noted, for it probably had effects upon the rankings of the abilities. It had to do with communication of the meanings of the abilities to the raters, both in the definitions and in the examples of relevant activities presented. The full significance of SI concepts had not come in time to influence the definitions. The ranking of DFT in first place by the research group and in second place by the nonresearch group could be attributed in part to the attractive statement:

"DFT: To abandon conventional problem-solving methods that have become unworkable and to think of original solutions. Example: Putting the eye in the point of the needle to make the invention of the sewing machine."

A restriction to figural information was not mentioned. The definition could well have applied to DMT also, since nothing restricts it to figural information. The example is of a figural problem, at least in part, but the reference is to a very important invention. On the other hand, the statement regarding DMU could have biased raters in the other direction:

"DMU: To produce many ideas where free expression is encouraged and where quality of ideas is not important. Example: Producing as many ideas as possible for the improvement of a product or new use of it."

To raters who habitually look for ideas of high quality, this definition, although descriptive enough in reference to DMU tests, would probably be less attractive than it should be. Thomas A. Edison would probably have rated DMU very high, since it was one of his reputed outstanding qualities. The two examples of biasing statements just given were probably the most extreme cases.

Another feature that may have had some biasing effects was the choice of kinds of activity suggested in the examples. Some examples pertained to engineering problems, some to social problems, and some to management problems, and so on. The rater may feel more kindly toward an ability for which the example is connected with his own field and therefore rate it higher. All these sources of possible bias are mentioned for the guidance of other investigators who might be inclined to apply the same approach. Better examples to give raters might be in the form of sample items from tests that rather clearly represent the abilities in question.

RELEVANCE OF SELECTED ABILITIES IN PERFORMANCES OF MILITARY OFFICERS

The study that provided the subject matter for Report No. 21 had the double objective of assessing both concurrent-predictive validity and construct validity. Alvin Marks, who was a Reserve Marine officer initiated the study and contributed most to the conduct of it. It was expected that a number of intellectual abilities then recognized should be relevant in the operations of Marine officers, extending possibilities of prediction over and above that obtainable from the customary military examinations.

The Predictor and Criterion Variable

The Tests After consultation with Marine officers, some degree of consensus led to the selection of the following abilities, given here in terms of their later SI specifications: CMU, CMS, CMT, CMI, DFT, DMU, DMC, DMT, EFI, and EMS.[6] The marker tests selected to represent these abilities are listed by title in Table 10.11. It should be noted that this study was done well before the SI model was introduced, and the abilities were then known by other labels that were often determined by the supposed nature of those abilities. It can also be noted that the choices of abilities from the much larger number and from their SI properties at a later time might have been different. In most cases, more than one test was selected for each ability, anticipating a factor analysis that would check upon the appropriate functioning of the tests in the Marine officer population and that would provide the basis for combining tests in order to obtain factor scores. In Table 10.11, both the latest SI designation and the original name of the ability are given in each case.

Criterion Variables Desiring a more analytical evaluation of the officers than is provided by the customary officer-fitness index, and evaluations that would include attention to signs of status on the selected abilities, the investigators attempted to develop a more pertinent rating system. Ratings were requested from both superior and peer officers with respect to each of the 11 supposed factor abilities plus a twelfth rating of the hypothetical trait of leadership. Each of four items for a variable was to be rated on a 5-point scale. The items were designed in multiple-choice form with five descriptive phrases for choices. In most items, a particular military duty or episode was described, with alternatives stating how the officer in question would probably handle the situation. Each item was designed to reflect individual differences in one of the SI-ability variables. From the standpoint of later placement of each ability in the SI model, some of the item episodes and alternatives were not logically very close to the mark. An example of a good item in this respect and one of a poor item will be cited; also cited is an item for the rating of "leadership."

An item that is very clearly in line with SI ability CMU is:

Considering the following words: EFFACE, FURTIVE, ADHESIVE, IRASCIBLE, and ESOTERIC, this officer would most likely know the meanings of:
  a. One of them
  b. All of them
  c. Two of them
  d. Four of them
  e. Three of them

---

[6] An eleventh ability was known as "sensitivity to problems," which, when the SI model became known, was first identified with EMI but later shown to be identifiable as CMI. Thus, in Table 10.17 there are two CMI abilities labeled, with CMI_2 corresponding to the sensitivity-to-problems variable of this study.

The lack of conformity to order of ability among the alternatives is in agreement with scrambled orders in other items, designed to avoid helping the rater to judge in terms of position of the alternative in a list. An item that missed the SI mark because of a drastic change in its interpretation after its placement in the SI model was written for "penetration," now CMT. It reads

> A group of officers is asked for suggestions to improve a training program. This officer would most likely suggest:
> a. Only immediate and obviously needed changes
> b. Mostly long-range and not too obviously needed changes
> c. Some immediate, some long-range, some obviously needed changes, and some not so obviously needed changes
> d. Only long-range and not too obviously needed changes
> e. Mostly immediate and obviously needed changes

Table 10.11 SI Abilities and the Tests to Represent Them Used in the Validation Study with Marine Officers

Ability	Test	Ability	Test
CMU	(verbal comprehension)	DMU	(ideational fluency)
	19. Verbal Comprehension		6. Consequences (obvious)
			11. Plot Titles (nonclever)
CMS	(general reasoning)		
	15. Ship Destination	DMC	(spontaneous flexibility)
			3. Brick Uses (shifts)
CMT	(penetration)		
			21. Alternate Uses
	16. Similarities		
	17. Social Institutions	DMT	(originality)
			5. Consequences (remote)
CMI_1	(conceptual foresight)		
			10. Plot Titles (clever)
	1. Alternate Methods		
	8. Pertinent Questions	EFI	(perceptual foresight)[†]
			4. Route Planning
CMI_2	(sensitivity to problems)[*]		
			12. Competitive Planning
	2. Apparatus Test		
	13. Seeing Deficiencies	EMS	(experiential evaluation)
	14. Seeing Problems		18. Social Situations
			20. Unusual Details
DFT	(adaptive flexibility)		
	7. Match Problems III		
	9. Planning Air Maneuvers		

[*]Originally thought to be SI ability EMI but later shown to be CMI (Report No. 32).
[†]Originally regarded as CFI but later shown to be EFI (Report No. 40).

Receiving points 5 to 1, respectively, would be responses d, b, c, e, and a. The responses fit the meaning of "penetration," but not nearly so well the meaning of cognition of semantic transformations (CMT), which deals with changes in meaning, as in understanding a pun.

The special "leadership" variable was presented, as in one item of four, as follows:

In your opinion, this officer is:
a. Not as good an officer as most other officers
b. One of the most outstanding officers I have ever known
c. An excellent officer
d. An average officer
e. A better-than-average officer

Forty-eight items were prepared for the criterion instrument. The items for different traits were mixed within the instrument and were presented without any trait names. Two superior officers and two peer officers rated each subject. The reliability estimates (Spearman–Brown) for the superiors' ratings ranged from .37 to .63 for the 12 variables, and for the peers' ratings, from .18 to .53. These low reliabilities should be taken into account in interpreting validity correlations to be cited later.

The Factor Analyses and Factor Composites

Three factor analyses were done, one for the 21 aptitude tests and one each for the 12 superiors' rating variables and the 12 peers' variables. The 11 expected aptitude factors were found, with the tests performing very much as anticipated. Except for the test Seeing Problems, the factor composites were constituted of the representative tests as shown in Table 10.11. That test divided its common-factor variance weakly on several factors.

The rating variables were factor-analyzed, not with the idea of deriving any new information about intellectual abilities, for those abilities had been verified from a better approach through analysis of test variables. Furthermore, each rating variable was aimed at a single ability factor, and there should have been as many factors as experimental variables. In general, analysis of rated traits may be expected to tell us more about what is in the minds of raters when they are making their ratings than about the nature of traits. For example, the raters may have discriminated a smaller number of dimensions of ability than 11. The advantage to be expected from analysis of the rating variables was a practical one: to find a number of criterion variables less than 11 that would represent what the raters were trying to say about the subjects. The intercorrelations of rating variables immediately showed this possibility, for they were all of substantial size, up to .74. One factor commonly expected in sets of ratings of traits is a general one, interpretable as "halo."

The two analyses of ratings gave very similar results. In both there was a quite general (completely general in one set) halo factor. Of the three other factors, one was interpreted as a "field-capability" composite. It was determined by the rating variables for adaptive flexibility (DFT), perceptual foresight (EFI), and general reasoning (CMS). Examination of the items rated for these qualities

Table 10.12 Correlations between the Aptitude-factor Composites and the Rating-factor Composites

	Rating Composites					
	Superior Ratings			Peer Ratings		
Aptitude Composite	Field Capacity	Leadership	Ideation	Field Capacity	Leadership	Ideation
CMU (verbal comprehension) (19*)	.07	.07	.17†	.01	.14†	.19‡
CMS (general reasoning) (15)	.08	.05	.22‡	.08	.07	.14†
CMT (penetration) (16, 17)	.09	.07	.19‡	.06	.07	.12
CMI₁ (conceptual foresight) (1, 8)	.06	.01	.08	.03	.00	.11
CMI₂ (sensitivity to problems) (2, 13)	.12	.17†	.27‡	.07	.11	.16†
DFT (adaptive flexibility) (7, 9)	−.03	−.07	.13	.09	.11	.19‡
DMU (ideational fluency) (6, 11)	.06	.05	.00	.03	−.01	.03
DMC (spontaneous flexibility) (3, 21)	.03	.08	.17†	.06	.13	.23‡
DMT (originality) (5, 10)	.18‡	.17†	.18‡	.07	.14†	.19‡
EFI (perceptual foresight) (4, 12)	−.04	.01	.12	.04	.00	.08
EMS (experiential evaluation) (18, 20)	.07	.00	.11	.12	.10	.10

*Number of the test used to represent the factor in its composite (see Table 10.11 for the names of the tests).
†Significant at the .05 level.
‡Significant at the .01 level.

shows that some of them pertain to situations of a stressful nature, as in combat, and they involve organizing and reinterpreting aspects of field situations. Another factor was headed by the leadership variable, along with that for experiential evaluation (EMS) and that for general reasoning (CMS). The rating items of these variables tended to emphasize decision making based upon experience. The third nongeneral factor was called "ideation," because the items emphasized having verbal knowledge and being flexible. The variables having significant loadings on this factor in both rater groups included verbal comprehension (CMU), originality (DMT), and spontaneous flexibility (DMC).

The rating composites to represent the three factors other than halo were composed of variables with highest loadings on each factor. Some variables were not included in any composite because they had very large loadings also on halo. No variable was included in more than one composite.

Correlations between Test Composites and Rating Composites

Table 10.12 gives the correlations between the test-factor composites and the three rating-factor composites for both supervisors' and peers' ratings. The coefficients are all quite small, attributable in part to the low reliabilities of the rating-scale variables. Of the 66 coefficients in the table, however, 17 were significant at least at the .05 level, a number well in excess of chance.

There is some degree of system in the locations of the significant rs. There were 12 instances of agreement between superiors' and peers' rating data, but there were five rs significant for one group and not for the other. The composite for field capability had one significant r (for DMT), and this was for the superiors' ratings. The leadership variable had two significant rs in the superiors' data (for CMI_2 and DMT) and two in the peers' data (for CMU and DMT). The great majority of the significant rs are found in the ideation column for both groups of raters. The two groups agreed on this point with respect to CMU, CMS, CMI_2, DMC, and DMT.

Considering the various aptitude composites, that for DMT had the most significant correlations, and CMI_2 was second. CMU, CMS, and DMC composites had two significant correlations each, and those for DMU, EFI, and EMS had none.

There proved to be little or no correspondence between the three rating-factor composites and the aptitude-test composites that were hypothesized to represent the same abilities. For example, the field-capability rating composite was supposed to represent abilities DFT and EFI, yet the correlations of this composite with the DFT and DFI test-score composite were close to zero for both groups of raters. The rating composite for leadership included the ratings designed for ability EMS, yet its correlation with the test-score composite for the same ability lacked statistical significance. The rating composite called "ideation" had components aimed at abilities CMU, DMC, and DMT. Although it correlated zero with the test score designed for CMU, its correlations were .17 and .23 with the composite score for DMC, and .18 and .19 with the score for DMT, for supervisors' and peers' ratings, respectively.

There is a real question of which variables, test-score or rating, should be the criteria to be predicted, and which should be the predictors. Assuming that the test variables had successfully run the gamut of construct validity in more than one factor analysis, the indications seem to be that the ratings of the officers were wide of the mark in the majority of the instances.

More direct indication of the same conclusion was found by estimating factor loadings for the 11 aptitude factors in the rating variables taken singly. This was done by extending the reference frame for the aptitude tests to include vectors for the rating variables, as described in Chapter 4. For the peers' ratings, correlations (extended factor loadings) between the rating variables and their intended factors ranged from −.12 to .18, with a median of .06. Corresponding correlations for the superiors' ratings ranged from −.07 to .14, also with a median of .06. What is more telling regarding the lack of relevance of both sets of ratings, the correlations between corresponding peers' and superiors' rating variables ranged from .08 to .40, for the 12 variables, with a median of .19. The highest correlation was for the trait of leadership. All that can be said is that there were no negative relationships, but ratings by peers and superiors for the same traits had very little in common.

One reason for these failures in the ratings might be the investigators' inability to communicate to the raters, through the rating items, the variables that were to be assessed. Another might be the raters' lack of observation of behavior to be evaluated, for lack of opportunity, or lack of attention to behavior that indicates status on the trait abstractions. The best that can be said for the rating composites is that they indicate abstractions that the raters distinguished to some extent. The three composites were not free from the halo effect, which might have contributed to the correlations in Table 10.12. The composites were not free from halo because almost all their components had some loadings for that variable. That the correlations in the table were not entirely due to halo is indicated by the fact that the number and location of significant rs in the table differ from one rating composite to another and from one aptitude variable to another. It may be said that the locations of significant rs within rows gives us some information as to what SI abilities the raters were emphasizing, whether they realized this or not. From this we could conclude that they had abilities DMT and CMI_2 on their minds, consciously or unconsciously.

RELATIONS OF SI ABILITIES TO OTHER PERSONALITY TRAITS, IN ADULTS

In the course of research events, questions arose concerning possible relations of some of the SI abilities to nonaptitude traits, in the categories of temperament and motivational traits, the latter category including needs, interests, and attitudes. There were several reasons for the appearance of these questions. They arose more particularly in connection with abilities in the divergent-production category, some of which had been given the nonsystemic labels "fluency," "flexibility," and "originality." There could be logical reasons for regarding these qualities as being temperamental in nature. It was for operational reasons that they were given status as abilities, for they were found in tests whose scores indicate *how well* a person performs when presumably he is trying his best.

Reasons for Expecting Relationships

There was empirical evidence regarding some apparently intimate connections, if not identities, for two kinds of flexibility and corresponding temperament traits. It had been found (Report 18) that tests designed to measure perseveration in thinking came out in substantial bipolar relations with tests of spontaneous flexibility, that is, with SI ability DMC. Tests designed for persistence in direction of thinking also came out in substantial negative relations with tests for adaptive flexibility, that is with SI ability DFT.

There were logical reasons for expecting some kinships between certain thinking abilities and certain factorially demonstrated interest traits. Three interest-in-thinking traits had previously been demonstrated (Guilford, Christensen, Bond, & Sutton, 1954); more specifically, interests in logical thinking, meditative thinking, and autistic thinking. It was thought that there might be others, and that some of them might be related on a one-to-one basis with certain thinking abilities that had been demonstrated by factor analysis.

There had been previous studies aimed at relations between interests and abilities, with generally very low correlations found between the two kinds of traits. Generally, however, there had been no utilization of measures of factor traits of either kind, because such studies had antedated knowledge about factorial abilities and interests. In more recent times, with at least the use of factorial scores for abilities represented by the Thurstone PMA tests, and of score variables from the Kuder interest inventory, some of which approach factorial status, and correlating pairs of profiles (one profile for abilities and one for interests) within persons, rather significant results have been obtained (Wesley, Corey, & Stewart, 1950).

Certain theoretical backgrounds should also lead to an investigation of the problem. From psychoanalytic theory we should expect motivational features to have much to do with development of abilities. If there are inter-individual differences in drive profiles, there should be inter-individual differences in ability profiles (Mayman, Schafer, & Rapaport, 1951). Hayes (1962) has more recently defended the thesis that profiles of motivational traits are inherited, from which corresponding profiles of aptitude traits develop.

A New Analysis of Thinking Interests and Other Traits

New Hypothesized Interest Traits Suspecting that three thinking interests do not cover the potential list of such motivational traits, the ARP made further explorations in that direction. Having knowledge of varieties of thinking abilities helped considerably in thinking of possible new interest-factor traits.[7]

The most expeditious route to assessment of interest variables is by way of questionnaire or inventory items. New items were written in accordance with

---

[7] See Report 20; also Guilford, Christensen, Frick, & Merrifield (1961), and Merrifield, Guilford, Christensen & Frick (1961).

hypotheses regarding interest factors to be expected. Since a distinction had been found between divergent and convergent production, two corresponding interest traits were hypothesized. The major distinction was thought to be an interest in working toward a generalized goal versus that toward a particularized goal. Two groups of items for interest in divergent thinking were labeled "Fanciful Thinking" and "Transitional Thinking" (dealing lightly with many ideas). Two other groups of items were called "Adaptive Divergent Thinking" (thinking of many ideas to meet a situation), and "Spontaneous Divergent Thinking" (unfocused production of many ideas). A fifth score variable that belongs in the divergent-production category was called "Whimsical Thinking" (including appreciation of puns, humorous incongruities, and comical activities). It may be noted that some of these variables emphasize fluency and others emphasize flexibility relatively more, suggesting that two factors might be found in the same divergent area.

For the hypothesized interest in convergent thinking, two emphases were applied, with the resulting variables of Decisiveness in Others (admiring decisive people), Decisiveness—Personal (liking to be decisive), and Goal-oriented Thinking (preference for direct, systematic approaches).

For the hypothetical factor for intolerance of ambiguity, the test variables were Black-White Thinking (preference for thinking in terms of absolutes) and Need for Definiteness (dislike for uncertainty).

The three older thinking-interest traits mentioned earlier were also represented by small sets of items for alternative hypotheses in each case. Some other motivational variables in the category of "needs" were also represented in order to verify their right to claim of factorial existence and their distinctness from the new interest variables. These need variables had been brought out by Guilford, Christensen, Bond, and Sutton (1954). Among the need traits were those for variety, freedom, cultural conformity, adventure, discipline, general activity, and precision.

Some Temperament Traits   A few temperament-factor traits were represented, having been selected for their theoretical relevance in connection with the kinds of thinking involved in the divergent and convergent categories of abilities. There were short inventory variables in the analysis for the traits of depression, nervousness, emotionality, ascendance, and self-confidence. Earlier, the trait of persistence was mentioned in connection with adaptive flexibility. To the knowledge of the investigators, a persistence factor had not previously been reported from analyses of inventory scores. Two score variables were included in the new analysis: Rational Persistence (preference for keeping on with one line of thought in solving a problem), and Irrational Persistence (continuation of thinking beyond requirements).

Some Hypotheses regarding Relationships   Some comments are in order to account for the choices of temperament and need variables that might show relations with certain aptitude variables. The bases were mostly purely rational, for there were only a few reports of connections between pairs of variables to provide empirical sources. Some nonaptitude traits that were expected to have negative relations with fluency and flexibility aptitudes were depression and nervousness (as represented in this study by the composite of neurotic tendency), N meticulousness,[8] N discipline, and N precision, all of which would seem to offer restricting influences on rate and diversity in production of ideas. Positive influences on abilities might be expected from certain other traits, including impulsiveness, self-confidence, tolerance of ambiguity, L aesthetic expression,[9] L originality, N general activity, N freedom, and N variety.

Among the aptitude traits, ideational fluency (DMU) and originality (DMT) were expected to be more generally influenced by status on the nonaptitude traits, with spontaneous flexibility a strong third in this respect. Word fluency (DSU) and adaptive flexibility (DFT) were expected to have the smallest numbers of significant relationships. Both seemed to be more specialized, being nonsemantic in terms of content. No predictions were made with respect to relationships with abilities outside the divergent-production category, but opportunities were afforded for finding such relationships.

The Factor Analysis   Altogether, the nonaptitude battery included 250 items in 40 small sets, to give as many score variables. The battery was administered along with selected tests of fluency and originality to 212 U.S. Coast Guard Academy students at the time of entrance examinations. The outcomes of the analysis are reflected roughly in Table 10.13. After considering the obtained factors and their loadings for the various score variables, the investigators drew up a list of nonaptitude factorial variables to be related to the aptitude-factor variables. Those nonaptitude variables and their basic score components are listed in Table 10.13.

The first variable, neurotic tendency, represents a combination of what have been considered two factor traits—depression and nervousness—which failed to separate in the analysis. Two divergent-production variables (traits 16 and 17) appear, since the experimental variables designed for that kind of thinking did not cohere in the analysis. Not all score variables were utilized to help give factor scores because of low factor loadings in some cases. No score variable represented more than one factor.

Aptitude Factors and Their Tests
At the time of this investigation, much attention was being given to divergent-production abilities, especially in the semantic category. A battery for factor analysis that emphasized fluency abilities was administered to 221 Naval air cadets (Report 17), and a battery primarily for flexibility abilities was administered to 208 Air Force cadets. The former group also took the complete inventory for nonaptitude traits, and the latter took a shortened form of it. It was stated earlier that the Coast Guard cadets had had some tests of fluency and flexibility along with the complete inventory. Tests of abilities outside the divergent-production category were also included in the three administrations, so it was possible incidentally to examine correlations of nonaptitude traits with

---
[8] For N, read "need for."
[9] For L, read "liking for."

some additional aptitude variables. In speaking of correlations between traits, it must be understood that it is empirical indicators of those traits that are correlated. The list of SI abilities represented in this study and their representative tests is given in Table 10.14.

Table 10.13   Nonaptitude Score Variables Used to Measure the Various Factors of Needs, Interests, and Temperament Traits

Factor Trait	Score Variables
1. Neurotic tendency	Pessimism, dejection, nervousness
2. N freedom*	Independence
3. N variety	Nonconformity, need for variety
4. L autistic thinking†	Famous person, wealth and power
5. L logical thinking	Logical processes, problem solving
6. Emotionality	Emotional immaturity, emotional excitability
7. N cultural conformity	Moral conformity–general; moral conformity–individual
8. N adventure	Risk taking
9. N meticulousness	Meticulousness, orderliness
10. Impulsiveness	Impulsiveness
11. L convergent thinking	Goal-directed thinking
12. N decisiveness	Decisiveness–personal
13. Ascendance	Ascendance
14. Persistence	Persistence–rational; persistence–irrational
15. N discipline	Discipline–general; discipline–individual
16. L divergent-adaptive thinking	Divergent thinking–adaptive
17. L divergent-spontaneous thinking	Transitional thinking, divergent thinking–spontaneous
18. Tolerance of ambiguity	Black-white thinking, need for definiteness
19. L aesthetic expression	Creative expression, interpretative expression
20. L originality	Fanciful thinking, whimsical thinking
21. L meditative thinking	Meditative thinking
22. N general activity	General activity
23. Self-confidence	Self-confidence
24. N precision	Precision

*The prefix "N" should be translated as "need for."
†The prefix "L" reads "liking for."

Interrelations between Aptitude and Nonaptitude Composites

One approach to seeing what is in common to the two kinds of traits would be to factor-analyze all basic aptitude and nonaptitude score variables together. But from an examination of the complete correlation matrices that included both kinds of variables, it was clear that the two sets of variables were close to orthogonal. A factor analysis would apparently not give the kind of answers that were desired. The choice was therefore to correlate aptitude-factor representatives with nonaptitude-factor representatives, in the form of composite scores from the two sources. The aptitude composites listed in Table 10.14 were correlated with all nonaptitude composites in Table 10.13, wherever this could be done.

The Aptitude and Nonaptitude Composites Each composite score for an ability was a simple sum of two or more test scores, except for SI ability CMU and except for certain tests being absent from one or more of the test batteries. Reliability estimates for these composites ranged from .53 to .89, with a median of .81. Reliability estimates for the nonaptitude variables were more roughly obtained. The Kuder-Richardson-21 estimates from the basic inventory score variables ranged from .20 to .83. Since communalities from the factor analysis ranged systematically higher, these values are generally underestimates. Reliabilities of composites of these scores should be even higher.

Intercorrelations of Composites

The correlations between the two kinds of composites were computed from the known intercorrelations of their components, applying the formula for correla-

Table 10.14 Aptitude Tests Representing the SI Abilities Investigated in Relation to Nonaptitude Traits

SI Code	Ability	Tests
CMU	Verbal comprehension	Verbal Comprehension
CMS	General reasoning	Ship Destination, Circle Square Triangle
DFT	Adaptive flexibility	Match Problems II, Squares
DSU	Word fluency	Rhymes, Suffixes, Word Listing I
DMU	Ideational fluency	Brick Uses (fluency), Plot Titles (nonclever), Riddles (obvious), Thing Listing II
DMC	Spontaneous flexibility	Brick Uses (shifts), Object Naming (cluster)
DMR	Associational fluency	Controlled Associations II, Controlled Associations IIIa, Simile Insertions
DMS	Expressional fluency	Expressional Fluency, Simile Interpretations, Word Arrangement
DMT	Originality	Cartoons, Consequences (remote), Plot Titles (clever), Riddles (clever)
NFT-NST		Hidden Figures, Camouflaged Words
NMR		Inventive Opposites, Vocabulary Completion
EMI	Logical evaluation	Logical Reasoning, Puzzles

tions of sums (Guilford, 1965, p. 545). Only Pearson rs or rational estimates of them were used between the basic score variables, some being biserial rs, some nonaptitude variables having been dichotomized near their medians. The majority of the correlations presented in Table 10.15 are means of the coefficients obtained in the three samples of subjects, i.e., where all three groups had provided the necessary data. Some coefficients represent two samples and some even only one. Some nonaptitude-trait scores were not available from the Air Force sample, as indicated by the blanks, where aptitude-test scores were also missing in the other two groups. The Navy and Coast Guard groups lacked scores for DFT, DMC, NFT-NST, and EMI variables, where the Air Force group lacked scores for traits 1, 2, 5, 8, 10, 13, 22, 23, and 24 (see Table 10.13).

Only coefficients with claim to statistical significance are presented in Table 10.15. Although formulas for significance of correlations of sums are unknown to the authors, for a rough guide, the standard error of a biserial r of zero was used, with summed degrees of freedom from the three sources. Under these conditions, the given rs may be regarded as significant at the .05 level. Although one-tail tests would have been justified where directions of correlations were predicted, two-tail tests were applied throughout.

Although the aptitude variables in Table 10.15 are listed in the order of appearance in the SI model, let us consider the divergent-production abilities first. We note first that the composite for DFT had no significant correlations with any trait composite, in spite of 14 opportunities to show such a correlation. Its failure to correlate with the trait of persistence is the most striking fact, since behavior tests aimed at persistence in thinking were strongly related (negatively) to DFT in an earlier analysis (Report 18). There are two possible reasons for this failure. The trait measured by the behavior tests could be a very different one from that measured by the inventory scores. It could be that the two traits are the same but different kinds of measurement (trait indicators) present poorly correlated evidence. This may be a case of variation due to instrumental difference, such as that pointed out by Campbell and Fiske (1959). The first interpretation is preferable. It would seem that if the trait is the same, and if both instruments are valid, their scores should show at least a significant correlation. The view adopted here is that not all traits are susceptible to measurement by all methods. Even when they are measurable by different methods, some are better measurers than others. The difference in persistence traits is suggested by the fact that the inventory items pertain to persistence in general; they are not confined to persistence in thinking activity. The behavior tests of persistence *were* aimed at the restricted area of thinking activity.

Word fluency (DSU) had two significant correlations, negative with N cultural conformity and positive with N freedom. The signs are in meaningful directions, but it is difficult to relate these traits to DSU logically, rather than to some fluency ability in the semantic category, for which significant correlations with those two traits did not appear.

DMU was correlated with six nonaptitude traits, negatively with neurotic tendency, as predicted, and positively with L logical thinking, impulsiveness, ascendance, L originality, L aesthetic expression, and self-confidence. The relation to L logical thinking was not anticipated, for the latter implies evaluation,

Table 10.15 Significant Intercorrelations between Aptitude Scores and Nonaptitude, Factor-trait Scores*

	Aptitude Variables (SI Abilities)											
Factor Trait	CMU	CMS	DFT	DSU	DMU	DMC	DMR	DMS	DMT	NFT NST	NMR	EMI
1. Neurotic tendency			—†		−14	—				—		—
2. N freedom			—	12		—				—		—
3. N variety												
4. L autistic thinking	−17											
5. L logical thinking		15			11							21
6. Emotionality			—			—				—		—
7. N cultural conformity	−21	−14		−14								
8. N adventure			—			—	13					—
9. N meticulousness	−33								−14	−20		
10. Impulsiveness			—		22	—		25		—		
11. L convergent thinking		23								−25		
12. N decisiveness											18	
13. Ascendance			—		16	—				—		
14. Persistence	−22											—
15. N discipline									−17			

16.	L divergent-adaptive thinking							16
17.	L divergent-spontaneous thinking	21						12
18.	Tolerance of ambiguity	25		15				26
19.	L aesthetic expression		—		16			—
20.	L originality					16		25
21.	L meditative thinking	18	22				21	
22.	General activity	−22	—					13
23.	Self-confidence		—	20				—
24.	N precision		—					20

*Decimal points omitted.
†Nonaptitude-trait scores not available.

333

which should place some restriction upon quantity of output of ideas. The relation to L originality might be due to the fact that most tests of DMU were also tests of DMT, e.g., Plot Titles, Consequences, and Riddles, all scored also for originality, and the tasks may look like tests of originality to Es.

DMC had only one significant correlation, and that was with L meditative thinking, where it was not expected. Of all the traits in the list, DMC should be related to N variety, since shifting from class to class is the essence of that ability. Meditative thinking does suggest freedom to roam about among ideas, and in that sense could be relevant. We shall see that L meditative thinking is related to a number of the SI-ability variables, and thus seems to have a *general* bearing upon intellectual activity. Es high on this trait may be more highly motivated for many intellectual tasks.

DMR shows two correlations in Table 10.15, with N adventure and tolerance of ambiguity, neither of which was predicted. A common leading test for DMR has been Associational Fluency, in which E is to list words meaning almost the same as a given word. E could gain longer lists if he can tolerate the uncertainty of answers doubtfully related to the given word. To say that the more the adventurous Es extend their searches to more risky answers may be only a metaphorical statement, since items for N adventure pertain to geographical explorations and risks of personal danger, not risks in thinking.

Three traits—impulsiveness, L aesthetic expression, and L meditative thinking—are reasonably related to the score for DMS. Tests for DMS commonly call for the composing of sentences, in limited time. In speed tests, it should pay to be impulsive, provided the probability of errors is low. Writing can be an art, associated with which L aesthetic expression is natural. The general applicability of L meditative thinking was mentioned earlier. It is related to 5 of the 12 abilities in the list.

DMT, which was first given the label "originality," would seem to be the epitome of creative-thinking endeavor, and evidence of it should be apparent to the average, educated person. In the SI model, also, it is lodged in both the divergent-production and transformation categories, thus having a double claim for its creative potentialities. The same distinction in SI placement applies also to DFT, which, it may be recalled, was rated highest by the research scientists. One might therefore expect a greater number of relations to nonaptitude traits for such abilities and their tests. DFT showed only two such relations (in single populations), but there were restrictions that probably prevented the appearance of others.

At any rate, DMT showed seven relationships, all reasonable. There were two negative relations, with N meticulousness and N discipline, both of which had been predicted. The strongest positive relations were with L aesthetic expression and L meditative thinking, both of which were expected. Other relations were with L divergent-adaptive thinking, tolerance of ambiguity, and self-confidence. One of the relationships most naturally expected, that involving L originality, did not materialize, at least in terms of an average correlation. A correlation of .27 did occur in one sample in which the two variables were present. It could be that the trait of L originality was misinterpreted and wrongly named. It did have a significant average correlation with DMU, whose composite score was derived from three tests also involving DMT, when scored differently.

The composite score that involved the two convergent-production abilities, NFT and NST, correlated negatively with two trait scores where positive correlations might seem more reasonable. The two traits were N meticulousness and L convergent production. It may be that, for E, the convergent-production aspect of the two tests for this composite is very much overshadowed by the transformation aspect. Both tests call for one right answer, but E has to make a detour, so to speak, in arriving at that answer, a detour that he dislikes to make, in his progress toward his goal, if he likes convergent thinking. The negative relation to N meticulousness is easier to rationalize. The meticulous person likes to keep things in order. Breaking up the obvious gestalt in order to achieve a new one in the NFT and NST tests leads the person through disorder. The meticulous person would probably prefer to keep the order he sees first.

N decisiveness was hypothesized to have a kinship with convergent production, and apparently it has, judging from the correlation with the composite for NMR. A correlation of .19 between the same aptitude composite and the score for N precision in one sample and an r of $-.18$ with L spontaneous divergent thinking in the same sample suggest some appreciation, however implicit, that the NMR tasks are convergent in nature.

The composite for EMI (which probably also involves EMR) correlates with L logical thinking, which could not be a more reasonable choice, and with L meditative thinking, the latter appearing to be a more general intellectual interest, as stated before. No traits had been hypothesized to go with evaluation abilities or their tests. N precision might be expected in that category, but there was no opportunity to test that hypothesis in this study.

Returning to cognition abilities CMU and CMS, we find that the measure of CMU showed eight significant correlations with the traits listed in Table 10.15. Three correlations were positive, and five were negative. The positive correlations were with tolerance of ambiguity, L aesthetic expression, and L meditative thinking. We have seen before the latter's inclination to go with a number of intellectual abilities. L autistic thinking does not seem to share that generality, as shown by its negative correlation with CMU. The other instances of negative correlation indicate that persons high in CMU are likely to be low in N cultural conformity, N meticulousness, N persistence, and N general activity. Since CMU ordinarily dominates measures of verbal IQ and verbal academic aptitude, these correlations lead to similar inferences regarding the concept of "general intelligence," as traditionally conceived.

The correlations with the CMS composite are less numerous. Persons high in the major ability in solving arithmetical problems also tend to like logical thinking and convergent thinking, which seems natural. Like those who are high on CMU, they are likely to be low on N cultural conformity. It is curious that, whereas low cultural conformity is popularly associated with creative persons, there is only one negative correlation with seven divergent-production abilities, and there are two with the two cognition abilities in the list.

Some General Implications

The general lesson in the correlational results is that there is very little relation between the SI abilities on the one hand and traits of temperament and motivation on the other, when the latter are measured by inventory scores. There is certainly not enough relation to support any theory that one set of traits develops systematically as a consequence of the other. Besides the very low correlations, there is no clear set of motivational traits that parallel the SI abilities on a one-to-one basis. Where there are significant correlations, it seems to the writers that the best interpretation is that some nonaptitude traits make very small contributions to variances in scores from some aptitude tests. It would be less reasonable to infer that the SI abilities make small contributions to variances in the nonaptitude score variables, although this inference cannot be excluded without having further evidence.

It might be thought that, because both kinds of measures fall short of perfect reliability, the obtained coefficients of intercorrelation do not represent very well the extent of relationships that actually exist. If the coefficients were corrected for attenuation, however, it is estimated that they would be increased in size by only about one-third. A coefficient of .15 raised by one-third is still a very small correlation.

Taking the coefficients at their face values, we can say only that the proportions of variances in common to the two kinds of variables are in the range of from 1 to 10 percent, with most of the overlaps being about 4 percent or less. It is quite possible that correlations between profiles of the two sets of traits within individuals would run higher than intercorrelations between traits do within populations. In correlating profiles, however, it would be very difficult to know which aptitude trait should be paired off with which nonaptitude trait. It might be that outside the test situation, and where conditions are less restricted, the nonaptitude traits would show higher relations with intellectual performances. But an expectation of such results is only conjectural.

And what of the substantial relations between test scores for abilities DMC and DFT on the one hand and behavior-test scores of perseveration and persistence, respectively, on the other, as shown in Report 18? In the study just given attention, there were results only in the form of correlations of inventory scores for persistence and scores for DFT, since no inventory items were prepared for perseveration. From the results available, it would seem best to conclude that persistence-in-thinking test scores measure DFT in reverse and that, by implication, perseveration-in-thinking test scores measure DMC in reverse. A shift in polarity of scales would give such tests positive loadings in both cases. Variables of perseveration and persistence assessed by inventories are probably different traits. One needs to be wary of the assumption that two variables that somehow acquire the same name are therefore the same thing.

RELATIONS OF SI ABILITIES TO OTHER PERSONALITY TRAITS, IN CHILDREN

A study similar to that just reported with adult males was conducted with boys and girls at the seventh-grade level (see Report 28). Besides the differences in age and in sex, the study with children was confined to the six semantic-divergent-production abilities. In addition to test scores for those abilities and scores from personality inventories for selected nonaptitude traits, ratings of the children made by teachers were obtained on a number of comparable, if not parallel, traits, both aptitude and nonaptitude. The variables involved thus included scores from aptitude tests and from personality inventories, and also ratings made by teachers with respect to many of the same traits, aptitude and nonaptitude. The relations between aptitude scores and ratings of aptitude variables were discussed in an earlier section of this chapter. Here we are concerned with relations between the aptitude scores and both scores and ratings for the nonaptitude variables.

The Variables and Their Measures

The tests used to measure the six SI abilities were listed in Table 10.2. It is necessary to describe the other variables here.

The Inventory Variables Preliminary to the selection of traits to be covered with inventory items, a series of four factor analyses of single items as experimental variables was carried out for each sex. Items were first selected because they seemed logically to represent traits that might be related to the SI abilities involved or to represent interests in different types of thinking. Results from the earlier study with adults were also taken into consideration (Report 20). Some of the resulting factors appeared to be the same for boys and girls, but others appeared to differ somewhat, so they were given different interpretations accordingly. Following are the lists of the interpreted, nonaptitude factors found in the inventory items for boys and girls. Where the factors were similar but not identical, they are listed with numbers in common.

1. *Persistence*—the disposition to stick to a task until it is completed, despite varying degrees of obstacles in the way.
2B. *Spontaneity*—the disposition to act without contemplation or planning, on the spur of the moment; to act without waiting for much information.
2G. *Initiative*—the disposition of desire for change, independence, and decisiveness.
3B. *Impulsiveness*—the disposition to act with poor conscious control over impulses, to be irresponsible, or to act with poor judgment.
3G. *Lack of restraint*—impulsive expression, resulting in unreflective acts, in inability to complete tasks, and in a lack of caution in social relationships.
4B. *Need for rules*—a need for explicit and absolute rules and laws, and for strict enforcement of rules.
4G. *Need for authority*—a need for explicit, absolute, strict, and inflexible external structuring, as well as an unquestioning respect for authority.
5. *Liking for originality*—a liking for wild, humorous, silly, and original ideas; a perception of one's self as a humorous person.
6. *Self-confidence*—confidence in one's ability, optimism about the future, and assurance that others are interested in and accept one.

Table 10.16 Significant Correlations between Inventory Scores for Nonaptitude Traits and Test Scores for Divergent-production Abilities*

Scored Trait Variable	Correlations, for boys, with:								Correlations, for girls, with:							
	DMU_1	DMU_2	DMC	DMR	DMS	DMT_1	DMT_2	DMI	DMU_1	DMU_2	DMC	DMR	DMS	DMT_1	DMT_2	DMI
1. Persistence	—	—	—	—	—	—	—	—	—	15	—	20	16	19	—	28
2B. Spontaneity	—	—	—	-15	-21	—	—	—	—	—	—	—	—	—	—	†
2G. Initiative	—	—	—	—	—	—	—	—	—	—	—	—	—	—	—	—
3B. Impulsiveness	—	—	—	—	—	—	—	—	—	—	—	—	—	—	—	—
3G. Lack of restraint	—	—	—	—	—	—	—	—	—	—	—	-18	—	-19	—	-13
4B. Need for rules	—	—	—	—	—	-14	-13	—	—	—	—	—	—	—	—	—
4G. Need for authority	—	—	—	—	—	—	—	—	—	-15	-28	-20	—	-15	-24	-22
5. L originality	—	—	—	—	—	—	—	—	—	-15	13	—	—	—	—	—
6. Self-confidence	—	—	—	—	—	15	14	—	—	—	15	18	—	20	17	18
7B. Adaptive flexibility	—	—	—	15	13	15	—	—	—	—	—	—	—	—	—	—
7G. Tolerance of ambiguity	—	—	—	—	—	—	—	—	—	—	—	—	—	—	—	—
8B. Fluency	—	—	—	13	—	—	—	—	—	—	—	—	—	—	—	—
8G. Moral relativism	—	—	—	—	—	—	—	—	—	-15	-15	-18	—	-18	—	-16

*Decimal points omitted.
†No correlations computed; trait does not apply.

7B. *Adaptive flexibility*—the disposition to be flexible in attitude and in problem solving, involving the belief that changing set is helpful in arriving at solutions.

7G. *Tolerance of ambiguity*—flexibility in attitudes; a willingness to consider alternative solutions and different approaches, with a belief that people do not need structure and restrictions.

8B. *Fluency of ideas*—the disposition to produce a quantity of ideas; a perception of self as an idea producer.

8G. *Moral relativism*—a desire for less strict, less absolute, and less restrictive authority, and a belief in leniency when conditions warrant a breaking of rules.

The resulting factor scales were restricted to from four to eight items each; hence internal-consistency reliabilities were not high. The estimates ranged from .28 to .56 for the boys' scales and from .19 to .64 for the girls' scales. These low reliabilities need to be kept in mind in interpreting the correlations of these scales with aptitude scores.

Rating Variables for Nonaptitude Traits   In the following list are given the seven nonaptitude traits and their definitions, as indicated in Report 28:

1. *Impulsiveness*—the tendency to act or to make decisions without first making a plan.
2. *Need for variety*—need for frequent change and for new experiences.
3. *Self-confidence*—assurance of one's own abilities.
4. *Liking for unrestricted thinking*—the tendency to produce ideas not directly or obviously related to situations.
5. *Persistence*—the tendency to maintain a course of thought or action until a task is completed.
6. *Need for structure*—a need for clear, explicit conceptions of situations and for knowledge of specific requirements of tasks.
7. *Liking for originality*—an appreciation of unique, clever, or unusual ideas, points of view, and activities.

Resulting Intercorrelations

Correlations with Inventory Scores   We consider first the correlations between inventory scores and aptitude-test scores. Such data were obtained for boys and girls separately.

The first impression given by Table 10.16 is that there are more significant correlations than should be expected by chance (an r of .13 should be significant at the .05 level, and one of .18 significant at the .01 level). A second general impression is that there were more significant correlations for girls than for boys. This result, indicating that the girls' aptitude-test scores were more predictable than the boys', is consistent with results shown in Table 10.3.

To generalize further, where a trait variable has negative correlations with test scores, all the given correlations are negative, except that the results are in opposite directions for boys and girls when the trait is persistence. Experience and logic should lead us to expect negative correlations also with the trait variable of need for rules, and for the boys they are negative. The similar trait for girls had negative correlations for all except ability DMS.

Table 10.17 Significant Correlations between Ratings of Nonaptitude Traits and Test Scores for Divergent-production Abilities*

	Correlations, for boys, with:										Correlations, for girls, with:					
Rated Trait Variables	DMU_1	DMU_2	DMC	DMR	DMS	DMT_1	DMT_2	DMI	DMU_1	DMU_2	DMC	DMR	DMS	DMT_1	DMT_2	DMI
Impulsiveness																
N variety		−13									13	14				
Self-confidence	16		17	19	22	26	20	20			26	27	13	28	21	
L unrestricted thinking			25	24	15	25	16	17		13	35	32	27	38	31	26
Persistence	19			21	22	19	15	19			26	31	28	28	21	25
N structure			−15		−23	−22	−17			−14	−15	−19		−29	−17	−23
L originality	13		15	21	20	22		22		19	37	34	27	41	30	29

*Correlations for ratings by homeroom teachers; decimal points omitted.

But, in addition to the unexpected reversal in direction of correlations with persistence in the case of girls, the variables of lack of restraint and moral relativism correlate negatively where there would be reason to expect positive relations. Freedom from restraint would appear to be a hindrance rather than a help in the case of girls. The boys had no significant correlations with impulsiveness. "Moral relativism" was defined as a desire for relaxation of moral requirements, which, according to popular belief, should lead us to expect positive correlations between that variable and divergent-production tests. These departures from expectation suggest the suspicion that girls regard persistence as a desirable quality, and the more able ones on the DP tests tend to answer the self-descriptive questions more in the direction of persistence. Girls tend to regard lack of restraint and moral relativism as unfavorable traits, and the more able ones on the DP tests tend to answer the questions more in those unfavorable directions.

It is of interest to compare the results from boys and girls with those from young-adult males, as reported in the previous section. This can be done only for five semantic-DP abilities (lacking DMI) and for such inventory variables as can be accepted as being logically equivalent or similar. The adults' samples showed no significant correlations for persistence, where both boys' and girls' samples did so, but with opposite signs. Impulsiveness and lack of restraint, two similar traits, had no significant correlations in the boys' sample; negative rs for DMR, DMT, and DMI in the girls' sample; and positive rs for DMU and DMS, in the adults' sample. For liking for originality the boys showed no significant rs; the girls had two rs, but of opposite sign; and the men had one positive r, for DMU. Self-confidence had a significant r with both DMT tests in the boys' data; rs with five abilities in the girls' data; and rs for DMU and DMT in the men's data. Tolerance of ambiguity was not assessed for boys, and girls showed no significant rs for it, but the men had rs with DMS and DMT. Thus, only for the trait of self-confidence were correlations similar in the three groups. For girls and men, correlations for similar traits were often opposite in sign, as they were in one case in comparisons of boys and girls.

Relations of Rated Traits to Aptitude Scores   Table 10.17 presents results from correlations of seven trait-rating variables with the eight DP tests for boys and girls. Here the numbers and sizes of coefficients are distinctly greater than when inventory scores were used. The secret for this trend is probably to be found in the halo effects of teachers' ratings, in which the temperament and motivational traits are generally confused with the DP abilities.

The lack of correlations for impulsiveness in the case of boys is entirely consistent with the results for the inventory trait of the same name in Table 10.16. For girls, however, the similar trait of lack of restraint measured by an inventory score correlated negatively with three abilities, whereas the two correlations in Table 10.17 are positive. Self-confidence again almost sweeps the board. Teachers must have noticed that self-confidence and divergent production, perhaps observed as superior performance in problem solving, are affiliated. Another tie must have been noticed between liking for unrestricted thinking and performances of the same type. The almost universal positive correlation between rated persistence and the aptitude scores may indicate a halo effect—an assumed tie between two other supposedly favorable qualities. On the other hand, a somewhat consistent tie of a negative kind seems to have been noted between DP performances and the rated need for structure. Perhaps the logical dissimilarity of unrestricted thinking and need for structure made the difference. For the first time, the rated variable of liking for originality correlated generally with the aptitude-test scores. Perhaps the halo was again at work, or a similarity was noted between the traits of liking for unrestricted thinking and liking for originality.

SUMMARY AND CONCLUSIONS

This chapter has been concerned primarily with validation problems, with interest in construct validity of SI abilities from evidence from outside the factor analyses themselves, but more interest in predictive validity, with academic performances and work performances as criteria. A special interest was in relations of the SI abilities to temperamental and motivational traits, in view of occasional expressions indicating persistent expectations of overlaps of this kind expressed by psychologists concerned with personality.

Two studies took the route of correlating tests and factor scores of selected SI abilities with ratings designed to assess the same abilities. One was in a seventh-grade population, and the other was in a population of U.S. Marine officers. The former was confined to the six semantic-divergent-production abilities; the latter sampled 11 abilities more broadly. In both cases the usual difficulties with ratings of abstractly defined qualities were evident—low reliabilities with high intercorrelations between assessed traits, the latter indicating strong halo effects. The correlations between SI-ability scores and ratings were very low, although the numbers of significant coefficients exceeded chance levels. Correlations between paired measures of the same traits were usually not noticeably higher than for the nonmatched measures. The net results from these two rating studies were clearly negative.

Efforts in determining relevance of certain SI abilities in connection with certain areas of academic achievement gave many positive findings. When the criterion variables were course grades at the U.S. Coast Guard Academy, a number of the SI-test variables correlated significantly, as high as .4, with grades. The test for any single factorial ability should not be expected to correlate very high with grades in any course, owing to the factorial complexity of grades. Best predictions of complex criteria are obtained by means of multiple-regression equations that weight the factors optimally.

In a study of aptitude for higher mathematics (calculus courses), four SI abilities stood out as most predictive of grades, ratings, or achievement-test scores, among nine abilities that were represented. They were spatial orientation (CFS), spatial visualization (CFT), divergent production of figural transformations (DFT), and evaluation of semantic implications (EMI). EMR was also probably involved in the last instance. Three of these abilities are in the visual-figural-content area, two of them involving transformations. It looks as if the calculus students depended very much for success on visual-spatial thinking and on flexibility of thinking. They may have resorted to semantic thinking when it came to evaluating results.

In a major study of mathematics achievement at the ninth-grade level, more than 15 SI abilities were represented by ARP tests and 4 SI abilities by part scores from three standard academic-aptitude tests. Four levels of instruction were involved, two of general mathematics and two of algebra. The criteria utilized were scores from two special achievement examinations administered at the end of the school year. Of 24 ARP tests, 23 correlated significantly with the general-mathematics criterion, and 13 did so with the algebra criterion. Using scores for 13 factorial abilities, the multiple correlations were .46 and .45 in the two general-mathematics courses and .39 and .75 in the algebra courses, the Rs being corrected for bias. With the scores from the three standard academic-aptitude tests included in turn in the regression equations, the multiple Rs ranged from .59 to .65 for general mathematics and .54 to .85 for algebra. Different factors were represented in the two sources, accounting for significant gains from combining tests from the two.

A discriminant-function analysis for predicting whether students were in the successful (with above-median achievement scores) general-mathematics group or the successful algebra group yielded predictions with about 90 percent accuracy. The predictors were composites of ARP SI-ability tests only.

Two other criterion studies were in the academic context, with special criteria of academic types of learning utilized. Since much school learning is devoted to the mastery of new concepts, three concept-learning tasks were devised, each involving efforts in mastery of four concepts (rules), one task each in the areas of figural, symbolic, and semantic content. The objective was to determine which of selected SI abilities were involved in those learning tasks. Loadings for 12 "stage" scores from each learning task were estimated on 15 factors for SI abilities.

Loadings and communalities were small. This fact, in connection with reliability estimates, indicated that abilities outside the 15 must also have had something to do with work on the learning tasks. Among the factors having the strongest loadings were those for memory, particularly for memory for semantic classes (MMC). Among the smallest loadings were those for divergent-production abilities, suggesting that if there were much trial-and-error behavior in the tasks, it was of little relevance for success. Among the next highest loadings were those for convergent production, especially among the stage scores later in learning. The cognition abilities gave the most interesting results. For both the symbolic and semantic tasks, in the earliest stage scores the loadings were negative for the respective factors. As learning progressed, loadings in both cases increased in linear relationship with practice, being strongest at the end of the experiment, where learning was still incomplete.

Two SI abilities that ordinarily dominate academic-aptitude tests, CMU and CMS, had few significant loadings in connection with learning scores. The general conclusion is that learning of this type is related most to cognition and memory abilities that deal with classes.

Another type of common academic-learning task is that of reading and remembering information. A reading-and-remembering task was used as a criterion in a study that emphasized transformation abilities. The hypothesis, derived originally from Gestalt psychology, was that much learning is in the form of revision of formerly held information. In a multiple-regression analysis, the factor score for CMU had the highest beta coefficient, but following it were scores for memory for semantic transformations (MMT) and cognition of the same (CMT), with other transformation abilities making significant contributions to prediction. The multiple R was .58, for a composite of seven predictors, all with significant contributions. The Gestalt hypothesis thus received strong support; much learning through reading is a matter of revising what is already known. It may also be true that remembering those changes helps one to remember other products of information as well.

A very different kind of study was aimed at determining how creative research scientists and other creative people evaluate different abilities for importance in their work. Twenty-eight selected SI abilities were defined for these subjects, who were asked to place them in ranked categories. The research people rated among the most important abilities some of those having to do with transformations—in other words, those involving flexibility. They rated convergent-production abilities generally higher than divergent-production abilities and cognition abilities. The nonresearch group, however, rated divergent-production abilities relatively higher.

In three studies with young-adult, male subjects, 12 SI abilities, with an emphasis upon divergent production, were correlated with 24 nonaptitude variables in the form of inventory scores. Traits of both temperamental and motivational qualities were involved. The motivational list included six traits of interest in different kinds of thinking. All 24 traits had been demonstrated by at least one factor analysis.

The intercorrelations across the two major groups of traits were quite low, typically under .20, but with a clear excess of significant rs. Five of the nonaptitude variables had 3 or more significant rs, out of 11 possible rs. Two of these traits had negative correlations only—N (need for) cultural conformity and N meticulousness. Thus, less able Ss in the SI abilities tend to be higher in these two qualities. The other three traits had only positive correlations with abilities—tolerance of ambiguity, L (liking for) aesthetic expression, and L meditative thinking.

In a study with seventh grade children, 13 inventory scores for factor traits were correlated with measures of the six semantic-divergent-production abilities. The girls had many more significant rs than the boys. For girls, there were four or five significant correlations with inventory traits for measures of four abilities, where boys had three such correlations each, for two abilities. Ability DMS had no significant r for either sex group, whereas DMR and DMT showed some relations for both sexes.

When seven defined nonaptitude traits were rated by teachers of the children, significant correlations with measures of the same six SI abilities were numerous, ranging up to .4. The ratings were obviously loaded with a halo, and that halo was strongly related to IQ. This fact suggests that teachers rated all qualities they regarded as good in line with what they knew of the IQ status of each child. As with the rating results cited at the beginning of this summary, ratings of abstract variables here proved to be of little value.

By way of general conclusions, it may be said that there is little or no evidence that would support the belief that different abilities are dependent genetically or otherwise upon motivational or temperamental dispositions. The small relationships that can be found between the two kinds of measures probably mean that the nonaptitude traits contribute differentially to performances on aptitude tests to an average extent of less than 10 percent.

The few studies reported here on relations of SI abilities to achievement in various academic courses indicate that there are many potential dividends to be expected by using predictors of achievement that go well beyond the restricted number of SI abilities now represented in academic-aptitude tests. Only a minor sampling of such abilities have as yet been investigated in relation to a limited number of courses. Using multiple predictions, with different combinations of SI abilities represented, seems to be the best answer to the academic-prediction problem.

In relation to learning exercises of types quite common in education, abilities other than those that now dominate standard aptitude tests appear to be equally relevant or even more relevant—for example, abilities pertaining to memory and other operations and to the products of classes and transformations. The way seems open to very searching investigations of learning events within wide educational contexts.

ELEVEN
SOME GENERAL CONSIDERATIONS

In order to make the story of the 20 years of investigation of intellectual abilities or functions by the Aptitudes Research Project more complete, it is desirable to give further thought to experiences gained from that undertaking. Most of the things considered here are of a general nature, such as the role of factor analysis as a scientific method, the importance of taxonomies in science, and implications of the ARP experiences for psychology and for testing policies and practices.

FACTOR ANALYSIS AS A SCIENTIFIC METHOD
Those who factor-analyze for the purpose of discovering fundamental, underlying variables in behavior or in mental functioning must recognize the circumstance that their findings have not made deep or far-reaching impressions on those who do not. In fact, there is much looking askance at their findings, and for sufficient reasons in too many cases—not always for the right reasons, however. The truth of the matter seems to be that some of those who

factor-analyze have expected too much and claimed too much for a method that cannot automatically yield compelling conclusions. And those who do not factor-analyze do not realize the sensitivity and suggestiveness regarding the nature of psychological events that the method has to offer. It can be an excellent hypothesis-testing device that can be very productive, as the preceding chapters should have demonstrated. Its best promise for psychology thus far has been in the development of taxonomies.

Need for Taxonomies of Behavior

Where some other sciences have given considerable attention to development of taxonomies in their own fields, psychology has been negligent in this respect. It has much too often proceeded to attempt to answer questions of "how" and "why," without first answering questions of "what." It has too often investigated on a kind of catch-as-catch-can basis, with "what" concepts of relatively short life. As one consequence, its poverty of enduring, general laws is notorious, in a society that cries out for behavioral principles needed in solutions of problems. A more localized consequence is the Tower of Babel atmosphere of the body politic of psychology, and its tendencies toward scientific schizophrenia.

Taxonomies in the Natural Sciences By contrast, we can readily see how other sciences have prospered, having given attention to taxonomies. Perhaps this subject suggests first the field of biology, with its hierarchical systems of plants and animals. To cite evidence of the value of this activity in biology, it is necessary only to mention one name—Charles Darwin.

In considering the logical consequences of taxonomies, it is interesting in passing to apply some structure-of-intellect concepts to what scientists do. Observations of similarities of *units* within a sphere of information lead to categories and *class* ideas. Observations of distinctions or differences of various kinds lead to *relations* and variables. Observations of regularities in complex phenomena lead to principles or *systems* of information. Observations of dependencies lead to laws of the type "Y is a function of X," or of the type "If X, then Y," which is an *implication*. Thus, the product categories of SI theory are involved in the scientist's construction of taxonomies and in deducing important consequences from them.

The physical sciences also have their taxonomies. Physics grew by the recognition of the various manifestations of energy and by the invention of the three variables of the CGS system. There is still apparent room for further taxonomic efforts. Chemistry gained enormously, obviously, by virtue of its systematic table of elements. Both sciences continue to gain through discoveries of kinds of nuclear particles and knowledge acquired about their properties.

Taxonomies in Psychology There have been a few historical attempts to construct taxonomies in psychology, of course, but some of the outcomes remain just that—historical. The earliest of these was made by the "faculty psychologists," with their small list of "mental powers." Faculty psychology gained such a bad reputation that more than one generation of psychology students have been unthinkingly conditioned against it. It was not the faculty psychologists' type of thinking that should have been condemned. Where they were wrong was in their choice of faculty concepts and for regarding them as unitary powers or functions when they are decidedly not. The main trouble with the faculty psychologists was that they lacked empirical methods for discovering unitary or unique functions and for checking up on their hypotheses regarding them.

Where the faculty of "memory" was hypothecated, SI theory calls for 24 kinds of ability, 18 of which have been investigated and demonstrated, as described in Chapter 8. Where a faculty of "reasoning" was traditional, SI theory calls for 24 cognition abilities, many of which can be regarded as unique cases of inductive-reasoning functioning, and for 24 convergent-production abilities, which are in the deductive-reasoning area. All 24 of the cognition abilities have been demonstrated and 15 of the convergent-production abilities, all that have been investigated (see Chapter 5). Where there was a faculty of "judgment," modern factor-analytic operations have shown 18 of the projected 24 evaluation abilities (see Chapter 7). Instead of a faculty of "creative imagination," we can now suggest a set of 24 divergent-production functions, 23 of which have been investigated and demonstrated (see Chapter 6).

To return to history, taxonomies of a very different nature were explored and suggested by Wundt and Titchener, who proposed three kinds of elements of consciousness—sensations, images, and feelings—and also Titchener's five dimensions of sensory experience. Titchener also emphasized geometric models to account for varieties of sensory content, in the areas of vision, taste, smell, and somesthetic experiences. Such taxonomies have been useful, within their limited spheres of relevance.

Another area in which taxonomies were attempted included varieties of instincts, taxonomies that found culmination in W. McDougall's pairings of instincts and emotions. Except for more recent dimensional studies of emotions, feelings, and moods, this kind of effort has been regarded as outmoded, too hastily so. Wundt's dimensional model for feelings seems to have been rediscovered by Osgood and his associates (Osgood, Suci, & Tannenbaum, 1957). Emotions may need some other type of model.

The psychoanalytic search for "mechanisms" and "complexes" should also be cited as efforts to find a list of taxonomic categories. To the knowledge of the writers, no rigorous hypothesis-testing procedures have been applied to determine the validity of such concepts. But the efforts in this direction are other examples of recognized needs for basic vocabularies.

Reflection upon the apparent relative lack of interest and the lack of concerted taxonomy-building activity on the part of psychologists suggests three possible reasons. Already mentioned is the lack of more natural empirical methods by which taxonomic hypotheses can be examined. The ways of observation and the ways of reduction of data in modern factor analysis and multivariate scaling procedures are now available. The increasing availability of computer services makes applications of such methods quite feasible.

A great distracting influence has been the preoccupation with the minutiae of stimulus-response psychology, and the kind of thinking that goes with it. The preference for the study of activity is understandable. Theory about ongoing behavior requires operational models rather than taxonomic models, but taxonomic concepts can be of prime value in the construction of operational models, as can be seen in Guilford's model for problem solving (Guilford, 1967).

Another deterring influence has been the very general urge to oversimplify. It is ridiculous to believe that the enormous range and variety of behavioral events can be accounted for with two or three concepts or principles, universally applied, whether it be in the form of classical conditioning, operant learning, or Spearman's g. Psychologists have taken the demand from Occam's razor much too seriously. Too many have been searching for the "philosophers' stone," without success. They must become reconciled to a multiplicity of concepts. No matter what the number, it will still be decidedly smaller than the number of psychological events for which those concepts stand. Any reasonable gap between the number of concepts and the number of events could still satisfy demand for parsimony.

Where Taxonomies Are Needed   In his book on personality, Guilford (1959a) attempted to show just how far factor-analytic procedures had gone toward distinguishing personality traits of all kinds. Factorial traits of personality were regarded as relatively permanent dispositions, each of a unique character. Such dispositions predetermine behavior of certain kinds, in conjunction with determiners in the form of relatively temporary dispositions, such as moods, feelings, and emotions, and of course, in response to immediate situations. Behavior traits were classified in the major modalities of aptitudes, including psychomotor abilities, perceptual abilities, and intellectual abilities; temperamental dimensions; and hormetic or motivational traits, including needs, interests, and attitudes. Taxonomic models were suggested in the areas of temperament and psychomotor abilities, as well as in the modality of intellectual abilities. Where the SI model for the latter is a three-dimensional matrix, those for temperament and psychomotor abilities are two-dimensional matrices or cross-classifications. No model was suggested for the motivational traits, but it appeared that one of a hierarchical type might be more realistic. These examples are cited to show that the possibility exists for integrating factor-isolated variables into meaningful and systematic models, which offer opportunities to generate further significance psychologically.

The multidimensional approach to the temporary dispositions of feelings, emotions, and moods was mentioned earlier. In this connection, however, there should be an openness to models other than dimensional ones, as being possibly more realistic. Other dispositions that have been investigated by factor analysis are known as "cognitive styles." There is little doubt that in the intellectual processing of information, to which many investigators apply the term "cognition," the management of such processes or abilities is something to be considered. There appear to be certain intellectual habits that have bearings on *how* an individual approaches problems of different kinds, as well as on *what* he thinks. Also calling for taxonomic study are kinds of strategies that individuals use in problem solving, including the solving of problems in taking various tests of intellectual abilities.

Intellectual abilities, cognitive dispositions, and strategies are involved in reaching decisions, but if behavior does not stop there, as it usually does not, there arise further steps in putting decisions into action. In this connection there may be a whole family of "executive functions," as mentioned in another place (Guilford, 1967). There was a possibility that such basic functions were brought out in a factor analysis of production of emotional expressions (Report 42).

Factor-analytic explorations need not stop with such more generalized dispositions as traits, styles, and strategies. Particular personal habits of many kinds might also offer a field in which taxonomic concepts and categories could be sought. Habits are responses to particular situations, which suggests that there could also be taxonomies of situations, and more broadly conceived, taxonomies of environments. In reporting behavioristic investigations, situations, even particular stimuli, are often poorly described. This is probably for lack of effective descriptive terms or concepts regarding stimulating conditions. Such descriptions as are given are generally unsystematic, without reference to variables or categories having behavioral significance. This investigative situation should be corrected. There have been occasional expressions of needs in this direction, but little has been done about the matter, except in educational research where home, school, and classroom environments have been more or less successfully measured and categorized in attempts to relate such conditions to educational achievements.

Need for Multivariate Methods

It is a truism that human behavior is exceedingly complex. The numbers of independent and dependent variables are very great, mostly unknown, unrecognized, and often improperly ignored. There is a generalization that has been dignified by calling it a "law" (van Heerden, 1968) to the effect that everything is more complicated than it seems. Analysis and further analysis bear out this assertion. Even nuclear particles may in turn be broken down. Van Heerden also mentions a counter law, to the effect that everything is simpler than it seems. It is probably safe to say that the simpler picture is more adequate when derived after the complex picture has been achieved.

Guilford (1967) has elaborated to some extent upon the relative advantages of multivariate-experimental approaches over bivariate-experimental approaches, where complex behavioral phenomena must be dealt with, and where knowledge of concepts and variables is limited or uncertain. It is sufficient to reemphasize this point here. In addition to its inadequacies for dealing with complexity, the bivariate approach is more likely to limit itself to overt variables, such as stimulus and response variables. This approach is thus likely to confine the investigator to a rank empiricism, without benefit of general theory, and too often to the discovery of trivia. By contrast, the multivariate approach offers opportunities for finding underlying variables, which are often the most relevant and most worth knowing, and which lend themselves more readily to basic-theory construction.

Optimal Uses of Factor Analysis in Basic Psychological Research

As noted in early chapters, factor analysis is not a magic method by which the "truth" can be wrung from numerical data. Such an expectation has much too often been apparent. The question as to where to rotate axes for extracted factors always leaves a margin of uncertainty. Thurstone proposed the concept of simple structure as a law of nature that could be applied in rotating axes. But experience shows that simple structure is not a safe guide, nor will it necessarily lead to replicability of rotated structures. Defining simple structure in terms of some mathematical model or criterion may only make matters worse (Guilford & Hoepfner, 1969). Oblique rotations may facilitate the finding of a better-looking simple structure in a solution, but it may only lead the investigator further astray psychologically.

It was stated earlier that factor analysis can be a hypothesis-testing procedure, and experiences in the ARP have contributed to confirmation in that belief. Obviously, one must recognize that it is not hypothesis testing of the kind that has become very common in analysis of variance and related statistical manipulations. For most purposes, one has to forego the advantages of making probability statements regarding numerical results of a factor analysis. But the discovery value of factor analysis offers more than a fair trade off for those privileges.

On a number of occasions Thurstone remarked that his research group spent more time in thinking about the nature of the domain in which the analysis was to be done and in planning the experimental variables and steps than they did in the reduction of the data in the factor analysis proper. Since present-day computers have cut the data-reduction time to only a small fraction of that formerly necessary, the division of time might well be on the order of 10 to 1, or even 100 to 1, in favor of hypothesis generation and test development needed to put the hypotheses to an empirical inspection. A reading of the preceding chapters should show the extent to which hypothetical abilities were given consideration, particularly before the structure-of-intellect model became available to serve as the source of hypotheses. Even with the availability of the model, the translation of the abstract conceptions of the abilities into the operational variables of measurement taxed inventive and evaluative skills. One might even say, then, that factorial abilities are discovered by the thinking of the investigators in advance of the factor analysis. Is this not typical of numerous discoveries in science? The experimental operations then test the discoveries for their plausibility. No amount of statistical hypothesis testing will generate new ideas about nature.

During the more recent years of the ARP research, the typical steps were essentially as follows. First, the question was asked, does an ability having such and such properties, as implied by its location in the SI model, exist as a unique function? Following this question there were others regarding particular tests, such as: Will this test reflect to a relatively high degree in its scores individual differences in that unique ability? Will it, at the same time, avoid showing to any appreciable degree differences in any other unique ability? The factor analysis is expected to yield information that should support yes-and-no answers to these questions. The practice of rotating factor axes toward target matrices, in which the target loadings represent the factor matrix to be expected if the hypotheses were true, however, qualifies the weight of the yes-no answers. The resulting factor loadings tell us that yes, we may tolerate the hypotheses with which we started, or no, we may not. The no answers are more decisive than the yes answers, but the fact that loadings of the same tests on the same factors time after time are of similar orders of magnitude augments confidence in the yes answers.

Thus, consistency with theory and invariance in factor structures, in spite of some variations in populations of individuals and populations of tests, became the criteria of successful demonstrations of unique intellectual abilities or functions, as noted in Chapter 3. Experience showed the great heuristic value of having a general theory or model, and it is strongly recommended that a theory of some kind be developed as early as possible in such investigations in various psychological domains. The SI theory was first constructed on the basis of about 40 recognized intellectual abilities. After it came into use in generating additional hypothesized abilities, in only one instance was there complete failure to demonstrate an explored ability, and this was because the wrong kinds of tests were developed for it. At the end of the 20 years of investigation, 98 of the cells of the model had been populated with demonstrated abilities. Abilities for the remaining 22 cells remained to be investigated.

SOME FINDINGS OF GENERAL PSYCHOLOGICAL SIGNIFICANCE

Discussions of how structure-of-intellect concepts have broad relevance in general psychological theory were presented in Chapter 2, and much more extensive discussions appear elsewhere (Guilford, 1967). In Chapters 5 through 9 may be seen the bases for the claims just mentioned. A point to be emphasized is that a taxonomy is not an end in itself. Its greatest value is that it leads to conceptions that have potency for understanding a great range of events. The taxonomic concepts in SI theory have the distinct advantage of possessing empirical referents, and as such, they should be welcome replacements for many time-honored concepts that have never had such definition.

Some Replaced Concepts

It happens that the replaced concepts are in the general category known as "mentalistic," but the historical persistence of those mentalistic terms has testified to the needs for descriptive vocabulary to cover phenomena that cannot be denied. No vocabulary derived from a supposedly completely objective source of observations from the behavioristic point of view has provided adequate coverage for those phenomena. It could probably never do so.

Reasoning: Inductive and Deductive   At the risk of some redundancy with discussions in Chapter 2, let us consider the major replacements of traditional concepts, in a general theoretical view that has been denoted as "operational-informational." It has been concluded that although "reasoning" is properly recognized in two varieties—inductive and deductive—the former is better conceived in terms of cognition functions and the latter in terms of convergent-production functions. In either operational category there are 24 functions because there are 24 kinds of items of information, in the SI *psychoepistemology*. This psychoepistemology is formed from the conjunctions of six kinds of products with four kinds of content. Psychologists who have preferred to use the terms "inductive" and "deductive" for the two kinds of

Association The most enduring and most pervasive concept of "association" has been replaced in large part by the SI product of "implication." Theorists who have given an "expectancy" feature to association have come very close to this view. The idea of "implication," however, goes a step further, placing the concept within a broader one of *psychologic*. The concept "association" has been called upon to carry too many theoretical burdens, in many places in which it is obviously incapable of bearing the load. Fortunately, the SI list of products includes five other concepts to take over duties formerly thrust upon "association." No longer need we conceive of more complex mental constructs as composites of glued pieces of elementary components, held together by associations. The products of classes, relations, and systems, for example, have their own wholistic characters that could be lost by efforts to reduce them, a position that Gestalt psychologists vigorously maintained.

Creative Thinking It cannot be maintained that "creative thinking" has been a widely used term in the psychological vocabulary. In earlier years there were references to "creative imagination," with almost no investigative efforts being devoted to it. Apparently, almost no one had operational hypotheses about its nature or saw how to go about investigating the phenomenon. Chapter 6 relates how the multivariate approach brought the phenomenon within reach of empirical research methods.

It turned out that creative activity can be described in terms of fluent production of items of information, flexibility in items of information, and elaboration upon what is given. Such processes come most conspicuously within a larger divergent-production category—the generation of logical alternatives—and flexibility is also accounted for in terms of a certain kind of product, which became known as "transformation." The latter is found involved in connection with every kind of SI operation. Although creative performance is dependent upon a richly stocked memory store, which in turn depends upon previously achieved cognitions and the fixation and retention of those cognitions, it is more critically dependent upon the operation of divergent production and the product of transformation.

Problem Solving "Problem solving" as a concept was discussed at greater length in Chapters 2 and 5. It is necessary here only to remind the reader of the exceedingly heterogeneous range of phenomena to which the term is applied. Problems vary from very simple to very complex. They arise in any of the four content categories, singly or in combination. The problem-solving event ordinarily involves all five SI operations. Guilford's SIPS model (where "SIPS" stands for "structure-of-intellect, problem-solving") shows how well all the SI taxonomic concepts can be effectively used in an *operational* model (Guilford, 1967).

Learning   It has been a common mistake to regard learning as a standard kind of activity or function in behavior. The total behavior observed when learning occurs is best described in terms of a number of SI operations, which was just said to be true of problem solving. Whatever happens in a learning episode, from an operational-informational point of view, new information is cognized and fixated so as to be retained. These two operations are minimum essentials. By being a little arbitrary, one could limit learning to the step of fixation, which would identify learning with the SI operation of memory. This would mean that there are 24 learning abilities, where the term "learning ability" has never heretofore been pinned down.

But "learning" is by custom more broadly conceived than that. Even the cognition-memory sequence just suggested does not always fully describe the event as generally known. Many recognized instances of learning are actually acts of problem solving. Much of the new information gained in problem solving comes about by operations of production, divergent and convergent. Woodworth and Schlosberg (1954) make a useful distinction between "learning a lesson" and learning in problem solving. The former involves merely memorizing (cognition and memorial fixation); the latter involves all the SI operations, including evaluation, which enters into self-checking as problem solving proceeds. In Chapter 10, some examples were given of determining which SI abilities play roles in learning concepts and in reading to gain remembered information. Both of these activities, particularly the former, offer occasions for problem solving. Both were shown to depend upon several SI abilities. In both it was noteworthy that memory abilities played very prominent roles.

Judgment   "Judgment" has never been well accepted as a systematic concept in psychology, yet it has cropped up in a number of connections. It was a phenomenon for study at Würzburg, it was a commonly used term by those dealing in psychophysics, and it entered into some of the earlier models proposed for problem solving. Only in the first instance was there serious interest in its psychological nature. The ARP undertook to gain some enlightenment regarding this phenomenon, but preferred to use the term "evaluation." The latter seemed to offer more ready suggestions of tasks that could be used in tests. With repeated analyses, this concept came into increasingly better focus, resulting in a conception that includes comparison of items of information, with one another or with specified standards. Evaluation proves to be a highly logical activity, in terms of what is to be evaluated (what product of information), with respect to what variable or variables, and with respect to what criterion. Personal preferences do not furnish sufficiently rigorous bases. Evaluation is not to be identified with decision making, but since decision making of any degree of complexity is in the category of problem solving (Guilford, 1969), evaluation does play a role in that phenomenon.

Logic and Psychology   The reference just made to logic calls attention to the more general question of the relation of psychology to logic. Formal logic has been traditionally regarded as a matter of man-made rules that are useful in guiding thinking to correct conclusions. Earlier references to divergent production as a generation of logical alternatives, and to convergent production as a generation of logical necessities, suggest relationships of logical principles to psychological functioning. Can such principles be discovered by empirical investigation?

It seems reasonable enough to conceive of a convergently produced item of information as being logical, since it is the "one right answer"; it is "correct." But some defense is needed for the expression *"logical* alternatives" in connection with divergent production. Examination of specific instances will show that tests of fluency call for producing class members in response to class specifications or producing relations in response to two given units, or correlates in response to given relations and units. Elaboration calls for producing implied items of information. In other words, these alternatives are products, and the products are logical concepts. We may extend this thinking to units, systems, and transformations, and it is on this basis that we may say that the six products provide the basis for an empirically derived psychologic. More has been said on this subject elsewhere (Guilford, 1967). In view of the strong implication of logic in connection with SI theory, *intelligence may be defined as the collection of abilities for processing information in accordance with principles of psychologic.* A suggestion derived from this definition might be that all behavior occurs according to principles of psychologic, and it is the responsibility of the psychologist to discover those principles.

THE FUTURE OF INTELLIGENCE TESTING

Readers who are concerned with assessment of intellectual levels of individuals, either by way of test administration or determination of assessment policies, will ask what effect the new knowledge of intellectual qualities will have on intelligence testing in the future. Some of the more obvious implications and some not so obvious will be mentioned, to help answer this question.

The needs for assessment of intelligence arose for Binet in the context of formal education, and this is the sphere in which intelligence tests (including academic-aptitude tests) have had their greatest use. Close behind have been their need and use in civil-service jurisdictions, in military contexts, and in business and industry. Whether or not the tests in such uses have had the label "intelligence," they have very often dealt with intellectual abilities as envisaged in the broader structure-of-intellect view.

Roles of Assessment in Education In approaching an answer to the question posed above, let us consider some of the apparent needs for knowing levels of basic intellectual talents of individuals. Let us begin with the context of education.

Traditional uses of tests in education have been concerned with admission of students to various critical levels along the educational ladder, where the practice of "promotion by chronological age" is not in vogue. Testing is expected to answer the question of whether or not the individual is ready to learn what has to be mastered in the new educational setting. Entrances to the first grade, to college, and to postgraduate instruction have been the most critical points, most dependent upon test information. At high school and college levels, admission to or choices of certain curricula are also occasions for decisions for which test results may be utilized. Choices need to be made between college-preparatory versus terminal curricula. If the choice is for a terminal curriculum, there is need to select one of several such avenues. In a four-year college, there need to be decisions between a liberal arts and sciences and a professional curriculum. If the former is the choice, there are decisions to be made among major fields. Although tests have not been utilized in connection with that type of decision, the much more detailed information regarding differential abilities should make this use of tests a real possibility. The same should be true for choice of specialization at the graduate level.

In addition to the use of test information to aid in decisions regarding admission to educational programs, the counselor could find further uses by way of diagnosing student difficulties in learning. It may be that such a difficulty is dependent upon special weakness in one or more of the SI abilities. If this is the case, a change of curriculum or of course may be the needed treatment, making a better match between student-aptitude profile and curriculum requirements. Or the treatment could be in the form of special intellectual exercises prescribed with the hope of strengthening the weak ability or abilities. There would be much value to the counselor in having a cumulative record of intellectual development for each of his counselees; a record that includes information on status and development with respect to all relevant abilities. Mary N. Meeker (1969) has already done much to relate SI abilities to educational practices.

Roles of Assessment in Personnel Management The uses of tests in selection, classification, and placement of personnel are generally known. In these connections, the needs for going beyond a single score from an intelligence scale have been more apparent, but still not sufficiently so. The eminent success of the U.S. Air Forces classification program is the best citable evidence to support this statement. In the selection and classification of trainees for aircrew assignments during World War II and since, and of trainees for technical training of nonflying personnel in recent years, relatively large batteries of tests have been used. Different combinations of scores are differentially weighted in order to obtain composite aptitude indices for various training assignments. It was pointed out (Guilford, 1948) that the 20 aircrew-battery tests covered eight factorial abilities (there was much redundancy in assessment of the abilities), most of which were in the intellectual category. The multiple correlations for the pilot-aptitude composite with the criterion of passing versus failing in training, for example, were in the neighborhood of .55. This result applied within the restricted range of trainees, half of whom had been previously eliminated by scores on a qualifying examination that emphasized some of the same abilities. It was estimated that if tests for additional factorial abilities, then known to have some relation to the pass-fail criterion, were added to the battery, or if they replaced some of the redundant tests, the multiple correlation could have reached the level of about .72. As it was, the elimination rate for pilots alone, which was about 35 percent at the beginning of World War II, shrank to about 10 percent at the end of the war, owing to selection on the basis of the tests. By setting the selection ratio even smaller, that rate could probably have been reduced to 4 percent.

The moral of all this is that, in testing for employment of personnel, the rational way in which to proceed is to make job and task analyses in ways that give full attention to SI abilities in the intellectual area, to other factorial abilities, and to factorial traits in other areas, and to use weighted composite scores as predictors. Such a goal and the operations needed to achieve it require expenditures of time and effort, with sophisticated psychometric personnel to man the proceedings. There should be adequate payoffs not only in terms of economic values but also in terms of values of human satisfaction.

Inadequacies of Present Tests

Consideration of present tests, including those labeled "intelligence tests" or "academic-aptitude" tests, shows many limitations, particularly when they are viewed in the broad frame of reference of SI theory. From the time of Binet, IQ tests were designed for one particular purpose: to tell school administrators which children could not progress normally in the elementary school. The fact that reading and arithmetic have been the critical school subjects has determined the emphasis on certain SI abilities in the tests. To this day, the predominantly verbal IQ tests have emphasized SI ability CMU overwhelmingly, with CMS next in importance—just two of the SI abilities.

The Stanford-Binet Scale The intelligence scale on which most reliance has been placed for many years has been the Stanford-Binet. Its most recent form, LM, was produced and published about a decade ago (Terman & Merrill, 1960). It contains 140 items or parts tests, covering a range of ages from 2.5 years to the superior adult level. Examination of the items can readily suggest the SI abilities probably emphasized, each item covering one or more abilities. A survey in terms of the SI parameters shows that the SI categories are very unevenly represented. Of the operation categories represented, cognition dominates in about two-thirds of the items. Memory abilities are featured in one-sixth of the items, with memory span the most popular form of memory test. The remaining one-sixth of the items are divided among the other three operation categories, with only 5 of the 140 items apparently offering clearly some measurement of divergent-production abilities.

As to content, about two-thirds of the items are in semantic form and one-fourth are visual-figural. Only 11 of the 140 items present tasks in symbolic form, a number of which are memory-span items. No items can be said to emphasize behavioral content; the area of social intelligence is thus untouched.

A survey of the items with respect to kinds of products of information shows that about half deal with units and a third deal with systems. The remaining one-sixth is divided among other products, including a few items dealing with transformations, for the ability for visualization (CFT) most often. Only 1 among the 140 items deals with classes, which seems to be a very serious oversight, in view of the logical importance of that category. It may be recalled from a report of a study of the learning of concepts in Chapter 10 that abilities dealing with classes were among the most relevant.

Looking at the Stanford-Binet from another angle, trusting only inspections, it can be said that 28 of the SI abilities are represented *somewhere* in the total scale, but many of them by only one item each. Such trivial representation is practically useless for giving such abilities weights of any consequence in a total score. As should be expected, CMU and CMS are most strongly represented, but they are entirely missing from some year levels of the scale. Other abilities with less representation appear irregularly, in one year and out the other in a seemingly haphazard manner. Such shifting representation means that different ability composites are measured at different age levels in the scale. Meeker (1969) has capitalized upon what meager opportunities there are to provide rough evaluations of a few SI abilities in addition to CMU and CMS, in a refined use of the Stanford-Binet Scale.

The Wechsler Scales: WAIS and WISC Although the two Wechsler scales (Wechsler, 1958)—the Wechsler Adult Intelligence Scale and the Wechsler Intelligence Scale for Children—present the same kinds of tests at all age levels, thus correcting one of the defects of the Stanford-Binet Scale, they are also limited to effective measurement of only a few SI abilities. With 11 tests in each scale, apparently 11 SI abilities are represented, but not on a one-to-one basis. There is some redundancy—for example, CMU is represented in two and possibly three tests—and there is some factorial complexity, in that, in some instances, each test represents two or more SI abilities. The emphases are generally similar to those in the Stanford-Binet Scale, with cognition the dominant operation, with semantic and figural information most featured as to content, and with units and systems the most represented products. Wechsler's two composite scores, verbal and nonverbal, are not well segregated psychologically, although the former emphasizes semantic content most, and the latter emphasizes figural content. There is some symbolic content in both scores, and there is one semantic test in the nonverbal list. It is possible that the latter (Picture Arrangement) involves some behavioral content as well.

Wechsler took a commendable step in the direction of differential measurement, which logically calls for a profile of scores rather than a single summation score. In spite of their unreliabilities, single scores from his 11 tests have been recommended for use, and they have been used (also misused), but clear interpretations in terms of SI abilities have not been generally possible, because of ambiguity that comes from factorial complexity. The latter condition arises from the fact that Wechsler also wanted tests in his scale that correlate strongly with one another so as to measure the traditional construct of "general intelligence," with a single composite score—IQ. His two objectives were flatly contradictory, operationally. One calls for low intercorrelations and the other for high intercorrelations. It is obviously impossible to have both.

For differential measurements, factorial scores are ideal. Their intercorrelations are very low, if not zero, so that differences of status in different abilities within persons stand out, and interpretations are relatively free from ambiguities, since one test measures one ability. Composite scores should be used after it has been shown that their weighted combination serves optimally to predict some specified, complex criterion, such as achievement in some particular course, task, or job assignment. If there is to be a composite score to represent a construct of "general intelligence," the factorial composition of that variable should be known and should be agreed upon by those who use it. It is to be expected that such a score, as is true of the present IQ, would not be equally useful in all uses and in all situations.

Suggestions for Testing Programs in Education

In accordance with the last statement, no single set of tests or no single policy for using tests will serve best in all educational situations. The wholesale application of standard IQ tests has been increasingly called into question, and their use has been discontinued in some places in recent years, mostly for the wrong reasons, however. Such a radical change is unfortunate, for, properly used and properly interpreted, the scores continue to be useful in some contexts. It is the occurrence of misinterpretations and misuses that should have been curbed, and needed supplementations should have been introduced. Where IQ tests have been banished, no doubt they will be missed; the time is ripe for new experimental uses of differential tests of intellectual abilities.

Preschool Testing Recent social circumstances have focused attention upon needs for contributing to intellectual development, particularly at the preschool level where development is most rapid and where apparently most can be done to overcome the depressing effects of unfavorable environments, at least. The notion that an IQ that is found by testing a child during his early years is a fixed quantity that will apply through life, and the self-fulfilling prophesies to which it has often led, is apparently giving way, as it should.

The focus on development in the preschool years calls for consideration of whether the SI abilities that are found at high school and adult levels also apply in the lower age levels. There have been an increasing number of analyses showing that there is, indeed, much differentiation of intellectual abilities, even down to the age of one year (see Stott & Ball, 1963, particularly). Furthermore, many of these factorial abilities can be logically identified as SI abilities. The general inference is that testing during the preschool years should be along the lines of demonstrated abilities, and it should be applied at intervals so as to follow the course of development in those abilities. The selection of abilities to be given most attention should be made in terms of values of knowing about status in those abilities. For example, as entrance into school approaches, it would be important to know how ready the child is for learning in reading and for number work.

Special School Subjects When the child faces new subjects—spelling or a foreign language—status in other abilities should be worth knowing about. At the junior high school level, algebra becomes a novel and critical subject. In Chapter 10 is an account of a study of relevant SI abilities that come into play in mastering algebra. That study was not complete in its coverage of possibly relevant SI abilities, for the latter were not all known and represented by tests at the time. But the study demonstrates how one could go about the derivation of a weighted composite of factor scores in order to predict achievement in a particular school subject. In senior high school, similar problems and similar kinds of solutions arise in connection with geometry and even higher mathematics, and other unique subjects.

Specialization in art, music, shop work, or commercial subjects undoubtedly calls for quite different combinations of SI abilities, and aptitude-score summations of different composition are called for. Further specializations in college and in the graduate school should call for still other unique predictors. It does not matter that such composite predictors overlap to some extent. The fact that they do not overlap completely makes some differential predictions possible. They may all have in them the very few components that are emphasized by present academic-aptitude tests, but that is not sufficient reason for limiting the testing to the common components. The overweighting of those components in the past has been highly unfair to students who seek entrance to the study of certain specializations, such as art and music. It is not known how many potential geniuses in such areas are denied entrance to college halls.

CONCLUSIONS

This condensed treatment of issues and of ramifications from SI theory and the abilities that it encompasses has attempted to stress a number of points. It pointed out the great value of taxonomies in science and the way in which multivariate-experimental approaches such as factor analysis can greatly facilitate the establishment and the testing of systematic concepts so badly needed in a complete psychology.

Consequences of the body of thinking involved in the SI model for general psychological theory and investigative programs have not yet been well appreciated. Concepts provide tools for thinking. SI concepts offer numerous opportunities for seeing new problems and for looking at old problems in new ways, particularly in the investigation of the "higher mental processes" in human behavior. Diversionary efforts from the purely behavioristic point of view have turned serious efforts away from "mentalistic" problems that have never gone away, and those efforts have never provided approaches that are at all adequate for their investigation. New objective approaches are made possible by regarding the brain as a processor of information of different kinds in different ways. SI concepts provide a convenient frame of reference and systematic catalog of the basic kinds of information and of the basic kinds of operations or functions.

For the first time, intelligence testing has a firm, broad foundation, and for the first time there is a genuinely operational definition for intelligence. The assessment of the intellectual resources of man can now take on features of a psychoengineering. It is likely that the comprehensive coverage of abilities that pertain to logical processing of information will account for needed resources in wide ranges of human activity. Talents of numerous kinds can be discovered in individuals, and their development can be promoted because their properties are known. Optimal development through education and optimal placement of the individual within the scheme of things can now be more nearly achieved, and those steps should contribute to satisfactions for all concerned.

APPENDIX A

NUMBERED LIST OF REPORTS FROM THE APTITUDES RESEARCH PROJECT[1]

1. Guilford, J. P., Comrey, A. L., Green, R. F., & Christensen, P. R. A factor-analytic study of reasoning abilities. I. Hypotheses and description of tests, 1950.
3. Guilford, J. P., Green, R. F., & Christensen, P. R. A factor-analytic study of reasoning abilities. II. Administration of tests and analysis of results, 1951.
4. Guilford, J. P., Wilson, R. C., Christensen, P. R., & Lewis, D. J. A factor analytic study of creative thinking. I. Hypotheses and description of tests, 1951.

[1]The general title for this series was "Reports from the Psychological Laboratory, University of Southern California." Reports 2 and 5 were not from the Aptitudes Research Project and consequently are not listed here. Except for those two Reports, copies in Xerox reproduction may be purchased from the Photo-Duplication Department of the University of Southern California Library, Los Angeles, 90007.

6. Guilford, J. P., Green, R. F., Christensen, P. R., Hertzka, A. F., & Kettner, N. W. A factor-analytic study of Navy reasoning tests with the Air Force Aircrew Classification Battery, 1952.
7. Guilford, J. P., Hertzka, A. F., Berger, R. M., & Christensen, P. R. A factor-analytic study of evaluative abilities. I. Hypotheses and description of tests, 1952.
8. Guilford, J. P., Wilson, R. C., & Christensen, P. R. A factor-analytic study of creative thinking. II. Administration of tests and analysis of results, 1952.
9. Guilford, J. P., Hertzka, A. F., & Christensen, P. R. A factor-analytic study of evaluative abilities. II. Administration of tests and analysis of results, 1953.
10. Guilford, J. P., Berger, R. M., & Christensen, P. R. A factor-analytic study of planning. I. Hypotheses and description of tests, 1954.
11. Guilford, J. P., Kettner, N. W., & Christensen, P. R. A factor-analytic study across the domains of reasoning, creativity, and evaluation. I. Hypotheses and description of tests, 1954.
12. Guilford, J. P., Berger, R. M., & Christensen, P. R. A factor-analytic study of planning. II. Administration of tests and analysis of results, 1955.
13. Guilford, J. P., Kettner, N. W., & Christensen, P. R. The relation of certain thinking factors to training criteria in the U.S. Coast Guard Academy, 1955.
14. Guilford, J. P., Kettner, N. W., & Christensen, P. R. A factor-analytic investigation of the factor called general reasoning, 1955.
15. Hills, J. R. The relationship between certain factor-analyzed abilities and success in college mathematics, 1955.
16. Guilford, J. P., Kettner, N. W., & Christensen, P. R. A factor-analytic study across the domains of reasoning, creativity, and evaluation. II. Administration of tests and analysis of results, 1956.
17. Guilford, J. P., & Christensen, P. R. A factor-analytic study of verbal fluency, 1956.
18. Guilford, J. P., Frick, J. W., Christensen, P. R., & Merrifield, P. R. A factor-analytic study of flexibility in thinking, 1957.
19. Guilford, J. P. A revised structure of intellect, 1957.
20. Guilford, J. P., Christensen, P. R., Frick, J. W., & Merrifield, P. R. The relations of creative-thinking aptitudes to non-aptitude personality traits, 1957.
21. Marks, A., Guilford, J. P., & Merrifield, P. R. A study of military leadership in relation to selected intellectual factors, 1959.
22. Merrifield, P. R., Guilford, J. P., Christensen, P. R., & Frick, J. W. A factor-analytic study of problem-solving abilities, 1960.
23. Guilford, J. P., Merrifield, P. R., Christensen, P. R., & Frick, J. W. An investigation of symbolic factors of cognition and convergent production, 1960.
24. Guilford, J. P., & Merrifield, P. R. The structure of intellect model: Its uses and implications, 1960.

25. Allen, M. S., Guilford, J. P., & Merrifield, P. R. The evaluation of selected intellectual factors by creative research scientists, 1960.
26. Guilford, J. P., Merrifield, P. R., & Cox, Anna B. Creative thinking in children at the junior high school levels, 1961.
27. Merrifield, P. R., Guilford, J. P., & Gershon, A. The differentiation of divergent-production abilities at the sixth-grade level, 1963.
28. Merrifield, P. R., Gardner, S. F., & Cox, Anna B. Aptitudes of personality measures related to creativity in seventh-grade children, 1963.
29. Gershon, A., Guilford, J. P., & Merrifield, P. R. Figural and symbolic divergent-production abilities in adolescent and adult populations, 1963.
30. Guilford, J. P., & Hoepfner, R. Current summary of structure-of-intellect factors and suggested tests, 1963.
31. Petersen, H., Guilford, J. P., Hoepfner, R., & Merrifield, P. R. Determination of "structure-of-intellect" abilities involved in ninth-grade algebra and general mathematics, 1963.
32. Nihira, K., Guilford, J. P., Hoepfner, R., & Merrifield, P. R. A factor analysis of semantic-evaluation abilities, 1964.
33. Hoepfner, R., Guilford, J. P., & Merrifield, P. R. A factor analysis of the symbolic-evaluation abilities, 1964.
34. O'Sullivan, Maureen, Guilford, J. P., and de Mille, R. The measurement of social intelligence, 1965.
35. Hoepfner, R., & Guilford, J. P. Figural, symbolic, and semantic factors of creative potential in ninth-grade students, 1965.
36. Guilford, J. P., & Hoepfner, R. Structure-of-intellect factors and their tests, 1966.
37. Brown, S. W., Guilford, J. P., & Hoepfner, R. A factor analysis of semantic memory abilities, 1966.
38. Tenopyr, Mary L., Guilford, J. P., & Hoepfner, R. A factor analysis of symbolic memory abilities, 1966.
39. Dunham, J. L., Guilford, J. P., & Hoepfner, R. Abilities pertaining to classes and the learning of concepts, 1966.
40. Hoffman, Kaaren I., Guilford, J. P., Hoepfner, R., & Doherty, W. J. A factor analysis of the figural-cognition and figural-evaluation abilities, 1968.
41. Hoepfner, R., Guilford, J. P., & Bradley, P. A. Identification of transformation abilities in the structure-of-intellect model, 1968.
42. Hendricks, Moana, Guilford, J. P., & Hoepfner, R. Measuring creative social intelligence, 1969.
43. Bradley, P. A., Guilford, J. P., & Hoepfner, R. A factor analysis of figural-memory abilities, 1969.

APPENDIX B

TESTS EMPLOYED BY THE APTITUDES RESEARCH PROJECT IN ITS ANALYSIS OF INTELLIGENCE

Abbreviations.   Choose one of three alternative words that a given abbreviation best implies.

Sample item: crnt   A. crescent   B. coronation   C. current

Answer: C.

Absurdities.   (From a test by Adkins and Lyerly, 1951.) Indicate whether given statements make sense, i.e., are internally consistent.

Sample items:
1. Mrs. Smith has had no children, and I understand the same was true of her mother.
2. While the businessman was eating his lunch, he was interrupted by a long-distance telephone call.

Answers: 2 is sensible; 1 is not.

Alterations. Indicate whether a new word can be made by reversing the order of any two adjacent letters in a given word.

Sample items. 1. SUE 2. BRAKE Baker

Answers: 1—yes; 2—~~no~~ yes

Alternate Additions. Using given numbers, produce a specified sum in different ways.

Sample item:[1]
Given numbers: 1 2 3 4
Specified sum: 7

Possible answers: 3 + 4 = 7; 1 + 2 + 4 = 7.

Alternate Cartoon Completions. Invent different endings for incomplete cartoon strips.[2]
The girl will say, "Dad, where did you get those shorts?"

Alternate Expressional Groups. Group pictured expressions in different ways so that each group expresses a common thought, feeling, or intention.

Sample item:

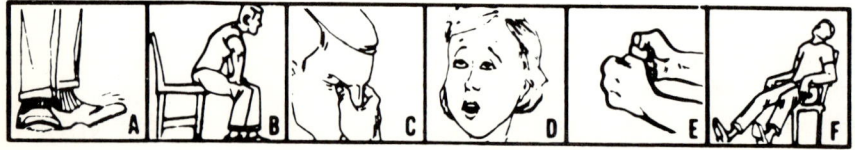

Possible groups: C, D, F; A, C, E.

Alternate Face Groupings. Group photographs of faces in different ways, each one expressing a common thought, feeling, or intention.

---

[1] Many of the sample items given in this Appendix are from the instructions for their tests and hence are ridiculously simple.

[2] Owing to copyright restrictions, it was not possible to reproduce sample items based upon cartoons owned by the United Features Syndicate. Sample items may be found in Report 34 for behavioral-cognition tests and Report 42 for behavioral-divergent-production tests.

Sample item:

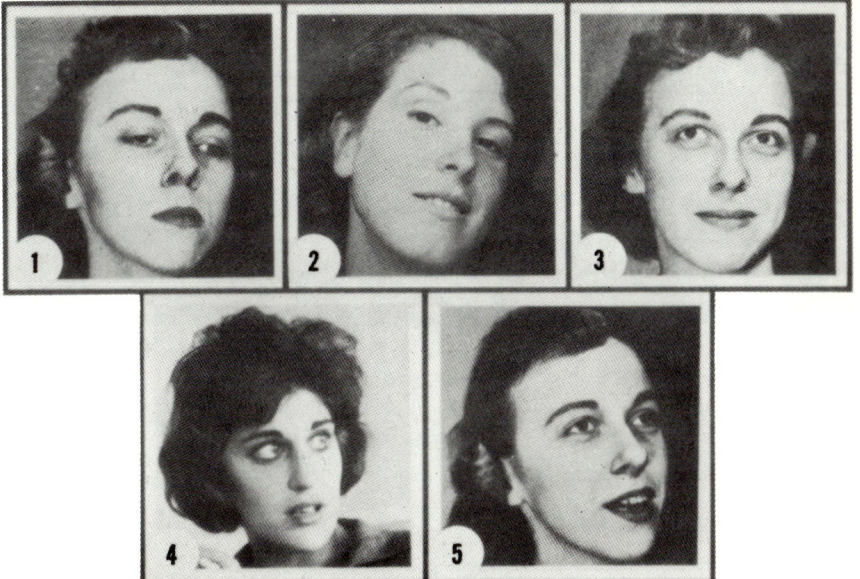

Possible groups: 2, 3, 5; 1, 3, 4.

Alternate Facial Relations. From a set of photographs of faces, choose pairs that fit interpersonal relationships indicated by a remark one person is saying to the other.

Sample item: "Wait, that isn't what I meant."

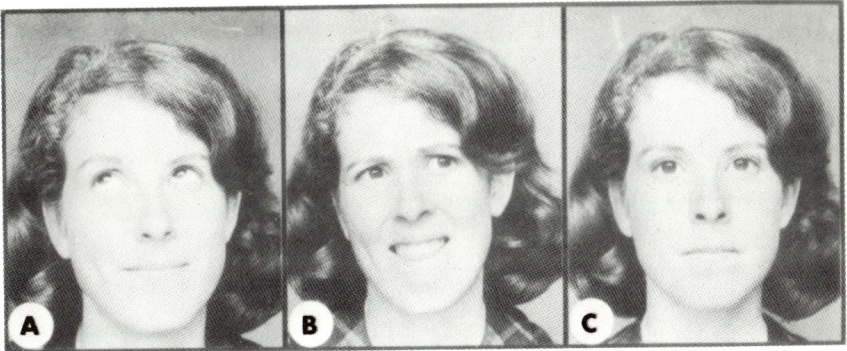

Possible pairs: B and C; C and A.

Alternate Headlines (arrangement). Rearrange elements in writing different versions of a headline.

Sample item:
Headline: MAN DROWNS IN VAIN EFFORT TO SAVE FIANCÉE

One rearrangement: In vain effort to save fiancée, man drowns.

Alternate Headlines (words). Substitute words in writing different versions of a headline.

Sample item:
Headline: MAN DROWNS IN VAIN EFFORT TO SAVE FINANCÉE

A substitute: Sea claims valiant husband-to-be.

Alternate Letter Groups. Group and regroup letters in classes on the basis of figural properties.

Sample item:
Given letters: A H V T C

Possible groups: A H V T (all made of straight lines); A H T (all contain horizontal lines).

Alternate Line Meanings. List names of different feelings or emotions represented by each given line.

Sample item:

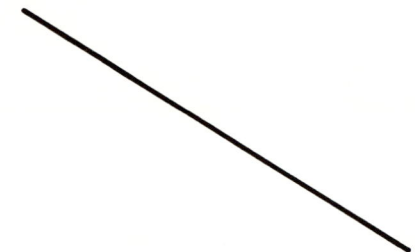

Possible meanings: Sad, quiet, gentle.

Alternate Methods. Give several methods for accomplishing each given task.

Sample item: A house located near a stream is on fire. Twenty men, each carrying a bucket, arrive to help put out the fire. The house is about 20 yards from the stream. In how many ways could you organize this bucket brigade to deal with the fire?

Possible methods:
Form two lines of 10 men each. The filled buckets are passed up one line and down the other.
Assign 5 men to fill the buckets, 10 men to run with the buckets, and 5 men to throw water on the fire.

Alternate Picture Meanings. Write different things that a person might say if he felt as the person in the given picture apparently does.

Sample item:

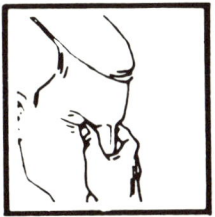

Possible responses:
"Let me see ... where was I?"
"I wish he'd shut up."
"Good grief! What have I done?"

Alternate Signs. Draw different signs to express the meaning of each given word.

Sample item:
Given word: HEAVY

Possible signs:

Alternate Social Meanings. Write different interpretations of stated actions of people.

Sample item: If one person winks at another, what could he (she) be thinking or feeling?

Possible responses:
"How about a date?"
"You and I know better."

Alternate Social Solutions. Give different social solutions appropriate to each given social problem.

Sample item: You are on a weekend trip with a group of friends. They want you to spend the day hunting with them but you want to go fishing instead. You could:

Possible responses:
Give in and go hunting with them.
Suggest deciding by tossing a coin.

Alternate Uses. List different uses for which common objects can be employed.

Sample item: NEWSPAPER (used for reading)

Possible uses: Start a fire, wrap garbage, stuffing for packing boxes, protection against cold.

Angle Estimation. Select the alternative angle that is closest in size to the given angle.

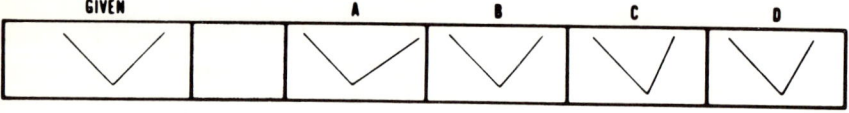

Answer: B.

Apparatus Test. Suggest two improvements each for common appliances.

Sample item: TELEPHONE

Possible improvement: A device that tells who is calling before you answer.

Aptitude—Spatial. (A Coast Guard Academy test.) Identify what a folded and punched piece of paper would look like when unfolded.

Aptitude—Verbal Analogies. (Coast Guard.) Choose one of five alternative words that complete each analogy.

Aptitude—Verbal Opposites. (Coast Guard.) Select two of four words most nearly opposite to a given word.

Arithmetic Achievement—Fundamentals. (A subscale of the California Achievement Test.) Choose correct alternative answers to problems in numerical computation.

Arithmetic Reasoning. (A U.S. Air Force test.) Solve short, verbally stated arithmetical problems.

Artistic Interpretations. Select the alternative artistic interpretation of a given object that is the least distorted artistically.

Sample item:

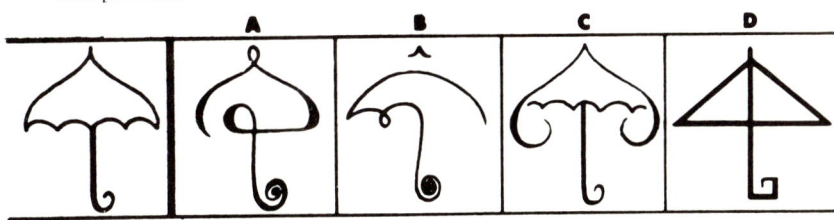

Answer: C.

Associational Fluency. Write a number of different synonyms for each given word.

Sample item: HARD

Possible synonyms: Difficult, solid, severe, firm.

Associations I. Write a word that is associated with each of two given words.

Sample item: Indian _____ money

Answer: Penny, or wampum.

Associations II. Think of a word associated with each of two given words, then encircle the initial letter of the word, to be found among given alternatives.

Sample item: TREE   a b g m s   DOG

Answer: b (for "bark").

Associations III. Write a word similar in meaning to two given words.

Sample item: nonsense _____ bed

Answer: Bunk.

Associations IV. (Essentially the same as Associations I).

Attribute Listing I. List attributes of given objects.

Sample item: CHEWING GUM

Possible answers: Comes in flavors; sticks to furniture.

Attribute Listing II. List attributes of objects needed to serve given functions.

Sample item: You wish to drive a long nail into a hard post. List the attributes that a usable object should have.

Possible attributes: Harder than the nail; flat striking surface; won't shatter.

Balances. Equalize the pans of a balance by adding weights selected from those given.

Sample item: The scale has 7 grams on the left pan and 1 gram on the right. Given weights are 2, 3, 4, and 10 grams.

Answer: Add the 2 and 4 grams to the right pan.

Behavioral Elaboration. Write different responses a person might have for a given stated action of another person.

Sample item: IF PERSON A WINKS AT PERSON B, WHAT WILL B DO?

Possible responses: Smile back timidly; get embarassed and blush; pretend that he doesn't see person A.

Best Figural Class. Assign figures to one of four figural classes so that it receives the most points.

Sample item:

Figural classes and their values: TANGENTS, 4 points; PARALLELS, 3 points, INTERSECTIONS, 2 points; and CURVES, 1 point.

Answer: Intersections.

Best Figural Class Separation. Select the pair of figural properties that best sorts a group of nine figures into two distinct classes.

Sample item:

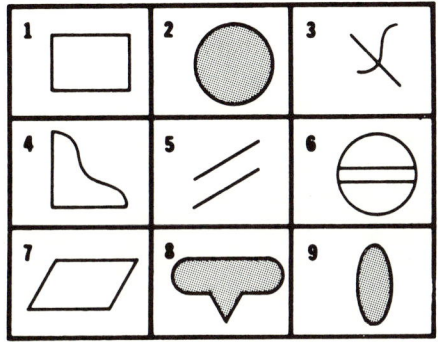

Given alternative pairs of figural properties:
A. Straight lines versus curved lines
B. Right angles versus shading
C. Parallel lines versus curved lines

Answer: C.

Best Figure Pairs. Select one of three pairs of figures that belongs to the most valuable of four figural classes.

Sample item:

A. △ △
B. □ Z
C. L T

Given classes and values: BEST, right angles; SECOND BEST, parallel lines; THIRD BEST, identical shapes; WORST CLASS, open figures.

Answer: C.

Best Letter Set. Choose one of three alternative letter sets that is most like a given set.

Sample item: EKN   A. JFT   B. PAQ   C. OBT

Answer: C.

Best Map Placement. Fit alternative insets into cut-out portions of each map.

Sample item:

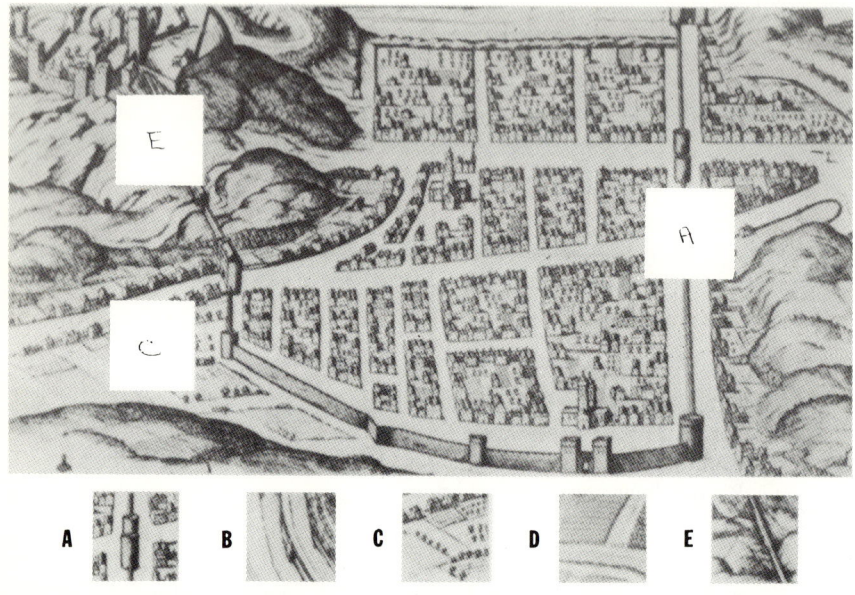

Best Move Selection. Decide which of four game pieces can cover all the given game-board squares in the fewest moves.

Rules:
Piece A can move horizontally, vertically, or diagonally, but only one square per move.
Piece B can move only diagonally, but any number of squares per move.
Piece C can move only horizontally or vertically, but any number of squares per move.
Piece D can move only in an L shape, in any direction, with either tail of the L having two squares, while the other tail has one square.
Sample item: Given the following game-board squares (X marks the starting point):

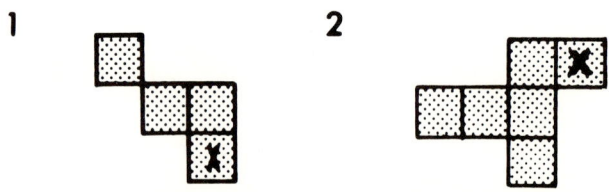

Answers: 1−A; 2−D.

Best Number Class. Judge into which of four classes each given number fits so as to receive the most points.

> Classes and their values: EVEN MULTIPLES, 1 point; ODD MULTIPLES, 2 points; SQUARES, 3 points; PRIMES, 4 points.
> *Given number:* 100
>
> *Answer:* Squares.

Best Number Pairs. Choose one of three number pairs that makes the best class.

> *Sample item:*   A. 2–7   B. 5–2   C. 7–5
>
> *Answer:* C (both are odd).

Best Trend Name. Select the word that best describes the order of four given terms.

> *Sample item:* horse–push cart–bicycle–car
> Alternative terms: A. speed   B. time   C. size
>
> *Answer:* B

Best Word Class. Select one of four given classes to which a given object best belongs.

> *Sample item.*   PALM   A. plant   B. tree   C. flower   D. leaf
>
> *Answer:* B.

Best Word Pairs. Select the pair of words that makes the best class.

> *Sample item:*   A. handsome–dark   B. handsome–man   C. man–dark
>
> *Answer:* A.

Block Rotation. Visualize what a block will look like when it is seen from a different point of view.

> *Sample item:*

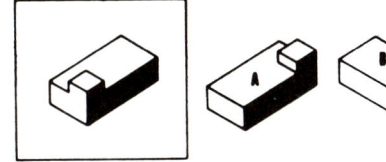

> *Answer:* E

Block Visualization. From a verbal description of a colored block of wood, imagine how the cut parts will look.

Sample item: The ends of a block 1 inch by 1 inch by 3 inches are painted black and the block is cut into 1-inch cubes.
1. How many cubes have one side painted black?
2. How many cubes have no painted sides?

Answers: 1—two cubes; 2—one cube.

Blocks. Count the blocks that each lettered block touches, in a neat pile.

Sample item:

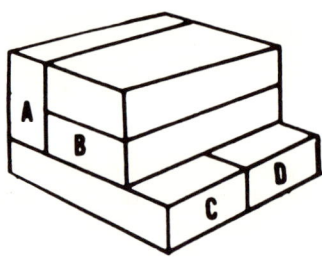

Answers: A touches 4 blocks; B, 4 blocks; C, 3 blocks; D. 3 blocks.

Books and Authors. Recall probable occupations for each given author after studying pairs of names with book titles.

Sample study items:
Brooks: Pictures I Have Painted
Adams: Great Moments in Baseball
Sample test items:
Adams: _____
Brooks: _____

Answers: Adams—baseball player; Brooks—artist.

Brick Uses (fluency). List many different uses for a common brick, the total number given being the score.

Brick Uses (flexibility). Same task as in preceding test, with the number of shifts of category of use being the score.

California Achievement Test—Arithmetic Reasoning. Select alternatives that represent numerical and arithmetical definitions, and solutions to simple arithmetical problems.

California Achievement Test—Reading Vocabulary. Select one of four alternative synonyms for the given word.

APPENDIX B   379

California Reading Test—Comprehension. Choose correct answers to questions about studied paragraphs, maps, and tables.

California Reading Test—Vocabulary. Select one of four alternative synonyms for the given word.

Camouflaged Words. Find within a sentence a group of consecutive letters that spells the name of a sport or a game.

> *Sample item:* I did not know that he was ailing.
>
> *Camouflaged word:* Sailing.

Cartoon Analogies. Choose the alternative expression that is related to the third given expression in the same way as the second is to the first.

> *Sample item:*

Alternative answers:

   1   2   3

Answer: 2.

Cartoon Exchange. Substitute an alternative cartoon frame for one of a given sequence of frames so that the meaning of the story is changed with respect to the intentions of the characters. (See footnote 2, p. 368.)

Cartoon Implications. Choose the alternative statement that describes what happened before or what will happen after the pictured situation. (See footnote 2, p. 368.)

Cartoon Predictions. Choose one of three alternative cartoon frames that can be most reasonably predicted from the given frame.

Sample item:

Answer: 1:

Cartoons. Write a punch line for each cartoon.

Sample cartoon:

Possible responses:
"I'd say "Z" but it's only a wild guess."
"What chart?"

Chain Association (cluster). Given a cue word, list many words, each associated with the one preceding it. The number of clusters is the score.

Sample cue word: RED

Sample chain: Sunset—weather—cold—beer—party.

Circle Continuations. Select a point that would fall on a circle, given only an arc and five alternative points.

Answer: B.

Circle Reasoning. (A test by Blakey, 1941.) Discover the principle by which one small circle is blackened in each of four rows of circles and dashes, then apply the rule to the fifth row.

Sample item:

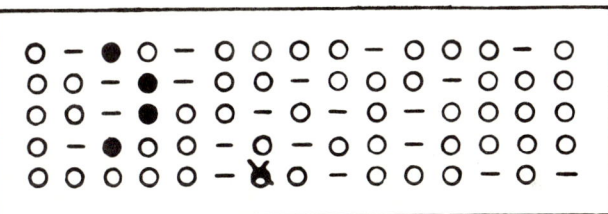

Circle-Square-Triangle. Associate three objects, each with a circle, square, or triangle; then place them according to instructions.

Sample item:
Given objects: BLOTTER   MARBLE   GRAPE
Make the most edible one the triangle. Put the hardest one on the outside and the softest one on the inside.

Alternatives:

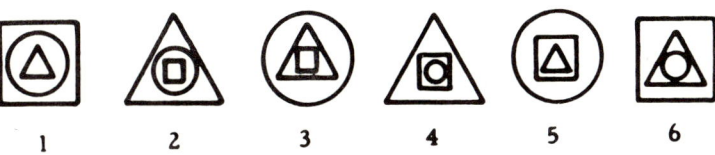

Answer: 5.

Class Name Selection. Select a class name that most precisely fits a group of four given words.

Sample class: cat   cow   mule   mare
Alternative names: A. farm animals   B. four-legged animals
C. domestic animals

Answer: C.

Classified Information. Recognize classes of meanings similar to those given on a previously studied page.

Sample class studied: SILK   WOOL   NYLON
Sample test classes:
1.   rayon   cotton   felt
2.   snow   ice   sleet

Answers: Class 1 was studied; 2 was not.

Close-ups. Identify the objects shown in close-up photographs.

Sample items:

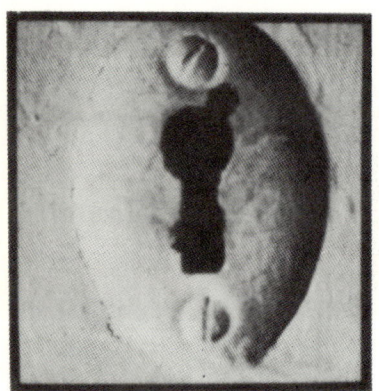 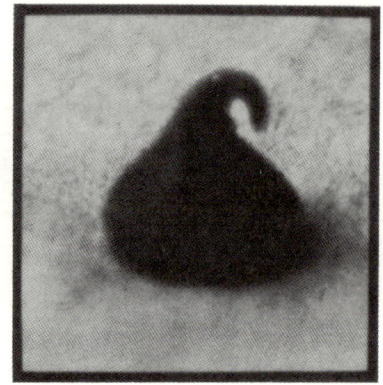

Answers: Keyhole and chocolate chip.

Closest Spatial Series. Choose the one end view of a series of photographs that is farthest away from the remaining three views.

Sample item:

A   B

Answer: A.

APPENDIX B   383

Code Analysis.   Decide which of five sets of five letters and numbers is a prescribed transform of a given set, following an elaborate set of rules.

Sample item: JG9A3
Alternatives: A. 97913   B. J61C7   C. G7BD4   D. 15DCF
E. 27JE1

Answer: C (under rules too lengthy to be given here).

Common Needs.   Select two objects that require the same preceding operation, or the presence of a third object, before they can be used.

Sample item: BANANA
Alternatives: A. book of matches   B. desk   C. mailbox   D. pull-toy

Answer: A (both must be opened before use).

Commonsense Judgment I.   Select the two best of five given reasons why a briefly described plan is faulty.

Sample item: A city wants to improve its streets and its sewer system. It decides to work on street improvement first.
Alternative faults:
A. The streets will have to be torn up again in order to work on the sewer system.
B. Street improvements can be done gradually, so might as well be done second.
C. Since street improvement is less important than sanitation, the sewer system should be installed first.
D. Since the street improvement is costly, the city might run out of funds before it can work on the sewer.
E. The homeowners would disagree with the council that street improvement comes before sewer improvement.

Answers: A and C.

Commonsense Judgment II.   Select the two best of five given methods to demonstrate the truth of a given statement.

Given statement: The light in an electric refrigerator goes out the moment the door is closed.
Given methods:
A. Feel whether the bulb is hot after the refrigerator door has been closed for some time.
B. Substitute a wire-socket arrangement leading to a bulb outside the refrigerator.
C. Utilize a delayed-shutter camera that would expose a film after the door is closed.
D. Disconnect all appliances except the refrigerator, close the door, then see whether the electric meter is running.

Answers: B and C.

Common Situations. List problems inherent in common situations.

Given situation: Washing an automobile at home

Possible problems:
Keeping run-off water off the grass.
Keeping streaks from remaining.

Competitive Planning. (Based upon an experimental U.S. Air Force Test.) Reconstruct the moves, according to rules, of two contestants (Black and White) in filling in incomplete squares so as to obtain the best solutions for both contestants.

Sample item:

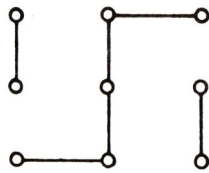

Rules:
1. Black always moves first.
2. When either Black or White completes a square, he must make one additional line.
   Alternative answers:
   A. Black 0, White 4
   B. Black 1, White 3
   C. Black 2, White 2
   D. Black 3, White 1
   E. Black 4, White 0

Answer: C

Complete Thoughts. Judge whether a statement expresses a complete thought.

Sample statements:
1. In the dawn as I was going.
2. Light breaks in secret places.

Answers: 1 is not complete; 2 is complete.

Completion of Figural Changes. Change a given figure according to instructions.

Sample figure:

Instruction: Change the circle to a square and add a cross inside.

Answer:

Concept Grouping. Given a target word and a list of words, group words from the list with the target word in different ways.

Given list: 1. tar 2. silver 3. raven 4. log 5. ink 6. copper 7. gasoline 8. gold 9. kerosene
Target word: COAL

Classes: 1, 3, and 5; 4, 7, and 9; and 2, 6, and 8.

Concept Recall. Supply one additional class member to previously studied classes.

Sample study classes:
FORD   PLYMOUTH   BUICK
BANANA   APPLE   ORANGE

Sample additional members: Grapefruit; Chevrolet

Concept Synthesis. Write the word for a concept suggested by two given words.

Given words: CLOTH   WOUND

Suggested concept: Bandage.

Consequences (obvious). List effects of a new and unusual event, with only obvious responses counted toward the score.

Sample event: People no longer need or want sleep.

Possible effects: Get more work done; alarm clocks not needed.

Consequences (remote). Same as preceding test, but only remotely connected responses counted toward the score.

Possible remote effects: No need for lullaby books; apartment rents based upon number of living rooms.

Consonant, Digit, and Nonsense Word Span. Recall and reproduce sequences of consonants, digits, or nonsense words presented visually or auditorially.

Sample sequences: G R Z M C Q   2 7 1 8 6 3   gup zar vif caj mof

Contingencies. State a condition that might require the use of a given object in a certain situation.

Situation: Sally and Jane go berry picking.
Given objects: 1. ointment   2. pins

Possible conditions:
1. Bitten by insects or scratched.
2. Ripped clothing.

Controlled Associations.   See **Associational Fluency.**

Controlled Associations II.   List three synonyms for each given word.

Sample given word: ODD

Possible synonyms: Usual, unique, queer.

Controlled Associations III.   See **Associational Fluency.**

Correct Figural Trends. Judge whether given figural series follow exactly stated rules.

Given rule: Originally closed figures become more open, and open figures become more closed, at each step.

Sample series:

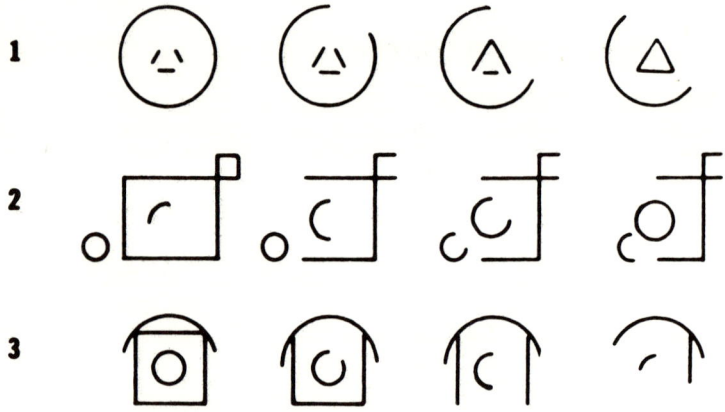

Answers: 1 follows the rule; 2 and 3 do not.

Correct Letter Orders. Judge whether the order of given letter sequences follows given rules.

Given rule: Alternate letters in the alphabet (skipping one)

Sample sequences: 1. M O Q S U W   2. P R S U W Y

Answers: 1 follows the rule; 2 does not.

Correct Number Series. Judge whether the order of given number sequences follows given rules.

>Given rule: Alternately add 1, multiply by 3.
>Sample sequences: 1.   2 3 9 10 30 31   2.   4 5 15 16 49 50

>Answers: 1 follows the rule; 2 does not.

Correct Spelling. Recognize whether common words are spelled correctly.

>Sample words: 1. experience   2. thier   3. seperate

>Answers: 1 is spelled correctly; 2 and 3 are not.

Correlate Completion. Complete analogies made up of words paired either for meaning or for letter composition.

>Sample items:
>1.   am—ma   not—ton   tool—
>2.   chair—arms   clock—hands   table— _____

>Answers: 1—loot; 2—legs.

Correlate Completion II. Complete analogies where words are paired as to letter compositions.

>Sample item: enrage—rage   correlate—late   about— _____

>Answer: bout.

Creating Social Relations. Given the expressions of two people, write appropriate comments one might be saying to the other.

>Sample item: What might the man be saying to the woman?

Possible responses:
"Oh brother! Here we go again."
"I'm sorry; I didn't mean it."
"Why do you think I did it?"

Creating Social Situations. Create different situations that account for the feelings of three interacting people.

Given People: A. a fearful woman   B. an angry man   C. an unhappy child

Possible situations:
1. C gets a bad report card; B, his father, is mad at C; and A, his mother, is afraid B will hurt C.
2. B comes home to find A with another man. He yells at her and C is unhappy his parents are fighting.

Critical Evaluation. Designate given statements as being based on emotion or prejudice or on reasoning and thought.

Sample statements:
1. All people who drink liquor should have their driver's licenses taken away.
2. The police should revoke the licenses of people who drive while drunk.

Answers: 1 is based on emotion; 2 on thought.

CTMM Language MA. (A subscale of the California Test of Mental Maturity.) Select correct answers to simple word problems, vocabulary items, syllogisms, and reading-comprehension items.

Daffynitions. Give new meanings to word sounds, using them in statements.

Given words: TREE   DECIDE

Possible new uses:
I have tree new pencils.
Decide of de barn.

DAT Abstract Reasoning. (A subtest of the Differential Aptitude Tests.) Choose one of five alternative figures that completes a four-figure series.

DAT Numerical Ability. (A subtest of the DAT.) Perform arithmetical operations and complete simple equations.

Decoding. Choose the word that would be easier to decode, if coded according to an ambiguous scheme.

Given code:
All double letters (oo, gg, etc.) = 1
All pairs of vowels (ea, ou, etc.) = 2
All pairs of consonants (bl, sh, etc.) = 3
All single vowels (a, e, i, o, u) = 4
All single consonants (b, g, p, etc.) = 5
Sample items:
1.   A. call   B. miss   C. (equally easy)
2.   A. strong B. trusty C. (equally easy)

Answers: 1–C; 2–B.

Decorations.   Adding lines, decorate two identical outline drawings of objects differently.

Sample decorated drawings:

Derivations.   Judge rapidly whether words can be derived from a given long word by using some of its letters

Given word: PROCRASTINATE
Sample items: 1. trap   2. percent   3. stamina

Answers: 1 can be derived; 2 and 3 cannot.

Descriptions.   Recognize whether given adjectives are implied by noun pairs presented on a previously studied page.

Sample study pairs: RING–CIRCLE   HOUSE–TENT   RATTLE–DIAPER   MOUSE–ELEPHANT

Sample test adjectives   1. livable   2. tired   3. round   4. big   5. spotted   6. infantile

Answers: 1, 3, and 6 are implied; 2, 4, and 5 are not.

Descriptive Completion. Write completions to simple sentences.

Sample item: The sky is _____ .

Possible completions: Blue, full of stars, a patchwork of clouds, milky.

Designs. Combine any or all of a given set of simple figural elements in many different ways to form patterns.

Given elements:

∧ ⌒ • —

Possible designs:

[figure of design patterns arranged in four rows]

Differences. List different ways in which two given objects differ.

Sample objects: BANANA–APPLE

Possible differences: long versus round; tropical versus cool climate; thick skin versus thin skin; ease of peeling.

Disarranged Words. Rearrange given letters to form words.

Sample letter sets: 1. odg   2. mabler

Answers: 1–dog; 2–ramble.

Disemvowelled Words. Recognize familiar words with vowels missing, then write in the vowels.

Sample words: 1. h___l   2. m___t___l___t___

Answers: 1–heal, or heel; 2–mutilate.

Dot Systems. Draw two copies of a given letter in different positions within a matrix of evenly spaced dots.

Sample item: Draw two T's in different ways.

Possible answers:

Double Descriptions. Select the one object of four that best fits two given descriptions.

Sample item: ROUND and HARD
Alternatives: A. gold   B. record   C. steel   D. coin

Answer: D.

Double Meanings. Recognize pairs of meanings to the same word from synonyms in new sentences.

Sample study sentences:
She carried food in a paper <u>bag.</u>
The hunter planned to <u>bag</u> a deer.
Sample test sentences:
1. John took his lunch in a <u>sack.</u>
   Mother wants to <u>obtain a</u> new chair.
2. He was asked to name the <u>letter</u> after S.
   The <u>beverage</u> can be either hot or cold.

Answers: 1—words were studied; 2—not studied.

Effects. Predict future events from specified present trends.

Sample trend: More girls than boys were born in the last 5 years. What will happen 20 years hence?

Possible effects:
More rivalry among women for husbands.
Agitation to allow polygamous marriages.
More women will take up careers.

Efficient Word Transformations. Combine four words by overlapping as efficiently as possible.

Given words: ENTER   LOOP   OPEN   POLO

Best transformation: POLOOPENTER.

Episodes. Write two explanations for a specified action.

Sample action: A man is sitting in his chair reading a magazine. Suddenly he closes the magazine and strides out of the room.

Possible explanations:
He realizes he is late for an appointment.
His wife called him to dinner.

Essential Maze Routes. (Adapted from a former Air Force test entitled "Route Planning.") Find the points in a printed maze through which one must go from specified starting points to a goal.

Sample maze:

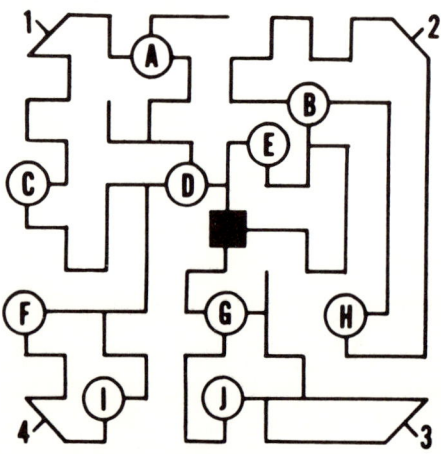

Answers: 1–D; 2–B; 3–G; 4–D.

Essential Operations. Choose one of five items of information that is irrelevant to the solution of a given problem.

Sample problem: How many miles apart will the two boats be when they run out of gas?
Alternatives:
1. Boats A and B each have 5 gallons of fuel.
2. They cruise together toward the same point.
3. Boat A uses 1 gallon in going 3 miles.
4. Boat B uses 2 gallons in going 1 mile.
5. Boat B is twice as heavy as Boat A.

Answer: 5.

Evaluation of Comparisons. Select the one of three comparisons between two given objects that is most justified.

Given objects (sports):   X—baseball   Y—football
Alternative comparisons:
A. X requires more teamwork than Y.
B. X draws bigger crowds than Y.
C. X has less men on a team than Y.

Answer: C.

Expressing Mixed Emotions. Write different things a person might say if he felt two given emotions.

Given emotions: both JEALOUS and DISAPPOINTED

Possible responses:
"You can have it; I don't want it."
"Yeah, Bill won; he always wins."
"He got it? But I expected to."

Expression Exchange. Choose one of three alternative facial expressions to go with a gesture, changing the latter most.

Given face and gesture:

Alternative facial expressions:

    1   2   3

Answer: 3.

Expression Grouping. Choose one of four expressions that belongs with a given group by virtue of common psychological dispositions.

Given group:

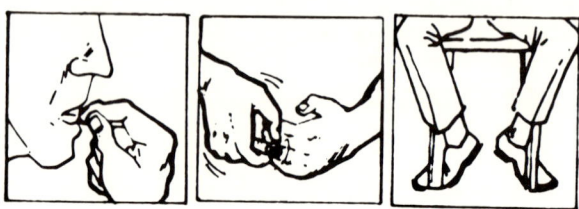

Alternatives:

 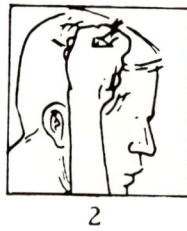  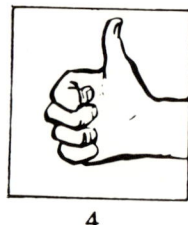
1   2   3   4

Answer: 2.

Expressional Fluency. Write different four-word sentences using a given set of initial letters for the words.

Given letters: K _____ u _____ y _____ i _____ .

Possible sentences:
Kill useless yellow insects.
Keep up your interest.
Kidnapping upsets young infants.

Expressions. Choose one of four expressions that indicates the same psychological state as another given expression.

Sample item:

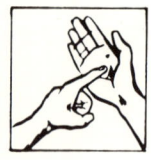 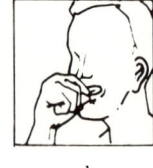 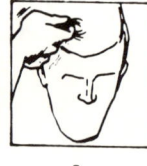  
     1   2   3   4

Answer: 4.

F Test. Given only sets of letters, words, numbers, and figures, see problems and solve them.

Sample items: 1. 4 1   2. H O U S E
                   1 4

1. 4 1 1   2. B A R N
   1 4 1
   1 1 4

Face-Shield Matching. Match faces with shields as previously studied in pairs.

Sample study item:

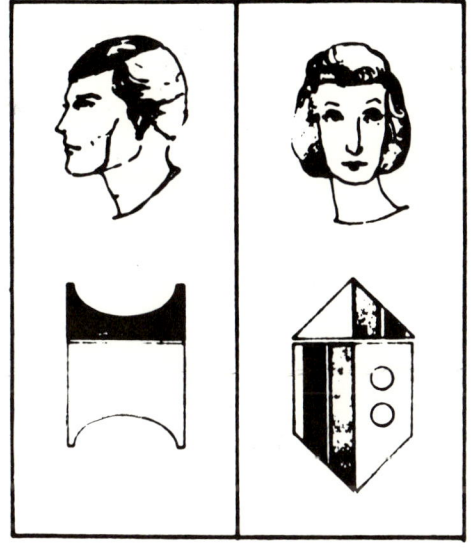

Sample test item:

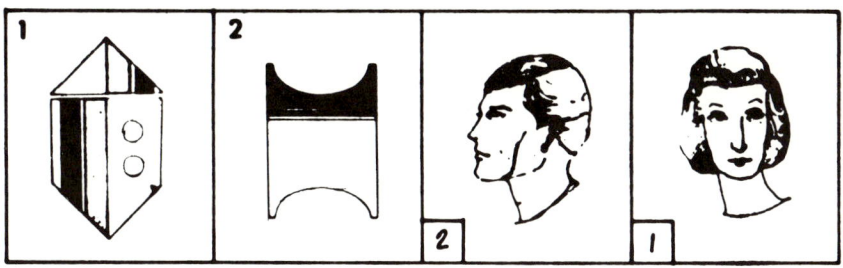

Faces[3]. Choose one of four facial expressions that indicates the same psychological state as a given expression.

Sample item:

Answer: 4.

Facial Situations. Choose one of three verbally described situations that fits the expressions in two photographs.

Given expressions:

Alternative situations:
1. He was told the child looks like him.
2. They have accepted the invitation.
3. He got the promotion.

Answer: 1.

Facts and Opinions. Designate given statements as being either facts or opinions.

Given statements:
1. In 1939 there were two World's Fairs held in the United States.
2. The Democratic party has done more for this country than the Republican party has.

Answers: 1–fact; 2–opinion.

---

[3] Adapted from the Frois-Wittman and Lightfoot pictures of emotional expression, obtained from the Brown University Photo Laboratory. Also true of Facial Situations, to follow.

False Premises. (From a Thurstone test.) Judge whether conclusions to given nonsensical verbal syllogisms are true or false.

Sample items:
1. All haystacks are catfish. All catfish are typewriters. Therefore all haystacks are typewriters.
2. Some lagoons are hilltops. All hilltops are hungry. Therefore, all lagoons are hungry.

Answers: 1–true; 2–false.

Figural Class Inclusion. Select from five figures the one that contains the same property as two given figures.

Sample items:

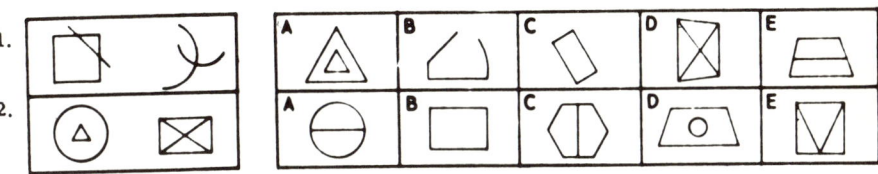

Answers: 1–D; 2–E.

Figural Class Recall. Recall (sketch) the common elements of members of previously studied figural classes.

Two sample study classes:

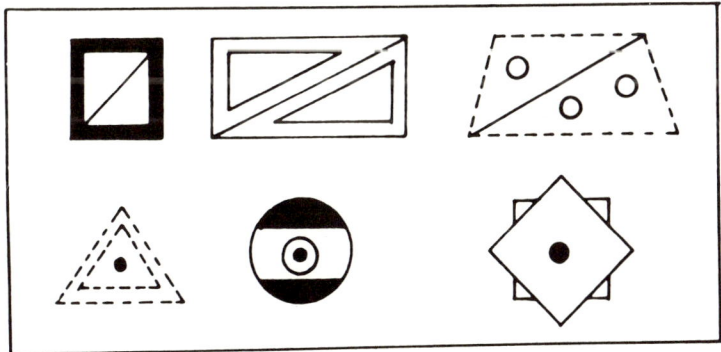

Sample responses:

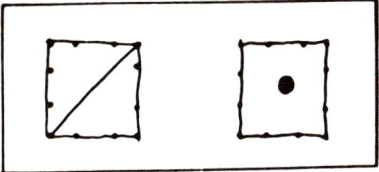

Figural Hierarchical Grouping. Place figures in a hierarchical system of classes.

Sample item:

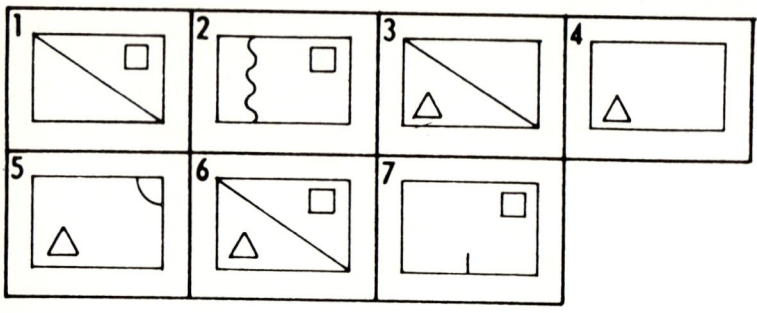

Answer:

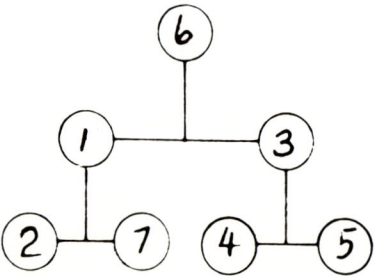

Figural Letter Recognition. Recognize type of faces for letters previously studied.

Sample study letters:

Alternative test letters:

	A	B	C	D
1.	*i*	*i*	*i*	*i*
2.	*n*	*n*	*n*	*n*

Answers: 1–B; 2–C.

Figural Relations Recall. Recall (sketch) the second figure of previously studied pairs of related figures.

Sample studied pairs:

Sample answers:

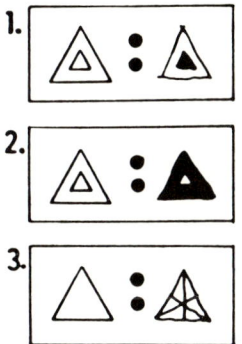

Figural Similarities. Say whether figural aspects of six complex figures can be used to form class sets of three figures each.

Given figures:

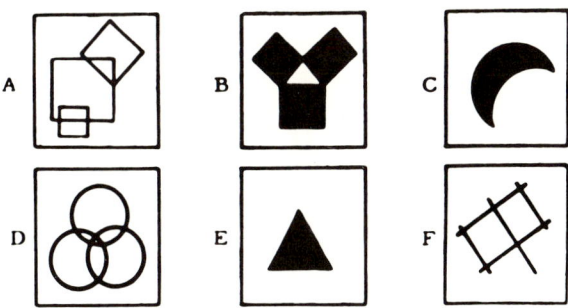

Alternative sets: 1. ABD   2. BCF   3. DEF

Answers: 1 can be used; 2 and 3 cannot.

Figural Subtraction Recall. Remember changes in pairs of subtracted figures and make similar subtractions on a test page.

Sample study pairs:

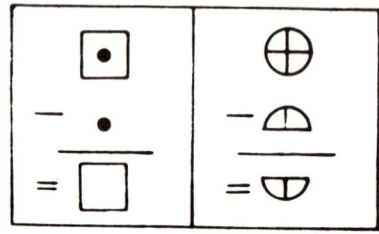

Sample test responses:

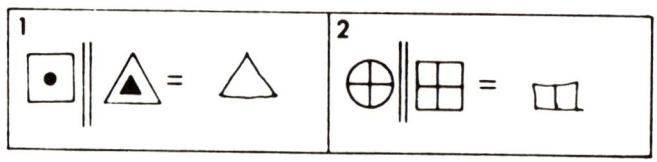

Figure Analogies. Select one of five figures to complete an analogy.

Sample item:

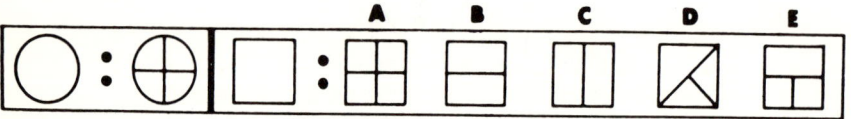

Answer: A.

Figure Analogies Completion. Draw a figure to complete an analogy.

Sample item:

APPENDIX B **401**

Figure Analysis. Name objects seen in a picture of jumbled, mutually embedded figures.

Sample item:

Possible answers: Ostrich, tree.

Figure Classification. Discover classes of figures and assign other figures to the classes.

Sample figure classes:

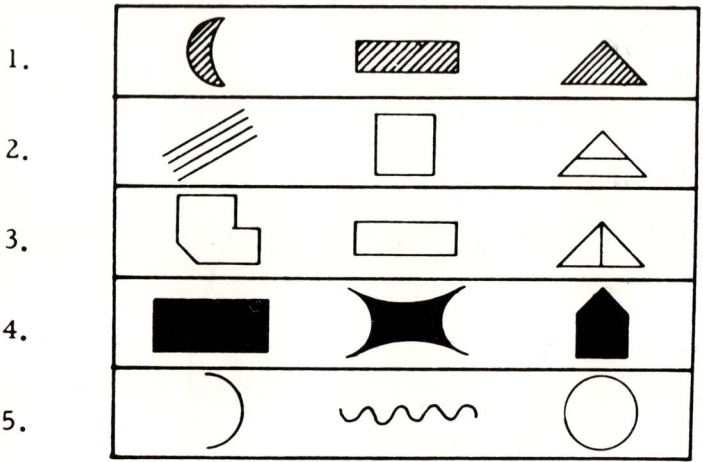

Alternative figures:

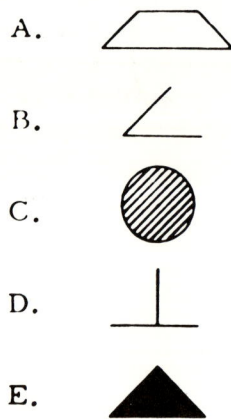

Answers: 1–C; 2–A; 3–D; 4–E; 5–C.

Figure Completion. Identify objects that are incompletely shown.

Sample items:

Figure Concept Grouping. Group given figures in classes so that a common attribute of each class is shared by a target figure.

Given figures:

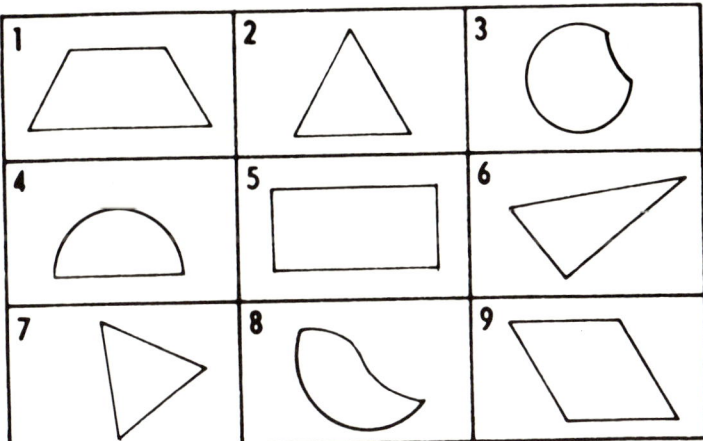

Target figure:

Possible classes: 1, 5, 9; 2, 6, 7; 3, 4, 8.

Figure Concepts Test (uncommon). Find characteristics in common to two or more of many pictured objects.

Sample objects:

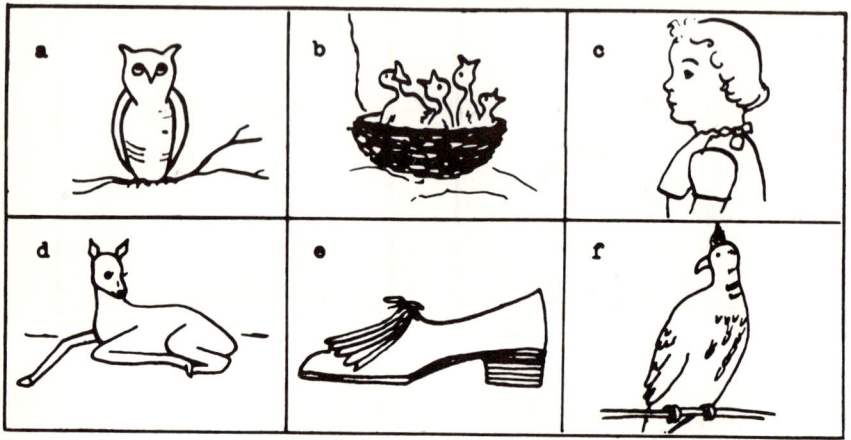

Possible groups: a and b (animals); b and d (youth); a and f (birds).

Figure Exclusion. Exclude one of five figures that does not belong in a class with the other four.

Sample item:

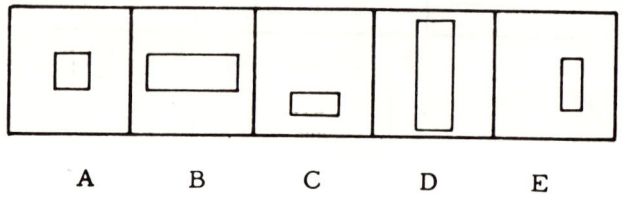

Answer: A.

Figure Grouping. Group 12 figures into four classes with three figures each, using each figure once.

Given figures:

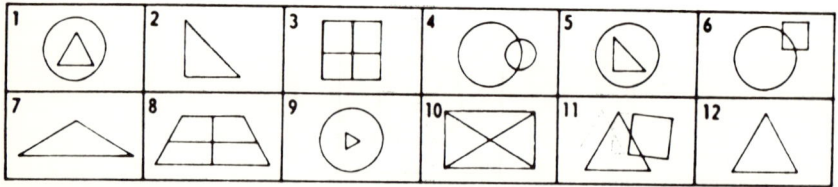

Correct classes: 1, 5, 9; 2, 7, 12; 3, 8, 10; 4, 6, 11.

Figure Matching. Select one of five figures having most in common with another given figure.

Sample item:

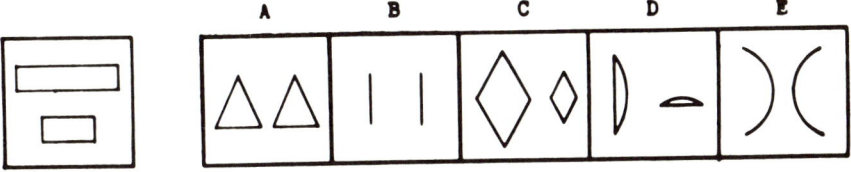

Answer: C.

Figure Matrix. Discover the trends in rows and columns of a 3 by 3 matrix of figures, and choose one of five figures to go in a specified cell.

Sample item:

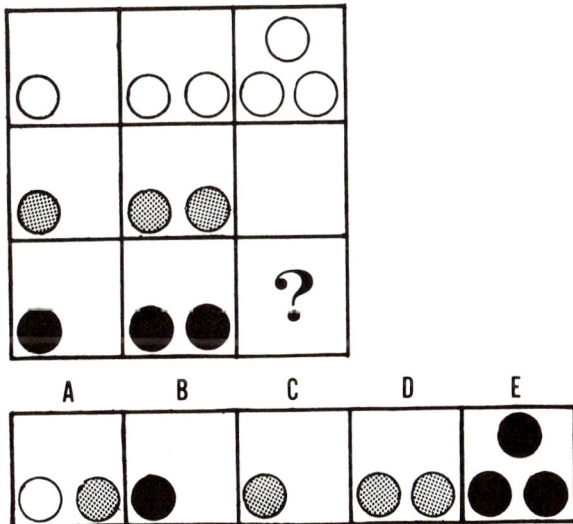

Answer: E.

Figure Production. Add lines to given lines in order to produce meaningful objects.

Given figure:

Possible productions:

Figure Recall. Recall (sketch) previously studied, simple figures.

Sample study figures:

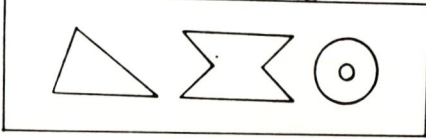

Sample test figures:

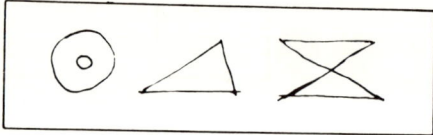

Figure Recognition. Recognize previously studied geometric figures.

Sample study figures:

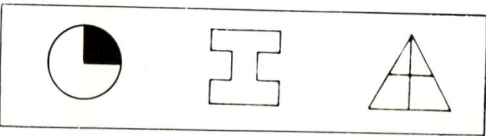

Sample test figures:

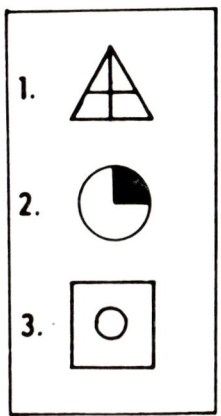

Answers: 1 and 2 were studied; 3 was not.

Figure Series. Continue each figure series by selecting one of five alternatives.

Sample item:

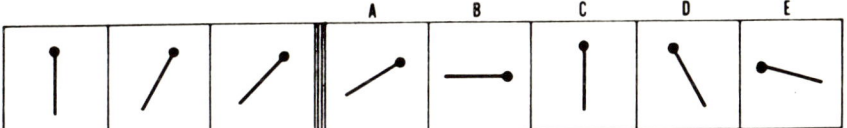

Answer: A.

Finding Letter Transformations. Describe the change that has occurred between a correctly and incorrectly spelled word.

Given words: 1. maneuver–manuever   2. citizen–citezin
3. calculus–calolus

Answers:
1. "u" and "e" are interchanged.
2. "i" and "e" are switched.
3. "cu" is changed to "o."

Form Reasoning. (A test by Blakey, 1941.) Solve equations stated in terms of figures, based upon a table of figure equivalences.

Table of equivalences:

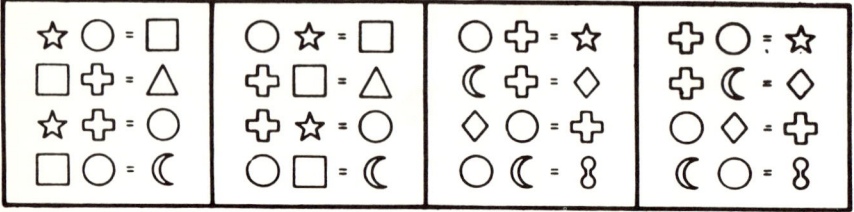

Sample items::

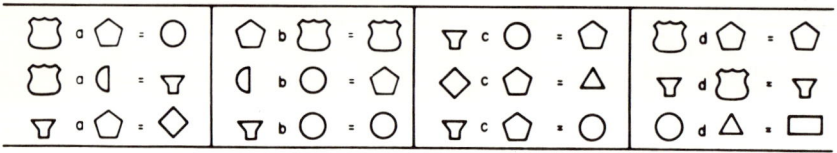

Form Reasoning II. Solve equations stated in terms of letters and figures, based upon a table of letter and figure equivalences.

Table of equivalences:

Sample item:

Do the operations in the order: c, d, b.
Alternatives:

  A   B   C   D   E

Answer: A.

Forming Alternate Faces. Match top and bottom halves of faces to make different expressions appropriate to stated situations.

Given situation: Ted has just heard bad news.
Movable face tops:

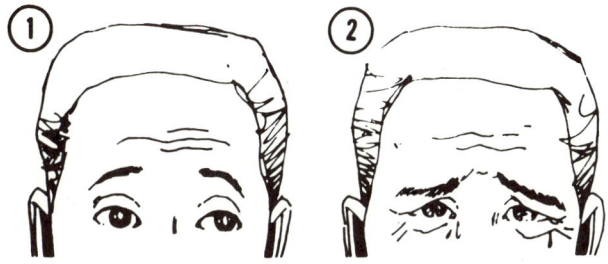

Given face bottoms:

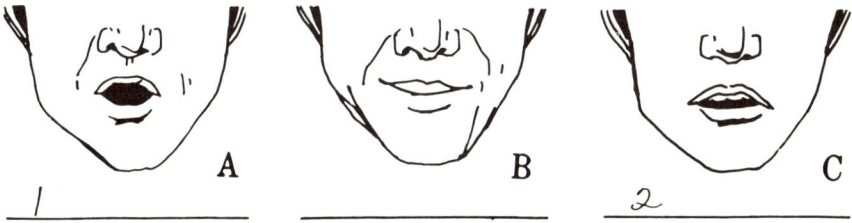

Possible answers: Top 1 with bottom A; top 2 with bottom C.

Four Letter Words. Find four-letter words in lines of letters.

Sample line of letters:
A M G E W I N D T E Y K Q C I R O C K W Z E H O W L P

Embedded words: Wind, rock, howl.

Front View Recognition. Recognize front view of drawing of a previously studied, three-dimensional form, observed from another direction.

Sample study forms:

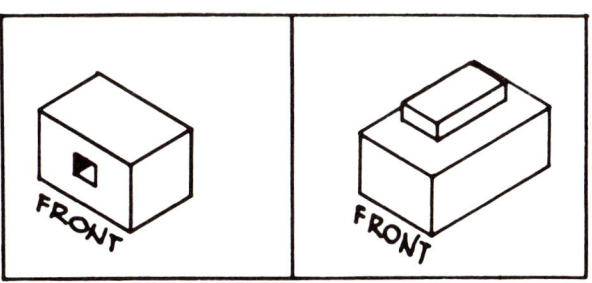

Sample test front views:

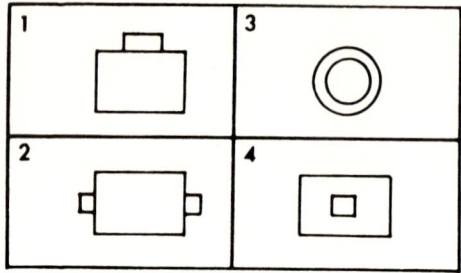

Answers: 1 and 4 are front views of studied objects; 2 and 3 are not.

Generalizations. Judge whether statements support or do not support given generalizations.

Sample generalization: The role of Hamlet was best acted by John Barrymore.
Sample statements:
1. The reviews of Barrymore's performance as Hamlet were always favorable.
2. Some of the qualities of the stage play have been lost in the filming of "Hamlet."

Answers: 1 is supportive; 2 is not.

Gestalt Transformation. Select one of five objects, a part of which could be adapted for some new and unusual purpose.

Sample purpose: To start a fire.
Alternative objects: A. fountain pen   B. onion   C. pocket watch
D. bottle top   E. bowling ball

Answer: C (crystal used as burning lens).

Group Classification. Classify groups of words so that one of two target groups belongs to each class formed.

Given target groups:
Target A: bargain, store, applaud, water
Target B: ruler, dog, bite, thimble
Given groups of words:
1. Radio, ocean, sextant, fear
2. Cloth, tear, consent, ice
3. Scale, cheap, plastic, record
4. Knife, agree, captain, cut
5. Sugar, like, scratch, cat

6. Hate, bumper, tool, clock
7. Cook, gauge, sew, button
8. Savings, approve, can, bank

Answers: Groups 2, 4, 5, and 8 belong with the "applaud" of target A; groups 1, 3, 6, and 7 belong with the "ruler" of target B.

Henmon-Nelson Vocabulary. (Subscale of the Henmon-Nelson Tests of Mental Ability.) Choose the alternative word that has the same meaning as a word that completes a sentence.

Hidden Figures. Choose one of five basic figures that is hidden in each complex figure.

Basic figures:

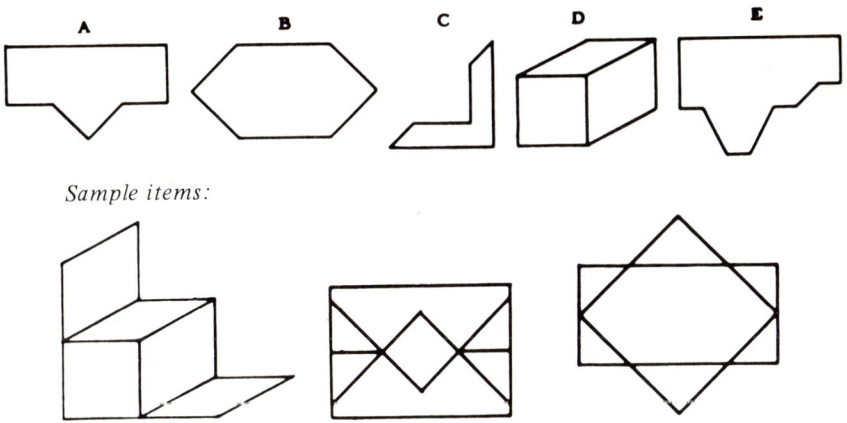

Sample items:

Answers: D, A, and B, respectively.

Hidden Print. Find letters or numbers concealed in squares of scattered dots.

Sample items:

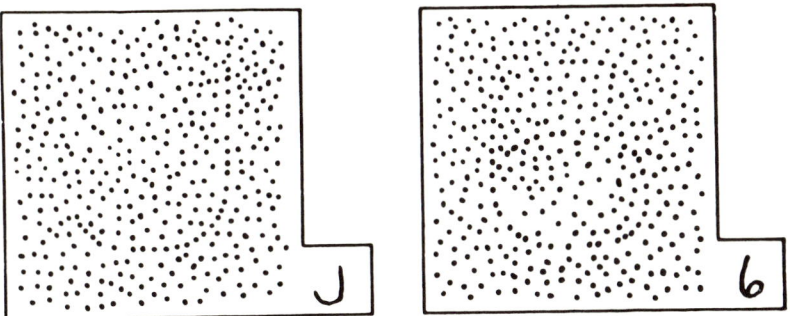

Hidden Word Production. Write phrases or sentences so as to conceal a given word in different ways.

> *Given word:* FORMER
>
> *Sample phrases:* <u>For mer</u>ely one dollar; In<u>form er</u>rors; Yoursel<u>f or Mer</u>vin; Arrest all in<u>former</u>s.

Homonyms. Recognize a definition that matches that of the "other element" in a pair of previously studied homonyms.

> *Sample study homonyms:*
> There is a *hole* in the wall.
> He ate the *whole* pie.
> Sample test definitions: ENTIRE   A. nut   B. ship   C. hollow space   D. operation
>
> *Answer:* C.

Ideational Fluency. List members of a broadly defined class.

> *Sample class:* FLUIDS THAT BURN
>
> *Possible responses:* Gasoline, kerosene, hydrogen, alcohol.

Identical Figural Relations. Judge which pairs of figures have relations like that of another pair.

> *Sample item:*

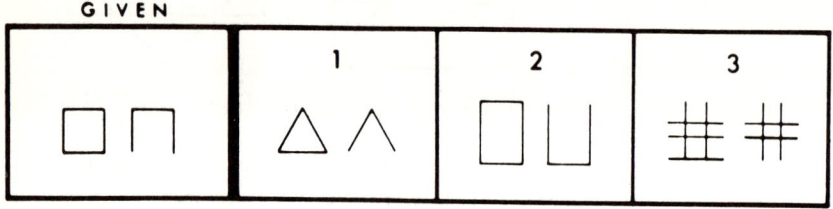

Answers: 1 and 3 have similar relations; 2 has not.

Identical Forms. (A Thurstone test.) Find one of five figures that is exactly like the key figure.

Sample items:

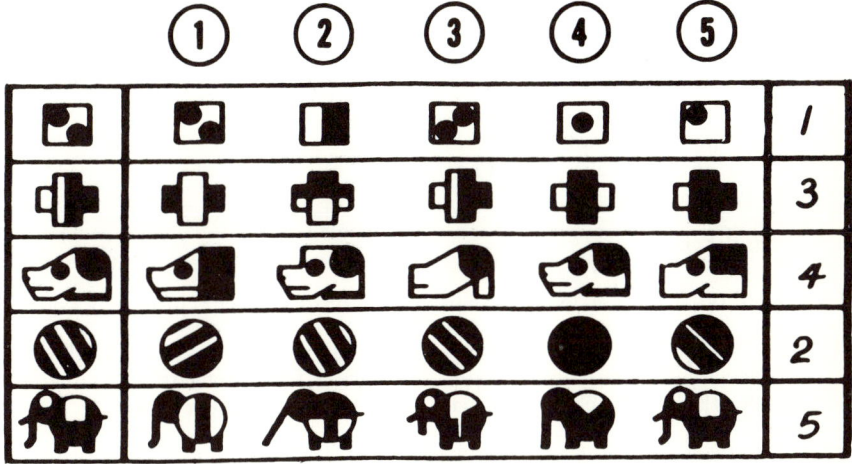

Identical Verbal Relations. Select one of four pairs of words having the same relation as a given pair:

Given pair: CANARY—SING
Alternative pairs: A. sparrow—wing B. dog—bark C. expression—song D. yellow—feather

Answer: B.

Implied Uses. Write phrases or sentences using secondary meanings of given words.

Given word: TAKE (to grasp or seize)

Possible responses: To take in marriage; to take for a ride; to take food; I'll take this coat.

Important Facts. Judge which one of four facts is most important and which least important in a problem situation.

Sample situation: You are to sing in an opera and must decide which costume to wear.
Alternative facts:
A. The opera is named "A Dutch Maiden."
B. The scenery is green and blue.
C. The spotlight is blue.
D. The theater is very small.

Answers: A is most important; D least important.

Impossibilities.   List things that are impossible.

Inference Test.   Choose one of five conclusions that follows from a factual, meaningful premise.

> *Sample premise:* Most of the trees in the forest are green.
> Alternative conclusions:
> A. There are no yellow trees in the forest.
> B. There are some yellow trees in the forest.
> C. Some of the trees in the forest are green.
> D. Green trees are the tallest in the forest.
> E. Pine trees are green.
>
> *Answer:* C.

Inferences II.   Write a logically correct, but informal, conclusion to a given statement.

> *Given statement:* No parachutes are available for passengers of commercial aircraft, but life jackets are usually available for passenger ships.
>
> *Possible conclusion:* Parachutes don't help much in aircraft emergencies.

Inflections.   Choose one of four facial expressions that goes with the inflection of a tape-recorded word or phrase.

> *Sample item:* Alternative faces for a tape-recorded "no."

1   2   3   4

Insight Problems.   Solve problems involving marked shifts in ideas.

> *Sample problem:* A board is 8 feet long and 3 feet wide. It is to be cut into only *two* pieces that will exactly cover a hole 12 feet long and 2 feet wide. Show by drawing on the diagram how to cut the board.
>
> *Given diagram* (The dotted line shows how to cut the board.):

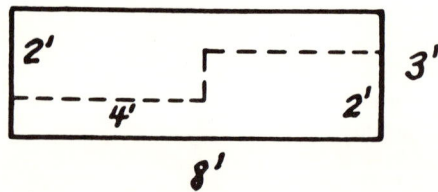

Internally Consistent Figures. Judge whether given two-dimensional representations of three-dimensional forms could exist.

Sample figures:

I 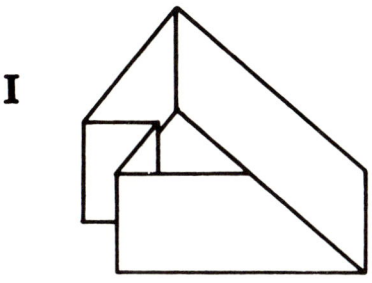 II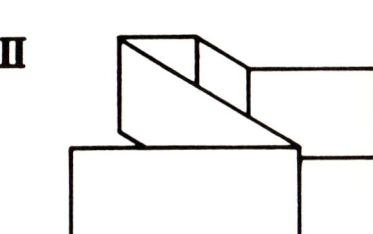

Answers: I does not make sense; II does.

Interpretations. Decide whether conclusions from a premise are correct, incorrect, or no decision is possible.

Given paragraph: The marriage ceremony of the Veddas of Ceylon is very simple, but it is absolutely binding, since cases of divorce or separation are entirely unknown. The women are jealously guarded by the men, who do not allow traders or other strangers to see them.
Sample conclusions:
1. It is easy for explorers to get photographs of Vedda men, women, and children.
2. Marriage ties are taken quite seriously by the Veddas.
3. Women are allowed no choice as to their marriage partners among the Veddas.

Answers: 1—false; 2—true; 3—no decision is possible.

Inventive Opposites. (A Thurstone test.) Write two antonyms for each given word, the first letters of the antonyms being given.

Sample item: NARROW   b _____ w _____

Answers: Broad, wide.

Inventive Verbal Relations. Write words that bear specified relations to given words.

Sample relation: (a) is the opposite of (b)
Sample items:
1. (a) black   (b) _____
2. (a) strong   (b) _____

Answers: 1—white; 2—weak.

Iowa Reading Comprehension. (Subscale of the Iowa Test of Basic Skills.) Answer questions on short reading selections.

Iowa Tests of Educational Development—Verbal. Select a word to insert in a fragmentary sentence.

Iowa Tests of Educational Development—Quantitative Thinking. Solve problems involving arithmetical reasoning, exponents, formulas, and interpretation of charts.

Judging Figural Balance. Determine which of three defined types of balance each given figure exhibits.

Types of balance:

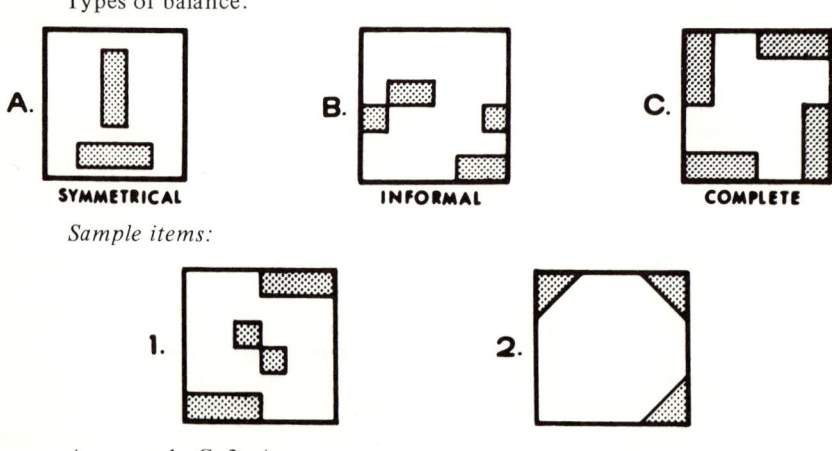

Sample items:

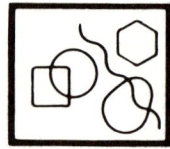

Answers: 1–C; 2–A.

Judging Figural Combinations. Judge whether only specified component figures are contained in each given figure.

Sample key figures:

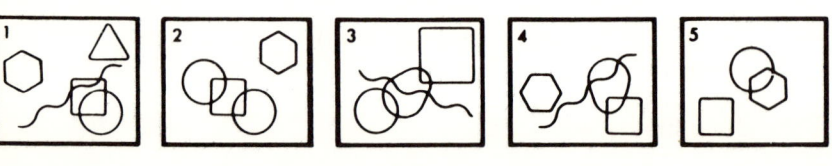

Sample items:

Answers: 4 and 5 have only key figures; 1, 2, and 3 do not.

Judging Figural Elaboration. Following given identification rules, judge whether figures are specified well enough to be identified.

Sample code box:

```
                    CODE BOX
    •      means a point at which two sides meet.
    →      means a side runs in the direction indicated.
    ×      means the midpoint of a side.
```

Given key figures:

Sample item:

Answer: Item can be none of the key figures.

Judging Mathematical Expressions. Judge whether mathematical expressions are equivalent alternatives of a given expression.

Given expression: $\dfrac{(2p + 4q)}{8r}$

Sample items:

1. $\dfrac{2(p + 2q)}{8r}$

2. $\dfrac{4(p + q)}{8r}$

Answers: 1 is equivalent; 2 is not.

Judging Object Adaptations. Select activities that illustrate the most unusual, ingenious, or clever use of given objects.

Sample object: TELEPHONE
Alternative uses:
1. To get help in an emergency
2. To pound a nail
3. To keep a dog near a tree

Answer: 3 (use the cord as a rope).

Judging Rearrangements.   Judge whether figures are rearrangements of parts of a given figure.

Given figure:

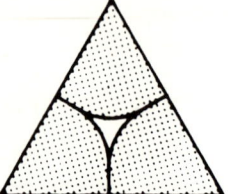

Sample items:

   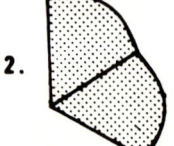   

Answers: 1 and 2 are not rearrangements; 3 is a rearrangement.

Judging Specified Figures.   Judge whether figures exhibit two stated properties.

Given properties: At least one dotted line and one square.
Sample items:

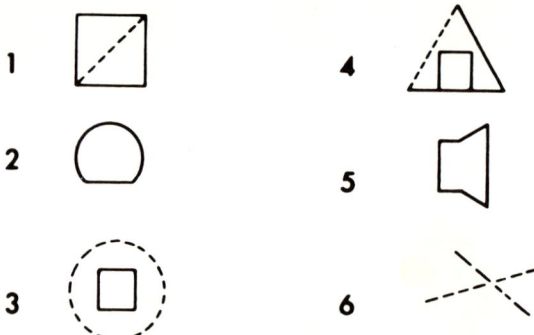

Answers: 1, 3, and 4 have both properties; 2, 5, and 6 do not.

Judgment of Size. Judge which of four simple outline figures is exactly the same as the center figure.

Sample item:

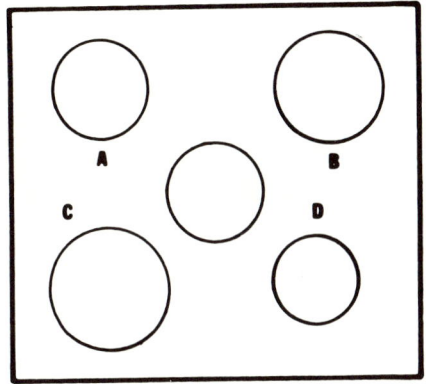

Answer: A.

Jumbled Words. Judge whether given words could be made just by rearranging the letters of a key word.

Key word: start
Item words: 1. stare   2. starts   3. tarts

Answers: 1 and 2 cannot be made; 3 can be.

Largest Class. Form the largest class possible from a given list of words so that the remaining words also make a class.

Given list: 1. button   2. staple   3. purse   4. zipper   5. filing cabinet   6. paper clip   7. mailbox   8. scotch tape   9. pocket

Answers: Largest class is 1, 2, 4, 6, 8.

Learned Information (classes). Reproduce the contents of a short essay, given several key terms; scored for proper classifications.

Learned Information (systems). Reproduce the contents of a short essay, mentioning given key concepts in correct order.

Least Movement. Select the photograph in which the object has been rotated least from its original position.

Sample item:

GIVEN  A 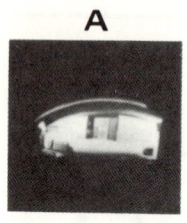 B 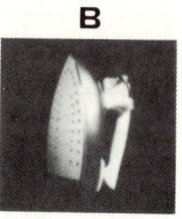 C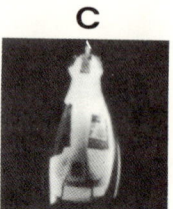

Answer: C.

Letter Analogies. Recognize a relation in each of two pairs of letters, then complete another pair having the same relation.

Sample item: m o   f h   j ?
Alternative answers: k l u i p

Answer: l.

Letter Classification. Recognize classes of nonsense words, then assign given nonsense words to the classes.

Given classes: 1. ALF OSTE IMBR   2. CFCO AQOQ HCHY
3. GMB RGAD OFGE
Alternatives: A. LSUG   B. WAWO   C. DXTE   D. OFMA   E. SZU

Answers: D goes with class 1; B with class 2; A with class 3.

Letter-Concept Grouping. Group nonsense words in classes so that each class shares an attribute with a target word.

Nonsense words: 1. AMK   2. SBN   3. TFT   4. QIP   5. BYS
6. GHH   7. RDB   8. LLS   9. CVO
Target word: TBLET

Answers: 1, 4, 9; 3, 6, 8; 2, 5, 7.

Letter Group Exclusion. Choose a group of letters that does not belong in the class of the other three.

Sample item: 1. AABC   2. ACAD   3. ACSH   4. AACG

Answer: 3.

Letter Group Relations. Determine whether a given triad of letters is similar in different ways to other triads.

Given triad: ABC
Given groups: 1. TTE   2. SUW   3. BRR

Answers: Given triad is similar to 1 (one vowel); similar to 2 (in alphabetical order, even if skipping two letters); but not similar to 3.

Letter Grouping. Group a list of nonsense words in four classes, using each word only once.

List: 1. LXD 2. GOG 3. LZQ 4. BCD 5. MAA 6. SUS
7. OPQ 8. EEB 9. RIR 10. LWP 11. KII 12. RST

Classes: 1, 3, 10; 2, 6, 9; 4, 7, 12; 5, 8, 11.

Letter-Number. Find the relations in two letter-number pairs and use it to find the number for a new letter-number pair.

Sample item: no = 56   po = 76   mo = ___?___

Answer: 46.

Letter Problems. Judge the difficulty with which letter problems can be solved, based upon a table of letter equivalences.

Table of equivalences:
TZ = U   YY = W   YX = T   ZY = V   TV = Z
VW = Y   XX = Z   ZU = W   UU = T

Alternatives: Problems in this test are of three kinds:
A. They can be solved with no changing of order.
B. They can be solved only by changing order.
C. They cannot be solved.

Sample problems: 1. TZU = _____   2. UVZ = _____

Answers: 1–A; 2–B.

Letter Series. Find the rule of order in a series of letters, then continue the series, following the rule.

Sample items:
1. E F E F E F E ___ ___
2. A R B R C R D ___ ___

Answers: 1–F E; 2–R E.

Letter Triangle. Choose one of five letters to appear in a given place in a triangular pattern of ordered letters.

Sample item pattern:

```
              a
         b        c
       d     e        f
     ___   ___   ___   ___
      ?
```

Alternative letters: A. f   B. g   C. h   D. i   E. j

Answer: C.

Letter "U".   Check all the words in a long list that contain the letter "U."

Sample list: ( ) sense   ( ) short   (✓) juice   ( ) special   (✓) jump   ( ) field

Answers: (Checked.)

Limited Sums.   Combine given digits to make specified totals by addition only.

Given numbers: 2 5 3 1 4
Sample items: obtain 7   obtain 6

Answers: 3 + 4 = 7; 1 + 2 + 4 = 7; 2 + 4 = 6; 2 + 3 + 1 = 6.

Limited Word Revisions.   Make one new word from each given word, using all the letters of the given word.

Sample given words: 1. gape   2. tale   3. elbow

Possible new words: 1–page; 2–late; 3–below.

Limited Words.   See **Word Pair Revisions.**

Line Continuations.   Decide which of four lines is the continuation of an interrupted given line.

Sample item:

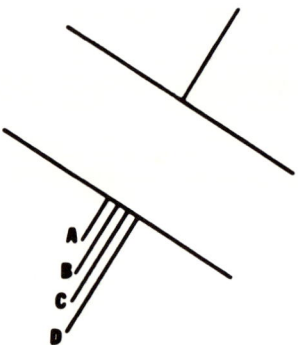

Answer: B.

Line Drawing.   Draw a simple line that expresses the feeling or emotion indicated by a given adjective.

Sample adjectives: SERIOUS   DELIGHTED   ANGRY

Logical Classification. Classify statements in specified categories of statement types.

> *Given statement:* You ought not to cross the street against the red light.
> Types: A. custom   B. completeness   C. utility   D. safety   E. welfare
>
> *Answer:* D.

Logical Reasoning. Choose one of four conclusions that follows logically from two premises.

> *Given premises:* No birds are insects. All swallows are birds.
> Alternative conclusions:
> A. No swallows are insects.
> B. Some birds are not swallows.
> C. All birds are swallows.
> D. No insects are birds.
>
> *Answer:* A.

Make a Code. Construct different number-letter codes.

> *Sample codes:*
> A = 1   B = 2   C = 3   etc.
> Z = 1   Y = 2   X = 4   W = 8   etc.

Make a Figure Test (fluency). Draw many different figures, using simple given lines. Score is total number drawn.

> *Given lines:*

> *Possible figures:*

Make a Figure Test (shifts). Same as the preceding test; scored by the number of changes in category of figures.

Make a Mark. Draw many different figures according to simple specifications.

Sample specifications: Use dotted lines.

Possible responses:

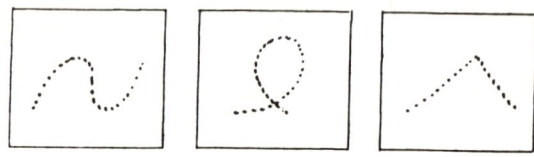

Making Objects. Combine figures in various ways to form named objects.

Sample elements:

Named objects: face lamp

Possible responses:

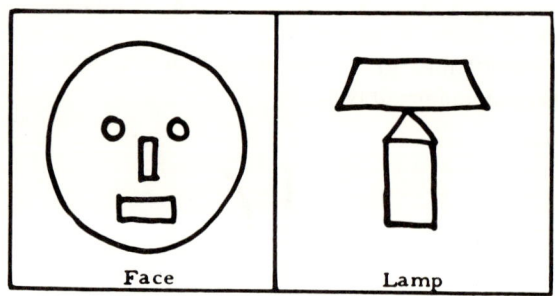

Marking Speed. Make as many Xs as possible in 2 minutes.

Match Problems. Remove a specified number of matches from a design to leave a specified number of complete squares or triangles.

Given design:

Sample problem: Remove three matches and leave four squares.

Answer:

Match Problems II. Same as Match Problems except that each problem is to be solved in several different ways.

Given design: Same as for Match Problems.

Sample problem: Remove three matches and leave four squares.

Possible answers:

 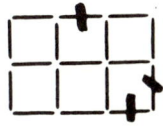

Match Problems III. Same as Match Problems II except more very unusual solutions are possible.

Sample item: Starting with the same design as for Match Problems, remove four matches and leave three squares.

An unusual solution:

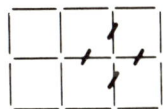

Match Problems IV. Remove any number of matches, leaving a specified number of squares.

Sample problem: With the same initial design, leave three squares.

Possible solutions:

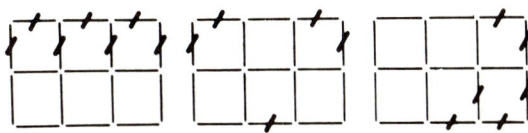

Match Problems V. Remove a specified number of matches, leaving any number of possible squares.

Sample problem: Cross out five matches, leaving any number of squares.

Possible answers:

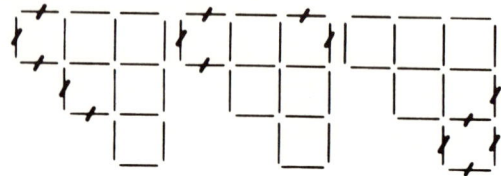

Matched Verbal Relations. Choose one of four pairs of words with a relation most like that in another given pair.

Sample given pair: FISH–WORM
Alternatives: A. pole–hook   B. crumb–bird   C. water–swim
D. mouse–cheese

Answer: D.

Matrix Order. Draw a line through the three-word sequence in a 3 by 3 matrix that is in the most meaningful order.

Sample matrix:
run	think	want
read	write	sleep
walk	publish	book

Answer: A line should be drawn down the center column.

Matrix Trend Recall. Complete figural matrices by remembering row and column trends from a previously studied page.

Sample study item:

Sample test item:

Alternative figures to use:

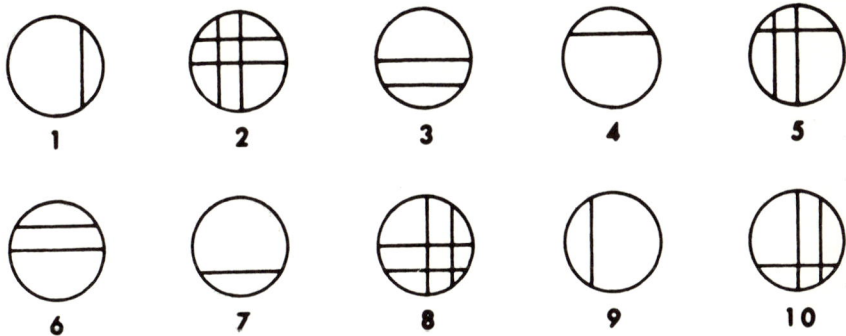

Completed test item:

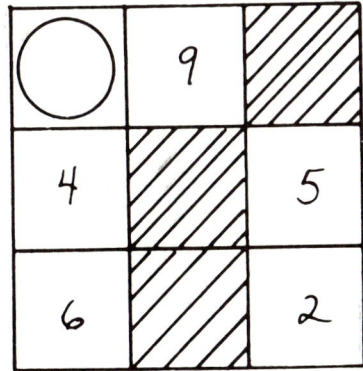

Mechanical Principles. (A U.S. Air Force test.) Select the correct responses to pictured problems, applying mechanical principles.

Memory for Decimal Point Shifts. Determine whether decimal-point shifts between pairs of the same numbers are the same as for the same pairs on a previously studied page.

    Sample study items:
    1.694   31.26
    169.4   312.6
    Sample test items:
    1. 31.26   2. 16.94
       312.6   169.4

    Answers: 1 is the same shift; 2 is not.

Memory for Definitions. Choose definitions that are similar to those given on a previously studied page.

    Sample study definitions:
    NEUTRAL—neither one thing nor another.
    SKIM—a kind of milk.
    Sample test items:
    1. SKIM   A. remove   B. a liquid   C. read rapidly   D. pass over
    2. NEUTRAL   A. not engaged   B. neither plus nor minus   C. not harsh   D. neither of two things

    Answers: 1—B; 2—D.

Memory for Digital Units. Say whether each of a list of numbers was in a list previously heard five times in varied orders.

    Sample items: Assume that only 71 and 24 had been read.
    Sample test items: A. 24   B. 32   C. 71

    Answers: A and C were read; B was not.

Memory for Facts. Answer questions regarding information presented in previously given sentences (a recall test).

    Sample sentences studied: Frogs are aquatic members of the animal kingdom. Soccer is an English sport.
    Sample test items:
    1. What sport was mentioned? _____
    2. What aquatic animal was mentioned? _____

APPENDIX B   429

Memory for Figural Analogies. Choose completion of a figural analogy consistent with a studied analogy.

Sample study pairs:

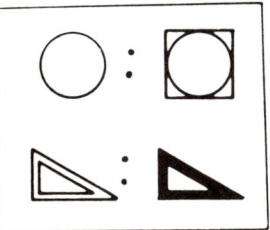

Sample test items:

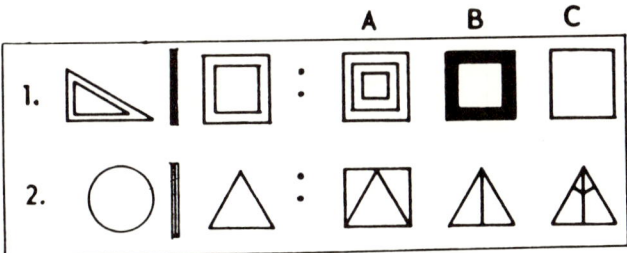

Answers: 1–B; 2–A.

Memory for Figural Classes. Indicate whether given test figures have a class property in common with sets of figures studied.

Two study classes:

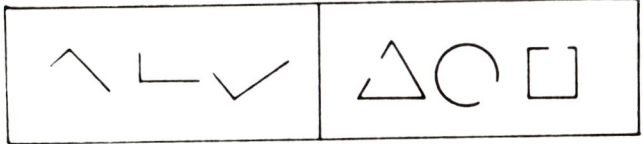

Sample test figures:

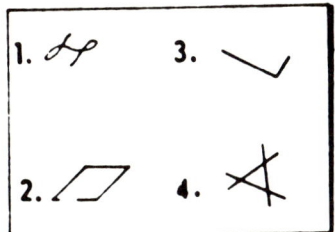

Answers: 2 and 3 belong to studied classes; 1 and 4 do not.

Memory for Hidden Figures. Remember (sketch) how simple geometric figures were hidden in complex figures previously studied.

Sample study figures:

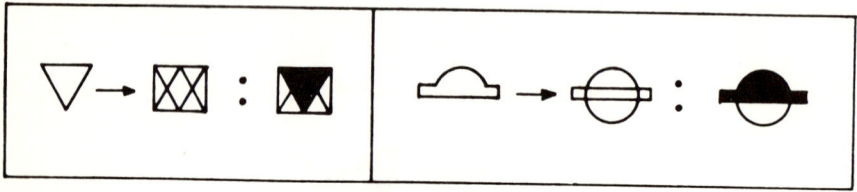

Sample test figures, with studied figures sketched in:

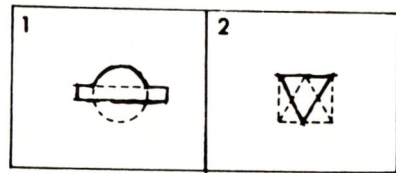

Memory for Hidden Transformations. Determine whether embedded words are hidden in the same manner as previously studied.

Sample study items:
Don't leap in before you look
You must not burden the teacher.
Sample test items:
1. They load entire trucks.
2. He will stop in the evening.

Answers: 2 has same hidden arrangement; 1 has not.

Memory for Letter Series. Choose one of four series composed of a given letter with the same rule as on the study page.

Sample study series:
z zz zzz zzzz zzzzz
xxxxxxxx xxxx xxxxxx xx xxxx
Sample test item:
1. A. z zzz zzzz zzzzzz
   B. zzzz zz zzz z zz
   C. zzz zzzz zzzzz zzzzzz
   D. zzzzzzzz zzzz zzzzzz zz zzzz

Answer: 1–C.

Memory for Listed Nonsense Words. Remember whether nonsense words are the same as those studied on a previous page.

    Sample study words: GAJ   DOF
    Sample test words: 1. DIJ   2. GAJ   3. DOF

    Answers: 2 and 3 were studied; 1 was not.

Memory for Meanings. Recognize whether or not words are close synonyms for previously studied words.

    Sample study words: LAMP   TO SEARCH   COURAGEOUS
    Sample test words: 1. toaster   2. brave   3. to write   4. lantern   5. to hunt   6. shy

    Answers: 2, 4, and 5 are synonyms; 1, 3, and 6 are not.

Memory for Misspelling. (See p. 247.)

Memory for Name and Word Classes. Remember whether names and words belong to classes studied on a previous page.

    Sample study classes:
    Iris   Irene   Irving
    test   pest   lest
    Sample test items: 1. Molly   2. West   3. Ira   4. list

    Answers: 2 and 3 belong to studied classes; 1 and 4 do not.

Memory for Name Relations. Choose from four pairs of names the one having an internal relation observed on a study page.

    Sample study pairs:
    Sam Martin   Tom McTavish   Pam Merton
    Robert Redding   Rose Reardon   Roger Renshaw
    Sample test items:
    1. Roy   A. Rollins   B. Revere   C. Radford   D. Young
    2. Tim   A. Thompson   B. Traver   C. Mensch   D. Tolman

    Answers: 1–B; 2–C.

Memory for Nonsense Word Classes. Tell which four nonsense words represents a class given on the study page.

    Sample study classes:
    NEC   NEP   NEF
    GUZ   GAZ   GYZ

Sample test items:
1. A. GIS   B. GOZ   C. LOZ   D. MOZ
2. A. NOP   B. NAR   C. NER   D. NUP

Answers: 1—B; 2—C.

Memory for Nonsense Word Order. Remember the order of a studied list of nonsense words.

Sample study list: GUJ   KER   NIK   BAS
Sample test items:
1. Did KER come before BAS?
2. Did NIK come before GUJ?
3. Did NIK come before BAS?

Answers: 1—yes; 2—no; 3—yes.

Memory for Nonsense Words—Free Recall. See **Recall of Nonsense Words.**

Memory for Number Classes—Recall. Write descriptions of number classes studied on a previous page.

Sample study classes: 5, 10, 25   307, 602, 704   621, 821, 521

Sample test responses: Contain a zero in the middle; divisible by 5; end in 21.

Memory for Numerical Relations. Describe remembered relations between pairs of numbers from a previously studied page.

Sample study pairs:
2—8   7—13
18—6   24—8
Sample test items:
1. The second is _____ the first.
2. The second is _____ the first.

Possible responses: 1. Six more than; 2. one-third of.

Memory for Order of Listed Numbers. Remember the order of numbers listed on a study page.

Sample list: 9 6 2 7 12
Sample test items: Which number in each group came first on the study page?
1.   A. 2   B. 6   C. 9   D. 12
2.   A. 2   B. 6   C. 7   D. 12

Answers: 1—C; 2—B.

Memory for Test Order. Indicate whether or not a given test preceded another in a test booklet just completed.

Sample items:
1. Was *Alternate Uses* before *Cartoons?*
2. Was *Consequences* before *Related Alternatives?*

Memory for Transpositions. Indicate whether or how pairs of four-digit numbers underwent transpositions between two tape-recorded presentations.

Sample test item: (3871 and 9148 were read the first time, and 3871 and 1948 the second time). In which number was there a transposition?

Answer: The second group.

Memory for Word Classes. See **Memory for Name and Word Classes.**

Memory for Word Meanings. Recognize whether given definitions match words presented on a previous page.

Sample study words: WINTER   KNIFE   WISH
Sample test definitions:
1. used to cut   2. a round object   3. a season of the year   4. victory
5. to hope   6. to trip or stumble

Answers: 1, 3, and 5 match studied words; 2, 4, and 6 do not.

Memory for Word-Number Relations. Select one of four numbers having a relation to a given word the same as a relation previously studied.

Sample study relations:
dead–285   read–785
neck–412   neat–419
Sample test items:
1. next   A. 312   B. 416   C. 482   D. 498
2. lead   A. 682   B. 784   C. 685   D. 786

Answers: 1–B; 2–C.

Memory for Word Relations. Choose relations that have the same sense and direction as ones given on a previously studied page.

Sample relations: scissors–hair   alley–highway
Sample test items:
1. highway   A. lion–kitten   B. creek–river   C. boat–river
   D. track–train
2. scissors   A. mower–lawn   B. nail–clipper   C. knife–cut
   D. break–hammer

Answers: 1–B; 2–A.

Memory for Word Transformations. Remember how groups of letters were previously divided to form words.

    Sample study words: BIND/ARE   EARN/ICE
    Sample test words: 1. EAR/NICE 2. BIND/ARE

Answers: 2 is divided the same way; 1 is not.

Missing Cartoons. Choose one of four cartoon frames to complete a given cartoon strip, making the best psychological sense. (See footnote 2, p. 368.)

Missing Links. Produce three words to complete a chain of associations between two given words.

    Sample items:
    1. work _____ _____ _____ orange
    2. red _____ _____ _____ beer

Possible completions: 1. job money food; 2. sunset weather cold.

Missing Pictures. Choose one of three photographed situations to complete a story, making the best psychological sense.

    Sample item:[4]

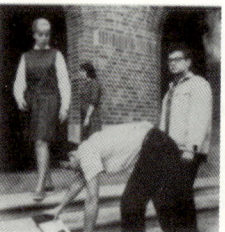

Answer: 3.

[4] Reproduced by permission of Sheridan Psychological Services.

APPENDIX B   435

Monogram Recall. Recall (sketch) various monographic arrangements of three given letters.

Sample study monographs:

Monograms. Construct different monogram designs from three given letters.

Sample given letters:

Possible responses:

Most Effective Path. (Adapted from the U.S. Air Force experimental test Planning a Circuit.) Find the path in a diagram that allows a round trip through certain points without retracings.

Sample item:

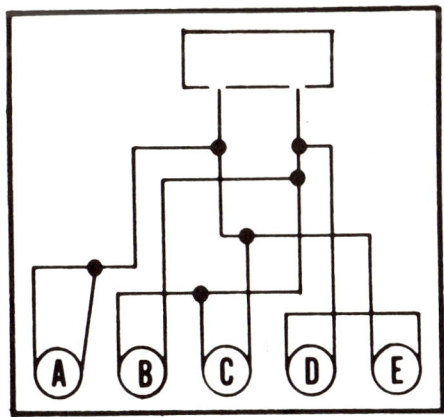

Answer: C (if certain rules are followed).

Multiple Analogies. Produce different relations between a given pair of objects, in completing analogies.

> *Sample items:*
> 1. MAN is to GIRL as BULL is to _____ .
> 2. MAN is to GIRL as STEEL is to _____ .
> 3. MAN is to GIRL as HORSE is to _____ .
>
> *Answers:* 1—cow; 2—wood; 3—colt.

Multiple Behavioral Grouping. Group comments into different sets according to psychological states they express.

> *Given comments:*
> 1. "You get out of here"
> 2. "Are you sure"
> 3. "What a bore"
> 4. "How could you do such a thing"
> 5. "Didn't you listen to me"
> 6. "I wonder what time it is"
>
> *Possible sets:* 1, 3, 4, 5 (anger or annoyance); 2, 4, 5 (disbelief).

Multiple Cartoon Fill-Ins. Explain in different ways the missing center frame in a three-frame cartoon strip. (See footnote 2, page 368.)

Multiple Emotional Expressions. Write different things that a person might say when he feels a specified emotion.

> *Given emotion:* ANGER
>
> *Possible responses:*
> 1. "Oooh, you make me so mad!"
> 2. "I hate you."
> 3. "One more word and I'll belt you."
> 4. "How many times have I told you . . ."

Multiple Expression Changes. Choose different sets of faces to show how a person might feel at three points in a story.

> *Given story:*
> 1. A man trips a lady who is walking by.
> 2. She falls, and the man apologizes to her.
> 3. The lady then becomes angry.

Given faces:

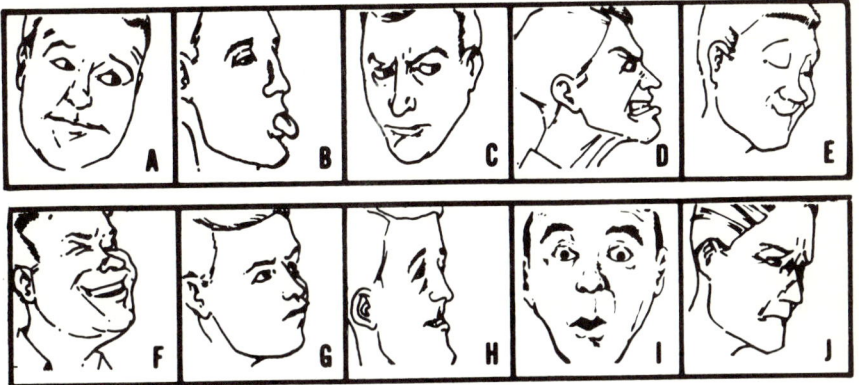

Possible sets of faces: IAC or FGE for the three steps.

Multiple Figural Similarities. Select different figures that can be classified with a given set of three figures.

Given class of figures:

Alternative figures:

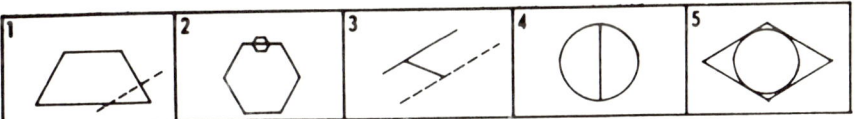

Answers: 3 (open figures); 1 (dotted line); and 2 (two figures of the same shape).

Multiple Grouping. Group and regroup words in several classes.

Given words: 1. arrow 2. bee 3. crocodile 4. fish 5. kite 6. sailboat 7. sparrow

Possible answers: 1, 2, 5, 7 (found in the air); 3, 4, 6 (found in the water); 2, 3, 4, 7 (animals).

Multiple Grouping of Figures. Group and regroup figures in different ways.

Given figures:

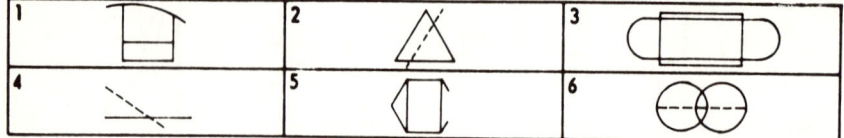

Possible classes: 1, 3, 6 (curved lines); 1, 2, 3, 5 (parallel lines); 1, 3, 5 (right angles).

Multiple Grouping of Nonsense Words. Form different classes from a list of nonsense words.

Given words: 1. RUATWS 2. FJOSUX 3. EJLORU
4. AAKNPB 5. BOOQIC 6. HIOSTV

Possible classes: 1, 4, 5, 6 (two adjacent vowels); 1, 4, 5 (first and last letters in alphabetical order); 2, 3, 6 (all letters in alphabetical order).

Multiple Letter Changes. Substitute a stated number of letters in each given word to make several new words.

Given word: FOLDER (change any two or three letters)

Possible new words: Finder, silver, fuller, softer, feeder.

Multiple Letter Similarities. From a list, find new members of a given class of letter sets.

Given classes:
UPOH   OKID   IFEC
HISV   TAMN   PEFOZ
List: 1. FOQI 2. ZHEM 3. IAO 4. MKICA 5. EIMCK
6. IJUME 7. NWRO 8. GOINU

Answers: 4, 5, and 6 go in the first class; 6 and 8 go in the second.

Multiple Social Problems. Suggest different personal problems that two given people could have with one another.

Given people: BROTHER   SISTER

Possible problems: Sister makes fun of brother's friends. They compete for attention of mother. Brother tries to dominate sister.

Multiple Story Plots. Develop different interpersonal situations involving all three given characters.

APPENDIX B   439

Sample of given characters: Two sisters, A and B, are romantically interested in the same young man, C. One day he comes to their home unexpectedly.

Possible developments: A and B praise each other to C, who becomes more confused than ever about which one he likes better. A tells C that B does not want to see him, which makes him all the more interested in B.

Multiple Symbolic Implications. Find different combinations of numbers that yield specified numbers by computations.

Sample items:
1. ____ + ____ + ____ = 10
2. ____ × ____ × ____ = 60
3. ____ ÷ ____ ÷ ____ = 2

Possible answers:
1—2, 2, 6; 3, 3, 4.
2—2, 3, 10; 2, 5, 6.
3—12, 3, 2; 20, 5, 2.

Multiple Word Extractions. Find short words concealed in two long words, using consecutive letters, but using no syllables as words.

Given words: e gal i tar i an   tick ing

Possible short words: Lit, it, ant, anti, antic, kin, king.

Mutilated Words. (A Thurstone test.) Identify words in which parts of each letter are missing.

Sample items:

house

football

Answers: House, football.

Name Grouping. Group and regroup a list of given names according to letter similarities.

Given names: 1. GERTRUDE   2. BILL   3. ALEX   4. CARRIE   5. BELLE   6. DON

Possible classes: 1, 3, 4 (two syllables); 2, 4, 5 (double consonants); 1, 4, 5 (initial consonant, terminal vowel).

Naming Meaningful Trends. Name or describe the meaningful progression in a group of concepts.

Sample trends:
1. mouse rat lion pig cow horse elephant
2. century year decade day week second

Answers: 1—animals become larger; 2—time units become smaller.

Nearest Figural Relations. Choose the pair of figures that has most nearly the same relation as a given pair.

Sample item:

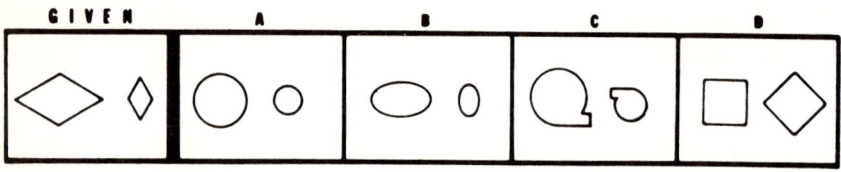

Answer: B.

Necessary Arithmetical Operations. Determine what numerical operations are necessary in solving arithmetic problems.

Sample problem: A city lot 48 feet wide and 149 feet deep costs $79,432.00. What is the cost per square foot?
Alternative operations: A. add and multiply   B. multiply and divide   C. subtract and divide   D. add and subtract   E. divide and add

Answer: B.

Necessary Facts. Determine what information necessary for a solution is missing from statements of arithmetic problems.

Sample item: The world's record for the 100-yard dash is 9.3 seconds. How many feet per second is that?

Answer: The number of feet in a yard.

New Uses. Make objects illustrated in photographs serve new given purposes.

Sample photograph:

Sample items:
1. Use as a curtain rod
2. Use to make a small kite

Answers: 1—lamp pole; 2—picture frame and curtain.

Non-Language Factors M.A. (Subtotal score of the California Test of Mental Maturity.) Multiple-choice items on immediate auditory recall, spatial orientation, visualization, picture interpretation, number series, and memory problems.

Nonsense Word Cross-Out. Cross out all nonsense syllables that have appeared earlier on a page filled with syllables.

Samples: 1. MYT   2. ZAR   3. POF   4. MYT   5. FUG   6. POF
7. RUP   8. SEY

Answers: 4 and 6 should be crossed out.

Number and Operations Changes I. Decide which equation is correct after a certain interchange of signs or numbers is made.

Given interchanges: $+$ and $\div$ 3 and 2
Alternative equations: A. $(2 + 3) - 5 = 0$ B. $(2 - 3) \div 2 = 3$
C. $(3 \times 3) \div 3 = 3$ D. $(3 \div 1) - 2 = 3$ E. $(4 \div 3) + 2 = 3$

Answer: E.

Number and Operations Changes II. Discover the interchanges of signs or numbers that will make given equations true.

>Possible interchanges:
>Of signs   Of numbers
>A. + and x   A. 0 and 2
>B. + and ÷   B. 0 and 3
>C. x and −   C. 1 and 2
>D. x and ÷   D. 1 and 4
>E. − and ÷   E. 2 and 3
>Given equation: $(2 + 3) + 1 = 4 \times 2$
>
>Answer: Sign change A only.

Number and Operations Changes III. Choose one of five equations made true using an interchange needed in preceding equation.

>*First equation:* $(4 + 2) = 8$
>Alternative equations:
>A. $4 + 4 = 16$
>B. $1 \div 1 = 2$
>C. $2 \times 2 = 2$
>D. $3 \div 3 = 6$
>E. $4 \div 8 = 4$
>
>*Answer:* A.

Number Associations (uncommon). Give many associations with specified numbers.

>*Sample number:* 4
>
>*Possible associations:* Quadruplets, quartet, four-leaf clover, the four horsemen of the Apocalypse.

Number Classification. Recognize classes of three numbers each, and then assign given numbers to them.

>*Sample classes:* 1. 44 55 33 2. 10 45 15
>Alternative members: A. 421 B. 53 C. 219 D. 22 E. 25
>
>*Answers:* D goes with class 1; E with class 2.

Number Combinations. Write different equations using only given numbers and rules.

>Given rules:
>A. Use *only* the numbers given.
>B. Use *only* addition (+) and multiplication (x).
>C. Use a given number only once in each equation.

Given numbers: 2 3 4 5 6

Possible equations: 5 = 2 + 3; 3 + 4 = 2 + 5; 2 x 3 = 6.

Number Group Naming. State what three numbers have in common.

Sample number groups: 1. 35 110 75   2. 676 65 161

Answers: 1—divisible by 5; 2—contain 6.

Number Grouping. Group and regroup numbers in several different ways to form classes.

Given numbers: 2 3 4 6 17 23 36

Possible groups: 3, 17, 23 (odd numbers); 17, 23, 36 (two-place numbers); 3, 6, 36 (divisible by 3).

Number-Letter Association. Recall (write) letters associated with numbers in previously studied pairs, when numbers are given.

Study associations: 88–U   67–K

Sample test items: 1. 67– _____   2. 88– _____

Answers: 1–K; 2–U.

Number Operations. See **Numerical Operations**.

Number Relations. Recognize a pair of numbers that does not belong with other pairs for lack of common property.

Sample item: A. 1–5   B. 2–6   C. 5–8   D. 3–7

Answer: C.

Number Rules. Arrive at a given number by performing simple operations upon other given numbers.

Sample item: Starting with 2, obtain 6.

Possible operations: + 4; x 3; x 2, + 2; + 5, – 1.

Number Series. State the rule for a series of numbers.

Sample series:
1. 15 18 21 24 27 30
2. 24 48 12 24 6 12 3

Answers: 1—add 3; 2—multiply by 2, divide by 4.

Number Series Correction. Cross out the number in a series that does not follow the rule.

Sample series: 2 4 8 18 32 64

Answer: Cross out the 18.

Numerical Operations. (Part III of the Guilford-Zimmerman Aptitude Survey.) Contains multiple-choice items of simple numerical computations.

Object Class Memory. Recognize whether objects fit into previously studied figural classes.

Sample study class:

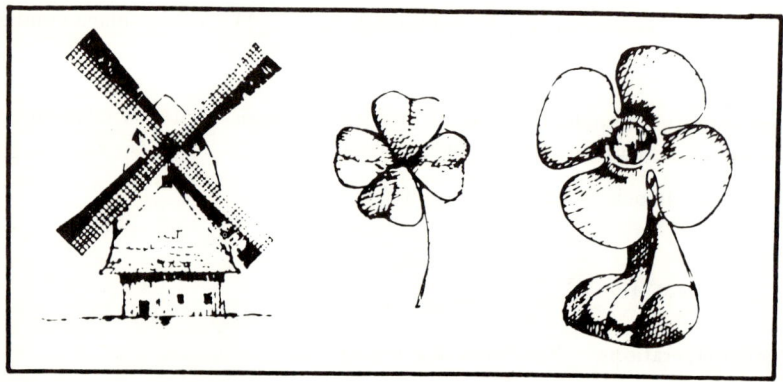

Sample test objects:

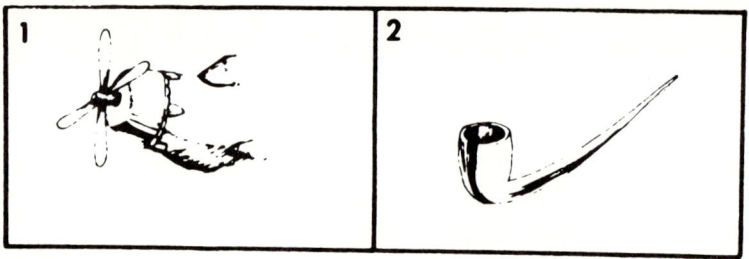

Answers: 1 fits the class; 2 does not.

Object Naming (cluster). Write a list of objects belonging to a very broad class. Score is number of types of objects.

Sample class: MINERAL

Object Naming (shifts). Same as above, but score is number of shifts of category.

Object Recognition.   Recognize previously studied objects.

Sample studied objects:

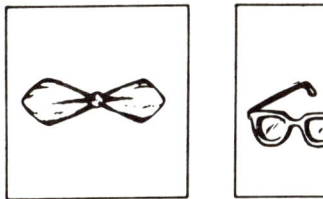

Sample test items:

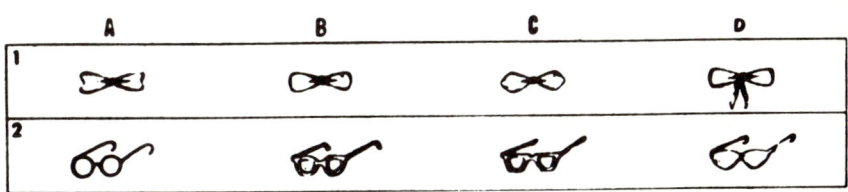

Answers: 1–C; 2–B.

Object Synthesis.   Combine two common objects to make a new one.

Given objects: PLIERS and SHOESTRING

Possible composite: pendulum; weapon.

Object Synthesis III.   List as many as five objects that could be made from a pair of given objects.

Given objects: SHEET OF PAPER and GLUE

Possible objects: Envelope, hat, lampshade.

Odd Strip Out.   Choose one of three cartoon strips in which the main character behaves differently. (See Footnote 2, p. 368.)

Omelet Test.   Rearrange sets of four letters to make familiar words.

Sample item: L C T O

Answer: Colt.

Operations Sequence.   Order three specified numerical operations to get from one number to another.

Sample item: Starting with 6, obtain 18.
Alternative operations: A. + 3   B. ÷ 2   C. x 3

Correct order: BAC.

Ordering I. Put a list of events into most reasonable time order.

Sample events:
A. Casey swung mightily but missed.
B. There was no joy in the hometown after the game.
C. The hometown stands roared as he came to bat.

Correct order: CAB.

Orientation Memory. Recall the locations of houses and other buildings on a previously studied city tract map.

Sample study map:

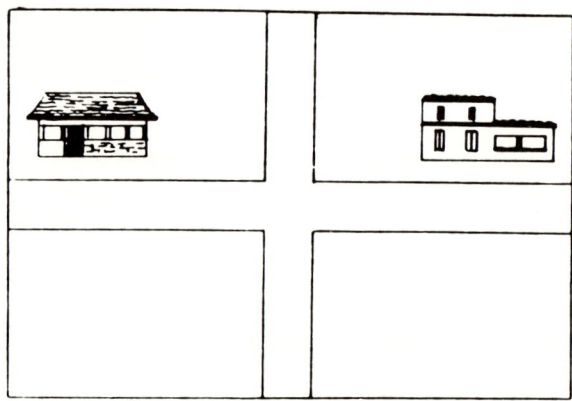

Sample test map:

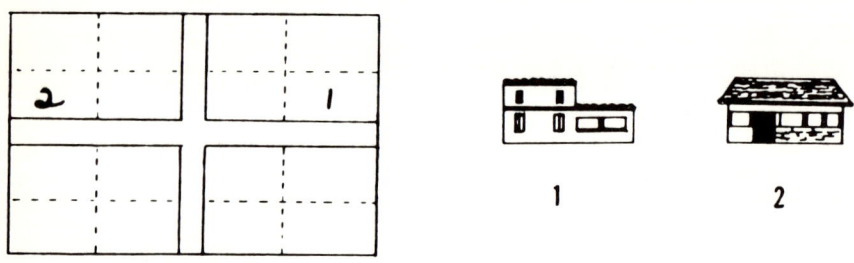

Outcomes. Choose similar fact-inference conclusions after studying a list of fact-inference statements.

Sample study statement: When a driver does not stop for a traffic signal, he usually gets a traffic citation.

Sample test item: Ted did not stop for that red light.
A. He probably didn't see the signal.
B. He must be in a hurry.

C. He got involved in an accident.
D. He will probably get a ticket.

Answer: D.

Outlining.   Arrange given statements in a logical, hierarchical outline.

Sample statements:
A. Cats are useful as mousers.
B. Dogs are fine as guardians.
C. Cows give milk.
D. Animals are useful in a variety of ways.
E. Some pets are useful and enjoyable.
F. Sheep furnish wool.
G. Farm animals are essential.

Solution: Main heading, D; major subheadings, G and E.

Paired Associates Recall.   Recall second words of previously studied word-word pairs, in response to given first words.

Sample study pairs: SUCCEED–HEAVY   BEVERAGE–NOW   PERFECT–WORD

Sample test items:
BEVERAGE– _____
PERFECT– _____
SUCCEED– _____

Answers (in order): Now, word, heavy.

Paired Figure Recall.   Recall (sketch) figures previously paired with given figures.

Sample study pairs:

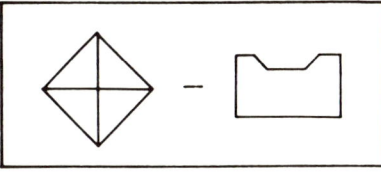 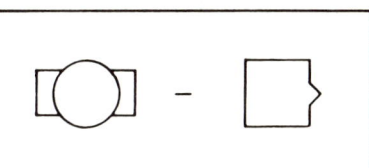

Sample test figures:

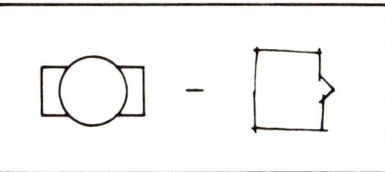 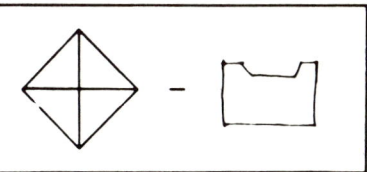

Paired Similarities. State one way in which words of a pair are similar.

Sample pairs:
1. QUARTER–FIFTH _____
2. NICKEL–QUARTER _____
3. LEAD–NICKEL _____

Answers: 1. Fractions; 2. coins; 3. metals.

Paper Folding. Visualize what a folded and cut piece of paper would look like when it is unfolded.

Sample item:

 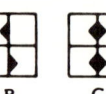
                                    A   B   C   D   E

Answer: C.

Paragraph Analysis. List the five basic ideas contained in each given paragraph.

Pattern Arrangement. Arrange black and white game pieces in the most efficient single pattern according to given rules.

Given rules:
1. No piece may be rotated.
2. Only *squares* of the same color may overlap.
3. Triangles may not overlap other pieces.
4. Two triangles may be joined to make a square.

Sample item:

1.   2.  3.  4.

Most efficient solution:

Penetration of Camouflage. (An experimental U.S. Air Force test.) Find as many hidden faces as possible in a complex scene.

Perceptual Relation Judgment. Judge the equivalence of figural relationships

Sample figures:

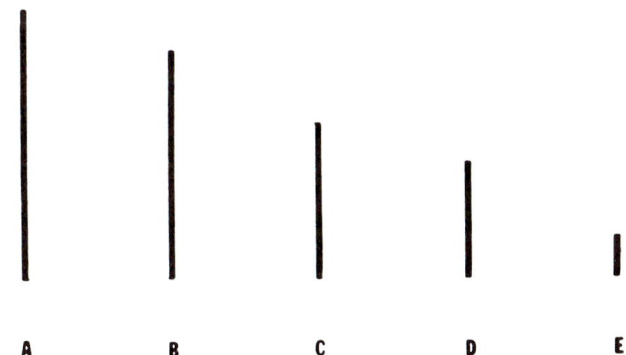

Sample items:
1. A : B :: C : D
2. A : B :: D : E
3. B : C :: D : E

Answers: 1 and 3 are true; 2 is not.

Perceptual Relations Naming. State the relation that the first figure of a pair bears to the second figure.

Sample pairs:

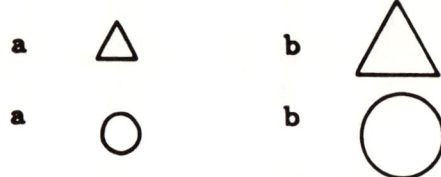

Answer: a is smaller than b.

Perceptual Speed. (Part IV of the Guilford-Zimmerman Aptitude Survey.) Find the pictured object that is identical with the given one.

Sample items:[5]

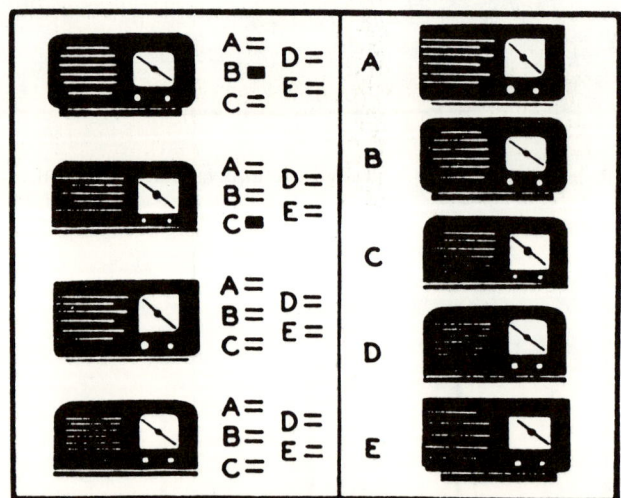

[5] Reproduced by permission of Sheridan Psychological Services.

Pertinent Questions. Write four questions, the answers to which would help one make a decision in a given problem situation.

Sample situation: Some teenagers want to build a clubhouse. Two vacant lots are available.

Possible questions: Which lot is nearer to where they live? Which lot has friendly neighbors?

Picture Arrangement. (From a test of Adkins and Lyerly.) Reorder the panels of a cartoon strip so that it tells a meaningful sequence of events.

Picture Class Memory. Indicate whether a given two-element class represents the same concept as appeared on a study page.

Sample study class:

452   THE ANALYSIS OF INTELLIGENCE

Sample test classes:

 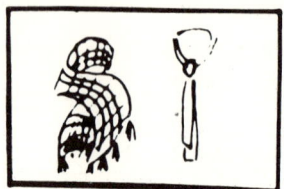

Answers: The first class represents the same concept; the second one does not.

Picture Classification.   Assign pictures to classes defined by groups of three pictures each.

Sample classes:

Sample test classes:

I

II

Answers: Figure I belongs in class B; II belongs in class A.

APPENDIX B 453

Picture Exchange. Select the photograph which, when substituted for a picture in a series, will change the meaning of the story.

Sample item:

Answer: 1.

Picture Exclusion. Select one photographed expression in four that does not belong to the class.

Sample item:

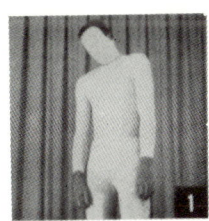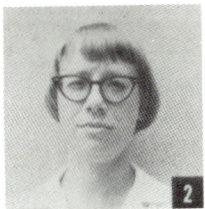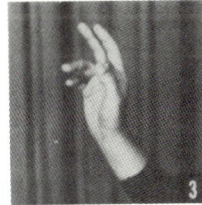

Answer: 3.

Picture Gestalt. See **New Uses** (p. 441), which replaced it.

Picture-Group Naming. Write a class name for each group of five pictured objects.

Sample groups:

Sample Responses: Hats, farm animals.

Picture Memory. Recall names of common objects pictured on a previously studied page.

Sample study pictures:

Sample responses: Iron, tricycle.

Planning a Circuit. See **Most Effective Path.**

Planning Air Maneuvers. (An experimental U.S. Air Force Test.) Indicate the most efficient path in "skywriting" letter combinations, following certain rules.

Sample item: (Composed of the letters L Z.)

Most efficient solution:

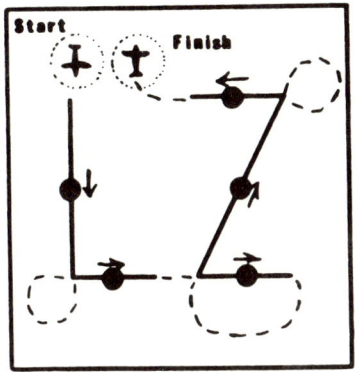

Planning Elaboration. List many detailed steps needed to make a briefly outlined plan work.

Sample plan: Your club is presenting a play. There will be three performances, Friday, Saturday, and Sunday evenings, in the school auditorium. You have been chosen as manager for the production, for which detailed arrangements must be made.

Possible details: Get tickets printed. Arrange for ushers. Advertise in the newspapers.

Planning Skills. Devise a complete plan for meeting a practical problem.

Planning Skills II. Devise a complete plan for meeting special conditions in a hypothetical complex situation.

Plot Titles (clever). Write titles for short-story plots, only clever ones being counted toward the score.

Sample plot: A new clerk in a department store, in anticipation of winter, ordered 100 dozen gloves, but forgot to specify that they should be in pairs. The store now has 100 dozen left-handed gloves.

Possible clever titles: "Southpaw's Delight"; "If Your Child Is Left-handed, Don't Worry"; "Left with a Lot of Lefts."

Plot Titles (nonclever). Same as preceding test, the nonclever titles being counted toward the score.

Possible nonclever titles: "What a Dilemma!"; "Clerk Fired"; "A New Clerk Makes an Error."

Possibilities. Name as many as four objects that could be used to perform a specified task.

Sample task: To leave a message

Possible objects: Letter, sketch, newspaper clipping.

Possible Jobs. Name as many as six occupations or groups of people that might be indicated by a pictured emblem.

Sample emblem:

Possible responses: Electrical engineer, light-bulb manufacturer, bright student, missionary.

Poster Judgment. Decide which of several different types and sizes of print could be used in making a sign that fits into a specified space.

Sample type styles:

Given poster area:

Sample signs: A. ROAD WORK   B. FALLING ROCKS

Answers: 1 or 3 will make sign A; 1 or 4, sign B.

Practical Judgment.   (An experimental U.S. Air Force test.)   Select from alternatives the best solution to a practical problem.

Predicaments.   Choose two of four objects to be adapted to an unusual use, in whole or in part.

Sample problem: To slice cheese for sandwiches, no knife being available. Given objects: harmonica   matches   thermos bottle   guitar

Solutions: Use thermos bottle to roll cheese thin enough for sandwiches. Hold wire from the guitar taut and use as a cutting edge.

Prescribed Relations.   Choose one of five figures that bears a described relation to another figure.

Sample item:

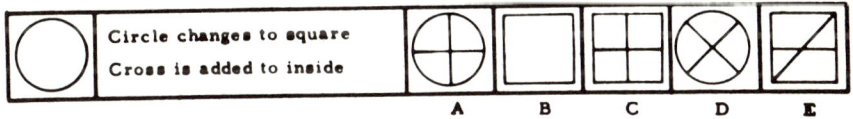

Answer: C.

Problem Solving.   A five-choice arithmetical-reasoning test.

Procedure Applications.   Describe as many as four tasks in which a certain general procedure would apply.

Sample procedure: Successive crystallizations in chemistry, to remove impurities from a substance.

An analogous task: Rinsing clothes repeatedly to remove soap and dirt.

Product Choice. Select best and worst of three objects that could be made by combining two stated objects.

Given objects: lace curtain   wire hanger
Alternative products: A. Christmas wrapping   B. mop   C. butterfly net

Answers: C is best; A worst.

Production of Figural Effects. Add details to a simple figure without drawing real objects.

Sample figure:

Possible details:

PSAT–Verbal. (Subscale of the Preliminary Scholastic Achievement Test.) Select words opposite in meaning to given words, complete analogies and sentences, and answer questions about paragraphs.

Punch-Line Comparisons. Judge which members of pairs of punch lines are more clever or unexpected for a given cartoon.

Given cartoon:

Pairs of punch lines:
1. A. "My hat is old enough to watch itself."
   B. "I've watched it so long it's last year's model."
2. A. "Do you think I have eyes in the back of my head?"
   B. "While I was watching my hat, someone stole my coat."

Answers: 1−A; 2−B.

Punched Holes. (A Thurstone test.) Draw circles where holes should be in an unfolded paper after it has been folded and punched.

Sample figure:

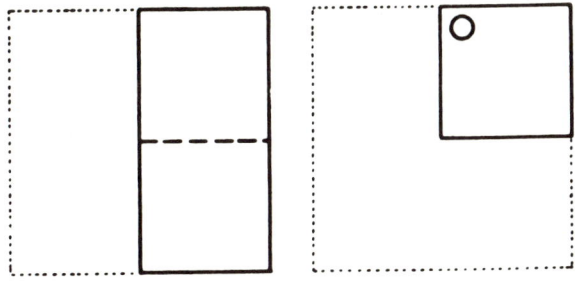

Answer:

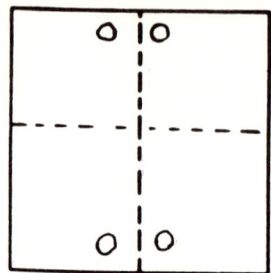

Puzzles. Solve problems requiring radical shifts of conceptions.

Sample problem: Two men applied for a job. Their last names were the same, and it was discovered that they were brothers, they had the same birthdate and the same parents, but they denied that they were twins. What was their relationship?

Answer: They were two of a set of triplets.

Questions II. Choose one of four questions about circumstances that might have resulted in the pictured expression.[6]

Sample expression:

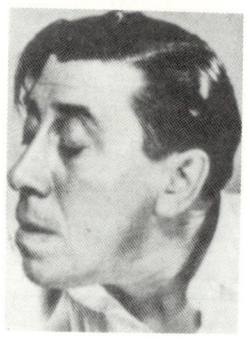

Alternative questions:
1. "Which way to the police station?"
2. "Were you glad to win all that money?"
3. "Do you hear something odd downstairs?"
4. "Isn't this lovely perfume?"

Answer: 4.

---

[6] Pictures in this test were adapted from a book by Halsman (1949) and were reproduced with permission.

Quick Response. Write the first word thought of in response to each of 50 words read aloud.

Sample words: table   soft   black

Reading Backwards. Answer simple questions that are printed backwards.

Sample items:
1. sthgie eerht etirw _____
2. nezod a ni selppa ynam woh _____

Answers: 1–888; 2–12.

Reading Comprehension. Answer questions about short passages.

Reading Confused Words. Write the correct words for given words in which letters and sounds are confused.

Sample items:
1. redboom _____
2. static airs _____
3. pots of wower _____

Answers: 1–bedroom; 2–attic stairs; 3–watts of power.

Reading Vocabulary–CAT. (Subtest of the California Achievement Test.) Select from four words one meaning the same as the given word.

Recall of Nonsense Words. Recall previously studied nonsense words.

Sample study words: GAJ   DUF   NYT

Recalled Analogies. Recall missing elements for previously studied incomplete analogies.

Sample analogies studied:
Native:tourist: :resident: ___?___
Police car:fire engine: :policeman: ___?___
Sample test items:
1. Policeman: _____
2. Resident: _____

Answers: 1–fireman; 2–visitor.

Recalled Words. Recall words presented on a study page.

Sample words: BABY   RABBIT   DARK

Recognition of Figural Classes. Recognize whether figures have the common class properties of sets previously studied.

Sample study sets:

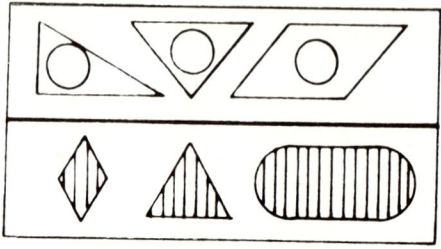

Sample test figures:

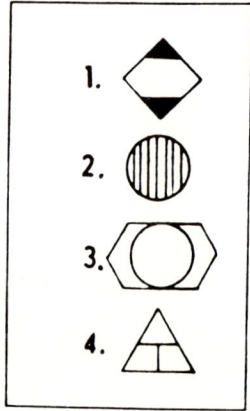

Answers: 2 and 3 have same class properties; 1 and 4 do not.

Reflections. Choose one of three statements that expresses the genuine attitude or feeling underlying given statements presented auditorially as well as in print.

Sample item: "I suppose if I did get work, I'd just bungle things—something would go wrong—at least I'd probably be pounding the streets again in a few weeks."

Alternative interpretations:
1. He wants work and yet he feels that if he does get it, something would go wrong anyway.
2. He feels his lack of self-confidence makes him incapable of holding a job even if he should get one.
3. He feels it's rather useless to try again.

Answer: 3.

Related Alternatives. Recognize items that are related to person's jobs, based upon studying a page of name-job pairs.

    Sample study pairs: Smith–bricklayer   Jones–radio announcer
    Sample test items:
    1. Jones   A. microphone   B. watch   C. tire   D. brick
    2. Smith   A. piano   B. microphone   C. brick   D. typewriter

    Answers: 1–A; 2–C.

Related Number Association. Given the first numbers of studied pairs, recall the second numbers of the pairs.

    Sample study pairs: 3–6   70–10
    Sample test items:
    1. 70–   A. 7   B. 10   C. 35   D. 140
    2. 3–   A. 6   B. 9   C. 12   D. 30

    Answers: 1–B; 2–A.

Related Words I. Choose the alternative word pair with a relation like that of the given pair.

    Sample item: GRAND–RAN   A. country–cot   B. respite–sit
    C. loving–log

    Answer: B

Remembered Relations. Complete sentences from alternatives in a manner consistent with previously studied relations.

    Sample studied relation: Diamonds are *harder than* coal.
    Sample test item: Coal is _____ than diamonds.
    A. softer   B. blacker   C. less valuable   D none of these

    Answer: A.

Remembering Classes. Recognize whether a given class name corresponds to one of the classes on a previously studied page.

    Sample study classes:
    BOOTS   SHOES   STOCKINGS   SLIPPERS
    ALGEBRA   GEOMETRY   ARITHMETIC   TRIGONOMETRY
    Sample test items: 1. foreign language   2. branches of mathematics   3. famous men   4. worn on the feet

    Answers: 2 and 4 correspond; 1 and 3 do not.

Remembering Faces. Recognize previously studied faces.

Sample studied faces:

Sample test faces:

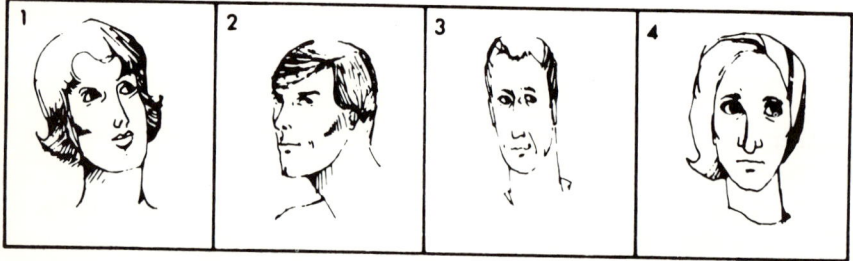

Answers: 1 and 3 were studied; 2 and 4 were not.

Remembering Figural Trends. Recognize which trends among circles have the same relations as studied trends among squares.

Sample studied trends:

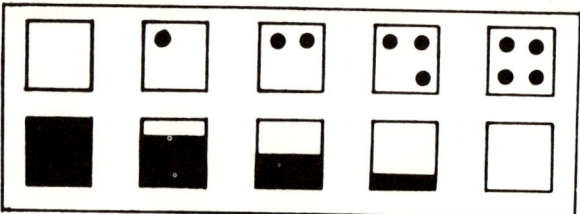

Sample test trends:

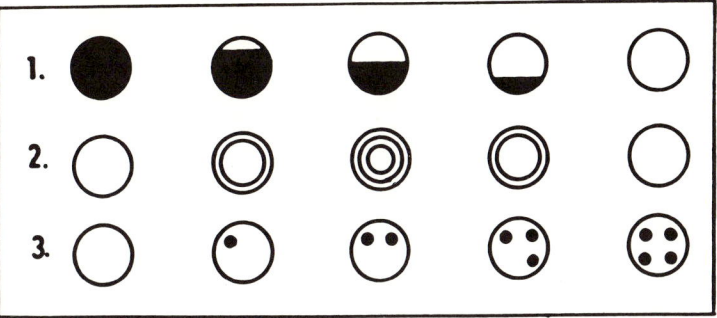

Answers: 1 and 3 were studied; 2 was not.

Remembering Flag-Letter Pairs. Match letters to flags as they were paired with each other on a previous page.

Sample study pairs:

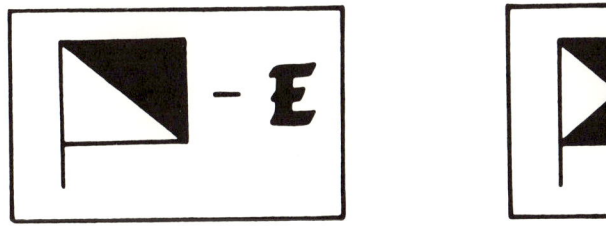

Sample test items:

Remembering Hand-Object Pairs. Match objects to hands as they were paired with each other on a previous page.

Sample study pairs:

Sample test item:

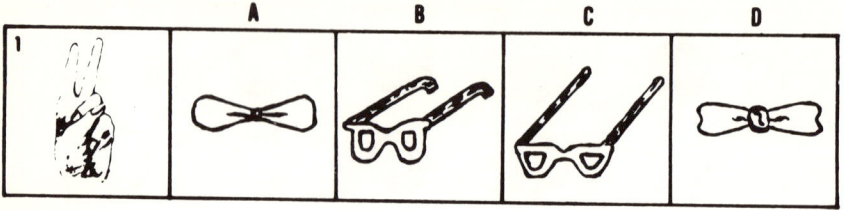

Answer: D.

Remembering Object Orientation. Remember the relative positions of pairs of objects from a 5 by 3 matrix on a study page.

Sample study matrix:

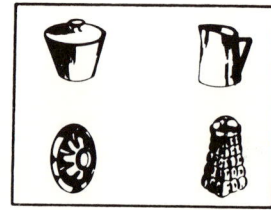

Sample test pairs:

Alternative directions for pairs of objects:

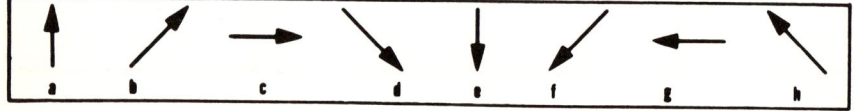

Answers: 1–D; 2–G.

Remembering Puns. Recall the word corresponding to a pun word presented on a study page.

Sample studied pun: The bird-loving bartender was arrested for contributing to the delinquency of a <u>mynah</u>.
Sample test item: MYNAH–_____

Answer: minor.

APPENDIX B   467

Remembering Spatial Changes. Select a repositioning of an object so that its change in position is the same as one undergone by a cue object on a study page.

Sample study items:

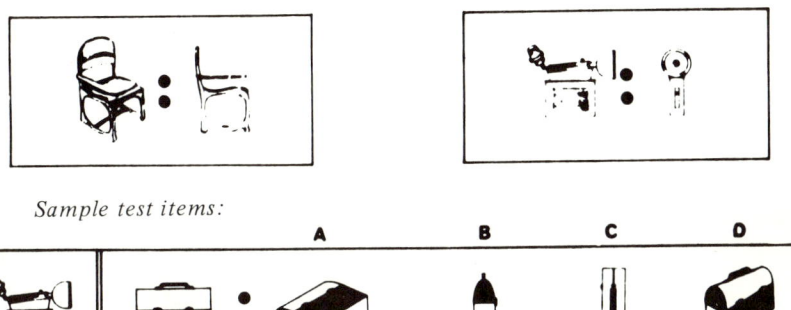

Sample test items:

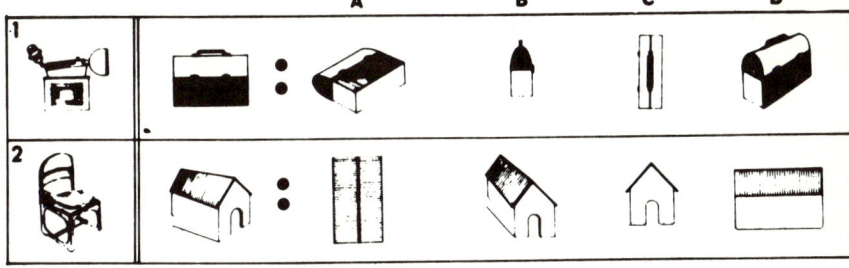

Answers: 1−B; 2−D.

Remembering Symbol Codes. Match symbols to the nonsense syllables with which they were paired on a study page.

Sample study pairs:

Sample test matching items:

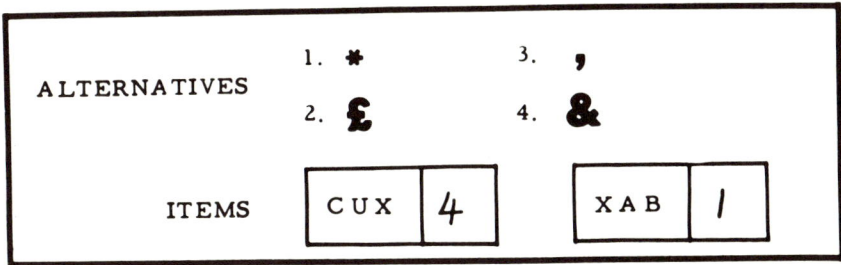

Remote Verbal Similarities. Select a word from five that has the most in common with a remotely connected word.

    Sample item: FATHER   A. candidate   B. second baseman   C. agitator   D. superintendent   E. salesman

    Answer: D.

Restricted Figural Classifications. Partition a set of figures so that each figure is a member of exactly two classes.

    Sample figures:

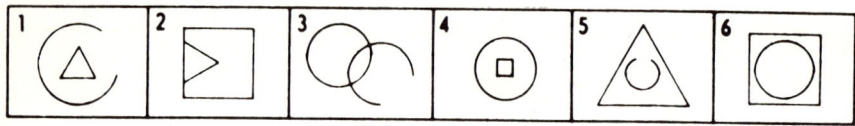

    Partitions: 1, 3, 5; 2, 4, 6; 3, 4, 6; 1, 2, 5.

Restricted Symbolic Classifications. Partition a list of nonsense words so that each word is a member of exactly two classes.

    Sample word list: 1. AVFB   2. SCPZ   3. MWDN   4. POYT   5. GXKH   6. WPIR

    Partitions: 1, 4, 6; 1, 3, 5; 2, 3, 5; 2, 4, 6.

Rhymes. Write words rhyming with a given word.

    Given word: MOON

    Sample responses: Soon, prune, June, lagoon, typhoon.

Rhyming Definitions. Produce two rhyming words expressing humorously a brief phrase.

    Sample phrases: 1. A pretty girl   2. A baby's finger

    Expressions: 1—slick chick; 2—midget digit.

Riddles (clever). Answer riddles in an imaginative way.

    Sample riddle: What city is best liked by actors?

    Clever response: Publicity.

Riddles (obvious). Same as preceding test, but realistic answers count toward the score.

    Realistic answer (to the same riddle): Hollywood.

Right Order Test. See **Operations Sequence.**

Route Planning. See **Essential Maze Routes.**

Rules. Find the rule by which one figure is selected from three.

Sample item:

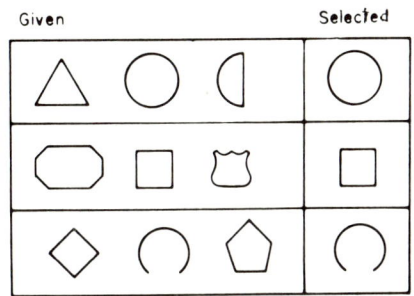

Answer: The middle figure.

S Test. Discover and solve problems in items composed of numbers, letters, and words. (See **F Test.**)

SCAT–Verbal. (Subtest of the School and College Aptitude Test.) Multiple-choice test of understanding words and sentences.

Secret Writing. Find the letter that corresponds to each number in a decoding task.

Sample words: to on no
Corresponding numbers: 36 68 86

Code system: $t = 3; o = 6; n = 8.$

Seeing Deficiencies. Explain how a plan or activity is faulty.

Sample plan: A city needs to improve both its streets and its sewer system. The council decides to work on the street-improvement program first.

Possible response: The streets would have to be torn up later for the work on the sewer system.

Seeing Different Meanings. Write as many as four different meanings for common words:

Sample word: SCALE

Possible meanings: A balance for weighing; fish scales; consecutive musical tones; scale the wall.

Seeing Letter Changes.   Match letter changes in pairs of short words.

Sample items: 1. cad–cod   2. cry–pry   3. tin–nit   4. aye–yea
A. die–lie   B. tan–ant   C. set–sit   D. cat–car   E. nap–pan

Matchings: 1–C; 2–A; 3–E; 4–B.

Seeing Problems.   Give as many as five problems that might arise in connection with each object.

Sample object: CANDLE

Possible problems: How to light it; how to keep it from falling over; how long will it burn? how to prevent fires.

Seeing Puzzle Meanings.   Solve rebus puzzles.

Sample puzzles:

I.   T   4   II

II.   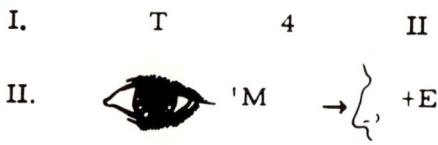 'M   →⎨ +E

Answers: I. Tea for two; II. I'm nosey.

Seeing Trends I.   See **Naming Meaningful Trends.**

Seeing Trends II.   Find the trend in a series of words, based on letter compositions of the words.

Sample trends:
1. anger bacteria camel dead excite
2. rated crate morning dearth separate

Answers:
1. First letters are in alphabetical order.
2. The "r" moves one position to the right each time.

Sensitivity to Order.   Determine whether a series of words is meaningfully ordered. If not, rearrange the series.

Sample series:
1. Key lock door room house
2. accident write-up reporter newspaper reader

Answers: A is in good order; in B, "write-up" should come after "reporter."

Sentence Analysis.   Write facts or assumptions contained in or implied by a given statement.

Sample statement: In Buna-Buna the game of ticky-ticky is played with the feet.

Possible facts: There is a game called ticky-ticky. Whoever plays the game must have feet. There is a place called Buna-Buna.

Sentence Classification. Designate sentences as conveying fact, possibility, or name.

Sample sentences:
1. The natives of New Zealand have wooden houses to meet the requirements of a cool climate.
2. The Rarotongan word *vari* means "mud."
3. The gods informed the people of the disaster.

Answers: 1–fact; 2–name; 3–possibility.

Sentence Evaluation. See **Sentence Classification.**

Sentence Gestalt I. Separate words in lines of pied type.

Sample line:
LIKESOMANYOFTHEPURSUITSWHICHHAVEBECOMEPARTANDPARCEL

Answer: Like so many of the pursuits which have become part and parcel.

Sentence Memory. Write the meaningful content of sentences immediately after hearing them.

Sentence Order. (Adapted from Adkins and Lyerly, 1951.) Arrange three statements of events in good order.

Sample sentences:
A. She bought some food at the market.
B. She cooked some of the food she had bought.
C. She went to the market.

Correct order: CAB.

Sentence Pairs. Choose two sentences that express the same kind of idea.

Sample items:
Lettered sentences:
A. Cats are real companions.
B. Deer are excellent game.
C. Exercise promotes good health.
D. The storm approached rapidly.
E. The picture sold for twice its true value.

Numbered sentences:
1. He walked home every night.
2. Some animals make good pets.
3. Artists are sometimes well paid.
4. The train gathered speed as it left the station.

Matchings: 1–C; 2–A; 3–E; 4–D.

Sentence Selection. Select a sentence that is most probably true, using only the information in a given statement.

Given statement: In the mid-Pacific on Buna-Buna, the game of ticky-ticky is played outdoors.
Alternative sentences:
A. People in Buna-Buna like to play games.
B. Ticky-ticky is a difficult game to play.
C. There is an island called Buna-Buna.

Answer: C.

Sentence Synthesis. Rearrange scrambled words to make a meaningful statement.

Sample item: testimony commission the the released

Answer: The commission released the testimony.

Sentensense. Judge whether given sentences express internally consistent thoughts.

Sample sentence: Johnny, who is seven, went with his mother to Europe ten years ago.

Answer: Inconsistent.

Sequential Association. Arrange four words in a sequence so that each word is associated with words adjacent to it.

Given words: PEN   PIG   READ   WRITE

Correct sequence: Pig–pen–write–read.

Series.   See **Figure Series.**

Series Relations. Choose one of three operations that best interrelates numbers in a series.

Sample item: $\underline{17}$–9–2   A. -8 B. $\div 2$ C. -7

Answer: A (taking the 17 to be a fixed number).

Ship Destination. Find the distances from ships to ports, taking into account an increasing number of variables. The distance between neighboring positions is 2 miles.

Sample item:[7]

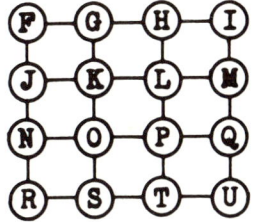

Sample variables: 1. Ship N to Port O   2. Ship J to Port G   3. Ship U to Port M

Answers: 1–2 miles; 2–4 miles; 3–4 miles.

Sign Changes. Solve simple equations, in which the operation signs are changed according to rules.

Given rules: Replace − with x.   Replace + with −.
Sample items: 1. 3 − 6 = _____   2. 6 + 2 = _____   3. 4 − 3 = _____

Answers: 1–18; 2–4; 3–12.

Sign Changes II. Choose changes that make expressions into equations.

Sample item: 3 + 1 = 6 x 2   A. Instead of + you −   B. Instead of + you x   C. Instead of x you −   D. Both A and C

Answer: C.

Silhouette Relations. (The silhouette figures adapted from R. H. Knapp, 1963.) Choose from sets of three photographs the face that expresses the psychological state portrayed in silhouette relationships.

Sample item:[8]

Answer: 3.

---

[7] Reproduced with the permission of Sheridan Psychological Services.
[8] The faces are from the Frois-Witman series and were reproduced by permission of the Brown University Photo Laboratory.

Similar Number Relations Cross-Out. Cross out pairs of numbers with relations that appeared earlier in the list.

Sample test page:
1. 6–36 2. 3–5   3. 6–18 4. 3–9
   5–25   8–10   7–21   4–16
5. 7–10 6. 4–32 7. 5–7   8. 10–5
   9–12   3–24   6–8   20–10

Answers: Pairs 4 and 7 should be crossed out.

Similar Orientations. Judge the similarity or difference in changes in direction or position of collections of objects.

Sample items:

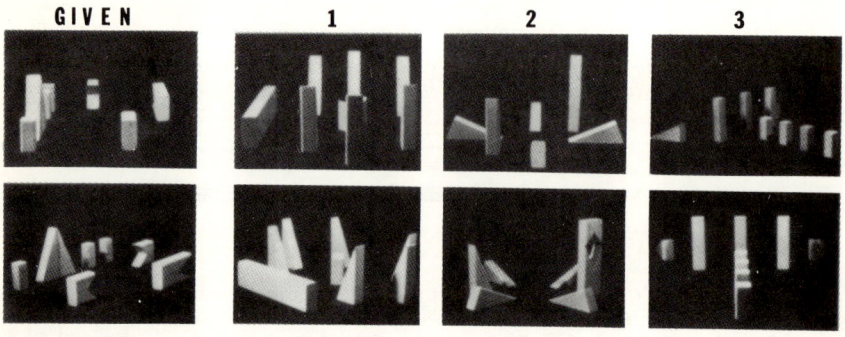

Answers: 1 and 2 have different changes in position; 3 has the same change as in the given pair.

Similar Pairs. Judge whether the relations in the second pairs of words are the same as those in the first pairs.

Sample items:
1. kire–lire   fora–gora
2. brake–rake   freed–reed
3. moan–noam   toes–seot

Answers: Pairs 1 and 2 have the same relations; 3 does not.

Similar Word Changes Cross-Out. Cross out pairs of words having the same literal relations as earlier pairs in the list.

Sample test page:
1. brink–brine 2. nit–tin 3. book–hook 4. sink–sine 5. lake–fake 6. bit–sit 7. rat–tar 8. mail–pail

Answers: Pairs 4 and 7 should be crossed out.

Similarities. Give as many as six ways in which two objects are alike.

> *Sample pair:* APPLE ORANGE
>
> *Possible responses:* Sweet, round, have seeds, are fruit, have skins, grow on trees.

Simile Completion. Name different objects having attributes in common with a given object.

> *Sample item:* The kitten's paws were as smooth as _____ .
>
> *Possible responses:* Ice, velvet, a baby's skin.

Simile Insertions. Give different adjectives as alternative completions to similes.

> *Sample item:* The fog is as _____ as a sponge.
>
> *Possible insertions:* Heavy, damp, full of holes.

Simile Interpretations. Complete in different explanatory ways sentences that contain similes.

> *Sample item:* A woman's beauty is like the autumn, _____ .
>
> *Possible interpretations:*
> It passes before it can be fully appreciated.
> It is enhanced by many changes in hue and color.
> It can be enjoyed with the eyes.

Sketches. Draw added lines to replications of a basic, simple design to produce a variety of recognizable objects.

> *Given blank figure:*[9]

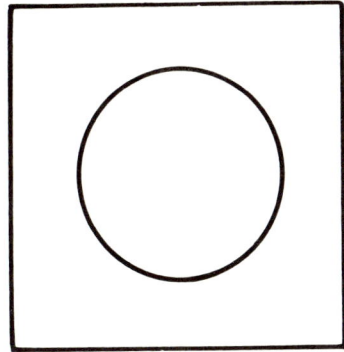

[9] Reproduced by permission of Sheridan Psychological Services.

Possible responses:

 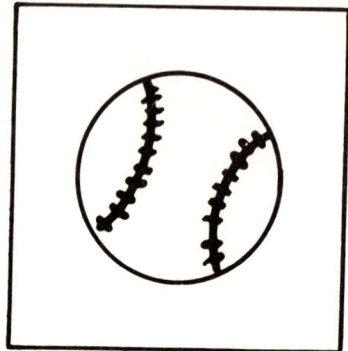

Social Institutions. Suggest two improvements for each of several institutions or customs.

Given institution: MARRIAGE

Possible improvements:
Courses on training for marriage in high school.
Introduce custom of women also proposing to men.

Social Relations. (The faces adapted by permission from Cline, 1956.) Choose one of three statements that express the feelings of a face that is interacting with another.

Sample faces:

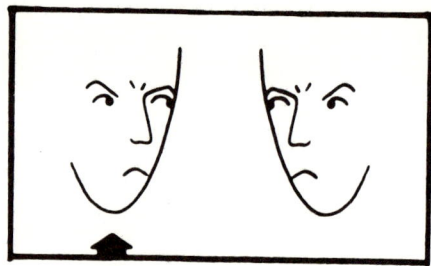

Statements:
1. "I didn't like that movie very much."
2. "What a bore."
3. "Who does he think he is, anyway?"

Answer: 3.

Social Relations II. See **Social Relations.**

Social Situations. Select actions leading to the most desirable consequences in given social situations.

Given situation: You are on a weekend trip with a group of friends. Most of them prefer to spend the day hunting, but you would prefer to go fishing. You should:
Alternatives:
A. Go hunting with them.
B. Tell them to go hunting, while you go fishing.
C. Try to convince them to go fishing.
D. Offer to toss a coin to decide the matter.

Answer: A.

Social Translations. Select an alternative pair of people between whom a given statement differs in meaning from that between a given pair.

Sample item: Boss to secretary: "Please."
Alternatives: A. beggar to stranger   B. father to son   C. chauffeur to boss

Answer: A.

Sound Grouping. (A Thurstone test.) Find a word that does not belong to a set of four because it sounds different.

Sample items:
1.   A. comb   B. foam   C. home   D. come
2.   A. phrase   B. chase   C. maize   D. phase

Answers: 1–D; 2–B.

Sound Meaning. Choose from four words the one that best names the common emotion in three vocalized expressions.

Alternatives (for a tape-recorded expression):
A. relief   B. loving   C. anger   D. sorrow

Space Positioning. Indicate the direction from which a photograph of a pattern of balls was taken.

Sample item:

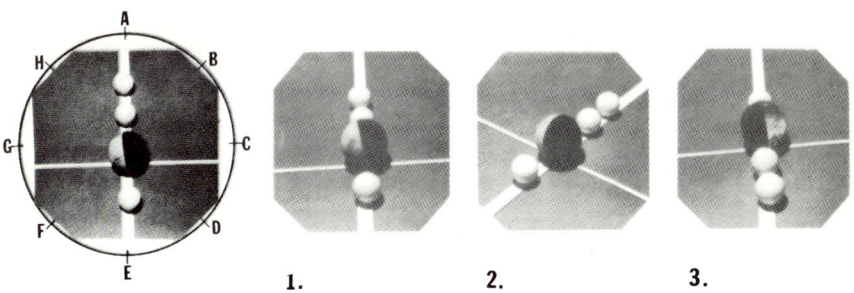

1.   2.   3.

Answers: 1–E; 2–D; 3–A.

Space Orientation. See **Space Positioning.**

Spatial Comprehension. On the basis of a verbal narrative, locate landmarks on a diagram.

Sample diagram:

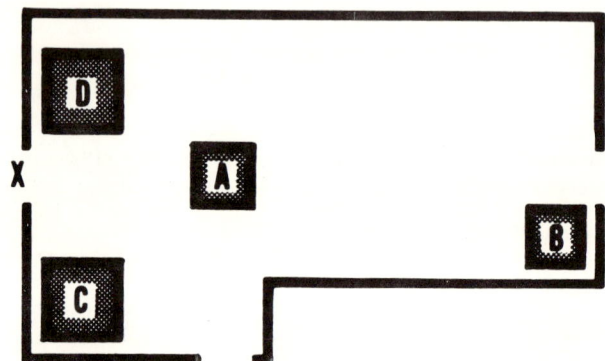

Given narrative: As you enter the General's library from the hall, you are met by a large statue of Napoleon. The left hand of the statue points down and backward to the General's desk, from which you can see the gun collection behind the door you entered. Diagonally across the room from the desk is a display of all the medals and honors of this great man.

Keyed objects: A–statue; B–desk; C–gun collection; D–medals.

Spatial Orientation. (Part V of the Guilford-Zimmerman Aptitude Survey.) Indicate the changes in direction and position that would account for changes in the orientation of one picture from a given one at the top.

Sample items:[10]

Answers: (As marked.)

[10] Reproduced by permission of Sheridan Psychological Services.

Spatial Orientation Test I. (A U.S. Air Force test.) Find where detailed photograph segments fit into aerial photographs.

Spatial Orientation Test II. (A U.S. Air Force test.) Locate area on a map that is shown in an aerial photograph.

Spatial Visualization. (Part VI of the Guilford-Zimmerman Aptitude Survey.) Visualize what a clock would look like after a given set of rotations.

Sample items:[11]

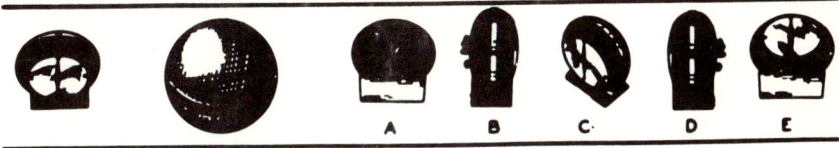

Answers: 1—B; 2—A.

Speed of Identification. (A U.S. Air Force test.) Select airplanes identical to given ones.

Squares. In several different ways, place a specified number of Xs on a checkerboard so that no two are in the same row, column, or diagonal.

Sample item: Place five Xs on a board of 36 squares.

Answer:

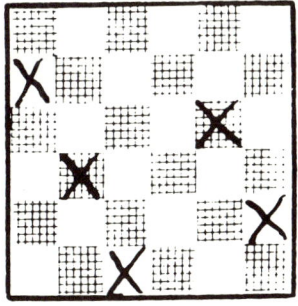

[11]Reproduced by permission of Sheridan Psychological Services.

Stick Figure Expressions. Choose one of four stick figures that expresses the same psychological state as a given figure.

Sample item:

Answer: 3.

Stick-figure Opposites. Choose one of three stick figures that expresses a feeling state opposite that of a given figure.

Sample item:

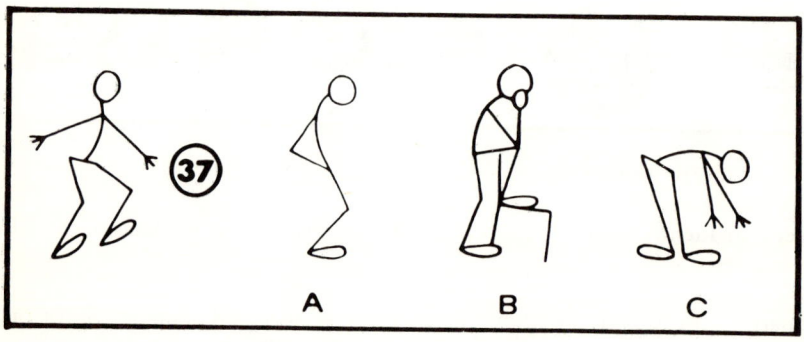

Answer: A.

Story Titles. Select the best and worst titles for given short stories.

Sample story: A fox came to a vineyard full of grapes, but there was a high fence around it. After trying for some time to climb the fence, the fox said, "I didn't want those grapes anyway; they're too sour for me."
Titles: A. "Fenced-out Fox" B. "Sour Grapes" C. "Story of a Fox"

Answers: B is keyed best, C worst.

Street Gestalt Completion. Identify pictured objects having missing segments.

Sample item, with identification written:

Studying and Remembering. Read a short essay and answer questions based on it after it is removed.

Substitutions. Recognize an object that may be adapted for an unusual use, as per information previously studied.

> Studied information:
> A gummed label may be used as a bandage.
> A cigarette filter may be used as a pin cushion.
> A mop may be used as a wig.
> Sample test alternatives: A. cigarette filter   B. gummed label   C. mop   D. none of these
> *Sample test items:*
> 1. To dress for Halloween
> 2. To clean a floor
> 3. To help straighten a sewing box
> 4. To dress a wound
>
> *Answers:* 1–C; 2–D; 3–A; 4–B.

Suffixes. Write words ending with a specified syllable.

> *Given ending syllable:* ABLE
>
> *Possible words:* Remarkable, likeable, sociable.

Suggested Feelings and Actions. Write names of different emotions and their concomitant actions arising in given situations.

Given situation: Late at night when A and his family are in their mountain cabin, he hears over the radio that a forest fire is raging a few miles away.

Possible feelings and actions:
Fear—pack up and leave.
Interest—tune in other stations to hear more.
Curiosity—pack a lunch and go to see the fire.

Syllables. Write a list of two-syllable nonsense words.

Syllogism Test. Decide whether conclusions drawn from two or three given statements are correct.

Given statements: All the hats sold in that shop are high priced; some of your hats are sold in that shop. Therefore:
1. All high-priced hats are yours.
2. Some of your hats are high-priced.
3. None of your hats are high-priced.
4. That shop sells some of your high-priced hats.
5. All your high-priced hats are sold in that shop.

Answers: Conclusions 2 and 4 are correct; 1, 3, and 5 are not.

Syllogisms I and II. Choose correct conclusions to premises, and judge whether the given conclusions are true or false.

Sample items:
1. All soldiers are men. Some citizens are soldiers. Therefore, some citizens are men.
2. All Americans are English-speaking. No Eskimos are English-speaking. Therefore:
A. No Eskimos are Americans.
B. Some Eskimos are Americans.
C. No English-speakers are Eskimos.

Answers: Conclusion to item 1 is true; the answer to 2 is A.

Syllogisms III. Write correct conclusions to two premises.

Given premises:
All living things breathe.
All insects are living things.
Therefore, _____ .

Answer: All insects breathe.

APPENDIX B 483

Symbol Comparison and Number Order. Turning pages as often as necessary, mark whether sets of numbers and letters are exactly the same as sets on the previous page.

  Sample sets: Z,397   53916

Symbol Elaboration. Write new equations derived from given pairs of simple equations.

  Given equations: $B - C = D$ $Z = 2A + D$

  Some new equations: $D = Z - 2A$ $B - C = Z - 2A$

Symbol Grouping. Rearrange scrambled symbols in a specified systematic order as efficiently as possible.

  Rule: Put all Xs first, all $-$s second, and 0s last.
  Given symbol set: $X - 0\ X - X$

  Solution: Move second $X -$ pair after the first X so that $X\ X - - 0\ X$ appears. Then move last X to follow $X\ X$, so that $X\ X\ X - - 0$ appears.

Symbol Identities. Judge whether members of pairs of words and numbers are same or different.

  Some sample pairs:
  2163 _____ 2163
  Hahn, Lorena _____ Hahn, Lorina
  Bob Ulm _____ Rob Ulm

  Answers: Pair 1 has identical members; 2 and 3 have not.

Symbol Manipulation. Judge whether symbolic conclusions are true or false, based upon given premises and definitions.

  Definitions:
  "l" means "is larger than."
  "s" means "is smaller than."
  "e" means "is equal to."
  "nl" means "is not larger than."
  "ns" means "is not smaller than."
  "ne" means "is not equal to."

  Sample items: If X s Y, then: A. X e Y B. X nl Y C. X l Y

  Answers: Conclusions B is correct; A and C are not.

Symbol Manipulation II. Judge the truth or falsity of various complex conclusions based upon given premises.

  Definitions: (Same as for the test above.)
  Each item presents two equations, with the same alternative answers:

A. Both parts are true.
B. One part is true, the other part indeterminate.
C. One part is true, the other false.
D. One part is false, the other indeterminate.
E. Both parts are false.
Sample main statement: If *X* e *Y* and *Y* ne *Z*, then:
Items:
1. *X* ne *Z* and *Y* e *X*
2. *X* s *Z* and *X* l *Z*
3. *X* ns *Z* and *X* nl *Y*

Answers: 1–A; 2–C; 3–B.

Symbol Production. Draw symbols to represent given activities and objects.

Given activities and objects (numbered):
Ring the *bell* and *open* the *door.*
 (1)   (2)   (3)   (4)

Possible symbols:

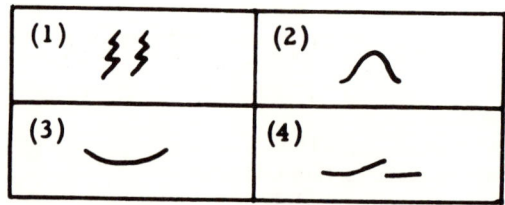

Symbol Reasoning. Decide whether symbolically stated conclusions are true, false, or uncertain, given certain relationships.

Given relationships: $2X < 3Y < 2Z$
Conclusions: 1. $2X = 2Z$ 2. $Y < Z$ 3. $X = Y$

Answers: 1–false; 2–true; 3–uncertain.

Symbolic Judgment. Judge which of four symbols is most appropriate for given words or phrases.

Sample item: ARC   A. a   B. +   C. O   D. C

Answer: D.

Symbols and Letters, Digits and Symbols. Rapidly mark symbol conversions with the conversion table in view.

Sample items:

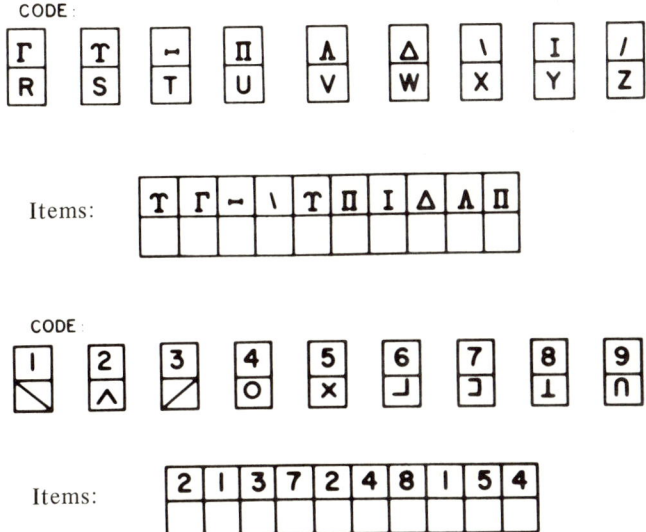

Synonyms. Select the synonym that is closest in meaning to a given word.

Sample item: LAMP   A. torch   B. wand   C. candle   D. lantern

Answer: D.

System-Shape Recognition. Recognize the positions and orientations of simple outline figures seen on a study page.

Sample study figures:

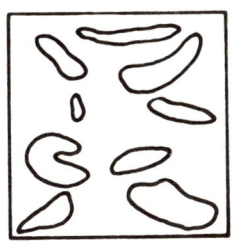

Sample test figures:

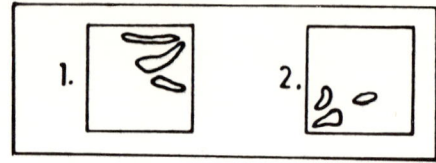

Answer: 1 is the same as studied; 2 is not.

Temporal Ordering. Order temporally disarranged steps in a described project.

Sample project: Changing a tire on a car.
Some steps:
A. Set out flares.
B. Tighten nuts.
C. Block wheels so car won't roll.
D. Raise car with jack.
E. Replace flat with spare.
F. Unlock trunk to get tools.
G. Take jack out of trunk.
Sample items:
1. What steps should precede D? _____
2. The first two steps, in order, are _____
3. The last step should be _____

Answers: 1—A, C, F, G; 2—A, F; 3—B.

Test Name Recall. Recall the titles of tests included in a test booklet just administered.

Thing Listing I, II, and III. See **Ideational Fluency**. The three differ in the number of class specifications given.

Titles. Judge which ones of pairs of titles, appropriate to given stories, are more clever.

Sample story: (Same as for Story Titles.)
Title pairs:
1. A. "The Fox Goes Hungry"
   B. "The Philosophical Fox"
2. A. "The Outfoxed Fox"
   B. "The Story of a Fox"

Answers: 1—B; 2—A.

Transitions (coherence). Write an account connecting the given initial and final situations in a short story, scored for rated degree of coherence.

Transitions (logical aspects). Same as the preceding test, but scored for logical connections.

Twenty Questions. Write questions, answerable by "yes" or "no," that help to identify objects given in broad categories.

Sample item: The object is a vegetable.

Possible questions: Is it alive? Is it edible?

Two- and Four-Word Combinations. See **Expressional Fluency.**

Typing Errors. Choose one of three correctly typed words that the given incorrectly typed word would most likely be. (A sketch of a standard typewriter keyboard appears on each test page.)

Sample item (misspelled word): WORM A. warm B. worn C. wars

Answer: B.

Unlikely Things. Select the two more unlikely or incongruous of four listed features for sketches in common situations.

Given situation:

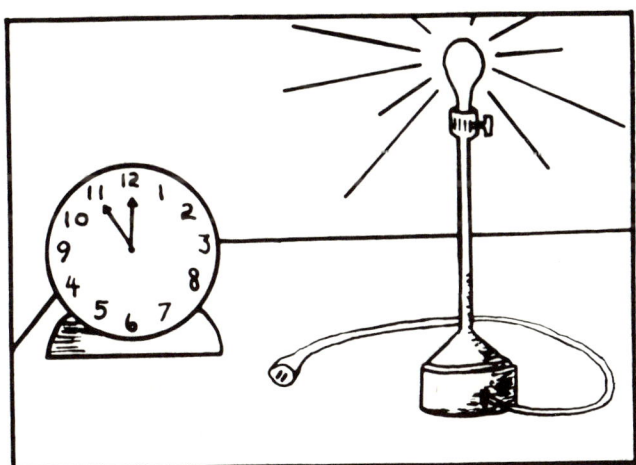

Listed features:
A. The hands of the clock are of the same length.
B. The lamp cannot give light when not plugged in.
C. The lamp plug has no prongs.
D. The numbers are reversed on bottom half of the clock.

Answers: B and D are most unlikely.

Unusual Answers. Recall questions in connection with previously studied riddles.

> *Sample riddle:* What can never be beaten? Answer: A broken drum.
> *Sample test item:* What is special about a broken drum?
>
> *Answer:* It cannot be beaten.

Unusual Details. Find two things that are unusual or do not make sense in sketches of common scenes. (Like Unlikely Things, except it is in completion form rather than multiple choice.)

Unusual Methods. Give two different, unusual, although usable, ways of dealing with a common problem.

> *Sample problem:* Relieve boredom and fatigue of doing work in business or industry.
>
> *Possible methods:*
> 1. Have employees change their tasks every hour.
> 2. Have 4-hour shifts instead of 8-hour ones.

Unusual Uses. See **Alternate Uses.**

Useful Changes. Select the object that can perform the specified task most adequately.

> *Sample item:* TO SLICE CHEESE   A. guitar   B. dinner plate   C. paper clip
>
> *Answer:* A.

Utility Test (fluency). List many different uses for common objects, scored for length of list.

> *Sample object:* TIN CAN
>
> *Possible uses:* A vase for flowers, for cutting round cookies, a cooking utensil, a drum.

Utility Test (flexibility). Same as in the previous test, but scored for number of shifts of category of uses.

Varied Emotional Relations. From a set of faces, choose different pairs that show social cause-and-effect relationships.

Sample faces:

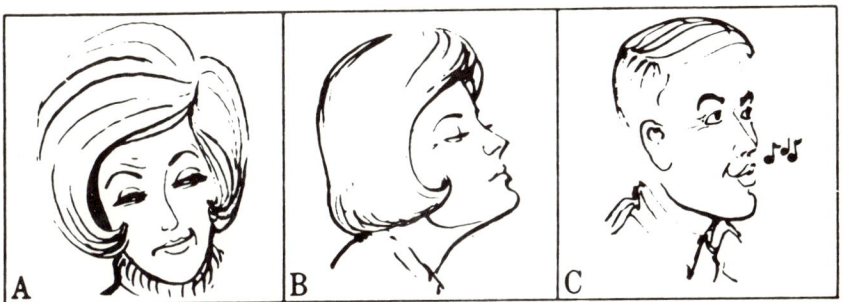

Possible pairs: C and A; C and B.

Varied Figural Classes. Assign the same figure to a number of different sets of figures to form classes.

Sample set:

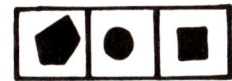

Sample figures:

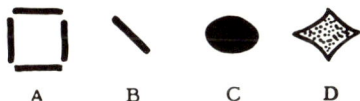

Answers: C (filled in); D (closed).

Varied Symbols. See **Multiple Letter Similarities.**

Verbal Analogies I. Choose words that complete analogies where the relation is difficult to see but choice is easy.

Sample item: CLOTH : DYE :: HOUSE : ___?___
A. shade   B. paint   C. brush   D. wood

Answer: B.

Verbal Analogies II. Choose words to complete analogies where the relations between given words are simple but choice of alternatives is difficult.

Sample item: NIGHT : DAY :: TIMID : ___?___
A. brave   B. bold   C. afraid   D. fearful   E. strong

Answer: B.

Verbal Analogies III. Choose words to complete analogies where the relationships are simple but choices among alternatives are difficult because they are so obviously associated.

Sample item: TRAFFIC : SIGNAL :: RIVER : ___?___
A. bank   B. dam   C. canal   D. sand bags

Answer: B.

Verbal Analogies Completion. A completion form.

Sample item: FOOT : SHOE :: HAND : _____

Answer: glove.

Verbal Classification. (A Thurstone test.) Assign words to one of two classes, or to neither, each class represented by four words.

Sample problem:

Class A	Words	Class B
COW	____ desk	____ TABLE
HORSE	____ sheep	____ CHAIR
GOAT	____ rocker	____ BOOKCASE
DOG	____ tree	____ LAMP
	____ cat	
	____ nose	
	____ dresser ____	
	____ donkey ____	

Answers: Desk, rocker, and dresser go with class B; sheep, cat, and donkey go with class A; others go with neither.

Verbal Comprehension. (Shortened form of the Guilford-Zimmerman Aptitude Survey, Part I.) Choose a word that means about the same as the given word.

Verbal-Picture Translation. Name objects, being given figurative descriptions of them.

Sample descriptions:
1. Men playing ball with a foot
2. A piece of furniture copying notes
3. A lawn that jumps about

Answers: 1–football; 2–writing desk; 3–grasshopper.

Verbal Relations Naming. Name the relation that the second word in a pair has to the first word.

Sample item: (a) dwarf—(b) giant   (a) bottle—(b) barrel

Relationship: (b) is larger than (a).

Verifications. Describe two different procedures for demonstrating aspects of common phenomena.

Given phenomenon: The inside of a large gas flame is not as hot as the outside parts.

Possible procedures:
Hold a stick in the flame and show that sections in outside parts of the flame burn first.
Show that temperature rise in an insulated thermometer is slower for center than for outer parts.

Visualization Memory. Recognize in new objects the rotational changes in previously studied three-dimensional objects.

Sample study objects:

 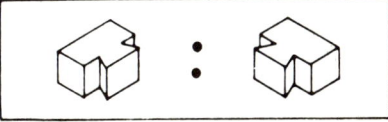

Sample test items:

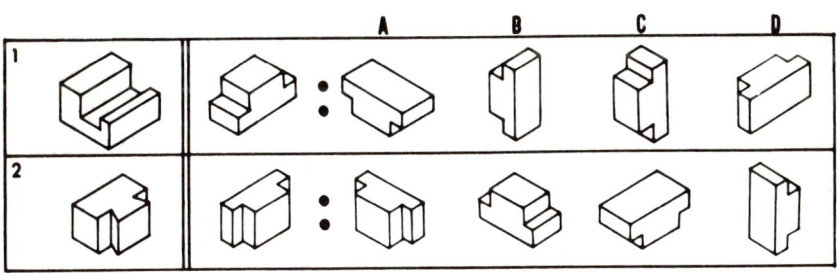

Answers: 1—C; 2—A.

Vocabulary. See **Verbal Comprehension.**

Vocabulary Completion. Write a word that fits a given definition and begins with a given letter.

Sample items:
1. A contest of speed: r _____
2. The wife of a king: q _____

Answers: 1—race; 2—queen.

Water Jars. Measure out a required amount of water, using only three jars of different capacities.

Sample item: Given jars of 1 quart, 4 quarts, and 5 quarts, measure out exactly 2 quarts.
Special feature: The first five problems can all be rather obviously solved by the same formula. The next five can be solved by the same formula or more simply.

Way-Out Numbers. Choose the number from four that is farthest in size from the other three.

Sample item: 31   35   45   47
                   A   B

Answer: A.

Who Said It? Choose the baby's expression that fits the caption.

Sample caption: "Oh no! I forgot my wallet."[12]

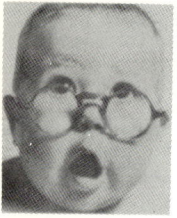 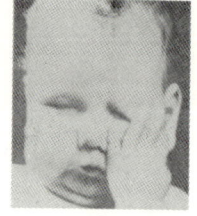 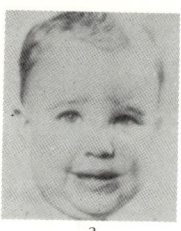 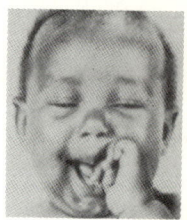

   1   2   3   4

Answer: 2.

Whoppers. List unusual things that a liar might claim to have seen at given places.

Given place: AUTO SHOW

Possible responses: Glass seats, gold steering wheel, flying station wagon, fur tires.

---

[12] Babies' faces were adapted from Bannister (1950) with permission.

Word Arrangement.   Write sentences each containing four specified words.

Given words: SEND   ALMOST   SHORE   LARGE

Possible sentences:
Almost all the large ships send ship-to-shore signals.
The large shore party was almost enough to send them flying.

Word Changes.   Arrange a list of words so that the first word is changed into the last one, one letter changed each time.

Sample item:
End words: BELL   ———   ———   ———   MAIN
Filler words: 1. BAIL   2. BALL   3. MAIL

Correct order of the fillers: 2, 1, 3.

Word Checking I.   Choose one of four words that fits a single criterion.

Given criterion: Object must be man-made.
Alternatives: A. valley   B. mountain   C. highway   D. river

Answer: C.

Word Checking II.   Choose one of four words that fits two given criteria.

Given criteria: Object must not be growing and smaller than a football.
Alternatives: A. frog   B. pebble   C. lake   D. fisherman

Answer: B.

Word Choice.   Choose one of three words that best fits into the given class, based upon letter compositions.

Given class: l<u>oy</u>alty empl<u>oy</u> anno<u>y</u>ance
Alternatives: A. payload   B. ontogeny   C. ivory

Answer: C (none fits exactly; C comes nearest).

Word Classification.   Select the one word of four that does not belong to the class on the basis of meaning.

Sample item: A. horse   B. cow   C. man   D. flower

Answer: D.

Word Combinations. Produce a new word from the ending of one word and the beginning of another.

> *Sample items:*
> Beginnings from: 1. bridge   2. beam   3. open
> Endings from: A. duress   B. zero   C. pledge   D. need   E. none of these
>
> *Answers:* 1–D (gene); 2–C (ample); 3–A (endure).

Word Completion. Write definitions for given words.

> *Sample item:* COURAGEOUS _____
>
> *Possible answer:* To be brave.

Word Extensions. Select the word for the thing that is most involved in or implied by a given thing.

> *Sample item:* A BOOK always has   A. words   B. pages   C. pictures   D. a story
>
> *Answer:* B.

Word Fluency. Write words, each containing a specified letter.

> *Sample item:* Write words containing the letter "O."
>
> *Possible responses:* Pot, load, over, too, oven, fought.

Word-Group Naming. Give class names to five-word groups.

> *Sample words:*   knife   pan   bowl   rolling pin   strainer
>
> *Class name:* Kitchen utensils.

Word Grouping. Assign 12 words to 4 mutually exclusive classes.

> *Given words:*   1. blue   2. cutter   3. driver   4. heavy   5. larger   6. light   7. little   8. long   9. opener   10. orange   11. redder   12. short
>
> *Classes:* 1, 10, 11; 5, 7, 8, 12; 4, 6; 2, 3, 9.

Word Groups. State the feature of letter combination or other letter property common to four words.

> *Sample words:*   read   retire   rearming   restless
>
> *Answer:* All begin with "re."

Word Linkage. Select from three words the one that is related to both of a given pair.

    Sample item: JEWELRY–BELL   A. ornament   B. jingle   C. ring

    Answer: C.

Word Listing 0.   Write just any words.

Word Listing I, II, and III.   See **Word Fluency**; forms differ in number of specified letters.

Word Matrices.   Arrange given words in a 3 by 3 matrix so that each row and each column show the same relationship.

    Given matrix:

minnow		net
		rod

    Given words to be added: lake   whale   ocean   bass   harpoon   pool

    Completed matrix:

minnow	pool	net
bass	lake	rod
whale	ocean	harpoon

Word Matrix Test.   Discover the trends in a 2 by 3 matrix of words, and choose one of five words to fill an empty cell.

    Given matrix:

ground	street	automobile
air	route	

    Alternatives: A. airplane   B. bird   C. kite   D. balloon   E. cloud

    Answer: A.

Word-Pair Revisions.   Make different pairs of words, using all the letters of a given word pair.

    Given pair: HIS   NOT

    Possible new pairs: sin hot   hit son   this no

Word Patterns. Arrange a list of short words efficiently in a crossword-puzzle design.

Given Words: bats easy hot tea the

Most efficient design:

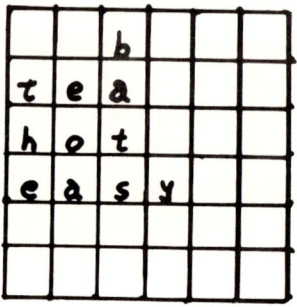

Word Recognition. Recognize whether given words were on a previously studied page.

Sample studied words: WHAT   US   USEFUL
Sample test item: 1. time   2. useful   3. what   4. us   5. find

Answers: 2, 3, and 4 were studied; 1 and 5 were not.

Word Relations. Recognize the same relation between words in each of two pairs, then complete a third pair from alternatives.

Sample item: on–no   top-pot   part-_____?_____
Alternatives: A. art   B. pat   C. rapt   D. tar   E. trap

Answer: E.

Word Selection. See **Word Extensions.**

Word Substitution. Select one of four words that would best serve in place of an underlined word in a sentence.

Sample item: He was a good doctor, but alcohol was his <u>ruin</u>.
Alternatives: A. plague   B. undoing   C. fate   D. destruction

Answer: B.

Word Synthesis (words). Write a story containing ten specified words.

Specified words: church   grass   fruit   square   sweet   dark   count   pick   meeting   quickly

Word Systems. Choose one of three word matrices that shows the best trends and one that shows the worst trends, in both rows and columns. (See **Word Matrices** for an example of a word matrix.)

Word Transformations. Separate letters of words in a phrase with lines to make a different set of words.

Sample phrases: RING SOFT HE   THE RED OLIVE

New sets of words: RING S/OF/T HE   THE RE/D O/LIVE

Writing Behavioral Stories. Write different stories describing how three people in a given photograph feel or what they are thinking and why.

Sample item:

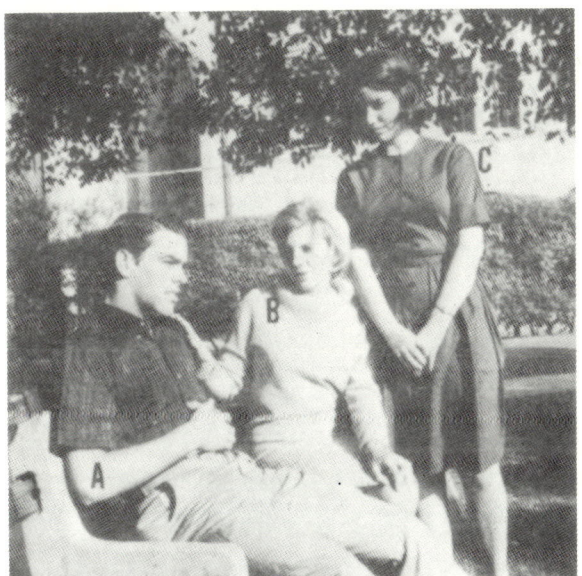

Possible story: The blond girl, B, feels sorry for A because she thinks he is sick. C thinks he is faking, but A likes the attention.

REFERENCES

ADKINS, D. C., & LYERLY, S. B. *Factor analysis of reasoning tests.* Chapel Hill: University of North Carolina, Department of Psychology, 1951.

ASCH, S. E. & LINDNER, M. A. A note on "strength of association." *Journal of Psychology,* 1963, **55**, 199−209.

BANNISTER, C. *Baby: A photographic inquiry into certain private opinions.* New York: Simon and Schuster, 1950.

BARTLETT, M. S. The statistical conception of mental factors. *British Journal of Psychology,* 1937, **28**, 97−104.

BECHTOLDT, H. P. Factorial investigation of the perceptual speed factor. *American Psychologist,* 1947, **2**, 304−305.

BERGER, R. M., GUILFORD, J. P., & CHRISTENSEN, P. R. A factor-analytic study of planning. *Psychological Monographs,* 1957, **71** (6, Whole No. 435).

BLAKEY, R. I. A factor analysis of a nonverbal reasoning test. *Educational and Psychological Measurement,* 1941, **1**, 187−198.

BOE, E. E., GOCKA, E. F., & KOGAN, W. S. The effect of group therapy on interpersonal perceptions of psychiatric patients. *Multivariate Behavioral Research,* 1966, **1**, 177–195.

BOTZUM, W. A. A factorial study of the reasoning and closure factors. *Psychometrika,* 1951, **16**, 361–386.

BROWN, S. W., GUILFORD, J. P., & HOEPFNER, R. Six semantic-memory abilities. *Educational and Psychological Measurement,* 1968, **28**, 691–717.

BURT, C. The structure of mind: A review of the results of factor analysis. *British Journal of Educational Psychology,* 1949, **19**, 100–111, 176–199.

BUTLER, J. M. Simple structure reconsidered: Distinguishability and invariance in factor analysis. *Multivariate Behavioral Research,* 1969, **4**, 6–28.

CAMPBELL, D. T., & FISKE, D. W. Convergent and discrimination validation by the multitrait-multimethod matrix. *Psychological Bulletin,* 1959, **56**, 81–105.

CANISIA, SISTER M. Mathematical ability as related to reasoning and use of symbols. *Educational and Psychological Measurement,* 1962, **11**, 105–127.

CARROLL, J. B. A factor analysis of verbal abilities. *Psychometrika,* 1941, **6**, 279–307.

CATTELL, R. B. *A universal index for psychological factors.* Urbana, Ill.: Laboratory of Personality Assessment and Group Behavior, 1953.

CATTELL, R. B. The scree test for the number of factors. *Multivariate Behavioral Research,* 1966, **2**, 245–276.

CHRISTAL, R. E. Factor analytic study of visual memory. *Psychological Monographs,* 1958, **72** (13, Whole No. 466).

CHRISTENSEN, P. R., & GUILFORD, J. P. An experimental study of verbal fluency factors. *British Journal of Statistical Psychology,* 1963, **16**, 1–26.

CLIFF, N. Orthogonal rotation to congruence. *Psychometrika,* 1966, **31**, 33–42.

CLIFF, N., & HAMBURGER, C. D. The study of sampling errors in factor analysis by means of artificial experiments. *Psychological Bulletin,* 1967, **68**, 430–445.

CLIFF, N., & PENNELL, R. The influence of communality, factor strength, and loading size on the sampling characteristics of factor loadings. *Psychometrika,* 1967, **32**, 309–326.

CLINE, M. G. The influence of social context on the perception of faces. *Journal of Personality,* 1956, **25**, 142–158.

CLINE, V. B., RICHARDS, J. M., JR., & ABE, C. The validity of a battery of creativity tests in a high school sample. *Educational and Psychological Measurement,* 1962, **22**, 781–784.

COOMBS, C. H. A factorial study of number ability. *Psychometrika,* 1941, **6**, 161–189.

CURETON, E. E. *A factor analysis of project TALENT tests and four other batteries.* Pittsburgh, Pa.: American Institutes for Research, 1968.

DAVIS, P. C. A factor analysis of the Wechsler-Bellevue Scale. *Educational and Psychological Measurement,* 1956, **16**, 127–146.

DE MILLE, R. Intellect after lobotomy in schizophrenia. *Psychological Monographs,* 1962, **76** (16, Whole No. 535).

DEWEY, J. How we think. Boston: Heath, 1910.

DIXON, W. J. Biomedical computer programs. Los Angeles: Health Science Computing Facility, University of California, 1965.

DUDEK, F. J. The dependence of the factorial composition of aptitude tests upon differences among pilot trainees. I. The isolation of factors. *Educational and Psychological Measurement,* 1948, **8,** 613–634.

DUDEK, F. J. The dependence of factorial composition of aptitude tests upon differences among pilot trainees. II. The factorial composition of tests and criterion variables. *Educational and Psychological Measurement,* 1949, **9,** 95–104.

DUNHAM, J. L., GUILFORD, J. P., & HOEPFNER, R. Multivariate approaches to discovering the intellectual components of concept learning. *Psychological Review,* 1968, **75,** 206–221.

DWYER, P. S. The determination of the factor loadings of a given test from the known factor loadings of other tests. *Psychometrika,* 1937, **2,** 173–178.

FLEISHMAN, E. A. Human abilities and the acquisition of skills. Washington, D.C.: American Institutes for Research, 1966.

FLEISHMAN, E. A. & FRUCHTER, B. Factor structure and predictability of successive stages of learning Morse code. *Journal of Applied Psychology,* 1960, **44,** 97–101.

FLEISHMAN, E. A., & RICH, S. Role of kinesthetic and visual-spatial abilities in perceptual-motor learning. *Journal of Experimental Psychology,* 1963, **66,** 6–11.

FRENCH, J. W. The description of aptitude and achievement tests in terms of rotated factors. *Psychometric Monographs,* 1951, No. 5.

FRENCH, J. W., EKSTROM, R. B., & PRICE, L. A. Manual for kit of reference tests for cognitive factors. Princeton, N.J.: Educational Testing Service, 1963.

FRICK, J. W., & GUILFORD, J. P. An analysis of a form of the Water Jars test. *American Journal of Psychology,* 1957, **70,** 427–431.

FRICK, J. W., GUILFORD, J. P., CHRISTENSEN, P. R., & MERRIFIELD, P. R. A factor-analytic study of flexibility of thinking. *Educational and Psychological Measurement,* 1959, **19,** 469–496.

FRUCHTER, B. The nature of verbal fluency. *Educational and Psychological Measurement,* 1948, **8,** 33–47.

GAMES, P. A. A factorial analysis of verbal learning tasks. *Journal of Experimental Psychology,* 1962, **63,** 1–11.

GARNETT, J. C. M. On certain independent factors in mental measurement. *Proceedings of the Royal Society of London,* 1919, **46,** 91–111. (a)

GARNETT, J. C. M. General ability, cleverness, and purpose. *British Journal of Psychology,* 1919, **9,** 345–366. (b)

GETZELS, J. W., & JACKSON, P. W. Creativity and intelligence. New York: Wiley, 1962.

GIBSON, W. A. Remarks on Tucker's inter-battery method of factor analysis. *Psychometrika,* 1960, **25,** 19–25.

GREEN, R. F., GUILFORD, J. P., CHRISTENSEN, P. R., & COMREY, A. L. A factor-analytic study of reasoning abilities. *Psychometrika,* 1953, **18,** 135–160.

GUILFORD, J. P. Factor analysis in a test-development program. *Psychological Review*, 1948, **55**, 79-94.

GUILFORD, J. P. Les dimensions de l'intellect. In H. Laugier (Ed.), *L'analyse factorielle et ses applications*. Paris: Centre National de la Recherche Scientifique, 1956. Pp. 53-74. (a)

GUILFORD, J. P. The structure of intellect. *Psychological Bulletin*, 1956, **53**, 276-293. (b)

GUILFORD, J. P. New frontiers of testing in the discovery and development of human talent. In *Seventh Annual Western Regional Conference on Testing Problems*. Los Angeles: Educational Testing Service, 1958. Pp. 20-32.

GUILFORD, J. P. *Personality*. New York: McGraw-Hill, 1959. (a)

GUILFORD, J. P. Three faces of intellect. *American Psychologist*, 1959, **14**, 469-479. (b).

GUILFORD, J. P. Basic conceptual problems in the psychology of thinking. In E. Harms (Ed.), *Fundamentals of psychology: The psychology of thinking. Annals of the New York Academy of Sciences*, 1960, **91**, Art. 1. Pp. 6-21.

GUILFORD, J. P. Factorial angles to psychology. *Psychological Review*, 1961, **68**, 1-20.

GUILFORD, J. P. Zero intercorrelations among tests of intellectual abilities. *Psychological Bulletin*, 1964, **61**, 401-406.

GUILFORD, J. P. *Fundamental statistics in psychology and education*. (4th ed.) New York: McGraw-Hill, 1965.

GUILFORD, J. P. Intelligence: 1965 model. *American Psychologist*, 1966, **21**, 20-26.

GUILFORD, J. P. *The nature of human intelligence*. New York: McGraw-Hill, 1967.

GUILFORD, J. P. Intellectual aspects of decision making. In A. T. Welford and J. E. Birren (Eds.), *Decision making and age: Interdisciplinary topics in gerontology*. Vol. 4. Basel: Karger, 1969. Pp. 82-102.

GUILFORD, J. P., CHRISTENSEN, P. R., BOND, N. A., & SUTTON, M. A. A factor analysis of human interests. *Psychological Monographs*, 1954, **68** (4, Whole No. 375).

GUILFORD, J. P., CHRISTENSEN, P. R., FRICK, J. W., & MERRIFIELD, P. R. Factors of interest in thinking. *Journal of General Psychology*, 1961, **65**, 39-56.

GUILFORD, J. P., DUNHAM, J. L., & HOEPFNER, R. Roles of intellectual abilities in the learning of concepts. *Proceedings, National Academy of Sciences*, 1967, **58**, 1812-1817.

GUILFORD, J. P., FRUCHTER, B., & ZIMMERMAN, W. S. Factor analysis of the Army Air Forces Sheppard Field Battery of experimental aptitude tests. *Psychometrika*, 1952, **17**, 45-68.

GUILFORD, J. P., GREEN, R. F., CHRISTENSEN, P. R., HERTZKA, A. F., & KETTNER, N. W. A factor-analytic study of the Navy reasoning tests with the Air Force Aircrew Classification Battery. *Educational and Psychological Measurement*, 1954, **14**, 301-325.

GUILFORD, J. P., & GUILFORD, R. B. A prognostic test for students in design. *Journal of Applied Psychology*, 1931, **15**, 335-345.

GUILFORD, J. P., & HOEPFNER, R. Creative potential as related to measures of IQ and verbal comprehension. *Indian Journal of Psychology*, 1965, **41**, 7–16.

GUILFORD, J. P., & HOEPFNER, R. Sixteen divergent-production abilities at the ninth-grade level. *Multivariate Behavioral Research*, 1966, **1**, 43–66.

GUILFORD, J. P., & HOEPFNER, R. Comparisons of varimax rotations with rotations to theoretical targets. *Educational and Psychological Measurement*, 1969, **29**, 3–22.

GUILFORD, J. P., HOEPFNER, R., & PETERSEN, H. Predicting achievement in ninth-grade mathematics from measures of intellectual-aptitude factors. *Educational and Psychological Measurement*, 1965, **25**, 659–682.

GUILFORD, J. P., KETTNER, N. W., & CHRISTENSEN, P. R. A factor-analytic study of the factor called general reasoning. *Educational and Psychological Measurement*, 1956, **16**, 438–453.

GUILFORD, J. P., & LACEY, J. I. (Eds.) Printed classification tests. *Army Air Forces Aviation Psychology Research Program Reports*. No. 5 Washington, D.C.: GPO, 1947.

GUILFORD, J. P., MERRIFIELD, P. R., CHRISTENSEN, P. R., & FRICK, J. W. Some new factors of symbolic cognition and convergent production. *Educational and Psychological Measurement*, 1961, **21**, 515–541.

GUILFORD, J. P., & ZIMMERMAN, W. S. Some variable-sampling problems in the rotation of axes in factor analysis. *Psychological Bulletin*, 1963, **60**, 289–301.

GUTHRIE, G. M. Structure of abilities in a non-Western culture. *Journal of Educational Psychology*, 1963, **54**, 94–103.

GUTTMAN, L. Some necessary conditions for common-factor analysis. *Psychometrika*, 1954, **19**, 149–161.

HALSMAN, P. *The Frenchman*. New York: Simon and Schuster, 1949.

HARGREAVES, H. L. The "faculty" of imagination. An enquiry concerning the existence of a general "faculty" or group factor, in imagination. *British Journal of Psychology Monographs*, 1927 (Suppl. 10).

HARMAN, H. H. *Modern factor analysis*. Chicago: University of Chicago Press, 1960.

HARRIS, C. W. On factors and factor scores. *Psychometrika*, 1967, **34**, 363–379.

HAYES, K. J. Genes, drives, and intellect. *Psychological Reports*, 1962, **10**, 299–341.

HERTZKA, A. F., GUILFORD, J. P., CHRISTENSEN, P. R., & BERGER, R. M. A factor-analytic study of evaluative abilities. *Educational and Psychological Measurement*, 1954, **14**, 581–597.

HILLS, J. R. Factorized abilities and success in college mathematics. *Educational and Psychological Measurement*, 1957, **17**, 615–622.

HOEPFNER, R., NIHIRA, K., & GUILFORD, J. P. Intellectual abilities of symbolic and semantic judgment. *Psychological Monographs*, 1966, **80** (16, Whole No. 624).

HOTELLING, H. Analysis of a complex of statistical variables into principal components. *Journal of Educational Psychology*, 1933, **24**, 417–441, 498–520.

HULIN, W. S., & KATZ, D. The Frois-Wittman pictures of facial expression. *Journal of Experimental Psychology*, 1935, **18**, 482–498.

KAISER, H. F. The varimax criterion for analytic rotation in factor analysis. *Psychometrika*, 1958, **23**, 187–200.

KARLIN, J. E. Music ability. *Psychometrika*, 1941, **6**, 61–65.

KARLIN, J. E. A factorial study of auditory function. *Psychometrika*, 1942, **7**, 251–279.

KELLEY, H. P. Memory abilities: A factor analysis. *Psychometric Monographs*, 1964, No. 11.

KELLEY, T. L. *Crossroads in the mind of man.* Stanford, Calif: Stanford University Press, 1928.

KETTNER, N. W., GUILFORD, J. P., & CHRISTENSEN, P. R. The relation of certain thinking factors to training in the U.S. Coast Guard Academy. *Educational and Psychological Measurement*, 1959, **19**, 381–394.

KLINE, W. E. A synthesis of two factor analyses of intermediate algebra. *Technical Report.* Princeton, N. J.: Educational Testing Service, 1956.

KLUEVER, R. C. A study of Guilford's memory factors in normal and reading disabilities children. Unpublished doctoral dissertation, Northwestern University, 1968.

KNAPP, R. H. Group and individual differences in the interpretation of diadic silhouettes. Paper read at the Western Psychological Association convention, April, 1963.

LEVY N., & SCHLOSBERG, H. Woodworth scale values of the Lightfoot pictures of facial expression. *Journal of Experimental Psychology*, 1960, **60**, 121–125.

LEYDEN, F. The identification and invariance of factors. *British Journal of Statistical Psychology*, 1953, **6**, 119.

LUCHINS, A. S., & LUCHINS, E. H. *Rigidity of behavior: A variational approach to the effect of Einstellung.* Eugene: University of Oregon Press, 1953.

LYKKEN, D. T. Statistical significance in psychological research. *Psychological Bulletin*, 1968, **70**, 151–159.

MACDONALD, R. P., & BURR, E. J. A comparison of four methods of constructing factor scores. *Psychometrika*, 1967, **32**, 381–401.

MAYMAN, M., SCHAFER, R., & RAPAPORT, D. Interpretations of the Wechsler-Bellevue Intelligence Scale in personality appraisal. In H. H. Anderson and G. L. Anderson (Eds.), *Introduction to projective techniques.* Englewood Cliffs, N.J.: Prentice-Hall, 1951.

MEEKER, M. N. *The structure of intellect: Its interpretation and uses.* Columbus, Ohio: Charles E. Merrill, 1969.

MEREDITH, W. Rotation to achieve factorial invariance. *Psychometrika*, 1964, **29**, 187–206.

MERRIFIELD, P. R., GUILFORD, J. P., CHRISTENSEN, P. R., & FRICK, J. W. Interrelationships between certain abilities and certain traits of motivation and temperament. *Journal of General Psychology*, 1961, **65**, 57–74.

MERRIFIELD, P. R., GUILFORD, J. P., CHRISTENSEN, P. R., & FRICK, J. W. The role of intellectual factors in problem solving. *Psychological Monographs,* 1962, **76** (10, Whole No. 528).

MICHAEL, W. B. Factor analysis of tests and criteria: A comparative study of two AAF pilot populations. *Psychological Monographs,* 1949, **63** (3, Whole No. 298).

MILLER, G. A., GALANTER, E., & PRIBRAM, K. H. Plans and the structure of behavior. New York: Holt, 1960.

MOONEY, C. M. A factorial study of closure. *Canadian Journal of Psychology,* 1954, **8**, 51–60.

MOSIER, C. I. Determining a simple structure when loadings for certain tests are known. *Psychometrika,* 1938, **3**, 149–162.(a)

MOSIER, C. I. A note on Dwyer: The determination of the factor loadings of a given test. *Psychometrika,* 1938, **3**, 297–299. (b)

OSBORNE, R. T., ANDERSON, H. E., JR., & BASHAW, W. L. The stability of the WISC factor structure at three age levels. *Multivariate Behavioral Research,* 1967, **2**, 443–451.

OSGOOD, C. E., SUCI, G. J., & TANNENBAUM, P. H. The measurement of meaning. Urbana: University of Illinois Press, 1957.

PEARSON, K. On lines and planes of closest fit to systems of points in space. *The Philosophical Magazine,* 1901, **6**, 559–572.

PEMBERTON, C. The closure factors related to other cognitive processes. *Psychometrika,* 1952, **17**, 267–288.

PIAGET, J. Logic and psychology. (Tr. by W. Mays and T. Whitehead.) Manchester: Manchester University Press, 1953.

PINNEAU, S. R., & NEWHOUSE, A. Measures of invariance and comparability in factor analysis for fixed variables. *Psychometrika,* 1964, **29**, 271–281.

RIMOLDI, H. J. A. The general intelligence factor. *Psychometrika,* 1951, **16**, 75–101.

ROFF, M. A factorial study of tests in the perceptual area. *Psychometric Monographs,* 1952, No. 8.

SCHLOSBERG, H. A description of facial expressions in two dimensions. *Journal of Experimental Psychology,* 1952, **44**, 229–237.

SPEARMAN, C. "General Intelligence," objectively determined and measured. *American Journal of Psychology,* 1904, **15**, 201–293.

SPEARMAN, C. Abilities of man. New York: Macmillan, 1927.

STOTT, L. H., & BALL, R. S. Evaluation of infant and preschool tests. Detroit: Merrill-Palmer, 1963.

TAYLOR, C. W. A factorial study of fluency in writing. *Psychometrika,* 1947, **12**, 239–262.

TENOPYR, M. L. A factor-analytic study of symbolic-memory abilities. Doctoral dissertation, University of Southern California, 1966.

TERMAN, L. M., & MERRILL, M. A. Stanford-Binet Intelligence Scale: Manual for the third revision, Form LM. Boston: Houghton Mifflin, 1960.

THORNDIKE, E. L. Intelligence and its uses. *Harper's Magazine,* 1920, **140**, 227–235.

THORNDIKE, E. L., et al. The measurement of intelligence. New York: Teachers College, 1927.

THURSTONE, L. L. Primary mental abilities. *Psychometric Monographs*, 1938, No. 1.

THURSTONE, L. L. A factor analysis study of perception. *Psychometric Monographs*, 1944, No. 4.

THURSTONE, L. L., & THURSTONE, T. G. Factorial studies of intelligence. *Psychometric Monographs*, 1941, No. 2.

THURSTONE, L. L., & THURSTONE, T. G. SRA Primary mental abilities technical supplement. Chicago: Science Research Associates, 1954.

TUCKER, L. R. A method for synthesis of factor analysis studies. *Personnel Research Section Report*, No. 984. Washington, D.C.: Department of the Army, 1951.

TUCKER, L. R. An inter-battery method of factor analysis. *Psychometrika*, 1958, **23**, 111–136.

TUCKER, L. R. Three-mode factor analysis of Parker-Fleishman complex tracking behavior data. *Multivariate Behavioral Research*, 1967, **2**, 139–151.

TUCKER, L. R., KOOPMAN, R. F., & LINN, R. L. Evaluation of factor analytic research procedures by means of simulated correlation matrices. Urbana: University of Illinois, 1967.

UNDERWOOD, B. J., & SCHULTZ, R. W. Meaningfulness and verbal learning. Philadelphia: Lippincott, 1960.

VAN HEERDEN, P. J. The foundation of empirical knowledge. Wassenaar, The Netherlands: Wistik, 1968.

VANDENBERG, S. G. The primary mental abilities of South American students: A second comparative study of the generality of a cognitive factor structure. *Multivariate Behavioral Research*, 1967, **2**, 175–198.

VERNON, P. E. The structure of human abilities. New York: Wiley, 1950.

WEBER, H. Untersuchungen über die Faktor Structur numerischer Aufgaben. *Zeit. f. exp. u. angew. Psychol.*, 1953, **3**.

WECHSLER, D. The measurement and appraisal of adult intelligence. (4th ed.) Baltimore: Williams & Wilkins, 1958.

WERDELIN, I. The mathematical ability. Investigationes IX, *Studie Psychol. e. Paed.* Lund, Sweden, 1958.

WESLEY, S. M., COREY, D. Q., & STEWART, B. M. The intra-individual relationship between interest and ability. *Journal of Applied Psychology*, 1950, **34**, 193–197.

WILSON, R. C., GUILFORD, J. P., CHRISTENSEN, P. R., & LEWIS, D. J. A factor-analytic study of creative-thinking abilities. *Psychometrika*, 1954, **19**, 297–311.

WOODROW, H. The common factors in fifty-two mental tests. *Psychometrika*, 1939, **4**, 99–108.

WOODWORTH, R. S., & SCHLOSBERG, H. Experimental Psychology. (2nd ed.) New York: Holt, 1954.

ZIMMERMAN, W. S. A revised orthogonal solution for Thurstone's original primary mental abilities test battery. *Psychometrika*, 1953, **18**, 77–93.

NAME INDEX

Abe, C., 314, 500
Adkins, D. C., 6, 90, 98, 142, 146, 367, 451, 471, 499
Allen, M. S., 365
Anderson, H. E., Jr., 37, 505
Asch, S. E., 235, 499

Ball, R. S., 38, 360, 505
Bannister, C., 264, 492, 499
Bartlett, M. S., 59, 316, 499
Bashaw, W. L., 37, 505
Bechtoldt, H. P., 6, 221, 499
Berger, R. M., 142, 189, 364, 499
Blakey, R. I., 6, 381, 408, 499
Boe, E. E., 37, 500
Bond, N. A., 326, 327, 502
Botzum, W. A., 6, 500
Bradley, P. A., 365
Brown, S. W., 230, 365, 500
Burr, E. J., 59, 504
Burt, C., 2, 3, 18, 21, 500
Butler, J. M., 35, 57, 500

Campbell, D. T., 37, 331, 500
Canisia, M., 292, 500
Carroll, J. B., 124, 500
Cattell, R. B., 2, 50, 144, 500
Christal, R. E., 10, 230, 250, 500
Christensen, P. R., 8, 14, 62, 90, 94, 97, 112, 124, 142, 150, 160, 189, 284, 326, 327, 363, 364, 499-506
Cliff, N., 35, 38, 39, 52, 308, 500
Cline, M. G., 261, 476, 500
Cline, V. B., 315, 500
Comrey, A. L., 9, 14, 62, 363, 501
Coombs, C. H., 6, 221, 500
Corey, D. Q., 326, 506
Cox, A. B., 365
Cureton, E. E., 50, 500

Darwin, C., 348
Davis, P. C., 242, 500
de Mille, R., 242, 365, 500
Dewey, J., 103, 501
Dixon, W. J., 58, 501
Doherty, W. J., 365
Dudek, F. J., 8, 501
Dunham, J. L., 12, 30, 37, 304, 365, 501, 502
Dwyer, P. S., 58, 501

Ekstrom, R. B., 41, 501

Fiske, D. W., 37, 331, 500
Fleishman, E. A., 30, 37, 307, 501
French, J. W., 41, 58, 231, 242, 243, 501
Frick, J. W., 103, 112, 160, 164, 326, 364, 501, 502
Fruchter, B., 8, 30, 132, 142, 501, 502

Galanter, E., 212, 505
Games, F. A., 37, 501
Gardner, S. F., 365
Garnett, J. C. M., 2, 124, 501
Gershon, A., 365
Getzels, J. W., 315, 501
Gibson, W. A., 40, 501
Gocka, E. F., 37, 500
Green, R. F., 9, 12, 62, 90, 363, 364, 501, 502
Guilford, J. P., 4, 5, 6, 8, 9, 11, 12, 14, 17, 25-28, 30-32, 36, 37, 46, 51, 54, 58, 62, 73, 90, 93, 94, 97, 103, 112, 124, 125, 142, 146, 150, 164, 176, 213, 220, 221, 227, 230, 242, 243, 250, 258, 275, 278, 284, 291, 304, 314, 326, 327, 331, 350, 357, 363-365, 499-506
Guilford, R. B., 146, 275, 502
Guthrie, G. M., 37, 503
Guttman, L., 50, 503

Halsman, P., 260, 460, 503
Hamburger, C. D., 35, 38, 500
Hargreaves, H. L., 124, 503
Harman, H. H., 46, 503
Harris, C. W., 59, 60, 503
Hayes, K. J., 279, 326, 503
Hendricks, M., 365
Hertzka, A. F., 90, 189, 364, 502, 503
Hills, J. R., 288, 364, 503
Hoepfner, R., 4, 11, 12, 30, 36, 37, 46, 54, 58, 93, 176, 205, 213, 230, 242, 291, 304, 352, 365, 501-503
Hoffman, K. I., 365
Hotelling, H., 2, 3, 504
Hulin, W. S., 260, 504

Jackson, P. W., 315, 501

Kaiser, H. F., 504
Karlin, J. E., 6, 504
Katz, D., 260, 504
Kelley, H. P., 10, 230, 504
Kelley, T. L., 2, 504

507

NAME INDEX

Kettner, N. W., 8, 90, 94, 97, 284, 364, 502-504
Kline, W. E., 292, 504
Kluever, R. C., 315, 504
Knapp, R. H., 262, 473, 504
Kogan, W. S., 37, 500
Koopman, R. F., 50, 506

Lacey, J. I., 6, 62, 142, 189, 221, 227, 243, 250, 503
Levy, N., 260, 504
Lewis, D. J., 124, 363, 506
Leyden, F., 38, 504
Lindner, M. A., 235, 499
Linn, R. L., 50, 506
Lorge, I., 145
Luchins, A. S., 162, 242, 504
Luchins, E. H., 242, 504
Lyerly, S. B., 6, 90, 98, 142, 146, 367, 451, 471, 499
Lykken, D. T., 38, 504

MacDonald, R. P., 59, 504
McDougall, W., 349
Marks, A., 319, 364
Mayman, M., 326, 504
Mays, W., 505
Meeker, M. N., 357, 359, 504
Meredith, W., 39, 504
Merrifield, P. R., 103, 112, 160, 326, 364, 365, 503-505
Merrill, M. A., 358, 505
Michael, W. B., 8, 505
Miller, G. A., 212, 505
Mooney, C. M., 186, 505
Mosier, C. I., 58, 505

Newhouse, A., 39, 40, 505
Nihira, K., 93, 205, 213, 365, 505

Osborne, R. T., 37, 505
Osgood, C. E., 349, 505
O'Sullivan, M., 365

Pearson, K., 2, 505
Pemberton, C., 6, 505
Pennell, R., 308, 500
Petersen, H., 11, 242, 291, 365, 503
Piaget, J., 28, 505

Pinneau, S. R., 39, 40, 505
Pribram, K. H., 212, 505
Price, L. A., 41, 501

Rapaport, D., 326, 504
Rich, S., 501
Richards, J. M., 315, 500
Rimoldi, H. J. A., 6, 505
Roff, M., 8, 505

Schafer, R., 326, 504
Schlosberg, H., 260, 355, 504-506
Schmadel, E., 169
Spearman, C., 1, 2, 4, 8, 22, 26, 71, 350, 505
Stewart, B. M., 326, 506
Stott, L. H., 38, 360, 505
Suci, G. J., 349, 505
Sutton, M. A., 326, 327, 502

Tannenbaum, P. H., 349, 505
Taylor, C. W., 6, 124, 505
Tenopyr, M. L., 246, 248, 365, 505
Terman, L. M., 358, 505
Thorndike, E. L., 10, 26, 27, 258, 505
Thurstone, L. L., 2, 3, 5-9, 12, 62-65, 68, 93, 119, 121, 124, 129, 130, 132, 190, 193, 197, 221, 224, 352, 397, 413, 415, 439, 459, 477, 490, 506
Thurstone, T. G., 5, 506
Titchener, E. B., 349
Tucker, L. R., 37, 40, 50, 506

Vandenberg, S. G., 37, 506
van Heerden, P. J., 351, 506
Vernon, P. E., 2, 18, 21, 506

Weber, H., 292, 506
Wechsler, D., 242, 248, 359, 506
Werdelin, I., 292, 506
Wesley, S. M., 326, 506
Whitehead, T., 505
Wilson, R. C., 124, 363, 364, 506
Woodrow, H., 6, 506
Woodworth, R. S., 355, 506
Wundt, W., 349

Zimmerman, W. S., 8, 9, 36, 132, 142, 502, 503, 506

SUBJECT INDEX

Academic achievement:
  prediction of, 284-303
  and transformations, 315-317
Adaptive flexibility:
  defined, 161
  hypotheses for, 162
  tests for, 162, 166
Aesthetic judgments and evaluation, 227
Algebra achievement:
  multiple prediction of, 299-301
  and SI abilities, 291-303
Analogies, tests of, 22-23
Analysis:
  ability of, 132
  hypotheses for, 129
Aptitudes:
  factor scores for, 336
  and nonaptitude traits, 325-342
Aptitudes Research Project:
  plans of, 9-11
  procedures of, 11-14, 44-60
Arithmetic achievement:
  factors in, 298
  multiple prediction of, 299-301
  SI abilities in, 291-303
Association:
  concept of, 354
  and implication, 29
Associational fluency:
  optimal tests for, 151, 154-155, 157-158
  tests for, 166
Associationism, 20-30
Associations:
  memory for, 235
  synonymous, 153

Behavioral cognition, analysis of, 265-269
Behavioral content, defined, 21
Behavioral divergent production:
  analysis of, 276-277
  tests of, 269-276
Behaviorism, 349-350, 361

Calculus achievement, SI abilities and, 288-291
Cartoons, as social stimuli, 263-264, 274
Centroid method, 3
Class, defined, 21
Classes:
  role in learning, 313
  tests for, 192-193, 305-306

Cleverness factor, 124
Coast Guard Academy, academic prediction in, 284-287
Coefficient:
  of invariance, 39
  of pattern similarity, 39
  of similarity, 39
Cognition:
  analysis of, 69-73, 90-93, 95-97, 100-103, 108-111, 115-121
  behavioral, 258-269
    analysis of, 265-269
    tests for, 258-265
  of classes, 305-306
  defined, 20
  figural: analysis of, 115-121
    tests of, 74-75
  hypotheses for, 62-69, 90-91, 93-94, 97-100, 104-108
  and learning, 308-309
  and memory, 229
  semantic, tests for, 78-83
  symbolic: analysis of, 115
    hypotheses for, 112-115
    tests for, 76-78, 112-114
  tests for, 65-68, 74-83, 91, 94-95, 104-108
  of transformations, tests for, 178-179
Cognitive styles, as factors, 350
Communality, estimation of, 48-49
Complexity, hypothesis for, 94
Concepts, learning of: SI abilities in, 304-315
  tasks for, 304
  verbalization in, 311-312
Content:
  abilities differing in, 22-23
  defined, 20
Contents, translations between, 314
Convergent production:
  analysis of, 69-73, 90, 91-93, 95-97, 100-103, 108-111, 115-121
  of classes, tests for, 306
  defined, 20
  figural: analysis of, 115-121
    tests for, 83-84
  hypotheses for, 62-69, 90-91, 93-94, 97-100, 104-108
  and learning, 308
  and memory, 230
  in science, 318-319
  semantic, tests for, 86-89

509

SUBJECT INDEX

Convergent production:
symbolic: analysis of, 115
hypotheses for, 112-115
tests for, 114-115
tests for, 65-68, 84-88, 94-95, 104-108
of transformations, 181-182, 185-186
Correlation:
of composites, 45-46
matrix, 3
Correlations:
distributions of, 56
zero, 54
Creative abilities:
ninth-grade, 164-169
sixth-grade, 169-171
Creative performance, SI abilities in, 317-319
Creative thinking:
cognition in, 186
divergent production and, 142
hypotheses for, 186-187
SI interpretation of, 354
Creativity:
hypotheses for, 125-131
and IQ, 282-283
SI abilities in, 31-32
teachers' ratings of, 280-283
tests for children, 281

Darwinism, 28
Decision making and evaluation, 220
Deduction:
SI concept of, 31, 73, 122, 353
Thurstone's, 63-64
Differential Aptitude Test (DAT), validity in mathematics, 299-301
Discriminant function for mathematics courses, 302-303
Divergent production:
in academic achievement, 285-286 289-290, 297-298, 301
behavioral: analysis of, 269-277
tests for, 269-276
of classes, tests for, 306
and creative thinking, 142
defined, 20
figural: analysis of, 175-177
tests of, 171-173
and learning, 308
and memory, 229-230
in military officers, 323-324
at ninth grade, 164-169, 176-177
in science, 318-319
semantic: analysis of, 132-133, 142, 148-150, 154-160, 163-164, 167-169, 170-171, 175-177
tests for, 126-129, 137-141, 150-154, 161-163, 165-167

Divergent production:
at sixth grade, 170-171
symbolic: analysis of, 175-177
tests for, 135-137, 147, 171-175
of transformations, 180-181, 184-185
Education, 22
abilities in, 67, 72, 92, 98-100
and SI theory, 32
Elaboration:
abilities, 149
figural, tests for, 166-167
hypotheses for, 145-146
nature of, 187-188
tests for, 145-146, 166
Empathy and social intelligence, 258
Environment, factors of, 351
Evaluation:
and academic achievement, 289-290, 297-298, 301
analysis of, 197-198, 204-205
defined, 20, 220, 228
figural: analysis of, 226-227
hypotheses for, 220-225
tests for, 198-199, 221-226
hypotheses for, 190-195
semantic: analysis of, 210-212
hypotheses, 205-210
tests for, 201-203, 205-210
symbolic: analysis of, 218-220
hypothesis for, 213-218
tests for, 199-201, 213-218
tests for, 192-196
of transformations, tests for, 182-185
Expressional fluency:
optimal tests for, 156-157
tests for, 152-153, 167

Facial expressions, 259-260
Factor:
analysis: operations of, 11-14
optimal use of, 351-353
origins of, 1-4
procedures in, 46-53
as scientific method, 347-353
loadings, 3
distributions of, 56
matrix, 3
extension of, 58-59
scores, 59-60
in multiple prediction, 316-317
prediction from, 299-301
structure, 3
Factorial invariance:
achievement of, 35-36
indices of, 38-41
as scientific goal, 34-35

SUBJECT INDEX

Factorial invariance:
  types of, 36-38
Factors:
  and faculties, 349
  first-order, 4
  interpretation of, 41
  number of, 50-51
  oblique versus orthogonal, 2-3
  and races, 8
  rotations of, 52-53
  second-order, 4
  and sex, 8
Faculty psychology, 348-349
Feelings, dimensions of, 349
Figural abilities in calculus, 290
Figural cognition, 115-121
  tests for, 116-119
Figural content, defined, 20
Figural convergent production, 115-121
  hypotheses for, 119-120
Figural evaluation, 220-227
Figural memory, 250-255
Flexibility:
  abilities for, 123-133, 163-164, 168
  hypotheses for, 127, 160-163
  intellectual, 160-164
  nature of, 187
  in science, 318-319
  tests for, 127, 160-163, 165-169
Fluency:
  abilities for, 25, 132
  expressional, tests for, 152-153
  factors for, 8-9, 154-160, 167-168
    hypotheses for, 126-127, 150-154
    origins of, 124
  nature of, 187
  tests for, 126-127, 150-154, 165-169
    restriction in, 151-152
  verbal, 150-160
Foresight, abilities for, 144-145, 149

g, Spearman's, 2, 4
General reasoning, 8
  analysis of, 93-97
  definition of, 96
  factor of, 95
  hypotheses for, 63-64, 70-71, 93-94
  tests for, 65-66, 94-95
Gestalt psychology, 29, 65, 130, 354
  and transformations, 315
Goal attainment, tests of, 194-195
Group factors, 2
Guilford-Zimmerman Aptitude Survey, 444, 450, 479, 490

Habit, factors of, 351

Ideational fluency, tests for, 165
Implication:
  and association, 354
  and belongingness, 29
  defined, 21
Induction:
  abilities of, 66
  SI concept of, 31, 72, 122, 353
  Thurstone's, 62, 64
Inference, tests of, 191-192, 204
Ingenuity:
  abilities for, 149
  hypotheses and tests for, 147
  nature of, 187
Integration factors, 7
Intellectual factors, sources of, 5-9
Intelligence:
  definition of, 356
  and nonaptitude traits, 335
  testing of: in education, 356-357, 360-361
    future of, 356-361
    inadequacies in, 358-360
    in personnel work, 357-358
    preschool, 360
    and school subjects, 360-361
Interests:
  and SI abilities, 326, 331-335
  in thinking, 326-327
Intuition in factor interpretation, 41
IQ:
  and creativity, 282-283
  and divergent production, 164-165

Judgment:
  commonsense, tests for, 210
  concept of, 190, 355
  factor of, 6-7
  of figural information, 195-196
  practical, 191-192, 195
  psychophysical, 227
  speed of, 196
  subjective, 226-227
  tests for, 193-194

Leadership and SI abilities, 323-325
Learning:
  ability, 355
  concept of, 355
  SI abilities in, 304-315
  theory of, 30
  transformations in, 315-317
Logic and psychology, 355-356
Logical reasoning, factor of, 212

Mathematics:
  higher, prediction in, 288-291

SUBJECT INDEX

Mathematics:
    ninth-grade, prediction in, 291-303
Mechanical-knowledge factor, 7
Memory:
    abilities of, and learning, 310
    for classes, tests for, 306
    defined, 20
    factors of, 7
    figural: analysis of, 254-255
        tests for, 238-239, 251-253
    rote, factors of, 243-244
    semantic: analysis of, 237-238
        tests for, 240-241
    span factors, 242-243
    store: and cognition, 230
        and production, 230
    symbolic: analysis of, 249-250
        tests for, 239-240, 244-249
    tests: nature of, 230-231
        weaknesses in, 256
    of transformations, tests for, 179-180, 184
    visual, 250-255
Military leadership and SI abilities, 319-325
Model:
    Burt's hierarchical, 18
    structure of intellect, 17-21
    Vernon's hierarchical, 18
Motion pictures and social cognition, 259
Motivation and SI abilities, 325-342
Multiple-factor theory, 2-4
Multiple prediction with factor scores, 316-317
Multiple regression, 58
Multivariate methods, needs for, 351

Nonaptitude factors, 329, 337-338
    and SI abilities, 331-336, 338-341
Number factors, 242

Operation:
    abilities differing in, 23-25
    defined, 20
Operational-informational psychology, 28
Ordering:
    ability, 150
    hypotheses and tests for, 146-147
Orientation, hypotheses and tests for, 144
Originality:
    factor for, 133
        origin of, 124
    hypotheses for, 127-129
    in military officers, 323-325
    nature of, 187
    and nonaptitude traits, 334
    tests for, 127-129, 166

Penetration:
    as cognition, 186-187
    factor for, 133-134
    hypotheses and tests for, 131-132
Perseveration, hypotheses and tests for, 160-162
Persistence, hypotheses and tests for, 162-163
Person perception and social intelligence, 258
Personality, theory of, 350
Phi, Tucker's, 40
Planning:
    abilities in, 142-150
    factors in, 7, 148-149
    hypotheses and tests for, 143-148
    nature of, 187-188
Predicting, abilities for, hypotheses and tests for, 144-145
Primary mental abilities, Thurstone's, 5
Principal-factor method, 3
Problem solving:
    abilities in, 110-111
    hypotheses and tests for, 104-108
    analysis of, 103-112
    model for, 103-104, 354-355
    in SI theory, 31
Product:
    abilities differing in, 24-25
    defined, 21
Psychoanalytical theory:
    of intelligence, 279
    taxonomies in, 349
Psychoepistemology, 28, 353
Psychologic, 28, 354
Psychological theory, 353-356
    operational-informational, 28
    from SI model, 28-31

Races and factors, 8
Ratings:
    of creativity, 280-283
    of personality traits, 341-342
    of SI abilities, 317-319
Reading, transformations and, 315-317
Reasoning:
    abilities, hypotheses for, 63-65, 90-91, 97-100
    analysis of, 97-103
    concept of, 31, 72-73, 352-354
Reasoning-A analysis, 62-90
Reasoning-B analysis, 90-93
Reasoning factors:
    Air Force, 62-63
    Thurstone's, 62-63

Reasoning I:
  hypotheses for, 63-64
  tests for, 65-66
Reasoning II:
  hypotheses for, 64, 71-72
  tests for, 66-68
Reasoning III:
  hypotheses for, 64, 72
  tests for, 68
Reasoning IV:
  hypotheses for, 64-65, 72
  tests for, 68-69
Redefinition:
  factor for, 133
  hypotheses and tests for, 130-131
  as transformation, 315
Relation, defined, 21
Rigidity, hypotheses for, 160-163
Rotations:
  of factors, 52-53
  oblique versus orthogonal, 3-4
  to targets, 52-53
  varimax, 54-55
Rote memory, factors of, 243-244

Science, abilities in, 317-319
Semantic content, defined, 20
Semantic evaluation:
  analysis of, 210-212
  tests for, 200-203, 205-211, 213-220
Semantic memory:
  analysis of, 237-238
  tests for, 230-236, 240-241
Sensitivity to problems:
  as cognition, 186, 211-212
  factors for, 133
  hypotheses and tests for, 125-126
Sex differences:
  in abilities, 8
  in trait organization, 338-339
SI (*see* Structure of intellect)
Simile tests, 153-154
Simple structure, 3, 53, 57
  and factorial invariance, 35-36
Social intelligence:
  nature of, 257-258
  unexplored abilities in, 277-278
Social sensitivity and social intelligence, 258
Space factors, 7
Spatial abilities and calculus, 290
Spontaneous flexibility:
  defined, 160
  tests for, 161, 165
Stanford-Binet scale, inadequacies in, 358-359

Structure of intellect:
  categories of, 20-21
  code system for, 21
  confirmed abilities in, 54-55
  development of, 25-27
  heuristic value of, 27-28
  hypotheses from, 10-11, 13, 352-353
  implications from, 27-32
  model, 17-21
  origins of, 21-25
  parameters of, 18-21
Summation method, Burt's, 3
Syllogism tests, 191, 204
Symbolic abilities, analysis of, 293-296
Symbolic content, defined, 20
Symbolic evaluation, abilities and tests for, 213-220
Symbolic memory:
  analysis of, 249-250
  tests for, 244-249
Synthesis:
  ability for, 132
  hypotheses and tests for, 129-130
System, defined, 21

Taxonomies:
  in natural sciences, 348
  needs for, 348-351
  in psychology, 348-350
Temperament and SI abilities, 325-342
Tests:
  combined in analysis, 44-45
  deleted in analysis, 46-48
  time limits for, 151, 154-155
Thurstone analysis, 5-6
Time, as test condition, 151, 154-155
Transformation:
  abilities, 177-186
  in science, 318-319
  analysis of, 183-186
  tests for, 177-183
  defined, 21
  role of, in learning, 315-317
Transformations:
  cognition of, 178-179, 183-184
  convergent production of, 181-182, 185-186
  divergent production of, 180-181, 184-185
  evaluation of, 182-183, 185-186
  memory of, 179-180, 184
Translation between contents, 314
Trial and error, hypotheses for, 94

Unit, defined, 21
U.S. Army Air Forces analyses, 6-8

Validity of SI tests:
    in academic achievement, 284-287
    in concept learning, 304-314
    for creativity, 280-283
    in higher mathematics, 288-291
    in military officers, 319-325
    in ninth-grade mathematics, 291-303
    in school learning, 315-317
Vectors:
    factor, 2
    test, 3

Verbal comprehension, role of, in learning, 289-290, 297-298, 312
Verbalization and SI abilities, 311-312
Visual-figural abilities, 115-121
Visual memory, 250-255

Wechsler scales, inadequacies in, 359-360
Word fluency:
    optimal tests for, 155-156
    Thurstone's, 125, 132